Barcode in Back

D1715185

THE FUTURE OF IDENTITY
IN THE INFORMATION SOCIETY

IFIP – The International Federation for Information Processing

IFIP was founded in 1960 under the auspices of UNESCO, following the First World Computer Congress held in Paris the previous year. An umbrella organization for societies working in information processing, IFIP's aim is two-fold: to support information processing within its member countries and to encourage technology transfer to developing nations. As its mission statement clearly states,

> *IFIP's mission is to be the leading, truly international, apolitical organization which encourages and assists in the development, exploitation and application of information technology for the benefit of all people.*

IFIP is a non-profitmaking organization, run almost solely by 2500 volunteers. It operates through a number of technical committees, which organize events and publications. IFIP's events range from an international congress to local seminars, but the most important are:

• The IFIP World Computer Congress, held every second year;
• Open conferences;
• Working conferences.

The flagship event is the IFIP World Computer Congress, at which both invited and contributed papers are presented. Contributed papers are rigorously refereed and the rejection rate is high.

As with the Congress, participation in the open conferences is open to all and papers may be invited or submitted. Again, submitted papers are stringently refereed.

The working conferences are structured differently. They are usually run by a working group and attendance is small and by invitation only. Their purpose is to create an atmosphere conducive to innovation and development. Refereeing is less rigorous and papers are subjected to extensive group discussion.

Publications arising from IFIP events vary. The papers presented at the IFIP World Computer Congress and at open conferences are published as conference proceedings, while the results of the working conferences are often published as collections of selected and edited papers.

Any national society whose primary activity is in information may apply to become a full member of IFIP, although full membership is restricted to one society per country. Full members are entitled to vote at the annual General Assembly, National societies preferring a less committed involvement may apply for associate or corresponding membership. Associate members enjoy the same benefits as full members, but without voting rights. Corresponding members are not represented in IFIP bodies. Affiliated membership is open to non-national societies, and individual and honorary membership schemes are also offered.

THE FUTURE OF IDENTITY
IN THE INFORMATION SOCIETY

Proceedings of the Third IFIP WG 9.2, 9.6/ 11.6, 11.7/FIDIS International Summer School on The Future of Identity in the Information Society, Karlstad University, Sweden, August 4-10, 2007

Edited by

Simone Fischer-Hübner
Karlstad University
Sweden

Penny Duquenoy
Middlesex University
The United Kingdom

Albin Zuccato
TeliaSonera
Sweden

Leonardo Martucci
Karlstad University
Sweden

 Springer

Library of Congress Control Number: 2008923749

The Future of Identity in the Information Society

Edited by Simone Fischer-Hübner, Penny Duquenoy, Albin Zuccato, and Leonardo Martucci

p. cm. (IFIP International Federation for Information Processing, a Springer Series in Computer Science)

ISSN: 1571-5736 / 1861-2288 (Internet)
ISBN: 978-0-387-79025-1
eISBN: 978-0-387-79026-8

Printed on acid-free paper

Printed in the United States of America.

9 8 7 6 5 4 3 2 1

springer.com

Foreword

The increasing diversity of Information Communication Technologies and their equally diverse range of uses in personal, professional and official capacities raise challenging questions of identity in a variety of contexts. Each communication exchange contains an identifier which may, or may not, be intended by the parties involved. What constitutes an identity, how do new technologies affect identity, how do we manage identities in a globally networked information society?

From the 6th to the 10th August 2007, IFIP (International Federation for Information Processing) working groups 9.2 (Social Accountability), 9.6/11.7 (IT Misuse and the Law) and 11.6 (Identity Management) hold their 3rd International Summer School on "The Future of Identity in the Information Society" in cooperation with the EU Network of Excellence FIDIS at Karlstad University. The Summer School addressed the theme of Identity Management in relation to current and future technologies in a variety of contexts.

The aim of the IFIP summer schools has been to introduce participants to the social implications of Information Technology through the process of informed discussion. Following the holistic approach advocated by the involved IFIP working groups, a diverse group of participants ranging from young doctoral students to leading researchers in the field were encouraged to engage in discussion, dialogue and debate in an informal and supportive setting. The interdisciplinary, and international, emphasis of the Summer School allowed for a broader understanding of the issues in the technical and social spheres.

Both IFIP and FIDIS take a holistic approach to technology and support interdisciplinary exchange. Contributions combining technical, social, ethical or legal perspectives were solicited. Keynote speeches provided a focus for the theme of the Summer School – Social and Political Dimension of Identity, Identity Management Architectures, Identity & Privacy in Social Communities, Transparency and User-Controlled Identity Management, Identity Theft, ICT Implants, eHealth and Ethical Challenges, Identity & Mobility – and the contributions from participants enhanced the ideas generated by the keynote speeches. The Summer School was a very successful event. More than 55 delegates from 20 countries actively participated. We succeeded in initiating intensive discussions between Ph.D. students and senior acknowledged researchers from different disciplines.

These proceedings include both keynote papers and submitted papers accepted by the Programme Committee, which have been presented at the Summer School. The review process consisted of two steps: First contributions for presentation at the Summer School were selected based on a review of submitted short papers by the Summer School Programme Committee. After the Summer School, authors had the opportunity to submit their final full papers, addressing also the discussions at the Summer School. These papers were again reviewed and the ones included in these proceedings were carefully selected by the International Summer School Programme Committee and by additional Reviewers according to common quality criteria.

It is our pleasure to thank the members of the programme committee, the additional reviewers, the members of the organising committee as well as all speakers. Without their work and dedication, this Summer School would not have been possible. Besides, we owe special thanks to the multidisciplinary research centre HumanIT at Karlstad University and the Municipality of Karlstad (Karlstads kommun) for their financial support.

Simone Fischer-Hübner   Albin Zuccato
Penny Duquenoy   Leonardo Martucci

Organisation

The Summer School was organized by IFIP Working Groups 9.2, 9.6/11.7, and 11.6 in cooperation with the Network of Excellence FIDIS.

Programme Committee Co-Chairs
Penny Duquenoy (Middlesex University/UK, IFIP WG 9.2 chair)
Simone Fischer-Hübner (Karlstad University/Sweden)
Albin Zuccato (TeliaSonera/Sweden, IFIP WG 9.6/11.7 vice chair)

Local Organising Committee Chair
Leonardo A. Martucci (Karlstad University/Sweden)

International Program Committee
Geoff Busby (British Computer Society/UK)
Brian O'Connell (Central Connecticut State University/USA)
Hans Hedbom (Karlstad University/Sweden)
Günter Karjoth (IBM Research Lab/Switzerland)
David-Olivier Jaquet-Chiffelle, (Berne University of Applied Sciences/Switzerland)
Elisabeth de Leeuw (Ordina/Netherlands, IFIP WG 11.6 chair)
Ronald Leenes (Tilburg University, NL)
Marc Van Lieshout (TNO/Netherlands)
Javier Lopez (University of Malaga/Spain)
Kai Rannenberg (Goethe University Frankfurt/Germany, IFIP WG 9.6/11.7 chair)
Rocío Rueda (Central University Bogotá/Colombia)
Kevin Warwick (University of Reading/UK)
Gunnar Wenngren (AB Wenngrens/Sweden)
Diane Whitehouse (The Castlegate Consultancy/UK)
Louise Yngström (Stockholm University/KTH/Sweden)
Jozef Vyskoc (VaF/Slovakia)

Additional Reviewers
Jacques Berleur, Mark Gasson, Leonardo Martucci, John Sören Pettersson, Charles Raab, Morton Swimmer

Table of Contents

Workshop: Legal Identity and Identification Aspects

Keynote Session 4:

Workshop: Privacy-Enhancing Technologies

Workshop: Social and Cultural Aspects of Identity

Workshop: Identifiers in eHealth

Workshop: Economical and Organisational Identity Aspects

Workshop: Economical Aspects of Identity Management

Keynote Session 1:

Social and Political Dimensions of Identity

1 Introduction

This paper points up a number of issues concerning the topic of identity, to stimulate further debate and discussion without, however, solving any of the intellectual and practical problems that are inherent in this subject. It dwells on some conceptual matters and also describes some current policy and legal developments that have important implications for the way in which we understand identity and identification, as well as privacy and other matters that are closely related to these.

'Identity' is a fashionable focusing concept that indicates a host of contemporary anxieties. Whether it will have long-lasting value as a concept that crystallises and expresses these, or whether it will be overtaken by the next wave of fashion, cannot be foretold. But concerns over personal, social, national, ethnic, cultural, religious and other identities, and problems involved with verifying the authenticity of persons' claims to be who they say they are, have long been with us, and are likely to live long. So, too, may the contemporary absorption with matters of selfhood and otherhood. In addition, there are political, economic, bureaucratic and security issues around identity theft, identity fraud, identity cards, identity management, and so on, which are also likely to persist.

Philip Agre notes that identity, as a 'public, symbolic phenomenon that is located in history, culture and social structure', and one that embraces national, ethnic, self-adopted or ascribed attributes, differs from information technologists' conception of identity as 'epitomized by proper names' or by mathematical denotations in which 'the identity of a thing is strictly separate from, and prior to, its attributes'[1]. This is one broad conceptual distinction that characterizes discourse about identity. It is apparent that both senses are 'political', albeit in different but partially convergent ways. The former is political in that national or ethnic identities play a major part in power relations in and among jurisdictional political systems (e.g., states), and because adopted or ascribed identities affect individuals' and groups' citizenship or participation rights. The latter is political in that the identification of unique persons has always been a task carried out by states for a host of reasons to do with taxation, movement, voting, and other functions. It is the latter that is particularly relevant to the present discussion, because – as we shall see later – the development of identity cards and means of identification by states (and also the commercial sector) involves, in the first instance, the ability to distinguish among people with unique identifying characteristics. But competing concepts make this far from straightforward.

---

[1] Agre (1997): 6-7.

Please use the following format when citing this chapter:

Raab, C.D., 2008, in IFIP International Federation for Information Processing, Volume 262; The Future of Identity in the Information Society; Simone Fischer-Hübner, Penny Duquenoy, Albin Zuccato, Leonardo Martucci; (Boston: Springer), pp. 3–19.

2   Issues in the conceptualization of 'Identity'

'Identity' and 'identification' are among the most elusive and difficult concepts confronting scholars and researchers in the broad field of information studies, reflecting a welter of discourse in many other fields, including philosophy[2], psychology[3] and sociology[4]. There are many interpretations and applications of these terms that arise from different and often discrepant perspectives, modes of thought, and disciplines, and they extend to some of the further reaches of metaphysics and social and political theory. Some of this is profound and quite far-reaching into the nature of what it is to be a human being. But identity and identification are not just specialist terms used only by researchers in our various technical discourses. They feature prominently in casual everyday use by citizens, consumers, politicians, legislators, the media, public and private organisations, and many more domains as well. People are asked, 'have you got any identification?' or 'show me your ID' in public places and shops. We normally have no practical difficulty understanding what is being requested. But in other circumstances, the kinds of information included or omitted from the documents we carry around, and especially the information resources that lie behind such casual transactions, can be challenged. They might misrepresent the nature of whatever it is that is referred to when processes of identification question or verify your or my identity, or the identity of the groups or categories to which we belong or to which we are assigned. But so, too, scholarly and technical usage can overlook important implications of the management, verification, encoding and other systematisations of identity, especially when the perspectives of the people whose identities are involved are sidelined or left out of account.

The enormous and diverse literature that surrounds the term 'identity' testifies to the growing importance of identity in the politics and social life of our time. Identities are lost, sought, denied, created, challenged, changed, played with, killed for, legislated, and abolished. Some identities are personal, others are group, with the 'group' ranging in scale and space from the very intimate to the national. National identity, relating often to nationalism, is a flourishing topic in the social and political sciences, overshadowing other adjectival identities, such as gender, class, and personal with which it intersects in complex ways, sometimes helping persons to define these latter identities in regard to themselves. Identities, where they are non-physical or non-institutional, may be categorical, denoting some 'us' or 'we', according to cultural, religious, 'ethnic', or other criteria, and the possibility of any social or biological factor or feature becoming shaped as an identifying criterion seems infinite; the question of categorization will be considered later on.

There have always been conflicts over identities. Political scientists would say that the working-out of conflicts over anything is a political process, involved with power relations. This politicizes the very subject matter itself: in this case, what it means to have or not to have a particular identity, to be given one or to be denied one or

---

[2] E.g., Olson (2007).
[3] E.g., Simon (2004); see also Raab (2005).
[4] E.g., Jenkins (2004); Bauman (2004).

perhaps many. But political scientists would also say that power is exercised even where there is no overt conflict, and even where a potential conflict is not entered into by people because they do not expect success as an outcome, or where it is suppressed as an issue that could be resolved through political processes. Power, it is said, is exercised when people's mind-set is so shaped that they do not understand that their life, and even their conceptions of themselves and others, could be different from what it is: that is, that the normal, day-in and day-out world can not be otherwise than it is, and that cultural, social and governmental habits, practices and systems are important forces shaping this state of consciousness. And so it might be when identities are considered to be fixed in certain patterns and not subject to negotiation or change by people themselves or by others, because alternatives are inconceivable[5].

The various social-scientific 'takes' on identity, although debated amongst sociologists, social and individual psychologists, or political scientists, and between different camps, make vital contributions to understanding human social and political phenomena. Let us look at some of this for a bit. Here we begin to touch on the concept of the 'self' and its relation to other facets of our identity, although this cannot be explored too far here. Susan Hekman takes the view that:

> each of us possesses a coherent, core self that allows us to function as mature adults in a social world and provides us with an individual identity[6].

She argues that:

> Each of us possesses a personal identity that is constituted by an array of influences and experiences that form us as a unique person. These forces are both public, the hegemonic discourses that define our social life, and individual, the character and situation of those who care for us as infants, and through whom the public concepts are transmitted to us. The result of these influences is…our core self. But in addition to possessing a personal identity, each of us is subsumed under an array of public identities: woman/man; white/nonwhite; middle class/ working class, and so forth[7].

Other discussions of the uniqueness, or otherwise, of the 'self', and how it relates to other forms of identity, are worth looking at as well. Sociologists and cognate scholars have debated the relationship, if any, between 'real' and 'virtual' identities, and between personal and social identities. Erving Goffman makes these distinctions in his cogent analysis of stigma and the management of 'spoiled' identity,[8] when discrepancies between who one 'is' and who one purports to be are publicly exposed, or in danger of so being. Richard Jenkins, on the other hand, finds these distinctions unhelpful, because 'all human identities are by definition social identities'[9]. For him, the adjective 'social' is redundant because:

---

[5] See Lukes (1974).
[6] Hekman (2004).
[7] Ibid.: 7
[8] Goffman (1968) [1963].
[9] Jenkins (2004): 73; emphasis in original.

'[i]dentifying ourselves or others is a matter of meaning, and meaning always involves interaction: agreement and disagreement, convention and innovation, communication and negotiation'[10].

And also because identity is a reflexive process, rather than a fixed attribute. Therefore, he argues that, '[a]s social scientists, keen to avoid reification, we should probably only ever talk about "identification"'[11].

Yet some analytical distinctions are necessary. There are, indeed, both individual and collective identities and identification processes, even though these are not empirically separate but, as Jenkins insists, 'are routinely entangled with each other'[12]. There is also an important distinction between the internal and external aspects of identification – self-definition and definition by others – that forms the crux of Jenkins' analysis, and that indeed is pervasive in Goffman's works as well as in a great deal of other social and psychological treatments, whatever position is taken on the 'self', 'reality', and other contested concepts[13]. Likewise, the parallel distinction (but reflexiveness) between groups and categories is also an important cutting tool. Jenkins wants to reserve the use of the term 'virtual' to refer not to the identity that the individual presents to the world, or which the world perceives (in contrast to her 'real' identity, which is arguably a spurious concept), but to the (different) experience of an identity that persons may have despite their sharing of a name, (that is, a 'nominal' identity), or where the name changes but not the experience[14]. Whether there is a true and singular 'self' lying behind the multiplicity of identities and presented selves has long been debated, for instance, by Anthony Cohen[15]. From an anthropological angle, Cohen sees identity as relating to what he calls the 'authorial self', whose self-consciousness is ignored in many research paradigms. People play roles and enact performances in daily life, but their identity is not merely an aggregate of these. There is a political edge to this, in terms of potential conflict between persons and authorities, as we may find that an authoritatively assigned 'personhood' is at odds with the sense of self that we wish to assert as our identity. Cohen argues that it is more common than we might realise for individuals to resist the pressures of imposed classification[16]. Such responses are not confined only to outstanding instances of resistance to the dehumanisation of life in what Goffman calls 'total institutions'[17], so we should not interpret as special heroism what persons are accustomed to doing when classified by external and authoritative sources.

This is where we can cast some light on categorization and its relation to the uniqueness of identity. When individuals freely declare their adherence to available collective categories (e.g., gender, nationality, ethnicity, religion etc.), Cohen sees this

---

[10] Ibid.: 4.
[11] Ibid.: 5.
[12] Ibid.: 15.
[13] See Raab (2008, forthcoming).
[14] Ibid.: 22.
[15] Cohen (1994).
[16] Ibid.: 71.
[17] Goffman (1961)

as a 'means of reappropriating their identities or of creating them anew'[18], rather than as giving in to pre-formed and imposed alien definitions, much less as a rejection of categorization as such as being somehow contrary to some inexpressible, solipsistic sense of a unique self. In other words, I can identify myself and tell you who I am using categories that are common and current, without feeling that I have somehow misrepresented my 'true' being. John Turner, a social psychologist, would remove the concept from the status of debatability: '[t]he self is a human universal. It is an undisputed given of human experience and life[19]'. But that remark does not intend to support a particular interpretation of 'self' amongst a welter of alternative approaches in social psychology[20], nor is it to underplay the role of social relationships and situations in understanding the processual nature of the self and the 'adaptive flexibility of human behaviour'[21]. In fact, Turner criticizes the 'evils' of individualism, reification, and reductionism that remain influential in his discipline. Individualism is

> the tendency to define the self as a unique, purely individual property of the person, the idea that it is about one's personal identity ...(rather than one's shared collective identities) and that it is defined by or closely related to one's personality traits or other individual-difference factors[22].

Reification 'is the tendency to define the self as a thing, a mental entity stored in the cognitive system, rather than as a dynamic social psychological process'[23], and reductionism is

> the tendency to seek to reduce the self-process to the functioning of simpler, more elementary processes. ...[such as] our self-interest, our motives, drives, traits, likes, dislikes, needs, fears, etc., as if these were fixed in our character independent of and prior to social interaction[24].

These sources and related ones help us to ask: how do we feel about our identity? We are sometimes in two minds about our identity: wanting to conceal it and not be noticed, or to present ourselves differently to different audiences. If we belong to a minority group that is subject to discrimination in employment or social ostracism, we may sense a conflict between loyalty and a self-interested denial of membership. People with an unsavory past may wish to have it forgotten in the present by disavowing who they were. At other times, however, it may be literally in our vital interest to be distinguished from others, and not be mistaken for them. One may want to claim credit for something praiseworthy, to 'stand up and be counted', and to assert one's personal identity proudly. A fixed identity may be necessary if we are to function in daily life, and history attests to the severe difficulties that befall persons whose 'papers' have been destroyed or confiscated, and who therefore need to construct an identity. In sum, at different times and in different situations, we have

---

[18] Cohen (1994): 178.

[19] Turner (2004): x.

[20] A comprehensive survey of these is Simon (2004).

[21] Turner (2004): xiii.

[22] Ibid.: xii.

[23] Ibid.

[24] Ibid.: xiii.

interests in both the concealment and the assertion of identity. But how do we use identity, shape it, or deny it? How do we convince others that we have a certain identity? How are identities shaped in interaction? And what scope do we have to define ourselves for ourselves?

We should not be led to thinking that it is only official, bureaucratic institutions that are engaged in information management, including the manipulation of processes for identification of unique individuals. States and companies work away at it, but so do we. Whether to offer a critique of the one is also to offer a critique of the other is a matter for debate. Everyone is in the business of information management, including the management of identity. Goffman's work shows this consistently at the level of interpersonal relations conducted in a variety of spatial and social contexts[25]. Goffman draws attention to 'personal identity' as the uniqueness of the individual, made up of a set of 'facts' about her that mark her off from anyone else. Personal identity is what differentiates her from others, by virtue of a 'positive mark' or 'identity peg', and her unique set of 'life history items'[26]. He goes on to say:

> Personal identity, then, has to do with the assumption that the individual can be differentiated from all others and that around this means of differentiation a single continuous record of social facts can be attached, entangled, like candy floss, becoming then the sticky substance to which still other biographical facts can be attached[27].

For Goffman, the marks and pegs in question may be, for example, images held in others' minds, or their knowledge of where the individual stands in kinship networks. They could be handwriting qualities, unique registration numbers, and the like, used in governmental organisations. Writing in the context of the quaint, but not now yet obsolete, prevailing bureaucratic technology of the 1960s, and apparently not interested to explain why the state in future would intensify its interest in identification, Goffman nonetheless had foresight of the modern, high-tech state:

> [o]nce an identity peg has been made ready, material, if and when available, can be hung on it; a dossier can be developed, usually contained and filed in a manila folder. One can expect that personal identification of its citizens by the state will increase, even as devices are refined for making the record of a particular individual more easily available to authorized persons and more inclusive of social facts concerning him, for example, receipt of dividend payments[28].

This brand of sociology makes us aware that the individual's control of the information she gives out, or of the impressions that others gain about her when in her presence, is tenuous and negotiated. Moving away from the micro level of interpersonal interaction, this is perforce true of the information, whether 'hard fact' or 'soft intelligence', that flows into and out of information systems and is thereby embellished, reduced, mixed and merged, and ripened into something new that, nevertheless, be false. What can be 'managed' by me in face-to-face interactions may

[25] E.g., Goffman (1959); Goffman (1968) [1963].
[26] Goffman (1968) [1963]: 73-4.
[27] Ibid.: 74-5.
[28] Ibid.: 75.

be impossible for me to 'manage' in the database, even if I were to be aware of what is located there, potentially to be managed. This, to, is of political significance. Management has to do with choice, or at least with the possibility of negotiating the terms on which choices will be made by others. But information processes and processing beyond the immediate interaction transfer most of the crucial choices from the individual to the organisation and the system. Individual voice and collective pressure have an important role to play in helping to restore these choices to the individual, but restoration can only be brought about by a system of rights and rules that, however, may simulate all or some of the conditions of personal choice, but cannot recreate them.

Contexts matter a great deal n all this. However, there are some identities that each of us cannot have (or claim), although the realm of impossibility is apparently smaller in online environments. Space makes a difference, too: what you can claim to be may be limited in small towns or villages where 'everyone knows everyone', but may be very wide in large cities, where 'no-one knows anyone'. Cities have been magnets for people who wanted to be unrecognized and anonymous or to change their identity. Time also makes a difference: who one is may not be who one was, although there are metaphysical complexities about this[29]; the networks within which one is known and in which one has an identity may change or dissolve over time, releasing one from the older identity (and from certain commitments) and making it possible to adopt a new one (and new commitments) in a newly-formed network. Because one is involved in many networks that do not dissolve simultaneously, or that do not have the possibility of completely disconnecting from one another, one cannot easily abandon one identity and take on a wholly new one without the risk of being caught out. Changes of place may reduce the risk; likewise the passage of time; likewise changes of appearance or behaviour. However, administrative records may close these escape-routes; this is an issue with regard to identity cards, and to the question whether information systems reduce the possibility of forgetting (and forgiving), which is an important element of social and individual life. But the decay-rate of identities, and the factors affecting it, need more systematic analysis.

Identities may be overt and socially or politically acknowledged, or they may be covert and cloaked in secrecy. This is historically true for certain religious groups, for example, over centuries, in circumstances where overt identification would result in persecution. Some identities are inclusive, in the sense that the threshold for adopting them is low, and dependent upon civil attributes such as residence, while others are rigidly maintained and exclusive, dependent on birth, historic or genetic factors. This is a distinction often drawn between certain national identities and others, and bears heavily on the question of citizenship, rights, and socio-cultural segregation or integration. Some identities are claimed, recognized by some or all others, but other identities cannot so easily be asserted, and may incite challenges to the claimant. Some identities are assigned, and may incite challenges by the assignee on the grounds of misclassification, and by the excluded on the same grounds. Thus, the interaction of 'objective' and 'subjective' identities is perennially created and re-

---

[29] The implications of time for identity are explored in Olson (2007).

created, such that they reflexively shape each other, although some would deny the conceptual soundness of those two statuses. We all have multiple identities, whether simultaneously or in the course of a lifetime, and are highly unlikely to share identical 'portfolios' of these. Once again, in different contexts, we may invoke different identities, or we may validate, or at least not challenge, the identities that others consider us to have. We may also reject them. All these options require the tacit or overt agreement of others; the scope for self-determination of identity is limited, to one degree or another.

3   'Identity' in Government Policy and Practice: UK Identity Cards

Moving now from the social scientific to the governmental and organisational dimension: there appears to be a marked disjuncture between the social-scientific perspectives on identity, whatever they may be, and the worlds of government and commerce in which unique identities are the currency of practice, and in which 'identity' is not problematical, but matter-of-fact. What 'identity' means appears straightforward in the practical matter of government policy on identity cards, and in identity management schemes. Of course, there may be an untidy administrative landscape because of the diversity of identification systems that have grown up in the public administration of particular countries, and this causes problems for the efficiency, effectiveness and equitable conduct of the state. Here the problem is not seen in terms of any profound conceptual dilemmas, but as something that can be ironed out and rationalized, for example, by identity-management practices. Thus an important UK report on public services laments the welter of departmental identification processes and numbers and urges the standardization of identity management, so that

> [c]itizens should reasonably expect that government should be able to easily connect to who they are at different points in service delivery. ... This can be delivered by better identity management, establishing a 'single source of truth' and be made more robust through the introduction of identity cards.[30]

This might be a governmental 'take' on Goffman's idea of 'identity pegs'.

A more detailed example of this emphasis on the facticity of identity can be found in the UK's Identity Cards Act 2006, which illustrates the construction of an identity through many pieces of information about a person, stored in a National Identity Register, each of which ostensibly contributes to the formation of a profile. Section 1(5) of the Act provides for the establishment of a record of 'registrable facts' about every person in the country. These are:

  (a) his identity;
  (b) the address of his principal place of residence in the United Kingdom;
  (c) the address of every other place in the United Kingdom or elsewhere where he has a place of residence;

---

[30] HM Treasury (2006): 39-40

(d) where in the United Kingdom and elsewhere he has previously been resident;

(e) the times at which he was resident at different places in the United Kingdom or elsewhere;

(f) his current residential status;

(g) residential statuses previously held by him;

(h) information about numbers allocated to him for identification purposes and about the documents to which they relate;

(i) information about occasions on which information recorded about him in the Register has been provided to any person; and

(j) information recorded in the Register at his request.

Note that the individual's 'identity' is a registrable fact, defined in Section 1(6) as

(a) his full name;

(b) other names by which he is or has previously been known;

(c) his gender;

(d) his date and place of birth and, if he has died, the date of his death; and

(e) external31 characteristics of his that are capable of being used for identifying him.

Other 'facts' about the person nay be imagined, but they are not considered 'registrable': for example, marital and employment statuses (and details), education, religious affiliation, medical history, and attributes by which the person is both well known and in good company with thousands or millions of others: a longstanding love of ice cream, of Ingmar Bergman films, or of Spanish holidays. These are evidently considered irrelevant to the purposes envisaged for the identity card scheme, yet I – and significant others – may consider that these facts are inherent parts of my identity, and sometimes more important to the way I identify myself, presents myself to the world, and is perceived by that world, than my other names or my facial geometry.

Schedule 1 of the Act further specifies a very long list of other recordable information. It construes these registrable five, plus previous and current residential addresses, as 'personal information', which is separate from 'identifying information' (but, confusingly, not from 'identity', as indicated in Section 1) about an individual, which is now described as

(a) a photograph of his head and shoulders (showing the features of the face);

(b) his signature;

(c) his fingerprints;

(d) other biometric information about him.

By implication, identification, curiously, here has to do with the body, and not with what is otherwise considered 'personal'. Other recordable information mentioned in Schedule 1 has to do with: one's UK residential status; thirteen personal reference numbers on various kinds of document; one's previously recorded details and any changes to those; nine different forms of particulars concerning one's identity card registration as well as its history; a further set of validation information relating to the

---

[31] The Bill that preceded the Act said 'physical'. The Act's Explanatory Notes, no. 19, explains that 'external' means, for example, biometric information.

latter; several kinds of security information; and information about the disclosure of register information to third parties. These total more than fifty pieces of information. Moreover, Section 3(6) gives the Secretary of State the power to modify the Schedule 1 inventory, with parliamentary approval. This may require further primary legislation, because the new information must be consistent with the Act's statutory purposes.

Thus the 'facts' about identity are seen to be those that are so construed through political decision-making processes and thus inscribed in the National Information Register as an administrative surveillance information system by which persons are identified and classified, and with which crucial decisions are to be taken about persons' rights and claims. It is normally very difficult or impossible for us to control the identities that are ascribed to us by the 'factual' categories in which information is collected, stored, and further processed. But note, once again, that the establishment of uniqueness and differentiation through these procedures involves decisions about what categories are to be used in the universal framework, thus pointing up the importance of categorization in identity processes. The 'facts' of identity are intended to establish the uniqueness of the individual, but we may observe that uniqueness is only one dimension of what we consider our identity. I may identify myself as a member of a very large number of groups, categories, collectivities, and so on, and these help to form my 'identity', however unique I may be.

4 'Identity' in Public Services

The public services, and so-called 'e-government', are important sites for observing the way identities and identification processes enter into daily life, and are managed. In many countries, public services are increasingly being provided within a 'citizen-focused' or 'citizen-centric' policy framework. It aims to abandon an impersonal mode of service provision that is held to have characterized a patronizing post-war welfare state, and to move towards a mode that tailors services to citizens and takes their views and needs into account. There is a mixture of individuation and classification or categorization in these e-government initiatives that prompts further discussion about the way persons are identified for services. In passing, we may note that 'services' are of different kinds. They include those that provide benefits, while others involve the application of sanctions and controls. Each of these types can apply universally to all, or they can be targeted on certain groups, categories, or persons. Some services are preventative, while others are remedial. This gives several somewhat different contexts in which identification may be required, and which are therefore different 'ecologies' for information and organisational systems and their effects.

These distinctions will not be developed here in any detail; they feature in other work[32]. But they indicate that we should perhaps explore the differences between what is needed for identification in different administrative settings, and how the identity management systems can be tailored to these different requirements, where the risks and consequences of misidentification vary. This is because the sharing of data on citizens in each of these settings features different patterns of opportunity for consent, objection, mandatory requirement, and so on, shaped by the legislation and the administrative or professional practices involved in each of these types: for instance, as regards information systems involved in the control of offenders, as contrasted with those involved in providing care for caring for unemployed single parents. Or shaped by whether the requirement is the predictive identification of those likely to commit certain offences, as contrasted with the predictive identification of those likely to become unemployed with dependent children.

The drive towards citizen-focused government is built upon ancient characteristics of bureaucracies, and include novel developments of technical systems for locating, identifying and recording individuals and for authenticating their claims. New information technologies are seen as the key to the prospect of personalising the claims and rights of citizenship or membership in a political community. The point is put in the following extract relating to this policy from a United Kingdom (UK) website[33]:

> Government is delivering services in a way and at a time that suits the needs of each person. ...Individualising public services delivery is not a new idea, but one that is slowly becoming a reality, thanks to technology. Monolithic, 'one size fits all' government is fast becoming obsolete. ...
>
> With technology everyone, in the eyes of the government at least, is equal. With technology your geographic location, your economic and social status, whether you are disabled, homeless, working nights, rich or poor, all that in theory, becomes irrelevant. ...
>
> Personalising citizen services goes beyond convenience. We can use them to confront the problems of inequality, an aging population, greater competition and global security with ideas, innovation and opportunity.

This is not an appropriate place to debate or rebut the premises or conclusions of citizen-centric government in its electronic version. There are certainly creditable social-policy ideals in this departure. Personalising services may be a considerable improvement in governmental provision, and may be a way of addressing deep-rooted problems of inequality and disadvantage. But it is important to note what is left out of consideration in such a statement, or what is rebuttable in the egalitarian premise about technology.

---

[32] By Perri 6, Christine Bellamy and the author in writing related to a completed ESRC-funded research project on 'Joined-up Public Services: Data-sharing and Privacy in Multi-agency Working', Grant No. RES/000/23/0158.

[33] http://www.govx.org.uk/communities/spaces/citizenservice/; accessed 15/4/07; the quoted item was created 25/8/06, and is hosted by GovXChange – A SOCITM Information Age Group (SIAM) Initiative. SOCITM is the Society of Information Technology Management, which relates to local government and the public sector in the UK.

5 Privacy and 'Personal Data': The Case of RFID

Here, another concept enters the picture: privacy. The very means of personalization, and therefore the crucial means and infrastructures for implementing citizen-centric policy, poses a potential danger to privacy that has consequences wider than the infringement of privacy itself, alongside the benefits that personalization, and indeed, certain kinds of surveillance, may bring to individuals and to state systems.

The statement quoted immediately above gives no indication that governments, which are often politically, legally and morally committed to protect citizens' privacy, including information privacy, have been grappling with the question of protection in their plans for personalized, proactive service provision for many years,[34] and that answers have been difficult to give and to enshrine in policy that would reconcile the tension between conflicting objectives. Yet it must also be said that the momentum of public-service policy, including perhaps especially the law-enforcement and sanctioning side, makes it tempting for governments to underplay or to ignore their privacy commitments and to seek to maximize, rather than to limit, the utilization of personal information and the surveillance techniques through which much of these data are gathered.

But 'privacy' itself is a further ambiguous concept, as is evident through several decades or more of scholarly debate, policy-making and legal rulings. There are many 'takes' on 'privacy', which are too well known to require elaboration here; they will be touched on again later. Conflicts over identity and identification are, in part, conflicts over the extent to which privacy should be respected. But what is protected or invaded when privacy is protected or invaded cannot be taken for granted, whether in one legal jurisdiction or across many jurisdictions. This has a bearing on critical approaches to surveillance and to several kinds of practical measures: for example, to make technologies 'privacy friendly', to provide privacy statements for online consumers, to avoid the use of personal details of individuals where possible by providing the means for anonymisation when it is only necessary to verify entitlement, and to assess the impact of new developments on privacy.

This brings us a little closer to the question of the characteristics that are thought to constitute our personal data. What, in fact, counts as 'personal data', and how the definition of this can be inscribed in legislation and therefore reflected in information processing, has been a matter of come uncertainty for a few years, at least in the United Kingdom but also within the European Union more generally.[35]

Radio frequency identification (RFID) is one development in which we can see how the definition of 'personal data' matters. A good source for this is the debate in and around the European Union's Article 29 Working Party, which was established under the Data Protection Directive 95/46/EC; illustrative quotations from its 2005 'Working document on data protection issues related to RFID technology' will be given at some length.[36] It argued that, depending upon the particular application in

---

[34] See for example, Cabinet Office (Performance and Innovation Unit) (2002).
[35] This is discussed further in Raab (2005).
[36] Article 29 Data Protection Working Party (2005a).

which RFID technology is used, personal data may or may not be involved; and if it is not, then the Directive does not apply. The Working Party said:

> In assessing whether the collection of personal data through a specific application of RFID is covered by the data protection Directive, we must determine (a) the extent to which the data processed relates to an individual and, (b) whether such data concerns an individual who is identifiable or identified. Data relates to an individual if it refers to the identity, characteristics or behaviour of an individual or if such information is used to determine or influence the way in which that person is treated or evaluated. In assessing whether information concerns an identifiable person, one must apply Recital 26 of the data protection Directive which establishes that 'account should be taken of all the means likely reasonably to be used either by the controller or by any other person to identify the said person'. (paragraph 4.1; original emphases removed)

Recital 26 will be mentioned again at a later point. But we can see that the question turns on the definition of 'personal data', and those who are eager to implement RFID technology, and those who are hostile to it, have each pressed for the kind of interpretation that would support their position. Following a period of consultation, the Working Party issued another paper that briefly reported on the consultation results, and that pointed out the clash in opinion over the definition of 'personal data' as between – broadly speaking – the IT industry and retailers, on the one hand, and universities, consumers and think tanks, on the other.[37]

More recently, the debate has been taken further within the European Union by means of a new paper produced by the Article 29 Working Party.[38] The Working Party's 'Opinion 4/2007 on the concept of personal data', adopted on 20 June 2007, aimed to resolve uncertainty among the diverse practices of EU Member States in which 'personal data' had different meanings, and to elaborate and justify a definition. They said that the definition of the concept had a deep impact on matters to do with identity management and RFID, and their paper argued for a wider definition in keeping with the Directive; by implication, not one that would favour industry. The Working Party put forward three alternative criteria for judging whether data 'relate' to an individual, as follows:

> …in order to consider that the data 'relate' to an individual, a 'content element OR a 'purpose' element OR a 'result' element should be present. The 'content' element is present in those cases where…information is given about a particular person, regardless of any purpose on the side of the data controller or of a third party, or the impact of that information on the data subject. …For example, the results of medical analysis clearly relate to the patient, or the information contained in a company's folder under the name of a certain client clearly relates to him. Or the information contained in a RFID tag or a bar code incorporated in an identity document of a certain individual relates to that person, as in future passports with a RFID chip. …That 'purpose' element can

---

[37] Article 29 Data Protection Working Party (2005b).
[38] Article 29 Data Protection Working Party (2007).

be considered to exist when the data are used or are likely to be used...with the purpose to evaluate, treat in a certain way or influence the status or behaviour of an individual. (p. 10; original emphasis removed)

...when a 'result' element is present. ...data can be considered to 'relate' to an individual because their use is likely to have an impact on a certain person's rights and interests. ... it is not necessary that the potential result be a major impact. It is sufficient if the individual may be treated differently from other persons as a result of the processing of such data. (p.11; original emphasis removed)

The Working Party then went on to clarify what it means for someone to be identified or identifiable, with regard to what the Directive said about this. They wrote:

...a natural person can be considered as 'identified' when, within a group of persons, he or she is 'distinguished' from all other members of the group. Accordingly, the natural person is 'identifiable' when, although the person has not been identified yet, it is possible to do it....Identification is normally achieved through particular pieces of information which we may call 'identifiers' and which hold a particularly privileged and close relationship with the particular individual. Examples are outward signs of the appearance..., like height, hair colour, clothing, etc... or a quality...which cannot be immediately perceived, like a profession, a function, a name etc. (p.12; original emphasis removed)

They went on to distinguish direct and indirect ways of identification. Direct identification typically involves a name, but perhaps with other corroborating direct information to distinguish a specific individual. Indirect identification relies on 'unique combinations' that may involve categories, such as age or regional origin. But the distinction between identifying someone and their identifiability is particularly interesting, because it illustrates the social, economic, policy and other processes that provide the context for this, and not merely the technical infrastructures. Let us recall that the Directive, in Recital 26, said that identifiability relates to 'all the means likely reasonably to be used either by the controller or by any other person to identify the said person'. Thus the Working Party said of this criterion:

This means that a mere hypothetical possibility to single out the individual is not enough to consider the person as 'identifiable'. If...that possibility does not exist or is negligible, the person should not be considered as 'identifiable', and the information would not be considered as 'personal data'. The criterion...should in particular take into account all the factors at stake. The cost of conducting identification is one factor.... The intended purpose, the way the processing is structured, the advantage expected by the controller, the interests at stake for the individuals, as well as the risk of organisational dysfunctions (e.g. breaches of confidentiality duties) and technical failures should all be taken into account. ...[T]his test is a dynamic one and should consider the state of the art in technology at the time of the processing and the possibilities for development during the period for which the data will be processed. Identification may not be possible today with all the means likely reasonably to be used today. …However, i[f] they are intended to be kept for 10 years, the controller should consider the possibility of identification that may occur also in the ninth year of their lifetime, and which may make them personal data at that moment. The system should be able to adapt to these developments as they happen, and to incorporate then the appropriate technical and organisational measures in due course. (p. 15; original emphases removed)

The reason that this rich example has been dwelt upon in this paper is that it points up the effect that the decisions taken by those who use information about identities or who design and implement information systems in social, business and government organisations has upon the construction of a definition, such that it comes within or remains outside the scope of the law. This is important in any attempt to understand the politics of personal identity; we need to know more about the way these decisions are taken, what the patterns of interests and pressures may be that influence the decisions, what the discourses are amongst decision-makers, and whether there are likely to be sufficient safeguards surrounding the identification of individuals, in view of the potential harms that may result. On the other hand, many would say that the question of harm from identification should not be pre-judged; or, in a related way, that surveillance, which is very closely connected with the identification and identifiability of persons, should not be seen only in negative terms.

6   Conclusion: The 'Public Interest' and Privacy

Finally, a further controversial and ambiguous concept comes into play in these circumstances in which information systems are involved in identifications: the 'public interest', which can be juxtaposed to 'privacy'. The concept of 'public interest' is increasingly invoked as part of the legitimizing justification for information systems, technologies and processes that form the infrastructure for citizen-centric government. The public interest is said to be served by more efficient and effective provision of public services, including the sanctions side of public services – for example, anti-fraud operations – through the intensive and extensive use of databases of personal information and by improved methods of identity management. It is also invoked in certain situations where public protection is thought to override the concealment of identity, as in cases where the geographical location of pedophiles is concerned. We also find a variation of it, in the form of 'public safety' or 'security', especially in contexts where national borders, immigration, terrorism and the like are the subject of policy-making. Identity cards are at the forefront of these safety and security contexts. The old (and discredited) slogan, 'if you have nothing to hide, you have nothing to fear', is often deployed and applied not only to information about persons, but about their very identity; anonymity is said to be the shield for untrustworthy or criminal elements in society, against whom the public interest lies in revealing who they are and what they are.

The problem with counterposing a value like the 'public interest' against privacy and anonymity is that, in the current political climate across many countries, it too easily becomes the trump card over those competing values. In situations of conflict, this arises when policy-makers argue that there should be a 'balance' struck between different values or purposes involving information collection and processing, including information about identities. Whether there really is a conflict, and whether it is best stated as a conflict between privacy and the public interest, depends on how we understand the concept of 'privacy'. Exploring this would take us too far afield here, but it is certainly high on an agenda for theoretical development in this field, for it has not yet been sufficiently addressed in theory or in policy discourse. It turns on whether privacy is only a matter concerning individual rights and claims, or whether the beneficiaries of privacy protection are societies as a whole, and indeed the 'public interest', and not just the individual citizen or customer. The social values of privacy, and its value to the maintenance of democratic political communities, have been recognized by many writers39, but have been largely ignored in policy discourse, and in much of the discourse on rights as well. It may well be that we are dealing with two competing conceptions of the public interest, and not a contest between the claims of the individual and the claims of society. That puts it at the forefront of political theory and the study of public policy. This issue, and the other ones reviewed in this paper, resonate with long-standing debates about human life, citizenship, and the state; these are, indeed, very big subjects.

References

1. Agre, P. (1997) 'The Architecture of Identity: Embedding Privacy in Market Institutions', Information, Communication and Society, 2,1: 1-25.
2. Article 29 Working Party (2005a) Working Document on Data Protection Issues Related to RFID Technology, WP 105, January 19, 2005, 10107/05/EN, available at: http://ec.europa.eu/justice_home/fsj/privacy/docs/wpdocs/2005/wp105_en.pdf, accessed 27 November 2007.
3. Article 29 Working Party (2005b) Results of the Public Consultation on Article 29 Working Document 105 on Data Protection Issues Related to RFID Technology, WP 111, 28 September 2005, 1670/05/EN, available at: http://ec.europa.eu/justice_home/ fsj/privacy/docs/wpdocs/2005/wp111_en.pdf, accessed 27 November 2007.
4. Article 29 Working Party (2007) Opinion 4/2007 on the Concept of Personal Data, WP 136, 20th June 2007, 01248/07/EN, available at: http://ec.europa.eu/justice_home/fsj privacy/docs/wpdocs/2007/wp136_en.pdf, accessed 27 November 2007.
5. Bauman, Z. (2004) Identity: Conversations with Benedetto Vecchi, Cambridge: Polity Press.
6. Bennett, C. and Raab, C. (2006) The Governance of Privacy: Policy Instruments in Global Perspective, 2nd edn., Cambridge, MA: MIT Press.
7. Cabinet Office (Performance and Innovation Unit) (2002) Privacy and Data-Sharing: The Way Forward for Public Services, available at: http://www.cabinetoffice.gov.uk/ upload/assets/www.cabinetoffice.gov.uk/strategy/piu-data.pdf, accessed 27 November 2007.
8. Cohen, A. (1994) Self Consciousness: An Alternative Anthropology of Identity, London: Routledge.

---

39 E.g., Westin (1967); Schoeman (1992); Regan (1995); Bennett and Raab (2006).

9. Goffman, E. (1959) The Presentation of Self in Everyday Life, New York, NY: Doubleday Anchor.
10. Goffman, E. (1961) Asylums: Essays on the Social Situation of Mental Patients and Other Inmates, New York, NY: Doubleday Anchor.
11. Goffman, E. (1968) [1963] Stigma: Notes on the Management of Spoiled Identity, Englewood Cliffs, NJ: Prentice-Hall.
12. Hekman, S. (2004) Private Selves, Public Identities: Reconsidering Identity Politics, University Park, PA: Penn State University Press.
13. HM Treasury (2006) Service Transformation: a Better Service For Citizens and Businesses, a Better Deal for Taxpayers (Review by Sir David Varney), available at: http://www.hm-treasury.gov.uk/media/4/F/pbr06_varney_review.pdf, accessed 27 November 2007.
14. Jenkins, R. (2004) Social Identity, 2nd edn., London: Routledge.
15. Lukes, S. (1974) Power: A Radical View, London: Macmillan.
16. Olson, E. (2007) 'Personal Identity', in Zalta, S. (ed.), The Stanford Encyclopedia of Philosophy (Spring 2007 Edition), available at: http://plato.stanford.edu/archives/spr2007/entries/identity-personal; accessed 27 November 2007.
17. Raab, C. (2005) 'Perspectives on "Personal Identity"', BT Technology Journal, 23, 4: 15-24.
18. Raab, C. (2008, forthcoming) 'Identity: Difference and Categorization', in Kerr, I., Lucock, C. and Steeves, V. (eds.), On the Identity Trail: Privacy, Anonymity and Identity in a Networked Society.
19. Regan, P. (1995) Legislating Privacy: Technology, Social Values and Public Policy, Chapel Hill, NC: University of North Carolina Press.
20. Schoeman, F. (1992) Privacy and Social Freedom, Cambridge: Cambridge University Press.
21. Simon, B. (2004) Identity in Modern Society: A Social Psychological Perspective, Oxford: Blackwell.
22. Turner, J. (2004) 'Foreword', in Simon, B. (2004) Identity in Modern Society: A Social Psychological Perspective, Oxford: Blackwell.
23. Westin, A. (1967) Privacy and Freedom, New York, NY: Atheneum.

Workshop: Privacy Exploits

A Forensic Framework for Tracing Phishers

Sebastian Gajek[1] and Ahmad-Reza Sadeghi[2]

Horst Görtz Institute for IT-Security
Ruhr University Bochum, Germany
sebastian.gajek@nds.rub.de[1], sadeghi@crypto.rub.de[2]

Abstract. Identity theft – in particular through phishing – has become a major threat to privacy and a valuable means for (organized) cyber-crime. In this paper, we propose a forensic framework that allows for profiling and tracing of the agents involved in phishing networks. The key idea is to apply phishing methods against phishing agents. In order to profile and trace phishers, their databases are filled with fingerprinted credentials (indistinguishable from real ones) whose deployment lures phishers to a fake system that simulates the original service.

1 Introduction

With the advent of the Internet and the continuous growth of electronic commerce, offering new commercial prospects and opportunities, criminals have also discovered the Internet as a ground for illicit business. Cybercrime has entered the digital world and prospered to a severe concern for Internet users. Digital crimes appears in many variations, however, online fraud has proliferated recently and become a major threat. A prominent method of fraud is phishing where, e.g., Internet users are lured to faked web sites and tricked to disclose sensitive credentials such as credit card numbers and passwords. The attacker steals these credentials in order to gain access to users' accounts and services. Federal law enforcement link organized crime to phishing attacks that involve various actors a part of a highly professional criminal network, and that deploy methods similar to those of money laundering. There is not much publicly known about these criminal networks, however, their impact is noticeable.

Phishing has grown to a lucrative criminal business model. A report issued by the Gartner Group [10] totals financial losses to $2.8 billion in 2006 whereas in previous studies Gartner approximated total losses to $1 billion [9, 10]. In comparison to identity theft in real world, phishing attacks are cheap and the potential gains are huge. A standard approach to counter phishing attacks apart from user education is to incriminate and isolate rogue (phishing) servers [13]. In general, the hosting provider is contacted and asked for taking down the site. As most rogue servers are hosted in foreign countries, it is time-consuming to make on-site forensic analysis, and to initiate criminal prosecution. Specifically, different international regulations delay rapid shutdowns, giving phishers enough time to steal vast numbers of identities. Thwarting phishing attacks has become a game of one-upmanship. That is, when a rogue site is taken down, phishers

Please use the following format when citing this chapter:

Gajek, S. and Sadeghi, A.-R., 2008, in IFIP International Federation for Information Processing, Volume 262; The Future of Identity in the Information Society; Simone Fischer-Hübner, Penny Duquenoy, Albin Zuccato, Leonardo Martucci; (Boston: Springer), pp. 23–35.

move to another server. The introduction of countermeasures on client side such as blacklisting phishing mails [7] or improved user authentication schemes have failed to alleviate the threat. Phishers modified the attack vector when new measures have been applied, using a large portfolio of social engineering techniques, mounting and illusion attacks (cf. [1]). Hence, a general belief is that efficiency of countermeasures may be measured in terms of increased costs and risks to mount the attack.

In this paper, we present and discuss aspects of applying methods of phishing against the agents involved in phishing attacks. We propose a forensic framework and discuss the related forensic information sources that can support investigators and service providers to pro-actively fight phishing by identifying and tracing the involved actors. The key idea is to fill phishers' credential databases with fingerprinted credentials (dubbed *phoneytokens*). Upon using phoneytokens, phishers are lured to a fake system (dubbed *phoneypot*). The phoneypot simulates the original service in order to profile phishers' behavior. This approach deters criminals from harvesting valid credentials and increases the risks to track phishers. Moreover, our proposal has much broader coverage since it makes first steps towards the design and realization of an architecture that is interoperable to commodity web applications.

The remainder sections are oganized as follows. Section 2 summarizes the basic idea. Section 3 discusses related work and Scction 4 presents an idea for a concrete solution. Section 5 discusses the aggregation of profiles. Section 6 puts into perspective measures which phishers could use to thwart our approach. Finally, Section 7 concludes the paper.

2   Preliminaries

2.1   Model

The main goal of phishing attacks is to gain access to financial assets through identity theft. For this purpose, phishers make use of spoofing attacks to trick users into disclosing their credentials. Phishers use the stolen credentials to impersonate users, and deploy strategies similar to those of money laundering in order to transfer the (electronic) financial assets to the real world. Phishing generally involves several collaborating agents as illustrated in Fig. 2.1.

Assume a customer U uses a credential A to get access to service S (step 1). S may be a financial institute (e.g., a bank) that allows U to make money transfers to other accounts (step 2). We define the following agents in a phishing attack.[1]: *Mounting attack agents* provide the technology required to lure Internet users to collection servers (e.g., by impersonating the bank in spam emails that contain links to a fake website). *Hosting attack agents* provide the technology for tricking Internet users to disclose their private information (e.g., by designing phishing sites or implementing malware). One main task of hosting attack agents is to hijack vulnerable web servers and turn them into *collection servers* that store the

---

[1]Note that in some instances, one actor may play several roles.

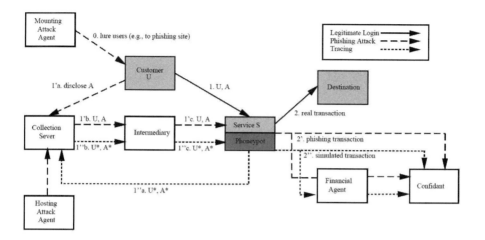

Fig. 1. Tracing the Agents of Phishing

stolen credentials of deceived users. Assuming U has been fooled by the mounting attack agent, and has disclosed credential A, then A is stored in the collection server (step 1'a). The stolen credential is then forwarded to an *intermediary* who is responsible for exchanging or moving financial assets through various entities in order to conceal their true origin and owner (step 1'b). For instance, the intermediary performs transactions on behalf of deceived customers (step 1'c). Transactions are made either to foreign accounts or to *financial agents* whose aim is to hide the illicit origin (step 2'). This is also known as *money layering*. Finally, *confidants* arrange the withdrawal of the money at the transaction's destination.

2.2   Basic Idea of our Approach

The objective of our approach is to deter phishing attacks by enabling the tracing of phishing agents and their associated criminal network, as well as to increase the cost and risks of phishing attacks. We concentrate on collecting information on intermediaries and financial agents that can then be provided to law enforcement for criminal prosecution. By feeding false credentials to phishers' collection server we increase the cost of the attack in two ways. First, the fact that their databases are filled with fake credentials means that phishers have to spend more time and resources in order to get some financial benefit; and second, the risk of a phishing attack is increased due to the tracing capabilities of our scheme.

The basic idea of fingerprinting credentials is analogous to using the serial numbers of bank notes or any other fingerprint to trace the circulation of money. We feed fingerprinted credentials which we call *phoneytokens* (*"phishing honeytokens"*), to the collection servers. A Phoneytoken is the application of honeytoken [18] to phishing, and represents some data that looks like a valid credential to the phisher, but is traced. To instantiate the phoneytoken approach, one has to detect active collection servers. This can be done by today's known methods such as bounces of phishing mails, alerts of phishing report networks[2], or reverse-engineering of phishing malware. After having sent different phoneytokens to the collection server, one can initiate the server's shutdown (as it is currently practiced). Alternatively, service providers such as financial institutes, may equip customers with phoneytoken credentials to be used when they detect a fake service. For user convenience, service providers may extend anti-phishing toolbars used to warn users when they are visiting a phishing site to submit phoneytokens.

Once we have identified a rogue web site used for phishing, we proceed as follows (see Fig. 2.1): We send phoneytokens to that site and thus insert a set of fake credentials at the collection server. We denote a fake credential with A^* (step 1"a). When the phisher—or more precisely the intermediary—harvests the credentials (step 1"b) and at some stage reuses A^* to get access to our service on behalf of a fake user U^* (step 1"c), we can distinguish U^* from a legitimate customer U and identify U^* as phisher. We then trap the phisher to a virtual system. We call the virtual system a *phoneypot* (*"phishing honeypot"*). The phoneypot simulates the original system and cherishes the illusion that phishers perform valid transactions on a real account; in fact, the phoneypot collects information about phishers' networking, browsing and service-specific behavior. Technically speaking, a phoneypot adapts the notion of honeypots to the problem of phishing; the data collected consists then of attributes typical for a certain intermediary. When the itermediary performs a transaction, the phoneypot simulates the service (step 2") in order for tracing the involved criminal network.

Based on the collected characteristics (see Section 5), we derive three classes of phishing profiles, namely, the *non-phisher*, the *definite phisher*, and the *potential phisher*. The non-phisher profile characterizes an honest user who legitimately authenticates to the service and accesses the real system. The definite phisher is unambiguously identified as an adversary according to the use of phoneytokens and is relayed to the phoneypot. The potential phisher is assumed to be an adversary according to some similarity to a definite phisher. Depending on the degree of similarity, the potential phisher is either relayed to the phoneypot or we delay the transaction and request for authorization (e.g., we call the account owner to confirm that transaction).

2.3   Assumptions

The primary difficulty in our approach is how accurately the phoneypot learns profile patterns. This ultimately affects the accuracy of the phoneypot framework both in terms of whether a non-phisher is flagged (false positive) and whether a phisher will be missed (false negative). In order to reduce false detections, we

---

[2]e.g., http://www.phishreport.net/

assume that some profiles have specific low-biased attributes that we apply to train the phoneypot:

1. The identification of definite phishers is accurate due to the use of phoneytokens. This enables us to use alternative fingerprinting techniques that enlarge the traceability of potential phishers.
2. Non-phishers are conservative regarding the use (and change) of security critical services. For instance, Internet consumers use banking services at a certain time of day and from a certain location. We get a false detection of a non-phisher, if the user changes usual behavior (e.g., requesting access to a service from abroad). However, we expect this behavior to rarely happen.
3. As with real-world organized crime, phishers change their strategy when the costs and risks of attacks increase; otherwise they keep and maintain the techniques and actors. Especially potential phishers address same intermediaries and financial agents since the number of agents is limited.

3   Related Work

Chandrasekaran *et al.* [5] use fake credentials which are submitted to phishing sites and may be seen as phoneytokens. The authors' key idea is to detect phishing sites according to the response of fake input. In contrast, our approach uses forensic methods to identify the involved actors and already assumes phishing sites to be identified. We use fake credentials in order to observe phishers' behavior.

McRae, McGrew, and Vaughn [11] make use of a "web bug", that is a specific kind of phoneytoken: The authors fill forms with HTML code, rather than filling out a phishing site's form with real or faked credentials. The HTML code will cause a web browser or email client to retrieve additional information in order to render the code. The request allows for forensic analysis. This approach is limited by the assumption that phishers render the HTML code. Most email clients prohibit the download of such code, and sophisticated phishers filter the information filled out. Hence, the use of web bugs may easily be foiled. We use phoneytokens that are indistinguishable to real credentials in order to avoid being detected by phishers.

The authors of the honeynet project [20] report on experiences with hosting a honeypot attacked by phishers. The goal of this project was to learn the strategies phishers deploy to mount a phishing attack. The project uses the standard definition of honeypots which is to deposit a "weak" system and wait until an intruder is attracted. This approach collects forensic information on techniques used by phishers and is aimed for thwarting on the technical part of phishing (e.g., setting up phishing sites, sending spam emails, controlling spam botnets). Our approach is different. We collect forensic information in order to trace the usage of stolen (and fingerprinted) credentials. By contrast, we are interested in tracing the phisher's agents and not in the technical means used by phishers.

Some financial institutes do fraud auditing which is closely related to our approach (see, e.g., [6]). However, fraud auditing is in general a post hoc method, i.e., after fraud has occurred investigations are initiated. Our approach is proactive. It helps to expose criminals without apriori knowledge of malicious activities. Further, our approach bears no financial risks, i.e., no customer becomes a victim of fraud. Hence, the presented approach may be used to complement existing fraud auditing mechanisms.

4   Framework

Fig. 2 illustrates our proposed framework in conjunction with a real system. The framework comprises two main components: The phoneypot that simulates the real system to infer phishing profiles and a phoneytoken machine that generates and distributes phoneytokens.

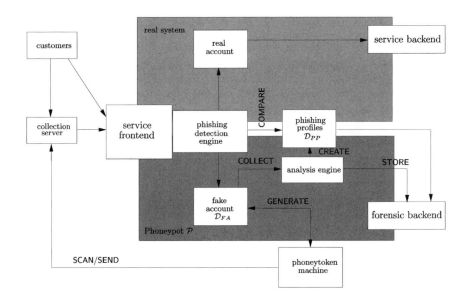

Fig. 2. The Architecture of a Phoneypot

4.1   Phoneytoken Machine

The interfaces SCAN, GENERATE and SEND constitute the phoneytoken machine. We use SCAN to analyze and extract the attributes required to fill a collection server with phoneytokens. We apply web crawling and form scanning techniques to extract attributes from phishing sites (e.g., [14]); in case of modern web technologies (e.g., Flash) or malware, an analyst has to manually look for the attributes. Typically, the attributes requested are email address, username, password and some service specific credentials, such as credit card number, PIN and

TAN or social number. Let $\mathcal{C}$ be the set of attributes requested by a collection server denoted by the address URL, then SCAN generates a new table in fake account database $\mathcal{D}_{FA} := (URL, \mathcal{C})$. We use GENERATE to create values for a fake account which ordinary users would normally submit (to a collection server). The phisher is unable to distinguish between user and machine-generated values. We call the entry of $\mathcal{D}_{FA}$ a *phoneytoken* $\mathcal{T}$ where $c_1, c_2, ..., c_n \in \mathcal{C}$ are the n attributes requested by a collection server URL.

In GENERATE we create random values of dictionaries or public lists for alphanumerical values, such as names, streets, cities. For (sufficiently long and randomly looking) numerical values, such as PIN, TAN, bank account number, we conceal sequence number and submission date to trace the time until the phisher applies this phoneytoken. The jitter time may be used to determine the submission frequency of phoneytokens. If f_k is a function that conceals the sequence number seq and the date of submission $date$, and k a secret key linked to a certain phoneytoken, then numerical values are calculated as concatenation of $date$ and seq. For example, let TAN be an integer, then $TAN = f_k(date\|seq)$. There are many possibilities to instantiate the function f (see e.g., [12]). The secret k also authenticates a phoneytoken $\mathcal{T}$. This prevents a phisher from creating a phoneytoken $\mathcal{T}^*$ and using $\mathcal{T}^*$ to fool the forensics. A further effect is that we do not have to store more information in a database where, e.g., only username and password pairs are queried in order to detect a phoney user. GENERATE also creates additional entries for each phoneytoken $\mathcal{T}$ that are mandatory to build up a fake user account (cf. Section 4.2).

We use SEND to submit the phoneytokens $\mathcal{T}$ to the collection server. The phisher should be unable to notice that $\mathcal{T}$ has not been submitted by phishing victims, as an unusual collection of phoneytokens may raise suspicion. Therefore, we require that SEND emulates the submission behavior of legitimate customers. We meet this requirement by inferring typical behavior profiles from log files of the real system (service frontend) and by sending the phoneytokens from different networks. To the authors' knowledge, service providers that are currently target to phishing attacks, especially financial institutes, have the capabilities to provide the phoneytoken machine with different IP addresses, allowing to send numerous phoneytokens from several addresses.

4.2   Phoneypot

The design goal of the presented architecture is to separate the real web application from the phoneypot. We isolate the phoneypot in order to ensure that our analysis do not negatively impact the original application. This design goal makes our approach appealing for high-performance and security critical applications where modifications to the backend are crucial (e.g., financial institutes). The phoneypot is coupled with a phishing detection engine to the service fontend of the web application. We integrate the phishing detection engine into the login and authentication mechanisms of the web application in order to recognize users logging in using a phoneytoken. The phishing detection engine then redirects this session to the phoneypot. This can be easily achieved with *load-balancing hardware*[3]

The phoneypot needs to exactly replicate the functionality and the look and feel of the real web application; otherwise phishers may raise suspicion. We call this a fake account. This seems at first an involved task, particularly because the modeling of the real web application has to be redone for every application which should be accompanied by a phoneypot. Fortunately, most security critical web applications have only very few interactive and dynamic elements as a result of non-interoperable browsers (e.g., the web application has to be completely renderable without active content). Therefore, most web sites are purely static and can simply be copied to the phoneypot. Requests for dynamic content is to be proxied by the phoneypot, however, with the slight difference that in order to complete the simulation of a fake user account (e.g., account balance, list of last activities) additional data is derived from the fake account database $\mathcal{D}_{FA}$.

For profiling, we log all traffic to and from the phoneypot. We use STORE to pass the data to the *forensic backend* which stores the data in a well documented and secure manner to meet with forensic standards (e.g., as specified by Scientific Working Group on Digital Evidence (SWGDE)[4]). Also, all components involved in evidence preservation must be thoroughly audited by independent parties.

5   Phishing Profiles

5.1   Data Collection

We use the interface COLLECT to collect information on phishers. This information is passed to the *analysis engine*, where we infer profiles of phishers. The profiles are stored in the *phishing profile database* $\mathcal{D}_{PP}$, using CREATE. To build our profiling information, we terminate the communication between the phisher and the phoneypot. We then have access to various link and application characteristics provided by ISO/OSI layers that we take into account to build phishing profiles. We apply standard passive fingerprinting techniques [21, 3, 17, 8]; we do not use active fingerprinting techniques to avoid being detected by phishers. Then we may fingerprint the phisher's geolocation, operating system, browsing application and user behavior.

In addition, we have access to characteristics provided by the service. Whenever a user—be it a phisher or be it an honest costumer—makes use of the service (e.g., make a donation), one can profile that behavior. As phishers prefer services that are appealing to clean digital goods into real funds, such as online-banking or auctions, we gain information dealing with aspects of money laundering (see e.g., [4]). For instance, in case of online banking, one can intercept the account

---

[3]Load balancers spread work between many computers, processes, hard disks or other resources in order to get optimal resource utilization and decrease computing time. The phishing detection engine instructs the load-balancer to transfer the session to the phoneypot.

[4]http://ncfs.org/swgde/index.html

number, amount due, the date and the recipient of an illicit transaction, where in case of online auctions, one can collect information about goods purchased or sold, contacted persons and messages exchanged using the internal instant messaging functionality, or the methods used to pay for the auction.

5.2 Profile Aggregation

In order to build a phishing profile, we need to find the distinguishing characteristics that allow us to distinguish a normal user from a phisher. Let $\mathcal{P}$ be the set of attributes stored in the phishing profile database $\mathcal{D}_{PP}$ that identifies known phishers. $\mathcal{P}$ includes both transaction information (e.g., destination accounts of financial agents and confidants), as well as network and application information.

Let $\mathcal{A}$ be the set of attributes that we infer on the customer U—be it a phisher or a legitimate user—who accesses the service S, and let $\Pi_i \in \mathcal{A}$ be a certain characteristic, then we use a simple rule as follows in order to instantiate the COMPARE function:

if U uses a phoneytoken $\mathcal{T}$, or if the remaining attributes $\mathcal{A} \setminus \{\mathcal{T}\}$ match the attributes $\mathcal{P}$ of one of the profiles, then we say U is a definite phisher.

As a phoneytoken is constructed such that $\mathcal{T}$ is indistinguishable from a real token, we can be sure that we unambiguously expose a phisher. Hence, the rule can be used to collect viable profile information on the phisher. This allows us to use supervised methods to infer profiles of potential phishers. Supervised methods are those where attributes of both definite and potentials phishers are present. Several techniques have been proposed in the literature for the construction of user profiles in different applications, such as intrusion detection, credit card fraud, telecommunications fraud based on statistical modeling like rule discovery, clustering, Bayesian rules, neuronal network classification, etc. (see e.g., [6] for an overview).

Similarly, we have a profile of each user U, containing information on her past behavior. If the attributes of the transaction match those of the user profile (e.g., money is transferred to a destination account already known by that user), the transaction is assumed to be legitimate. Note that, if U claims that a given transaction has not been performed by herself, the attributes of that transaction will be added to $\mathcal{D}_{PP}$. This would still leave a gray area of transactions with attributes that neither identify the user as a definite phisher, nor correspond to known behavioral patterns of the owner of the credentials that are being used. We note that, given the high volume of transactions processed by financial institutions, it is very important that the phishing detection engine is efficient in telling apart legitimate from illegitimate transactions.

Let us assume that we use the information collected from a given user U to define the probabilities $\Pr(\Pi_i|U)$ of U performing a transaction with attribute values $\{\Pi_i\}$. Note that these probabilities will vary for each user; for example, a user U_1 who travels often and makes transactions from different locations is much more likely to initiate a transaction from a new location than another user U_2 who has always made transactions from the same computer at her home address.

Analogously, we can define the probabilities $\Pr(\Pi_i|\mathcal{P})$ of how likely a phisher is to perform transactions with attribute values Π_i. For example, let us assume that Π_1 stands for the destination account on a financial transaction. $\Pr(\Pi_1|\mathcal{P})$ will be higher if Π_1 corresponds to a bank operating in a country with regulations that phishers can take advantage of, and which they have consequently used in the past. Based on this information, we can use Bayes' theorem to find the probability of a transaction having been made by the user or by a phisher. Given the probabilities $\Pr(\Pi_i|U)$, and given that the transaction has a set of attributes $\{\Pi_i\}$, we can compute the probability $\Pr(U|\{\Pi_i\})$ of those attributes belonging to a transaction made by U. Similarly, we can compute the probability $\Pr(\mathcal{P}|\{\Pi_i\})$ of those attributes being part of a phishing transaction.

We can thus define a "phishiness" metric σ for determining whether a transaction has been initiated by U or by a phisher impersonating U. Based on ideas from the field of anomaly detection [2, 16], we choose the odds ratio as metric for measuring "phishiness." The odds ratio is computed as:

$$\sigma = \frac{\Pr(\mathcal{P}|\{\Pi_i\})(1 - \Pr(U|\{\Pi_i\}))}{\Pr(U|\{\Pi_i\})(1 - \Pr(\mathcal{P}|\{\Pi_i\}))}$$

If $\sigma > 1$, that means that it is more likely that the transaction was made by a phisher than by the user. Conversely, if $\sigma < 1$, then the transaction is likely to have been initiated by the user U. The rationality behind odds ratio is that it is fast to compute (i.e., it does not require expensive computations and can therefore be used in a context where high throughput is required) and takes into account both the (independently derived) profile information of the phisher and of the credential owner. Especially taking into account attributes of the real credential owner allows to reduce false positives. These attributes are uncorrelated with the phisher's behavior and may reliably be inferred from past sign ons.

6   Security Considerations

We are aware that phishers are not completely defenseless against phoneytokens and phoneypots. In the following, we discuss the measures that phishers may apply to foil our approach.

6.1   Strategies to Counter Phoneytokens

Let us assume the phisher is aware that his credential server may be filled with phoneytokens. We see two ways he might strike back:

First, the phisher might analyze the network traffic, identify the phoneytoken machine (using methods, we discussed in Section 5), and launch a denial-of-service attack. However, this countermeasure can be prevented by using adequate anti-flooding mechanisms (e.g., [15]) to protect the phoneytoken machine or by simply changing the machine's IP address.

Second, the phisher might personalize mounting attacks. These attacks are called *context aware phishing* [19]. The attacks have in common that they are unique and address individuals, i.e., context aware phishing is tailored to attack a certain user. For instance, the phisher could encrypt a pattern, consisting of the recipient's email address and the time, and use the cryptogram as nonce in a phishing mail. In order to feed the phishing collection server with sufficient phoneytokens, we would have to collect numerous phishing mails (since the mails are fingerprinted). This is not crucial. As mentioned before, many phishing report networks and warehouses exist that might help us to collect a vast number of fingerprinted phishing mails.

6.2   Strategies to Detect Phoneypots

In our model, we assume that phishers know the existence of phoneypots and try to detect and avoid them. A countermeasure for a phisher would be to first test for phoneypot presence, we call the *phoneypot oracle attack*. The phisher queries the phoneypot and observes each interaction with the system to extract hidden data or implementation details. The test may be done with the same methods we described in Section 5.1 in order for enabling the phisher to distinguish the real system from the phoneypot. The queries yield no meaningful results (under the assumption that the phoneypot has been correctly implemented) since the phoneypot is hidden behind the same frontend as the real system is. Therefore, the phisher infers indistinguishable characteristics from and is incable of deciding whether he is on the real system or the phoneypot.

A more realistic countermeasure would be to query the phoneypot oracle whether it really provides the real service by observing the outcome. For instance, one strategy would be to initiate a small transaction as a donation to some organization which lists its donators online. The phisher could use this action to verify that a transaction was successful without revealing his identity or the identity of one of his agents. Nevertheless, such a test would mean considerable time and increase the probability that the deceived customer notices the fraud and the bank freezes the account. There might be a good argument for actually allowing the phoneypot to carry out the simulated service requests to the real world. While the service would have to bear the costs, the prospect of luring criminals into extensively usage of the phoneypot which would allow to collect enough data and to catch them more easily, might out-weight the associated costs. Therefore, there should be a way to allow near real-time review of the service requests initiated on the phoneypot by an analyst empowered to approve certain activities.

7   Conclusion

We have introduced an approach to proactively deter phishing-based identity fraud and proposed a forensic framework of luring, trapping and analyzing phishers in order to profile their sources. We have argued how to trace the agents involved in phishing, and identified the measures criminals may employ to thwart our approach. Even with the constraint that the phoneypot is detected in the long run, it will be able to collect considerable amount of information on phishing activity, and thus forces the phishers to commit resources to detecting phoneypots. Based on this, we believe that phishers who detect the use of phoneypot techniques by an organization will avoid its accounts in future.

Currently, we implement the framework and evaluate methods used to conduct meaningful statistical results in order to define phishing profiles and to achieve accurate detection rates. An interesting topic for future work would be to tweak the profiles to detect freeriders. Freeriders are dishonest customers who claim to be a victim of phishing attacks in order to get back the loss from the service provider.

Acknowledgement

We would like to thank Claudia Diaz, Maximillian Dornseif, Dominik Birk and Felix Gröbert for fruitful discussions.

References

1. A. Adelsbach, S. Gajek, and J. Schwenk. Visual Spoofing of SSL Protected Web Sites and Effective Countermeasures. In *Information Security Practice and Experience Conference*, 2005.
2. D. Agarwal. An empirical bayes approach to detect anomalies in dynamic multidimensional arrays. In *ICDM '05: Proceedings of the Fifth IEEE International Conference on Data Mining*, pages 26–33. IEEE Computer Society, 2005.
3. R. Beverly. A robust classifier for passive TCP/IP fingerprinting. In *Passive and Active Network Measurement*, LNCS, pages 158–167, 2004.
4. D. Birk, S. Gajek, F. Gröbert, and A.-R. Sadeghi. Phishing phishers—observing and tracing organized cybercrime. In *ICIMP'07: Proceedings of the Second International Conference on Internet Monitoring and Protection*. IEEE Computer Society, 2007.
5. M. Chandrasekaran, R. Chinchani, and S. Upadhyaya. Phoney: Mimicking user response to detect phishing attacks. *wowmom*, 0:668–672, 2006.
6. T. Fawcett and F. Provost. Fraud detection. In W. Kloesgen and J. Zytkow, editors, *Handbook of Knowledge Discovery and Data Mining*. Oxford University Press, 2002. CeDER Working Paper #IS-99-18, Stern School of Business, New York University, NY, NY 10012.
7. D. Florencio and C. Herley. Stopping a Phishing Attack, Even when the Victims Ignore Warnings. Technical Report MSR-TR-2005-142, Microsoft Research (MSR), 2005.
8. T. Kohno, A. Broido, and K. C. Claffy. Remote physical device fingerprintin. *IEEE Trans. Dependable Sec. Comput*, 2(2):93–108, 2005.
9. A. Litan. Increased Phishing and Online Attacks Cause Dip in Consumer Confidence. Gartner Study, June 2005.

10. A. Litan. Phishing Attacks Leapfrog Despite Attempts to Stop Them. Gartner Study, November 2006.
11. C. M. McRae, R. W. McGrew, and R. B. Vaughn. Honey tokens and web bugs: Developing reactive techniques for investigating phishing scams. *Digital Forensic Practice*, 1(3):193–199, 2006.
12. R. Molva and G. Tsudik. Authentication method with impersonal token cards. In *SP'91: Proceedings of the Symposium on Research in Security and Privacy*, pages 55–65, May 1991.
13. T. Moore and R. Clayton. An empirical analysis of the current state of phishing attack and defence. In *Workshop on the Economics of Information Security*, 2007.
14. M. Najork and A. Heydon. On high-performance web crawling. Technical report, Compaq Systems Research Center, 2001.
15. V. Paxson. An analysis of using reflectors for distributed denial-of-service attacks. *SIGCOMM Comput. Commun. Rev.*, 31(3):38–47, 2001.
16. S. L. Scott. A bayesian paradigm for designing intrusion detection systems. *Computational Statistics & Data Analysis*, 45(1):69–83, 2004.
17. M. Smart, G. R. Malan, and F. Jahanian. Defeating TCP/IP stack fingerprinting. In *USENIX Security Symposium*, 2000.
18. L. Spitzner. Honeytokens: The Other Honeypot, 2003. `http://www.securityfocus.com/infocus/1713`.
19. M. J. T. Jagatic, N. Johnson and F. Menczer. Social phishing, 2007. To appear in Communications of the ACM.
20. The Honeynet Project and Research Alliance. Know your Enemy: Phishing, Identifying remote hosts, without them knowing, 2005. `http://www.honeynet.org/papers/phishing/`.
21. M. Zalewski and W. Stearns. Passive os fingerprinting tool, 2006. `http://lcamtuf.coredump.cx/p0f/README`.

On the Internet, Things Never Go Away Completely

The growing problem of Internet data persistence

Thomas P. Keenan

Faculty of Environmental Design, University of Calgary
2500 University Drive NW Calgary, AB T2N 1N4
Canada
keenan@ucalgary.ca

Abstract. The problem of information "getting into the wrong hands" has existed since the first stored data computer systems. Numerous companies and government departments have been embarrassed by data left on un-erased media such as magnetic tape and discovered by inquiring minds. The advent of data communications brought the problem to a whole new level, since information could be transmitted over long distances to places unknown. The phenomenal rise of the Internet elevated the problem of Internet Data Persistence (IDP) to a public issue, as the "private" emails of public figures such Oliver North and Bill Gates were introduced in court proceedings, and when Delta Airlines fired a flight attendant for her in-uniform blog posting. In a significant way, the digital trail that we leave behind is becoming a new form of "online identity," every bit as real as a passport, driver's license or pin number. New technologies, from virtual worlds, to camera phones to video sharing sites, give the question of "Where Has My Data Gone and How Do I Really Know?" some new and frightening dimensions. Future developments like "signature by DNA biometric" will make the issue even more urgent and more complex. Coping with it will require new policies, technical tools, laws, and ethical standards. It has even been suggested that a whole new profession, sometimes called the "e-scrubber," will arise to assist in tracking down and deleting unwanted online remnants.

1   Introduction

Even casual computer users know that simply deleting a file from their computer may not completely erase the data from the machine's disk system. While the file may become invisible to application programs, data clusters often remain, awaiting reallocation, and open to unauthorized inspection. Increasingly, additional copies of user data are found in slack space, swap files, recovery files, etc. Modern operating systems are so complex that only a very sophisticated user would have any idea how to find and delete *all* copies of their data. Law enforcement investigators use this technical quirk to great advantage, pouring over seized computers with programs such

Please use the following format when citing this chapter:

Keenan, T.P., 2008, in IFIP International Federation for Information Processing, Volume 262; The Future of Identity in the Information Society; Simone Fischer-Hübner, Penny Duquenoy, Albin Zuccato, Leonardo Martucci; (Boston: Springer), pp. 37–50.

as EnCase and FTK (Forensic Tool Kit.) The truly paranoid, or at least privacy sensitive users, often try to counter such sleuthing with programs such as Wipedisk, PGP Shredder and Evidence Eliminator.

The advent of the Internet has vastly complicated the whole problem of controlling user data. Search engine spiders, caching sites (both documented and hidden) mirror sites, web mail and web storage have led to a situation where, unless specific precautions are taken, one should essentially assume that data placed on the Internet can never be completely recaptured and may be viewed by others.

1.1 Historical perspective – single user and timeshared computers

In the earliest days of computer use, controlling user data was really not a problem. Scientists took turns using a computer on "booked time" and entered their programs either physically with wires and switches, or via removable media such as punched cards or paper tape. Output was either displayed on evanescent display screens or printed on a teletypewriter, so it could be torn off and taken away. When the author entered the world of computing, in 1965, instructions were clearly posted on the IBM 1620 computer console to zero out the entire 20,000 digits of memory before attempting to use it. This was good advice since the machine might "hang" or "loop" if it accidentally encountered improper data in memory. Reaching a block of zeros stopped the processor, allowing time for sober thought about programming errors. Anyway, we were so eager to run our own programs that it never occurred to us to snoop on the previous user's data.

The move to interconnecting computers raised the question of "where is my data?" to new levels. In the 1960s, the author worked on one of the earliest time-sharing systems (SHARER,) on a CDC 6600 computer at New York University. This system pioneered the concept of dividing up the power of a large (and then very expensive) mainframe computer among several users, and introduced the "exchange jump" instruction [1] which caused the computer to switch context between two users. A subsequent project carried out on a similar computer at the University of Calgary in 1972 demonstrated some of the vulnerabilities inherent in switching from one user to another. A prankster calling himself "The Missionary Unmasker" discovered other users' passwords and posted them around the campus. The author had to modify the operating system's code to clear out the relevant password fields between users.

1.2 Email as an example of vulnerability by data proliferation

Single-system email systems such as IBM's Professional Office System (PROFs) brought the issue of data deletion to the front pages of the world's newspapers. In the Iran Contra scandal, Reagan administration official Oliver North was embarrassed to find that PROFs emails that he thought he had deleted were produced as evidence. The matter went to several courts, and, according to a chronology [2] on White House emails, assembled by the Federal of American Scientists:

"January 19, 1989…At 6:10 pm, on the eve of George Bush's inauguration, U.S. District Judge Barrington D. Parker issues a Temporary Restraining Order, prohibiting the destruction of the backup tapes to the PROFs system."

Other high profile instances of emails coming back to haunt the originator include the Jan. 5, 1996 memo from Microsoft chairman Bill Gates that was introduced as evidence in the company's antitrust trail. As reported by CNN [3] this email led to an interrogation of Gates about possible illegal business practices. And who could forget the posting, on the illmob.org website, of private phone numbers, photos, email addresses and notes belonging to celebrity Paris Hilton. (It is still unclear if this was done by social engineering or by a T-Mobile technical exploit such as the one posted at [4].) What makes that case particularly relevant is that, although illmob.org is a fairly obscure "hacker" website, the information rapidly proliferated to higher profile sites such as engadet.com and gizmodo.com.

IBM's ancient PROFs system had an interesting feature that many modern day email users would dearly love -- the ability to "recall" an ill-considered email message after it was sent. This was accomplished by simply deleting it from the delivery queue. Of course, if the recipient had already read, stored or forwarded the message, it was too late.

It's important to note that Jon Postel's original RFC 821 for SMTP (Simple Mail Transfer Protocol) [5] is silent on the issue of recalling mail, as is RFC 2821 which replaced it in 2001. [6] Some vestiges of this "unsend" concept remain in proprietary systems including Microsoft Outlook Exchange Server and AOL, but it's increasingly considered an archaic idea. It may well be impossible to implement now because of technical issues involving POP3 and IMAP servers, the use of web mail systems like Hotmail and Gmail, and a nasty security issue involving bogus recall requests that is described on www.whynot.com [7]

1.3   Web pages have become a treasure trove of information

The introduction of the Mosaic web browser in 1993 caused a flood of Internet activity. Now, it would be unthinkable for a major company not to have a webpage. Yet those web pages may contain seeds of the company's own destruction. In a simple experiment, conducted by the author and taking less than two minutes, high quality images of the corporate logos of the "big six" banks in Canada were obtained from in June 2007 :

- http://www.cibc.com/ca/img/default-logo.gif
- http://www.tdcanadatrust.com/images/TDCTLogo_big.gif
- http://www4.bmo.com/vgn/images/ebusiness/logo_financialgroup.gif
- http://scotiabank.com/static/en_topnav_logo.gif
- http://www.nbc.ca/bnc/files/bncimage/en/2/im_logo.gif
- http://www.rbcroyalbank.com/banners/oce/logo_rbc_bankng.gif

A repetition of this experiment five months later, again using the Firefox browser, disclosed that, while some of the image locations had changed, they were all obtainable by simply right clicking on the appropriate bank's webpage and clicking

"Save Image As." It should come as no surprise, then, that criminals preparing "phishing" schemes have little trouble creating very credible looking bogus bank web pages. In fact, they have reached the level of sophistication where the majority of their fake page is actually the real, functional code of the bank, with only a small portion of fraudulent content. It's also worth noting that, barring a significant change of their names and/or logos, (which for marketing reasons almost never happens,) once these images are available they will remain usable practically forever.

Though banned by some laws, such as the UK's anti-fraud statute that came into force in 2007 [8] "Phishing Kits" remain for sale in numerous online venues. These give even an inexperienced, non-technical user the tools to create false websites and launch large volumes of spam. Various techniques such as Anti-DNS Pinning can be brought into play to make the recipient of these emails think that they are in fact coming from the legitimate website of a financial institution.

Another significant development is the advent of "Google Hacking," which uses the leading search engine to find information that was never intended to be found, including passwords, internal printer addresses, even logs of security vulnerabilities produced by commercial security scanning products. There are excellent online references such as [9] to explain Google Hacking.

Lest it be thought that all Internet Data Persistence (IDP) is connected to malicious computing, there are countless examples of innocent archiving, which may still have embarrassing consequences. The "Wayback Machine," found at www.archive.org is an obvious example of unintended (to the webpage creator) archiving. Surely the webmasters of 1997 never intended to be judged by their old work which is easily viewable a full decade later!

2   The present state of data persistence on the Internet

2.1 Data storage by government agencies

This is an area shrouded in some mystery. Rumors and urban legends describe vast disk farms in basements near Washington, D.C. archiving every email, web page change, Usenet postings and even conversations by VoIP telephony. Internet users in China experience strange delays and "page not found" messages that lead them to believe they are being watched online. There is an excellent report on this subject from the Open Net Initiative which portrays the Chinese surveillance situation, at least as it existed in 2004-2005. [10]   Based on actual testing, this report notes that "China's Internet filtering regime is the most sophisticated effort of its kind in the world. Compared to similar efforts in other states, China's filtering regime is pervasive, sophisticated, and effective. It comprises multiple levels of legal regulation and technical control. It involves numerous state agencies and thousands of public and private personnel. It censors content transmitted through multiple methods, including Web pages, Web logs, on-line discussion forums, university bulletin board systems, and e-mail messages."

Many other governments have done some form of clandestine monitoring of the Internet. One early example is ECHELON, a secretive and controversial system operated by a number of governments to intercept and analyze communications of interest. It was publicly discussed in an article by Duncan Campbell [11] where he details various Signal Intelligence projects operating in the UK and the US, with code names like MOONPENNY, VORTEX and BIG BIRD.

Then came the US Federal Bureau of Investigation's CARNIVORE system, which became public knowledge in 2000. According to an internal FBI memo, obtained, in censored form, under the Freedom of Information Act by the Electronic Privacy Information Center [12] "Carnivore was tested on a real world deployment [deletion] having recently come back from a deployment...This PC could reliably capture and archive all unfiltered traffic to the internal hard drive (HD) at [deleted]." The general consensus is that the FBI and its partners eventually replaced Carnivore with commercially available tools. This trend is consistent with the author's own experience with another law enforcement agency. It is reasonable to assume that even better tools for data capture have been developed in the intervening years, and are now being deployed. It is also worth noting that the cost of data storage has plummeted, allowing the archiving of vast amounts of information at very low cost.

For many years, Usenet news groups were of special interest to governments and law enforcement because they were used for many questionable purposes, from trading pornographic images (legal and illegal) to planning drug deals and terrorist activities. That Usenet groups have been the subject of governmental attention is indisputable. According to a report prepared by the Electronic Privacy Information Center [13]:

"CompuServe, an on-line service of H&R; Block, based in Columbus, Ohio, removed from all of its computers more than 200 Usenet computer discussion groups and picture databases that had provoked criticism by a federal prosecutor in Munich." The "banned" newsgroups were still available to CompuServe users who used the service to connect to computers that carried the newsgroups. Information on how to do this circulated quickly through the CompuServe system. Three days later, the Chinese government echoed the Germans' actions by calling for a crackdown on the Internet to rid their country of pornography and "detrimental information."

2.2 Data storage by companies and individuals

Whether or not any governments were systematically monitoring Usenet group postings is somewhat moot, because they can just go do their data mining right now in a number of Usenet archives. The most famous was DejaNews, which allowed anyone to retrieve old postings. The author once accidentally embarrassed a teaching assistant by searching her name on DejaNews, only to find some fiery and radical political postings. They weren't actually her views, she pointed out; she was just trying to "infiltrate" a radical group to do an anthropology paper. Aside from the ethical questions there, the fact is that her (rather distinctive) surname remained attached to what may be an illegal (because of incitement to violence) posting.

DejaNews was bought by Google in 2001 and rolled into Google Groups. It contains postings back to 1981 (some with earlier dates like 1971 are undoubtedly the result of incorrect date setting) on predictable subjects like "Star Trek." One has to wonder if Chip Hitchcock, now a Fellow of the New England Science Fiction Association, would want to be reminded that 25 years ago someone bearing his name wrote this:

Date: 17 Jun 1981 10:40:32-EDT
From: cjh at CCA-UNIX (Chip Hitchcock)
…Certainly her proportions were extreme enough to satisfy most people; was it that she refused to do a nude scene (which I find thoroughly unlikely for an unknown in present-day filmmaking)? …And do you think that one mark of a good actress is willingness to strip for the camera?

Yet it's up there, in Google Groups, for all to see. And probably always will be.

3   Emerging threats

There are many, many ways to let data out, and essentially (except for encryption or some kind of encryption-based "data expiry" and "rights management" schemes) no effective way to get it back. So it is prudent to consider the data proliferation risks inherent in new technologies, and how they may affect us.

Observers of young people born between 1980 and 2000, have commented that "for Generation Y, communication is all about MySpace and Facebook." [14] One might add that it's also about blog postings, sharing videos on YouTube, Instant Messenger Chat and phone-to-phone SMS messages. While the seemingly ephemeral nature of such communications might seem to minimize the risk of data dissemination and persistence, actually the opposite is true. Briefly, here are some of the emerging issues:

3.1   IM logging

Chats are now routinely logged on the computers of both parties. This provides an opportunity for unauthorized parties to read them, unobtrusively, at a later date. They can also be sent by email, and in fact, in Google's Gmail system, chat entries that occur while you are offline are automatically sent to you by email. So all the data persistence problems of email are becoming replicated in the chat universe. The line between telephones and computers is also being blurred. SMS messages can be sent from computers using sites such as www.blueskyfrog.com.au, which links to certain mobile telephony providers in Australia. Whether such data is being logged at the computer, the cell phone, or somewhere in between is an interesting question to which most people don't know the answer. Few people realize that their (anonymized) search queries are being displayed on giant screens in Google's California headquarters, as well as on websites like www.metaspy.com.

The November 2007 announcement by Google and partners of the Open Handset Alliance, based on open source technology, will further eliminate the distinction between computing and telephony. If you use your phone to access Google Maps there are ample places that might retain the details of just where you were going.

3.2   Video sharing

Despite the intention of sites like YouTube to force viewers to watch videos in real-time, there are numerous free available programs to store them (KeepVid, YouTube Downloader, SnagIt) as well as the option of simply connecting the video stream via hardware to a device such as a DVD Recorder.

Every day, YouTube and similar sites receive numerous "takedown requests" from copyright holders and those who find particular videos offensive or invasive of their privacy. There is a formal procedure for handling these applications, as well as a process for getting a video re-posted if in fact it should not have been taken down under the company's policy. YouTube's broadly written "inappropriate content" clause [15] mentions material that is "unlawful, obscene, defamatory, libelous, threatening, pornographic, harassing, hateful, racially or ethnically offensive, or encourages conduct that would be considered a criminal offense, give rise to civil liability, violate any law, or is otherwise inappropriate."

Some videos just keep re-appearing and causing problems. According to Rabbi Abraham Cooper, Associate Dean of the Simon Wiesenthal Center, [16] a Nazi propaganda film called "Hitler Builds a Village for the Jews" is frequently re-posted on video sites by Holocaust deniers, forcing repeated takedown requests. The major video posting sites are now implementing "digital signature" technology to assist in automating the takedown process, but new video posting sites keep springing up all over the world. Some of them don't have the same level of scrutiny as Google-owned YouTube.

3.3   Blog sites

Delta Airlines became famous, in a negative way, for firing flight attendant Ellen Simonetti "for posting inappropriate pictures (of herself) in uniform on the Web." [17] Many other bloggers have suffered in real life because of their virtual lives. Blogspot, created by Pyra Labs and acquired by Google in 2003, stores blog entries on Google's servers. According to Google's Privacy Policy for this service [18], "If you delete your weblog, we will remove all posts from public view." However, it goes on to say that "because of the way we maintain this service, residual copies of your profile information and other information associated with your account may remain on back-up media."

That, in itself, is an understandable consequence of the technical architecture of the system. However, many aspects of that residual information are poorly defined. Who has access to it? Can it be subpoenaed? Can law enforcement just drop by and take a look? How long will it be retained? Cities that have installed surveillance cameras in public areas have needed to wrestle with these problems. However, private companies have much greater leeway in crafting and enforcing their privacy policies.

Blogging has taken an interesting public twist, politicians and political candidates now using this technique to "get closer to the voters." Bill Clinton has a blog, and uses it to talk about his recent trip to Africa. Barack Obama's site, www.barackobama.com, features a "group blog" written by campaign staffers. The risk of course is that their words may come back to haunt them. Old election promises may be archived and resurrected. Speeches given to a group of students may be compared against those given to senior citizens. The net result may be more transparency. It may equally result in more obfuscation and even more oblique speeches.

3.4   Skype and other VoIP products.

In its Privacy Policy [19] Skype distinguishes between your Personal Data (name, address, billing information) Traffic Data (who you call) and Communications Content (actually voice or data transmitted.) They of course note that they may be obliged to disclose any or all of these to law enforcement officials upon lawful request. However Skype also reserves the right to "share your Personal and Traffic Data with carriers, partner service providers and/or agents, for example the PSTN-VoIP gateway provider, distributor of Skype Software and/or VoIP Service and/or the third party banking organization or other providers of payment services."

Vonage [20] has a substantially similar privacy policy but also includes this warning about VoIP communications, "…no system or service can give a 100% guarantee of security, especially a service that relies upon the public Internet. Therefore, you acknowledge the risk that third parties may gain unauthorized access to your information when using our services."

3.5   Social networking (Facebook, MySpace, Nexopia)

Facebook suffered a major user backlash in 2006 when it launched new features called NewsFeed and MiniFeed. These programs sent all Facebook users information about the activities of their friends. An online protest group called "Students Against Facebook Newsfeed" was launched and attracted over 300,000 members, and the company modified its policy somewhat.

Most Facebook account holders believe that when they delete something (a wall posting, a photo, a compromising video) it's gone. But Facebook's own privacy policy (which few users have probably read) states "You understand and acknowledge that, even after removal, copies of User Content may remain viewable in cached and archived pages or if other Users have copied or stored your User Content." [21]

In any case, it is dead easy to right click on an interesting Facebook photo, capture a video, or make note of personal information provided when something is offered for sale in Facebook Marketplace. There's a good reason why certain law enforcement officials ruefully refer to it as "StalkerBook."

The public's awareness of Facebook privacy issues has been raised by a provocative video "Do you have Facebook" posted on YouTube and now viewed over 125, 000 times. Essentially, it is a reading of the Facebook terms of service, combined with a conspiracy theory about possible links between the site and certain US government agencies. As noted in the video, "all of the above raises more questions than answers."

MySpace, and Nexopia, provide free accounts to anyone who says they are 14 years of age or older. There is some review by human moderators to ensure that obscene or highly offensive images are not posted. Some fairly intimate personal details are requested, and freely given, though perhaps not always with 100% honesty.

A recent Nexopia search displayed several hundred Calgarians who list themselves as being between 14 and 17 with "homosexual" as their sexual orientation. Most have photos and many have some personal information attached in blog entries. The site also lists the nicknames of their friends, allowing for social network profiling. Of course, many of these boys and girls are just amusing themselves, but they run the risk of information they disclose voluntarily on Nexopia causing them embarrassment and perhaps even serious problems later in life.

3.6   Unsolicited data collection (ChoicePoint and ZoomInfo)

ChoicePoint (Alpharetta, GA) is one of the largest data brokers in the world. It collects personal data ranging from social security numbers to real estate holdings, and is not above sending people into courthouse basements to copy out divorce judgments. According to an online trade press article "it also offers businesses, government agencies and nonprofit organizations software technology and information designed to anticipate and respond to economic and physical risk, and it analyzes information for the insurance sector. Its database contains about 19 billion records." [22]

Most people in that database didn't ask to be there, and may well be unaware that they are. Whole government agencies such as the New York City's Office of Vital Records, have outsourced birth and death record processing to VitalCheck, a ChoicePoint company. Whether or not they guard the personal information with the same care as a government office is, of course, open to debate. It is known that when the Alberta provincial government moved Drivers License processing to private sector vendors, serious security flaws such as fake driver's license on official license blanks were reported.

An even more subtle form of unsolicited data collection is typified by the site www.zoominfo.com. This company has data on almost 39 million people, much of it obtained by scanning the Internet for web pages, press releases etc. The vast majority of the records are described as "automatically generated using references found on the Internet" and "This information has not been verified." When I checked my own profile, which had a great deal of correct information, I was surprised to learn that I was on the board of a defense contractor that I had never heard of.

3.7   Second Life and other virtual worlds

Virtual worlds are nothing new, dating back at least to The Palace that legendary virtual reality community created in 1996. It introduced many people to the idea of avatars, and conversing in a virtual world through chat bubbles. Now, Second Life claims to have 7.5M "residents" with 1.6M of them logging on in the last 60 days. There are virtual products and services, virtual real estate, and the ability to exchange Second Life's internal currency (Linden dollars,) for U.S. dollars.

Like, Facebook, the Second Life privacy policy cautions against expecting privacy with respect to information you disclose in the virtual world, i.e. "Please be aware that such information is public information and you should not expect privacy or confidentiality in these settings." They also note that they permanently retain the "registration file" of former customers even after they have ceased to use Second Life. They are silent on what happens to your other digital data, but it's a fair bet that your fuzzy little avatar and online transactions will be sitting on at least one backup file somewhere on the planet.

Ironically, the major concern about Second Life and similar systems may be the non-persistence of your data. As one writer recently noted in an online trade journal [23], "There are no standards that let you move your avatar, your virtual shop, or any of your innovations between virtual realities…if Linden goes down or bust, what happens to your Second Life shop?"

3.8   RFID and Bluetooth data

An experiment [24] at the MIT Media Lab demonstrated that Bluetooth-enabled cell phones produce enough data to track the movements of individuals as well as determine who they are spending their time with. Researchers outfitted willing subjects with "always on" phones that could discover each other and log precise locations through GPS technology. The findings included the concept of "familiar strangers," people you are often near but do not actually know, and suggested that it might benefit a company to introduce them to each other.

While this data trail was purely voluntary, one could easily imagine devices of this nature being used for social control purposes such as keeping track of who met with whom in a hallway at a busy conference. Indeed at the 2003 World Summit on the Information Society (WSIS) that took place in Geneva, Switzerland, rumors were rampant that delegates were indeed being tracked electronically through the RFID tags embedded in their badges. There have been numerous accusations that the procedures for handling personal data at WSIS 2003 may have violated legislation including the European Union Data Protection Directive. [25]

RFID tags have been controversial, with the Brittan Elementary School in Sutter, California seeking to have all children tagged and parents opposing it on privacy grounds. [26] The use of the RFID in passports is also highly contested for reasons of privacy and security. [27]

3.9   IP and MAC address logging

An underappreciated aspect of digital trail we leave is the logging of addresses such as our Internet Protocol (IP) and MAC (Media Access Control) addresses. The former is assigned by an Internet service provider and can vary over time. However, as more people move to services that assign IP addresses for a long time (such as cable providers) the IP address becomes more useful for tracking. As one example, if you forget your password on the Second Life site, your IP address is included in the email reminding you of your password. This is intended to provide tracking information for bogus password reset requests, but it also provides some degree of tracking information on innocent people. In fact, in a court case in Alberta, Canada, evidence was introduced in an "Internet defamation" case that included the IP addresses used to post on stock discussion sites.

MAC addresses are unique to individual Network Interface Cards, so they would seem to be the perfect identifier for a machine, and to be a dream come true for those trying to do computer forensics and trace people on the Internet. However, because of the design of TCP/IP, the protocol underlying the Internet, MAC addresses are only transmitted up to the Data Link Layer so they are not generally available across routers. The net effect is that retrieving the MAC address of a remote computer is generally only possible if it is on the same host. Also, there are techniques for "spoofing" MAC addresses. MAC addresses are sometimes used for the generation of license keys for proprietary software that is authorized to run only on a specific computer. A mathematical comparison is made of the computer's MAC address to what it is supposed to be, as encoded in the license key.

3.10   Public and shared computers

Who hasn't used an Internet café, or a hotel business center's computers or those in an airport lounge? We typically do that without regard for the fact that we have no control over the hardware, software or network that we are using. What better target for unscrupulous hackers than Business and First Class passengers?

There are numerous exploits that could be placed on public computers. A press article [28] reported that malicious software ranging from keystroke loggers to Back Orifice was reported on airport lounge computers. Even without hacker attacks, there are some simple problems relating to things like sending email using a common product. "Outlook Express is probably not configured to allow emails to be sent from these machines, so any message created simply moves to the system's 'outbox' where it remains indefinitely after the user clicks 'send'." This allows the next user to come in and review those messages. In fact, unless you explicitly clear your "Sent Mail" folder before leaving the airport computer, you are probably leaving all that juicy information in there as well.

3.11   Things we haven't invented yet

A consideration of Internet Data Persistence should contemplate future technologies. As just one example, it is entirely conceivable that we will soon be signing documents and authorizing online transactions using biometric data, perhaps even our DNA signature. Very few jurisdictions have comprehensive laws governing the handling, storage, exchange and sale of biometric data. Aside from its highly personal nature and status as an identifier with non-repudiation characteristics, genetic data may also disclose health information about the subject and even other family members. This, in turn, could have adverse consequences in areas such as health care, employment and insurance.

Other trends include the phenomenal decline in storage costs, leading many to believe that the costs will approach zero and all data will be retained because it is uneconomical to get rid of it. Couple this with ever-improving search technology, pioneered by firms like Google, and the ability to find the proverbial "needle in a haystack" and to embarrass a company with it, is a very real threat.

3.12   An emerging profession: the e-scrubber

In a provocative blog posting [29] from the firm Social Technologies, a number of "New Jobs for 2020" were postulated. One was the E-scrubber, who "Works to undo or minimize the indiscretions that people accumulate on the Web." Given the volume of embarrassing photos, off color jokes and other content posted every day, it seems that this might indeed be a growth industry. Of course, the same tools that would allow e-Scrubbers to track down indiscretions could, in the wrong hands, be used to find them.

An even bigger question arises, "How Would the E-scrubber Know When the Job is Done?" After all, there are many "Deep Web" Internet databases that are not visible to the general public, and not indexed by search engine spiders. There could always be one more place where a given piece of data is stored, perhaps in an encrypted form. So, the real answer to the question is not "the Job is Finished" but, sadly, "We've Done All We Can for You."

4   Conclusion: setting a balance before the technophobes do it for us

Whether through government snooping, corporate data retention, personal hoarding or just plain accident, more and more of our data is being permanently stored away. Much of it can be traced back to us, either by name, IP address, or pseudonym. As storage cost goes to zero, there will be no technical or economic reason to ever delete anything. In fact the human cost of figuring out what to delete already exceeds the cost of buying another 500GB hard drive for most people. So we keep everything.

The problem is exacerbated by the relentless improvement of search engine technology. Soon, not only will there be an embarrassing thirty year old video clip of you out there; anyone will be able to find it armed simply with a current photo of you and "reverse aging" software!

The risks are very real, and no-one is immune. Even the United States Air Force was a victim of Data Persistence, leaving sensitive data on un-erased magnetic tapes that were sold as surplus. [30]

Governments and companies that deal with the public will need to continually re-consider their policies on data use and retention. All of us should think carefully about every word, video and photo that we put into cyberspace, asking "would I want my mother or my prospective employer to see this?

If we don't set smart policies as a society, we might find ourselves moving in the technophobic Luddite direction suggested by a company called AlphaSmart. They're capitalizing on the fears of parents about their kids being online, and possibly leaving behind some digital footprints by selling the "Neo laptop." It's a computer with "versatile learning software for developing writing, keyboarding and quizzing skills." But, as their online brochure [31] explains, "Neo purposely does not include Internet capabilities. Students stay on task without Internet distractions — Web surfing, online games, or instant messaging."

It's not clear if the Neo is named as some sort of tribute to the heroic hacker Keanu Reeves plays in the "Matrix" movies. Whether it is or not, it points to the fact that we all need to see beyond the illusion that our data goes away when we think it does. It's time to prepare intelligently for a world where everything we ever say, do, or perhaps even, think, may someday come back to haunt us.

References[1]

1. Los Alamos Scientific Laboratory, Semiannual Atomic Energy Commission Computer Information Meeting, May 20-21, 1968, report LA-3930-MS, available online at http://www.fas.org/sgp/othergov/doe/lanl/lib-www/la-pubs/00320743.pdf
2. Federation of American Scientists, White House Email Chronology, http://www.fas.org/spp/starwars/offdocs/reagan/chron.txt
3. CNN, "Gates Deposition Makes Judge Laugh in Court," Nov. 17, 1998, available at http://www.cnn.com/TECH/computing/9811/17/judgelaugh.ms.idg/
4. Rootsecure.net, http://www.rootsecure.net/?p=reports/paris_hilton_phonebook_ hacked
5. Postel, J.B., Simple Mail Transfer Protocol, http://www.ietf.org/rfc/rfc0821.txt
6. Klensin, J., ed., Simple Mail Transfer Protocol, http://tools.ietf.org/html/rfc2821
7. http://www.whynot.net/ideas/902
8. http://www.opsi.gov.uk/acts/acts2006/pdf/ukpga_20060035_en.pdf
9. http://johnny.ihackstuff.com/
10. Open Net Initiative, "Internet Filtering in China in 2004-2005: A Country Study, http://www.opennetinitiative.net/studies/china/, accessed Dec. 7, 2007.
11. Campbell, D., They've Got It Taped, New Statesman & Society; Aug 12, 1988, pg. 10
12. Electronic Privacy Information Center, press release, November 16, 2000, http://www.epic.org/privacy/carnivore/11_16_release
13. Electronic Privacy Information Center, "Silencing the Net – The Threat to Freedom of Expression On-line, Human Rights Watch, Vol. 8, No. 2, May, 1996, http://www.epic.org/free_speech/intl/hrw_report_5_96.html

---

[1] All online citations accessed June 24, 2007 except as noted

14. Holland, A., Does Generation Y Consider Email Obsolete? http://www.marketingsherpa.com/article.php?ident=30010
15. http://www.youtube.com/t/terms
16. Cooper, A., Simon Wiesenthal Center, Private communication, May, 2007
17. Simonetti, E., "I Was Fired for Blogging," CNET News, Dec 16, 2004, http://news.com.com/I%20was%20fired%20for%20blogging/2010-1030_3-5490836. html
18. http://www.blogger.com/privacy
19. http://www.skype.com/intl/en/company/legal/privacy/privacy_general.html
20. http://www.vonage.com/help.php?lid=footer_privacy&article=399
21. http://ucalgary.facebook.com/policy.php
22. Campanelli, M, "Checkpoint to Divest Three Units," DMNews, July 13, 2006, http://www.dmnews.com/cms/dm-news/database-marketing/37474.html,   accessed December 9, 2007.
23. ZDNet, "Virtual Worlds, Real Problems," June 11, 2007, available online at http://news.zdnet.co.uk/leader/0,1000002982,39287486,00.htm, accessed Dec. 9, 2007.
24. http://reality.media.mit.edu/researchmethods.php
25. http://europa.eu.int/comm/internal_market/privacy/index_en.htm
26. Electronic Privacy Information Center, "Children and RFID Systems," http://www.epic.org/privacy/rfid/children.html
27. Zetter, K., "Feds Rethinking RFID Passport," Wired, online edition, Apr. 26, 2005, http://www.wired.com/politics/security/news/2005/04/67333
28. http://www.theregister.co.uk/2005/09/21/airport_pc_security_lax/
29. http://wcpl-businessbriefs.blogspot.com/2007/09/new-jobs-for-2020.html,   accessed October 27, 2007
30. Neumann, P., "Illustrative Risks to the public in the use of computer systems and related technology," ACM SIGSOFT Engineering News, Vol. 21, No. 6, pp. 16-30, 1996.
31. http://www.alphasmart.com/k12/K12_Products/neo_K12.html

Privacy in Danger: Let's Google Your Privacy

Emin Islam Tatli

University of Weimar, Faculty of Media, Chair of Media Security
`emin-islam.tatli@medien.uni-weimar.de`

Abstract. Protection of personal data is a requirement from both ethical and legal perspectives. In the Internet, search engines facilitate our lives by finding any searched information within a single-click time. On the other hand, they threaten our privacy by revealing our personal data to others. In this paper, we give concrete examples of Google personal data exploits against user privacy, discuss the countermeasures to protect our privacy and introduce a penetration testing tool called *TrackingDog* checking and reporting privacy exploits over Google.

1 Motivation

Privacy is both an ethical and legal requirement for the Internet users. Protection of personal data against unauthorized access and exploits is inevitable for the users. Different legacy systems in many countries define strict laws to prevent illegal use of personal data [2,3,13–15]. Unlike legacy systems, safeguarding user privacy is not an easy task from the technical point of view. The users share their personal data with third parties, but they can not control whether their data is used for other purposes or forwarded to others. They need to trust the data receivers. P3P (Platform for Privacy Preferences) [12] and Appel (A P3P Preference Exchange Language) [1] projects are two attempts in this direction to build a trust relation between data owners and data receivers.

Web crawlers threaten personal privacy by indexing more and more private data for unauthorized access. The biggest threats can result from the "indexing anything" features of the Internet search engines like Google, Yahoo, Lycos, etc. Especially, Google with its huge index size threatens our privacy. Today, a special research area called *Google Hacking* that focuses on finding vulnerable servers, applications, various online devices, files containing username-password pairs, login forms, etc. exists. We, as the individual users, need to take user-centric countermeasures in order to protect our privacy. In this paper, we illustrate real life examples of privacy exploits via Google hacking, discuss its social aspects and the countermeasures for Google hacking and illustrate our penetration testing tool *TrackingDog* for the user-centric privacy control.

The paper is organized as follows: Section 2 focuses on the real life examples of privacy exploits from Google hacking area. Section 3 explains the possible security countermeasures for Google privacy hacking and introduces our privacy penetration testing tool TrackingDog. Finally, Section 4 discusses the privacy policy of Google and proposes some enhancements for better privacy management.

Please use the following format when citing this chapter:

Tatli, E.I., 2008, in IFIP International Federation for Information Processing, Volume 262; The Future of Identity in the Information Society; Simone Fischer-Hübner, Penny Duquenoy, Albin Zuccato, Leonardo Martucci; (Boston: Springer), pp. 51–59.

2   A Case Study: Google Hacking for Privacy

Google is the most popular web search engine in the Internet. It indexes any information from web servers thanks to its hardworking web crawlers. But sensitive personal data that should be kept secret and confidential are indexed by Google, too. This threatens our privacy. Personal data like name, address, phone numbers, emails, CVs, chat logs, forum and mailing list postings, username-password pairs for login sites, private directories, documents, images, online devices like web cameras without any access control, secret keys, private keys, encrypted messages, etc. are all available to others via Google. In addition to the privacy risks, there might exist other security threats that can be revealed by Google. There exists even an online database [6] which contains 1423 different Google hacking search queries by November 2007.

2.1   Google Advanced Search Parameters

In addition to the basic search operators (i.e. +,-,.), Google supports other parameters for the advanced search and filters its results according to these parameters provided by users.

The *[all]inurl* parameter is used to filter out the results according to if the given url contains a certain keyword or not. If more keywords are needed to filter, the *allinurl* parameter should be used. *[all]intitle* filters the results according to the title of web pages. *[all]intext* searches the keywords in the body of web pages. With the parameter *site* you can apply host-specific search. *filetype* and *ext* parameters have the same functionality and are needed to filter out the results based on the file extensions like html, php, pdf, doc, etc. The minus sign (-) can be put before any parameter and reverses its behavior. As an example, a search query containing the parameter *-site:www.example.com* will not list the results from www.example.com. The operator `"|"` or the keyword `"OR"` can be used for binding different searches with the *logical OR*.

2.2   Privacy Searches

Google can be queried for revealing sensitive personal data by using its advanced search parameters. We have grouped private data searches into four different groups according to the privacy level. These are *identification* data, *sensitive* data, *confidential* data and *secret* data searches.

Identification Data The identification data is related to the personal identity of users. Name, surname, address, phone number, marital status, CV, aliases, nicknames used over the Internet, etc. are the typical examples of the identification data. Some private data searches would focus on a certain person and we choose the name "Thomas Fischer" which is a very common personal name in Germany.

Name, Address, Phone, etc. You can search for the web pages and documents which contain keywords like name, surname, address, phone numbers, birthdate, email, etc., optionally for a certain person or within certain document types.

```
allintext:name email phone address intext:"thomas fischer" ext:pdf
```

Twiki[1] is a wiki-based web application that is commonly used for project management. Inside TWiki, user data like name, address, phone numbers, web pages, location, emails, etc. are stored. If the required authentication techniques are not enforced, unauthorized people can also access this data.

```
intitle:Twiki inurl:view/Main "thomas fischer"
```

In addition to Google search, other search engines with the "people-find" capability can also be very helpful for gaining the identification data. Yahoo's People Search[2], Lycos's WhoWhere People Search[3] or eMailman's People Search[4] connecting public ldap servers are examples of such services. Similarly, the Firefox plug-in "People Search and Public Record Toolbar"[5] gives you many facilities to search for the identification data.

Curriculum Vitae You can search for the keyword CV (curriculum vitae) that can contain the identification data. This search can be extended by searching CV in different languages. For example, Lebenslauf can be used within the search query as the german translation for CV.

```
intitle:CV OR intitle:Lebenslauf "thomas fischer"
intitle:CV OR intitle:Lebenslauf ext:pdf OR ext:doc
```

Login Names Webalizer application[6] collects statistical information of web sites about their visitor activities. The most commonly used login names are also stored by Webalizer.

```
intitle:"Usage Statistics for" intext:"Total Unique Usernames"
```

Sensitive Data The sensitive data means that the data which is normally public but its reveal may disturb its owner under certain cases. The examples

---

[1]Twiki: http://twiki.org

[2]Yahoo People Search: http://people.yahoo.com

[3]Lycos People Search: http://peoplesearch.lycos.com

[4]eMailman People Search: http://www.emailman.com/ldap/public.html

[5]People Search and Public Record Toolbar, https://addons.mozilla.org/en-US/firefox/addon/3167

[6]Webalizer: http://www.mrunix.net/webalizer/

are postings sent to forums, emails sent to mailing lists, sensitive directories and Web2.0-based social networking applications.

Forum Postings, Mailinglists PhpBB[7] is a widespread web forum application. It enables to find out all postings sent by a particular user. The following search finds out all postings sent with the alias thomas to different phpBB-based forums.

```
inurl:"search.php?search_author=thomas"
```

Mailman[8] is a well-known mailing list manager. The following search gives all email postings which are sent to mailman-based lists and related to *Thomas Fischer*.

```
inurl:pipermail "thomas fischer"
```

Sensitive Directories Backup directories can contain also some sensitive data about users, organizations, companies, etc.

```
intitle:"index of" inurl:/backup
```

Web2.0-based Applications The next generation Internet Web2.0 introduces more privacy risks. People share more personal data with others within Web2.0-based social networking and blogging applications. The following searches are based on the favorite Web2.0 services like Yahoo's Image Sharing[9], Google's Blogger[10], Google's Video Sharing[11] and Facebook[12]. Instead of searching through Google, searching directly on the original sites would give more efficient results.

```
"Thomas Fischer" site:blogspot.com
"thomas" site:flickr.com OR site:youtube.com
"thomas fischer" site:facebook.com
```

Confidential Data The confidential data is normally expected to be non-public for others except for a group of certain people, but Google makes it possible to access such private data as well.

Chat Logs You can search for chat log files related to a certain nickname.

```
"session start" "session ident" thomas ext:txt
```

---

[7]PhpBB Forum: http://www.phpbb.com

[8]Mailman List Manager: http://www.gnu.org/software/mailman/

[9]Yahoo Image Sharing: http://www.flickr.com

[10]Google's Blogger: http://www.blogspot.com

[11]Google Video Sharing: http://www.youtube.com

[12]Facebook-Social Networking: http://www.facebook.com

Username and Password Username and password pairs can be searched within sql dump files and other documents.

```
"create table" "insert into" "pass|passwd|password" (ext:sql |
ext:dump | ext:dmp | ext:txt)
"your password is *" (ext:csv | ext:doc | ext:txt)
```

Private Emails Microsoft Outlook and Outlook Express store personal emails within single files like incoming messages as inbox.dbx. The following searches target the email storage files stored by Outlook Express or Microsoft Outlook.

```
"index of" inbox.dbx
"To parent directory" inurl:"Identities"
```

Confidential Directories and Files Confidential directories and files can be revealed with the following query.

```
"index of" (private | privat | secure | geheim | gizli)
```

In order to prevent web crawlers to list private directories, Robot Exclusion Standard [9] is used. But it also enumerates a number of private directory paths within world-readable robots.txt files.

```
inurl:"robots.txt" "User-agent" ext:txt
```

Not only directories but also private documents and images can be searched through Google.

```
"This document is private | confidential | secret" ext:doc |
ext:pdf | ext:xls
    intitle:"index of" "jpg | png | bmp" inurl:personal |
inurl:private
```

Online Webcams Online web cameras come along with their software for the remote management over the Internet. Based on the type of the webcam, you can filter the url and the title as listed in [6] and access to the online webcam devices without any access control. As an example;

```
intitle:"Live View / - AXIS" | inurl:view/view.shtml
```

Secret Data Secret keys, private keys, encrypted messages compose of the secret data which is expected to be accessible *only* to its owner.

Secret Keys Normally the secret keys are generated as session keys and destroyed after the session is closed. They are not permanently stored on the disks. But there are certain applications like Kerberos [8] that still need to store a secret key for each principal. The following query searches for the dumped Kerberos key databases.

```
"index of" slave_datatrans OR from_master
```

Private Keys The following search reveals the private keys that must be normally kept private.

```
"BEGIN (DSA|RSA)" ext:key
```

Gnupg [5] encodes the private key in secring.gpg files. The following search reveals secring.gpg files.

```
"index of" "secring.gpg"
```

Encrypted Messages The encrypted files with Gnupg have the extension *gpg*. Signed and public key files have also this extension. The following query searches for files with gpg extension and eliminates non-relevant signed and public key files.

```
-"public|pubring|pubkey|signature|pgp|and|or|release" ext:gpg
```

The encryption applications mostly use the extension *enc* for the encrypted files. This query searches for the files with the extension enc.

```
-intext:"and" ext:enc
```

In XML security, the encrypted parts of messages are encoded under *Cipher-Value* tag.

```
ciphervalue ext:xml
```

3   Countermeasures

Google hacking can be very harmful against user privacy and therefore the required security countermeasures should be taken. The protection methods can be grouped as *user-self protection* and *system-wide protection*.

As its name implies, user-self protection requires the users to safeguard themselves against the possible threats. If we enumerate some points which the users should take care of:

- Do not make any sensitive data like documents containing your address, phone numbers, backup directories and files, secret data like passwords, private emails, etc. online accessible to the public.
- Provide only required amount of personal information for the Wiki-similar management systems.
- Instead of using a single username over the Internet, try to have more pseudonyms which make linkability of user actions through a single username more difficult.
- Considering the forum postings and group mails, try to stay anonymous for certain email contents. Do not mention any company or organization name inside the postings if not required.
- Do not let private media get shared over social networking and blogging services.

As an administrator, you should focus on system-wide protection for the privacy of the users as well. The first method you can enforce is using automatic scan tools [7,10,17,18] that search possible Google threats and test privacy risks within your system. The tools mostly use the hack database [6] when they do the scans. Another method is integration of robots.txt (robots exclusion standard) [9] files into your system. Web crawlers (*hopefully*) respect the directives specified in robots.txt. Providing this, you can prevent the crawlers from indexing your sensitive files and directories. In addition to this method, you should never put database backups that contain usernames and passwords accessible over your system. The most advanced but also complicated method is installing and managing Google honeypots [16] in your system and trying to figure out the behavior of attackers before they attack your *real* system.

3.1 TrackingDog - A Privacy Tool against Google Hacking

To help the users to protect their privacy, new privacy enhancing tools are needed. For example, the users can be equipped with a penetration testing tool that would search automatically for the possible privacy threats and report its results. Providing this, the users can be aware of the privacy risks which threaten them. We have already implemented such a tool namely *TrackingDog* [17] which searches Google mainly for the privacy exploits mentioned in this paper for a given person and/or a given host. Besides, the tool has the support of finding cryptographic secrets as explained in [19] in details. *TrackingDog* helps the individuals to detect if any of their confidential data have become public over the Internet via Google. It supports both English and German language-specific queries and enables the users to edit raw search queries. Fig. 3.1 illustrates the main GUI of TrackingDog.

4   Discussion

Considering the privacy exploits explained in the previous sections, one can ask himself if such exploits are also misused by Google itself to profile people and

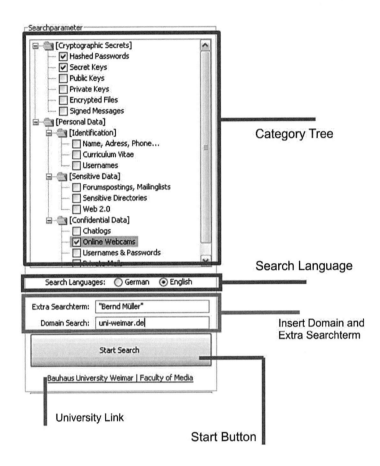

Fig. 1. TrackingDog Main GUI

track their activities. Even though Google replies this question as *no* and claims to respect our privacy, we can not be sure about this dilemma.

On the other hand, we see some good approaches to privacy by Google. Lately, they have declared that they would take steps to further improve privacy. By searching in Google, your query, your IP and cookie details are stored on the Google servers and that information can identify you uniquely. But now Google has decided to anonymise this collected data within a 18-24 month period [11]. You can even apply other means to remove your cookies from Google servers as explained in [4].

We believe, Google can do more for our privacy. The privacy exploits mentioned in this paper should be taken into consideration by Google. The personal data should not be collected by the Google crawlers. Internet users are careless and easily make their personal data public unintentionally. This should not be misused by Google. While we hope more respect to our privacy from Google, we also need to have the users get equipped with the powerful user-centric privacy enhancing tools like TrackingDog to get to know the threats and protect themselves.

References

1. A P3P Preference Exchange Language (Appel). http://www.w3.org/TR/P3P-preferences/.
2. EU Directives 2002/58/EC. http://www.dataprotection.ie/documents/legal/directive2002_58.pdf.
3. EU Directives 95/46/EC. http://www.cdt.org/privacy/eudirective/EU_Directive_.html.
4. Five Ways to Delete Your Google Cookie. http://googlewatch.eweek.com/content/ five_ways_to_delete_your_google_cookie.html.
5. The gnu privacy guard. http://www.gnupg.org.
6. Google Hacking Database. http://johnny.ihackstuff.com/index.php?module=prodreviews.
7. Goolink- Security Scanner. www.ghacks.net/2005/11/23/goolink-scanner-beta-preview/.
8. Kerberos: The network authentication protocol. http://web.mit.edu/Kerberos/.
9. Robots exclusion standard. http://en.wikipedia.org/wiki/Robots.txt.
10. SiteDigger v2.0 - Information Gathering Tool. http://www.foundstone.com/index.htm?subnav=resources/navigation.htm&subcontent=/resources/proddesc/sitedigger.htm.
11. Taking steps to further improve our privacy practices. http://googleblog.blogspot.com/2007/03/taking-steps-to-further-improve-our.html.
12. The Platform for Privacy Preferences. http://www.w3.org/2006/07/privacy-ws/.
13. Bundesdatenschutzgesetz (BDSG), Germany. https://www.datenschutzzentrum.de/material/recht/bdsg.htm, 1978.
14. Data Protection Act,UK. http://www.opsi.gov.uk/acts/acts1998/19980029.htm, 1998.
15. Bundesgesetz ber den Schutz personenbezogener Daten(Datenschutzgesetz 2000 - DSG 2000), Austria. http://www.dsk.gv.at/dsg2000d.htm, 2000.
16. Google Hack Honeypot Project. http://ghh.sourceforge.net, 2007.
17. Martin Kessler. Bachelorarbeit: Implementation of a penetration testing tool for searching cryptographic secrets and personal secrets with Google. Bauhaus Universitaet Weimar, Medien Fakultaet, October 2007.
18. Johnny Long. Gooscan Google Security Scanner. http://johnny.ihackstuff.com/modules.php?op=modload&name=Downloads&file=index&req=getit&lid=33.
19. Emin Islam Tatli. Google reveals Cryptographic Secrets. Technical Report of 1. Crypto Weekend, Kloster Bronbach, Germany, July 2006.

Workshop: Social and Philosophical Aspects of identity

Self, Script, and Situation: identity in a world of ICTs

Bibi van den Berg

Erasmus University, Faculty of Philosophy
Room H5-13, P.O. Box 1738
3000 DR Rotterdam, The Netherlands
vandenberg@fwb.eur.nl

Abstract. In this paper I will elucidate why 'situation' is a constructive unit of analysis for the study of both identity and the impact of technologies (particularly ICTs) on identity. Further, I will use a situational perspective to show some of the ways in which the 'definition of situations' may be affected by such technologies. I will conduct a conceptual analysis of the 'definition of a situation', looking into the notion of 'scripts', to show how alterations in scripts lead to changes in the 'definition of the situation', and these in turn lead to shift in the development and expression of identity.

1   Introduction

There are many ways of approaching the study of human identity. One of them is to focus on the relationship between human interaction and identity. This approach has been used by symbolic interactionists such as George Herbert Mead [14], and Erving Goffman [9]. In *The presentation of self in everyday life* [9] Goffman develops what has come to be known as the 'dramaturgy metaphor' [11] or the 'dramaturgical perspective' [4]. In search of an answer to the question 'what is identity?' Goffman turns to everyday, small-scale social engagements between people. His point of departure is the idea that the complex question of what identity is, is best tackled by studying its expression and formation in concrete micro-social interactions between people. For Goffman, identity literally *comes about* in and through social interactions – it is the '*dramatic effect*' of such interactions [4, 9]. In the eyes of Goffman, identity is simply the sum of all the roles we play in our lives. Thus, identity is not some innate quality, nor a physically localizable property. Also, identity is not an essence in itself. Rather, Goffman views identity as the socially constructed result of all our engagements with others.

Goffman's central thesis is that when people engage in social interactions with one another, they conduct '*performances*' – they assume a '*role*' and try to create as favorable an '*impression*' as possible [9]. He argues that identity is the "*...result of publicly validated performances.*" [4]. There is a distinction between the roles people play when they are in a '*front region*', i.e. before an audience, and the way they

Please use the following format when citing this chapter:

van den Berg, B., 2008, in IFIP International Federation for Information Processing, Volume 262; The Future of Identity in the Information Society; Simone Fischer-Hübner, Penny Duquenoy, Albin Zuccato, Leonardo Martucci; (Boston: Springer), pp. 63–76.

behave when they are in a '*back region*' or '*backstage*', i.e. in spaces where no one is watching them, e.g. within the privacy of their home environment. In such back regions they can rehearse for future performances, rest, relax and let their 'mask' down [9].

2   Goffman on situations

But how do people come to choose what 'role' to play when interacting with others? How do they know what behaviors to display when placed in a given situation? According to Goffman people entering a social interaction make use of a '*definition of the situation*', a concept that dates back to the American sociologist William Isaac Thomas [21]. A 'definition of the situation' emerges when people – in the words of Joshua Meyrowitz – "ask themselves: '*what is going on here?*'" [16, 17]. The 'answer' a person will come up with forms the basis for the particular action pattern, chosen from a whole range of possible action patterns, he or she will adopt within that setting. Thus, people use the 'definition of the situation' to ascribe *meaning* to the situation at large and give and interpretation of their specific part to play (i.e. their '*role*') within that situation.

It is important to observe that using a 'definition of the situation' is *not* (necessarily) a rational, conscious process. More often than not, 'answering' the question 'what is going on here?' is not done in an explicit, analytical or logical way, but rather in an immediate, automatic, implicit, un- or pre-conscious manner. The 'answer' to the question becomes visible in the choice of a role and its accompanying actions, but emerges in such an instantaneous, automatic way that the agent oftentimes won't even be aware of the fact that he or she is using a 'definition of the situation' at all to assume a role within the given context. The 'definition of the situation', one could argue, comes about by using what Bourdieu calls 'practical knowledge', which he describes as "...*based on the continuous decoding of the perceived – but not consciously noticed*..." [3][1].

How people come to define a situation exactly is the topic of the next paragraphs. One preliminary point to be made here is that the definition of the situation always comes about in the interplay between individual interpretations and socialized, internalized cultural meanings. They are the result of two components: on the one hand they stem from the learnt and internalized definitions a person has come to incorporate throughout his upbringing and the socialization processes that continue throughout his life. On the other hand they depend in part on the spontaneous individual interpretation of the current setting by a unique agent, incorporating his or her past experiences and definitions. This explains why individual differences in the 'definition of the situation' may exist.

---

[1] Although Bourdieu cannot be labeled a symbolic interactionist, he worked on many of the same themes as symbolic interactionists. It is clear from his writings also that he found great inspiration in Goffman's work. See also: [10].

By approaching identity as the performance of different roles in different situations Goffman achieves two goals. Firstly, it enables him to accommodate for the fact that people display different 'sides of themselves' under different circumstances. Secondly, by looking into identity as it is developed, experienced, and expressed in different settings, Goffman can make the notion of 'situations' into the central unit of analysis of his research. Thus, he can analyze, compare and differentiate aspects of identity across different settings, places and times – 'situation' is used as the entity of investigation into which the complexity of social life is dissected. This is why Goffman has been labeled the "quintessential sociologist of the 'situation'" [11].

However, a burning question at the heart of Goffman's line of thinking remains: how does the person come to a 'definition of the situation' in the way he or she does? What 'cues' does he or she use to interpret 'what is going on'? Goffman's theory starts from the assumption *that* people use definitions in each situation they enter, but does not explain *what such definitions are based on*. I argue that it is useful to explicate the 'cues' people use to define what the situation is, because by explaining the elements that have an impact on such a definition, it becomes possible to analyze whether fundamental changes in the environments we live and work in, such as the advent of information and communication technologies, will have an impact on the way we define situations and, if so, what form and shape that impact will take. Therefore, we will now turn to Goffman's starting point, the 'definition of the situation', and see if we can clarify the mechanisms at work in the construction of such a definition.

3   Scripts and situations

When entering a situation a person uses a 'definition' to establish 'what is going on'. But how does a person come to such a 'definition'? Which elements in the environment, be they physical or social in nature, play a part in the ascription of meaning that arises in this manner?

I argue that each situation contains 'scripts' that human beings use to come to a 'definition of the situation'. I define a script as *a set of 'contextual cues' explicitly or implicitly governing (courses of) action in connection with a situation*[2]. Scripts provide an indication of the range of appropriate behaviors that apply in the situation. They allow us to quickly distill 'what is going on' and what roles we may choose from, thus allowing us *"to do less processing and wondering about frequently experienced events"* [20]. My definition of scripts deviates from the meaning ascribed to the same term within the field of Science and Technology Studies (S&TS). To show in which ways my own definition differs from the one used in S&TS we will look into their use of this term first.

---

[2] A situation, in turn, can be defined as *an ensemble of a specific meaningful locale (place), and a specific moment in time in which agents, their behaviors, and scripts come together to create a single 'slice of social reality'*.

3.1   Scripts in Science and Technology Studies

In S&TS much research has been conducted regarding the images of and presuppositions concerning '*users*' and '*use*' that become incorporated into technological artifacts during the design process [1, 2, 7, 12, 18, 19]. In 'script analysis' the term 'script' denotes all the ideas concerning prospected users and practices that are embedded in technological artifacts. Researchers in ST&S have shown convincingly that such scripts abound in even the most simple and straightforward technological artifacts. For example, Van Oost conducted research on 'gender scripts' and focused on electric shavers developed by Philips Electronics [18]. She found that there are significant differences in the way female and male shavers are designed and marketed – differences expressing conceptions of gender in the minds of the designers. The scripts that are thus embedded in the shavers, Van Oost points out, reify gendered behavioral distinctions. She concludes that "...*Philips not only produces shavers but also gender.*" [18]

A second example of script research in S&TS is that conducted by Gjøen and Hård on the electric car (EV) and its use and social acceptance in Norway [7]. Gjøen and Hård show that, besides the scripts embedded in the electric car by its designers, users sometimes add their own scripts ('*user scripts*') to an artifact. One of the users, named Sylvia, created her own script by naming the car 'Barbie' (because it is small and cute). With this feminine name, Gjøen and Hård argue, Sylvia turns existing cultural scripts concerning cars, labeling them as gendered, masculine vehicles, upside down.

3.2   An alternative approach to scripts

As these examples show research in Science and Technology Studies predominantly focuses on (a) the *design and development process* of technological artifacts, and (b) the scripts that are embedded in *singular* technological artifacts, as opposed to the multitude and variety of scripts that may be present in *contexts* or *environments* (of which technological artifacts may be part). Although this approach is valuable for studying the ways in which human-technology interaction is shaped regarding individual artifacts, my use of the notion of 'scripts' broadens the perspective to accommodate the interactions users may have with the *milieus* they find themselves in. In contradistinction with the approach used in S&TS I focus on what happens once technological artifacts enter our everyday environments, particularly looking into their 'scriptal influence' in concert with other objects and influences present in a given situation. From this point on, we will therefore see scripts as elements of everyday situations, operating as a variety of 'signs' that together give off suggestions for the ascription of meaning pertaining to 'what is going on' in that situation.

4   Script characteristics

Let us explore the meaning of the notion of 'scripts' as proposed here. From my definition of 'scripts' as 'contextual cues' it follows that they are bound up with the environments or situations that we find ourselves in or move between. Scripts may be present explicitly within a given situation, and thus guide behaviors in a conscious manner, for example when a sign in the park says we are not allowed to walk on the grass. But scripts often do their work in more implicit and unconscious ways. A railway platform with an escalator and staircases leading to the main entrance of the building has implicit scripts concerning the way the flow of passengers should move from the train to the main hall and vice versa. When entering the office building in which one works, there are implicit scripts that guide us in adjusting to the environment, not just in a literal way (we enter the offices in the building through the door and not through one of the windows; we sit on chairs, not on top of our desks), but also in more symbolic ways – we instantly, automatically, and without conscious awareness assume roles appropriate for interactions with colleagues, clients, and superiors, instead of roles we would play in front of friends, spouses or family members. The scripts contained in the environment help us make these transitions from one situation to the next.

Scripts arise on the basis of *shared cultural meanings*. They are the result of processes of cultural dynamism, in which people create ways of interacting, rules of conduct, legal prescriptions, and so on and so forth to facilitate the relations among participants in social connections and exchanges. Most of these processes of cultural dynamism have been ingrained in our interaction patterns through gradual and unconscious socialization and have been integrated into our repertoire of roles in such a way that we cannot view our exchanges with others apart from them. Meeting and interacting with the world and the other people in it presupposes shared cultural meanings, and precisely these are expressed in the 'cues' we take from the situations we enter: scripts.

Scripts, then, are *social constructs*. They are created and preserved in and through social processes. Scripts can only be sustained by their affirmation in everyday practices. Goffman calls such affirmations '*everyday-life interaction rituals*' [4]. Such rituals consist of all kinds of "...*unspoken social traffic rules that pervade everyday existence*" [4]. To Goffman, the 'social order' is simply the totality of all of the interaction rituals of a group or culture [8].

Scripts are not arbitrary or without obligations. They call forth a certain level of *engagement* with the particular situation and create a framework within which a person may choose his or her course of action, so to speak. Also, one could argue that scripts *structure situations*, in the sense that they provide guidelines for choosing a role befitting the environment a person has entered. 'Scriptal cues' enable us to pick a course of action that is deemed 'appropriate' within the situation. At the same time, however, their structuring capacities are not exhaustive, in the sense that there is room for variation in interpretation and, therefore, room for maneuvering through social traffic with unique personal patterns and courses of actions. Scripts leave room for interpretation, so that the same scripts may not give rise to the same responses in different people – on the one hand because every person brings a different set of previous experiences to his interpretation of the situation, which affect the way he or she will 'read' the current one, and on the other hand because every situation is in fact a new one, which means that persons always need to 'improvise' to some extent within the given circumstances. Scripts are *non-determinate* in this sense. They could be labeled as '*strategy-generating principles*', to use a term by Bourdieu [3], principles that accompany people's actions within given situations, but don't determine these actions completely. As Van Oost argues with regards to the scripts embedded in technological artifacts: "*Obviously, scripts cannot determine the behavior of users, their attribution of meaning or the way they use the object to construct their identity, as this would lead to the pitfall of technological determinism. Users don't have to accept the script, it is possible for them to reject of adapt it.* […] *…but scripts surely act invitingly and/or inhibitingly…*" [18]

As guidelines in action one could argue that scripts *condition* us to some degree within the situations we enter, since they point us in clear directions. Thus, one might argue, scripts have a repressive effect on our action patterns. They can be seen as expressions of political/power strategies used by some (viz. those in power) to control the behavior of others (viz. those without power). Simultaneously, though, scripts can be conceived of as *aides* or guidelines that facilitate the burden of having to choose a role in every given situation. Scripts help us select a course of action from a whole range of possible options. So while scripts may indeed be labeled as restrictive, they can also be viewed as supportive, assisting mechanisms. Scripts, therefore, can be said to be both *limiting* and *enabling*.

Another characteristic of scripts is that they are *interactional* mechanisms emerging in a situation. A script is not something that is simply embedded in the environment as a rule etched in stone, to be interpreted and used by every passer-by in the same exact way. Rather, as argued above, scripts leave room for interpretation – they are taken to mean one thing by one individual and may be taken to mean something else by someone else. One could argue that the script even *comes about* only in being a cue for whomever sees its meaning, for whomever takes it *to be a cue*. This is where my perspective of scripts diverges from that of Roger Schank and Robert Abelson [20]. In *Scripts, plans, goals and understanding* Schank and Abelson attempt to uncover some of the structures of human knowledge in order to use the outcomes to further research in Artificial Intelligence. Schank and Abelson introduce the notion of a *script*, which they define as "*a predetermined, stereotyped sequence of actions that defines a well-known situation.*" [20] A script, for them, is a form of 'specialized knowlegde' that allows people to quickly determine what is going on in a specific situation and choose a pattern of action appropriate within the limits of that situation. Schank and Abelson's definition of scripts strongly resembles my own approach – we fully agree on the role scripts play in everyday life (i.e. "*scripts handle stylized everyday situations*" [20]) and the way in which they are used (i.e. facilitating answering the question 'what is going on here?'). However, whereas Schank and Abelson view scripts as *knowledge* structures, thereby placing them in the human mind, in my perspective scripts are emergent properties of situations, which come about in the *interaction* between an agent and the situations he enters. Scripts are not elements of the human episteme, but rather situational components.

5   Script forms and functions

Scripts come in different forms and fulfill different functions. Most of our everyday interactions are governed by a host of *implicit* social scripts. Some scripts, though, have been made more *explicit* and formal – these are expressed, for example, in the legal rules that groups and societies create. In case of an offence such formalized legal scripts are often backed by institutionalized fines or penalties. Unspoken, implicit social scripts lack such official penalties, but violating them may still have severe social implications: crossing the boundaries of what is deemed 'socially appropriate' within a group or culture may result in breaking taboos, which in turn can lead to the social exclusion or shunning of the perpetrator by that social group. Such ostracizing behaviors may last a short time, but can also be of a more permanent nature, depending on the seriousness of the breach caused by the doer, and also on the amount and type of 'repair work' [5] the perpetrator may do.

Then there are scripts that have a *physical expression* in the environment of the situation. Doors, walls, windows, and traffic lanes are simple examples thereof. Such scripts guide our actions (e.g. entering or leaving a room, driving on the right side of a road) through their material form – they enable certain action patterns, while disabling others. Physical script cues may be conveyed in the space and size of rooms, in the placement of doors and windows, in the ways in which movement is affected through for example the position of barriers and the arrangement of furniture and other physical objects within a spatial plan.

In some cases such materialized scripts have a *moralizing* property. In his brilliantly funny and insightful article entitled *Where are the missing masses? The sociology of a few mundane artifacts* [12] Bruno Latour uses the example of seat belts in a car to explicate this point. In some cars, Latour states, the seat belt is connected to the door and gently buckles the driver up automatically once he closes the door. In this type of car the driver cannot *choose* to *not* buckle up – the responsibility for buckling up has been removed from the user and delegated to the artifact. Thus, the scriptal influence of the seat belt is absolute.

In most cases, though, the script cues expressed in physical form are not absolute. Entering a room through the door is not as binding a script as the seat belt example described above – we may choose instead to enter through a window (provided there is one), but usually refrain from doing so for reasons of practicality on the one hand, and for reasons social suspiciousness on the other. So although we generally follow the physical script prescribed to us by the shape and placement of a door (e.g. use this hole in the wall to enter or leave a room) this type of script leaves room for maneuvering.

Broadly speaking, one could say that scripts bring about the emplacement of social regulations, legal rules, political prescriptions, symbolic formulations etc.[3] However, making a clear distinction between the social, legal, physical, political and symbolic aspects of scripts that may be present in situations is impossible. In the reality of everyday situations different constellations of scripts may be present, working in concert and reinforcing (or combating) one another. It is impossible to untangle these assemblages.

6   Adding technologies to situations

The next question to be addressed is: what is the impact of the addition of technologies (in particular ICTs) to existing situations? In which ways does the addition of such technologies to existing situations affect the scripts in that situation and, in turn, the 'definitions of situations'?

Before looking into the changes brought about in the 'definitions of situations' by the advent of new technologies, we need to establish what *kind* of situational changes technologies cause: do they interfere with situations on a script level, e.g. do they create new situational action cues within given contexts? Or are they rather physical and informational additions to the environment that may affect existing scripts but do not function as such themselves? In order to answer this question I would like to use Roger Silverstone's notion of 'double articulation'. According to Silverstone technologies always have '*double articulation*': they are both "*material objects located in particular spatio-temporal settings*" and "*symbolic messages located within the flows of particular socio-cultural discourses*" [13]. Thus, communication technologies have both a material expression, they are objects like any other, but at the same time they enable communication with and information regarding the outside

---

[3] Scripts show a certain amount of overlap with what in common sense language we call '*rules*'. An extensive field of study has developed in a wide range of scientific fields, ranging from philosophy, to Artificial Intelligence, and to law, as to what the precise nature of 'rules' and 'rule-following' is. The common sense meaning of a 'rule' refers to either explicit (and even codified) instructions with regard to the *fulfillment* of actions, or explicit (and even codified) instructions with regard to the *limitations* of actions. Comparing this notion of rules to my conception of scripts, one could argue that rules are *declarative* (i.e. they refer to a correlation between a specific state of affairs and an action pattern to be taken), scripts are more *procedural* in nature: they refer to implicit or tacit knowledge that we may use within a contextual frame of reference. However, within modern philosophy an extended debate between such prominent scholars as Wittgenstein, Ryle, and Searle, has led to a different perspective on 'rule-following'. In this conception 'rule-following' refers to socially constructed, contextual, and (most importantly) rather implicit knowledge which is adopted in specific instances. Within this debate 'rules' are highly similar in meaning as 'scripts'. Solving this conceptual confusion unfortunately falls far outside the limits of this paper. We will leave the issue by concluding that both 'rules' and 'scripts' are complex, diffuse concepts, whose precise definition and demarcation, both separately and in relation to each other, deserves further attention in a separate paper.

world to enter the domestic environment. When translated to the current problem at hand, one could say that they function both as objects in a situation, and as situational scripts.

Thus, technologies have the ability to change situations, either as script forces, or as situational elements. But how does this happen precisely? I argue that there are *four ways* in which technologies have a bearing on the 'definition of the situation'.

6.1   Boundedness

First of all, the presence of ICTs alters the *boundedness* of situations, as Joshua Meyrowitz argues [15-17]. Electronic media have an impact on the permeability of a situation's boundaries. Whereas situations traditionally may be said to link up with bounded, physical places, electronic media break through this boundedness, and even dissolve it [17]. Meyrowitz writes: *"The pre-electronic locality was characterized by its physical and experiential boundedness. Situations were defined by where and when they took place and by who was physically present – as well as by where and when they were not taking place and by who was not physically present at particular events. [...] Now such boundedness requires some effort: Turn off the mobile phones, PDAs, and laptops; banish radio and television. [...] In most settings in a post-modern society [...] the definitions of the situation are multiple and unstable, able to shift with the ring or buzz of a telephone or with the announcement of a 'breaking story'"* [17] And Meyrowitz concludes: *"By changing the boundaries of social situations, electronic media do not simply give us quicker or more thorough access to events and behaviors. They give us, instead, new events and new behaviors."* [16]

According to Meyrowitz, the advent of electronic media leads to the destabilization of the 'definitions of situations' since we are 'always connected' through such media. This means that our 'definition of the situation' may change the instant the phone rings or an email is received on the PDA. Whereas only a few decades ago physical seclusion meant social seclusion as well, in the days of mobile and ubiquitous computing this is no longer the case.

Meyrowitz compares electronic media to traditional ones, like books and clay tablets. He points out that print media always had to be moved physically from place to place and usually traveled with the person who owned them, at the speed of human travel [16]. Electronic media have changed all of this. Whereas in the pre-electronic age the amount of information that entered or left a situation was bound up with rules of access for (groups of) people on the one hand and with physical carriers, such as books, papyrus roles, or clay tablets on the other, electronic media have dissolved this link. Walls, doors and fences are of no consequence in the social insulation of a place that is electronically mediated. The physical transportation of messages and communications in the digital age is infinitely faster than that of the human traveler (and becoming faster every day), and digital media have no need for material carriers, such as books or scrolls, nor do they depend on human beings literally bringing them from one location to the next. All of this has enhanced easy access for electronic media and their contents to situations and localities.

6.2   Physical place and social place

Second of all, the spread of technologies has lead to the disconnection of '*physical place*' and '*social place*'. This point, too, derives from Meyrowitz's *No sense of place*. Before the age of electronic media, he argues, 'physical place' and 'social place' coincided: in order to have specific social interactions, one had to go to specific physical places. Access to and presence in these physical places enabled certain social interactions, whereas those who did not have access or were not present in them were excluded from participating in the interaction. Let me illustrate this with an example. In the past, members of an exclusive 'Gentlemen's Society' would visit meetings with other members ('social place') at a specific physical location, viz. the society's Club House ('physical place'). Non-members did not have access to this physical place, and therefore had no access to the 'social place' of a Gentlemen's Society. Electronic media, Meyrowitz argues, have had a profound impact on situations such as these. Non-members of a distinguished club may now gather information about what it means to be in such a club by browsing the club's website or perhaps by viewing a documentary about it on television.

Of course, there is still a lot of social information that is actually closely tied to specific physical place – the uncoupling of 'physical place' and 'social place' has not made 'physical place' completely irrelevant as a category of experience, nor do we have access to any and all physical places, simply because we may be able to gain access to (a wide variety of) social places. Rather, Meyrowitz's point is that the connection between 'physical place' and 'social place', which was complete in pre-electronic times, has been greatly *weakened* ever since the introduction of electronic media.

Since information and communication technologies have come to pervade physical settings at any given moment and thus have turned literally physical places into technologically mediated ones, this has a bearing on the 'definition of the situation': 'what is going on' is no longer strictly bound up with the physical place one finds oneself in; a person can be physically present in one place, and yet be 'socially' absent from it, for example because he or she is on the phone talking to someone who is not physically present – this person thus really 'is' somewhere else entirely. Kenneth Gergen calls this notion '*absent presence*', being somewhere, yet not being there at the same time [6]. Gergen writes: "*One is physically present but is absorbed in a technologically mediated world elsewhere. Typically it is a world of relationships, both active and vicarious, within which domains of meaning are being created or sustained. Increasingly, these domains of alterior meaning insinuate themselves into the world of full presence – the world in which one is otherwise absorbed and constituted by the immediacy of concrete, face-to-face relationships.*" [6]

This means that there is a decreased relevance of our physical presence in situations. 'Being present' in a situation literally is no longer related to one's physical location, but has rather become an *informational* property: being 'present' means being 'tuned-in'. Note once more, that because of the disconnection between physical and social place the 'definition of the situation' has become more instable: it can change in the blink of an eye as a result of the 'social interference' that electronic media may cause. As we have seen above, a situation that was defined as one type of setting by its participants may change instantly as a result of a technological artifact's 'intrusion'.

6.3   Middle region behaviors

A third point, again put forth by Meyrowitz, refers to Goffman's distinction between 'front region' behaviors and 'back region' behaviors [9]. As stated at the beginning of this article, Goffman points out that people play out 'performances' when they are in front of an audience, for which they want to create a favorable 'impression'. Such performances are labeled as 'front region behaviors'. When there is no audience present individuals (or teams of players) can relax, let down their guard, and rehearse for future performances. Goffman calls this 'back region behavior'. With the advent of electronic media, Meyrowitz argues, the clear distinction between 'front region' and 'back region' as separate regions, each with their own repertoire of behaviors, starts to crumble [16]. He concludes that the merging of front region and back region behaviors leads to a host of new behavioral practices, which he labels as '*middle region behaviors*': "*In middle region behaviors, the extremes of the former front region are lost because performers no longer have the necessary backstage time and space; the control over rehearsals and relaxations that supported the old front region role is weakened. The new behaviors also often lack the extremes of the former backstage behavior because the new middle region dramas are public (that is, performed before an 'audience') and, therefore, performers adapt as much as possible to the presence of the audience, but continue to hide whatever can still be hidden.*" [16]

Meyrowitz has an ecological conception of situations and the behaviors we may find in them. He argues that when formerly separate situations merge, this does not result simply in the combination of both of these formerly disconnected situations, but rather in a *new* merged situation, with new behavior patterns.

Electronic media, Meyrowitz argues, may also give rise to the merging of formerly separate situations. For example, using a home telephone to conduct work-related business opens the private 'back region' of the home temporarily into a 'front region'. Similarly, displaying 'private' ('back region') behaviors on television in front of a large audience turns them into 'front region behaviors'. Also, television, the internet and other ICTs allow formerly distinct social groups (divided by age, gender, etc.) to gather information about each other. This, Meyrowitz suggests, leads to homogenization of knowledge, in the sense that more people have access to the same types and contents of information. Again, the emergence of a middle region is the result: since the strict distinction between social groups lessens, new behaviors emerge that correspond to the fusion of these groups and their situations.

Technologies, then, clearly affect the 'definitions of the situation'. Who we are in each situation, and what we show of ourselves, has become more fluid in the current age of information and communication technologies, and all the more so with the recent emergence of mobile technologies, that have aided in further destabilizing the boundaries between public and private behaviors.

6.4   Situational function

Lastly, I argue that ICTs, particularly mobile technologies, have changed the *function* of the situations we find ourselves in. As we have seen, Meyrowitz argued that the link between 'physical place' and 'social place' has been weakened by the advent of electronic media. Specific situations, that used to be bound up with particular locations in space and time, such as visiting a movie theater, attending a church service or going to a store, have become uncoupled from their former physical locations (although one can still go to their respective locations to get such experiences) – we can now watch a movie on television or on our iPods, download it from the internet or rent it from a video store; we can watch a church service on television, listen to it over the radio, or download the latest service as a Podcast; and we can shop for virtually anything through catalogues and on the internet. However, it is not just physical and social place that become separated; we may say the same of physical place and spatial function.

In the pre-digital age there was a close connection between a physical place and the function it fulfilled. For example, a train functioned as a public space, which one entered to travel from A to B, a park was a space used to relax and enjoy the weather or the green surroundings, an office was a semi-public space used to work etc. Although physical places could fulfill more than one function, their functions were usually limited in scope. With the advent of information and communication technologies, particularly mobile technologies, some of these limitations were lifted. A park may now function in the same 'traditional' ways, as a meeting place, a place to relax, a place to do exercise etc., but it may also be used as a place to work, using a laptop, a mobile phone, a PDA, or all of these combined. Information that was previously unavailable in the park, such as one's personal computer files or webpages on the internet, are now available in those green surroundings (or basically anywhere, anytime). This means the function a space like a park may fulfill in our everyday lives has expanded: on top of the 'traditional' functions a park had, it may now include a work function, a technologically mediated communication function, a technologically provided entertainment and information function, etc. Thus, the clear tie between physical place and spatial function of the pre-electronic age has weakened.

As a consequence, the clear situational divisions of old days, for example between public and private situations, have become blurred. For example, a train may function as a (semi-) personal space when we use it to have intimate discussions over the phone, and a park may function as (semi-) public one when we sit on a bench to work on a laptop. While such situations were previously seen as either private or public, they now may be both of these at the same time, or one or the other in rapid succession. It is obvious that alterations in the function of places and spaces again leads to a destabilization, or at least an immense expansion of the 'definition of the situation': since the range of possible patterns of action has expanded as a result of our being always-on and always-connected through mobile technologies, there is more variation in how we define 'what is going on' in each situation we enter.

7   Situations, technologies and identity

In which ways do these four types of destabilization affect human identity? At the beginning of this chapter I argued that we use 'definitions of situations' to come to terms with 'what is going on' in a specific context, to ascribe meaning to that context, and to choose an appropriate course of action, a role, within that context. With Goffman I stated that identity might be viewed as the totality of all of the roles we play throughout our lives. Thus, I argued, the 'definition of the situation' forms the starting point for role choices, and hence for the construction and expression of identity. As we have seen in this chapter, scripts play a fundamental role in establishing 'what is going on' in each situation, and changes in situations or scripts, for example brought about by the addition of information and communication technologies to these situations, have an impact on how we define them.

We may conclude that changes in the 'definition of the situation' have a direct and profound impact on identity. After all, when the 'definitions of the situation' change, role choices and cues are affected, which in turn has an effect on identity. ICTs may function as situational change factors, therefore have a bearing on identity. They affect identity because they change situations, either as situational elements or as scripts, and thus impinge on the 'definitions of the situation' we formulate.

We may conclude that the emergence of information and communication technologies, particularly the more recent development of mobile technologies, has led to a tremendous expansion of the possible definitions we may use to come to grips with role choices in each situation. Since the amount of roles to choose from is destabilized and increased in each specific situation, the bandwidth for choosing stretches as well, thereby creating a double effect: on the one hand individuals get more freedom and flexibility to choose roles in given situations. This means they may choose more freely what they want to do (and in turn, by effect, ultimately who they are). At the same time, however, this places an ever-bigger burden of choice on these individuals. The sum total of all the roles we may play in life is enlarged, thus dramatically expanding the necessity for human beings of merging the vast amount of separate roles they play into some form of a combined self. ICTs thus function both as mechanisms of liberation yet at the same time also helps corrode coherent and simple senses of self. Therefore, it is too simplistic to view the effects of ICTs on situations as 'good' or 'bad' – their complexity calls for a more nuanced analysis.

References

1.   M. Akrich, in: Shaping technology/building society: Studies in sociotechnical change, edited by W.E. Bijker and J. Law (MIT Press, Cambridge, Mass., 1992), 205-224.

2. M. Akrich, in: Managing technology in society: The approach of constructive technology assessment, edited by A. Rip, T.J. Misa and J. Schot (Pinter Publishers: Distributed in the United States and Canada by St. Martin's Press, London; New York, 1995), 167-184.
3. P. Bourdieu, *Outline of a theory of practice* (Cambridge University Press, Cambridge, New York, 1977).
4. A. Branaman, in: The Goffman reader, edited by C.C. Lemert and A. Branaman (Blackwell, Cambridge, Mass., 1997), xlv-lxxxii.
5. T. Burns, *Erving Goffman* (Routledge, London ; New York, 1992).
6. K.J. Gergen, in: Perpetual contact: Mobile communication, private talk, public performance, edited by J.E. Katz and M.A. Aakhus (Cambridge University Press, Cambridge, UK; New York, 2002), 227-241.
7. H. Gjøen and M. Hård, Cultural politics in actions: Developing user scripts in relation to the electric vehicle, *Science, Technology & Human Values* **27** (2), 262-281 (2002).
8. E. Goffman, *Relations in public: Microstudies of the public order* (Harper Colophon Books, Harper & Row Publishers, New York, 1972).
9. E. Goffman, *The presentation of self in everyday life* (Doubleday, Garden City, N.Y., 1959).
10. R. Jenkins, *Social identity* (Routledge, London; New York, 2004).
11. O.B. Jensen, 'Facework', flow and the city: Simmel, Goffman, and mobility in the contemporary city, *Mobilities* **1** (2), 143-165 (2006).
12. B. Latour, in: Shaping technology/building society: Studies in sociotechnical change, edited by W.E. Bijker and J. Law (MIT Press, Cambridge, Mass., 1992), 225-259.
13. S.M. Livingstone, On the material and the symbolic: Silverstone's double articulation of research traditions in new media studies, *New Media & Society* **9** (1), 16-24 (2007).
14. G.H. Mead and C.W. Morris, *Mind, self & society from the standpoint of a social behaviorist* (The University of Chicago Press, Chicago, Ill., 1934).
15. J. Meyrowitz, in: Mobile democracy: Essays on society, self and politics, edited by K. Nyíri (Passagen Verlag, Vienna, 2003), 91-102.
16. J. Meyrowitz, No sense of place: The impact of electronic media on social behavior (Oxford University Press, New York, 1985).
17. J. Meyrowitz, in: The global and the local in mobile communication, edited by K. Nyíri (Passagen Verlag, Vienna, 2005), 21-30.
18. E.v. Oost, in: How users matter: the co-construction of users and technologies, edited by N. Oudshoorn and T. Pinch (MIT Press, Cambridge, Mass., 2003), 193-209.
19. N. Oudshoorn and T.J. Pinch, *How users matter: The co-construction of users and technologies* (MIT Press, Cambridge, Mass., 2003).
20. R.C. Schank and R.P. Abelson, *Scripts, plans, goals, and understanding: An inquiry into human knowledge structures* (L. Erlbaum Associates; distributed by the Halsted Press Division of John Wiley and Sons, Hillsdale, N.J. New York, 1977).
21. W.I. Thomas and M. Janowitz, *W. I. Thomas on social organization and social personality: Selected papers* (University of Chicago Press, Chicago, 1966).

Moral identification in Identity Management Systems

Noëmi Manders-Huits and Jeroen van den Hoven

Department of Philosophy,
Delft University of Technology, Netherlands
N.L.J.L.Manders-Huits@tudelft.nl
M.J.vandenHoven@tudelft.nl

Abstract. Identity has become a central theme in modern philosophy. In this paper we are not concerned with the logic and metaphysics of identity, nor with questions of personal identity. We address a part of the ethics of identity in the light of ubiquitous modern technologies of identity management. In many practical contexts it is a 'forensic' and 'biographical' notion of identity and identification that is often prominent and morally problematic. Persons identify themselves and are identified by others; they present themselves as having certain properties, others scrutinize their self-presentations and form alternative representations of them, either in- or outside formal or administrative systems. Persons are consequently dealt with in legal and administrative contexts (and increasingly also in private spheres) on the basis of formal representations and sets of characteristics or statistical profiles. In this paper we articulate a basic moral justification for constraints on how persons may be represented and identified in identity management systems by explicating Bernard Williams' suggestion that respect for persons implies a particular form of identification, which we term "moral identification". Moral identification in this sense implies the identification of a person as someone who engages in self-identification.

1 Introduction[1]

There is an increasing need for identification and identity management. Globalization, mobility, and international terrorism have recently added to the desire of many to be clear about individual identities in order to know "who is who" on the internet, on the road, at airports, and in business transactions. Considerable investments are being made by governments and businesses around the world to unambiguously establish identities of citizens and customers and to learn as much as possible about them. Both in the public and in the private sector "identity management technologies" are used for that purpose. They allow one to manage identities of persons in two different

---

[1] This article builds upon previous work by the authors, i.e. Manders-Huits en Van den Hoven, 'Het Managen van Identiteiten en Morele Identificatie', *Algemeen Nederlands Tijdschrift voor Wijsbegeerte*, 98 (2), 111-128 (2006).

Please use the following format when citing this chapter:

Manders-Huits, N. and van den Hoven, J., 2008, in IFIP International Federation for Information Processing, Volume 262; The Future of Identity in the Information Society; Simone Fischer-Hübner, Penny Duquenoy, Albin Zuccato, Leonardo Martucci; (Boston: Springer), pp. 77–91.

senses. First, they manage the access of persons to physical spaces, to knowledge, information and communication infrastructures and to a broad range of services. They do so on the basis of the identity of individuals and their associated authorizations for access. Secondly, identity management technologies enable the storage of elaborate digital representations of individuals in databases for a broad range of uses. Individuals are now increasingly treated on the basis of these representations; The treatment they receive, the things they are entitled to, their rights, accountabilities, the opportunities they are given and the limitations that are imposed upon them are shaped by the way their identities are construed and used. The example of an identity management system used in this paper is the Electronic Health Record that is being developed in the Netherlands for regulating data streams between caregivers in the health sector.[2] There are also numerous databases and future (commercial) identity management systems which collect and store data for various purposes, including some not yet envisioned.

Hundreds of agencies and thousands of databases in the Western World and in the East (e.g., as a result of off-shoring in the world of medical image processing) keep files on citizens in the West. The digital representations of them are assumed to be good enough for a rapidly growing number of practical purposes. More and more often organizations act upon what a record, a file, a data set or a profile leads them to believe about a particular person. Categories, descriptions and models are routinely imposed on individuals' identity information. We know what dramatic consequences the availability of labels like 'Jew', 'Hutu' and 'Tutsi' and 'white', 'black' , 'honorary white', 'colored people' in administrative identity management systems can have for those concerned. In political, military and racial conflicts, but also in everyday practices in the insurance and the financial world, profiles, postal codes, income data, educational records, and a wide variety of behavioral indicators are used to sort and classify people [1,2].

Neuro-images, genetic information and other biometric data may in the future be included as an annex to the biography of individuals or even directly linked to computer networks, architectures and databases. Government agencies understandably want to know who the tax evader is, who the serial rapist is, and who has a tendency to become one, but also - on a more positive note - they want to know who is among worst off in society and in need of assistance or services.

In this paper we set out to articulate moral reasons for constraining the management of identity by others than the person whose identity is at stake. What do we owe to people when we are dealing and tinkering with their identities by representing them, changing their representations and self-presentations, or acting on the basis of these representations? In the first half of the paper we will discuss what kind of identity we are talking about in identity management. Next, we discuss the shortcomings of thinking about personal data and the protection thereof in light of the possibilities of modern identity management. We claim that it is necessary to extend

[2] This identity management system is carefully designed for a specific purpose, confining the span of control over data to the health domain. Our argument, needless to say, is on a more general level towards identity management systems. Therefore the example may not cover our argument in full depth, though it will illustrate our main point.

the category of data worthy of protection in relation to persons and their identity in two directions and we therefore prefer to speak of "identity related data" instead of "personal data". In the first place identity related data does not need to be linked to specific natural persons to be worthy of protection, as most discourse and legislation concerning the protection of personal data presupposes. Identification in a morally relevant sense can occur without the referential use of descriptions. Descriptions need neither be tied to the perception of individuals. Even without a unique reference and linkage to specific individuals there can be practically relevant and important strategies to get to know more about persons, whoever they may be and to structure interaction with them in an electronic environment accordingly. This is what is morally relevant.

In the second half of the paper we will give four reasons for the protection of identity related data in this broader sense. The fourth moral reason, pertaining to moral autonomy, implies epistemic modesty with respect to knowing the identity of persons and respect for persons as "self-presenters". This moral consideration leads up to the formulation of the demand for "moral identification" as put into words by Bernard Williams.

1.1   The Electronic Health Record[3]

An example of an identity management system now being developed is the Electronic Health Record in The Netherlands. Ministries, government agencies and others are working on a national identity management system – as is the case in many other countries - that will enable caregivers to share patient data via electronic communication. Different health organizations can add and exchange health related data using a pointer system, the National Switch Point (LSP), routing and authorizing data demands. This information is kept and filed under a national identification number, the Citizen Service Number4. Although the design of this identity management system is still ongoing and the architecture hasn't yet reached its final form, it can be assumed from pilot tests that are now being done that the architecture will be designed handling data in a decentralized way and providing patients appropriate control over their own data. The Electronic Health Record will be individually accessible for patients, e.g. by using their Citizen Service Number in combination with a personal code. As we will argue, 'moral identification', the moral concern with identity management discussed in this paper, is something to be kept in mind when completing the design of this particular identity management system.

---

[3] In Dutch: Elektronisch Patiënt Dossier (EPD), for more information see http://www.minvws.nl/images/fo-dutch-approach_tcm20-146105.pdf
[4] In Dutch: Burger Service Nummer (BSN)

2   Biographical identity

Identity management, in the sense given above, is concerned with 'identity' and 'identification' in a practical, biographical or forensic sense. John Perry calls the biographical and the forensic elements of our identity "objective representations" of persons. They are called objective since there is nothing that makes their content depend on who created them: they do not necessarily contain expressions with the first person pronoun "I". Some of these representations cannot be changed by the person, e.g. address or nationality. Take for instance Rip Van Winkle, an old Dutch Settler who falls asleep in the mountains before the American revolution. He wakes up twenty years later, after the revolution, and upon his return in the village he claims to be loyal to the British King, without realizing he is American Citizen now.

David Velleman [3] argues that these representations of persons are often and in part self made, in which case he refers to them as the "self-images" that persons present. Self-images are just among a number of different aspects or guises of selves. By means of a self-image "a person represents which person and what kind of person he is-(…) how he looks, what he believes in, what his personality is like, and so on". Velleman thinks, like Perry, that this self-image is not intrinsically reflexive, since "it picks out the one he is, thus identifying him with one of the world's inhabitants". It is a way of conceiving of oneself as the potential referent of the pronoun 'who', which ranges over persons in general". It is the representation of a person "considered non-first-personally but identified as the subject by some other, extrinsic means".[3]

Identity management does not only concern objective representations, but also concerns unique references to persons by means of descriptions proper names, passwords, personal ID-numbers and user names. We use these descriptions even if we don't know the person or do not see the person, when there are no de re-thoughts. According to John Perry and Kent Bach thinking of a person by means of a description or name should be reconstrued in terms of 'calling up a file on that individual'.[4,5] They give a description of "singular reference" in terms of so-called "files". Perry argues that we receive information on an individual from within a role. Objects and persons can play an "agent relative" role in someone's life, for instance by "standing in front of someone" or "being on the phone with someone". Epistemic and pragmatic methods are attached to these "agent relative" roles, e.g. 'methods for finding out about the object and methods for doing things to the object (…), the success of which depends on facts about the object'.[4] Introducing yourself to someone and shaking that person's hand is an example of applying the information that is attached to the "being in front of someone"-role and what coordinates acting. This is part of the standard information game that people play.

Another important activity in this respect is referred to by Perry as the "detach and recognize information game". Perry gives an example of a business card, but another example could be the checking of a municipal database a "customer relationship database" on the laptop of a travelling sales man or the electronic patient health records of a local hospital. When someone hands over his or her business card, the objective representations on the card (such as name, address, profession, birth date, resume, etc.) are tied/linked to a person.. When one is no longer together, the objective representations are separated from perception. The next time one meets this person again, one can re-attach the information to a perception, recognize the person from the card and re-apply one's own convictions about this person. This procedure of separation and recognition is crucial for communication where separated information is exchanged in a way in which others can re-attach their own perceptions to this person or object'. The objective representations and their separated supplement are "agent relative" perceptual ways of thinking and acting. Perry stresses that 'an objective representation with no possibility of being reattached to its source via some agent-relative role that supports pragmatic techniques is quite useless'.[4]

3   Identity related information and data protection constraints

Descriptive phrases can be said to form partial identities in the sense that they can all figure in tags or contents of mental, physical or electronic files on people: "The man next door", "my best colleague", "the guy with the awful aftershave", "John", "John Smith", "the guy who always takes the 9 o'clock train and gets off at central station", "the owner of a blue ford", "the person who collected 200 Euro at the teller machine in the Centre of Amsterdam at 14:21:11 at August 1 2005", "the person on the cctv tape who put two orange boxes in the trunk of a blue Ford", "the owner of a bank account 1234567", "the person on Flight Q1 from Sydney to London on October 2 2005 in seat 55c", "the idiot with the baseball cap", "the guy who dumped Alice". These description could all be about different persons, they could also be about the same person (in which case the characterizations provide already a lot of information about John Smith), or they could fail to refer, since there is no one who satisfies this list of properties.

Keith Donellan distinguished between referential use of descriptions and attributive use of descriptions. "The owner of a blue ford living in postal code area 2345" could have more than one individual satisfying the description and the user of these descriptions may not have a particular individual in mind; he just thinks about the owner of a blue Ford 'whoever he is'. "The owner of a blue Ford" could also be used referentially, when we have a particular person in mind or in attendance. "The man sipping his whisky" (pointing to the person at a party) is used referentially, and is about the person the speaker mistakenly thought was drinking whisky, even when it turns out he is actually having ice-tea instead of whisky, and there is, strictly speaking, no one over there sipping his whisky.

Both attributively used and referentially used descriptions figure in epistemic and doxastic strategies to collect information on people and to expand our knowledge and belief sets on them. Both represent identity relevant information. One may open a mental or another type of file on a person under the label "the murderer of Kennedy", as crime investigators do. The history of their criminal investigation is at the same time the history of filling the file with identity relevant information. The police has a good deal of freedom to fill the files on suspects and establishes the identity of the criminal. They can use biometric techniques such as fingerprinting, DNA evidence,

Internet traffic data, they can use logistic and travel data, Closed Circuit Television tapes, stories told by eye witnesses and combinations of these.

The moral and legal constraints in the data-protection and privacy laws and regulations that are in place all over the world apply primarily to referentially used descriptions of persons. It should be clear however that both usages of descriptions can play an important role in keeping tabs on people and in managing their identities. The international laws on privacy and data-protection define personal data as follows [6]:

"'personal data' shall mean any information relating to an identified or identifiable natural person ('data subject'); an identifiable person is one who can be identified, directly or indirectly, in particular by reference to an identification number or to one or more factors specific to his physical, physiological, mental, economic, cultural or social identity"

The referential reading of 'identity' and 'identifiable' leads to an unduly narrow construal of moral constraints on identity management techniques. and attributively used descriptions could go unprotected. This seems a major weakness of data protection regimes, since we know that large amounts of data are used attributively, in marketing, security and profiling domains for example. One could have a file on an owner of a blue Ford, and add a long list of descriptions, all used attributively. Adding one piece of information to the rich and anonymous file could suddenly make the data set uniquely referring. Consider Ruth Gavison's anecdote in her article "Privacy and the Limits of Law"[7]:

"Consider the famous anecdote about the priest who was asked, at a party, whether he had heard any exceptional stories during confessionals. "In fact", the priest replied, "my first confessor is a good example, since he confessed to murder". A few minutes later, an elegant man joined the group, saw the priest, and greeted him warmly. When he asked how he knew the priest, the man replied: "Why, I had the honour of being his first confessor".

Did the priest violate the privacy of the elegant man? Gavison thinks that the first piece of information was anonymous and did not violate the confessor's privacy in and by itself. The second piece was about a specific individual, but was volunteered by the person whose privacy is at stake and could therefore also not have violated the man's privacy. Gavison however claims that the latter piece of information "turned what was previously an anonymous piece of information into further information about the individual" [7]: there is "a translation from anonymous information to information about X"

Gavison presents this anecdote in the context of a listing of problems associated with the clarification of the notion of privacy. It all starts with the requirement "that for a loss of privacy to occur, the information must be "about" the individual.

It may well be the case that given the prominence and importance of identity management techniques and technology we need to have a new look at this requirement and instead of defining the object of protection in terms of referentially used descriptions, we need to define the object of protection in terms of the broader notion of "identity relevant information", even if it is not 'about' a particular person, since we know it can be equally useful as a part of an epistemic strategy or doxastic policy to get to know more about particular individuals eventually.

Perry focused on recognition and the importance of reattachment of objective representations to some perception, preparing the information for use ("recognition is a prelude to action"). In recognition, according to Perry, a comparison takes place between the attributes of the person perceived with the attributes of the person one has on file. No matter how vast the files and records and detached objective representations are, since all perception and action takes place by agents at certain times, they need to be (re)attached to perceptions.

This seems again to point in the direction of another narrow construal of the scope of moral constraints on identity management techniques and technology. Recognition may also take place on the level of files of beliefs regarding detached representations, without them being necessarily tied to perceptions. Think e.g. of an insurance agent, who is handling and evaluating insurance declarations. He knows the dossiers, numbers, and names and is looking at a case of a stolen bicycle in one of the big cities. During his lunch break he suddenly realizes that this very same person has had his bicycle stolen last year. The identities our insurance clerk processes are descriptions or objective representations, detached, but the most relevant form of recognition does not seem to require reattachment by him to a perception. As a matter of fact many of the acts of recognition and (re)identification in information rich work environments dealing with identities of individuals are about detached representations which are unlinked to any perception of the data subject.

Many acts of identification in the field relevant for identity management involve descriptions that are used attributively and do not involve re-attachment in Perry's sense.

They are attempted identifications of whoever satisfies the description, without ever being in a position to attach or reattach this in a perceptual context to a particular person. Still these identifications play an important role in epistemic strategies and doxastic policies to learn about persons. We need to think about the moral constraints that may apply to these new practices.

4   Data protection from the perspective of moral autonomy

We will now discuss four types of moral reasons for constraining the management of identity relevant information.

4.1   Information-Based Harm

The first type of moral reason for thinking about constraining identity management by others is concerned with the prevention of harm, which is done to persons by making use of identity related information. Cyber criminals and malevolent hackers are known to have used computerized databases and the Internet to get information on their victims in order to prepare and stage their crimes. One of the most important moral problem is 'identity theft' and identity Fraud, with brings high risk of financial damages and emotional distraught. One's bank account may get plundered and one's credit reports may be irreversible tainted so as to exclude one from future financial benefits and services. Stalkers and rapists have used the Net and on-line databases to track down their victims and they could not have done what they did without tapping these electronic resources and finding out about some of the most intimate details of their victim's lives. In the information society there is a new vulnerability to harm done to one on the basis of identity –theft, identity fraud or straightforward harm using identifying information. Justifications of constraining the freedom of persons who cause, threaten to cause, or are likely to cause, harms to people using identity related information can be justified by invoking Mill's Harm Principle [8]. Protecting identifying information, instead of leaving it in the open, diminishes the likelihood that people will come to harm, analogous to the way in which restricting access to fire arms diminishes the likelihood that people will get shot in the street. In information societies, identity relevant information resembles guns and ammunition.

4.2   Informational Inequality

The second type of moral constraint on identity related information is concerned with equality and fairness. More and more people are keenly aware of the benefits the market for identity information can provide them. If a consumer buys coffee at the modern shopping mall, information about that transaction is generated and added to his file or profile. Many consumers now begin to realize that every time they come to the counter to buy something, they can also sell something, namely, the information about their purchase or transaction, the so-called transactional data. Likewise, sharing information about ourselves on the Net with web sites, browsers, and autonomous agents may pay off in terms of more and more adequate information (or discounts and convenience) later. Many privacy concerns have therefore been and will be resolved in quid pro quo practices and private contracts about the use and secondary use of personal data. But although a market mechanism for trading personal data seems to be kicking in on a global scale, not all individual consumers are aware of this economic opportunty, and if they do, they are not always able to trade their data in a transparent and fair market environment, so as to get a fair price for them. Moreover they do not always know what the implications are of what they are consenting to when they sign a contract. We simply cannot assume that the conditions of the developing market for identity related information guarantees fair transactions by independent standards. Constraints for Identity Management need to be put in place in order to guarantee equality and a fair market for identity relevant information.

4.3   Informational Injustice

A third and very important moral reason to justify constraints on identity management by others is concerned with justice in a sense which is associated with the work of Michael Walzer. Michael Walzer has objected to the simplicity of Rawls' conception of primary goods and universal rules of distributive justice by pointing out that "there is no set of basic goods across all moral and material worlds, or they would have to be so abstract that they would be of little use in thinking about particular distributions" [9] . Goods have no natural meaning; their meaning is the result of socio-cultural construction and interpretation. In order to determine what a just distribution of the good is we have to determine what it means to those for whom it is a good. In the medical, the political, the commercial sphere, there are different goods (medical treatment, political office, money) which are allocated by means of different allocation or distributive practices: medical treatment on the basis of need, political office on the basis of desert and money on the basis of free exchange. What ought to be prevented, and often is prevented as a matter of fact, is dominance of particular goods. Walzer calls a good dominant if the individuals that have it, because they have it, can command a wide range of other goods [9]. A monopoly is a way of controlling certain social goods in order to exploit their dominance. In that case advantages in one sphere can be converted as a matter of course in advantages in other spheres. This happens when money (commercial sphere) could buy you a vote (political sphere) and would give you preferential treatment in healthcare (medical), would get you a university degree (educational), etc. We resist the dominance of money -and other social goods for that matter (land, physical strength) - and we think that political arrangements allowing for it are unjust. No social good x should be distributed to men and women who possess some other good y merely because they possess y and without regard to the meaning of x.

What is especially offensive to our sense of justice is the allocation of goods internal to sphere A on the basis of the distributive logic associated with sphere B, second, the transfer of goods across the boundaries of separate spheres and thirdly, the dominance and tyranny of some goods over others. In order to prevent this from happening the 'art of separation' of spheres has to be practiced and 'blocked exchanges' between them have to be put in place [9]. If the art of separation is practiced effectively and the autonomy of the spheres of justice is guaranteed then 'complex equality' is established. One's status in terms of the holdings and properties in one sphere are irrelevant -ceteris paribus- to the distribution of the goods internal to another sphere.

Walzer's analysis also applies to information. The meaning and value of information is local, and allocation schemes and local practices that distribute access to information should accommodate local meanings and should therefore be associated with specific spheres. Many people do not object to the use of their personal medical data for medical purposes, whether these are directly related to their own personal health affairs, to those of their family, perhaps even to their community or the world population at large, as long as they can be absolutely certain that the only use that is made of it is medical, i.e. to cure people from diseases. They do object, however, to their medical data being used to classify them or disadvantage them socio-economically, to discriminate against them in the workplace, refuse them commercial services, deny them social benefits, or turn them down for mortgages or political office on the basis of their medical records. They do not mind if their library search data are used to provide them with better library services, but they do mind if these data are used to criticize their tastes, and character. They would also object to these informational cross-contaminations when they would benefit from them, as when the librarian would advise them a book on low-fat meals on the basis of knowledge of their medical record and cholesterol values, or when a doctor asks questions on the basis of the information that one has borrowed a book from the public library about AIDS.

We may thus distinguish a third moral reason to constrain identity management: "informational injustice", that is, disrespect for the boundaries of what we may refer to, following Michael Walzer, as 'spheres of justice' or 'spheres of access'. I think that what is often seen as a violation of privacy is oftentimes more adequately construed as the morally inappropriate transfer of personal data across the boundaries of what we intuitively think of as separate "spheres of justice" or "spheres of access."

4.4   Moral autonomy

Even though there are multiple reasons to support data protection, in this paper we focus on moral autonomy – and especially moral identification. It is argued by some that privacy is a necessary condition for (the development of) moral autonomy [10]. It provides a safe place as well as the freedom to experiment in order to develop and protect a personal identity. The development and continuous adaptation of who we want to be and who we want to become are both fundamental to and expressions of our moral autonomy.

We argue that moral autonomy, i.e. the capacity to shape our own moral biographies, to reflect on our moral careers, to evaluate and identify with our own moral choices, without the critical gaze and interference of others and a pressure to conform to the 'normal' or socially desired identities, is one of the moral reasons for constraining identity management by others. A moral person is engaged in self-definition and self-improvement, and experiences the normative pressures which public opinion and moral judgements of others exert on the person to conform to a socially desired identity. Information about Bill, whether fully accurate or not, facilitates the formation of judgements about Bill. Judgements about Bill, when he learns about them, when he suspects that they are made, or fears that they are made, may bring about a change in his view of himself, may induce him to behave and feel differently than he would have done without them.

To modern contingent individuals, who have cast aside the ideas of historical necessity, living in a highly volatile socio-economic environment, and a great diversity of audiences and settings before which they make their appearance, the *fixation* of one's moral identity by means of the judgements of others is felt as an obstacle to 'experiments in living' [8], as Mill called them. This is what happens when one is applying for a job and confronted with - possibly even judged or pre-screened on the basis of - personal experiments on the Internet, by means of chat boxes, You Tube videos, gaming and other activities that pop up when 'googled'[5] by the potential employer. Or, in the case of the Electronic Health Record, data is stored

---

[5] Term used in popular everyday language referring to the use of the Google search engine (www.google.com) to get to know more about a person (or subject).

in the record and directly retrievable revealing preferences of the past that one does not (fully) support any longer or wishes to be associated with, e.g. a visit to the general practitioner concerning the treatment of an infected piercing.

The modern individual wants to be able to determine himself morally or to undo his previous determinations, on the basis of more profuse experiences in life, or additional factual information. As Newton Garver aptly put it:

Contemporary freedom and choice go farther than Mill suspected – we all chose our identities, and make that choice from among a heterogeneous set of data, (…) we rarely choose our nationality, sex or religion, but we do choose to make these data part of our identity"[11]

The conception of the person as being morally autonomous, as being the author and experimenter of his or her own moral career, provides a justification for constraining others in their attempts to engineer and directly or indirectly shape the subjects identity. The fixation of one's moral identity by others than oneself should be prevented in the design of identity management systems and their regulatory framework. This is done by holding on to the requirement of informed consent and notification for the processing of the individual's data. If there are domains where for obvious reasons individuals in well-ordered societies cannot be allowed to write their own biographies from cover to cover, they at least should be allowed to write those parts that are amenable to it and to be given an opportunity to authorize the parts that were or had to be written by others.

For the example that we use of the Electronic Health Record, this works out as follows: Patients should be notified and/or asked for their consent when adding/collecting/processing their data in the system. Moreover, they should have individual access in order to control what information is being kept so that they can become aware what the possible implications of data exchange may be. Imagine for example cases where sensitive information regarding psychological health or birth control is available and accessible. The fixation of one's moral identity could concern categories such as: 'depressed', 'accident prone', 'unstable', 'hysterical', 'quarrelsome' or 'promiscuous' , but also risk categories concerning a particular disease.

4.5   Moral identification

In his analysis of privacy and shame, Velleman states that individuals have a fundamental stake 'in being recognized as a self-presenting creature, an interest that is more fundamental, in fact, than your interest in presenting any particular public image'.[12] Events can be shameful for someone if the person in question is not able to present him- or herself as he or she wishes. This undermines his or her status as a self-presenting individual.[12] 'When something private about you is showing, you have somehow failed to manage your public image, and so an inadequacy in your capacity for self-presentation is showing as well, potentially undermining your standing as a social agent'.[12] Privacy norms are – according to Velleman – implicitly 'norms of competence at self-presentation'.[12]

This is also the case with victims of stereotyping: they are being characterized in a way 'that leaves no room for self-presentation.'[12] Someone being characterized for example on the basis of ethnicity, doesn't have to feel ashamed because of his or her (ethnic) background, but rather because he or she feels represented as 'less than the master of his self-definition and therefore less than a socially qualified agent.'[12] Shame is 'the anxious sense of being compromised in one's self-presentation in a way that threatens one's social recognition as a self-presenting person.'[12] Velleman's analysis of shame suggests that interventions in the identity management and self-presentation of a person by others can compromise the status of a person as a social agent.

A further explanation for the importance of respect for moral autonomy may be provided along the following lines. Factual knowledge of one person by another is always knowledge by description. The person himself however, does not only know the facts of his biography, but is the only person who is acquainted with the associated thoughts, desires, emotions and aspirations. However detailed and elaborate our files and profiles on Bill may be, we are never able to refer to the data-subject as he himself is able to do. We may only approximate his knowledge and self-understanding.

Bernard Williams has pointed out that respecting a person involves 'identification' in a very special sense, which we refer to as 'moral identification'.

"(...) in professional relations and the world of work, a man operates, and his activities come up for criticism, under a variety of professional or technical titles, such as 'miner or 'agricultural labourer' or 'junior executive'. The technical or professional attitude is that which regards the man solely under that title, the human approach that which regards him as a man who has that title (among others), willingly, unwillingly, through lack of alternatives, with pride, etc. (...) each man is owed an effort at identification: that he should not be regarded as the surface to which a certain label can be applied, but one should try to see the world (including the label) from his point of view"[13].

Moral identification thus presupposes knowledge of the point of view of the data-subject and a concern with what it is for a person to live that life. Persons have aspirations, higher order evaluations and attitudes and they see the things they do in a certain light. Representation of this aspect of persons seems exactly what is missing when personal data are piled up in our data-bases and persons are represented in administrative procedures; compare the categories one can be assigned to by combining health data from the Electronic Health Data without the appropriate contextual data.

The identifications made on the basis of data on persons fall short of respecting the individual person, because they will never match the identity as it is experienced by the data-subject. It fails because it does not conceive of the other on his own terms. Respect for privacy of persons can thus be seen to have a distinctly epistemic dimension. It represents an acknowledgement that it is impossible to really know other persons as they know and experience themselves. Even if we could get it right about moral persons at any given point in time, by exhibit of extraordinary empathy and attention, then it is highly questionable whether the data-subject's experience of himself, as far as the dynamics of the moral person is concerned, can be captured and adequately represented. The person conceives of himself as trying to improve himself morally. The person cannot be identified, not even in the sense articulated by Bernard Williams, with something limited, definite and unchanging. This point was by the French existentialist Gabriel Marcel:

"(...) a person should definitely not in any way be compared to an object, which we can say is there, i.e., is given and present before us, and is part of an inherently denumerable collection, or even is a statistical element (...)"[14][6]

The person always sees itself as becoming, as something that has to be overcome, not as a fixed reality, but as something in the making, something that has to be improved upon:

"The person sees him- or herself much less as a being than as a will to transcend the totality of what he or she is and is not, i.e., a reality which he or she feels genuinely committed to and involved in but which fails to satisfy her, because it falls short of the aspirations he or she identifies with"[14][7].

As Marcel puts it, the individual's motto is not sum (I am) but sursum (higher). The human person has a tendency not to be satisfied, but he or she is always aspiring to improve him or herself. Always on his or her way, Homo Viator. This is also suggested by Berlin: "what I may seek to avoid [is to be] insufficiently recognized,… a statistical unit without identifiable … purposes of my own."[15] Because we feel we have inaccessible qualitative aspects of our own private mental states, i.e. that we have hopes and purposes and there is something that it is like to have them, which cannot be known from the outside, we insist on epistemic modesty on the part of others in claiming to know who we are or to be actively involved in the management of our identities. Moreover, we see ourselves as our own moral projects, subject to moral development and capable of moral improvement, so the result of the management of our identities seems a premature fixation of what is an essentially dynamic project.

Respect for persons in the field of identity management involves epistemic modesty in explicit or implicit claims to know who someone is. Individuals resist quite understandably the pretense which seems to be ingrained in the identity management technology and implied in its very idea, to the effect that they can be fully known.

"…the apprehension of the mind of another person may thus only count as knowledge to the extent that it can approximate to this kind of awareness... such an approximation can never be more than a very distant one."[16]

---

[6] Translated by Manders-Huits. Original quote: "(...) il faudra dire que la personne ne saurait être assimilée en aucune maniere a un objet dont nous pouvons dire qu'il est la, c'est-a-dire qu'il est donne, present devant nous, qu'il fait partie d'une collection par essence denombrable, ou encore qu'il est un element statistique (...)".

[7] Translated by Manders-Huits. Original quote: "Elle se saisit bien moins comme etre que comme volonte de depasser ce que tout ensemble elle est et elle n'est pas, un actualite dans laquelle elle se sent a vrai dire engagee ou implique, mais *qui ne la satisfait pas*: *qui n'est pas a la mesure de l'aspiration avec laquelle elle s'identifie*".

When a person is considered as 'one person among others', his attitude and self-directed reactive attitudes (his shame or shamelessness) expresses the kind of person he is. It is the sort of thing we take into account in determining how we feel about him. Moran argues that not doing so would be wrong since it would be failing to respect the "total evidence" of the case. For responding to what he did with shame, pride or gratitude constitutes a new facts about him, which are morally salient and provide part of the total evidence of who he is. Anything less would not only be wrong, but also epistemically irresponsible [16].

5   Conclusion

Through the availability of information technology identities of persons have become objects of manipulation by others than the ones whose identity is at stake. We have argued that all identity related data, also when it concerns descriptions that are not used referentially, but attributively, or descriptions which are not reducible to a unique and perceivable natural person, is worthy of protection and access should be made dependent of the informed consent by the person in question.

We have articulated four moral reasons for the justification of this protection. Constraining the freedom of others to assimilate, process or aggregate data can be justified on the basis of the following considerations: (1) the prevention of harm to the person or data subject, (2) fairness and transparency in the market of identity related data, (3) the separation of social spheres where identity related data has different connotations and practical meanings, and (4) moral autonomy.

Respect for moral autonomy in the meaning defined by us, implies (a) epistemic modesty in knowledge based claims about persons and (b) respect for persons as "self-presenters". The pretense which seems to be ingrained in identity management technologies and implied in the very idea thereof, to the effect that the identity of persons can be fully known, quite understandably stirs up resistance of data subjects involved who appeal against this epistemic arrogation, often by appealing to his or her "privacy".

Therefore, where we cannot leave it completely up to individuals to write their own autobiographies and design their own identities in identity management systems, since some facts about individuals need to be standardized and cannot be under the control of the subject, we argue that they have a right to authorize and correct, when and where appropriate. Moreover, the parts of individuals' identities that need to be managed by others for reasons alluded to above, require not only careful and thorough identification strategies for the sake of accuracy and completeness, but also require attempts at 'moral identification' in Williams' sense. Returning to the example of the Dutch Electronic Health Record, we endorse that patients are to be given the opportunity of control over their data as intended. They should be encouraged to verify and manage their data, in order to keep control over their (perceived) identities and to prevent the patients as persons in this identity management system to become patients as numbers.

Acknowledgements

I wish to thank Bjørn Jespersen for assisting with French translation and Michael Zimmer for commenting on earlier drafts of this paper. I also thank the faculty and students attending the IFIP Summer School for their valuable feedback.

References

1. O. Gandy, The Panoptic Sort, (Westview, Boulder (Colorado), 1993)
2. O. Gandy, 'Dividing practices: segmentation and targeting in the emerging public sphere' in Lance Bennett & Robert Entman (eds), *Mediated Politics: Communication in the Future Democracy*, (Cambridge University Press, New York, 141-159, 2001)
3. D. Velleman, *Self to Self. Selected Essays*, (Cambridge University Press, Cambridge, 2006)
4. J. Perry, *Identity, Personal Identity and the Self*, (Hackett, Indianapolis, 2002)
5. K. Bach, *Thought and Reference*, (Oxford University Press, Oxford, 1987)
6. Directive 95/46/EC on 'The protection of individuals with regard to the processing of personal data and on the free movement of such data', (Official Journal L 281, pp. 31-50, Brussels, 1995)
7. R. Gavison, 'Privacy and the Limits of Law', in F. Schoeman (ed.) *Philosophical Dimensions of Privacy*, (Cambridge: Cambridge University Press, 346-402, 1984)
8. J.S. Mill, *On Liberty,* edited by H.B. Acton (Everyman edition, London, 1972)
9. M. Walzer, *Spheres of Justice*, (Basil Blackwell, Oxford, 1983)
10. B. Roessler, *Value of Privacy* (Polity Press, Amsterdam, 2004)
11. E. Garver, Why pluralism now?, *The Monist* **73**, 388-410 (1990)
12. D. Velleman, 'The Genesis of Shame', *Philosophy and Public Affairs* **30**, 27-52 (2001)
13. B. Williams, *Problems of the Self*, (Cambridge University Press, Cambridge, 1973)
14. G. Marcel, *Homo Viator*, (Aubier, Editions Montaigne, Paris, 1944)
15. I. Berlin, *Four Essays on Liberty*, (Oxford University Press, Oxford, 1969)
16. R. Moran, *Authority and Estrangement. An Essay on Self-Knowledge*, (Princeton University Press, Princeton (NJ), 2001)

Keynote Session 2:

Privacy in the Metaverse

*Regulating a complex social construct
in a Virtual World*

Ronald Leenes

TILT – Tilburg Institute for Law, Technology, and Society,
Tilburg University, the Netherlands,
r.e.leenes@uvt.nl

Abstract. Second Life by many is considered to be more than just a game. It is a social microcosmos in which fairly normal people behave normally and where (complex) social behaviour develops. As such it is an interesting environment to study social and legal phenomena. In this chapter we will look at the privacy and how privacy is regulated within Second Life. The analysis will point out shortcomings of the current mode of governance within Second Life and point at near future changes therein.

1 From Snow Crash to EPIC yearbook

In 1992, some years before the Internet entered the sphere of ordinary people, Neil Stephenson published the sci-fi novel Snow Crash. In this book, Stephenson sketches a bleak future where the US government is almost completely replaced by private organizations and entrepreneurs who run sovereign suburban enclaves, 'Burbclaves'. Other notable features of Stephenson's projection are the perfection of pizza delivery, finally, by 'pizza deliverators' – pizza delivery guy meets Terminator – and that people, besides taking drugs (the title's Snow Crash), have found distraction in the Metaverse. The Metaverse is a computer generated 3D environment where the players move around as Avatars. Central to the Metaverse is 'the Street' which is '... subject to development. Developers can build their own small streets feeding off the main one. They can build buildings, parks, signs, as well as things that do not exist in Reality, such as vast hovering overhead light shows, special neighbourhoods where the rules of three dimensional spacetime are ignored, and free combat zones where people can go to hunt and kill each other.' [1, p.23].

Snow Crash is an interesting novel, not only because it inspired Linden Lab to model what is now known as Second Life (SL) on the Metaverse[1], but also because of the model of governance it offers. The novel depicts a world void of the governance structures common to the Western world. Instead, it shows a libertarian society where traditional government responsibilities are subsumed by corporations and private interest, both offline and online (the Metaverse). Interestingly, Second Life is slowly moving to such a model of governance, where the corporation Linden Lab governs the

---

[1] http://www.usatoday.com/printedition/money/20070205/secondlife_cover.art.htm

Please use the following format when citing this chapter:

Leenes, R., 2008, in IFIP International Federation for Information Processing, Volume 262; The Future of Identity in the Information Society; Simone Fischer-Hübner, Penny Duquenoy, Albin Zuccato, Leonardo Martucci; (Boston: Springer), pp. 95–112.

whole virtual world and a multitude of private entities will govern 'estates'. What Stephenson introduced as a though experiment[2] in the book is in a sense the operating mode of Second Life.

Since 2003, Second Life has evolved into one of the popular massively multiplayer online role-playing games (MMORPGs), with at present some 11 million Residents.[3] Contrary to many other MMORPGs, SL lacks a content-driven plot, enabling it to be used for a multitude of different purposes, such as a platform for social interaction, design, manufacture and delivery of objects and services, or just for exploring a 3D environment.

Perhaps because SL lacks a plot and allows the Residents to define what SL is, the idea has been coined that SL could be perceived as a social microcosmos in which the players exhibit real(istic) social behaviour, which would potentially make it a unique research platform for the social sciences and clinical therapy [2]. This would offer interesting opportunities, not only for the study of people's behaviour, but also for the study of social phenomena and for the experimentation with legal constructs and instruments, including governance.

Whether studying SL behaviour makes sense, and whether drawing conclusions from the virtual world for the real world are valid, or even credible, depends on the extent to which social behavior and norms in SL are comparable to those in the physical world [2]. I will argue that this is the case to some extent. I will do so by exploring some of the information available on the demographics of SL Residents and their behaviour. This includes data about more complex (automatic) social behaviour, such as maintaining interpersonal distance and gaze. The tentative conclusion that can be drawn on the basis of this material is promising: there is congruency of social norms in Second Life and the real world.

Given these results we can then move on to explore one of the more complex social needs, privacy, and explore how this is handled in a relatively novel environment. Because SL is relatively new, relatively anarchistic and highly malleable, it could provide an ideal environment to study whether and how privacy evolves over time. Will privacy be regarded as an outdated social need, or will a genuine need for privacy in this brave new world arise? How do different forms of governance affect privacy in the virtual world? Because the rules of the online environment are flexible, SL could be an ideal test bed to explore a social value such as privacy [3]. EPIC and Privacy International have even gone as far as include Second Life as a jurisdiction in their annual privacy and human rights report 2006 [4].

Privacy may seem an odd social construct to explore in an environment that is aimed at offering its user almost unlimited means to expose themselves. There are inworld (privacy) concerns, such as anonymity, reputation and control over who is watching, and when [4]. These are not only 'game' concerns, but because of the fact that value is created within the game, valued in Linden$, and that these L$ can be

---

[2] See for instance the interview in Reason, February 2005, with the author, http://www.reason.com/news/show/36481.html

[3] http://secondlife.com/whatis/economy_stats.php states that there are 11.234.792 as of 4 December 2007, in the 7 days preceding this date, 332.904 Residents had logged into the virtual world.

exchanged against US$ at the Linden Exchange (the LindeX), they also become real-world concerns. Furthermore, SL Residents not only have Second Lives but also Real Lives. Inworld activities may have Real World ramifications. The interaction between SL and RL creates specific privacy issues. And to make the situation even more complex, the inworld perception of privacy issues are likely to be inspired by the perceived real-world implications of inworld actions. The inworld/real-world border is highly permeable. Given these issues, there may be a privacy need at least on the level of individuals. Whether the social value of privacy will be acknowledged is a different question.

In this chapter we will look at SL as a social microcosmos, privacy issues and privacy regulation in SL, how Residents and game creators (Linden Labs) handle (or mishandle) privacy and how the virtual world permeates the real world. Finally we will look at the state of governance in the game and the outlooks for near future governance and what this may mean for privacy as a social value.

2   Microcosmos or just a game?

Hiro Protagonist, Stephenson's hero in Snow Crash spends considerable time in the Metaverse. His business card reads "Last of the freelance hackers and the Greatest swordfighter in the world". Not your average person, and certainly when one considers that his swordfighting is practiced in the Metaverse as well as in the real world. What about Second Life's Residents? Who are they and what do they online?

A rich data source on MMORPGs is Nick Yee's Daedalus project, which aims at collecting empirical data about "the psychology of MMORPGs".[4] The data reported on in this project, as well as in similar studies, have to be taken with a grain of salt because they are prone to self-reporting and selection biases. Nevertheless, they are indicative for the demographics of MMORPG-gamers. For MMORPGs in general the current statistics show the average age of players to be around 26, about a quarter of them being teenagers. About half of the players have a full-time job, slightly over a third is married and about a quarter have children. MMORPG players, on average, spend about half a working week (22 hours) playing their games, a number not related to their age. This would suggest MMORPG gamers take their games very seriously. Most players (80%) play with someone they know in Real Life (RL) (a romantic partner, family member, or friend).

A large proportion of gamers consider themselves to behave the same in the game as in RL – 72% of the female gamers versus 68.8% of the males, or even better than in RL – 25.8% for the female and 31.8% for the males. This means that only a small percentage says to misbehave and lie online, which is contrary to popular opinion.[5] Other interesting findings of Yee's studies are that many gamers are very social and befriend people they meet online. This is especially the case for the female gamers, of which some 75% report to have a few or a bunch online friends, while only about

---

[4] http://www.nickyee.com/daedalus/gateway_demographics.html
[5] http://www.nickyee.com/daedalus/archives/000193.php

19% has no online friends. Male gamers are more solitary; 33.8% report to have no online friends or just one (7.2%). The distribution of a few and a bunch of friends among male gamers resembles that of female gamers, albeit that the overall joint percentage is lower at 60%. More telling than the number of online friends is whether gamers consider their online friendships real in the sense that information that very few other people know is shared with friends. The female gamers, unsurprisingly, turn out to be more social than the male gamers. 52.9% of the female gamers says to have real deep friendships online. The males score much lower. Only 38.6% of them consider their online friendship deep.

Dutch studies conducted by EPN focus on SL players in the Netherlands. EPN conducted a survey in 2006 [5], when there were some 17.000 Dutch SL Residents, and in 2007 [25].[6] The Dutch data corroborates the intensity of game play found in Nick Yee's studies. More than half of the gamers spend 18-30 hours a week (24%), or even more than 30 hours per week (33%) in Second Life. The 2007 study shows a slight decrease in time spent on the game. Follow up in-depth interviews in 2006 revealed that playing was real playing, and not just 'chair camping' – being online and parking the avatar somewhere, while doing something else, such as watching tv, in the meantime. People play in breaks, evenings, and weekends, basically every free minute. With respect to age distribution among the respondents, the 25-40 group is most strongly represented (50%), while the 16-25 and over 40 groups are about equal in size.

One of the frequent heard claims is that there are many gender experiments within SL. In the 2006 EPN study, this turns out not to be the case for the female players. Female players claim to have female avatars, while only 1 (out of 246) claims to have a male avatar and 2 change their gender occasionally. Among the male players the situation is slightly different. The large majority of male gamers has a male avatar (112), while 15 have a female avatar and 6 change their online gender occasionally. The conclusion here is therefore twofold. Firstly, the gender distribution in the sample is about equal, and secondly, only 10% of the respondents conducts gender experiments, men more than women.

The educational level in 2006 was high, about half of the female respondents has a university degree or even a PhD. For the male players the level is slightly lower. The 2007 study shows a more normalised picture, the overrepresentation of academics has dropped from 48% to 38%. A remarkable finding is that the average income of the players is positively correlated to the amount of time gamers spend online. In other words, heavy players have a higher average income. Here we find a large proportion of IT professionals and creative individuals. Students and public servants generally spend less than 17 hours a week in Second Life.

Based on this limited survey of demographic data we may conclude that the gamers take their games seriously and devote much energy to it. MMORPGs appear to be highly social environments where new relationships are forged and existing relationships are reinforced. Although the game populations, both of MMORPGs in

[6] The 2006 survey was conducted in August/September 2006 and involved 273 gamers, of which 246 completed the questionnaire. The 2007 study was conducted in the summer of 2007 and comprised over 500 respondents.

general and SL in specific, are not representative, there also is not a clear bias towards a particular gender, age, or educational group, apart from SLers by definition being over 18 years of age. Second Life Residents appear to be fairly normal people.

2.1 Inworld social behaviour

Second Life has no plot line, and therefore the Residents themselves define what SL is used for. One way of decomposing SL usage is by distinguishing between SL as a game environment and SL as a functional platform. Yee [6], building on Bartle, provides a comprehensive decomposition of the game aspects of SL (see figure 1).

Table 1. Motivations for gameplay as distinguished by Yee [6].

achievement	social	immersion
advancement progress, power, accumuluation, status	**socializing** casual chat, helping others, making friends	**discovery** exploration, lore, finding hidden things
mechanics numbers, optimization, templating, analysis	**relationship** personal, self-disclosure, find and give support	**role-playing** story line, character history, roles, fantasy
competition challenging others, provocation, domination	**teamwork** collaboration, groups, group achievements	**customization** appearance, accessories, style, color schemes
		escapism relax, escape from RL, avoid RL problems

Yee's study focuses on all MMORPGs and some motives, most notably the motives related to role playing and adventure, will be lacking in SL. According to the EPN studies [5, 25], having 'fun', which is undefined in the studies, followed by 'doing things I can't do in real life' and social motives, such as meeting friends and learning are the primary reasons to adopt a Second Life within the Dutch sample. Mapped onto Yee's ontology, most (Dutch) players have social (socializing, relationship) and/or immersion (discovery, customization, escapism, and a specific kind of role-playing) motives. An interesting observation is that 16 out of 246 respondents indicated that they have a disability in the real world and that this is a motive for them to be in Second Life [5].

Next to game playing, SL can also be used as a functional platform. In this case the environment's rich audio-visual capabilities, as well as the possibility to have group meetings and group interactions are the main drivers. Uses that belong in this category are inworld lectures, courses, and meetings. SL overcomes some of the disadvantages of other computer mediated forms of online learning and online meetings because of the richer visuals cues provided by the avatars as we will see below. SL is also used as a training environment for social interactions. For instance, the Dutch Tax authorities have used SL as a training ground for company search and seizure operations.[7]

Social interaction in both major types of uses is important. But how realistic is the social behaviour exhibited in SL? One interesting anecdote regarding emerging social norms within the game relates to 'virtual laptops', animated laptops to be used within the game. Residents started taking these functional devices with them to inworld bars, restaurants and disco's and using them while within these (social) environments.[8] This behaviour was seen as anti-social and a social norm, netiquette, emerged disproving it. As with all social norms, people have to learn the rules and they may be pointed out to newcomers in blunt or subtle ways.

But also on a deeper level inworld behaviour appears to be guided by real world social norms. Yee et al. [2] studied social norms of gender, interpersonal distance (IPD), and eye gaze transfer in Second Life. They found that even though the modality of movement is entirely different (i.e., via keyboard and mouse as opposed to eyes and legs), that IPD and eye gaze in virtual environments is similar to that in the real-world. Inworld, like in the real world male-male dyads stand further apart than female-female dyads. Furthermore, male-male dyads maintain less eye contact than female-female dyads, and finally, when the interpersonal distance between two avatars decreases this is compensated by averted gaze, which is predicted by the Argyle's Equilibrium Theory. The results on gaze as an indicator for turn-taking is interesting because this visual cue can help improve ICT mediated meetings, which are often plagued by inertia, multiple participants talking at the same time and difficulties assessing who is talking to whom [7].

Another interesting experiment relating to social behaviour in Second Life is the replication of the famous Milgram experiments by Slater et al. [8]. In the original Milgram experiments, people were instructed to inflict (apparently) lethal electric shocks to a stranger on the command of an authoritive figure. A staggering number of people appeared to obey to these commands. The Slater replication [8] features the test subjects to administer a series of word association memory tests to a female virtual human (the learner). When the learner gives a false answer the subject is instructed to administer an 'electric shock' with increasing magnitude. The learner responds with increasing discomfort and protests. Even though the test subjects knew that neither the learner nor the shocks were real, those who saw and heard the learner (23 out of 34) tended to respond to the situation at the subjective, behavioural and physiological levels as if it were real. Their own discomfort with sounds and images of a (virtual) person in distress caused them to behave differently than people who lacked these signals.

The experiments and research reported here do not provide a definite answer to the question whether SL is to be taken as a real social microcosmos, but they do illustrate that people can immerse in virtual environments in a way that resembles their real world behaviour. This, according to Yee et al. 'has significant implications for using virtual worlds to study human social interaction. If people behave according

---

[7] Private communication during a lecture the author gave on SL on June 21, 2007.

[8] I am not making this up, people access SL on their laptops to play on virtual laptops. Where will this recursion stop?

to the same social rules in both physical and virtual worlds even though the mode of movement and navigation is entirely different (i.e., using keyboard and mouse as opposed to bodies and legs), then this means it is possible to study social interaction in virtual environments and generalize them to social interaction in the real world.' [2].

3   Privacy - past tense?

Social interaction is an important motive for people to assume a Second Life. Social interaction involves sharing information with others. Yet information sharing is not unconditional. People have a need to control who has access to what information and they need to be able to play different roles in different arenas. Audience segregation [8] is an essential part of everyday life. Does this also hold for Second Live?

On first sight, Second Life seems to be based on openness and transparency as some of the default settings in the game illustrate.

The players move their avatars around in a 3-D environment and the scene is observed by the player who can take either a first person perspective (called *mouse look* in SL) and look through the eyes of their avatars, or a third person perspective where the camera is detached from the avatar allowing the player to watch both their own avatar as well as the environment. In third person perspective, which is the default in SL, the camera can move independently of the avatar and can be taken to locations different from the avatar's. This practically allows the player to use the camera as a spying device to unobtrusively observe other avatars and their interactions. The camera can even be attached to another avatar without this avatar's awareness. This act comprises virtual stalking. Especially the third person view allows the player to observe much more of their avatar's environment than is the case in the real world which may also infringe on other's privacy because they may be unaware of the observation.

Another difference with the real world is that moving about anonymously is more difficult. Although players can easily, and radically, adapt the appearance of their avatars to make it difficult or even impossible to recognize them, this does not really help, because the avatar's name is clearly visible; by default it hovers above the avatar.

Not only the Resident's name provides information about them. One can also find out more about a particular Resident by inspecting their profile. This can either be done by right-clicking on the avatar, or from within the search function. In the latter case the Resident in question needs not be in the vicinity, but their name is sufficient to pull up their profile. The profile reveals what the Resident wants to reveal about their identity. It contains sections about the Resident's 2nd Life – including photo, date of birth, partner, group memberships, and a 500 char description of the Resident –, websites of interest, inworld interests, and 1st life, where one can provide information about one's real world identity. Many Residents only provide sparse information, especially about their RL identity, but the amount of information available up for grabs surpasses that in RL easily.

In default mode it is also difficult to keep the location of one's Resident hidden from others. The game features an extensive directory that allows any nameable item to be found. Residents and places can be found by entering partial names or words. The location of the item requested can be shown on the map, and the Resident can be teleported right to it. The search results also show whether a requested Resident is online. Residents can keep a list of their inworld friends. This SL address book will also show whether friends are online.

The basic mode of communication in SL is by means of typed text; voice support has only recently been introduced in the game. Residents can either chat to other Residents, or use instant messages. In chat mode, the communication of every Resident within a radius of about 20 meters is visible to the player. This means that Residents can listen in on the communication between other nearby Residents, much like in the real world. Instant messaging resembles RL phone conversations. These are more private and don't require the recipient to be anywhere near.

3.1   Regaining privacy

The preceding section illustrated that, in default mode, SL Residents can learn much about their fellow Residents and their interaction by using the tools provided by the gaming environment. In practice the players have control over the personal data that gets disclosed to other gamers. Furthermore, privacy provisions are also included in the game's regulatory framework, the Terms of Service (ToS) and the Community Standards (CS), which are enforced by Linden Lab. Linden Lab's Privacy Policy, finally, outlines the way in which Linden handles the user's personal data.

Privacy comes into play as soon as a individual enrolls in the game. During registration, the user has to choose a name for their avatar, comprised of a freely chosen first name and a surname to be selected from a list of predefined surnames. Article 2.1 of the ToS requires the user to provide accurate information about their real name, gender, date of birth, and country of residence during registration. Because the user enters into a contract with Linden Lab during registration, article 2.1 of the ToS is binding. The information entered during registration is only available to Linden Lab, unless the user discloses it to other Residents in conversation or includes it in their profile (under the 1st life tab). If a user wants to own land, then additional data has to be provided during registration. This includes payment data (credit card data or PayPal data). In this case also an age check is performed.

Once a user has created a primary avatar, they can also create Alternate accounts, or Alts. These Alts allow a user to engage in the game under a different identity and therefore allow users to segregate audiences. They can go to one island as their normal avatar and switch to an Alt when visiting another. The different identities are unlinkable for the Residents, but Linden can make the connection between the various identities belonging to a particular user account. Alt accounts are used for various reasons. They offer a kind of anonymity and are therefore popular among users who want to misbehave, for instance because they want to grief other Residents (inworld this means making other Residents' SL miserable by acts such as trolling, flaming, and spamming). Linden Lab reports [10] that the number of abuse reports has not increased since the option to create Alts was opened for users with basic – unverifiable – accounts. Audience segregation is also a genuine need for normal users. IBM has a significant presence in Second Life. Their employees with a Second Life do not always want to be associated with the company or be recognizable as IBM employees, and therefore many of them have Alts for private purposes. The 2007 EPN study [25] shows that the Dutch respondents on average have 1.6 avatar, although almost three quarters only has one avatar [25].

The user can change user preferences that affect data disclosure and the Resident's privacy. For instance, users can toggle whether their name is visible to other Residents, whether their profile shows up in search, and whether their online status is visible to friends. It is also possible to manipulate the avatar's status, for instance by setting their status to offline while being online, or by setting it to busy, both suggesting unavailability of the avatar.

Linden on their support pages [12] state that users can create their own private islands, also called private estates, where they have control over who can get to the island by teleporting (which is the principal way to get to an island). The private islands therefore are really enclaves where only the 'happy few' can go and which therefore offer a maximum level of privacy. A final option for gaining some privacy is creating a skybox [12]. A skybox is a private home that lives up high in the sky and that can only be reached by avatars equipped with flight assist scripts. This does not seem to be a very relevant or serious way to get some privacy in SL, but nevertheless.

3.2   Privacy infringements

In principle real world privacy breaches have their counterpart in SL due to the fact that Second Life resembles real life. People are curious and nosy in SL as they are in RL. Whenever Residents are interacting, by text or voice chat, there will also be Residents around that can listen in on the conversation and based on what they hear or see conclude that they want to know more. The various tools outlined earlier allow them to do so. The knowledge that can be acquired by listening in on conversations will often be confined to inworld knowledge. Judging from my own experience, many people use SL as a virtual market square where conversations will cross the SL/RL border. Many people are (also) interested in other Resident's real lives. The distinction between SL and RL easily blurs. And hence information about a Resident's 1st life can often also be obtained easily. From here, Google helps to fill in the blanks.

Inworld, people's curiosity can also be satisfied by calling virtual detective agencies to help. Famous inworld detective agencies are those run by Markie MacDonald's respectively Bruno Buckenburger [14]. Like in the real world, these detectives are employed for various covert operations, including surveillance and spying on people. Well known examples of their line of work are 'honey pot' operations to uncover inworld infidelity.

Residents have inworld relations and also the concept of marriage exists in Second Life, which includes a commitment not to be unfaithful. So, there are Residents who want to know whether their partner is unfaithful. Hamlet Linden [14] reports of the case of Laura Skye who hired Markie MacDonald to set up a honey trap, involving a gorgeous woman or a handsome man hired to approach the target of an infidelity investigation, lay down some seductive pattern on him or her, and see if the suspected philanderer takes the bait. This clearly invades the private sphere of the Resident being investigated. It would be easy to consider this kind of behaviour as part of the game or as confined to the game, but it goes beyond this. As the following section of Hamlet Linden's interview with Laura Skye, who happens to have a relation with the 'suspect' in real life as well as in SL, illustrates:

> "If you had found out he was cheating on you in Second Life," I
> ask her, "how would that effect your real life relationship?"
> "It would be the end of the relationship."
> "You would break up with him in real life?"
> "Oh yes." [14]

An interesting question is whether the activities of the private detectives are legal (within the game). Article 5.1 sub ii of the Terms of Service state:

> "[You shall not] impersonate any person or entity, including, but not limited to,
> a Linden employee, or falsely state or otherwise misrepresent your affiliation with
> a person or entity."

The target of covert operations will often be unaware of who the agent is and what their true affiliation is (i.e., I am not here to befriend you, I am here to try and trap you) [15]. This could be considered as a case of impersonation as meant in ToS article 5.1 sub ii meaning that it is illegal and that Linden could suspend the detective.

There are also numerous devices – bugs – to listen in on conversations and chats on sale in SL which can be used to spy on other Residents [16]. These bugs can be placed anywhere within SL, including on Residents. As we shall see later on, these devices are also illegal within the game, but his does not stop people from using them, like in the real world.

3.3   Crossing borders

Another kind of device that poses privacy concerns, are devices that make SL behaviour visible outside the realm of the game. One example is the SLstats watch [17]. This device, a wrist watch available for free in SL, reports the location of the watch wearer, plus any other avatars in the vicinity to a database outside the SL realm, namely one hosted at SLStats.com. This site constructs a list of the watch wearer's friends on the basis of avatar proximity and duration. This in itself is a privacy infringement for these 'friends' because they often will be unaware of the watch's function. But, because the database is hosted on a website outside SL, it is within reach of search engines such as Google. This makes inworld associations available outside the realm of the game.

There are more ways in which (personal) data flows from Second Life into the Real World. For instance, Linden is implementing a new search feature. On their support Blog they state:[9]

"Be aware that the new search results will be available to the public, once it's released, anyone with a web browser can view them from the Second Life website. The search results may also be picked up by other external search engines such as Yahoo and Google, although we are not explicitly asking search engines to crawl them at this time. It's important to remember that this information is not tied to your real life identity and is the same information that anybody could see with a free Second Life account."

The latter statement may be true, but there is a difference between Residents and the rest of the world. One has to register to SL in order to become a Resident, which means signing up to the game's terms and conditions. These contain privacy protection provisions to which Residents are contractually bound and non Residents are not. Privacy breaches inworld by people with a free SL account can therefore be addressed inworld while this is much harder on the internet at large.

A final area of privacy concerns pertains to the role of Linden Lab in Second Life. Linden by virtue of the Second Life software and infrastructure in principle has access to everything that happens in SL. The Second Life Terms of Service state:

"6.1 Linden Lab uses your personal information to operate and improve Second Life, and will not give your personal information to third parties except to operate, improve and protect the Service."

This provision seems to guarantee the Residents' privacy, as it states that personal information will only be used for the sake of the virtual world itself. The lines following this provision in the ToS, however, sketch a completely different picture:

"Linden Lab can (and you authorize Linden Lab to) disclose any information about you to private entities, law enforcement agencies or government officials, as Linden Lab, in its sole discretion, believes necessary or appropriate to investigate or resolve possible problems or inquiries, or as otherwise required by law."

This is a very open provision. Not only law enforcement and government may receive personal information, but also private entities. Does the provision as it stands exclude any possible recipient? Furthermore, the request may not only pertain to the usual legitimate law enforcement purposes, but to 'investigate or resolve inquiries'. This may include a request by a private party to have the names of all Residents who live in the Netherlands (for instance for sending them ads).

The extent and amount of data possibly collected by Linden is large. Article 6.2 of the ToS reads:

"6.2 Linden Lab may observe and record your interaction within the Service, and may share aggregated and other general information (not including your personal information) with third parties.

---

[9] http://blog.secondlife.com/2007/10/19/new-search-currently-under-development/

You acknowledge and agree that Linden Lab, in its sole discretion, may track, record, observe or follow any and all of your interactions within the Service. Linden Lab may share general, demographic, or aggregated information with third parties about our user base and Service usage, but that information will not include or be linked to any personal information without your consent."

Linden defines personal information in their Privacy Policy [19] as:

"'… any information that may be used to identify an individual, including, but not limited to, a first and last name, home or other physical address, an email address, phone number or other contact information, whether at work or at home."

According to this policy, Linden considers IP addresses not to be personal data. In Europe, the Article 29 Working Party on Data Protection considers IP addresses to be personal data in most cases [18]. This judgment is even more likely in the case of Second Life because most users will use the software at home. But apart from this, article 6.2 of the ToS in itself opens the possibility to collect behavioral patterns and even construct profiles of the Residents. It is easy for Linden to track who goes where and when. Users may be stereotyped on the basis of these data, for instance because there are numerous types of islands in the game. The following names are telling: Camp Darfur, Virtual Dublin, Neufreistadt, Nymphos Paradise. And then there are gay islands, islands with sex clubs, etc. Profiles created on the basis of tracking behaviour may be used by Linden and shared with others.

The data Linden collects of Second Life users includes [19]:

"… a variety of data to monitor system and simulation performance, and to verify your unique identity. This includes specific and general information about your computer hardware and Internet connection, which are stored together but are not personally identifiable. We track usage of customer-service resources in order to ensure high quality interactions. This is in addition to the personal data and billing information collected during the registration process."

This is not very specific. On various SL discussion forums there has been concern about Linden possibly storing every word spoken in Second Life via chat or instant messages [20]. According to Neal Stewart [20], when requesting more information about the Linden data retention policy regarding chats and IM, Robin Linden replied "Logs for chat and IM aren't permanent, although I can't say how long we keep them". That Linden keeps track of conversations would be in line with their statements about handling abuse reports filed by Residents (see below).

Whether or not Linden actually operates as Big Brother in SL is unclear. Their developer level access to the game's infrastructure makes it possible [4] and there is some anecdotal evidence that conversations are being monitored [20].

4   Regulating the Metaverse

We have looked at some of the privacy issues related to Second Life, both within the game as well as outside of the realm of the game. The role of the Terms of Service, Community Standards, and the Linden Lab privacy policy in relation to this have been addressed somewhat in passing. In order to understand how privacy issues are handled in SL we need to look closer at the modalities of regulation regarding Second Life.

Lessig [21] distinguishes four modalities of regulation: social norms, law, market and architecture ("code", ie software). Within Second Life we see all forms of regulation at play, but law and code are the most prominent forms.

Second Life is operated by a US corporate entity with computing facilities in various countries. Linden Lab therefore has to comply with US and foreign law. With respect to privacy and data protection, this creates a number of difficult issues, such as to what extent does the game comply with EU data protection regulation? European citizens active in the game will move from server to server (islands are generally hosted on a dedicated computer) located in different countries.

I will leave this issues aside here and instead focus on inworld regulation and on what is coined "Linden Law": the Terms of Service, Community Standards and Privacy Policy. These codify the social norms (as Linden sees them fit) into written rules and provide for effective enforcement of these rules [22]. The participants in Second Life enter into a contract with Linden Lab when they register for the game. By entering into an agreement the participants agree to be bound to the provisions in the various documents outlined. Linden Law therefore provides Linden Lab with an instrument to regulate the behaviour of the players in Second Life.

Apart from the rules set out in Linden Law, there is also regulation at the code level. Irrespective of the question whether monitoring of conversations by bugs is permissible according to Linden Law, Linden can make the act of creating bugs or attaching them to objects possible or impossible. By changing the software Linden can control all sorts of behaviour. Teleporting, creating skyboxes, attaching camera's to other Residents, the possibility of storing conversation, are all controlled by the (implicit) rules embedded in the software.

Enforcement of the rules in Second Life is handled in two ways, both ultimately involving code. When rules are (implicitly) embedded in code, such as in a hypothetical ban on bugs, the enforcement will be automatic. In this case the software will simply make the impermissible behaviour impossible. In the case where rules in ToS or CS are at play, punishment involves code. The three most important forms of punishment in Second Life are warnings, suspension (temporary or permanently) and banishment to "the Corn Field". The Corn Field is a moonlit environment that only contains rows of corn, two television sets, an aging tractor and a one-way teleport terminal allowing no escape.[10] Suspension is implemented by the impossibility to log into the game by means of one's username and password for the period of the ban. In

---

[10]http://www.secretlair.com/index.php?/clickableculture/entry/hidden_virtual_world_prison_r
evealed/

the case of banishment to the corn field, the software prevents the Resident from escaping from it for the duration of the punishment.

4.1   Regulating privacy

Inworld, the primary privacy framework consists of the Community Standards (CS) and the Terms of Service. The CS sets out six behaviours, the Big Six, that may result in suspension, or even expulsion from the game. Rule 4 of the Community Standards addresses privacy in the form of a data protection clause:

"4. Disclosure
Residents are entitled to a reasonable level of privacy with regard to their Second Lives. Sharing personal information about a fellow Resident including gender, religion, age, marital status, race, sexual preference, and real world location beyond what is provided by the Resident in the First Life page of their Resident profile is a violation of that Resident's privacy. Remotely monitoring conversations, posting conversation logs, or sharing conversation logs without consent are all prohibited in Second Life and on the Second Life Forums."

Residents can file abuse reports using a comprehensive form available within the Second Life application. Each abuse report will be investigated by the Community Affairs Committee, which is the Linden team. According to [12], the Abuse Team investigates each abuse report on the basis of screenshots, chat logs (remember Linden storing conversations) and other tools to make sure that the claim is valid. On the basis of this evidence it will determine whether an offense is committed and if so, action will be taken against the wrongdoer. The reporter will be notified and the suspension will be reported publicly (without providing details with respect to reporter and wrongdoer) on the Police Blotter website.[11]

For serious misbehaviour, defined as warranting a two-week suspension, a *Review for Ban* procedure will automatically be triggered [13]. The Linden staff reviews the offender's entire disciplinary history to determine whether a permanent expulsion is in order. In this process the advice of the Resident Review Panel on the specific case is taken into account. The Resident Review Panel consists of 25 active Residents, chosen anonymously and at random. The panel reviews the, anonymised, case history and voices their opinion.

The Community Standards are subsumed under the Terms of Service, which provides a more abstract privacy provision. Article 4.1 sets the stage by providing a blanket clause for (im)proper conduct within SL. It reads:

"4.1 You agree to abide by certain rules of conduct, including the Community Standards and other rules prohibiting illegal and other practices that Linden Lab deems harmful."

---

[11] http://secondlife.com/community/blotter.php

The scope of 'other rules' is not specified and could include much more than what is defined in the sub-articles of Article 4.1 ToS, most notably sub-article iv, which states:

"you agree that you shall not: ... (iv) take any action or upload, post, e-mail or otherwise transmit Content as determined by Linden Lab at its sole discretion that is harmful, threatening, abusive, harassing, causes tort, defamatory, vulgar, obscene, libelous, invasive of another's privacy, hateful, or racially, ethnically or otherwise objectionable;"

This provision is interesting because, unlike CS rule 4 which defines a complaints based offense, it defines behaviour that can be addressed by Linden at any time, even without prior complaint by a Resident. Furthermore, Linden, by virtue of 'as determined by Linden Lab at its sole discretion', provides itself with unlimited powers to define behaviour as offensive. Residents can be 'prosecuted' for privacy offenses on the basis of ToS article 4.1 and the CS (Rule 4). Punishment can take place on the basis of article 2.1 ToS, which states that:

"Linden Lab may suspend or terminate your account at any time, without refund or obligation to you. Linden Lab has the right at any time for any reason or no reason to suspend or terminate your Account, terminate this Agreement, and/or refuse any and all current or future use of the Service without notice or liability to you."

4.2   Governance?

The combination of Linden Law, code and the procedures Linden has put in place provide a mode of governance within the game. But what kind of governance? The ToS and procedures places much emphasis on Linden acting on their own discretion. They are open to suggestions, but making decisions about the rules and their enforcement are considered to be their call. Linden acts as a 'benevolent dictator', doing what is best for the community, without democratic participation or assurance of transparency [22].

Second Life is not the first virtual environment facing a democratic deficit. LambdaMOO is a famous example of a system that in the early 1990s was run by a small group of system administrators (the Wizards) who decided on issues within the game [reported on in 22]. In 1992 the Wizards decided to institute a form of self-governance by means of ballots in the game. Because proper means of enforcement of decisions made through the ballot system lacked, LambdaMOO turned into a rough place where '[t]he level of inter-player strife and harassment rose and rose, slowly but inexorably' [23]. This is precisely what the Lindens try to prevent.

Here now is an interesting dilemma. On the one hand Linden does not want to interfere in the game and play judge and jury, yet on the other hand it acknowledges that some form of global governance is needed to prevent the game from becoming an anarchy that will deter users.

Philip Linden has stated that "We will not restrict Second Life by adding constraints which might make it more compelling to a specific subset of people but have the effect of reducing the broadest capabilities it offers to everyone for communication and expression." [24]. Instead, Linden is looking for means of local control. Linden is gradually implementing tools that help groups control their members.

"Groups have new features that allow them to fine tune the rights and responsibilities of their members. Individuals are better able to manage their personal experience of Second Life using features like improved mute. Parcel owners have a no-push setting and a larger ban list. Estate owners can assign a Covenant to their land that explains the rules they wish visitors and Residents to abide by, rules that reflect their values and goals." [24]

Linden foresees a role for themselves on the "problems that threaten the stability of our technical, economic and social structures" and they will police on these matters. "But when it comes to deciding what behavior should be allowed in a particular place or social group, those rules and their enforcement will be decided by the people involved—those who understand the context of the situation and have a stake in its outcome. Linden Lab is carefully planning the move to this federated model ..." [24].

The first steps towards this federated model were taken early in 2007. It involved introducing an "Estate Level Abuse program, designed to allow estate owners to receive and resolve their own abuse reports in the method in which they best see fit."[12] The Local Governance Study Group[13] endorses Linden's proposals and devotes considerable energy to further develop these ideas. The LGSG has made a proposal outlining procedures for entities to create a new group-like abstraction called "government" (or "state') for a fee (higher than that for instituting a group, which is L$ 1000). Each government should have a name, flag or symbol, national anthem, government type (monarchy, democracy), constitution, details about land and citizens and details about decision making. Furthermore, it proposes that any parcel of land should be allied to one specific government or no government, in which case "anarchy" or "ungoverned" should appear in the "About>Land" box.

Governments are to have jurisdiction over certain parcels of land and within these jurisdictions the governments could experiment with forms of governance, including means for defining and enforcing rules.

The system of local governance allows for different kinds of estates to be created suiting the different needs of the participants. One could imagine:

"a large corporation buying a series of islands as a showcase for its products or services might want a system whereby misbehaviour on its lands can be punished by banishment without it having to do any of the hard work, but where it retains ultimate control; a commercial landlord might want a full-fledged system of civil

[12] http://blog.secondlife.com/2007/04/20/introducing-estate-level-governance/
[13] http://lgsg.wetpaint.com/page/LGSG+Proposed+Tools+-+2nd+Draft, last consulted on Dec 10, 2007.

law; including contract and covenant enforcement to entice serious businesses and consumers at once; a group of aspiring businesspeople and artisans wishing to start their own community and share resources might want a democratically elected local council; and an individual who wants an island for creating whimsical artistic follies might want no government at all." [27]

5 Conclusion

We have now come full circle. Snow Crash depicted a world run by corporate entities that set and enforce the rules within their own territories. Linden Lab's move towards Estate Level governance and the Local Governance Study Group's proposal for governance tools go a long way into creating these Burbclaves. This seems an apt move in a social microcosmos. Local governance alleviates many of the problems inherent in the Linden's original model [26]. Linden, for instance simply does not have the resources to address conflicts relating to inworld contracts. As outlined in the previous section it also allows for models of governance to fit the needs of groups of users.

The analysis in this chapter aimed to show that privacy is inadequately handled in the current governance model. It will be interesting to see local governance develop. Different governance models are likely to develop within the game and some will certainly address privacy needs of the individual (think of estates aiming at certain vulnerable subgroups). Whether privacy as a social value will be acknowledged and handled within these diverse forms of governance is a different question.

References

1. Stephenson, N. Snow Crash. London: Penguin, 1992.
2. Yee, N., Bailenson, J. N., Urbanek, M., Chang, F., & Merget, D. (2007). The Unbearable Likeness of Being Digital: The Persistence of Nonverbal Social Norms in Online Virtual Environments CyberPsychology and Behavior, 10(1), 115-121.
3. Bradley, Caroline. M. & Froomkin, A. Michael. (2003) Virtual Worlds, Real Rules, State of Play I conference.
4. EPIC and privacy International, Privacy and Human Rights 2006, Washington: EPIC, 2007. Availble at <http://www.epic.org/phr06/>
5. Nood, David de, Attema, Jelle, Second Life, the Second Life of Virtual Reality, the Hague: EPN, 2006. Available at <http://www.epn.net/interrealiteit/Second_Life-Het_Tweede_Leven_van_Virtual_Reality.pdf>
6. Nick Yee, Motivations of play in online games, Journal of Cyberpsychology and Behaviour, 9, 772-775.
7. Roel Vertegaal, Look who's talking to whom: mediating joint attention in multiparty communication and collaboration. PhD thesis, University of Twente, 1998.
8. Erving Goffman, The presentation of self in everyday life, Edinburgh, University of Edinburgh, 1956.

9. Slater M, Antley A, Davison A, Swapp D, Guger C, et al. (2006) A Virtual Reprise of the Stanley Milgram Obedience Experiments. PLoS ONE 1(1): e39. doi:10.1371/journal.pone.0000039

10. Linden Lab, Alt Accounts and Griefing, Second Opinion, Oct 2006, http://secondlife.com/newsletter/2006_10/html/police_blotter.html

11. http://secondlife.com/knowledgebase/article.php?id=358

12. Linden Lab, Police Blotter: Dealing with Assault in Second Life, Second Opinion, June 2006, http://secondlife.com/newsletter/2006_06/.

13. Linden Lab, Police Blotter: Getting terminated - How it happens, Second Opinion, Feb 2006, http://secondlife.com/newsletter/2006_02_15/.

14. Hamlet Linden, Watching the Detectives, New World Notes, March 22, 2005, http://secondlife.blogs.com/nwn/2005/03/watching_the_de.html

15. Hamlet Linden, Spy Game, New World Notes, 13 Feb, 2007, http://nwn.blogs.com/nwn/2007/02/spy_game.html

16. Cienna Samiam, Linden Lab Supports Invasion of Your Privacy?, The Second Life Herald, 25 Mar 2005, http://www.secondlifeherald.com/slh/2005/03/linden_lab_supp.html.

17. Pixeleen Mistral, SLStats: Is Big Brother Watch-ing?, The Second Life Herald, 3 Aug, 2006, http://www.secondlifeherald.com/slh/2006/08/slstats_is_big_.html

18. Article 29 WP, Opinion 4/2007 on the concept of personal data, 01248/07/EN WP 136.

19. http://secondlife.com/corporate/privacy.php, accessed on 17 June 2007.

20. Neal Stewart, Big Brother Linden is Watching You!, http://nealstewart.blogspot.com/2005/08/linden-lab-all-knowing_22.html

21. Lawrence Lessig, Code and other Laws of Cyberspace, New York: Basic Books, 1999.

22. Viktor Mayer-Schönberger and John Crowley, Napster's Second Life? The Regulatory Challenges of Virtual Worlds, Northwestern University Law Review, 100.4 (Summer 2006): 1775-1826.

23. Pavel Curtis, the Incredible Tale of LambdaMOO, Jun 19, 2002, http://www.g4tv.com/techtvvault/features/38666/The_Incredible_Tale_of_LambdaMOO.html

24. Linden Lab, Civic Center: Bigger and Better, http://secondlife.com/newsletter/2006_12/

25. Nood, David de, Attema, Jelle, Residents in analyse – De feiten over Second Life na de hype (Residents analysed - the facts on Second Life after the hype), the Hague: EPN, 2007. Available at http://www.epn.net.

26. Local Government Study Group, Benefits of Local governance, http://lgsg.wetpaint.com/page/Benefits+of+local+governance+in+virtual+worlds

Young People's Gender and Identity Work in a Swedish Internet Community

Malin Sveningsson Elm

Karlstad University, Sweden
malin.sveningsson@kau.se

Abstract. One of the most popular Swedish online meeting places is the community portal Lunarstorm, which is visited above all by young people. During the last years, media has described how teenage girls have been contacted at Lunarstorm and lured into sexual activities. This in turn has led to further discussions on the way teenagers present themselves online. The adolescence is a time to explore identity and to find out who one really is. The way to an independent identity goes through experimenting, and it is important to find places where this can be done away from the surveillance of the adult generation. Here, online meeting places may have an important part to fill. This paper is a presentation of a research project (2005-2007) that sets out to study what role Lunarstorm plays in the identity work of young Swedes. It presents the methodological and theoretical points of departure, and summarizes the main findings of the project.

1 Introduction

One of Sweden's most frequented meeting places is the community portal Lunarstorm[1]. Lunarstorm is especially popular among young people, and it is the web site where young Swedes spend most time – on average 45 minutes a day. Half of the users are under 18 years old, the single largest group found among 15 to 20 year-olds. Within this group, 85% of all Swedes visit Lunarstorm at least once a week and 29% every day[2]. In other words, Lunarstorm is a place where young people hang out together and thus a place where much identity work is done.

Young people's use of meeting places online implies that the means for adults, such as parents and teachers, to get insight into and control what young people do may decrease. This, in turn, has often lead to moral panics [1]. Popular culture has often been interpreted as threats towards young people. The reason being that it is often associated with the leisure time of the young or with the borderlands between family, school and work upon which the fosterers have limited possibilities to exercise control [2]. The mass media play an important part in this process, and to a great extent create it by describing the phenomenon in a stereotypical, exaggerated or even erroneous way. During the last years, Swedish media have addressed the issue of youngsters' doings in Lunarstorm. Girls and young women have been reported to be

---

[1] www.lunarstorm.se
[2] Statistics available at: www.lunarworks.se, Nov. 2005.

Please use the following format when citing this chapter:

Elm, M.S., 2008, in IFIP International Federation for Information Processing, Volume 262; The Future of Identity in the Information Society; Simone Fischer-Hübner, Penny Duquenoy, Albin Zuccato, Leonardo Martucci; (Boston: Springer), pp. 113–126.

contacted in Lunarstorm, and persuaded to pose in pornographic pictures, or lured into sexual contacts. These stories have caused discussions on the way young women and teen age girls present themselves in their personal pages in Lunarstorm, where presentations of self are often said to be sexually provocative[3].

The discourse on young women's presentations of self in Lunarstorm evokes questions on girls' and women's sexuality, which has often been seen as a threat, both to society and to the women themselves [3]. It is often not even acknowledged, but women are rather seen as victims being abused by male predators. Media discourse affects public ideas, and many parents and educators think of internet use as a potential danger to their girls [4]. The question, however, is how true these images are. Of course it does occur that young women are abused and persuaded into doing things they would rather not have wanted to do, but the point is that media coverage is quite one-sided. On the whole, it reproduces the image of women as weak and (sexually) passive and of men as strong and (sexually) active. Furthermore, for those with personal experiences of Internet communication and -communities, the image depicted in media appears quite unfamiliar. In general, online communities are not fora where all inhibitions are dropped and users engage in wild orgies of pornographic exposures of self (unless the forum is explicitly focused on pornography and sexual activities of course).

However, I had no previous experience of the specific web community Lunarstorm, and decided to see what things really looked like there. Other questions I had in the start of this project were how young women's attitudes towards sexuality really look today, and what part meeting places on the Internet, such as Lunarstorm, play in these attitudes, as well as in the social practices of young women. Could the Internet be seen as a space where they can, in a relatively safe way, experiment with sexuality and gender identity, and where an exposure of the body can be done in another way, perhaps with a different meaning, than in offline environments? Another side of the problem is that media stories were all about young women, while young men's presentations of self were not discussed at all. However, meeting places like Lunarstorm imply new means for young men too to develop identity, experiment with sexuality and try out new, alternative gender identities - identities that they might not otherwise have been able to explore, due to constraints and expectations put on them from society [cf. 5 , in her study on bisexual young men living in a small town].

This project takes as point of departure the assumption that meeting places on the Internet may play an important part in both men's and women's gender- and identity work. The aim of the project was to look at the function Lunarstorm fills in young Swedes' gender- and identity work.

---

[3] Paradoxically enough, Lunarstorm is known to be a relatively secure web community, with much social control and regulated behavior among its users. The owners of Lunarstorm also cooperate with the Swedish police, in order to prevent crimes such as for example prostitution and child pornography.

2   Identity and identity work

In society today, the individual has increasingly come to be seen as creating him/herself [6]. This view of identity as "doable" is one of the premises of this analysis, which is also revealed by my choice of the phrasings "identity work" and "identity construction". I here side with the view of identity not as a stable and static entity, but rather as a dynamic and changeable property, which, in its making, needs to be performed in front of others, and is elaborated in dialogue with others. I.e., individuals construct their identities in the interaction with other human beings [cf. 7, 8].

As Giddens [9] says, modernity confronts individuals with a complex abundance of choices, but at the same time, it offers little guidance as to what they should choose. This dilemma is perhaps especially difficult for young people. The adolescence is a period of exploring identities, where the eternal question seems to be "Who am I?" Young people of today are not bound by the constraints of rules and norms of old patterns of life, which implies a freedom to find their own way of life [10]. However, it also implies that they stand without the support that traditions used to be for the individual's choices of life. They are expected to make decisions and form identities on their own, in a world where the power of authorities have diminished, and where, at the same time, there is an abundance of different roles and ideals to choose between. This may be especially difficult for young women, who have to deal with many conflicting ideas of what femininity is, and what it means to be a woman [11], but neither for young men is it an easy task to relate to the often contradictory ideals of masculinity [cf. 12, 13].

The way to independence goes through experiments. Therefore, says Ganetz [10], one of the distinctive marks of youth culture is the seeking for places where one can decide for oneself, and be on one's own with peers, without the interventions from either parents or grown up representatives of authorities. These places, says Ganetz, are absolutely necessary for the individual to seek, experiment with and create an own identity. The free spaces of boys have traditionally been territories set up in public places. For girls and women, on the other hand, streets and other public spaces have often been experienced as dangerous places to be in, and visibility in public has therefore often been the privilege of boys and men [14]. Girls have instead mainly sought their free spaces in the home, at shopping malls, or other places that offer some security, but which on the other hand also are supervised in one way or another. The Internet could here have an important part to play, being a public, unsupervised arena, although visited from secure places like the home, school or library. Even though researchers and media alike have pointed at harassment and inequalities online [15-17], the internet has also frequently been called a "safe haven" for women, and for girls engaging in identity work [4, 18-20]. Here, they can try out various roles and identities, in safety at home, while at the same time the medium provides them with an audience in which to mirror themselves in their identity work. However, the aspect of security is important not only for women – men who display alternative gender identities may also profit from the absence of physical reprisals as a consequence of their performances.

3   Gender as created and performed

This project has a constructivist perspective, which holds that gender properties are not inherently written into individuals' minds. A male body is not necessarily followed by a male gender. Rather, gender is created, or "done". Gender is created by being performed: it is not a cause of, but rather an effect of different sorts of actions [21] Enacting and displaying certain properties that are generally associated with one specific gender thus becomes the means through which gender is created. People constantly "do" gender, i.e., they make performances that display characteristics that are thought of as masculine or feminine, and in doing so; they construct themselves to fit into one of the categories men or women. As Goffman [22: 7] puts it:

"What the human natures of males and females really consists of, then, is a capacity to learn to provide and to read depictions of masculinity and femininity and a willingness to adhere to a schedule for presenting these pictures, and this capacity they have by virtue of being persons, not females or males. One might just as well say there is no gender identity".

Individuals always play different roles in different contexts [8]. When an activity takes place in the presence of other people, the actor performs so as to accentuate some aspects of self, while suppressing others. The aspects of self that are accentuated typically correspond to norms, conventions and ideals that are embraced in the group that the actor belongs to, or wishes to belong to. In all groups, some norms have higher status than others, implying that some behavior gives more "rewards" than others, typically in the form of positive (or lack of negative) responses from the audience. This means that characteristics that are highly valued within the group are likely to be displayed more frequently than characteristics with lower value.

This is also applicable to gender performances, as some kinds of masculinities and femininities get more rewards than others. There are many co-existing kinds of masculinity that relate to each other [23]. The concept *hegemonic masculinity* is defined as "the configuration of gender practice which embodies the currently accepted answer to the problem of the legitimacy of patriarchy, which guarantees (or is taken to guarantee) the dominant position of men and the subordination of women" [23: 77]. Hegemonic masculinity is the form of masculinity that is the most valued in a certain society at a given time. What is valued depends on the societal context, and what is hegemonic is therefore changeable in time and space. However, it is important to note that far from all men fit into the ideals of hegemonic masculinity, which should be seen more as an ideal to relate to. As Connell [23: 78] says, "hegemony relates to cultural dominance in the society as a whole. Within that overall framework there are specific gender relations of dominance and subordination between groups of men". Some masculinities are for example seen as complicit, i.e., consisting of men who take advantage of men's privileged position without themselves living up to the ideals of hegemonic masculinity. Other masculinities are seen as subordinated, i.e., those that are associated with femininity, among which homosexual men are the most obvious [23].

There is no equivalent – no hegemonic femininity – that can be directly applied to women. Because hegemonic masculinity implies men's superior position relative to women, the notion of hegemony is difficult to translate to processes and power relations between women [24]. Inspired by Beverley Skeggs, Fanny Ambjörnsson states that there still exist different kinds of femininity, which are valued differently and which hold different positions relative to each other. Ambjörnsson calls the most highly valued femininity "normative femininity" [24: 29].

4 Presentation of self

Besides theories on gender and identity I have also been using theories on the presentation of self, most notably Goffman's concepts of back stage and front stage, and audience segregation [8]. The concept 'front stage' refers to when the actor is involved in doing a performance. The concept can be divided into two aspects: the 'setting', which is the place where the performance takes place, and the 'personal front', which can refer either to the equipment or items needed to perform, or to the personal characteristics of the actor. 'Back stage', on the other hand, is when the performing person, the actor, is present but the audience is not. The actor is either alone, or in a group in which the members cooperate around the performance - a team. Back stage is a place or a situation, in which the actor can relax and step out of character, and it can be used for preparing and rehearsing the role until it is time to step out before the audience again[4].

The sections above have hinted at how norms and ideals may differ between various settings. This is something that the socially skilled individual always has to deal with when performing in front of others, because the different roles played by the same individual in different contexts may, most probably, sometimes be inconsistent. Actors therefore try to keep contexts and audiences apart, in order to be spared from embarrassment resulting from conflicting roles. This process is called 'audience segregation' by Goffman.

5 Method

In Lunarstorm, users create "krypin" (or "dens", in English), which are their own personal sites on Lunarstorm, where they present themselves. Here, I looked at how young men and women represent themselves. How is femininity and masculinity performed? Are gender identities expressed in a stereotypical way or does the medium encourage users to express new, alternative forms? And if so, what do they look like?

Lunarstorm has a friend finder facility where users can specify the characteristics of other users they wish to find. To get a sample of users, I used this friend finder facility, specifying age and gender, while letting city of residence vary with users.

[4] It should be noted that 'back stage' is a relative term and exists only in relation to a *specific* audience. Whenever performers are not alone, they are in a performance. In the back region, another performance may be given before the other team members, although typically, the roles that the actor performs before different audiences will be different.

This was done in turn for female users 15, 16, 17, 18 and 19 years old, and for male users of the same age groups. This resulted in a sample of 50 users from each age and gender group, i.e., 500 in total[5]. At the time I collected my data (2004-2005), nests could have 13 sub-pages: pres, guest book, diary, friends, clubs, roots, hot, quiz, lists, collage, stuff, party and status. In this study, I chose to delimit the scope of study to three sub-pages: pres, stuff and collage pages[6].

A quantitative content analysis was made of the "pres", "stuff" and "collage" pages of all 500 nests. Quantitative content analysis has been described as the objective, systematic and quantitative presentation of the manifest content of a message [25]. As other quantitative methods, it is supposed to be independent of who is doing the analysis, and so the units of analysis (i.e., what parts of the content are to be counted) are usually decided and fixed before the analysis takes its start. In other words, content analyses are usually deductive. However, in this study, the approach was inductive. In the analysis, I looked for what aspects of self the young people expressed in their nests, but I did not know beforehand which aspects these would turn out to be. I therefore let the data gradually give rise to the categories for analysis. The method used could thus be described as a hybrid - quantitative content analysis with streaks of thematic analysis or grounded theory [26], or the other way around: a thematic analysis where the resulting categories became subject to a statistical analysis.

The analysis started with the pres page of each nest. There, all components such as texts, links, pictures and other graphical elements, as well as the graphic design were described. Similar inventories were made for the stuff and collage folders. I wrote brief descriptions of 50-250 words of each nest, and classified them according to what aspects of self each user emphasized. These aspects of self will in the following text be referred to as "themes". I chose not to limit myself to a certain number of themes, but all themes that were expressed were included. The number of themes per nest therefore ranges from 0 to 23, with a mean of 4.28 and a median of 4. When classifying the themes, no consideration was taken into how large extent a certain theme was stressed, but data were treated on a nominal scale where all cases of occurrence were given the value one and the rest of the cases the value zero.

---

[5] Information about age and gender is acquired automatically by Lunarstorm's software in the registration process, i.e. when the users provide their personal number. Even if this decreases the risk of gender crossing, it is of course still possible that some of the users have provided fake numbers to appear to be of another gender or age than is actually the case.

[6] The pres is where visitors arrive when clicking other users' name links. Here, first impressions are created, and visitors decide whether to proceed to look at the other sub-pages, sign the guest book or take other initiatives to contact. Pres pages vary greatly in how much information users provide. Some do not give any information at all, besides the user name. Others write detailed descriptions about themselves, their background, interests and relationships to other people. On "stuff" pages, users publish material such as photos, texts, drawings, sound files, video clips, links to web sites and other material. "Collage" pages work like photo albums. The main difference from the stuff page is that the material is more clearly organized and that users have more disk space at their disposal and can thus publish more material.

Analyses have been made on the whole as well as on parts of this material, where I used the large study as a point of departure and entered more deeply into aspects that I saw as specifically interesting. I have here used different types of sample procedures and analysis methods. Quantitative analyses (frequencies and crosstabs) were made with SPSS. Qualitative analyses included thematic analyses, case studies, and analyses of pictures, done on material strategically chosen with respect to its content.

6   Results

A survey of the material resulted in 94 different themes that were grouped into 20 categories. The categories with least number of occurrences (i.e. those stressed by less than 2% of both men and women[7]) were sorted out, leaving us with 16 categories as shown in table 1.

Table 1. Categories of orientations

	Men %	Women %	Men Sum	Women Sum	Significance[8]	N
Relationships	58,4	79,2	146	198	***	344
Culture	47,2	47,2	118	118	-	236
Feelings	18,4	30,4	37	76	***	113
Sport	25,2	18	63	45	-	108
Animals	7,6	29,2	19	73	***	92
Humor	21,6	14,4	54	36	*	90
Exposure of Body	14,4	20,8	36	52	-	88
Party	12,8	20,8	32	52	*	84
Motorvehicles	23,6	7,6	59	19	***	78
Work & Education	11,2	18,4	28	46	*	74
Exposure of Status	14	5,2	35	13	***	48
Technology	14,4	6	36	15	**	51
Politics	6,8	6,4	17	16	-	33
Heterosexuality	8,4	2,8	21	7	**	28
Ethnic origin	3,6	3,6	9	9	-	18
Cooking	1,2	5,2	3	13	*	16

Juxtaposing the presentations of young men and women, we see that the young men are in the majority in the categories humor, motor vehicles, exposure of status, technology, and heterosexuality. The young women, on the other hand, are in the majority in relationships, feelings, animals, party, work and education, and cooking. Hence, even though differences were not significant for the categories culture, sport,

---

[7] Those were nature, hunting and fishing, religion and gambling.
[8] The asterisks * mean that the difference is significant. *p<0.05 **p<0.01 ***p<0.001

politics and exposure of physical body, in the rest of the categories we see that the expressed interests follow a strongly gender stereotypical pattern as described by authors such as Connell [23], Davies [27], Frosh et al, [28], Skeggs [3], Svahn [29] and Walkerdine [30].

Practising and displaying one's interests can be seen as one type of gender work [cf. 6], and of doing gender. Frosh et al (2002), for example, saw that for young men in Britain, it was important to display and stress an interest in football in order to be seen as properly masculine. The young men who did not have this interest (or pretended to have it) often ran into problems with their peers, being considered feminine (and thereby put under suspicion to be homosexual and as such seen as non-men, or at least subordinated (Connell, 1995)). This strong polarization was not found in my data, at least not in relation to sport, which is quite evenly distributed among men and women. In general other aspects seem to be seen as more gender specific than sport.[9] The categories that host the biggest gender differences are motor vehicles (76/24), heterosexuality (75/25), exposure of status (73/27), technology (70/30), feelings (33/67), animals (21/79), and cooking (19/81). It is thus likely that these aspects are seen as more important to stress in order to appear as 'proper' young men respectively women. On the other hand, however, the number of users who do stress aspects belonging to these categories is in many cases not very large, so it does not seem to be compulsory in the way the interest in football seemed to be in Frosh et al.'s study (2002). One could perhaps turn it the other way around and say that in the Lunarstorm material, users rather tend to not display interests that are associated with the other gender, since this could put their gender identities into question.

7 Analyses on parts of the material

Within the project, analyses have also been done on parts of the material. In Young men's gender- and identity work in a Swedish Web community[31], the sample consisted of 250 male users, and was a quantitative overview of what aspects of self was presented and displayed. The gender representations of the boys were found to be quite stereotypical, as defined by authors such as [23, 24, 28, 29, 32], and represented in the users' spheres of interest and personal characteristics displayed. However, exceptions were found in the young men's' strong focus on social relationships and romantic feelings Similar tendencies were found in statistics on offline conditions [33], implying that it may be a question of changing masculinities rather than the

---

[9] It should, however, be noted that sport was one category, and not divided into several subcategories according to different branches of sport. It is likely that there are some differences here, whereas more young women would be more attracted to sports like aerobics, gymnastics and horseback riding, and more men to sports such as football and ice hockey. Even if this was not analyzed, there were a good deal of young women who displayed a strong interest in football and ice hockey, both as practisers and as fans. However, no young men displayed an interest in aerobics and gymnastics, and extremely few in horseback riding.

medium making a difference, although the medium and the specific community may further encourage these changes.

The study Young people's presentations of relationships in a Swedish Internet community[34], dealt with the users' presentations of relationships. Here, the sample was one whole category, or more exactly the dens of the 339 users who had addressed relationships. The aim was to look closer at how, and by whom various types of relationships were addressed. In many respects, the presentations of relationships follow a gender stereotypical pattern, and this goes for all types of relationships included in the material: friendships, family relationships and romantic relationships. More women than men emphasize relationships, and they also express stronger feelings about them. However, one exception was found in the way romantic relationships were addressed, where both men and women expressed strong feelings towards their relationships and partners. All of the addressed romantic relationships were heterosexual, and in the whole sample, only one user explicitly claimed to be other than straight. This was somewhat surprising – it does not reflect the fact that a certain percentage of the population is bi- or homosexual. Some of this can probably be explained by the users being too young to have tried out and felt their way vis à vis their sexual orientation, or if they have, not be willing to come out with it. But the most important explanation probably lies in norms and ideals of what is accepted, what implies status and what is seen as stigmatizing within the community. Heterosexual relationships are generally seen as desirable, while non-heterosexual desires, activities and identities are generally seen as stigmatizing, especially for boys (Frosh et al., 2002; Connell, 1995).

In the study Doing and undoing gender in a Swedish Internet community [35], I took a closer look at how stereotypes may be transgressed. I here used a strategic sample, and made a thematic analysis of 2 cases, corresponding to users who deviated from the pattern and transgressed gender stereotypes. The analyses illustrate how complex young people's presentations of self may be, where various characteristics, interests and orientations intertwine, carrying with them different, sometimes contradictory and conflicting images of masculinity and femininity that have to be balanced against each other. It was, for example, found that even though the users on a conscious level try to break free from constraining stereotypes, it seems as they still at least partly end up in traditional patterns of gender, where some structures seem to be more difficult to get rid of than others. There seems to be some fundamental and tenacious structures that largely remain unchanged and which express themselves in what individuals communicate about themselves without thinking about it (c.f. Goffman's [8] concepts expression given and expression given off[10])

The study Young people's exposure of bodies in a Swedish Internet community[36, 37] aimed at looking at young men's and women's presentations of

---

[10] "Expression given" involves verbal symbols or their substitutes, which are used deliberately to convey the information attached to these symbols. "Expression given off", on the other hand, consists of a wide range of actions that others can treat as symptomatic of the actor, where the purpose is other than conveying information. It can for example consist of tone of voice, body language, facial expressions, blushes, etc, and it often provides a great deal of information about the actor that s/he never intended to convey.

self, focusing specifically on how and by whom bodies were displayed. The sample consisted of a whole category, exposure of physical body, or more exactly, the 941 photographs of the 88 users included in the category, which depicted the users alone. The method was mainly quantitative. Results showed differences in what parts of their bodies the young men and women show: women tend to focus on faces, while the men on torsos. Results also contradicted the image depicted by media, as very few photos could be described as provocative. An explanation is here offered by the specific internet community's lack of anonymity and lack of means of audience segregation, meaning that the interaction is steered by the same mechanisms and social pressure as in offline environments, and that the users must balance their presentations of self so as to fit several possible audiences at the same time.

In Exploring and negotiating femininity: Young women's production of style in a Swedish internet community[38], the aim was to look at how teenage girls use their production of style in their identity work in their dens. Here, a strategic sample was employed, using the dens of 11 girls, who, in comparison with the majority of the 500 users of the first sample seemed to experiment much with looks and styles online, i.e., these girls had published a large number of photos of themselves, where they wore different outfits and accessories, and showing many different postures and facial expressions. Results showed how girls can explore and experiment with different sides of femininity, but also how they may balance between undesired extremes. In this way, the girls' room online may serve as a tool for identity construction.

In Taking the girls' room online: Similarities and differences between traditional girls room and computer-mediated ones[39], I compare the traditional girls' room offline with girls' dens at Lunarstorm. Despite many similarities as concerns what activities are performed, the differences in terms of publicity and privacy makes it impossible to talk about the den as an equivalent to the traditional girls' room. Or, in Goffman's terminology [8], the traditional girls' room can be seen as a back stage region while the computer mediated girls room, with all its potential spectators, is more properly described as front stage.

8   Conclusions

The findings have contradicted some commonly held assumptions: Lunarstorm, being an online arena, would offer opportunities for more experimenting and exploration with gender identity and sexuality than offline environments; users would feel freer to abandon traditional gender stereotypes and more likely to expose alternative gender identities and sexualities, a plentitude of exposures of bodies, perhaps being done in different conditions than in offline settings. None of this turned out to be true. Instead, the youngsters' presentations of self turned out to follow quite stereotypical patterns both in terms of gender and of sexuality. However, the gender representations showed some interesting exceptions and contradictions, especially in the young men's strong focus on relationships, especially romantic ones. There are also exceptions that consist of single users' more or less conscious attempts at transgressing norms and stereotypes. But the analyses also show that presentations of self are complex, with different markers of masculinity and femininity co-existing in each presentation of self, sometimes conflicting with and contradicting each other. Often users end up in stereotypical ideals anyway, even though they may try to avoid it. However, one interesting discovery was that the dens are used in a way that is much reminiscent of how traditional girls' rooms are used, where girls, alone or more often together with friends, work out and experiment with style and appearance, and thereby explore their relation to femininity. The dens can thus be an important part in their elaboration and acquiring of a female gender identity.

As for the issue of sexuality, it can be argued that the absence of references to queer identities is not surprising, considering the fact that there are other online communities that specifically address such target groups. However, considering the fact that 85 per cent of all Swedish youngsters in the chosen age group are members of Lunarstorm, it is likely that at least some of them have other sexual orientations than heterosexual, and the sample of 500 Lunarstorm users should thus include at least a few such individuals. The point here is not to find out exactly how many these may be. Rather, it is to point to the lack of references to other romantic relationships, practices and desires than heterosexual as a sign of the heteronormative character of Lunarstorm, where the absence of such references clearly shows that queer, or non-heterosexual, identities are not highly valued within the community.

As for the ways bodies are presented, contrary to the image being shown by popular media, the analyses show that very few of the photos that the youngsters display classify as sexually provocative.

There are several explanations to these results. The fact that Lunarstorm follows such a gender stereotypical and heteronormative pattern and that users appear so sexually moderate may have at least three explanations. First, we have the culture of a specific Internet community. The managers of Lunarstorm have taken measures to make it a safe and friendly place – they cooperate with the Swedish police and organizations that aim at protecting children, to prevent prostitution and pornography, but also other harassment. The culture of the overarching community can be described as mainstream and decent.

The second explanation lies in the lack of anonymity and the connections between users' online and offline identities. Even if being a large community, members mostly use Lunarstorm to hang out with friends and interact with people they already know from their local offline environments [40, 41], meaning that despite its size, Lunarstorm is clearly locally anchored. Due to the connections between on- and offline identities (i.e., that users mainly interact with people from their offline lives), everything that users do at Lunarstorm will cause repercussions in their daily life offline, in school for instance.

A third explanation can be found in Lunarstorm's attraction of a large and wide audience. Previous research has pointed at the difficulties that users of online arenas may experience in their presentations of self, due to the variety and heterogeneity of their audiences [see, for example, 42, 43, 44]. In many online arenas, such as publicly accessible personal web sites or blogs, the heterogeneity of the audiences comes with the open interface. As for other arenas, which require registered membership, as boyd and Heer note, users may not have foreseen the dramatic growth of these arenas into unexpected audiences. This is clearly the case for Lunarstorm users too, only that they are fully aware of the possibility of getting their presentations read by unintended audiences. The users show a clear awareness of that audience segregation is not possible. Since users know it is impossible to keep audiences apart in this specific forum, they tend to form their presentations of self so as to fit into several different contexts at the same time. It would likely take quite some competency for the young people to, in their minds, position themselves in various situations, contexts and groups, and designing a presentation of self that manages to fit into all of them, while at the same time not transgressing the norms and standards of conduct of any of them. Not only do the young men and women have to balance between undesired polarities of gender ideals, but they also have to foresee situations where people from their different spheres of life may come and watch their presentations. As Lunarstorm is so widespread among youngsters, parents and teachers, for example, often register as members to be able to see what their children are doing during their leisure time[11].

Bearing this in mind, the absence of alternative gender identities, sexualities and provocative material is perhaps not surprising after all – this kind of material is probably rather found in arenas that are more anonymous and that allow more of audience segregation, i.e., which are not so openly available. It would be interesting to do a comparison with such communities, because it is probably in such arenas that more progressive presentations of self can be found, both in terms of gender and of sexuality. There are however methodological issues for such studies: the researcher has to get access to the secluded places and must be able to conduct the research without violating people's right to privacy. But that's another question.

References

1. S. Cohen, Folk devils and moral panics: the creation of the mods and rockers, MacGibbon & Kee, 1972.
2. U. Boëthius, "Ungdomar, medier och moraliska paniker," Ungdomar i skilda sfärer5, J. Fornäs, et al., eds., Bruno Östlings förlag Symposion, 1993, pp. 257-284.
3. B. Skeggs, Att bli respektabel, Daidalos, 1997.
4. S.M. Thiel, "IM me," Girl wide web. Girls, the Internet, and the negotiating of identity, S. R. Mazzarella, ed., Peter Lang, 2005, pp. 179-202.
5. H. Bertilsdotter, "Att fetischera det "normala". Bisexualitet utifrån några unga mäns berättelser," Sexualitetens omvandlingar. Politisk lesbiskhet, unga kristna och machokulturer, T. P. Johansson & Lalander, ed., Daidalos, 2003, pp. 239-270.
6. K. Drotner, At skabe sig - selv. Ungdom, aestetik, paedagogik, Gyldendal, 1991/1996.
7. G.H. Mead, Mind, Self, and Society, University of Chicago Press, 1934.
8. E. Goffman, The Presentation of Self in Everyday Life, Penguin books, 1959/1990.
9. A. Giddens, Modernity and self-identity. Self and society in the late modern age, Polity Press, 1991.

[11] Boyd & Heer [43] noted similar issues in another online social forum, but boyd and Heer's concern was how users had not foreseen that their employers would enter into the same community and thus get access to information and in-jokes that were shared between them and their friends.

10. H. Ganetz, "Butiken, hemmet och kvinnligheten som maskerad. Drivplatser och platser för kvinnligt skapande," Unga stilar och uttrycksformer, J. Fornäs, et al., eds., Bruno Östlings förlag Symposion, 1992, pp. 203-240.

11. A. Göthlund, Bilder av tonårsflickor. Om estetik och identitetsarbete, Linköping studies in Art and Science, 1997.

12. J. Andréasson, "Brudar, bärs och bögar - maskulinitet och sexualitet i en enkönad miljö," Sexualitetens omvandlingar. Politisk lesbiskhet, unga kristna och machokulturer, T. Johansson and P. Lalander, eds., Daidalos, 2003, pp. 25-46.

13. N. Hammarén, "Horor, players och de Andra. Killar och sexualitet i det nya Sverige," Sexualitetens omvandlingar. Politisk lesbiskhet, unga kristna och machokulturer, T. Johansson and P. Lalander, eds., Daidalos, 2003, pp. 95-124.

14. L.A. Lewis, "Being Discovered: The Emergence of Female Address on MTV," Sound and Vision: The Music Video Reader, L. Grossberg, et al., eds., Routledge, 1993, pp. 129-152.

15. L. Cherny and E. Reba Weise, eds., Wired women : gender and new realities in cyberspace, Seal Press, 1996.

16. S. Herring, "Gender and democracy in computer-mediated communication," Electronic Journal of Communication, vol. 3, no. 2, 1993.

17. S. Herring, "Gender Differences in Computer-Mediated Communication: Bringing Familiar Baggage to the New Frontier," Proc. American Library Association annual convention, June 27, 1994.

18. S.R. Stern, "Adolescent girls' expression on web home pages. Spirited, sombre and self-conscious sites.," Convergence, vol. 5, no. 4, 1999, pp. 22-41.

19. S.R. Stern, "Expressions of identity online: prominent features and gender differences in adolescents' world wide home pages," Journal of Broadcasting & Electronic Media, vol. 48, no. 2, 2004, pp. 218-243.

20. A.D. Grisso and D. Weiss, "What are gURLs talking about? Adolescent girls' construction of sexual identity on gURL.com.," Girl Wide Web. Girls, the Internet, and the Negotiation of Identity, S. R. Mazzarella, ed., Peter Lang, 2005, pp. 31--50.

21. J. Butler, Gender Trouble. Feminism and the subversion of identity, Routledge, 1990.

22. E. Goffman, Gender Advertisements, Macmillan, 1976.

23. R.W. Connell, Masculinites, University of California Press, 1995.

24. F. Ambjörnsson, I en klass för sig. Genus och sexualitet bland gymnasietjejer, Ordfront, 2004.

25. H. Østbye, et al., Metodbok för medievetenskap, Liber, 2003.

26. A. Strauss and J. Corbin, Basics of Qualitative Research. Grounded Theory Procedures and Techniques, SAGE, 1990.

27. B. Davies, Hur pojkar och flickor gör kön, Liber, 2003.

28. S. Frosh, et al., Young masculinities, Palgrave, 2002.

29. M. Svahn, Den liderliga kvinnan och den omanlige mannen. Skällsord, stereotyper och könskonstruktioner, Carlsson, 1999.

30. V. Walkerdine, School Girl Fictions, Verso, 1990.

31. M. Sveningsson Elm, "Young men's gender- and identity work in a Swedish Web community," AoIR Internet Annual Volume 4, M. Consalvo and C. Haythornthwaite, eds., Peter Lang, 2006.

32. M. Bäckman, Kön och känsla. Samlevnadsundervisning och ungdomars tankar om sexualitet, Makadam, 2003.

33. SCB, Undersökningarna av levnadsförhållanden., 2003.

34. M. Sveningsson Elm, "Young people's presentations of relationships in a Swedish Internet community," YOUNG, vol. 15, no. 2, 2007.

35. M. Sveningsson Elm, "Doing and undoing gender in a Swedish Internet community," Cyberfeminism in Northern lights. Gender and digital media in a Nordic context, M. Sveningsson Elm and J. Sundén, eds., Cambridge Scholars Publishing, 2007.

36. M. Sveningsson Elm, Young people's exposure of bodies in a Swedish Internet community, submitted.

37. M. Sveningsson Elm, "Att visa sin kropp på Nätet. Om ungdomars självpresentationer på Lunarstorm.," LOCUS, no. 1, 2006.

38. M. Sveningsson Elm, "Exploring and negotiating femininity: Young women's production of style in a Swedish internet community.," Book Exploring and negotiating femininity: Young women's production of style in a Swedish internet community., Series Exploring and negotiating femininity: Young women's production of style in a Swedish internet community., ed., Editor ed.^eds., 2007, pp.

39. M. Sveningsson Elm, "Taking the girls' room online: Similarities and differences between traditional girls room and computer-mediated ones," Proc. INTER: A European Cultural Studies Conference in Sweden, ACSIS, 2007.

40. E. Dunkels, "Nätkulturer - vad gör barn och unga på Internet?," Tidskrift för lärarutbildning och forskning, no. 1-2, 2005, pp. 41-49.

41. A. Enochsson, "Ett annat sätt att umgås: yngre tonåringar i virtuella gemenskaper," Tidskrift för lärarutbildning och forskning, no. 1-2, 2005, pp. 81-99.

42. D. Boyd, "Sexing the Internet: Reflections on the role of identification in online communities," Proc. Sexualities, Medias, Technologies, 2001.

43. D. Sevick Bortree, "Presentation of self on the web: an ethnographic study of teenage girls' weblogs," Education, Communication & Information, vol. 5, no. 1, 2005, pp. 25-39.

44. D. Boyd and J. Heer, "Profiles as conversation: Networked identity performance on Friendster," Proc. Hawai'i International Conference on System Sciences (HICSS-39), Persistent Conversation Track., IEEE Computer Society, 2006.

Workshop: Ethical and Privacy Aspects of RFID

Privacy implications of RFID: an assessment of threats and opportunites

Marc van Lieshout and Linda Kool

TNO Information and Communication Technologies,
Brassersplein 2, PO Box 5050, 2600 GB
Delft, the Netherlands
{marc.vanlieshout, linda.kool}@tno.nl

Abstract. European citizens consider Radio Frequency Identification (RFID) to be the most intrusive technology of the past two decades. Safeguarding privacy requires specific action that needs attention of all parties involved. European citizens consider legal instruments to offer insufficient guarantees for safeguarding privacy. `Privacy by design´ offers interesting opportunities to build in privacy guarantees in the technology, not as an end-of-pipe solution but as an integral design parameter. Notwithstanding the commercial focus on RFID in logistic processes and – eventually – in the retail sector, the first grand scale uses of RFID will be in public domain applications. These application domains are perfect 'niches' to stimulate a 'privacy by design' approach, both to academic researchers and application engineers.

1. Introduction

The Big Brother Award in the Netherlands has this year (2007) been awarded to the Dutch railway organisation (NS). The award was given to the NS for its intentions regarding the introduction of the RFID-based public transport card in the Netherlands. These intentions were suspect, not transparent and at the cost of the privacy of passengers travelling with the card. Since the card will be the single transport ticket throughout the entire Dutch public transport system, use of the data for a variety of purposes which are not known to the data subjects (the passengers) may impact on the privacy of the passengers. At the same event the Dutch public was awarded with a Big Brother Award as well, for being totally absent in the debate on privacy these days. While the magazine Time had identified 'You' as the person of the year in 2006, the Dutch organisation Bits of Freedom in co-operation with the Amsterdam cultural centre De Balie identified 'You' as the person who is co-responsible for privacy violations. While Time's You was heralded because of his or her contributions to today's ICT revolution in which innovation is democratised and in which all kind of new services are developed by users themselves, Bits of Freedom considered the contribution of these same users to defending their own privacy as overtly insufficient and factually absent.[1]

Please use the following format when citing this chapter:

van Lieshout, M. and Kool, L., 2008, in IFIP International Federation for Information Processing, Volume 262; The Future of Identity in the Information Society; Simone Fischer-Hübner, Penny Duquenoy, Albin Zuccato, Leonardo Martucci; (Boston: Springer), pp. 129–141.

The Dutch railway organisation is one of the many organisations that are implementing Radio Frequency Identification as means to re-organise their services. RFID is an enabling technology that may be used in many different situations for many different purposes. RFID is one of the cornerstones of the so-called Internet of Things [2] It is a technology that enables objects to identify themselves wirelessly by means of radio frequency. The objects are usually tagged with an RFID chip, encased with a small antenna, and – depending on the kind of application – sometimes with a battery as power source. Together with developments as the new Internet Protocol (IPv6) RFID enables a total coverage of the physical world and a complete linking of all conceivable objects to each other by means of unique labels. Having access to the labels enables parties to construct links between seemingly separated objects and events and link these to persons as well. With the advent of a unified coding scheme such as the Electronic Product Code (the successor of the bar code) each object will be uniquely determined and – if linked to another object – unique profiles may be created that may be composed of many millions of data events of all kind of objects.

This Panopticon in a modern form (totally decentralised in contrast to Jeremy Bentham's original idea of a totally centralised panopticon) will have severe privacy implications.[3] But to get a proper understanding of the issues at stake it is necessary to start at a more modest level, by looking at the privacy implications that can be straightforwardly perceived in today's RFID applications. There is no need to wait until RFID has reached the state of the item-level tag, in which each separate item is tagged. Today, most of us carry an RFID-based object, such as a public transport card, an electronic identity card, an electronic health insurance card, or simply an access badge for the buildings we work in. The pets we have can be implanted with an RFID-chip, in order to identify them in case of loss. In short, RFID is already with us and is here to stay, whether we like it or not. In order to guide its introduction such that one of the success factors is appropriately taken care of, namely privacy, we will pay due attention to the privacy impact of RFID.

2. The concept of privacy

The modern approach of privacy, and the use of it today has much to owe to the seminal contribution of Samuel Warren and Louis Brandeis in 1890 in which they argued for the need to have a separate law for what they called 'the right to be let alone'. Their plea for a right to privacy has not lost much of its power today. They refer to modern equipment that allows the intrusion of privacy: 'Recent inventions and business methods call attention to the next step which must be taken for the protection of the person, and for securing to the individual what Judge Cooley calls the right 'to be let alone'. Instantaneous photographs and newspaper enterprise have invaded the sacred precincts of private and domestic life; and numerous mechanical devices threaten to make good the prediction that 'what is whispered in the closet shall be proclaimed from the house-tops.' [4] But Warren and Brandeis are remarkably modern in identifying the backgrounds of the need for privacy as well: 'The intensity and complexity of life, attendant upon advancing civilization, have rendered necessary some retreat from the world, and man, under the refining influence of culture, has become more sensitive to publicity, so that solitude and privacy have become more essential to the individual; but modern enterprise and invention have, through invasions upon his privacy, subjected him to mental pain and distress, far greater than could be inflicted by mere bodily injury.' [4] Warren and Brandeis mention solitude separate from privacy. We propose to perceive solitude as one of the 'spheres of privacy', starting from the most outward sphere anonymity working inwards to reserve, intimacy and, finally, solitude. In public we may have a need for anonymity, we sometimes want to be able to withdraw from the public (reserve), we have an intimate circle in which we share our thoughts with those who are most intimate to us and finally we may have a need for contemplation just by ourselves in order to free our minds from the pressures of everyday life. The four spheres refer to the cornerstone of privacy, the right to be let alone. This right, which essentially is a social right based on social norms, values and conventions, is usually safeguarded by means of some kind of juridical regime. This, unfortunately, has led to a rather juridical notion of the panopticon. We will return to this issue.

Next to the four spheres – which as onion shells run from very intimate to very anonymous – we define two dimensions on privacy. We can distinguish between informational or relational privacy, spatial privacy and bodily privacy as the three main dimensions. Informational or relational privacy relates to information transferring something about ourselves or our relations to other persons, organisations or objects and thus revealing information about our personal relations to these persons, organisations or objects. Spatial privacy relates to the physical boundaries which we safeguard, such as our house, but also the spatial distance we keep to other people. Bodily privacy relates to the integrity of our body, which no one is allowed to touch or to invade except when granted access. These dimensions of privacy are laid down in the Universal Declaration of Human Rights and in other laws and have led to specific juridical regimes, such as the European Privacy directive (95/46/EC). We will return to the question how adequate these regimes are for safeguarding our privacy in relation to the dissemination of RFID. Before doing so, we will first present the technology at stake, RFID.

3.   RFID – the technology

The basic elements of RFID have been known for many years and go back to the Friend or Foe devices that were in place during the Second World War. Airplanes had an identification signal which enabled the ground stations and other airplanes to identify whether the airplanes belonged to the 'friends' or to the enemy. The concept of Radio Frequency Identification has been adopted to enable a chip to communicate wirelessly with a device, and to identify itself by transmitting a unique number to the identifying device. An antenna is used to create the energy that can trigger the chip to read out its number and to send it via the antenna back to the reader. These passive RFID-chips are delivered in all kind of frequency classes, where each frequency class has its own distinct characteristics. Overall, one could say that the higher the frequency used, the higher the energy and thus the higher the distance that the signal with the number can travel and the higher the complexity of data that can be transmitted. The lay-out of the antenna (a small one or a larger sophisticated one) plays a role as well. Simple passive tags only have a number to be read out which identifies the tag itself. Usually this number is 'printed' in the chip during fabrication. More sophisticated chips have processing capacities which enable the storage of more information and processing the information before it will be released. Usually, these more sophisticated chips have an external energy source (a battery) to power them for their processing capacities. When a sensor is attached to the RFID-chip, sensor information can be stored next to the identifying number. Processing capacity can also be used for encryption facilities. In case the battery is only used for internal processing capacities, the tag is called a 'semi-active' tag. When the energy source is used to increase the read range, the tag is called an 'active tag'. Read ranges from passive tags range from a few millimetres (proximity tags, such as those in electronic identity cards) to a few metres. Active tags can have a read range of up to hundred metres.

RFID tags come in different sorts and casings. Sometimes they are encased in plastic (such as access cards for buildings), sometimes they are embedded in paper labels, and today antennas become printed (printed electronics) in order to reduce costs of the tags. Chipless tags (which work on different physical principles which we will not spell out in this paper) are part of research into different modalities that may be cheaply produced in massive quantities.

The privacy implications of RFID tags will differ, depending on the kind of tag that is used and the circumstances in which it is used. We will now turn to discuss the privacy impact of RFID.

4. Privacy impact of RFID

The relation between RFID and privacy has been acknowledged by several organisations and institutes. The OECD states that : '[W]ithout addressing privacy related issues carefully, appropriately and transparently ... backlash by consumers and citizens is a potential risk that could limit long-term benefits and development.' [5: p. 15]. The European Article 29 Working Party on Data Protection emphasises several problems with the introduction of RFID and stresses the importance of indicating what kind of data should be processed under what conditions. Especially the notion of 'personal data', a pivotal concept in data protection legislation, is difficult to define unambiguously with respect to RFID, according to the Working Party. When a wristwatch carries an RFID tag, this by itself does not turn the RFID number into personal data. The number identifies the wristwatch, not the person who wears the wristwatch. But when the number is used to identify the person because one assumes the same person to carry the same wristwatch in different situations, the RFID number turns into personal data, i.e. in data that can be traced down to a specific person. This feature of RFID is very problematic in the context of privacy laws. It will not be a surprise that the position of the Article 29 Working Party that *any* RFID number may turn into personal data has met fierce resistance.[6,7]

Given the fact that RFID relates to data, we could assume the privacy impact of RFID being mainly within the realm of informational or relational privacy. And indeed, the gathering of information about someone's travel behaviour on the basis of my use of the public transport card with an RFID chip can be seen as impacting on his informational privacy (information about him) and on his relational privacy (it may be used to relate him to other travellers who exhibit the same travelling pattern as he does). The fact that these travel patterns may reveal *where* he has been may impact on his spatial privacy, as can be illustrated by the case of using access control badges. Access control badges can be seen as devices that limit the spatial privacy of a person since they enable tracking him down in buildings. RFID-based access control badges have an impact on spatial privacy since they enable people to survey *where* other people are. The bodily dimension of privacy is at stake when RFIDs themselves are inserted in the body. A well-known example of this situation is the use of embedded RFIDs in the Baja Beach clubs in Barcelona and Rotterdam. Since these chips are inserted on a voluntary basis this specific use of RFID is not a real intrusion of bodily privacy. Many other examples can be given, especially the attempts of VeriChip, the first organisation in the USA that is licensed by the Food and Drug Administration to implant RFID chips in humans. VeriChip has offered several opportunities to use implanted RFID chips, for instance to tag illegal Mexican workers that trespass the USA borders and are trapped, or American soldiers who in specific events can not be identified anymore and who have lost their identification badge.[8] Again, when these chips are implanted on a voluntary basis, one can not proclaim that bodily privacy has been intruded. But the VeriChip examples show it is a thin line to walk.

A recently performed survey by the Dutch Rathenau Institute in cooperation with the Dutch Consumers Organisation and the Dutch ICT interest organisation ECP.NL details the opinion of people towards RFID.[10] 2000 respondents filled in the internet-based questionnaire. The results of the internet based survey are presented in Table 1.

Table 1: Attitude of Dutch population with regard to introduction of RFID [10]

Statement	Possession [%]	Agree/ (very) positive [%]	Not agree/ (very) negative [%]
RFID based access card at work	21		
Opportunity to show work attitude		40	20
Employer should not register everything that is possible		55	
Public transport card	7		
Personalised card (possession)	80		
Use of data by intelligence services		72	16
Use of data to track witnesses		61	25
Limit possibility to travel anonymous		58	32
Transborder use by intelligent services of collected travel data		52	26

Biometric identity card	23		
Biometric card will be illegally copied		71	
Centralised registration of finger print data		66	20
Centralised registration of facial recognition data		56	26
Use of facial scan to track people of video images		62	14
Shopping and commercial products			
Prices will rise due to introduction of RFID		62	
Use of RFID at Point of Sale (direct payment)		70	
Need for transparency and killer option		85	
Need for opt-in system		62	
Trust in appropriate use of RFID-data			
By medical services		62	8
By police, justice and intelligence services		51	18
By commercial entities		10	50

Overall, the Dutch population exhibited the feeling that the introduction of RFID and RFID-based applications can not be stopped. 47% expressed concerns with the kind of data that will be collected and used by RFID-systems, 25% did not express concerns in this respect. When asked for advantages and disadvantages of RFID, the following top 5s were mentioned:

Table 2: Advantages and disadvantages of the introduction of RFID [10]

Advantages		Disadvantages	
1.	Fighting criminality	1.	Difficult to correct mistakes
2.	Ease of use	2.	Function creep
3.	Determining identity	3.	Misuse of data
4.	Need for fewer cards	4.	Criminals will circumvent the system
5.	Prevention of theft	5.	Use of data for direct marketing purposes

The results of the survey show that people welcome the opportunities RFID offers for surveillance purposes and do not oppose centralised systems that can be used to track down criminals or to search for people. Interestingly, they are less positive when the system will be used to track down witnesses (who of course can be everybody) in case of specific situations (a case of molestation in a train for instance). The Dutch survey shows that there may be two domains of discussion: a public domain, dealing with the applications and the opportunities of use and misuse, and a technological domain that deals with the underlying technological threats and opportunities (linking of systems, opportunities for eavesdropping, security measures, developing opt-in systems and the like).

4.1   Towards a more detailed analysis of the privacy impact of RFID[1]

In the assessment on RFID which we have performed for the Institute of Prospective Technology Studies (IPTS, Seville, one of the Joint Research Centres of the European Commission) we have identified a set of threats to privacy. We based our assessment on previous research of Sarah Spiekermann of the Humboldt University in Berlin.[11] In Table 3 we indicate the threats that can be related to RFID, based upon a distinction between the threats that can be linked to the RFID reader-tag system and the threats that can be linked to the back-end systems (the data processing equipment).

Table 3: Direct and indirect privacy threats, related to RFID

Privacy threats	Reader-tag system	Back-end
Individual	Unauthorised reading of personal information Real-time tracking of individuals	Combining personal information Using data for purposes other than originally specified
Collective/Group	-	Profiling and monitoring

Unauthorised reading of tags: Simple RFID tags do not contain much more than a number. The number can be read out by readers that have access to the tag. Without specific security mechanisms (such as encrypting the data stored on the tag, or using a handshake protocol to recognise readers that are enabled to have access to a tag), all readers in the appropriate frequency range are able to read data from the tag. Reading ranges are dependent on frequency used: the higher the frequency the higher the read distance. Active tags (with batteries for energy supply) tend to have longer read out distances than passive tags (which are dependent on the energy of the transmitted waves for data processing and communication). Juels *et al.* have demonstrated that ranges for eavesdropping outpace the nominal read range which is specified in standards. UHF-tags, with frequencies in Mega- or Gigaherz domain, have nominal read ranges of 7-10 meters, but Juels *et al.* have demonstrated that they can be read out at a distance of several tens of metres [12]. Proximity cards work at close distance (a few millimetres) but can be accessed from greater distances as well. Especially in case of sensitive data (for instance the identification of specific nationalities in a row of tourists) unauthorised reading of tags can have severe consequences. Security measures, such as encrypting the data stored in the tag or authentication handshake protocols, may prevent unauthorised reading of tags. Not all tags will be interesting to read, since they will not reveal much (if any) personal information of the holder. Still, the principal position holds that one should be able to determine by oneself what

---

[1] The following sections are based on a previous paper 'Little sisters are watching you' which we have submitted as pre-conference paper to the IFIP Summerschool 'The Future of Identity in the Information Society' that was held 6-13 August 2007 in Karlstad, Sweden.

information under what circumstances will be communicated to other people and organisations. Unauthorised reading of tags is an infringement of this position.

Real-time tracking of individuals: On the basis of a single tag one can trace people. All that is needed is a unique tag that is linked to that person. An RFID tag attached to a wristwatch could be used. This wristwatch identification could be used to track a specific individual. Purposeful monitoring of people is used in hospitals, in schools and in prisons. In hospitals one experiments with RFID tags to identify new born babies, to locate people with Alzheimer diseases but also to locate doctors and nurses. In the USA a board of school has suggested to tag children so that the school could meet its juridical obligation to know whether a child left school yes or no. While this was seriously opposed by the parents these kind of practices are much less disputed in Japanese schools.[13] RFID based systems are used as an alternative to electronic handcuffs. Several of these applications are contested since they impinge on personal freedom and on the right to be let alone. In situation of electronic imprisonment, a small and relatively invisible RFID-tag may however be more humane than a much more visible scaffold. In principle, the purposeful real-time tracking of people against their will poses privacy problems. In case of new born babies (to prevent kidnapping of babies and accidental exchange of babies) the privacy infringements are less clear. Tracking people with serious forms of Alzheimer disease is more difficult to judge as well. RFID can be of use to offer these people more freedom, and to save costs in searching for them. In case of the school children the parents protested against this use of RFID; the company responsible for the trial backed off eventually [13]. The absence of communication with the parents about the benefits and pitfalls of use of RFID showed to be a showstopper. Use of RFID to track people in real time will have to be weighted against the infringement on privacy but it would be wrong to deny beneficial uses of RFID in all situations.

Combining personal information: At the back-end of RFID systems privacy infringements are comparable to 'ordinary' data collection systems that aggregate information about people from different sources. RFID is no exception to this situation, but the amount of data to be aggregated will explode. Having billions of RFID tags means that the back-end system will have the opportunity to aggregate data that belong to one and the same person by combining specific data. Once item-level tagging has become commonplace, the accompanying model to label all products in one encompassing mode will release an enormous amount of correlations between previously separated sets of data. The prime example here is the supermarket that identifies its customers by one specific item, an RFID tagged wristwatch for instance. Each time the customer enters the supermarket, all items that will be purchased will be linked. This information can be more detailed than the data that are now collected by loyalty cards, since also the route through the shop and the items that have been picked up but have not been taken can be monitored. There are numerous other places where this information can be aggregated such as libraries, on the road, in public transport, or in hospitals. The Article 29 Working Party has expressed its concern for these practices since it presupposes an increasing number of controllers that should audit all these situations.[6]

Using data for purpose other than originally specified: Function creep, the extension of the functionality of systems, lurks around the corner. Datamining technologies enable tracing specific patterns within large data heaps and revealing social networks on the basis of these patterns. Since the introduction of the Oyster card in London public transport, the Metropolitan Police has multiplied its request for specific travel data. In January 2006, it had requested travel information of Oyster card users 61 times, compared to only seven times over the whole of 2004 (before introduction of Oyster card). In March 2006 the frequency had risen to 243 times. By comparing travel patterns with travel patterns of suspect people, the Metropolitan police tried to identify social networks of suspect people [14, p.251]. The data that were collected for public transport purposes were not collected with the aim of surveying behaviour of people. Though in this situation data retention acts and lawful decisions support the attempt of the Metropolitan Police, one can also argue that with a different design of the data system function creep could be prevented.

Profiling and monitoring of people and behaviour: By analysing the various sources of data one can construct profiles of people. The more detailed and fine-grained the analysis is, the more difficult it will become to prove the incorrectness or impreciseness of the profile. Though this is not a new threat RFID may intensify the construction and use of profiles.

5   Strategies to cope with RFID privacy issues

Using RFID poses threats to privacy, especially but not exclusively related to the informational or relational dimension of privacy. Protecting the informational dimension of privacy is the purpose of the European privacy directive. Given the special classes of privacy threats of RFID we have to investigate the adequacy of the existing legal framework to safeguard our informational privacy. Commercial entities usually adhere more to schemes of self-regulation than to legal instruments. Self-organisation enables a more flexible approach that hinges on the recognition of specific threats and the need to build up a trust relation between commercial entities and their customers. Self-regulation is in the interest of all parties and thrives on well-understood self-interest of the commercial entities, seriously taking into account the needs and attitudes of their customers. Finally, but surely not in the last place, technology itself may be applied to safeguard privacy. When information or data sharing architectures are designed such that it is technically impossible to exchange personal data, privacy is best safeguarded. Immobilising an RFID tag when it is outside a predefined area may be such a technical solution.

These three approaches, the legal one, self-regulation and technology itself as counterforce, are discussed in more detail in the following sections.

Legal instruments: Whenever personal data are collected by RFID based systems they have to comply with the privacy regulations and laws at hand. In case of the European Union this implies compliance with Directive 95/46/EU and its adjacent national privacy laws. Dispute is arising around the appropriateness of the legal framework. The legal framework itself is based upon the OECD Guidelines on the

Protection of Privacy and Transborder Flows of Personal Data, which was published in 1980.[15] The OECD Guidelines comprise eight principles for fair information practices, of which the most important ones are: do not collect more than strictly necessary and only for well-described purposes; be sure that the data collection is transparent and that data subjects have appropriate instruments to check the validity of what has been collected. With respect to RFID two issues come to the fore: the first one relates to the notion of 'personal data'. When an RFID tag contains nothing more than a number, for instance the number that identifies a wrist watch, the borderline between whether this is information that can be attributed to a person or not, is very thin. In the future, when item-level tagging will have become commonplace, items will be classified according to a specific categorization such as the Electronic Product Code, which is yet under development. By means of the Electronic Product Code (EPC) classification (to stick to this example) each item tagged with an EPC tag will get an identifier, which uniquely identifies the category to which this item belongs (watches), the producer of the item and the unique serial number of the item. This unique tag number could be associated with a specific person (for instance, the tag of his/her wristwatch or of his/her glasses). In this way, the RFID tag becomes a tag which can be used to identify a person and is thus susceptible to the Data Protection Act. According to the Article 29 Working Party, *all* RFID tags have data which may sooner or later turn into personal data. All RFID tags thus should be treated as susceptible to the European privacy directive [6]. This position has met severe resistance of market parties which consider this position to be detrimental for the market potential of RFID [7]. A second problem is the informed consent which is required when collecting personal data. Consent should be freely given, should be specific, should entail an indication of the individuals effective will, should be informed and should be unambiguous. Information about the possible collection of personal data will have to be communicated, in all places where this is appropriate. Given the highly unspecific manner of data collection this may be problematic as well, especially given other elements of the privacy directive which requires transparency in data processing, openness to the data subject (right of access, right of refusal), the quality of data collected, etc. The Working Party warns of the danger that all these measures 'will cause a boost in data to be processed by a wide variety of controllers, giving cause to concern' [6: p. 6].

Self-regulation: Market parties point at the opportunity to regulate uses of RFID data by means of self-regulation which prescribes use of RFID data, of informing customers, of raising awareness for RFID tags and of offering choice to consumers. Various guidelines are available, mostly if not all US-based. EPC Global has released guidelines in which they point at the need of notice (marking objects which are tagged), choice (offering consumers the possibility to de-activate or remove the tag), security, record use and retention (relates to the assurance not to process personal data) and educating the public [16]. The American Centre for Democracy and Technology (CDT) has developed guidelines in cooperation with American technology suppliers and RFID users (Microsoft, Procter and Gamble, VISA USA) and the Consumer League [17]. Their approach is comparable to EPC's set of guidelines. CDT has identified five guidelines: give notice, choice and consent, onward transfer (in case of third party transfer of data the third party must comply with at least a similar privacy regime or even better), access, and security. Though sympathetic in its approach, there is widespread agreement that self-regulation is not sufficient to safeguard privacy (see next section).

Privacy by design: The European Commission held an RFID Consultation process in 2006 in which it has consulted European citizens and companies about, amongst others, the privacy consequences of RFID [18]. Almost 2,200 participants delivered input to the consultation process. 65% of them were interested citizens, 15% were related to the RFID industry, and remaining respondents came from university and governments. Privacy was among the top level concerns (together with health and environmental risks). The questionnaire entailed a number of questions in which respondents were explicitly asked to rank measures to protect privacy. The respondents considered the development of technological solutions to allow or disable tags the best safeguard for privacy (67%). Legislation to regulate uses (50%) was ranked second, while self-regulation (15%) scored far less (more than one answer was possible).

Technological solutions relate to de-activating tags and removing them. Solutions are removal of antennas, creating Faraday cage to prevent transmission of data, removal of the tag from the object, and putting tags into 'deep sleep mode'. These are so-called 'end-of-pipe' solutions, they are add-ons instead of fully integrated at the early stages of development. The technological approach to safeguard privacy can however also be embedded in the design of the RFID system itself. The Article 29 Working Party 'considers that technology may play a key role in ensuring compliance with the data protection principles ...' and continuous referring to using specific design to enforce minimisation of collection and use of data [6: p. 12]. The OECD refers to this as the privacy by design approach. It considers this 'to be more effective in the long run', referring to legislation and self-regulation as other measures [5: p. 19]. Floerkemeyer et al [19] have demonstrated that the OECD privacy guidelines which are basic to the European privacy laws can be used as design criteria for EPC data collection systems. The design criteria relate to how specific Fair Information Principles (FIP) can be realised, such as collection limitation by an appropriate tag selection, use limitation by creating specific collection types, and purpose specification by identifying a specific set of possible purposes. Part of Floerkemeyer's approach is the empowerment of consumers by means of a so-called 'watchdog tag', a tag plus screen that identifies readers nearby and provides information about the reader. This idea of a watch dog has been developed by other parties as well.[20]

This EPC-based approach can be broadened to other domains as well. Within public transport, use of encryption technologies to decipher data that are stored on the public transport chip, may enforce compliance with the FIP. Technically, this is possible. Not all technical features to encrypt the data or to minimise data storage are however used. Given interests of companies to use the data for a broad range of purposes, there is a clear need for enforcement of using privacy enhancing technologies in all design stages of the RFID system. The example of the embeddedness of privacy principles in the RFID technologies itself, transferring privacy protection from end-of-the-pipe approaches to integrated privacy enhancing technologies, poses interesting challenges to the academic community, public and private privacy commissioners and designers.

6. Conclusions

Awareness of RFID applications is growing and is reaching a level where the focus changes from mere informing the general public on what is going on towards addressing specific issues and debating the privacy consequences of these issues. RFID is considered to be a highly intrusive technology that will have severe impacts on our privacy. On the other hand, results from a Dutch survey show that in the trade-off between protecting one's own privacy and safeguarding society against criminal acts or terrorist threats the balance tips in the direction of sacrificing personal freedom. The underlying maxim seems to be that as long as people have nothing to hide they have nothing to fear as well. RFID is impacting on all dimensions of personal privacy, i.e. on the informational/relational dimension, the spatial dimension and the bodily dimension. This re-enforces the status of RFID as a highly intrusive technology. By gathering and disseminating information about objects and relating them to each other, unique profiles can be constructed that are difficult to deny. RFID enable locating people's physical location and thus impact on their spatial privacy. Finally, RFID implants are promoted heavily by specific parties who have beneficial business cases for specific implant applications.

The means to counter the privacy threats can be classified in legal instruments, self-regulation and technological means. The legal approach is still considered to be very worthwhile, though some very persistent problems are defined with respect to RFID. First, all RFID data may become personal data in the end, by means of some kind of linking of objects to persons. Second, because of the widespread dissemination of RFID it will become increasingly difficult to get informed consent about applications (of which it is difficult to predict whether and under what circumstances they will enter into the personal realm). The technological approach is considered to be very promising, as is indicated by specialist parties such as the Article 29 Working Party and which is supported by the results of the European consultation process on RFID. This is a very interesting outcome that lends support to the activities around Privacy Enhanced Technologies. The main challenge is to involve privacy considerations in the design process from the start on, in order to prevent end-of-pipe solutions but to include privacy as design criterion in any RFID-based information system.

References

1. See http://www.bigbrotherawards.nl/
2. ITU 2005. The Internet of things.Geneva: ITU.

3. Whitaker, R. 1999 The End of Privacy – how total surveillance is becoming a reality. New York: The New Press.
4. Warren, S.& Brandeis, 1890.The Right to Privacy.Harvard Law Review,15 December 1890.
5. OECD. 2006a. Radio-frequency identification (RFID): Drivers, challenges and public policy considerations. Report DSTI/ICCP(2005)19/FINAL, published on 27 February 2006.
6. Article 29 Working Party on Data Protection. 2005a. Working document on data protection issues related to RFID technology. 10107/05/EN, 19 January 2005.
7. Article 29 Working Party on Data Protection. 2005b. Results of the Public Consultation on Article 29 Working Document 105 on Data Protection Issues Related to RFID Technology, 1670/05/EN, 28 September 2005.
8. For illegal immigrants see http://scaredmonkeys.com/2006/06/01/i-am-sure-the-aclu-will-approve-of-this-proposal-to-implant-tracking-chips-in-immigrants/#more-2655; for using RFID in soldiers, see http://www.techweb.com/wire/ebiz/192203522
9. Capgemini. 2005. RFID and Consumers – What European consumers think about radio frequency identifications and the implications for businesses. Capgemini report
10. Heuvel, E.van den, Nagel, K.Hof, C.van 't, Schermer, B 2007.RFID-bewustzijn van consumenten: hoe denken Nederlanders over Radio Frequency Identification?. ('RFID awareness of consumers: how do Dutch people think about RFID?') http://www.rathenau.nl/showpageBreed.asp?steID=1&ID=2963
11. Spiekermann, S., Ziekow, H. 2006. 'A systematic analysis of privacy threats and a 7-point plan to address them'. Journal of Information System Security, vol. 1, no. 3.
12. Juels, A., Rivest, R. and Szydlo, M. 2003. The blocker tag: selective blocking of RFID tags for consumer privacy. CCS'03, October 2003, Washington.
13. See http://ubiks.net/local/blog/jmt/archives3/004343.html for a description of the Japanese pilot, see http://www.rfid-weblog.com/50226711/tagging_of_school_ students_halted.php for a description of the objections in a USA pilot and http://www.epic.org/privacy/rfid/children.html for an overview of pilots and objections.
14. Lieshout, M. van, Grossi, L., Spinelli, G., Helmus, S., Kool, L., Pennings, L., Stap, R., Veugen, T., Waaij, B. van der, Borean, C. 2006. RFID Technologies: Emerging Issues, Challenges and Policy Options. Sevilla: IPTS, EN22770. http://www.jrc.es/publications/pub.cfm?id=1476
15. OECD Guidelines for the protection of privacy and transborder flows of personal data. See http://www.oecd.org/document/18/0,2340,en_2649_34255_1815186_1_1_1_1,00. html
16. EPC global, 2005. Guidelines on EPC for Consumer Products. Revised Sep. 2005 www.epcglobalinc.org/public_policy/public_policy_guidelines .html
17. Centre for Democracy and Technology. 2006. Privacy Best Practices for Deployment of RFID Technology – Interim draft, May 2006.
18. European Commission .2006c. The RFID Revolution: Your voice on the Challenges, Opportunities and Threats, Online Public Consultation. 16 Oct. 2006.
19. Floerkemeier, C., Schneider, R., Langheinrich, M. 2005. ,Scanning with a purpose – Supporting the Fair Information Principles in RFID Protocols'. Lecture Notes in Computer Science, Vol. 3598, pp. 214- 231.
20. Rieback, M.R.,Crispo, B. Tanenbaum, A.S. 2005. 'RFID Guardian: A Battery-Powered Mobile Device for RFID Privacy Management'. Lecture Notes in Computer Science, vol. 3574. pp. 184-194.

Identification and Tracking of Individuals and Social Networks using the Electronic Product Code on RFID Tags

Markus Hansen and Sebastian Meissner

Independent Centre for Privacy Protection Schleswig-Holstein
markus.hansen@privacyresearch.eu
meissner@datenschutzzentrum.de

Abstract. Recent studies claim that RFID transponders containing only an Electronic Product Code (EPC) do not carry person-related data. This paper describes how to use EPCs on RFID transponders to identify individuals and track their consumer habits and locations. In addition, it is shown how these mechanisms can be used to identify social networks. An overview of the relevant legal aspects is given; in particular the article elaborates under what circumstances EPC item level tagging entails the processing of personal data, thus resulting in the applicability of data protection legislation.

1 Introduction: The Electronic Product Code

EPCglobal Inc. is a non-profit organisation founded by GS1 (formerly EAN – European Article Numbering International) and Uniform Code Council (UCC), the two main barcode issuing associations.

EPC, the Electronic Product Code standardized by EPCglobal, is intended to replace EAN or UPC (Universal Product Code) numbers when Radio Frequency Identification (RFID) tags replace barcodes as identifiers on products. EPC is a set of coding schemes for RFID tags, originally developed by MIT AutoID centre.

When an EPC is read, the reading system can identify the object via the internet using the Object Name Service (ONS) to locate data related to a certain EPC within the EPCglobal Network community. EPC Information Services (EPCIS) are then used to exchange available information. The EPCglobal Network aims at exchanging data in real time to allow tracking of products. EPC allows for unique identification of tagged objects (as opposed to identification of object classes with barcodes) [7].

2 Identification of Individuals

As EPC, ONS, EPCIS and the EPCglobal Network have been designed with tracking of products as a feature, the idea to use the same infrastructure to identify and track people who have bought products with EPCs attached suggests itself.

Please use the following format when citing this chapter:

Hansen, M. and Meissner, S., 2008, in IFIP International Federation for Information Processing, Volume 262; The Future of Identity in the Information Society; Simone Fischer-Hübner, Penny Duquenoy, Albin Zuccato, Leonardo Martucci; (Boston: Springer), pp. 143–150.

The EPCglobal Public Policy Steering Committee Frequently Asked Questions (FAQ) states that "EPC tags do not contain any personally identifiable information about consumers. [...] The only information that is contained in the EPC tag relates to the product, not the purchaser" [11]. In addition, legal examinations of RFID and EPC applications also come to the conclusion that EPCs do not allow identification of a person (c.f. [9]).

While it is true that EPC tags only contain data related to the product, to conclude that these data are not person-related means missing certain aspects such as each item has an owner. Therefore, to show that assumptions that EPCs do not allow identification of a person are false, we have a look at biometric identification and transfer the mechanisms to identification of individuals using EPCs.

2.1   Lessons from Biometrics

Biometric identification uses non-binary functions to determine if a gathered set of characteristics matches a reference set from previous enrolment. Not all biometric information is of use for identification purposes. For example, in case of fingerprints, the minutiae and their relative positions are regarded as highly characteristic, while plain ridges are not.

As there are variations between each gathering of a print from the same person, the set of characteristics to be compared with the reference sample varies. In addition, there may be similarities between prints from different individuals, and it is also possible that only partial prints1 are available. Therefore, the "true" and "false" values of an identification (ID) test are determined by probability functions. As a result, false acceptance and false rejection rates need to be handled. [10]

2.2   Classification of Products

Some products have a high probability of being used by a single person only during the product's lifetime, e.g. a frame for a pair of glasses, or a pair of shoes, while others are used once only or often by different individuals. Apart from these extreme values, there are "shades of grey". It should therefore be possible to define a classification scheme of products reflecting the probability of always being used by the same person.

Tags containing EPCs identify what kind of object they are attached to. This information can be mapped to the before-mentioned classification scheme. In addition, a serial number within EPC allows for unique item identification.

---

[1] For an example of severe problems resulting from false positives due to latent/partial prints c.f. http://en.wikipedia.org/wiki/Brandon_Mayfield.

2.3   Identification: The EPC Cloud

According to the classification suggested in 2.2, it is possible to define a set of EPCs that can be used as characteristics to identify individuals. We call the set of EPCs that a person reveals when being scanned as his or her "EPC cloud". As fingerprints, the EPC cloud will contain elements that are highly characteristic (such as minutiae) or less characteristic (such as ridges) for identification.

A scanning system will look up the read EPCs within ONS and retrieve related information via EPCIS or from local databases, e.g. at a shop's cash register to determine which products customers will have to pay for and which ones they had already brought with them when entering the shop.

In contrast to biometric identification, there is not just an initial enrolment. Rather, each scan and database lookup is a kind of incremental enrolment, as new characteristics are added to or dropped from the reference set.

2.4   Consumer Habits

Again in contrast to biometric identification, the low-characteristic elements of the EPC cloud do not complicate identification, but have a certain significance themselves: As these EPCs are likely to be attached to consumer goods, they indicate consumer habits. However these EPCs will usually show up within a cloud for a rather short time frame (until consumption of the related goods occurs).

2.5   Tracking

With each scan and subsequent database lookup, a dataset containing the EPC cloud, a timestamp and the ID of the querying system (and therefore the location of the person identified by a certain cloud) will result.

Tracking of EPCs is a design feature of EPCglobal: "A fundamental principle of the EPCglobal Network Architecture is the assignment of a unique identity to physical objects, loads, locations, assets, and other entities whose use is to be tracked." [4]. Therefore, EPCs will also allow global tracking of individuals by 'following their cloud'.

Despite stating that "the only information that is contained in the EPC tag relates to the product, not the purchaser" [11], EPCglobal obviously is aware of the possible privacy implications of EPC tags: "Licensing agreements for the EPC specifically prohibit its use for tracking or identifying people, except in very specific cases and with full transparency relating to patient or troop safety" [12].

Furthermore, it is rather irrelevant what data are encoded into a unique ID and stored in a tag, as the privacy implications arise not only from the tag but even more from the data processing systems that contain information linked to that ID. To verify if data contained in an EPC tag are not related to a purchaser, it is therefore insufficient to not also look at the data processing systems.

2.6   Social Networks

Apart from highly characteristic elements and single-use items, it is also of interest to analyse EPCs that are interchanged from one EPC cloud to another. Such "cloud hopping" is an indicator of a link (tie) between two individuals (nodes).

When a unique EPC appears with a different EPC cloud than it has been with before, an interaction (sale, gift, theft, …) between the two individuals identified by their clouds is probable. Analysing the data that can be collected as described in this paper, it is feasible to assume that patterns of cloud hopping will be found that are characteristic and can therefore be mapped to types of interaction and social relation.

This will allow for a qualification of links between individuals and therefore for identification of social relationships such as family, friendship, employment, etc., that in combination – at least partially – represent their social networks.

3   Infrastructure Aspects

Once RFID transponders have reached a certain market penetration, reading systems to access the data stored onto them will become common as well. As a first step, RFID readers will be installed at supermarket cash desks and other points-of-sale. As shown in 2.5, log files with item identifiers of products purchased will occur.

These readers will not only read tags on items that are yet to be paid for, but for any readable transponder the customer is carrying. The readers will not be able to distinguish between items that the customer already brought into the shop and new goods in the store itself prior to a database lookup.

The EPCglobal Network provides services to identify the types of items by looking up the EPC in a database using the ONS and then retrieve related information via EPCIS.

As mentioned in 2.5 in relation to tracking, EPC Licensing agreements explicitly prohibit the use of EPC for tracking people (with defined exceptions, proving that it is possible to do so). Licensing agreements are rather weak precautions that are more likely to be designed to protect EPCglobal from liability claims than to protect consumers from privacy invasion.

The security precautions found in EPCglobal documents have as their main foci authentication and authorization when using EPCIS [5]; they are therefore probably not intended to secure consumer privacy, but rather the business model of EPCglobal. Further on, [4] explicitly states that tag level security is yet to be implemented in the future: "The EPCglobal Architecture Framework does not currently discuss how these features affect the architecture above the level of the Reader Protocol, nor is there any architectural discussion of how the goals of security and privacy are address[ed] through these or other features."

So, in order to implement the described scenario an attacker only needs the following items: a subscription to EPCglobal to retrieve information about certain EPCs from other community members of the EPCglobal Network; a database to store gathered data; and an initial contact to EPC clouds – and therefore individuals – he or she wants to track. In case of the larger supermarket chains with customer discount cards, it would further be feasible to add a name to an EPC cloud, even though names are not necessary for the unique identification of consumers and the resulting privacy invasion.

4   Legal Aspects

When dealing with EPC tags, one fundamental question is if the current data protection legislation is applicable. This is of particular importance because it is relevant for the lawfulness of the data processing and for the existence of certain legal obligations, such as informing individuals about the presence of EPC tags and readers or enabling the deactivation of tags. According to Article 3 Section 1 of Directive 95/46/EC, European privacy law is only applicable if personal data are processed. The question of whether personal data are concerned in relation to RFID and EPCs cannot be answered across the board, but has to be examined in each individual case.

4.1   Introduction to the Concept of Personal Data

A legal definition of the term personal data is provided by Article 2 a) of Directive 95/46/EC. Pursuant to this provision, personal data shall mean any information relating to an identified or identifiable natural person (the so-called data subject). In the sense of this provision, 'identified' means that a person who belongs to a group of persons is distinguished from all other members of this group [2] whereas an identifiable person is one who can be identified, directly or indirectly, in particular by reference to an identification number or to one or more factors specific to his (or her) physical, physiological, mental, economic, cultural or social identity [6]. Even if the name is the most common identifier, this definition implies that knowledge of the name of an individual is not an indispensable precondition to identify that person [2]. This understanding is underpinned by a judgement of the European Court of Justice in which the court elaborates that "the act of referring, on an internet page, to various persons and identifying them by name or by other means … constitutes the processing of personal data" [3]. To assess whether a person is identifiable, one has to be aware of Recital 26 of Directive 95/46/EC which stipulates that "account should be taken of all the means likely reasonably to be used either by the controller or by any other person to identify the said person" [6].

4.2   The Concept of Personal Data within the EPC Context

When dealing with the applicability of data protection legislation within the EPC context, three scenarios are usually distinguished:
- Scenario I: Only the Electronic Product Code is stored on the tag;

- Scenario II: Again only the Electronic Product Code is stored on the tag, but within the business transaction it is linked to personal data of the customer (e. g. if paying with a loyalty, credit or cash card);
- Scenario III: Not only the Electronic Product Code, but also other personal data are stored on the tag.

Concerning the two latter scenarios, it is beyond dispute that in both cases personal data are processed and therefore data protection legislation is applicable. In contrast, when dealing with Scenario I, it is a controversial issue whether EPC item level tagging (usually) entails a processing of personal data [8]. There are a number of explanations which elaborate on this issue:

It is true that EPC tags only contain data related to the respective product. However, from this explanation, one cannot draw the conclusion that data protection legislation is only applicable if the customer pays for the product with his or her loyalty, credit or cash card or if personal data are stored directly on the tag.

When focussing on EPC clouds, and considering the above explanation on the concept of personal data, one has to be aware of the fact that a person might be identifiable even though no traditional identifiers are available. As has already been elaborated in 2.2, some products have a high probability of being used by only a single person. Shops scanning and storing the EPCs of such products, and that subsequently identify a customer's EPC cloud, can easily recognize the customer every time he/she enters the premises. This means that such stores are able to distinguish this person from all other customers visiting them, and are thus able to identify the person by using his/her EPC cloud as a key for identification.

Shops are able to use the customer's EPC cloud for tracking consumption habits, and thus for setting up a consumer profile. By acting in this manner, shops are processing personal data. Thus, data protection legislation is applicable [1-2]. As one has to act on the assumption that an increasing number of objects will be tagged with EPCs in the future, tracking via EPC clouds will become an easy task. EPC item level tagging will usually entail a processing of personal data, and thus data protection legislation will be applicable.

4.3   Consequences

The applicability of data protection legislation in particular leads to the following consequences:

- Personal data may only be processed if this can be based on one of the legal grounds for processing listed in Article 7 of Directive 95/46/EC (e.g., the data subject's unambiguously given consent);
- Further processing which is incompatible with the purpose of collection is prohibited (cf. Article 6 (1) (b) of Directive 95/46/EC);
- According to Article 10 of Directive 95/46/EC, the data controller must provide certain information to the data subject (particularly the controller's identity and the processing purposes);

- The data subject has the right of access i.e., of checking the accuracy of the data and ensuring that the data are kept up to date (Article 12 of Directive 95/46/EC);
- Finally, pursuant to Article 17 of Directive 95/46/EC, the data controller is obliged to implement appropriate technical and organisational measures to protect personal data against accidental or unlawful destruction or unauthorised disclosure.

5 Conclusions

RFID transponders with EPCs on them that are used as tags on everyday use products allow for the identification of individuals. EPCs on RFID tags allow a new type of privacy invasion: it is no longer necessary to know the names of individuals to identify, track, and target them for advertising purposes.

As legal regulation inherently cannot prevent misuse, but just sanction it, the technical designs of systems will have to provide precautions to protect the privacy of individuals by enforcing purpose-binding and deletion of collected data, and to prevent misuse by private or public entities.

As of now, licensing agreements seem to be the only – yet insufficient – protection against this scenario.

References

1. ARTICLE 29 Data Protection Working Party: WP 105 - Working document on data protection issues related to RFID technology, 19 January 2005, http://ec.europa.eu/justice_home/fsj/privacy/docs/wpdocs/2005/wp105_en.pdf
2. ARTICLE 29 Data Protection Working Party: WP 136 - Opinion 4/2007 on the concept of personal data, 20 June 2007, http://ec.europa.eu/justice_home/fsj/privacy/docs/wpdocs/2007/wp136_en.pdf
3. Judgement of the European Court of Justice C-101/2001of 6.11.2003 (Lindqvist).
4. EPCglobal: EPCglobal Architecture Framework Final Version, 2005, http://www.epcglobalinc.org/standards/Final-epcglobal-arch-20050701.pdf.
5. EPCglobal: Electronic Product Code Information Service Frequently Asked Questions, 2007, http://www.epcglobalinc.org/standards/FINAL-EPCIS_FAQ042707.pdf.
6. Directive 95/46/EC of the European Parliament and of the Council of 24 October 1995 on the protection of individuals with regard to the processing of personal data and on the free movement of such data, 1995, http://eur-lex.europa.eu/LexUriServ/LexUriServ.do?uri=CELEX:31995L0046:EN:NOT.
7. Benjamin Fabian, Markus Hansen: Technische Grundlagen des Ubiquitous Computing, in: ULD, HU Berlin: TAUCIS – Technikfolgenabschätzung Ubiquitäres Computing und Informationelle Selbstbestimmung, Studie im Auftrag des BMBF, 2006, https://www.datenschutzzentrum.de/taucis/ita_taucis.pdf.

8.   Eleni Kosta, Michael Vanfleteren: Data Protection legislation, in: FIDIS - Future of Identity in the Information Society Deliverable 7.7: RFID, Profiling, and AmI, 2006, http:// fidis.net/fileadmin/fidis/deliverables/fidis-wp7-del7.7.RFID_Profiling_AMI.pdf.
9.   Bernd Holznagel, Mareike Bonnekoh: Rechtliche Dimensionen der Radiofrequenz-Identifikation, Untersuchung im Auftrag des Informationsforums RFID, 2006, http://www.info-rfid.de/downloads/rfid_rechtsgutachten.pdf.
10. Andreas Pfitzmann: Biometrics - how to put to use and how not at all?, Talk at ISC 2005, 2005, http://dud.inf.tu-dresden.de/literatur/Duesseldorf2005.10.27Biometrics.pdf.
11. EPCglobal Public Policy Steering Committee: Frequently Asked Questions on Guidelines on EPC for Consumer Products, no date given, http://www.epcglobalinc.org/public/ppsc_faq/.
12. EPCglobal Public Policy Steering Committee: Fact Sheet Electronic Product Code – An Overview, no date given, http://www.epcglobalinc.org/public/ppsc_factsheets/epc_overview.

Implantable RFID Chips
Security versus Ethics

Vikas Kumar

Asia-Pacific Institute of Management,
3 &4 Institutional Area, Jasola, Sarita Vihar,
New Delhi - 110025, India
vk_aggarwal@rediffmail.com

Abstract. Implantable RFID chips are being seen as a potential security device for the very near future with the availability of these chips already in the marketplace. The applications are presented in a broadly positive light in their use in contexts that range from health monitoring to emergency solutions. But there is a darker side to RFID chips: with their implantation, there may be an erosion of privacy and a breach in bodily integrity. In this paper, a variety applications of implantable RFID chips are discussed by taking a look at the particular technologies concerned. The legal and ethical aspects vis-à-vis the high-end security offered by such implants are compared with concerns about maintaining a democratic and sensitive society. Broadly, the paper contrasts the usefulness of RFID in industrial and other processes, with the ethical and health issues that are involved in human-implantable RFID.

1.   Introduction

Commercially, there are some exciting and interesting new technological developments on the market today. Radio Frequency Identification (RFID) is a new automatic identification method using wireless technology. With the growing need of automatic identification procedures, there has been a tremendous revolution in the applications of RFID technology with RFID tags replacing bar-code tags in the fast-growing retail industry [1]. The technology has really helped in the total management of the supply chain as well as in product outlets by using less human support and as a result of their high speed. With a predicted $US10-billion market over the next decade, RFID is a booming new wireless technology with an eager new market – retailers. The technology is transforming the way retailers receive, distribute, execute and merchandise goods to customers. Retailers today are embracing RFID as an enabling technology that will provide them with value beyond the supply chain. The commercial focus is now on transportation and logistics, healthcare and medical devices, pharmaceuticals, manufacturing, aviation and automotive sectors and the food supply chain. Successful RFID implementations have already been achieved in cars for moving through the toll gates, RFID-enabled credit cards (e.g. MasterCard's Paypass or Shell Oil's easypay) to speed up purchases or RFID-enabled transit passes

Please use the following format when citing this chapter:

Kumar, V., 2008, in IFIP International Federation for Information Processing, Volume 262; The Future of Identity in the Information Society; Simone Fischer-Hübner, Penny Duquenoy, Albin Zuccato, Leonardo Martucci; (Boston: Springer), pp. 151–157.

like London's Oyster card. RFID is used in all areas of automatic data capture that allow contactless identification of objects using radio frequency. From the global giant Wal-Mart down to other smaller companies, RFID is being adapted to track inventories *via* microchip-tagged products.

With applications that range from secure internet payment systems to industrial automation and access control, RFID technology solutions are receiving much attention in the research and development departments of large corporations. As a result, the technology is being seen as a major application in automotive identification and production automation, allowing emergency vehicles to trip traffic signals safely and providing the technology behind examples such as contactless smart cards that "auto pilot" cars. RFID certainly appears to be proving itself a technology booster for the smart electronic society.

In the present work, characteristics of the RFID technology have been discussed first with a focus on human body implants. Applications of the technology have been listed in the present scenario and in particular with respect to the security. Along with this, an effort has been made to see the harmful health effects of the technology as a result of high frequency use. Finally a closer look has been taken to the ethical challenges raised by the technology concerning human society.

2.   Implantable RFID Chips

Apart from their commercial use, direct applications of RFID technology to the human body are now seen as a potential future application; implantable RFID chips are now available in the marketplace [2][3]. Implantable RFID chips are already present in society with their practical use in hospitals and well as industry. An implantable RFID chip, which is durable and about the size of a grain of rice, can hold or link to information about the identity, physiological characteristics, health, nationality, and security clearances of the person concerned. We can imagine situations where your hand could start your car or unlock your front door or, if you were unconscious and in an emergency situation, could let a physician know about the vital characteristics.

RFID technology [4][5] works on the principle of radio frequency transmission-reception. An RFID system is made up of two components:

– A *transponder*, which is located on the object to be identified;
– A detector or *reader*, which, depending upon the design and the technology used, may be a read-only or a write/read device.

A transponder, which represents the actual data carrying device of an RFID system, normally consists of a coupling element and an electronic microchip. When the transponder, which does not usually possess its own voltage supply (or battery), is not within the response range of a reader, it is totally passive. The transponder is only activated when it is within the response range of a reader. The power required to activate the transponder is supplied to the transponder through the contactless coupling unit as is the timing pulse and data.

A reader typically contains a high frequency module (transmitter and receiver), a control unit and a coupling element to the transponder. In addition, many readers are fitted with an additional interface to enable them to forward the data received to another system (like a personal computer).

3.   Applications of Implantable RFID Chips

RFID technology applications are moving fast ahead towards human society. Human-centric applications of RFID [6] began in 1997 when a US patent for a "Personal Tracking and Recovery System" was registered [7]. The number of applications is increasing day by day, and has been reported widely in the literature [8-15].

At present, implantable chips are seen as a potential application for a form of permanent identity card that implies no need to carry personal documents. Once implanted, they could serve as the anytime, anywhere identity of the person concerned, and could serve as a single replacement of a number of identity cards. The chips have all been used for commercial, military as well as research applications. Implantable RFID chips have been designed and implanted successfully for animal tagging, and are now being used in some human beings, mainly experimentally. An early experiment with RFID implants was conducted by a British professor of cybernetics Kevin Warwick [16-17], who implanted a chip in his arm in 1998. Nowadays a number of night clubs in Barcelona, Spain, and in the Netherlands are using implantable chips to identify their very important (VIP) customers, who in turn use them to pay for drinks. The VeriChip Corporation [18] is a major company that deals in implantable or attachable chips. It has customized the devices for at least seven applications like (a) secure patient identification helping at-risk patients to get the right treatment when they need it most, (b) infant protection, (c) wander prevention to keep wander-prone residents safe, (d) an Assetrac system for locating different assets, (e) a tool and equipment management system that allows construction, maintenance and repair organizations to control their tools and equipment inventory, (f) vibration monitoring, and (g) emergency management solutions that allow users to manage, track, and inventory remains and evidentiary items accurately that are associated with small incidents, crime scenes, or mass disasters. The company claims a number of successful implementations of these implantable devices.

These implantable ICT devices represent the possible solution to a great need, with the rising demand for health services, increased mobility of the patients, and the need to limit occupational accidents and diseases [19]. For example, even though it did not explicitly or directly fund any RFID-related work, the European Commission in its fifth framework programme co-funded projects covering intelligent systems for health professionals, for patients and intelligent environments for the health of citizens [20] and, more recently, in its seventh framework programme, the Commission is funding a study that explores the use of RFID wireless technologies in hospitals in Europe.

When looking at these overall scenarios, the potential applications could seem to be really wonderful and to provide a huge step towards the world of automation. However there are a number of problems associated with them that we will be discussing in the upcoming sections.

4.   Security Applications

The most important applications of implantable chips still lie in the field of security management. These chips can have a potential role in the development of anti-terrorist security tools with automatic identification. For example, they are the most suitable means for keeping a watch on criminals in custody. As an illustration, most of the big criminals tend to free themselves from custody or prison; this has been seen a number of times in India as well as other countries [21]. Implantable RFID chips may offer great success in keeping sound security watch over such criminals. Also, RFID chips may be of good use for finding any security breach in the personal security of very-very important persons by reporting automatically their presence and activities. So, there are numerous of fruitful applications that can be explored in terms of RFID implantable chips technology and can be used for the welfare of society.

But the most commonly used technologies always pose a security threat as the result of the work of hackers as they follow the advancing technology trends. This type of security hazard, when applied to RFID chips, can lead to drastic irreversible implications as the sensitivity of the relevant data or information tend to be very high particularly in relation to security applications. Thus the security applications of implantable chips must be used or applied with greater care.

However there are still a number of problems associated with the implantable chips, and the most significant of these are the health effects associated with radiation.

5.   Health Effects

Normal RFID readers radiate electromagnetic field and magnetic fields in the close proximity of the tag. These fields activate circuitry on the tags and the data stored in the tag is retransmitted to the reader. The frequencies used are 13.56 MHz and 915 MHz (UHF). A lot of research work has been carried out to see the effect of electromagnetic radiation on human body (even complete journals have been devoted to this field [22]), but no consistent results have been reported for radiation in the range of frequencies being used by RFID. Also a study has been undertaken to see the effect of radiation on the drug products that use RFID tags for retail marketing. The results [23] show that the energy supplied by these is not sufficient to give rise to a chemical change. Thus, presently, there is no suitable evidence of the possible health hazards. A lot of research work is still needed to explore the possible health hazards of this technology [24]. However considering human beings as social beings, social health is of even greater importance than personal health. Hence, social issues need to be considered in the implementation of this technology.

6.   Ethical Issues

Ethics form the basis of effective human existence, and hence must be considered in the human centric applications of technology. The important, main concerns about the implementation of implantable RFID technology are the ethical and societal issues concerning the identity of human beings. As a specific example, with the growing need of identification, some educational institutes have installed biometric systems for the attendance of teachers in India, but the professors have taken a strong stance against this approach, since they see it as disregarding a highly respected profession [25].

In such a sensitive society, are we really ready to have identity chips implanted directly in our body? The situation may indicate that people are like 24-hour slaves rather than employees, and the universal law of 8 hours of work will not be valid. This will be an erosion of our privacy and our right to bodily integrity. Does anybody really want to be required to have a foreign object implanted in his/her arm just to either get or keep a job? And does the employee want the employer to know whenever s/he leaves the office? Also, should every RFID reader-equipped supermarket checkout counter note your presence and your purchases? Thus the personal life of people may always be at risk with continuous monitoring.

Implantable devices have serious ethical consequences as these devices are accessible via digital networks. This may lead to a situation where you are always insecure in your own secure home [26]. Subcutaneous RFID implants make people-tracking possible without the need for any correlation of profiling data or misuse of data. Consequently, this threat may cause a direct conflict with individual liberties. Such implants have the potential to form a basis for cyber-racism; they may be used to change the identity, memory, self perception and perception of others. The misuse of information certainly create ethically unacceptable instances as per the opinion of European Group on Ethics of Science and New Technologies, 2005. However this needs a further elaboration in particular with reference to the implantable RFID technology. In the worst case, they may be used to enhance capabilities in order to dominate others. Such applications, similar to human cloning, may tend to degrade the whole social system.

In the opinion of the European group on ethics [27], the implantation of ICT devices in the human body should be governed by the three principles that
  (a) The objective is important, like saving lives, restoring health and improving the quality of life.
  (b) The implant is necessary to achieve this objective.
  (c) There is no method that is less invasive and more cost effective for achieving the same objective.

The European group on ethics makes a general point that non-medical applications of ICT-implants are a potential threat to human dignity and democratic society.

Therefore, such applications should respect in all circumstances the principles of informed consent and proportionality. Such implants are a potential threat to human dignity when they are used for surveillance purposes, as they may be used by state authorities, individuals or groups to increase their power over others. Hence the surveillance applications of ICT implants may only be permitted if the legislator considers that there is an urgent and justified necessity in a democratic society.

Thus society really needs a brainstorming exercise so as to decide on the applications and usability of RFID technology while maintaining the dignity and integrity of individuals.

7.   Conclusion

Privacy advocates raise the issue of public awareness and aid in ensuring that technology is deployed responsibly, but ultimately consumers will drive the use of technology through their behaviours, preferences and demands. This paper summarizes the key applications of implantable RFID chips, by taking a closer look at the ethical and legal aspects of such implants in relation to human society. It is concluded that implantable RFID chip technology certainly has the potential to address the security concerns of present-day information society. But at the same time, the social and ethical issues (including privacy and health issues) must be taken care of before implementation. Technology has always been a leader in taking human society ahead of imagination. A careful constructive approach to RFID, used with increased awareness and perception, will certainly help society with tremendous applications.

Acknowledgement

The author is thankful to the reviewers of the paper for their comments and suggestions. They have certainly helped a lot in improving the quality of paper.

References

1. "euroRFID - your guide to RFID & GDS solutions", [Available at www.escinst.org]
2. Kenneth R.Foster and Jan Jaeger,"RFID Inside", IEEE Spectrum Magazine, March 2007
3. Amal Graafstra,"Hands On", IEEE Spectrum Magazine, March 2007
4. Sandip Lahiri, "RFID Source Book", IBM Press 2006
5. http://rfid-handbook.de/
6. Masters A and Michael K, "Humancentric applications of RFID implants: The Usability Contexts of Control, Convenience and Care", proceedings of 2nd International workshop on Mobile commerce and Services, July 19, 2005, pp 32-41
7. Paul A Gargano et al., "Personal tracking and recovery system", United States Patent Number 5629678, 1997

8.   D. Icke, "Has The Old ID Card had Its Chips?" Soldier Magazine, April, 2001
9.   C. Murray, "Injectable Chip Opens door to Human Bar Code", EE Times, January 7, 2002
10. J. Scheers, "New Body Art: Chip Implants", Wired News, March 11, 2002
11. J. Black, "Roll Up your Sleeves for a Chip Implant", Business Week Online, Business Week Magazine, March 21, 2002
12. L. Grossman, "Meet the Chipsons", Time, New York, 159(10), March 11, 2002 pp. 56-57
13. D. Stretfeld, "Chips To Be Implanted in Humans", Los Angeles Times, May 10, 2002
14. B. Gengler, "Chip Implants Become Part of You", The Australian, September 10, 2002
15. R. Woolnaugh, "A man with a chip in his shoulder", Computer Weekly, June 29, 2000
16. http://www.kevinwarwick.com/
17. Mark Gasson, "ICT Implants", Presentation at IFIP Summer School, Karlstad, 2007
18. http://www.verichipcorp.com/
19. Diane Whitehouse, "Information communication technologies and health: past, current and future directions", Proceedings of IFIP Summer School pp. 211-218
20. European Communities 2000-IST Programme. Report of the IST advisory group concerning trust, dependability, security and privacy for IST in FP6
21. http://in.news.yahoo.com/071024/43/6md4a.html
22. Bioelectromagnetics, John Wiley & Sons
23. H. Bassen, S. Seidman, J. Rogul at al.,"An Exposure System for Evaluating Possible Effects of RFID on Various Formulations of Drug Products", IEEE Applications and Practice Magazine, April 2007, pp. 17-23
24. European Commission Report, "User Needs in ICT Research for Independent Living, with a Focus on Health Aspects", European Communities, 2006
25. Asia-Pacific Institute of Management, New Delhi (2007)
26. Simon Garfinkel, "Database Nation: The Death of Privacy in the 20th Century", O'Reilly & Associates, Inc., 2000
27. European Commission Report, "Opinion on the ethical aspects of ICT implants in the human body (Opinion No. 20)", European Communities, 2005

Workshop: Privacy and identity in Online Social Networks and Communities

The Need for a Paradigm Shift in Addressing Privacy Risks in Social Networking Applications

Stefan Weiss

Johann Wolfgang Goethe-University
Gräfstrasse 78, 60054 Frankfurt am Main/Germany
stefan.weiss@m-lehrstuhl.de,
WWW home page: http://www.m-lehrstuhl.de

Abstract. New developments on the Internet in the past years have brought up a number of online social networking applications within the so-called Web 2.0 world that experienced phenomenal growth and a tremendous attention in the public. Online social networking services build their business model on the myriad of sensitive personal data provided freely by their users, a fact that is increasingly getting the attention of privacy advocates. After explaining the economic meaning and importance of online social networks to eCommerce in general and reiterating the basic principles of Web 2.0 environments and their enterprise mechanisms in particular, this paper addresses the main informational privacy risks of Web 2.0 business models with a focus on online social networking sites. From literature review and current expert discussions, new privacy research questions are proposed for the future development of privacy-enhancing technologies used within Web 2.0 environments. The resulting paradigm shift needed in addressing privacy risks in social networking applications is likely to focus less on access protection, anonymity and unlinkability type of PET-solutions and more on privacy safeguarding measures that enable greater transparency and that directly attach context and purpose limitation to the personally identifiable data itself. The FIDIS/IFIP workshop discussion has resulted in the idea to combine existing privacy-enhancing technologies and protection methods with new safeguarding measures to accommodate the Web 2.0 dynamics and to enhance the informational privacy of Web 2.0 users.

1 Introduction

In the last few years, the Internet has seen new developments that not only changed the structure of some of the online business models as we know them but they will also change the way we see and use the World Wide Web in the future. Dale Dougherty coined the term Web 2.0 in 2004 and Tim O'Reilly[1] popularized the term later in 2005 as the "participatory Web" [1]. Compared to Web 1.0 (to apply the same terminology) when the Internet was used as a pure information source for consuming

---

[1] Both Dale Dougherty and Tim O'Reilly are leading the publishing firm O'Reilly Media Inc.

Please use the following format when citing this chapter:

Weiss, S., 2008, in IFIP International Federation for Information Processing, Volume 262; The Future of Identity in the Information Society; Simone Fischer-Hübner, Penny Duquenoy, Albin Zuccato, Leonardo Martucci; (Boston: Springer), pp. 161–171.

content, the Web 2.0 is now providing users with functionalities to actively participate and create content. Research and survey data [2-4] as well as anecdotal evidence in the form of newspaper articles or blog entries [5-8] see in these developments both opportunities and risks. This paper addresses the potential misuse of personal information in online social networking applications, referred to in this paper as informational privacy risk. After explaining the economic meaning and importance of online social networks to eCommerce in general and reiterating the basic principles of Web 2.0 environments and their enterprise mechanisms, important privacy research questions in online social networks are derived by aligning new privacy approaches specifically to the new dynamics of Web 2.0 applications. With the privacy research questions derived from the following discussion, this paper intends to raise awareness in enterprises and in the research community for the growing need to view and research privacy in the Web 2.0 environment differently than before and in developing new privacy-enhancing technologies to address informational privacy risks.

2   The economic value of online social networks

Online social networking websites such as MySpace, LinkedIn, Xing or Facebook typically provide applications for users to set up individual profiles, create virtual networks with friends and business partners, share articles, photos and videos, create content such as stories and blog entries, or to share opinions or preferences by giving online votes or setting search tags. Increasing online collaboration, interaction and personalization is the result – something that an online advertiser values as the source for more targeted marketing initiatives using sophisticated data mining capabilities.

Major acquisitions of social networking providers by investors in the past two years underpin the potential economic value of these firms. After News Corp. bought the social networking site MySpace for about half a billion US$ in 2005, Google acquired the video sharing site YouTube for 1.65 billion US$. Those acquiring firms see the commercial value of social networking sites like MySpace or YouTube not only in their attractive user base, the 18-30 year olds, but also in their potential influence on online retail growth overall. According to eMarketer Inc., online sales analysis data from last year's holiday shopping season in the U.S. for example supports the increasing commercial importance of social networks, blogs and user preference tags as word-of-mouth buying suggestions for small businesses [9]. Members of social networking sites become more active online buyers in response to preferences and "best of" lists displayed for example for music CDs within their community groups.

The online analyst company Hitwise underpins this trend by the growing percentage of online retail traffic coming directly from social networking sites – 6.2 % in the pre-holiday season in 2006 up from 2% in the same period in 2005. Hitwise sees in this data a clear proof that social networking sites such as Google's YouTube and News Corp.'s MySpace.com have begun displacing portals such as Yahoo Inc. as the new home base for Internet users. Social networking websites have emerged in the US market to become an integral part of web activity for many Internet users – in

September 2006, one in every 20 Internet visits went to one of the top 20 social networks, nearly double the share of visits compared to a year ago [10].

Analysts such as Forrester point out the attractiveness of users of social networking sites in more detail. In their report on "How Consumers Use Social Networks" from June 2007 [11], social networking site users come from households with an average household income of US$ 62,000 and above – quite an attractive consumer group. 50% of adult users and 67% of young users between the ages of 12 and 21 specifically state that they often tell their friends about products that interest them. Once all marketers have realized the potential of this user group and how to turn their online activities on social networking sites into their own benefit, it can be expected that the value of the users' profiles, their online behaviour and in turn the amount of all of their personally identifiable information will increase.

Attractive users have attractive personal data. As a result, the informational privacy especially for users of social networking sites is at risk. The following chapters will look at the challenge of assuring security and privacy for personal data on social networking sites and will also identify new research areas that can help to minimize these privacy risks in online social networks.

3 New privacy challenges and risks in Web 2.0

The increasing risk of misuse of personal data processed by online social networking applications is evident from computer science research [2-4] as well from anecdotal evidence in the form of newspaper articles or blog entries [5-8]. One example for the privacy risks users of Web 2.0 services see was expressed by a blogger named Jamais Cascio in October 2006 on the personal site Freds House which dedicates most of its blog topics to mobility, media and ubiquitous life topics. His blog entry reads as follows: "I'm feeling increasingly uneasy about my dependence on Google services. [...] I look around my desktop and I see Google Reader, Google Mail, Google Talk, Google Toolbar, Google Maps, Google Calendar, Google News, Google Analytics, Google Earth, and of course Google Google. [...] I think I need a new Google product to drop into beta. That would be, let's see, Google Data Privacy (GDP). GDP would allow me to review all of the information that Google retains on me across all services, from all devices, and from all sources. GDP would allow me to determine the maximum data retention period for each of my services. GDP would allow me to selectively opt out of cross-service data mining & correlation, even if it reduced the quality of the services I receive. GDP would allow me to correct any inaccurate data in my profile. And GDP would log and alert me when my data was queried by other services. [...] This is exactly the kind of thing that Google could do, should do, to maintain its "Don't Be Evil" motto, while compiling better -- more accurate and more useful -- information."

This blogger has described in length the main functionality that a privacy-enhancing solution in a Web 2.0 environment should provide, namely the self-control of one's personal data. It is clearly understood that more personal data collected, displayed, stored and processed in a decentralized environment and across multiple devices causes all sorts of concerns, one being the feeling to loose control. Risks associated with this situation range from identity theft to online and physical stalking, from embarrassment to price discrimination and blackmailing [12]. The following table (Table 1.) lists a selection of privacy risks for the specific categories of social networking sites accumulated largely from published privacy breaches or from public discussions on the fears of such risks during the last 12 months.

Table 1. New Risks for Informational Privacy Emerge on Social Networking Sites

Category	Examples	Informational Privacy Risks
Business	LinkedIn Monster XING	Blackmail, Breach of Confidentiality, Data Reuse/Secondary Use, Discrimination, Aggregation (i.e. Pre-Screening for Recruiting, Harvard Business Case on Mimi Brewster)
Personal	MySpace Orkut Hi5 Classmates Bebo	Intrusion, Breach of Confidentiality, Data Reuse/Secondary Use, Aggregation, Identity theft, Abuse by Cyberbullies or Predators, Badmouthing, Pedophilia
Publication	YouTube Xanga Broadcaster Last.fm LiveJournal	Unwanted Exposure, Distortion, Data reuse/Secondary Use, Abuse by Cyberbullies or Predators, Video-bullying, Objectionable material, Pedophilia, Child pornography
Special Interests	BlackPlanet Cyworld Mixi WAYN Care2	Discrimination, Data reuse/Secondary Use, Aggregation, Intrusion, Exposure, Breach of Confidentiality
Individual	SecondLife Gaia Online	Exposure, Appropriation, Identity theft, Breach of Confidentiality, Insults, Cyberbullying

Considering the potentially differing interests of the data subject (here meaning the user providing personal data) and the receiving party in a commercial setting such as a social networking application, a definition of informational privacy that best describes the challenge to be solved is the following: "Privacy can be defined as an interaction, in which the information rights of different parties collide. The issue is of control over information flow by parties that have different preferences over information permeability." [13] In this context, the individual user typically has particular socioeconomic motivations for a certain degree of privacy. According to Gary T. Marx, one of the leading privacy researchers in computer sciences, users may want to be protected from an unwanted intrusion of their time, space and person, they may want to see protection from discrimination or they may want to avoid "type casting" [14]. On the other hand, the provider of an online social network may have the interest to receive as much personal data as possible from an individual, including links to as many other people as possible, in order to increase the value of advertisement to his members. The more personalized the member profiles are, the more targeted and – in consequence – valuable adverts can be.

Looking back at traditional viewpoints on privacy protection in information and communication technology, technical privacy solutions tried to satisfy the socioeconomic privacy motivations of individuals predominantly through the use of privacy-enhancing technologies and identity management solutions [15]. Whereas those solutions address the user's anonymity, unlinkability, unobservability, or pseudonymity in form of a "protection and disguising" mode, these solutions may not address new privacy challenges a user faces when he openly and willingly displays a whole data set of personal information in form of his personal profile for example on a social networking website. In fact, hiding and disguising the personal data in the person's profile would most likely contradict with the purpose and perceived benefit of providing the personal information in the first place.

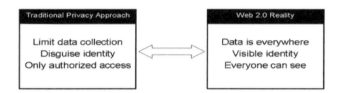

Fig. 1. Web 2.0 reality contradicts with the traditional privacy approach

Considering the general failure of the Web to satisfy requirements such as privacy protection, a balanced approach to intellectual property rights, and basic security and access control needs [16], additional privacy research in computer sciences will need to address solutions within the new "participatory Web". The Web 2.0 reality calls for a privacy paradigm shift adding privacy safeguarding measures for an open and decentralized environment. In this environment, the person whose data is at stake, may decide on a case-by-case basis if he wants to provide a certain set of personal information about himself in a specified context and if he only wants to provide it for a specific purpose and for a specific data receiver. In order to make those control features workable, the processes around those decisions and on what happens to the data need to be completely transparent.

Solutions for a policy-aware web such as the Platform for Privacy Preferences (P3P) or the Enterprise Privacy Authorization Language (EPAL) try to assure that personal data is being processed according to specified rules and policies. They offer the kind of tools that are needed to encode rules into web applications. On the other hand, they fall short on giving the actual control to the user, at least in their current application. If a user actual does set his privacy preferences using P3P, the system only checks against defined policies of the web site provider without any enforcement mechanisms. The actual control must be set down at the level of personal data.

Personal data is at the core of any online social network service's business model. That is why especially for this kind of application, privacy researchers need to go into more depth, looking at privacy safeguarding measures along the whole data processing life cycle, addressing the control and accountability of that data especially at the use end [17].

4   Privacy Research to Address the Web 2.0 Reality

Tim O'Reilly has defined the Web 2.0 as a "[...] platform, spanning all connected
devices; Web 2.0 applications are those that make the most of the intrinsic advantages
of that platform: delivering software as a continually-updated service that gets better
the more people use it, consuming and remixing data from multiple sources, including
individual users, while providing their own data and services in a form that allows
remixing by others, creating network effects through an 'architecture of participation',
and going beyond the page metaphor of Web 1.0 to deliver rich user experiences."
[18]. In such an environment of decentralized systems and infrastructures that enable
the quick and efficient development of systems, it is difficult to implement control
features such as traditional security or privacy measures. Nevertheless, the rapid
growth of Web 2.0 services is a reality and security and privacy research needs to
adapt to it.

In order to derive relevant and specific privacy research questions in the new Web
2.0 environment, it is helpful to use the four principles and enterprise mechanisms of
'Wikinomics' [19], defined by Don Tapscott and Anthony D. Williams. There are a
number of other more elaborate models and principles that could be used in the
context of defining Web 2.0 dynamics, for example the "Web 2.0 Meme Map" [20]
developed at a brainstorming session during a conference at O'Reilly Media.
However, the author has purposefully chosen the Wikinomics principles here because
they describe the relevant dynamics at work in the Web 2.0 somewhat more
simplistically and they can easily be used to conceptualize the resulting privacy
challenges and privacy research questions on a high level. While matching the
principles of 'Wikinomics' and the respective privacy issues in this paper, the author
has focused on the situation for an online social networking application and has not
viewed different scenarios for example at video sharing sites or services that provide
search and tagging functions. The case scenario of an online social networking
service was identified earlier in this paper as being extremely vulnerable to privacy
risks due to the nature of its business model dealing with personal data.

The principles of 'Wikinomics' are (1) Openness, (2) Peering, (3) Sharing and (4)
Acting globally. Each of those principles motivate specific economic mechanisms
within enterprises providing Web 2.0 services but each principle can also be related to
specific privacy approaches discussed or recommended in current research papers as
shown in the following table (Table 2.).

Table 2. Relating the principles of 'Wikinomics' and described enterprise mechanisms to
privacy approaches

Principle	Enterprise Mechanism	Privacy Approach
Openness	Transparency	Accountability for data
Peering	Marketocracy	Informational self-determination
Sharing	Collaboration	Personal data property and usage rights
Acting globally	Multinational	Non-legal rules and policies

4.1   Evaluating each principle on its implication for the privacy of users of online social networks:

(1) Openness: If personal data is exchanged and processed openly in applications that are based on open standards and it is transparent who the involved parties are, privacy safeguarding measures need to assure accountability for the data and its authorized usage. It needs to be transparent to the user (transparency-enhancing technology) what happens to his data and it needs to be possible that each data process can be accounted for later on. The assumption here would be that data is being exchanged openly, thus, the requirement calls for a completely open process where the various parties can be made accountable for what they do with the data if necessary.

(2) Peering: The principle of "peering" builds on self-organization by a group of individuals. Applied to the case of an online social network service, individuals and groups of individuals determine the success or failure of the particular site by actively engaging for example in the linking of friends, building interest groups and communities and setting preferences that determine the exponential growth of the site. When thinking of the influence of the individual within a group and aspects of privacy, it is apparent that the individual needs to be provided with a function to determine what should happen with his personal data.

(3) Sharing: Sharing in the online social network setting means that the individual willingly wants to share data with others. That means for the service provider that he needs to provide collaborative tools to enable the sharing of data. However, when it comes to sharing sensitive personal data or providing data in a specific situation or context only, the individual might be reluctant to share with everyone and for any purpose. For this reason, privacy safeguarding measures need to attach something like a property or usage right to the personal data set. Lessons from digital rights management techniques or the concept of "sticky policies" for the Web might be useful to address this requirement.

(4) Acting globally: And finally the principle of "acting globally" brings up a range of issues when looking at privacy challenges in online social networks. Without legal boundaries of Web applications and even in some cases without any cultural boundaries and rules, it is a tremendous operational challenge that service providers face. How can rules for privacy aspects be set by each individual and how can they be enforced automatically? Legal and public policy regulations alone certainly cannot solve privacy challenges within those applications. Technology and privacy standards in the future may help to work on a common ground. Progress in the area of the web technology standards and the semantic web may also have some answers to privacy challenges in online social networks that are largely related to the specific context and usage.

The following table (Table 3.) attempts to give a brief overview of some of the privacy research questions that can be derived from the preceding discussion. The list of privacy research questions does not claim to be complete and, at this point in time, simply has the intention to raise awareness in enterprises and in the research community for the growing need to view and research informational privacy in the

Web 2.0 environment. In fact, it can be expected that interested readers, security and privacy experts can immediately add additional questions and topics to this list which should fulfil the underlying purpose of this paper to initiate discussions and thought processes around the topic.

Table 3. Inferring privacy research questions in the context of online social networks

Principle	Privacy Approach	Privacy Research Questions
Openness	Accountability of data use	• Is the definition and general perception of privacy in our networked world changing and how will privacy be defined in the future? • Do users see their privacy safeguarded if the data processes will be more transparent? • How do user groups and their behavioural patterns differ in open vs. closed online communities in relation to the type and extent of public display of their identity? • How can context-based data usage be integrated in existing Semantic Web concepts?
Peering	Privacy self-control	• How do group dynamics influence the attitude towards privacy? • Can we use existing literature on social network theory to explain aspects of trust and intimacy in online networking? • What is the commercial benefit of peer networks to eCommerce? • Would privacy self-control features in an online social networking site be perceived as a benefit and used as a solution to privacy concerns?
Sharing	Personal data property rights	• Under which circumstances and in what context are social network users willing to limit the usage of certain types of personal data (risk awareness)? • What kinds of gratification and cost models can show the value of sharing sensitive personal data with specific individuals or groups? • How can DRM technology be used by an individual for protecting his/her personal data from unauthorized access, copying, usage, or transfer?
Acting globally	Non-legal rules and policies	• What set of rules would users of online social networks see as essential to protect their privacy? • How can those personal, non-legal rules be converted into automated policies and attached to the personal data sets? (sticky policies concept) • Is it possible to derive general rule sets on privacy by studying different user groups attitudes toward privacy in different cultures and in different contexts or technology environments? • How can privacy standardization help to automate a privacy policy-aware Web?

4.2   Considering existing technologies for solving privacy issues in a Web 2.0 environment

Further research should evaluate and develop new solutions and methods that are able to ensure the informational privacy of individuals when using applications in the Web 2.0 environment. Privacy perceptions in the Web 2.0 have changed and will change further with the introduction of new information and communication methods. Besides researching those changing perceptions in terms of their social, psychological or economical roots, it should be of great value to look at existing privacy or security technologies and how they might contribute as a whole or in part to new privacy 2.0 solutions.

The following list of technologies or methods to be considered for evaluation against possible privacy 2.0 solutions (Table 4.) should be seen as work-in-progress. It served the audience of the FIDIS/IFIP workshop session on "Privacy and identity in social networks and online communities" as a source for discussion and could possibly be extended with ongoing work or planned work by the research community. The discussion during the workshop session led to the idea that combining existing privacy safeguarding measures with new methods to accommodate the Web 2.0 dynamics and bundling those into a packaged privacy 2.0 solution might have its greatest value by addressing an easier usability of privacy solutions at large, especially in an environment where users themselves increasingly participate.

Table 4. List of technologies and methods to be evaluated for their fit to solve privacy 2.0 issues

Privacy 2.0 Issues	Technology or method to consider for evaluation
Transparency and Accountability	• Audit trails and logs on data processes • Monitoring of pre-specified data usage • Privacy assurance methods (compliance) • Semantic techniques such as topic maps
User control model	• Trusted computing • Third-party service to manage personal data as a mediator • EPAL
Assuring the authorized usage of personal data	• Semantic web technologies adding usage context to personal data (tagging data) • Techniques from DRM solutions to be applied to personal data (Privacy Rights Management) • Watermarking techniques to mark the data owner (data provenance)
Managing privacy regulations and individual preferences	• Sticky policies concept (Semantic web) • Web site privacy with P3P • PRIME technology

The FIDIS/IFIP workshop session discussions have resulted in the viewpoint that besides the economic, social and legal questions around privacy protection in the Web

2.0 environment and particularly with online social networks, detailed technical research should be extended towards using semantic web languages, DRM technology and technology standardization to assure the informational privacy of individuals on the Web and the protection of personally identifiable information from misuse.

5 Conclusion

The growing economic value of online social networking sites in particular and Web 2.0 applications in general brings about new security and privacy risks that have not been adequately addressed by software developers, researchers and privacy advocates so far. Informational privacy risks such as identity theft, online or physical stalking, personal embarrassment, price discrimination or blackmailing differ widely among individuals and depend on the specific context. In the case of using online social networking services, the dominant approach to collect sensitive personal data at the outset makes it necessary to rethink traditional privacy approaches that were directed mainly at the protection and disguise of the user's identity information in the past. New privacy approaches need to direct their efforts to privacy safeguarding requirements that give control to the user. Data processes need to be transparent to the user, audit and monitoring methods need to be able to account for each data process and the pre-set privacy preferences of the user need to be managed and controlled diligently so that only authorized entities use the personal data for the specified purposes.

Research questions derived from the exercise of linking privacy approaches directly to the principles and enterprise mechanisms of Web 2.0 environments have shown that the pre-eminent goal for privacy research and PET development is likely to shift from access protection, anonymity and unlinkability type of solutions to privacy safeguarding measures that enable greater transparency and that directly attach context and purpose limitation to the personally identifiable data itself. Whereas specific research in this area needs to validate the need for new privacy approaches as described here, it can surely be concluded that the growth of online social networks and the systems that get developed around them need to get a stronger attention from the research community and from enterprises. It is clear that a number of new risks to information privacy arise where more personal data is collected, displayed, stored and processed in a decentralized environment and across multiple devices. More control, transparency and accountability can minimize those risks if all stakeholders put more attention on developing solutions in that direction.

References

1. O'Reilly, Tim, "What is Web 2.0", published on the O'Reilly website on September 30, 2005.
2. Nissenbaum, Helen, New York University, "Privacy as Contextual Integrity", Washington Law Review, v79 #1, Pages 119-158, 02-04-04.

3. Madden, Mary and Fox, Susannah, Pew Internet Project, "Riding the Waves of Web 2.0", October 5, 2006.
4. Cranor, Lorrie F., AT&T Labs-Research, "'I Didn't Buy it for Myself' – Privacy and Ecommerce Personalization", WPES'03, October 30, 2003, Washington DC, USA.
5. Heise Zeitschriften Verlag, Roth, Wolf-Dieter, „Tod im Netz: Wenn das Profil einer Social Networking Site zum Steckbrief wird", 09-19-06.
6. Wired News, Lynn, Regina, "The Internet makes us naked", March 9, 2007.
7. Time Magazine, Cox, Ana Marie, "Making mischief on the Web", 12-16-06.
8. Süddeutsche Zeitung Wissen, Stirn, Alexander, "Das soziale Netz: Ende der Privatsphäre", Ausgabe 13/2007.
9. eMarketer Inc., "Social networks influence online holiday shopping", Computerworld, December 25, 2006.
10. Hitwise Pty. Ltd., "Hitwise US Consumer Generated Media Report", November 2006.
11. Forrester Research Report, "How Consumers Use Social Networks", June 2007, Forrester Research Inc., Figure 6.
12. Gross, Ralph, Acquisti, Alessandro, H. John Heinz, III, Information revelation and privacy in online social networks, Proceedings of the 2005 ACM workshop on Privacy in the electronic society, November 07-07, 2005, Alexandria, VA, USA.
13. Noam, E.M., "Privacy and Self-Regulation: Markets for Electronic Privacy, in Privacy and Self-Regulation in the Information Age", 1997, US Department of Commerce.
14. Marx, Gary T., "What's in a Name? Some Reflections on the Sociology of Anonymity Title", Massachusetts Institute of Technology, 1999.
15. Hansen, Marit and Pfitzmann, Andreas: Anonymity, Unlinkability, Unobservability, Pseudonymity, and Identity Management - A Consolidated Proposal for Terminology, Version 0.28, May 29, 2006.
16. Weitzner, Daniel J., Hendler, Jim, Berners-Lee, Tim, and Connolly, Dan, "Creating a Policy-Aware Web: Discretionary, Rule-based Access for the World Wide Web" in Web and Information Security, Idea Group Inc., forthcoming.
17. Report in the 2006 TAMI/Portia Workshop on Privacy and Accountability, Massachusetts Institute of Technology, June 28-29, 2006.
18. O'Reilly, Tim, Founder and CEO of O'Reilly Media Inc., October 1, 2005.
19. Tapscott, Don, Wikinomics – How Mass Collaboration Changes Everything, Portfolio, Pages 20-30, December 2006.
20. O'Reilly, Tim, "What is Web 2.0? – Design Patterns and Business Models for the Next Generation of Software", Section 1. The Web As Platform, O'Reilly Media Inc., September 30, 2005.

Keynote Session 3:

Authentication and Transaction Security in E-business

Lorenz Müller

AXSionics AG, BFH Spin-off Park
c/o Hochschule für Technik und Informatik
Seevorstadt 103b, CH - 2501 Biel

Abstract. E-business is one of the driving factors for the growth of the worldwide economy. But in parallel to the upsurge of the digital trade the cyberspace became also a main attraction for criminals. Today main parts of the Internet are still outside of traditional national legislation and law enforcement. Security is therefore a task that can not be delegated to the government only. Each party in an E-business operation has to care about the threats and the effective countermeasures. This paper introduces in the theme of online security and presents at the end a technical system that helps to defeat many of the actually most dangerous threats to a trusted E-business world.

1   Introduction

Neither the bursting of the Internet bubble nor the recent boost of online criminality stopped the ascension of electronic business in the last few years. Almost all industries have developed business models which rely on so called E-business processes that use the communication facilities of the Internet. The growth rates of this new economic sector are impressive. The corresponding economic indicators show that online retail sales in 2006 (B2C) reached a value of $148 billion in North America and $102 billion in Europe with an expected CAGR of 20 % or more [1,2]. The already much larger ICT-based business to business (B2B) market (projected $2.3 trillion in US and €1.6 trillion in Europe in 2006) still continues to rise substantially above the total market growth (CAGR of 13.9 % in US [1] and 19 % in Europe) and represents already today a substantial fraction of the total worldwide economy.

E-business is now an important opportunity to extend the range and the productivity of existing and new companies. Customers appreciate the convenience and the expanded offering of the Internet shopping. Companies need the improved possibilities for their supply chain management to cut cost and to move rapidly in the global market. However this new Eldorado also attracts criminals and the Web technologies, originally designed for maximum availability and connectivity, offer numerous possibilities for abuse and attacks on the digital economy. Investigations showed that the fraud rate in online transactions is at the level of 2.1% (2004) rising to 3.7% (2005) [3] of the total transaction volume. This value is more than an order of magnitude higher than in conventional transactions and already now leads to

Please use the following format when citing this chapter:

Müller, L., 2008, in IFIP International Federation for Information Processing, Volume 262; The Future of Identity in the Information Society; Simone Fischer-Hübner, Penny Duquenoy, Albin Zuccato, Leonardo Martucci; (Boston: Springer), pp. 175–197.

substantial losses especially in the financial industry [4]. Identity theft, which is a preferred way to commit online fraud, caused over $2 billion damage to the US financial industry in 2006 [3]. These facts have also changed our view on security.

1.1   The Changing Landscape of Security

A big building with a vitreous facade and a prestigious lobby with secured entry doors still represents our classic picture of a secured enterprise. However this is an idea of the past. Within the digital economy, corporations have become increasingly virtual organizations distributed over many countries and interacting with a rapidly growing community of collaborators, clients and partners. In parallel to this evolution the classical concept of secured zones inside clearly defined borderlines has been replaced by new strategies to cope with fraud and crime.

1.1.1   Security is on the radar of all industries
Such new security needs have triggered a whole security industry in the IT sector. Although the classical security market is still dominant, the newer market for logical access control grows much faster and will reach US$ 9.3 billion this year with CAGR of 20% [5]. The growing importance of security is also reflected in the spending behavior of the IT departments of F1000 companies. In 2006 about 88 % of these departments allocated constant or growing budgets for IT security compared to the budgets in previous years. Some of them intend to spend as much as 25 % more on security [6].

1.1.2   Security in the physical and the digital world
Improved security concepts now not only include physical security (buildings, labs, rooms) but increasingly have to include logical security: protecting the knowledge and information space of an enterprise and the digital transaction processes with their clients. In the traditional approach, we defined a borderline with inside and outside infrastructure and well guarded gates between the two zones, using armed doors, firewalls, virus scanners, VPNs and other protective measures.

1.1.3   Three lines of defense: the new paradigm
This borderline security approach was well adapted for classical organizations but is not sufficient in a world of virtual and widely distributed organizations. To protect a complex network organization we have to introduce an in-depth defense at staggered perimeter lines. Border security, authentication and authorization build together three layers of defenses that allow secure user access and robust security.

1.2   Security requests in online transactions

We may represent an E-commerce transaction between a person and an operator of a value service schematically by a triangular relationship. On one side we have the physical person that intends to take advantage of the operators offer. To get in contact with the operator the person needs a certain digital identity, which in some way defines the social situation of the person and its business relation with the operator e.g. a proof of the capability to pay for a service. The operator administers the access rights to his value services and allocates these rights through his identity and service management system to the authorized users or customers. A person intending to use the operator's service must present some identity credentials to show that she really has the claimed identity with the corresponding social rights (e.g. possession of a personal credit card). On the backward step the operator then grants access or allowance to the person after having checked the presented identity credentials.

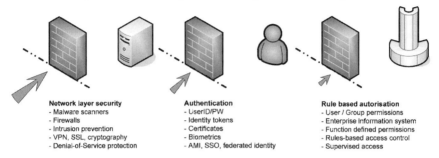

Fig. 1. Authentication is a central keystone in a layered defense system. Its strength has to match the strength of the typical border line security measures. The lines represent the three steps in an in depth security system.

2   Threats to e-business

The threats to the digital economy can be roughly put in three categories:
- Threats originating from criminals who intend to harm the welfare of others to gain financial, competitive or political advantages.
- Threats originating from reckless promoters of their online offering using unwished marketing means.
- Threats originating from software or product pirates that offer their fraudulent copies over the Internet.

All these threats target the digital economy and, in the same time, use the technological means of the digital economy. Typical methods to execute an attack within one of the above threat categories include the application of malware that is introduced to the users Internet access device, the operation of malicious Web sites or the infection of innocent Web sites with malicious codes, the pushing of unwanted information content to the user (spam, adware etc) and the distribution of illegal copies of digital content or values [12]. We will concentrate here on the threats of the first category in which the identity theft in all its forms is a major vector for the execution of an attack.

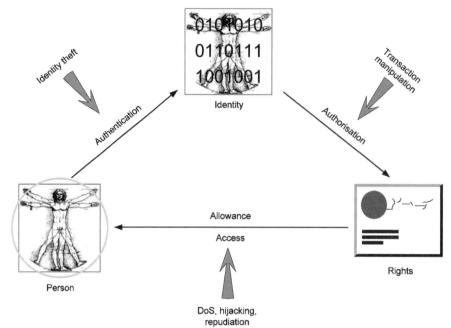

Fig. 2. The processing steps to conclude an E-commerce transaction are schematically represented by the above triangular relation between the physical person, its social identity and its rights that are administered by an operator. Each processing step is endangered by some specific threats, namely identity theft compromises the authentication, transaction manipulation jeopardizes the authorization step and any kind of threats to the use of the rights endangers the exercise of the rights through the authorized person.

2.1   What is new in online criminality

In reality the cyberspace is not so much different from the real world. Behind the entire complex infrastructure are human beings with more or less the same ethic behaviour as in the physical world. They interact with each other, make business and form social networks or build even common new living spaces. At the end we find similar threats in the cyberworld and in the physical world. Criminals still intend to rob or cheat others with the goal to enrich themselves or virtual violence can often end in real physical violence or sexual abuse. So the basic threats are not new in the cyberworld. There are however important differences that change the balance between threats and risks in the cyberspace [13].

2.1.1   Automation
Automation enabled by the digital technology overcomes the limits of single unit production of traditional attacks. A classical bank robbery needs a very high success rate to be profitable for the bank robber. He has neither the time nor the resources to rob thousands of banks with the same method. This is different for a cyberspace attacker. He simultaneously can attack thousands or millions of victims and he needs

only a tiny success rate to make the attack profitable. Typical phishing attacks have at best a few percent responding victim candidates but the absolute number of victims may be in the thousands or even more [14].

2.1.2   Remote action

A second difference comes from the very nature of the cyberspace. A personal and therefore risky presence on site of the crime is no more necessary. A cyberspace criminal may rob a bank in Norway easily from his home computer somewhere in Korea or elsewhere. The risk to get caught on the spot is quite high for a classical bank robber. For a cyberspace criminal the risk to be dismantled and caught however is at the per mille level [15].

2.1.3   Access to crime supporting technology

A further difference comes from the openness of the Internet. It leads to a rapid spread of new knowledge on security breaches and to a wide distribution of instruments to take advantage of such security holes. This is a further advantage for the cyber criminal over the classical criminal. Digital 'arms' are easy to procure and there is no real dissemination control. The attacker community has undergone a fundamental change in the last years. Highly skilled professionals produce the attacking tools and offer them on the Internet for moderate fees [16]. Organized crime but also so called script kiddies can use such tools to perform efficient attacks on persons and institutions. But such technology can also support the cheating of thousands of individual customers which may jeopardize even big companies or whole industries. The cracking of pay TV decoders or the distribution of illegal software copies are typical examples of such low level fraud at large scales.

2.2   The weak spots in online transactions

For a better understanding of the threats to online business transactions we need a closer look on the different weak spots of the end-to-end communication channel between user and operator and the way the transaction can be attacked. With 'user' and 'operator' we use the typical notation for an E-commerce transaction which is naturally the most exposed type of E-business transactions. But the same discussion holds for other forms of E-business relations e.g. for partners in internal business processes or in enterprise communication acts.

2.2.1   Attacks against the operator

A typical communication channel starts within a secure zone at the operator's site where the value services, the access rights and the user identities are administered. Such secured zones have in general a high level of logical and physical protection against intruders or malware. Their security is often assessed and defined through some sort of certification procedure. The entry threshold for an attacker into the heart of the IT infrastructure of a value service operator is rather high but can never be completely excluded [17].

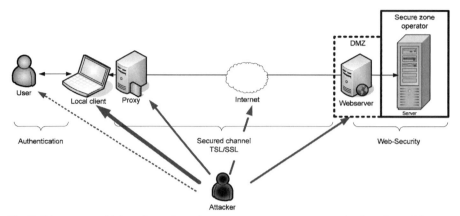

Fig. 3. There are multiple points of attacks on a user-operator communication channel in an e-business transaction scenario. The scheme is strongly simplified. In reality the communication channel is a complex technical system that bears many known and still unknown points of attacks.

The Web, mail and DNS servers of organisations are directly accessible from the outside. They reside normally in the so called DMZ (Demilitarized) zone of the internal perimeter security arrangement. Therefore they are less secure and often a target for malware attacks e.g. with the aim to infect visiting browsers. The main threats for the Web infrastructure come from attacks against the availability of the service. In so called DoS (Denial of Service) or even DDos (Distributed Denial of Service) attacks the attacker sends a huge amount of phoney service requests to the Web portal of an organisation. The resulting overload of the Web infrastructure may lead to a breakdown of the service.

2.2.2   Attacks against the connecting channel
Another potential weak point is the infrastructure of the Internet itself. Any gateway, router or data bridge can be used to eavesdrop on the passing data traffic. If the communication between the webserver and the Internet access device is secured by a SSL/TLS connection this kind of attack is marginally important. But there is the possibility that an attacker can manipulate the configuration of the local infrastructure to accept a self created SSL certificate and to connect to his webserver whenever a specific IP address is called. In this case the attacker becomes an impostor. He deviates the whole traffic to run through his machine and acts as a so called Man-in-the-Middle (see below).

2.2.3   Attacks against the user Internet access device
The most vulnerable zone in the channel is the user Internet access device and the local infrastructure of the user. Personal computers are often insufficiently protected against new types of malware. In addition local users are subject to social engineering attacks that may support the installation of malware at different levels of the local operating system, the Internet applications or even in HW device drivers. Identity theft, MITM (Man-in-the-Middle) and session hijacking attacks most often happen at

this level. There is a last but very important weak point in the end-to-end communication which is the authentication of the user itself. A simple UserID/PW authentication is highly insecure. New 2- or 3- factor authentication should be in place to protect from impostor attacks.

2.2.4   Insider attack

An insidious attack is the so called insider attack. A legitimate user for instance may run an E-commerce process and later he may deny that he had done so. This kind of cheating undermines the trust in E-business relations and it is very harmful for a proper functioning of E-business relations. It only works if the user can create reasonable doubt that he was not the author of a certain transaction. If the transactions are secured through provable and auditable mechanisms such attacks become ineffective.

2.2.5   Identity theft

The above briefly discussed attacks are only a strongly reduced summary of the threats to the end-to-end communication channel. But they already illustrate the huge task to provide real security in E-business and especially in E-commerce relations. There is an almost unforeseeable zoo of known and still to be discovered attacks on the complex IT communication infrastructure. The most dangerous ones for the further E-business development are the identity theft attacks. Today these kinds of attacks are already predominant and cause high damage to individuals and the economy [15]. Therefore we concentrate our further discussion on identity theft related attacks. Other threats like online extortion or protection code cracking are not covered in the further discussion.

3   Security requests for e-business

Security means that all the threats have to be disabled up to a certain level of remaining and acceptable risks. To improve the security situation of E-business transactions a set of security requests have to be fulfilled and the corresponding protective measures must be integrated in the ICT infrastructure [7].

3.1   Authentication

Probably the most important security problem to solve in the digital economy is the authentication of the business partners. Authentication in a transaction setting means that both partners can prove to each other that they have the identity under which they have addressed each other. Very often the authentication process is a mutual authentication between two Internet access devices with the assumption that the physical or legal persons using the corresponding computers have been authenticated beforehand locally (e.g. SSO solutions). In a typical E-commerce setting however the machine authentication is not sufficient. The value service requesting person has to deliver some additional identity credential to authenticate her at some point in the transaction process. There are three basic concepts called authentication factors that can be used for the identity verification of a person

- Proof that the person knows a secret
- Proof that the person has a personal token
- Proof that a person has a certain biometrics

The three concepts are used alone or in combination to construct an identity credential that can be delivered by the person. The factors also serve to qualify the strength of identity verification. 1-factor systems based on the knowledge of a password or PIN-Code are still the most common but the least secure authentication method. Many institutions now move to 2- or 3-factors systems that are considered to be sufficiently secure by the extranet access management community. The drawback of such multifactor or multimodal[1] authentication schemes is that they are more expensive and complex to deploy and often costly to operate. 3-factors systems all incorporate biometrics. They have the advantage that a negative proof becomes possible e.g. the proof that a certain person is not the one she claims to be.

Fig. 4. The verification of the correct assignment of a digital (partial) identity to the physical (or legal) person is a weak point in all security systems. There are three different concepts (called factors) to establish a link between a physical person and its digital identity.

Closely related to the authentication problem of person is the authentication of machines and messages. One needs the guarantee that only the assumed sender has created a certain message. This can be achieved through a digital signing of messages with a secret key that can only be used by the authorized person or network entity.

3.2   Privacy and anonymity

The complementary request to authentication is the need for privacy and anonymity. Nobody wants to be completely transparent for any alien persons or organizations. Therefore persons tend to disclose as little as possible about their identity when they enter in a simple business relationship. This need for privacy is naturally transaction dependent. Nobody cares that the neighboring bakery knows what kind of bread he or she is consuming. But people certainly like to remain anonymous if they access an adult service. On the other side there may be a substantial commercial interest to

---

[1] A multimodal authentication credential includes several proofs of the same concept type e.g. different biometric qualities.

break the anonymity of consumers and to profile their habitudes for marketing or even criminal purposes. There are methods available that allow anonymity without losing trust in the existence of a correct identity of the business partner [8]. The below presented personal identity management assistant from AXSionics also provides mechanisms to protect the card holder from profiling attacks. The AXS-Authentication System delivers to each business partner unique trusted credentials for its identity which can not be linked one to the other by a third party without additional information.

3.3   Integrity and freshness

To know the origin of a message is not sufficient. It is equally important that the message was not altered afterwards by any attacker. The validity and the actuality of the exchanged messages within a transaction context is a further security request. This requirement leads to the notion of data integrity. The assurance of data integrity is an important part of an E-commerce transaction as it is the basis of the trust both parties will have in the transaction contract. Data integrity is threatened in various forms. Intentionally or unintentionally a message or a document may be changed on the way from the sender to the receiver. This is especially true if the communication channel includes a communication over a larger time gap with an intermediate storage of the data. Especially with non symbolic data (pictures, sound tracks etc) the question if data is unaltered may often be difficult to answer. Data integrity can be protected by checksums or hash codes which are mathematical or cryptographic transformations of the original data. Such codes accompany the original data as so called digital fingerprints.

A special quality of a message is the freshness. A message is often linked to some context and it could mean something completely different if the same message is exchanged in an other context. Freshness means that there is some guarantee that a message has been generated and received in a special actual context. This can be achieved by a time stamp, if the messages are exchanged over a permanent channel, or by a unique identifier that is added to the digital fingerprint of the message.

3.4   Confidentiality

The basic information security goals are confidentiality, integrity and availability. Often information security is identified with confidentiality alone although this is just one of the security goals that can be achieved by protective measures like cryptography. Confidentiality is always necessary when valuable data are implied. This can be a credit card number but also data on a persons health condition or a trade secret of a company. Almost in all business relations there are numerous information that have to remain confidential in between a restricted group. Today in any research project with some commercial interest the partners have to sign a so called non disclosure agreement. The purpose is to protect know-how or intellectual property from disclosure to third parties and urges the partner to protect the confidentiality of the common data. The protection of secrets is the classic origin of cryptographic technologies. It is vital for military forces, governments, competing corporation but it may also be important for individuals. Confidentiality is a key issue to protect the privacy of a person. The usual way to achieve confidentiality of critical data is to encrypt such data. This reduces the need for physical protective measures for the whole data library to the need for the protection of the encryption key which in general is much smaller and easier to lock. But the breaking of the key is still a security risk that can never be completely eliminated. There are other methods to keep confidentiality of data like steganography [9] or scrambling [10]. But these methods do not allow a mathematical estimation of the remaining disclosure risk and are therefore seldom used in business applications.

3.5   Non repudiation, accountability and auditing

In E-business relations with high value transactions it is important that some additional security request have to be integrated in the underlying security scheme. It is certainly a need that neither party can deny to have agreed on the contract after the conclusion of a transaction. Therefore it must be possible to prove that the mutual transaction confirmations have really been intentionally submitted by both parties and no party had the possibility to alter the content afterwards. For this the exchanged messages need a non reputable proof that the sending party really meant what has been agreed and the receiving party accepted the message content. Such a prove may be delivered through a so called digital signature of a document. Such a signature can be provided by a business partner that has a private signature key and a certificate for the corresponding public key. The authenticity of the certificate has to be guaranteed by a trusted third party [11]. The digital signature consist of a footprint of the document encrypted with the private key of the contract signing party and the corresponding certificate contains the public key for the signature verification and the certified link to an registered identity. This non repudiation quality of a transaction system relies on two underlying security concepts. Persons are accountable for their acts. This means that the system can resolve the true identity of the transaction partners and it must be possible to proof that the system worked correctly in the specific case. This means that the correct working of a system can be verified at a later moment (auditability).

3.6   Availability

The last but not least security request is the availability of a service and the necessary communication channel to execute a transaction in the context of this service. To secure the availability always a combination of logical and physical actions are necessary. Attacks against the availability of a system undermine the trust of the transaction partners in the reliability of the system and can cause huge damage to the operator of the system.

4   The business case for cybercrimes

If we speak about criminals that move in the business of Internet fraud we have to understand their motivation. The basic explanation is given by the Willie Sutton's law [18]. The Internet today is a place where people can win and loose a lot of real money. For organized crime the cyberspace is therefore attractive. The winning perspectives are now as high as in the narcotic trade scene [19,20] and the risks to get shot are much lower. The times of the romantic hacker are definitely gone. Today's attackers intend identity theft, fraud, scam, money laundering, extortion, intellectual property and brand theft, political damage, inflicting a loss to a concurrent or ambush marketing.

4.1   Figures and facts about online fraud and phishing

There are overall statistics on the number of phishing attacks [21] and numerous compilations for losses due to Internet fraud and identity theft [3,4,22]. Typically there are 20-30 thousand phishing attacks per month all over the world and the success rate varies from less than one per mille to a few percent in the case of very sophisticated attacks. The targets of such attacks are now predominant in the financial industry. Identity theft is the most prominent form of fraud in the Internet [30]. In the US identity theft touches up to 7 % of the online banking users with an average reported loss of 1200$ [20]. For Europe similar numbers are reported [23].

4.2   How phishing works

Phishing is a method to conduct an identity theft. Let's have a closer look on a phishing attack on a banking institution.

4.2.1   Money Mules
In a first step the attacker has to prepare the environment for the collection of the stolen money. For this he needs so called money mules. These are legitimate holders of a bank account at the targeted institution or in the vicinity of it. The attacker sends out hiring e-mails offering an easy auxiliary income for people that have a bank account and are willing to make occasionally some transactions. Individuals that believe this offer get a phony contract with some offshore financial institution with the duty to transfer received money within a short time to a foreign place using a money transfer institution like Western Union.

4.2.2   Fake Web site
In a further preparation step the attacker creates a web page that looks like a legitimate web page of the targeted institution. He then sends e-mails that look like an e-mail coming from the targeted company to a large amount of Internet users. In the e-mail the attacker asks the receiver to update his identity credentials of the targeted institution for some security reason and provides a wrong link to his fake web page.

Some of the addressed users have indeed an account at the targeted institutions and connect bona fide to the fake site. There the attacker asks for the actual credentials for the original bank account contract. With the stolen credentials the attacker has access to the user's bank account and is able to make transactions in his name. Such a phishing attack was made recently on the Scandinavian Nordea bank and caused a loss of € 1 million within a week [4]. A variant of such an attack with an online use of the stolen credentials was tried against the US Citibank fooling even their 2-factor authentication system [24]. Not all phishing attacks are so successful but even with a much lower return on investment they are still profitable (see below).

4.2.3   Channel breaking MITM

In a more sophisticated scenario the attacker just attracts the legitimate users on a web site and installs a trapdoor Trojan (drive-by-infection) that allows the attacker to redirect all future sessions of the user with the bank institution's home page to a server that is under the attacker's control. He then installs a botnet and redirects the infected users to different nodes of his botnet. For the bank such a scenario looks like different independent normal E-banking users logging in from many different sites. Defensive traffic profiling programs of the bank will not register an unusual situation. The advantage of such an online channel breaking MITM attack is evident. The attacker does not need to steal the credentials the user will submit the real credentials at the begin of the session. He just modifies the transaction content in the background when the user tries to make his own online banking. Few such attacks have already been observed in the wild [25]. They can not be defeated by any of the traditional authentication or transaction security systems. The sole countermeasure is to confirm the transactions over a secure and trusted communication channel (see below).

4.2.4   Getting the money out from the financial system

Making a fake money transaction is not beneficial yet. If detected in time the transfer may be cancelled by the bank. Therefore the attacker needs the money mules that provide their ordinary bank account to receive the fraudulent transaction money. Once the money is on the account the naive helper has to go to the bank institution and take the money out. The money mule then takes his commission and sends the rest to the attacker who generally resides in a foreign country with an inefficient law enforcement system. The money mule will not be happy with his commission for a long time. As soon as the fake transmission is detected the bank will withdraw the full transferred amount from his account. In addition the money mule risks charges for money laundering. In the whole system the money mule is the person that suffers real losses. The hiring of new money mules is today's bottleneck for the attacker community. If the attackers find new ways to get the money out of the system the losses from identity theft online fraud may escalate.

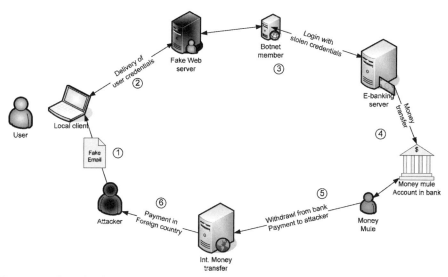

Fig. 5. Running of a phishing attack: 1. The attacker starts the process with the distribution of a phishing Email that draws the user to the fake webserver. 2. The fake webserver simulates a credible scenario of the targeted bank and extracts the authentication credentials from the user. 3 The credentials are used to access the user's bank account, most often from distributed nodes within a botnet. 4. The attacker transfers money to one of the money mule's account. 5. The money mule withdraws the transferred money and sends it via international money transfer (e.g. Western Union) to the attacking organisation (often in a country with inefficient law enforcement). 6 The attacker gets the stolen cash at his place.

4.3   Limitations and countermeasures

Classical offline phishing attacks can be averted by challenge response protocols for the user authentication or time dependent credentials that are only valid for a short time. The online MITM attacks can't be defeated with the sole authentication of user. The attacker just forwards the true authentication messages between user and bank operator without any intervention. He interferes only later with the exchanged messages and changes some transaction parameters. To get in such a MITM position the attacker has to insert himself in the encrypted communication channel (usually communications between a user and an operator run over an SSL/TLS connection). For this he has two possibilities. He may simultaneously establish a SSL/TLS connection to the bank and to the user simulating against both sides to be the expected communication partner or he can install a Trojan program on the local terminal of the user that acts as a MITM after the end of the SSL/TLS encrypted channel. The first attack can be avoided by the installation of a VPN connection between operator and user based on mutual and trusted certificates (e.g. on a smart card). The second attack is more difficult to counter. The user can't trust his local machine and needs an independent communication with the operator to discover such an attack or he must be capable to create a transaction dependent TAN number that can not be influenced by the attacker. This needs to be done in a physical independent device with an own secure processing capability.

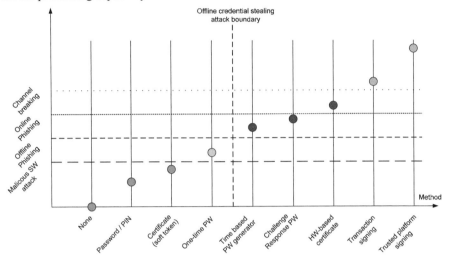

Fig. 6. Internet authentication and transaction security methods qualitatively ordered according their security level. The dashed horizontal lines show the minimum level of security to defeat a certain attack method. The dashed vertical line separates the methods which are vulnerable to classical offline phishing (left side) from the ones which can not be defeated by classical phishing (scheme adapted from [26]).

4.4   The business case

To better understand the attackers we need a closer look at the financial outcome of an average successful phishing attack. As explained above the market of malware production and distribution has reached a certain level of maturity. There is an established task sharing between developers of crimeware, programmers of fake web sites, collectors of valid e-mail addresses, managers of botnets, money mule hiring agencies and the organized crime as attack coordinator and investor.

An attacker can purchase almost all necessary tools and support service for his attack over the Internet at moderate prices. The main problem of the whole attack scenario is the question how to get hold of the money of the deviated transactions. For this the attacker has to find and hire money mules that provide their bank account for the reception of the fake fund transfer and that are willing to pick up the money in cash from the bank and forward it to the foreign receiver. In general a commission of 10 – 30 % is offered to money mules, which makes this part the most cost intensive item for the attacker. The revenue comes from the successful deviated transactions. On the average the single amount of such a transaction is in the range of a few hundred to a few thousand dollars. Higher values are unlikely to pass the banks fraud monitoring system. A phishing attack targets a few 10k to 100k Internet users. Only a small fraction of them have a business contact with the targeted bank and within this group only a few will fall In on the phishing attack. The attacker may end up with a few dozens to a few hundred successful deviated transactions which gives him total revenue in the range of $50 to $100 thousand dollars. After paying all furnishers and the money mules he remains still with a net benefice which is a multiple of the investment. This interesting business case combined with the very low risk to get caught by the police makes phishing a very lucrative business.

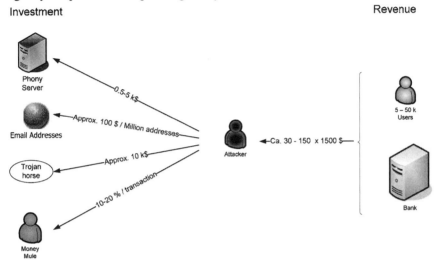

Fig. 7. An attacker has to invest for the crimeware and the customisation of the fake web site approx. $10 to $20 thousand depending on the quality of the tools. In addition he needs e-mail addresses with a good coverage of the targeted user population. All these components for an attack are available on specialised sites of the Internet. The most difficult part is the hiring of the money mules. It is a lengthy and costly process to hire persons with the wished bank connection who believe in the suspicious offer.

5   The secure channel approach

The effective loss and damage caused by cyber criminals is only one side of the medal. On the other side are the investments and costs for the security technology and their operation and the loss of confidence and trust in the E-business market. Operators have to add to the lost money of fake transactions the security bill and the loss of not realized business cases due to a growing lack of trust of the consumers or merchants. Actually the total worldwide cost for extranet access security technology is estimated to exceed $500 million per year and the rate of refused transactions due to security considerations is in the US between 6 % (domestic) and 13 % (foreign) [20,22]. The attackers in general have a leading edge on the defenders as long as the defenders just try to repair the detected weakest spots in the communication channels and the E-business protocols. Continuing in this way the arms race in the cyberspace will continue and the related costs will rise the confidence of the users will decline with a serious risk to damage the whole E-economy.

5.1   Dedicated trusted platform

There is however a quite radical concept that defeats most of the actual attacking tools and bans the dominating threats to the Internet access device of the user. The idea is to bridge the most insecure components of the communication infrastructure and install a direct uninterrupted communication channel from the secure zone of the operator directly in a dedicated secure data terminal of the user.

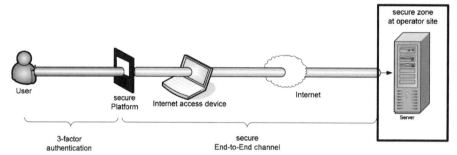

Fig. 8. The AXS-Authentication System provides a secure and tamper resistant communication channel between the operator and the personal AXS-Card of the user. The AXS- Card also verifies the identity of the owner of the token with a strong authentication protocol.

Any real secure digital system has to build up its security onto a tamper resistant hardware platform. Pure software solutions will never guarantee a strong anchor for the security measures. One approach for the realization of this idea is the so called Trusted Computing (TC) technology which is propagated by the Trusted Computing Group [27]. It is a concept that allows a certain degree of control of the hardware and software running in a computer. Although this technology is probably efficient against most of the malware attacks it is strongly disputed by privacy defending organizations. Another drawback of this technology is its limited flexibility for configuration changes that are approved by the authorized user. For real world applications it turns out that a PC system is often too complex to be controlled efficiently. TC is therefore not (yet) adapted for the home computing domain. We propose a different approach that combines the advantage of the TC technology with the requests for an easy accessible and privacy respecting computing for everybody. In fact secure transactions are needed only within a tiny fraction of our Internet activities. We therefore propose to create a secure end-to-end channel between the user and the service operator introducing a dedicated simple device that is linked but not integrated in the insecure local computing system. This personal trusted transaction assistant runs on every computer without any local installation whenever a secure communication is necessary. It assures secure transactions even over completely corrupted systems and tampered Internet connections. An attacker has no chance to enter in the strongly protected private end-to-end channel. The fact that the user needs an additional device for the security operation is even beneficial. It underlines the special situation of a secure and trusted transaction and makes the user more alert and vigilante.

5.2   The AXS-Authentication System

The AXS Authentication System™ (AXS-AS) [28] provides a secure channel between the protected zone of the operator and a dedicated tamper resistant personal device in form of a thick smart card.

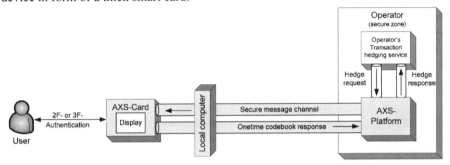

Fig. 9. The AXS-AS establish a secure ad hoc communication channel from the secure zone of the operator with the AXS-Platform into the personal AXS-Card. The message together with the possible response codes is only visible to the user on the integrated display of the AXS-Card. The local computer serves only as a transmission relay for the encrypted messages. The AXS-Card authenticates its user before it shows the message to him.

The device, called AXS-Card, is personalized to its owner and remains always in his possession. The AXS-Card contains numerous digital identity credentials that can be used to establish independent connections to different operators that run an AXS-AS. The AXS-Card controls the access to the credentials through a 2- or 3-factor authentication of the user.

The security level of the authentication protocol that verifies the identity of the card owner may be adapted according the transaction type on request of the operator. The biometric authentication factor is realised by an on-board fingerprint recognition system. On the highest security level the AXS-Card asks for a combination of biometrics and secret knowledge. For a normal authentication the user has just to present one of the enrolled fingerprint biometrics. There are two main differences relative to other token based authentication or transaction hedging systems.

5.2.1   Optical interface

The first and often surprising novelty is the way the token receives messages from the operator. The AXS-Platform, installed at the operators place, sends an encrypted message over any IT infrastructure to the screen display of the local computer. On the display appears a window with flickering fields in form of a stripe, a trapeze or a diamond. The user holds the activated AXS-Card directly on the display with the flickering window and the card reads the message over its optical interface. Only the authentic AXS-Card that was addressed by the operator can read and decrypt the displayed flickering code. This one way communication channel is sufficient to transmit a one-time password, a transaction receipt, a voting list or any other kind of short document that is needed to hedge a transaction. The AXS-Card shows the user the message content on the internal display together with some one-time codes for the possible responses. The user returns the chosen one-time code over the keyboard to the operator. A potential attacker has no chance to interfere with this communication protocol as he will not know anything about the semantic meaning of the message or the return codes. This communication scheme needs no electrical or radio connection between the AXS-Card and the local computer and no local SW or HW infrastructure has to be installed. This makes the AXS-AS mobile, flexible and simple to roll out. Any computer that is connected to the Internet can be used to establish a secure channel between the operator and the user.

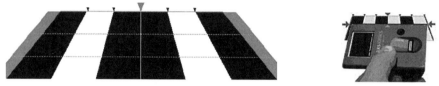

Fig. 10. The optical interface of the AXS-AS consist of a window that opens in the browser of the local computer. It shows flickering fields in the form of a trapeze. The user holds the AXS-Card directly on the flickering pattern on the computer display and receives the encrypted message from the operator. The local computer only serves as a transmission device and has no clue about the encrypted message.

5.2.2   User side identity federation

The second unique selling proposition is the identity credential management within the AXS-AS. Each AXS-Card contains a practically arbitrary number of secured channels that can be activated whenever necessary. The user decides which operators get access to the identity credentials in his AXS-Card. For this he submits a unique identifier (AXS-Card number) to the operator. The AXS-AS of the new operator and the AXS-Card of the user then allocate automatically a channel using predefined credentials for the new connection. The operator can modify the cryptographic parameters of the allocated channel in the AXS-Card already at the first message exchange. After this first registration step the allocated channel is controlled by the operator but the user decides to whom he wants to allocate the pre-initialized channels in his AXS-Card. This shared control of the communication channels allows a very flexible realization of identity federation. The trust is established and shared only between user and operator. No additional agreements between different operators or the sharing of identity information are necessary.

The advantage of such a personal identity management assistant is evident. Today a typical user of computer systems and Internet services has to memorize and manage over 50 UserIDs, passwords and PIN-codes. It is a well-known fact that users don't handle such identity credentials as valuable secrets. Users choose either simple passwords or simple rules to memorize passwords. Dictionary attacks can break most of such alleged password secrets within seconds [29]. To augment the authentication security operators move now to 2-factor authentication and distribute passive or active tokens (cards, OTP-lists, time dependant pass code generators, digital certificates etc). The handling of all these physical and virtual identity credentials makes life not easier for their owner. Many Internet services are just not used any more because users forgot how to access the site. Users restrict their business relations to fewer operators which naturally reduces the business opportunities for E-commerce. While many systems offer identity management functions for operators the problem of the user side identity management remains unsolved. Operator arranged federated identity management (FIM) and single-sign-on (SSO) systems are ineffective to solve this problem. Both actions are taken on the wrong side of the user-operator relation. Only a user side identity management can handle the proliferation of identity credentials for the user. The AXS-Card assumes the administration of the multiple identity based relations of the typical E-business user.

5.2.3   Encapsulated biometrics

A further innovation of the AXS-AS is the way biometrics is implemented. The storage of the biometric reference template, the measurement and the comparison process are completely integrated in the AXS-Card. The card keeps the biometric data encapsulated under the full control of the owner. All the fears about irreversible corruption of biometric data become obsolete. The privacy of these data in the AXS-token is fully protected which differentiate the AXS-AS solution from most other biometric identification or verification systems. The operator only knows what kind of biometric processing is performed in the card.

First attempts in such a direction have been done with biometric reference templates on smart cards carried by the user or even cards with match-on-card functions. But a real secure and privacy protecting implementation of a biometric authentication puts all biometric data handling, including the measurement process, into the user's hand.

The shared control, biometric data controlled by the user and biometric processing controlled by the operator, allows mutual trust in the biometric identity verification and guarantees the necessary privacy and protection for the non revocable biometric data of the user. This type of shared control implementation of biometrics is recommended by the privacy protection community [30].

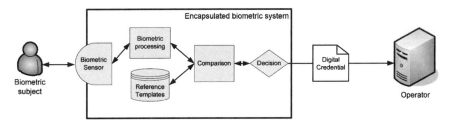

Fig. 11. In the AXS-AS all biometric processing and data are enclosed in the tamper resistant AXS-Card that remains in the possession of the user. The biometric data are encapsulated and protected in the secure processor memory of the device. Any outside instance gets only digital identity credentials with no information about the biometrics of the user. The biometric data are

controlled by the user and the way biometrics are processed and evaluated is defined and controlled by the operator.

5.3   End-to-end transaction security

The key element of the AXS-Authentication System is the AXS-Card. It is the platform over which a secured end-to-end communication can be established. Each message that is sent from the operator to the AXS-Card runs over a separate channel allocated to the specific operator – user relationship. The communication content is enveloped in a cryptographically secure message container. Its security mechanisms assure confidentiality, mutual authentication of the operator and the user, the freshness of the message and the correct display of the message on the internal screen of the card. The message also contains parameters that define the one-time response codes that the user may send back to the operator. There are protocols for different applications like onetime PW login, financial transaction hedging, voting, transaction signing, license checks, recovery of a previously stored secret and many more.

An important part of the security of such a mutual trusted communication platform is the initialization and roll out step. Special protocols make sure that only the authorized user can enroll his biometrics in the dedicated card and that only the authorized operator can take possession of one of the secured communication channels in the card. The AXS-Card can therefore be regarded as a secure container and reader of an almost arbitrary number of virtual smart cards that each operator has distributed in a secure way to the user. The advantage of the concept is the very high level of security achieved and the sharing of the infrastructure between operators without the need to establish connections and trust mechanisms between the different identity management systems.

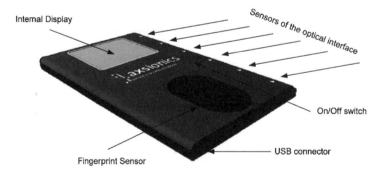

Fig. 12. The AXS-Card is the mutual controlled and mutual trusted device that allows a secure communication link between the operator and the user. All the typical security requests are realized and attackers have no possibility to make remote or automated attacks on such a system.

6 Conclusion

The E-business sector is forced to find a solution against the growing importance of Internet related crimes. The need to secure the communication between operators and users of a value service has been recognised on a broad scale [31]. However there is not yet a consensus about the way how to face this challenge. More or less all agree that the necessary secure channel needs some kind of additional infrastructure. There are communities which see the mobile phone and the SIM-Card as a carrier of this infrastructure [32], others see a solution in the Trusted Computing approach or in an extensive use of smart cards as identity credential [33]. On a longer time scale the community expects a convergence of the personal mobile communicator with an identity assistant. But independent of all the possible strategic technologies that the industry may develop and roll out on a large scale in the future, immediate efficient solutions are requested now. The presented AXS-Authentication System has the potential to defeat most of the actual MITM and identity theft attacks on financial services. It could become the requested secure platform that runs already on the present IT-infrastructure.

References

1. The Digital Economy Fact Book, 8.ed, The Progress ¬ Freedom Foundation, 2006;
2. Europe's eCommerce Forecast:2006 to 2011, Jaap Favier, Forester Research, 2006
3. Identity theft: A new frontier for hackers and cybercrime, Claudio Cilli, Information Systems Control Journal, 6, 2005Online fraud costs $2.6 billion this year, B. Sullivan, 2007 MSNBC.com, http://www.msnbc.msn.com
4. The Scandinavian bank Nordea equipped with a two-factor authentication system was victim of a malware MITM attack: http://www.nytimes.com/2007/01/25/technology/25hack.html?ex=1327381200&en=58990497ce27b2b2&ei=5088&partner=rss nyt&emc=rss (visible 18.07.2007). A similar attack on the Nederlands ABN Amro bank was also successful: http://www.theregister.co.uk/2007/04/19/phishing_evades_two-.factor_authentication/ (visible 18.07.2007)
5. Access Control Technologies and Market, Forecast 2007, RNCOS online Business research; http:/www-the-infoshop.com (visible 4.11.07)
6. Thursday's security tip 2/2/06, The Infopro Corp; www.theinfopro.net
7. An Introduction to Information, Network and Internet Security, The security practioner; http://security.practionier.com/introduction/infosec_2.htm
8. PRIME – Privacy and Identity Management for Europe; https:www.prime-project.eu FIDIS – Future of Identity in the Information Society; http://www.fidis.net

9. Hede and Seek: An Introduction to Steganography; N.Provos and P.Honeyman; IEEE Security and Privacy, May/june 2003; http://computer.org/security/
10. Data Scrambling Issues; White Paper; Net 2000 Ltd. http://www.datamasker.com/datascramblingissues.pdf
11. Introduction to Public Key Technology and the Federal PKI Infrastructure; NIST pub. SP800-32; 26.2.2001. See also on wikipedia: http://en.wikipedia.org/wiki/Public_key_infrastructure
12. Melani report, Informationssicherung, Lage in der Schweiz und international, 2007/1; ISB, Schweiz. Eidgenossenschaft
13. Secrets & Lies; B. Schneier; Wiley Computer Publishing, J. Wiley ¬ Sons, Inc., ISBN 0-471-25311-1
14. Identity Fraud Trends and Patterns; G.Gordon et al.; Center for Identity Management and Information Protection, Utica College- cimip US Dept. of Homeland Security
15. ID-Theft: Fraudster Techniques for Personal Data collection, the related digital evidence and investigation issues; Th. Tryfonas et al.; Onlinejournal, ISACA, 2006
16. Web server exploit Mpack: http://reviews .cnet.com/4520-3513 7-6745285-.html
17. At least 45.7 million credit and debit card numbers were stolen by hackers who accessed the computer systems at the TJX Cos. at its headquarters in Framingham and in the United Kingdom (discounter that operates the T.J. Maxx and Marshalls chains) over a period of several years, making it the biggest breach of personal data ever reported; see also:http://www.boston.com/business/globe/articles/2007/03/29/breach_of_data_at_tjx_is_called_the_biggest_ever/ (visible 8.11.07)
18. Willie Sutton's law: The law is named after the bank robber Willie Sutton, who supposedly answered a reporter inquiring why he robbed banks by saying "because that's where the money is".
19. Organized Crime and Cyber-Crime, P. Williams, CERT Coordination Center, preprint (visible 10.11.07):http://www.crime-research.org/library/Cybercrime.htm
20. McAfee North America Criminology Report: Organized Crime and the Internet 2007, McAfee Inc.
21. Phising Activity Trends, monthly report, 5/07; Anti Phishing Working group – APWG: http://www.antphising.org
22. Consumer Fraud and Identity theft, complaint data, FTC-report, Jan 2006, http://www.ftc.gov
23. Security report online Identity theft, Feb 2006; http://www.btplc.com/onlineidtheft/onlineidtheft.pdf
24. Washington Post Online (visible 10.11.07): http://blog.washingtonpost.com/securityfix/2006/07/citibank_phish_spoofs_2factor_1.html
25. Private communication, Security officer of a international bank (source remains confidential)
26. Secure Internet Banking Authentication, A. Hiltgen, Th. Kramp, Th. Weigold; IEEE Security & Privacy, March/April 2006
27. Trusted Computing Group; http://www.trustedcomputinggroup.org/home
28. AXSionics homepage: http://www.axsionics.ch
29. MySpace Passwords aren't so dumb, Bruce Schneier, in Wired, 14.12.06 http://www.wired.com/politics/security/commentary/securitymatters/2006/12/72300
30. Biometrics in identity management, FIDIS EU-NoE FP6; D3.10; (to be published), http://www.fidis.net
31. Information Security is falling short, it is time to change the game; A. Coviello, Keynote speech at the RSA Conference Europe 2007, London

32. The smart and secure world in 2020, J. Seneca, Eurosmart Conference, 2007
33. Establishing a uniform identity credential on a national scale; Bearing Point White Paper and Protecting future large polymorphic networked infrastructure; D. Purdy, US solution for a national governemental electronic ID-Card; presented at the World e-ID conference in Sophia Antipolis, Sep. 2007

Marrying Transparency Tools with User-Controlled Identity Management

Marit Hansen

Unabhängiges Landeszentrum für Datenschutz
Schleswig-Holstein, Germany

Abstract. User-controlled identity management systems assist individuals in managing their private sphere. An individual's privacy can be supported by transparency on processing of personal data. After giving an overview on transparency properties as well as its relation to privacy and data protection regulation, this text introduces different transparency tools: Prior to an interaction, information on the interacting party should be made transparent. During the interaction, privacy policies have to be communicated. Afterwards, users should be helped in exercising their privacy rights such as, among others, the right to access own personal data. In addition information on security and privacy incidents provides complementary data for the user's perception of the level of privacy. Although transparency tools alone are no panacea for maintaining the private sphere, the combination of transparency tools and user-controlled identity management systems yields viable functionality to empower users to protect their privacy.

1 Introduction

The world we live in becomes more and more complex. This is also true for data protection:

- In former times, personal information on individuals, so-called data subjects, were stored in few central databases. It was pretty much clear who processed personal data.
- The current situation is characterized by storage of personal data in many centralized and decentralized databases from various organizations in all sectors, often processing the data in a globalized context. In particular in the digital world, users accidentally or intentionally disclose a huge amount of personal data to others. Most people have difficulties to track who is processing what personal data.
- In the emerging world, not only organizations store, possibly link and analyze personal data of individuals, but also peers, e.g., in their e-mail folders or via social networks. In ubiquitous computing, sensors and thereby data processing can be everywhere. Every user may turn into a fully equipped data processing entity for own personal data and for those from others. The computing power in the hand of users can be used to assist them in maintaining their privacy.

Please use the following format when citing this chapter:

Hansen, M., 2008, in IFIP International Federation for Information Processing, Volume 262; The Future of Identity in the Information Society; Simone Fischer-Hübner, Penny Duquenoy, Albin Zuccato, Leonardo Martucci; (Boston: Springer), pp. 199–220.

The underlying challenge for privacy in a democratic information society is to prevent steep rugged power imbalances. In fact, society needs a fair balance of power (which is not equivalent with evenly distributed power). Transparency is a well-known necessary, yet not sufficient mechanism for achieving fair balances because it enables to discuss openly the power distribution [6]. Power balance is not only relevant on the societal or political level on a large scale, but also in each privacy-related transaction.

Since several years, in many areas of life there are increasing demands for transparency so that individuals are empowered to take appropriate action, cf. Table 1. While areas such as food, cosmetics or pharmaceuticals in industrialized countries have to comply with manifold regulations and standards concerning transparency, the current practice for handling personal data and privacy issues still seems to be underdeveloped.

Table 1: Trend towards transparency in various application areas

	Throughout processing	**For individuals**
Food	Coloring rotten meat; thaw checks for frozen food	Nutrition overview
Cosmetic care products	Tests	Indication of ingredients and important properties
Pharmaceuticals	Marking components; tests	Patient Information Leaflet
Personal data and privacy issues	Today: mainly internally handled	Today: partially via privacy policies

This text is organized as follows: Section 2 introduces identity management, focusing on the user's perspective. The next section concentrates on transparency and transparency tools, setting the scene by illustrating the scope when considering privacy-relevant issues as well as the legal background. Section 4 explains how user-controlled identity management can be enhanced by transparency tools. Further, Section 5 discusses limitations of transparency tools and ways to deal with them. Finally, Section 6 concludes the text and gives an outlook.

2 Identity Management

This section introduces the concept of partial identities and identity management. Taking the user's perspective, a focus is put on user-controlled and privacy-enhancing features of user-centric identity management. Important mechanisms of user-controlled identity management systems are outlined for the example of the project "PRIME – Privacy and Identity Management for Europe".

2.1 The manifold facets of identity

"Who are you?" the border guard asks me. It is a difficult question – it is probably not appropriate to inform him that I am a caring parent traveling without my kids, a person who seems to be creditworthy enough to get a loan to buy a house, an employee of a big company, a person open to new challenges, a jazz fan (in particular of Louis Armstrong's songs), a former resident of a quaint village near a national park who is now used to living in a big city, the best runner in the ninth grade at school, the treasurer of the district sports club, a lover of hot spicy meals. ... He interrupts my chain of thought: "Please show your ID. I need to see your passport." Sure, he is not interested in me as a person, but as – right now – an international traveler. He checks my citizenship as well as the validity of my passport and estimates the risk of me being a terrorist by looking at me and searching for my name in a database. "Okay, please proceed to the gate."

Indeed, the identity of an individual is a complex entity with many facets. In each situation only a subset of this complete identity is needed – in essence, a **partial identity** [11]. Individuals learn to manage their partial identities intuitively, telling others only what they are willing to disclose and separating contexts from each other where appropriate. Some people have nicknames which are only used within a specific scope: at the sports club or in their personal relationship, for example. It would be out of place to be called by that nickname in a business meeting. Nobody gets to know the complete identity of a person – instead, only specific partial identities can be perceived.

Digital representations of partial identities are data sets comprised of attributes and identifiers. In our information society, organizations and individuals are working with those digital partial identities in all areas of life. Identity management means managing various partial identities (usually denoted by identifiers such as pseudonyms), developing and choosing partial identities and pseudonyms appropriate to specific contexts, and administering identity attributes. Figure 1 illustrates some of the partial identities that an individual may employ in daily life.

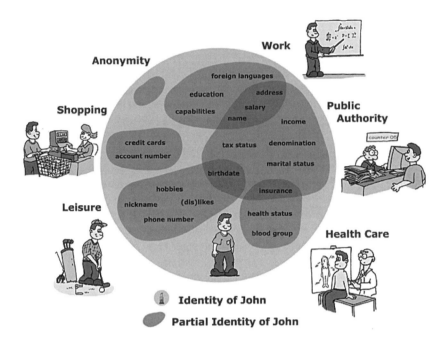

Fig. 1: John's partial identities (as shown in the PRIME tutorials [29])

2.2 Identity management: user-controlled and privacy-enhancing

Identity management is an overloaded term, associating various meanings. Starting from the notion of partial identities, "**identity management** means managing various partial identities (usually denoted by pseudonyms) of an individual, i.e., administration of identity attributes including the development and choice of the partial identity and pseudonym to be (re-)used in a specific context or role" [28].

From the service's perspective, account management systems and profiling systems are typical types of identity management [4].

Here we take the user's perspective and limit our view to **user-centric identity management** "that focuses on usability and cost effectiveness from the user's point of view" [21]. We highlight two main properties of user-centric identity management systems:

1. A **user-controlled** identity management system makes the flow of identity attributes explicit and gives its user a large degree of control [13]. The guiding principle is "notice and choice". These systems support users "to control, edit, manage, and delete information about them[selves] and decide when, how, and to what extent that information is communicated to others" [31]. This is also the essence of the "right to informational self-determination" which stems from the ruling of the German Federal Constitutional Court on the 1983 census and demands that each person can at any time ascertain who knows what about him or her.

2. A **privacy-enhancing** identity management system aims at data minimization, in particular unlinkability [28]. Preservation of unlinkability can be achieved by choosing the pseudonyms (and their authorizations such as private credentials [8]) denoting the partial identities carefully, especially by keeping discrete contexts separate over the course of time.

The combination of these two properties yields **user-controlled privacy-enhancing identity management** which strives for user-controlled linkability of personal data, i.e., accomplishing control by the user based on thorough data minimization [28].

2.3   The prototype of PRIME – Privacy and Identity Management for Europe

The EU-funded FP6 project "PRIME – Privacy and Identity Management for Europe" aims at developing solutions for both user-controlled and privacy-enhancing identity management that supports individuals' sovereignty over their private sphere and enterprises' privacy-compliant data processing.

The guiding principle of PRIME is to put individuals in control of their personal data, based on three main components which are explained in the following subsections: pseudonyms and private credentials, enforcement of privacy policies, and a history function for transactions (cf. also [23]).

2.3.1 Pseudonyms and private credentials
In interactions with others, often the real name of a user is not required. Instead, distinct identifiers, i.e., pseudonyms, could be used to prevent undesired context-spanning linkage and profiling by unauthorized parties. Organizations can support this by skillful design of their workflows, separating different tasks – and the corresponding databases – from each other.

As a special feature, PRIME's approach uses "private credentials" which enable proving one's authorization (e.g., to be over 18 years old) without revealing information that may identify the individual [8]. These private credentials are derived from certificates issued on different pseudonyms of the same person. Multiple private credentials can be created from a single certificate that are neither linkable to each other nor to the issuance interaction in which the master certificate was obtained. Private credentials provide accountability combined with data minimization – only in the case of misuse the user's anonymity can be revoked.

2.3.2 Enforcing privacy policies at all times
For an organization, presenting a privacy policy on its website is usual practice. But providing privacy policies which are really understood by users and at the same time serve as rules for the automated data processing within the organization is a challenge tackled by the PRIME project. Its work encompasses both "before" and "after": the provision of privacy policies before a transaction takes place, e.g., in a stage when the user has to give consent to data processing, and after the transaction when the policy still sticks to the data disclosed. These so-called "sticky policies" enforce the rules

how the data may be processed even after they have been disclosed and thereby have left the user's area [22, 9].

2.3.3 Logging transactions in the "Data Track"

The right to informational self-determination demands the knowledge who knows what about oneself. This is supported by a history function of the user's online transactions. In principle this "Data Track" – as it is called within PRIME's Internet browsing prototype (cf. Figure 2) – stores in the user's trusted area which personal data the user has disclosed to whom at what time. Currently the "Data Track" is limited to structured information being disclosed, e.g., forms filled in or identifiers such as pseudonyms [27]. In addition to the personal information the conditions for the disclosure are being stored. This comprises also the privacy policy of a service requesting data. Further, it could cover additional obligations the service promises to fulfill. The "Data Track" helps to (re-)use the appropriate accounts – pseudonymous and passwords – in different contexts, keeping them apart unless otherwise desired.

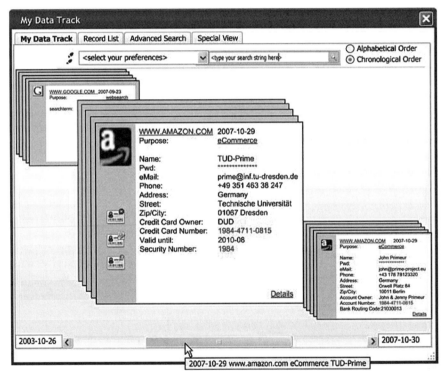

Fig. 2: The "Data Track" in the PRIME prototype

2.4   Other prototypes for user-controlled identity management

Various approaches have been studied for user-controlled identity management (beginning with [10]) and – at least partially – implemented in a prototype, e.g.,

"Dresden Identity Management (DRIM)" [12] focusing on role management, "iJournal" keeping track of transactions as part of MozPETs (Mozilla Privacy Enhancement Technologies) [7], "iManager" which is designed for mobile use via a PDA or mobile phone [20], and the "Personal Identity Assistant" for managing authorized access to user profiles [32].

As pointed out in [25], history functionality for logging transactions is an essential feature in DRIM, in the "iJournal" and – as presenting the most sophisticated concept – in the PRIME prototypes. For those user-controlled identity management systems without a history function, this transparency-enhancing feature could be added. As we will see later in Section 4.5, PRIME's "Data Track" plays a central role for integrating and orchestrating other transparency tools.

3 Transparency

In this section, basing on the definition of transparency different kinds of related tools are briefly introduced. The scope of transparency with respect to an individual's private sphere is illustrated. Finally the current legal baseline in the European Union for transparency issues with respect to privacy is outlined.

3.1   Defining transparency and transparency tools

Transparency is an ambiguous term: Especially in computing it depends on the context whether it should express that *all details* of a system or a process are being shown or on the contrary *none at all*. Indeed if transparency is meant to enhance understanding of a person, the amount of given information as well as the way of presenting it are important – if this is not performed appropriately, the level of understanding may even decrease, and in addition the person may even be demotivated to deal with the given information.

> *Transparency*
> *From Wikipedia, the free encyclopedia (2007)*
> "Transparency is the property of allowing transmission of light through a material. It is the noun form of the word *transparent* (for example, glass is usually transparent.)
> Metaphorical meanings can amount to clear visibility, but also the opposite, invisibility (in particular of irrelevant details)."

When dealing with personal data and privacy, **transparency tools** are tools which can provide to the individual concerned clear visibility of aspects relevant to these data and the individual's privacy. This comprises, among others, the data flow, the privacy policy, actual methods of data processing, offered services, used software, reputation of interaction partners, guarantees of trustworthiness and security of all data processing and also all actual or possible vulnerabilities and security breaches.

The objective of transparency tools in this context is to empower users to act in an appropriate way on this information which requires understanding as well as the possibility to take action.

When discussing transparency tools, it has to be clear *what* should be *transparent* (or the other way round: *not transparent*) to *whom* [6]. Table 2 shows what a person typically favors considering transparency in the relation of oneself to others, distinguishing **transparency-supporting** and **transparency-preventing tools**. The presented dichotomy is shown from a personal perspective, not the perspective from society. In any case transparency and its inverse, opacity, are possible properties for personal data or actions of an individual (which should be opaque against unauthorized parties from the privacy point of view) as well as for data processing mechanisms used by the data controller (which should be transparent for data subjects concerned).

Table 2: Categorization of tools concerning their effect on transparency (based on [6])

	Supporting tools	Preventing tools
Favorable from the personal perspective	Tools that help *ME* see what *OTHERS* are up to	Tools that prevent *OTHERS* from seeing what *I* am up to
Unfavorable from the personal perspective	Tools that help *OTHERS* see what *I* am up to	Tools that prevent *ME* from seeing what *OTHERS* are up to

In the context of profiling – in particular in the "Ambient Intelligence world" – **transparency-enhancing technologies (TETs)** are being discussed:

"TETs (transparency enhancing technologies) anticipate profiles that may be applied to a particular data subject. This concerns personalized profiles as well as distributive or non-distributive group profiles, possibly constructed out of anonymous data. The point would be to have some idea of the selection mechanisms (application of profiles) that may be applied, allowing a person adequate anticipation. To be able to achieve this, the data subject needs access – in addition to his own personal data and a profiling / reporting tool – to additional external data sources, allowing some insight in the activities of the data controller. Based on this additional information the data subject could perform a kind of counterprofiling." [18]

We do not build our discussion on the concept of transparency-enhancing technologies defined in [18] because we consider it too focused on counterprofiling. On the one hand this approach seems too narrow compared with the various flavors of transparency mechanisms. On the other hand it is problematic to rely on counterprofiling on the user's side only because it can (probably) never give an accurate estimation of what the other parties can or will do with personal data being processed. In particular this is the case in a potentially "hostile" environment refusing to disclose information on data processing to the data subject [17].

3.2   The scope of transparency tools concerning privacy

According to [5] transparency is an important privacy principle: "The design principles should ensure that the individual may check at any desired moment regarding what personal data he/she has given to the data systems, with the possibility to peruse, supplement, alter and delete personal data. ... Control empowers people to stipulate the information they project and who can get hold of it, while feedback informs people when and what information about them is being captured, and to whom it is being made available."

Transparency is not only an important prerequisite for the users' control over their private spheres. Also for enhancing trust in privacy-enhancing technologies, users should feel in control of the technologies concerning them, which can be achieved if procedures are transparent and reversible [1].

When discussing transparency of privacy issues, it is necessary to explore different stages of the typical workflow for observing, linking, and analyzing personal data, cf. Figure 3. This generic workflow illustrates different actors in different stages of the information gathering and linking process. This process can lead to decisions about, e.g., receptiveness to marketing information, creditworthiness, suitability for a specific job, or probability of contracting a particular disease in the next decade. The decisions made on the basis of these analyses may affect a group of people or a single individual.

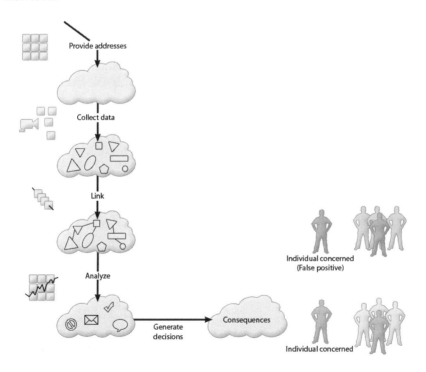

Fig. 3: Workflow of data enrichment influencing an individual's privacy [16]

As Figure 3 demonstrates, the individual whose information is processed is not necessarily well-equipped to either find errors in the case of wrong inferences or to ensure that corrective measures are applied [16]. Here, the power distribution obviously adversely affects the individual. Thus, considering the level of an individual's privacy, transparency would be needed in all these stages, about all data processing involved, about the responsible actors performing data processing, and about used algorithms and tools when enriching personal data. This would demand "transparency throughout processing" as well as "transparency for individuals" (cf. Table 1 in Section 1) and shows the wide scope of transparency tools.

3.3   Legal background on the EU level

The privacy principle of transparency of personal data processing is a key to informational self-determination. For this reason, the EU Data Protection Directive 95/46/EC guarantees individuals extensive information and access rights:

According to Art. 10 of the Directive, individuals from whom personal data will be collected have to be informed at least about the identity of the controller, the purposes of the data processing, and possible recipients or categories of recipients. In addition, a clear indication must be given as to how the individual can access additional information.

Under the terms of Art. 12 of Directive 95/46/EC, every individual has the right to access, i.e. the right to obtain from the controller a confirmation whether data relating to him are being processed and information at least as to the purposes of the processing, the data concerned, and possible recipients or categories of recipients. In addition, Art. 12 grants every individual the right to obtain from the controller the rectification, erasure, or blocking of data concerning him as far as the processing does not comply with the requirements of the Directive, in particular when the data at issue are incomplete or inaccurate.

Further, Art. 14 ensures that individuals are aware of the existence of the right to object, e.g., to processing of personal data for direct marketing.

In specific application contexts there may be other transparency and information obligations. Moreover there are proposals to change the EU electronic communications regulatory framework including improving transparency and publication of information for users and the introduction of security breach notification [19]. These recommendations are currently taken up in a proposal for amending Directive 2002/22/EC on universal service and users' rights relating to electronic communications networks, Directive 2002/58/EC concerning the processing of personal data and the protection of privacy in the electronic communications sector, and Regulation (EC) No 2006/2004 on consumer protection cooperation.

4 Enhancing identity management by transparency tools

After having seen already the history function as one potentially integrated transparency tool for user-controlled identity management, this section explains four main areas of related transparency tools: information on interaction partners, understanding privacy policies, exercising privacy rights online, and a news feed on security and privacy incidents. Further, the orchestration of the described transparency functions is sketched.

4.1 Information on interaction partners

For users in the digital world, trustworthiness and reliability of potential interaction partners are important not only when commercial transactions take place, but also when other processing of personal data is involved. Having this information at hand, a user may decide beforehand not to interact with the other party at all.

In principle there can be two different sources for information on potentially interacting parties: the party itself or some third party, such as an organization, a peer or a group of peers. In most cases statements from the party itself will neither be considered impartial nor comprehensive, so only self-statements may be not sufficient to convince users that a party can be trusted. However, a big organization such as a company with long history, no known scandals and the aim of staying in the market may be considered trustworthy because of a famous and widely acknowledged brand. In addition, with cryptographic trusted computing chips servers may prove to the client that they fulfill certain security requirements and give guarantees for enforcement of policies.

In any case the judgment from third parties will also play a major role when estimating trustworthiness and reliability, in particular if those third parties are independent and avow for the party under consideration with their own name or base the judgment on transparent processes. Positive information statements on the data handling of an interacting party may be audit certificates, privacy seals or other trust marks which could be issued by a data protection authority (DPA)[1]. An example for a negative statement is the blacklisting of that party, such as the blacklist from the Swedish consumer protection organization Konsumentverket[2].

Further, reputation systems can be used which inform on experiences from peers with the party to interact with[3]. However, many reputation systems do not enable a reliable judgment because the descriptions of experiences from other peers may not be accurate – i.e., too positive or overcritical – and usually cannot be considered

---

[1] E.g., the established privacy seal "ULD-Datenschutz-Gütesiegel", https://www.datenschutz zentrum.de/guetesiegel/, or in the European context the project EuroPriSe, https://www.european-privacy-seal.eu/.

[2] "Svarta listan" from Konsumentverket Sweden, http://www.radron.se/templates/ blacklist ____1936.asp.

[3] E.g., the reputation system used in eBay.

impartial. In addition, in most cases it cannot be excluded that the rating peers have been invented or bribed by the party itself.

4.2   Understanding privacy policies

Users are often not aware of their privacy rights [14]. But even if they are, it is not easy for them as lay people to understand privacy policies provided by services. There are different proposals to enhance the transparency of what is expressed in the privacy policy, as shown below.

The Article 29 Working Party has recommended a multi-layered format of privacy policies to improve the readability and focus on what users need in different steps to make decisions [2]. Further they propose to use language and layout that is easy to understand.

With development of P3P – Platform for Privacy Preferences[4], the World Wide Web Consortium aimed at machine-readability of privacy policies. This requires a harmonization of what can and should be expressed and how it should be interpreted. As a global harmonization of diverse privacy concepts is currently out of reach, the P3P vocabulary can only be a simplified compromise. Still even this less-than-ideal solution can help users understand privacy policies in foreign languages which have been expressed in P3P because their client can transform the machine syntax into their mother tongue. Further, parties such as data protection authorities could provide configuration files or wizards which express the national law both to users and service providers. If it turns out that the service does not work with a legally compliant configuration, users or supervisory authorities could make a complaint.

In a multimedia environment, a restriction to textual privacy policies seems to be old-fashioned and more difficult to grasp. In the complex world with information and communication technologies (ICT) we need short cuts for common concepts. The simplification as attempted in P3P could also be performed for audio- or video-enhanced privacy statements. In particular icons expressing data protection-relevant issues (as shown in Figure 4 [24, 30]) are currently under discussion.

---

[4] http://www.w3.org/P3P/.

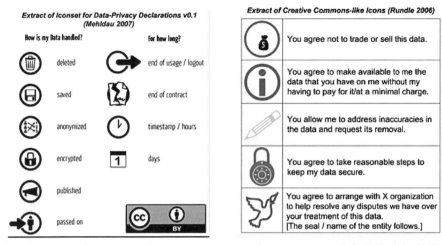

Fig. 4: Excerpts from proposed icon sets to express privacy statements (left: [24], right: [30])

4.3   Exercising privacy rights online

Whenever personal data of users are processed, they have specific rights in the European jurisdiction, as depicted in Section 3.3: Users have the right to request access to their personal data, rectification of inaccurate personal data and erasure of illegally stored data. In addition they can withdraw a formerly given consent.

Currently most services do not offer an interface to assert one's privacy rights online even if all other user communication takes place in digital networks. These days, providers usually offer users the possibility to access and correct data only for the benefit of the data controllers, e.g., to change the address after having moved. As a rule, users do not get online access to personal data processed by profiling, scoring or data mining systems.

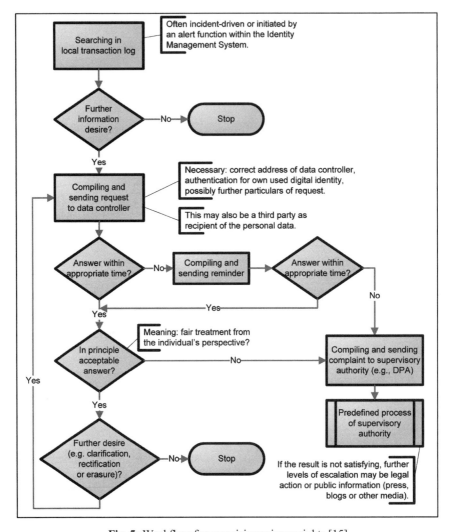

Fig. 5: Workflow for exercising privacy rights [15]

There are two ways to support users in exercising their rights: The service provider lowers the threshold for this by offering easy and convenient ways to access own data and request changes or erasure of data. Or the user gets tools which assist them to send requests to the data controller or – if necessary – complaints to a supervisory authority. An online function for requesting information related to one's personal data should help the user to specify all information needed for a data access request, which comprises:

- The contact address of the recipient.
- The personal data requested: Even though every individual has the right to request access to all information that can be linked to oneself, one might often only be interested in data that were released or collected about oneself in a

specific context. Hence, the online function should help the user to specify that context, which might also make it easier for the service's side to retrieve the data in its databases. If a user has released data under a certain pseudonym, a proof has to be given that the requesting user is actually the right holder of this pseudonym.

Additional information revealed by the request should be minimized; e.g., if the user's e-mail address has not been released yet, the user may choose another channel instead of e-mail communication or make use of one-time e-mail addresses or other anonymizing services.

The flow chart in Figure 5 gives an overview of essential steps to be taken into account when implementing an assisting function [15]. If the data controller offers a direct interface instead of posting letters, the process may be run through much faster. If no or only an incomplete answer is received from the service's side, a reminder process should start which may end in compiling a complaint mail to be sent to the supervisory authority in charge.

Meanwhile some public services, in particular citizen portals as gateway to the public sector, consider offering online access for citizens. In a few countries it is already possible for citizens to see their own profile data from the national register file, including the logfile containing who has accessed their data (except for law enforcement and other security agencies). This is implemented in, e.g., Belgium ("mijndossier/mondossier"[5]) and Norway ("minside"[6]), and a kind of "transparency portal" is planned in Germany as well[7].

4.4   News feed on security and privacy incidents

The user's privacy depends on security and data protection guarantees for all ICT systems involved in processing the user's personal data as well as organizational processes. This means that especially all information on security and privacy threats or incidents concerning the user's data is relevant. This comprises all mechanisms and implementations in use such as protocols, applications, cryptographic algorithms, or also the identity management system software itself. In particular users have to be informed about the risk to their private sphere, i.e., who definitely or potentially has unauthorized access to personal data, and about the consequences, e.g., options to take action.

In case of security breaches, transparency is legally demanded by Security Breach Notification Acts in several jurisdictions, in particular in the USA. Here any business that releases accidentally or otherwise personal information of any resident must

---

[5] https://www.mijndossier.rrn.fgov.be / https://www.mondossier.rrn.fgov.be / https://www. meindossier. rrn.fgov.be.

[6] http://www.norge.no/minside/.

[7] Information from the German Federal Ministry of the Interior, 16 March 2007: "IT-Projekte im Überblick: Bundesmeldereg ister" and the presentation from M. Schallbruch on 19 March 2007: "Das Deutschland Online-Vorhaben – Meldewesen", both available via http://www. deutschland-online.de/.

disclose such within a reasonable period. The intention of this obligation to notify residents is to ensure they are made aware when their data is received by unauthorized persons.

Today, security breaches and vulnerabilities are reported by a variety of providers, such as national Computer Emergency Response Teams (CERTs) or manufacturers of security tools. As in many cases vulnerabilities are only announced when there is already a patch available (which means that a certain percentage of vulnerabilities remains unreported), services such as VulnWatch inform on all threats submitted by security researchers or product vendors to alert the Internet community of security issues that may effect them[8].

Currently, comparable information in the area of privacy risks, e.g., relating to what can be observed or linked by others, is not available, or at least not in a structured way. This kind of information comprises, among others, the possible linkage of personal information by joining two formerly separated databases (e.g., if one company takes over another company), the possible linkage with other (publicly) available data, or the possible analysis of personal data according to other (publicly) available rules or knowledge (cf. Figure 3 in Section 3.2).

Feeding information on security and privacy threats or incidents directly into an identity management system can support the user to take action related to, e.g., configuring the system beforehand, administering the partial identities, using the identity management system within a transaction, or asserting privacy rights afterwards. The potentially presented options for users' activities comprise, e.g.,

- "Don't use that partial identity anymore."
- "Don't establish further communications or perform further transactions concerning this mechanism / party."
- "Patch the system (the identity management system itself or the environment, e.g., operating system)."
- "Don't use mechanism <mechanism_name> anymore."
- "Tag related transactions in the history logfile that there may has happened an incident (if possible: describe consequences)."
- "Assert right to access to own personal data or information on the data processing ICT system with respect to party <party_name>."
- "Assert right to delete personal data."
- "Revoke consent."
- "Inform peers."

In a prototype for PRIME, an RSS feed was designed to transport information on security incidents [26]. This feed is regularly polled by the user's system. For convenience reasons related warnings are grouped, and priorities assigned to the feed items are evaluated together with the user's estimation of reliability of the respective feed provider (i.e., a "trust level" "low", "medium" or "high", cf. Figure 6).

---

[8] http://www.vulnwatch.org/.

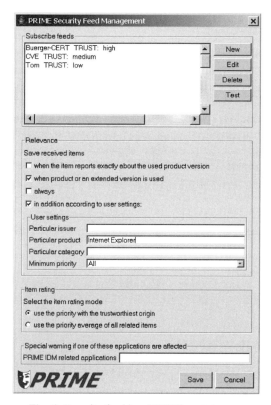

Fig. 6: Security feed in a PRIME prototype

The news items are formatted in XML, containing among others data on

- Product concerned (incl. version) and its issuer;
- Description of the vulnerability (incl. priority), since when it exists and the date of its detection;
- Recommendation for action (e.g., countermeasures or specific checks) with information on the effectiveness of the proposed solution;
- Digital signature for authenticity check.

For a wide use and the possibility of machine interpretation, e.g., by identity management systems, the format of news items and the way for interpretation by the user's system should be standardized. This is especially important when extending the information scope to data protection issues, leaving the traditional area of security vulnerabilities from CERTs and others which already base on structured formats.

4.5 "Data Track" as control center

The transparency tools showed in the previous sections can be used within any ICT system, but they are especially interesting in combination with a user-controlled identity management system.

In PRIME the main control center which can orchestrate the different transparency tools is the "Data Track" (cf. Section 2.3.3) together with the function to check which personal data to disclose in a specific context. Here the information on potential interaction partners and the privacy policy information can be shown even prior to the interaction or any disclosure of personal data. In addition, the "Data Track" would not only serve as a history function for user-side logging of data transaction records, but also would enable users to ask data controllers later on whether they really treated the data as promised. Moreover, information from security and privacy news feeds which is relevant for the user could be stored at the user's side and displayed when the user is going to disclose personal data. This information is also valuable for investigating potential risks related to former transactions in the "Data Track".

5 Limitations of transparency tools

The value of transparency tools depends on how accurate, comprehensive and understandable the information is. Obviously this is a challenge especially in a hostile environment where the reliability of available information is questionable and where adversaries would not make attacks transparent. In particular breaches of confidentiality can hardly be noticed. Hidden spying technologies are meanwhile available for everybody [16]. Partial remedy can be achieved by integrating findings of third parties or other peers on possible surveillance, linkage or profiling. People should be able to choose from a plurality of information providers whom to trust that they offer reliable information.

Without standardization, information being made transparent often is hard to understand for humans and cannot easily be interpreted by machines. In a globalized world this would require hard-to-achieve international harmonization, at least with respect to important aspects. Again, peers or organizations trusted by the individual can be of help when deciding on proper actions.

Providing transparency by offering information bears a great responsibility as inaccurate information may be harmful. In particular if news feeds for security and privacy information are automatically interpreted, rumors may lead to build-up processes with undesired consequences which are hard to revoke. Related are liability issues.

Transparency is not sufficient for achieving a high level of privacy: Giving all necessary information to individuals does not mean that they have a real and fair choice to maintain their privacy. In fact, data minimization with minimal disclosure of personal data is usually more effective than relying on "notice and choice". Also transparent privacy-invasive processes are still privacy-invasive. In this case, people concerned should be empowered to complain via other ways, as offered by today's democratic state mechanisms, e.g., informing supervisory authorities, bringing the case to court, or using political influence.

Further, transparency tools may be privacy-invasive themselves, in particular when they require to process personal data themselves. This is especially true if personal data from others are involved. But also a huge storage of own personal information is a risk as it represents yet another data silo which would have to be safeguarded against unauthorized access.

Finally, companies may not be willing to provide more information and enhance transparency because they would have to reorganize internal processes. In addition, this information would have to be kept apart from potential trade secrets or personal data from others. However, the people interested in transparency may be an own customer segment which could be attracted. Here it should be taken into account that according to a study, consumers who desire greater information transparency are less willing to be profiled, i.e., the demand for transparency and the need of privacy seem to be correlated [3].

6 Conclusion and outlook

In many areas of life in our increasingly complex world there is a trend towards transparency. Similar approaches are needed for privacy-related issues as well. Transparency is a precondition for an informed decision on aspects related with processing of personal data, e.g., which data to disclose, which data processing methods to allow and which additional conditions to demand. Not only in the European regulatory context it is legally required to offer data subjects transparency on processing of their personal data.

As user-controlled identity management systems assist individuals to manage their privacy, they can function as a perfect basis for transparency tools which pursue the same objective. In particular this means giving information to individuals in an understandable way and empowering them to act accordingly.

Transparency tools can enhance user-controlled identity management in many facets. Users can profit from their use at all times: before an interaction when checking the other party's trustworthiness and reliability, during an interaction when policies are being displayed and consent has to be given, and also after an interaction to control. The information can either be displayed directly on the spot or asynchronously, depending on the context.

Transparency can help users to get an idea which knowledge on the own person other parties may have gained. This is important to support them in determining (re-) use of partial identities, taking into account, e.g., the assumed or stated trustworthiness of the service and its already compiled knowledge. Moreover, it may provide information for deciding whether and how to act after data have been disclosed.

However, transparency tools are no panacea for achieving a high level of privacy. As a matter of fact, they may convey privacy problems, e.g., if the information to be made transparent to an individual belongs to other persons. Even in workflows which separate data from different persons, sometimes intermingling of multiple data subjects' personal data cannot be fully excluded, e.g., in interactions between natural persons or in reputation systems which base on linking ratings from others on former interactions.

Implementing transparency tools bears several challenges. In particular it is challenging to provide understandable information, not too little and not too much, otherwise individuals will be overwhelmed by the complexity of data processing and privacy. Also, precaution should be taken that individuals neither overestimate nor underestimate security and privacy risks. Further, if transparency information is sensitive itself, it is a challenge to protect these data silos which are set up for transparency purposes against unauthorized access.

The "marriage" of transparency tools with user-controlled identity management can result in a full "privacy suit" for users, providing only one user interface and gateway to the outside world. We do not have to start from scratch – information and services out there can be integrated to a certain extent. Standardization and harmonization of transparency tools and their interpretation is needed so that transparency-enhanced user-controlled identity management can come into full blossom – provided that interaction partners and parties within the infrastructure are also able and willing to support both identity management and transparency demands. For the sake of privacy and sovereignty of every user, transparency tools should be implemented on top of data minimizing functions and be combined with possibilities for users to track back data processing involving multiple parties to be able to find errors in the case of wrong inferences and to ensure that all necessary corrective measures are applied.

Thereby increased transparency will enable a further societal discussion on how to shape privacy and data processing on individuals in our information society, aiming at a fair power balance between individuals, companies and States.

Acknowledgments

This work was partially done within the context of two European research projects: the Network of Excellence FIDIS – Future of Identity in the Information Society (http://www.fidis.net/) which works among others on identity, identity management and transparency enhancing tools and the Integrated Project PRIME – Privacy and Identity Management for Europe (https://www.prime-project.eu/) where concepts and prototypes for user-controlled identity management are being developed. I am grateful for helpful comments on this topic and related issues from and constructive discussions with Mike Bergmann, Laurent Beslay, Katrin Borcea-Pfitzmann, Caspar Bowden, David Brin, Sebastian Clauß, Stephen Crane, Simone Fischer-Hübner, Riccardo Genghini, Markus Hansen, Mireille Hildebrandt, Xavier Huysmans, Katja Liesebach, Christian Krause, Holger Krekel, Martin Meints, Sebastian Meissner, Jan Möller, Antje Nageler, John Sören Pettersson, Andreas Pfitzmann, Stefanie Poetzsch, Thomas Probst, Hartmut Pohl, Charles Raab, Maren Raguse, Martin Rost, Jan Schallaböck, Sandra Steinbrecher, and Stefan Weiss. The FIDIS Network of Excellence and the PRIME project receive research funding from the European Union's Sixth Framework Programme and the Swiss Federal Office for Education and Science.

References

1. Andersson C, Camenisch J, Crane S, Fischer-Hübner S, Leenes R, Pearson S, Pettersson, JS, Sommer, D (2005) Trust in PRIME. In: Proceedings of the 5th IEEE Int. Symposium on Signal Processing and Information Technology. Athens, Greece, 552-559
2. Article 29 Working Party (2004) Opinion on More Harmonised Information Provisions. WP 100, 11987/04/EN. http://ec.europa.eu/justice_home/fsj/privacy/docs/wpdocs/2004/wp100_en.pdf. Accessed 2 Dec 2007
3. Awad, NF, Krishnan, MS (2006) The Personalization Privacy Paradox: An Empirical Evaluation of Information Transparency and the Willingness to Be Profiled Online for Personalization. MIS Quarterly 30 (1): 13-28
4. Bauer M, Meints M, Hansen M (eds) (2005) Structured Overview on Prototypes and Concepts of Identity Management Systems. FIDIS Deliverable D3.1. Frankfurt am Main, Germany. http://www.fidis.net/fileadmin/fidis/deliverables/fidis-wp3-del3.1.overview_on_IMS.final.pdf. Accessed 2 Dec 2007
5. Borking JJ, Raab CD (2001) Law, PETs and Other Technologies for Privacy Protection. In: Journal of Information, Law and Technology, Vol. 1. http://www2.warwick.ac.uk/fac/soc/law/elj/jilt/2001_1/borking. Accessed 2 Dec 2007
6. Brin D (1998) The Transparent Society: Will Technology Force Us to Choose Between Privacy and Freedom? Addison-Wesley, Reading, Mass.
7. Brückner L, Voss M (2005) MozPETs – a Privacy Enhanced Web Browser. In: Proceedings of the Third Annual Conference on Privacy, Security and Trust (PST05), Canada. http://www.ito.tu-darmstadt.de/publs/pdf/BruecknerVoss_Mozpets.pdf. Accessed 2 Dec 2007
8. Camenisch J, Lysyanskaya A (2000) Efficient Non-Transferable Anonymous Multi-Show Credential System With Optional Anonymity Revocation. IBM Research Report RZ 3295 (# 93341), extended abstract in: Advances in Cryptology – Eurocrypt 2001, revised full version available at http://eprint.iacr.org/2001/019. Accessed 2 Dec 2007
9. Casassa Mont M, Pearson S, Bramhall P (2003) Towards Accountable Management of Identity and Privacy: Sticky Policies and Enforceable Tracing Services. Trusted Systems Laboratory, HP Laboratories Bristol, HPL-2003-49. http://www.hpl.hp.com/techreports/2003/HPL-2003-49.pdf. Accessed 2 Dec 2007
10. Chaum D (1985) Security without Identification: Transaction Systems to Make Big Brother Obsolete. CACM 28 (10): 1030-1044
11. Clauß S, Köhntopp M (2001) Identity Management and Its Support of Multilateral Security. Computer Networks, 37 (2): 205-219
12. Clauß S, Kriegelstein K (2003) Datenschutzfreundliches Identitätsmanagement. Datenschutz und Datensicherheit 27 (5): 297
13. Clauß S, Pfitzmann A, Hansen M, Van Herreweghen E (2002) Privacy-Enhancing Identity Management. The IPTS Report 67: 8-16. http://www.jrc.es/home/report/english/articles/vol67/IPT2E676.htm. Accessed 2 Dec 2007
14. Eurobarometer (2003) Data Protection. http://ec.europa.eu/public_opinion/archives/ebs/ebs_196_data_protection.pdf. Accessed 2 Dec 2007
15. Fischer-Hübner S, Pettersson JS, Bergmann M, Hansen M, Pearson S, Casassa Mont M (2007) HCI Designs for Privacy-Enhancing Identity Management. In: Acquisti A, Gritzalis S, Lambrinoudakis C, Di Vimercati S (eds) Digital Privacy: Theory, Technologies, and Practices, Auerbach, in press

16. Hansen M, Meissner S (eds) (2007) Verkettung digitaler Identitäten. Report commissioned by the German Federal Ministry of Education and Research. https://www. datenschutzzentrum.de/projekte/verkettung/. Accessed 2 Dec 2007

17. Hildebrandt M, Koops B-J (eds) (2007) A Vision of Ambient Law. FIDIS Deliverable D7.9. Frankfurt am Main, Germany. http://www.fidis.net/fileadmin/fidis/deliverables/ fidis-wp7-d7.9_A_Vision_of_Ambient_Law.pdf. Accessed 2 Dec 2007

18. Hildebrandt M, Meints M (eds) (2006) RFID, Profiling, and AmI. FIDIS Deliverable D7.7. Frankfurt am Main, Germany. http://www.fidis.net/fileadmin/fidis/deliverables/ fidis-wp7-del7.7.RFID_Profiling_AMI.pdf. Accessed 2 Dec 2007

19. Hogan & Hartson, Analysys (2006) Preparing the Next Steps in Regulation of Electronic Communications – A Contribution to the Review of the Electronic Communications Regulatory Framework. http://ec.europa.eu/information_society/policy/ecomm/doc/libra ry/ext_studies/next_steps/regul_of_ecomm_july2006_final.pdf. Accessed 2 Dec 2007

20. Jendricke U, Gerd tom Markotten D (2000) Usability meets Security – The Identity-Manager as your Personal Security Assistant for the Internet. In: Proceedings of the 16th Annual Computer Security Applications Conference, 344-353

21. Jøsang A, Pope S (2005) User Centric Identity Management. In: Proceedings of AusCERT, Australia. http://sky.fit.qut.edu.au/~josang/papers/JP2005-AusCERT.pdf. Accessed 2 Dec 2007

22. Karjoth G, Schunter M, Waidner M (2002) Platform for Enterprise Privacy Practices: Privacy-enabled Management of Customer Data. In: Proceedings of 2nd Workshop on Privacy Enhancing Technologies (PET 2002), LNCS 2482, Springer, 69-84

23. Leenes R, Schallaböck J, Hansen M (eds) (2007) Privacy and Identity Management for Europe – PRIME White Paper V2. https://www.prime-project.eu/prime_products/ whitepaper/. Accessed 2 Dec 2007

24. Mehldau M (2007) Iconset for Data-Privacy Declarations v0.1. http://netzpolitik.org/wp-upload/data-privacy-icons-v01.pdf. Accessed 2 Dec 2007

25. Meints M (2006) Protokollierung bei Identitätsmanagementsystemen – Anforderungen und Lösungsansätze. Datenschutz und Datensicherheit 30 (5): 304-307

26. Nageler A (2006) Integration von sicherheitsrelevanten Informationen in ein Identitätsmanagementsystem. Diploma Thesis, Christian-Albrechts-Universität zu Kiel

27. Pettersson JS, Fischer-Hübner S, Bergmann M (2006) Outlining "Data Track": Privacy-Friendly Data Maintenance for End-Users. In: Advances in Information Systems Development – New Methods and Practice for the Networked Society, Proceedings of the 15th International Conference on Information Systems Development (ISD 2006), Springer US, 215-226

28. Pfitzmann A, Hansen M (2007) Anonymity, Unlinkability, Undetectability, Unobservability, Pseudonymity, and Identity Management – A Consolidated Proposal for Terminology v0.30. http://dud.inf.tu-dresden.de/Anon_Terminology.shtml. Accessed 2 Dec 2007

29. PRIME Tutorials (2007). https://www.prime-project.eu/tutorials/. Accessed 2 Dec 2007

30. Rundle M (2006) International Data Protection and Digital Identity Management Tools. Presentation at Internet Governance Forum 2006, October 2006, Athens. http://identityproject.lse.ac.uk/mary.pdf. Accessed 2 Dec 2007

31. Westin AF (1967) Privacy and Freedom. Atheneum, New York

32. Wörndl W (2003) Privatheit bei dezentraler Verwaltung von Benutzerprofilen (Privacy in Decentral Management of User Profiles). PhD Thesis at Technische Universität München. http://tumb1.biblio.tu-muenchen.de/publ/diss/in/2003/woerndl.pdf. Accessed 2 Dec 2007

Workshop: Identity Management

Identity Deployment and Management in Wireless Mesh Networks

Leonardo A. Martucci[1], Albin Zuccato[2], and Simone Fischer-Hübner[1]

[1] Karlstads University, Department of Computer Science
{leonardo.martucci, simone.fischer-huebner}@kau.se
[2] TeliaSonera, R&D Informations Security
albin.zuccato@teliasonera.com

Abstract. This paper introduces the problem of combining security and privacy-friendly provisioning in wireless mesh network environments. We present a set of non-functional requirements for a privacy-friendly identity management (IdM) system suitable for wireless mesh networks and derive another set of security and privacy properties for digital identifiers to be used in such networks. Later, we compare two existing identifiers, anonymous attribute certificates and anonymous credentials, and verify if any of those conforms to our set of defined properties. A business model and some business cases are presented to support and justify the need for a privacy-friendly IdM system not only from the security and privacy perspective, but also from a business-enabler perspective.

1 Introduction

Mesh networking is an elegant and affordable technical solution for extending the range and the provisioning of services that are deployed in an infrastructured network behind an wireless access point, such as a private network or even the Internet. The extension of the radio range of access points is achieved using nodes called wireless relays. Wireless relays can be mobile or stationary, and usually belong to telecommunication service provides (TSP). Ad hoc routing protocols are used when the wireless relays are mobile, especially if mobile clients can operate as intermediary nodes to forward packets from users that are located beyond the radio range of a wireless access point or a wireless relay. Therefore, a mobile client can also operate as wireless relay to other clients.

In Figure 1, we illustrate a wireless mesh network scenario. There are many research problems shown in this figure. In this paper we focus the technical and economical problems arising from the presented scenario. We divided those problems into three areas:

- performance aspects regarding hybrid ad hoc routing, QoS, transport layers, power-efficiency, and roaming between relays for instance[3]. In this paper we do not deal with performance aspects;

---

[3]The IEEE 802.11 task group S is currently working on the standardization for wireless mesh network based on the IEEE 802.11 standard [2].

Please use the following format when citing this chapter:

Martucci, L.A., Zuccato, A. and Fischer-Hübner, S., 2008, in IFIP International Federation for Information Processing, Volume 262; The Future of Identity in the Information Society; Simone Fischer-Hübner, Penny Duquenoy, Albin Zuccato, Leonardo Martucci; (Boston: Springer), pp. 223–233.

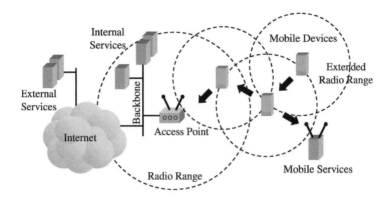

Fig. 1. A wireless mesh network with one gateway connected to the backbone of the telecommunication / service provider and also to the Internet, and one wireless relay connecting 3 nodes through a mobile ad hoc network. Services are provided directly from the provider's backbone, from the Internet and also from the mobile network.

- the security and privacy aspects, especially on the problems of identity management, user untraceability against other network participants and other privacy and security problems arising from lack of identification or Sybil attacks [10]. The security and privacy aspects are the main focus of this work;
- the economic and business problems involved, especially regarding the business models and business cases involved and how to stimulate and reward the cooperation among mobile nodes. In this paper we present a business model and some business cases regarding services that may be deployed by a TSP.

The organization of the paper is as follows. Section 2 sets the objective of this paper and stresses the importance of selecting proper identifiers when the provisioning of privacy is one of the goals of a TSP. In Section 3 we present the security threats in a wireless mesh network scenario, the trivial solution and the implications to users' privacy. Section 4 presents the basic structure of an identity management system, the privacy rights of each entity and the requirements for the deployment of digital identifiers in a wireless mesh scenario. Section 5 discusses the available techniques to issue anonymous identifiers, while Section 6 presents the business model of the system. Finally, Section 7 concludes the paper.

2   Digital Identifiers and Privacy

User privacy could be largely improved simply by distributing non-revocable anonymous credentials to end-users. However, for the TSP point of view, complete anonymous access to the network is usually undesirable for several reasons, such as: billing, impossibility of identifying malicious insiders (i. e., subscribed users misbehaving in the network into an impossible problem) and, in a wireless mesh network scenario, it is hard to reward subscribers collaborating into the network (e. g., for actions such forwarding packets from other users in the mobile ad hoc network).

The TSP needs to identify its subscribers for the purposes of billing and network security, nevertheless it is also a goal of the TSP to protect its users against privacy abuses coming from malicious insiders and outsiders i. e. user anonymity against other network users, but not towards the TSP. Revocable anonymous identifiers are a possible solution for protecting the TSP's customers privacy in a wireless mesh network scenario.

The goal of this work is the specification of these revocable identifiers that allows the identification of users by the TSP, but not does not permit a user to uniquely identify another network user. Therefore, the TSP is able to deploy security services (e. g., authentication, authorization, access control, accounting) to protect the network against malicious users and attacks, such as a Sybil attack, and provide user privacy simultaneously. We describe the system requirements, suggest an adequate solution and evaluate its advantages and disadvantages.

The first step for the provisioning of anonymity towards other network users is to distribute untraceable identifiers to the network subscribers. Despite the property of being anonymous apparently contradicts the possession and disclosure of a unique identifier to other parties, this is not true for deploying privacy in network environments where users may join or leave as they wish, such as a wireless network. Unique identification is a requirement for the provisioning anonymity. Without protection against identity-based attacks, the network may be compromised by Sybil attacks[4] [10]. The need for unique identification for the provisioning of anonymity in wireless network environments is referred as the identity-anonymity paradox [12].

Therefore, the TSP has to distribute network identifiers that will be used for the provisioning of anonymity against other network users[5]. Preferably, those identifiers should also allow pseudonimity. Pseudonyms are valuable for the provisioning of personalized network services, especially when those services are provided by third party service providers.

The Pfitzmann and Hansen terminology [13] is followed in this paper for following terms: anonymity, unlinkability and pseudonimity. The term untraceability is used to describe the property of a subject to be protected against electronic stalking (i. e., tracking) by an (omnipresent) attacker eavesdropping the wireless network.

---

[4]A Sybil attack occurs when a malicious user influences the network by controlling multiple logical identifiers from a single physical device. The distribution of identifiers (by a trusted third party) that guarantee the one-to-one relationship between logical identifiers and network devices can prevent Sybil attacks.

[5]In this paper we assume that the data link and IP addresses also change when the electronic identifier changes. We disregard other forms of electronic stalking using physical or application layer information.

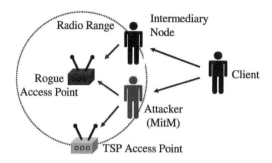

Fig. 2. Possible threats related to impersonation and man-in-the-middle (MitM) attacks in wireless mesh networks. In the figure, a client has her data being forwarded either by a honest intermediary node to a rogue access point or by an attacker towards a rogue access point or to an authentic access point that belongs to the TSP.

3 Security Threats, the Trivial Solution and Privacy

The threats involved in this scenario include privacy and network security threats. Network security threats include impersonation and man-in-the-middle attacks, as depicted in Figure 2. In an ad hoc network, the total absence of identification may lead to a Sybil attack [10], since honest users are not able to detect that the relationship between logical identifiers (e. g., IP addresses) and physical devices is actually one to one. In the absence of trustable identification, network security services, such as authentication, authorization and access control, cannot be guaranteed, and those security threats can affect the network performance and functionality, leading to denial of services attacks that deny the usage of the network by honest users [12].

Preventing the security threats described could be trivially achieved with the deployment of a Certification Authority (CA) and authentication servers (AS) on the TSP side (using two-way authentication), distribution of X.509 public key certificates [1], mutual authentication and end-to-end secure channels between network entities. Users and servers would then be able to univocally identify other network entities and verify the authenticity of their communication partners. There are many details involved even within this trivial solution, such as: decisions regarding the end-to-end secure communication protocol suite between users and servers, and users and users; the authentication protocols and data link security between wireless relays and access points; the use of on upper layer encryption, such as VPN connections, for users' transactions; and the security properties of the ad hoc routing algorithms (to be used in the extended radio range).

However, the presented solution does not address the privacy threats. Privacy threats include profiling, monitoring and stalking of devices using the provided identifiers as source of information[6]. X.509 public key digital certificates are not privacy-friendly since it is possible to track users using the serial number information of those certificates. Data link and network layer information (i. e., $\{MAC, IP\}$ pairs) could be used as privacy-friendly identifiers because they can be changed regularly [11], but this information cannot provide trustable identification [12] and makes the system vulnerable to Sybil attacks. Thus, the usage of privacy-friendly certificate-like identification, issued by a Trusted Third Party (TTSP), is a solution for both privacy and security threats in a wireless mesh network scenario.

4   Identities and Identity Management System

The identity management (IdM) system in the wireless mesh network scenario follows the general three type categorization for IdM [3]: *account management*, *profiling* and *management of own identities*. The account management – for authentication, authorization and accounting (AAA) purposes – is done by the TSP. The management of own identities is performed by each network user, who is able control her partial identities using an IdM tool. Profiling is done by the service providers (SP), especially for the purpose of service customization and / or customer relationship management. Therefore, identifiers are used in different ways in a wireless mesh network.

A privacy-friendly wireless mesh network must offer the following non-functional requirements for users and other parties during the life-cycle of a user's identifier[7] into the system:

a) users may remain anonymous against other users.
b) users may choose to be anonymous against a SP, or to be able to reuse pseudonyms. Pseudonyms may be used to obtain personalized services and are usually associated to the disclosure of a user's partial identity.
c) privacy-friendly does not only mean the TSP protecting the users' identity and identifiers, but also that users have control over their personal information and can share it if they wish so.
d) TSP can identify users and eventually revoke their identifiers, thus these identifiers cannot be used any longer, and also disclose user anonymity if necessary[8].

---

[6]Some threats related to physical and routing layer attacks are not going to be considered in the scope of this paper. Such threats include network jamming and radio device tracking using radio fingerprints and signal to noise (S/N) ratio techniques.

[7]The life-cycle of a user's identifier starts when the identifier is created by the IdM system, eventually hosted by the TSP, and ends when the identifier expires, is revoked by the IdM system or deleted by the user.

[8]The disclosure of user anonymity is needed for pinpointing malicious users and for the provisioning of some network security services, such as authentication, authorization and accounting (AAA) for instance.

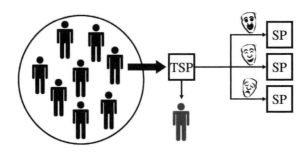

Fig. 3. Users are anonymous among their peers and at the same time are uniquely identified by the TSP and may have different identities towards different SP.

e) TSP must be fair and trusted regarding the disclosure of identities, and the rules for doing so must be well-defined and well-described. The TSP duties and rights on handling personal data are regulated according to the legislation regarding data protection[9].

f) SP may retain and process (anonymized) users' related information according to the applicable legislation.

Thus, a user has many identifiers: a single identifier towards the TSP, one or more pseudonyms towards different SP, and one-time identifiers (transaction pseudonyms) towards other users. Figure 3 provides an illustration of the multiple identifiers described in this paragraph. The security and privacy properties for digital identifiers in a wireless mesh network scenario are:

i) Identifiers must be unique. This is needed to guarantee the 1-to-1 relationship between logical identifiers and physical devices, especially in the extended radio range of the wireless mesh network. Uniqueness is needed for preventing Sybil attacks [10] in the wireless mesh network.

ii) Identifiers must be anonymous against all other entities, except the TSP. This is required for the provisioning of user untraceability against other network entities (e. g., other mobile users, SP).

iii) Re-identification of anonymous identifiers must be supported. The TSP shall be able to identify users and eventually revoke users' identifiers to disclose their anonymity and prevent them to be used any longer.

iv) It must be possible to authenticate peer devices without the interference of the TSP's AS (running in the TSP's AAA servers). This is needed for supporting mobile ad hoc services or peer-to-peer (P2P) applications that can be provided without the support of the TSP's telecommunication infrastructure.

A simplified network topology depicting the basic infrastructure and services supported or connected to the TSP is shown in Figure 4.

---

[9]In Europe, this includes the Data Protection Directive 95/46/EC and the Directive 2002/58/EC on privacy electronic communications.

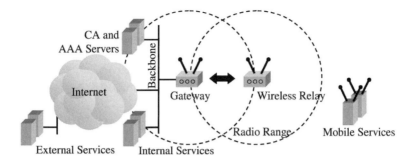

Fig. 4. The basic infrastructure provided by the TSP includes the wireless mesh network, CA and AAA servers and other internal and external services.

5   Anonymous Credentials in a Wireless Mesh Network

The usage of either anonymous attribute certificates (ATC) [4] or anonymous credentials [6–8] is recommended since they might provide untraceability to the user if used correctly. Untraceability is provided by preventing unauthorized identification of network clients by distinguishing multiple appearances of a given node into the wireless mesh network. Thus, each appearance of a user in the network must be unlinkable to a previous appearance. The set of potential attackers include other (colluding) nodes in the mobile ad hoc network or a SP.

ATC are based on zero-knowledge (ZK) proofs of knowledge[10] and are structured as a composition of a group certificate and an X.509 attribute certificate [1]. There are mechanisms associated with ATC that allow users' identities to be disclosed, traced or revoked by an identity escrow [4]. ATC do not offer guarantees to the 1-1 relationship between identifiers and devices (item "*i*" – Section 4) since there are no means to prevent or detect ATC sharing.

Anonymous credentials can be constructed using either blind signatures or ZK proofs. Anonymous credentials based on ZK proofs can, beyond providing anonymity, be used multiple times (multiple show) [8], be revocable [5] and can be built to detect sharing of credentials, as shown in [6]. Therefore, anonymous credentials have the potential to fulfill all the basic security and privacy requirements for identifiers in a wireless mesh scenario presented in Section 4.

6   Business Model for Privacy-Friendly IdM

To discuss a business model for a privacy-friendly IdM system we have to clarify the general conditions in which such a model need to exist. The TSP's key assets are the following three: (*i*) its customers, (*ii*) its technical infrastructure, and (*iii*) its technical competence. For the further discussion the first two are of significance.

---

[10]ZK proofs of knowledge are interactive proofs in which the verifier learns nothing besides the fact that the statement that is proven is true [14, 9].

The customer is a utterly important asset for the TSP. To maintain customers' loyalty and trust significant resources are required from the TSP (i. e., customer relationship management). The TSP aims to protect and strengthen its customer relationships and is reluctant to put it at risk. A SP must not receive enough "identifying" information that allows it to deal with the TSP's customers directly. Customer satisfaction decreases with inappropriate handling of personal information. The TSP is interested to act in a privacy-friendly way, so that the customer is satisfied and do not consider to move to another TSP.

The second important factor is the network infrastructure (i. e., networking hardware). The TSP has to invest heavily into infrastructure to provide a broader range of services to more customers. Wireless mesh networks are a way to reach more customers (by extending the network range) without infrastructure investments. A drawback is that wireless mesh networks imply that the TSP loses the control over part of the network. From a security point of view, this loss of control requires that the operator (a) do its uttermost to maintain security by investing into security mechanisms and (b) informing the customer about the risk.

A customer's identity can be divided in partial identities that enable the customer and the TSP to use only a subset of the personal information for the purpose at hand. Partial identities can be far better tailored to the purpose of the SP and the TSP does not risk to lose control of its customer's identities. By deploying an IdM system the TSP allows its customers to control their partial identities. Moreover, an IdM is an value-added service that increases the market attractiveness of the TSP to keep and attract more customers, and also offers new business opportunities (e. g., the customer pays for the service, 3rd parties pay for obtained information), which allow the creation of new income sources. The dilemma with market attractiveness effects is that they fade out over time as the competitors adapt them as well. This means they are very beneficiary in the beginning but are not reliable as income source. The business opportunities on the other hand allow to generate new income sources and we shall discuss some of them as business cases for privacy-friendly IdM. These business cases, which are presented in the following sections, are also viable requirement sources for the subsequent solution.

6.1   Business Case - IdM for Wireless Mesh Networks

Wireless mesh networking allows more customer to use the TSP network. This creates revenue from more user subscriptions (i. e., more customers are in range for using the service) and service usage (i. e., data traffic in the TSP network).

It is crucial that the parties are identifiable to guarantee some network security functions and also for billing / compensation payments and rewarding. The use of persistent identifiers can affect the privacy and risk the customers' privacy. Therefore, an IdM must be able to provide privacy-friendly identifiers that can be used to fulfill the requirements presented in Section 4.

6.2 Business Case - Distributed IdM Service

In this business case we assume that an operator charges for its IdM service. It is possible to charge different parties (e. g. the identity owner, active identity verifier) for the IdM activities that they consume. To be able to do that the IdM system has to support identity creation and validation activities. In addition value adding management functions (e. g. policy management for automatic identity use) should be provided to the user.

6.3 Business Case - Provide an IdM Infrastructure to 3rd Parties

Many projects (e. g. smart home) would like to use the identity of the user to customize the service they offer. This implies that each service would need to collect and maintain identity information of the user which it does not need most of the time. The costs and risk involved with that can be omitted with a 3rd party IdM. The operators role in this business case is to provide an IdM infrastructure that only delivers the personal information necessary for the service and encapsulates so that it is not linked to the identity. The difference to the business case above is that the operator not only provides a service via its own infrastructure but opens the infrastructure for others to provide their services upon it.

For instance, in an automobile example, starting a car engine should only be allowed upon the availability of a valid driver's license. The preferences for the adjustment of a car seat could be set using another identifier. And in the case of an accident it should still be possible to retrieve the driver's and passengers' identities and medical information (i. e. sensitive personal information). Naturally, the automobile could also hold this information – but it would need to collect, protect, maintain and communicate it. If the same information could be stored somewhere else and provided only as partial identity containing the purpose related information (e. g. the driver's licence, seat adjustment preferences) the automobile would not need any sophisticated IdM mechanisms. In addition, in an emergency situation, meaningful identification information would be obtained not from the vehicle but from the personal IdM system.

Our idea is to have a communication device in possession of the individual as an identity broker which delivers the right kind of information to the party which needs it at the moment. The broker would not need to have all identity information accessible at all time. In fact we imagine an online and offline capability where predictable identity information is stored locally (offline) in a protected form (e. g. credentials) and additional credentials, which are protected and partial for the new purpose, received on demand (online) from an online repository – maybe by a mesh network. The offline capability can also come handy in a mesh scenario because we cannot assume that a central connection is available at all time (e. g. when the end node in Figure 1 takes contact with the intermediate node the intermediate does not have online connection either but both must be able to identify each other).

6.4 Business Case - Customer Goodwill by Privacy Activities

Internal studies indicate that customers expect their operator to respect privacy. Engaging in an IdM platform would be a clear sign to the market that a TSP cares about its customers' privacy. Therefore the investment may deliver returns also in this segment and therefore provides a business case there.

7 Summary and Future Work

In this paper we introduced the problem of combining security and privacy-friendly identifiers in wireless mesh networks. We presented six non-functional requirements for users and other parties (TSP, SP) during the life-cycle of a user's identifier in a privacy-friendly wireless mesh network environment. From those requirements we derived four security and privacy requirements for digital identifiers in these environments. We compared two existing solutions for anonymous identifiers, anonymous attribute certificates and anonymous credentials, and concluded that anonymous credentials fulfill the imposed requirements: the provisioning of anonymity, uniqueness, revocability and independence of a central authentication server.

We also presented a business model that justifies the economic need of anonymous identifiers and wireless mesh network from a telecommunication provider viewpoint. We support our business model with two business cases.

A multiple-show, revocable, anonymous credential system, with credential sharing detection, derived from the periodic n-times spendable e-token scheme [6] is a work-in-progress initiated within the EU FIDIS Project[11]. As a future work, we plan the development of a prototype which will provide a proof-of-concept implementation of the selected scheme.

Acknowledgements

This research was partially funded by the European Network of Excellence Future of Identity in the Information Society (FIDIS), under the 6th Framework Program for Research and Technological Development within the Information Society Technologies (IST) priority. The authors also thank the reviewers that helped to improve this paper with insightful comments.

References

1. ITU-T Recommendation X.509, The Directory: public-key and attribute certificate frameworks. Recommendation X.509 - International Telecommunications Union, The International Telegraph and Telephone Consultative Committee, Data Communication Networks: Open Systems Interconnection (OSI); Security, Structure and Applications, Aug 2005.

---

[11]See http://www.fidis.net

2. IEEE P802.11 TGs. Status of Project IEEE 802.11s, Mar 2007. See `http://www.ieee802.org/11/Reports/tgs_update.htm`.

3. Matthias Bauer, Martin Meints, and Marit Hansen. D3.1: Structured Overview on Prototypes and Concepts of Identity Management Systems. Technical report, FIDIS – Future of Identity in the Information Society, 15 Sep 2005.

4. Vicente Benjumea, Javier Lopez, and Jose Maria Troya. Anonymous Attribute Certificates based on Traceable Signatures. *Internet Research: Electronic Networking Applications and Policy. Special Issue on Privacy and Anonymity in the Digital Era: Theory, Technologies and Practice*, 16(2):120–139, 2006.

5. Jan Camenisch. Efficient Private Credential Systems and Applications: Cryptography for Privacy – Credential$^+$ Systems. 3rd FIDIS Doctoral Consortium Event, Stockholm, Sweden, 9–13 Aug 2006.

6. Jan Camenisch, Susan Hohenberger, Markulf Kohlweiss, Anna Lysyanskaya, and Mira Meyerovich. How to Win the Clone Wars: Efficient Periodic n-Times Anonymous Authentication. In *Proceedings of the 13th ACM Conference on Computer and Communications Security (CCS 2006)*, 30 Oct–3 Nov 2006.

7. Jan Camenisch and Anna Lysyanskaya. An Efficient System for Non-transferable Anonymous Credentials with Optional Anonymity Revocation. In *Proceedings of the International Conference on the Theory and Application of Cryptographic Techniques (EUROCRYPT 2001)*, volume 2045 of *Lecture Notes in Computer Science*, pages 93–118. Springer, 2001.

8. Jan Camenisch and Anna Lysyanskaya. A Signature Scheme with Efficient Protocols. In *Security in Communication Networks: Third International Conference (SCN 2002)*, volume 2576/2003 of *Lecture Notes in Computer Science*, pages 268–289, Amalfi, Italy, 12–13 Sep 2002. Springer Berlin/Heidelberg, LNCS 2576.

9. Jan Camenisch and Markus Stadler. Proof systems for general statements about discrete logarithms. Technical Report TR 260, Institute for Theoretical Computer Science, ETH Zürich, Mar 1997.

10. John R. Douceur. The Sybil Attack. In P. Druschel, F. Kaashoek, and A. Rowstron, editors, *Peer-to-Peer Systems: Proceedings of the 1st International Peer-to-Peer Systems Workshop (IPTPS)*, volume 2429, pages 251–260. Springer-Verlag, 7–8 Mar 2002.

11. Marco Gruteser and Dirk Grunwald. Enhancing Location Privacy in Wireless LAN Through Disposable Interface Identifiers: A Quantitative Analysis. In Parviz Kermani, editor, *Proceedings of the 1st ACM International Workshop on Wireless Mobile Applications and Services on WLAN Hotspots (WMASH 2003)*, 19 Sep 2003.

12. Leonardo A. Martucci. The Identity Anonymity Paradox: on the Relationship between Identification, Anonymity and Security in Mobile Ad Hoc Networks, Licentiate Thesis, Karlstad University Studies 2006:36, September 2006.

13. Andreas Pfitzmann and Marit Hansen. Anonymity, Unlinkability, Undetectability, Unobservability, Pseudonymity, and Identity Management - A Consolidated Proposal for Terminology v0.30, 26 Nov 2007. See `http://dud.inf.tu-dresden.de/literatur/`.

14. Claus P. Schnorr. Efficient signature generation for smart cards. *Journal of Cryptology*, 4(3):239–252, 1991.

Automating Identity Management
and Access Control

Rieks Joosten[1] and Stef Joosten[2,3]

[1] TNO Information and Communication Technology,
P.O. Box 1416, 9701 BK Groningen, the Netherlands
`rieks.joosten@tno.nl`
[2] Open University of the Netherlands,
P.O. Box 2960, 6401 DL Heerlen, the Netherlands
`stef.joosten@ou.nl`
[3] Ordina B&E Solutions,
P.O. Box 7101, 3430 JC Nieuwegein, the Netherlands
`stef.joosten@ordina.nl`

Abstract. The problem that we address is the inability of businesses to correctly and completely specify what an automated Identity Management and Access Control (IMAC) solution must do within their organisation. This paper reports on experiments with a tool that, from a given set of business rules, generates a functional specification as well as code for a software component that provably enforces each rule. This tool allows a business architect to experiment with different sets of IMAC rules (policies) so as to find the most appropriate set of rules for the business context. Creating a demo around the generated software component provides hands-on proof to the business that they can understand. New to our work is the use of relation algebra, which provides a way to build and prove IMAC policies simultaneously. On a larger scale, this approach may help to solve cross-domain identity issues e.g. between governmental organizations.

1 Introduction

Identity Management and Access Control (IMAC) is already a major challenge for the (larger) businesses and governmental organisations. The gap between the business and IT has been demonstrated e.g. at the Identity 2006 seminar by various businesses [1–3], technology vendors [4,5], and independent organisations [6]. There does not seem to be a consistent way for facing such challenges, given the contradictory statements that are made, e.g. "the business does not understand RBAC" [2] and "the business should be in control rather than the IT" [1]. Unsurprisingly, projects take long to implement and are not required to be first-time-right [2].

This article describes research that has been done to find new ways for handling such challenges. The work consisted of defining the meaning of IMAC for a specific business in terms of formalized business rules, and subsequently using

Please use the following format when citing this chapter:

Joosten, R. and Joosten, S., 2008, in IFIP International Federation for Information Processing, Volume 262; The Future of Identity in the Information Society; Simone Fischer-Hübner, Penny Duquenoy, Albin Zuccato, Leonardo Martucci; (Boston: Springer), pp. 235–243.

these rules to create a service layer that enforces them. Then, a demonstrator was created with different applications (business processes), each of which used the service layer for all IMAC services. As a consequence, each of the applications cannot do otherwise than comply with the set of IMAC rules from which the service layer was generated.

The importance of the demonstrator is twofold. First, it makes IMAC issues, as well as consequences of IMAC rules, tangible to the business. Rather than discussing technicalities (e.g. standards or vendor products) as is currently often done, this work allows business people to focus on what it is they want IMAC to do for them and have them express this in terms of business rules. Secondly, it shows that formalizing such rules may lead straight toward the enforcement thereof in the automated systems of that business.

The scientific contribution of this work lies in the formalization of IMAC, which yields a thorough understanding of its issues. A compliant service layer has been specified and built as an embodiment of this result.

As the method we use and the associated tooling become mature, we will be in a better position to also address cross-domain Identity issues such as those that governmental agencies struggle with.

2   IMAC Rules

Creating rules for IMAC is a creative process that captures the essence of IMAC. Both this work and its results are comparable to legislative processes: discussions, negotiations and compromise ultimately lead to rules (laws) that, once formulated and approved, are meant to be obeyed. Different sets of IMAC rules may exist in different contexts, as different laws exist in (different parts of) different countries. Interoperation between contexts (business units, businesses, or countries) requires that rules are attuned or harmonized, which is basically the same process, albeit that existing rules in specific contexts should be changed in order to remain consistent with the harmonized set.

While judicial laws are to be processed by humans, our rules must be processable by computers. Therefore, we require that our IMAC rules are expressible in natural language (NL) for use with humans, and also have a formal representation (FR) such as relation algebra or predicate logic. Because FR is more precise than NL, the FR of the IMAC rules is authoritative in our work. FRs allow us to do formal reasoning with the IMAC rules or rule sets. For example, when trying to harmonize two IMAC rule sets, the consistency proof eliminates the need of discussions, whereas any proof of inconsistency precisely defines an issue to be discussed. This alone makes the harmonization process much more efficient.

After having created the rules, they must be put to use, which is to say: they must be complied with. As an example, consider the following (subset of the real) IMAC rules:

1. Any service (function, or method) that requires a permission may only be executed from sessions in which that permission is available.

2. A permission is available within a session if and only if that session has activated a role to which this permission has been assigned.
3. A role is activated within a session if and only if (a) sessions of this type are designed to activate this role and (b) the session's user has been assigned this role.
4. Every contract must have been signed by all contract parties.

Now consider the situation where we have a user, John, who wants to review a contract, and digitally sign it after having agreed to it. Suppose an application called CRM exists that he might use to do this, as CRM is programmed to activate roles such as "Customer" which has been assigned permissions P1 and P2, where P1 is the permission required by the service "get_contract" which retrieves contract information and P2 is required by "approve_contract", the service used for the digital signing of contracts. Also assume that CRM uses the IMAC service "AuthUser" for authenticating a user's credentials (e.g. username and password).

The first thing the CRM application does when John requests a session with it, is that it invokes "AuthUser" to check John's credentials and verify that John is really John. However, as soon as John's credentials have been authenticated, rule 3 calls for the activation of the "Customer" role in the session as the session was designed to activate this role and the session's user (John) has been assigned this role. As soon as this role is activated, rule 2 demands that permissions P1 and P2 are made available within the session, as the role of "Customer" has been activated in that session and both permissions are assigned to this role. From this we see that IMAC rules such as 2 and 3 not only specify functionality that systems should exhibit, but that this functionality can be automatically provided by "AuthUser". Rules of this type are called "Automatable Operative Rules", which is a further distinction from the notion "Operative Rules" as defined in [7].

Now that the invocation of "AuthUser" has made permissions P1 and P2 available within the CRM session, John requests CRM to show his contract information. To do this, CRM invokes "get_contract". This service starts by checking whether P1 exists in the session it is called from because it must comply with rule 1. As the permission exists, "get_contract" returns the required information. Here we see that rule 1 specifies constraints on behavior rather than the behavior itself as rules 2 and 3 did. Rules of this type are called "Structural Rules".

Note that all this time, the contract existed and had not been signed by all contract parties, implying that rule 4 was being violated all this time. We want rules like this to exist as they specify a desirable business situation, and violations of such rules signal that (manual) work needs to be done; that is why we call them "Manual Operative Rules"[1]. In fact, rules like this can be used to drive a process engine [8]. The fact that John's contract has not been signed yet may trigger John to review and sign the contract, and may trigger other parties

---

[1] This term is a another distinction derived from the term "Operative Rules" as defined in [7].

involved to either get other parties to sign, or to destroy the contract as either outcome would satisfy rule 4.

3   A Rule-based IMAC Demonstrator

Once a business has established its set of IMAC rules, a service layer for IMAC services can be specified directly from the (FR of) these rules. This rule-based specification has the property that it includes all functions the business may ever need to become and remain compliant to these rules, and all functional requirements in the specification can be traced back to one or more rules. Also, it can be proved that any information system built to these specifications will maintain all IMAC rules when each service complies to its specification and all specified services have been realized, and non compliance can be proved from the specification.

We have created an IMAC demonstrator in which

1. portals are simulated: one for a financial context, another for the business or enterprise context (EM) and the third for the consumer context (CM).
2. business services may be called: one for on-line bill checking (OLBC), another one for SOx[2] accounting.
3. an IMAC service layer provides all necessary IMAC functionality.

The IMAC service layer has been generated directly from a set of both IMAC and SOx rules, and consists of a PHP functional layer on top of a MySQL database. The business services have been programmed in PHP by hand, and run on an Apache web server. Figure 1 shows the home page of the demo, which has been created such that clicking on the OLBC-box in the CM portal invokes the OLBC business service logic as if it were called from the consumer portal. Using this demo, we show that one business service is capable of dealing with identities from different businesses in different contexts. For example, the OLBC service is equally capable of dealing with the creation of a new customer in a business context as it is in the consumer context. Also, in the business context it is equally capable of providing functionality to the business (e.g. for creating/deleting a customer) as it is for customers (e.g. for creating or deleting additional customer accounts. In fact, the demo shows that decisions with respect to how the OLBC service should operate in the CM context do not affect its operation in the EM context, even though it is the same service.

The demo cannot show rule violations, as all rules are upheld by the IMAC service layer and both business services use this layer for all IMAC (and SOx) functionality. It can however show the consequences thereof: a customer that is logged in to the EM portal can only see its own data and its own users, whereas a properly authorized user from the business can see all customer accounts.

The demo also shows what happens when functions that are available to the financial people within a large organization, such as inspection of a SOx-log, are

---

[2] SOx refers to the Sarbanes-Oxley act of 2002 [9], which establishes stringent financial reporting requirements for companies doing business in the United States.

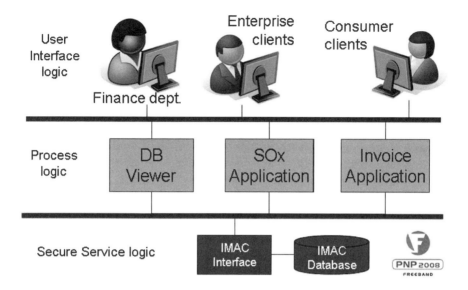

User
Interface
logic

Enterprise
clients

Consumer
clients

Finance dept.

Process
logic

DB
Viewer

SOx
Application

Invoice
Application

Secure Service logic

IMAC
Interface

IMAC
Database

PNP 2008
FREEBAND

Fig. 1. IMAC Demonstrator

made available to other business units. If for example the EM-administrator is given permission to access the SOx application of the financial department, one might think that the EM-administrator could see all log records, including those of other contexts such as CM. However, the fact that the application cannot violate the rule: "financial information may only be seen either by the domains that have a direct interest, or the financial administration" guarantees that the EM-administrator can only inspect SOx log records that are relevant to the EM context, and none other than that.

Similarly, and this is new for many businesses, this functionality can be made available in exactly the same way to customers. The rules enforced by the IMAC service layer ensure that each customer can only see or do things within the room defined by these rules. Businesses can now easily provide customers with information that is relevant for their SOx report.

4   Rules used in the demonstrator

In order to give the reader an idea of what rules look like, we provide most of the IMAC rules that we used for our demonstrator. These rules define how responsibilities are modeled in relation to performing actions, a simple form of authentication using "tokens" (a generic notion, covering username/passwords as well as certificates) and authorizations based on RBAC [10] and a rule implementing "Chinese walls":

1. Every domain, i.e. a named set of responsibilities, has at least one domain-manager that bears all domain responsibilities.

2. Whatever happens in a session is the responsibility of precisely one domain.
3. Every session is of precisely one type (the sessiontype).
4. Sessions of a given type may only run within a domain if there exists a valid sessiontype approval within that domain for this sessiontype.
5. A tokenadministration consists of entries, each of which is uniquely characterized by a token, the type of that token and the token's issuer.
6. Each entry in the tokenadministration has precisely one userid.
7. Each entry in the tokenadministration has precisely one "responsible domain", i.e. the domain that bears all responsibility for every use of the token.
8. If one userid is associated with multiple tokenadministration entries, each of them has the same responsible domain.
9. Logging into a session means providing a token, its tokentype and its issuer.
10. A sessiontoken is a login-token where the provided token, tokentype and issuer identify an entry in the tokenadministration.
11. A sessionCoactor is the userid associated with a sessiontoken.
12. A sessionCodomain is the domain that is responsible for every use of a sessiontoken.
13. There is at most one sessionCoactor and one sessionCodomain at any time.
14. Whenever a token, tokentype and tokenissuer combination is presented in a session that already has or has had a sessiontoken, this token shall only become a sessiontoken if its associated userid equals the sessionCoactor.
15. A session shall only access dataobjects containing a list of Codomains if the sessionCodomain appears in that list. Note that this access always requires a valid login. (This rule helps to define so-called "Chinese walls").
16. Every action whose execution implies taking a risk, must require a permission.
17. An action that requires permissions may only execute in sessions that have all such permissions.
18. The permissions a session has is the union of all permissions of all sessionroles.
19. A sessionrole for a session of a certain type is any role that (1) has been assigned to the sessionCoactor, and (2) has been defined as a role that may be activated for sessions of this type.
20. A role may only be assigned to existing userid's.
21. A token can only become a sessiontoken (i.e.: you may only login) in a session of a certain type if the userid associated with that token has been assigned at least one role that is relevant for sessions of that type.

5   Results

We have applied the above approach to define business rules for an IMAC service layer for a large Telco in the Netherlands. Talking to people from various business departments made us particularly aware of how diverse the ideas with respect to IMAC really are. For example, for the business unit Enterprise Market (EM), IMAC is equivalent with a part of customer care, where EM-customers can create accounts and accompanying permissions for their own employees. The finance department however sees IMAC primarily in the context of having to be compliant with the Sarbanes-Oxley act [9].

Abstracting from the use-cases provided by the business people and reconciling their needs, resulted in a set of business rules which we could both represent formally and in a way that the business could understand. In our experience, good rule sets tend to remain stable, meaning that each time they are used, only slight variations occur. Judging by this criterion, the demonstration rules have some good parts, whereas other parts still need work. Earlier versions of this work are documented in [11], [12].

Experimental tooling for generating a PHP service layer on top of a MySQL database allowed us to evaluate various rule sets "hands on". Such exercises have been invaluable in discovering which rules we need, how they should be formulated, and how to conceptually think about identity management.

From a reasonable rule set (described above) a service layer was generated allowing us to demonstrate the effects such rules would have for the business. A service layer such as ours, that guarantees compliance with a set of rules, goes a step beyond work as described e.g. in [13] where a tool only checks compliance.

Also, the ability to create functional specifications for the rule set, allows us to give the business a pretty good estimate of what actual implementation of the service layer is going to cost in terms of function points, which is the basis on which IT organizations make their offerings. For example, the functional specification for the demo has 118 function points. With a price of say 1000 EUR per function point, a business implementation of the service layer would cost about 118.000 EUR.

While creating the demo, we noticed that the application programming required limited knowledge of the rules (as we expected): programmers only need to know how to use the IMAC service interface. For the business, this means that rules may be changed at will as long as this does not affect the functional interface specification.

We also noticed that programming actually becomes easier as programmers no longer need to calculate permissions from roles or check whether or not a function might be executed. All such concerns are hidden, and taken care of in the IMAC service layer. This not only limits the amount of code to be written, but also frees the minds of programmers of IMAC concerns, allowing them to keep their attention focused on the actual business service to be programmed.

The demo shows that it is possible to share the same IMAC functionality in contexts that did not use to do this before. The reason for this is that instead of implementing IMAC for a particular context using the context's particular vocabulary and views, we have abstracted from use-cases of multiple contexts, and created rules that describe all of them. Then, obviously, a service layer implementing such rules is useful for every such context.

Showing the demo in workshops with business architects puts the message across that if identity situations similar to Arabic marketplaces are to be avoided, cross-domain IMAC issues are to be considered as a coherent set of issues rather than individual sets of concerns. Also, the demo helps discussions to stay much more focused on what the business wants rather than on technicalities such as the systems or standards to use for implementation.

6   Conclusions and future work

Abstracting from multiple use-cases in multiple business contexts, we have derived a set of formal Identity Management and Access Control (IMAC) rules, from which we have generated IMAC service layer software that enforces these rules. We have built a demonstrator on top of this, consisting of multiple applications and simulated portals that are provably compliant with these IMAC rules. We have found that the short turnaround time for building a demo for a set of rules is an invaluable instrument for fine tuning of the IMAC rule set. We also found that the final demonstrator helps the business to focus on the real IMAC issues (rather than on technicalities), putting them in a position to commit to such rules. This work shows that it is practically feasible to reconcile different business needs in such a way that a single set of automatable services can do the job, which is what is not only needed for IMAC within large businesses, but also for Identity management over multiple countries.

Future research will work towards IMAC rule sets that address other issues such as privacy, token management and claim based access control. Also, further work needs to be done to address interoperability issues across businesses, in particular where businesses have decided to use different rules, or are forced to use different rules, as is the case within multinationals or intergovernmental interoperability. Another focus will be on making the relation explicit with areas such as process architecture and/or commercial products. Additional research is required to professionalize the tools we have been working with, in an attempt to provide all necessary artifacts that state-of-the-art software factories need to produce commercial products.

7   Acknowledgement

The work presented here has partly been carried out in the collaborative project PNP2008 [14], which is supported by the Freeband Communication technology program of the Dutch Ministry of Economic Affairs.

References

1. Kruit, M.: Role Based Access Control bij ABN AMRO - Een lange en heuvelachtige weg. In: Identity 2006, IIR (October 2006)
2. Wijnschenk, A., Willigenburg, S., van Andel, K.: Implementatie bij AEGON NL. In: Identity 2006, IIR (October 2006)
3. Kotteman, D.: Access control, role based? In: Identity 2006, IIR (October 2006)
4. Bus, R.A.: Role based access control implementation strategy. In: Identity 2006, IIR (October 2006)

5. van den Branden, E.: Identity 2006. In: Identity 2006, IIR (October 2006)
6. Gebel, G.: The importance of role management for compliance and user provisioning. In: Identity 2006, IIR (October 2006)
7. OMG: Semantics of business vocabulary and business rules specification (2006)
8. Joosten, S., Joosten, R.: Specifying business processes by means of rules. In: Proceedings European Business Rules Conference, Amsterdam (June 2005)
9. United States Code: Sarbanes-Oxley Act of 2002, HR 3763, PL 107-204, 116 Stat 745. Codified in sections 11, 15, 18, 28, and 29 USC (2002)
10. American National Standards Institute: ANSI INCITS 359-2004 for information technology - role based access control (2004)
11. Joosten, R., Beute, B.: Requirements for personal network security architecture specifications - PNP2008 D2.4. Technical report, Freeband PNP2008 (april 2005)
12. Joosten, R.: RBAC Specification for Personal Networks - PNP2008 D2.5. Technical report, Freeband PNP2008 (October 2005)
13. Höhn, S., Jürjens, J.: Automated checking of SAP security permissions. In: 6th Working Conference on Integrity and Internal Control in Information Systems (IICIS), Lausanne, Switzerland (Nov. 13–14 2003)
14. Freeband PNP2008 project: http://pnp2008.freeband.nl (2005)

Privacy-friendly Identity Management in eGovernment

Xavier Huysmans

K.U.Leuven ICRI, Sint-Michielsstraat 6 B-3000 Leuven - Belgium
`xavier.huysmans@law.kuleuven.be`

Abstract. This paper starts from the empirical finding that privacy principles are not rated very high in current eGovernment architectures. This is problematic because it leads to a substantial *privacy erosion* and undermines the existing power relations between a government and its citizens with regard to a particularly valuable asset: *personal data*. Precisely because of these power relations, there are very few incentives for government managers to implement Privacy-Enhanced Identity Management Systems *on a large scale* in an eGovernment architecture. Hereafter we introduce a less far-going alternative to Privacy-Enhanced Identity Management in eGovernment: "Privacy-Friendly Identity Management". We conclude with a brief analysis of one important driver for government managers to choose for Privacy-Friendly Identity Management: *risk management*.

1 Introduction

A recent field study performed in assignment of the Danish government on the usage of privacy enhancing technologies shows that across Europe, today's governmental processes only include limited **privacy protecting functionality** [19]. Also, where governmental processes are re-engineered to eGovernment services, these new developments seem to follow this trend by not rating **privacy principles** high in the basic architecture design.

In the article "Implications of profiling practices on democracy and rule of law" by [10] we read that **personal data** plays a very important role in regulating the power balances between the citizen and his/her government. Finally, as we will see below, **personal data** is a strategic resource for eGovernment.

If we tie these 3 elements together it is not unreasonable to state that a *potential* large scale usage, aggregation, exchange, data mining,... of personal data in eGovernment *may* have a negative impact on the power balances between the citizen and the State and result in privacy erosion. Several scenarios can be imagined to tackle this privacy erosion varying from blunt acceptance ("you have zero privacy, get over it")[1]

---

[1]Famous words spoken by SUN's CEO Scott McNealy in Jan 1999 (http://www.wired.com/politics/law/news/1999/01/17538) They illustrate an interesting approach to deal with the mentioned erosion that focuses on transparency and

Please use the following format when citing this chapter:

Huysmans, X., 2008, in IFIP International Federation for Information Processing, Volume 262; The Future of Identity in the Information Society; Simone Fischer-Hübner, Penny Duquenoy, Albin Zuccato, Leonardo Martucci; (Boston: Springer), pp. 245–258.

As Mr. Lessig explained in his book "Code version 2.0", *code* can be used to implement privacy features [4].

Current research on the topic of identity management and privacy, such as the EU funded PRIME project[2]

In this paper we explain that this might be a tad too much for eGovernment, because (1) privacy is not an absolute right, (2) the existence of competing interests in eGovernment and (3) of the general lack of incentives for governments to restrain their technical capabilities on the personal data they are processing.

The underlying idea (which is not further developed in this paper[3]

Before that, we first explain what eGovernment, identity management and privacy / data protection in IDM for eGovernment is about (sections 2, 3 and 4) and clarify the terms *FIDIS type 1* and *type 3*).

In the European research project FIDIS, researchers came to the conclusion that there are three main types of IDM systems, namely:

- the ones used for account management (FIDIS type 1), in which case we can speak of an assigned identity.
- the ones used for profiling of user data (FIDIS type 2) and
- the ones used for user-controlled context-dependent role and pseudonym management (FIDIS type 3).

---

accountability: don't put too much energy in keeping your personal information unknown to the world – make sure instead that you can verify what is being done with it (transparency) and hold people accountable if needed. See [17], to legal constructs (e.g., qualifying privacy as a sort of intellectual property right which can be negotiated and traded) and technical measures. It is this third approach we are writing about here.

[2]PRIME develops a *privacy enhancing identity management system* (PE-IMS), which means that via the PRIME tools, the user is empowered to decide on the release of data and on the degree of linkage to his or her personal data within the boundaries of legal regulations. More information on the PRIME project can be found at http://www.prime-project.eu, usually suggests to implement code in the identity management (IDM) architecture in a *privacy enhancing* way, which means that the IDM architecture is (1) user centric and (2) focuses on context-dependent role and pseudonym management.

[3]It is work being done in Work Package 16 of the EU funded Network of Excellence, FIDIS (http://www.fidis.net) is that it is possible to outline and fully describe the requirements of:

- an organizational IDM system (FIDIS type 1)[4]
- that especially addresses the interest of natural persons to control, or at least significantly influence the processing of data about him/her-self, and
- incorporates at least some degree of privacy and data protection requirements in the basic IDM architecture design.

We've provisionally called this a "privacy-friendly" IDM system. In section 5 of the paper we further explore the reasons why government managers should implement privacy-friendly IDM systems in their basic eGovernment architecture design.

These three types have been consolidated in the FIDIS academic community and accepted as a final deliverable by the European Commission (FIDIS deliverable 3.1 referenced below).

2   eGovernment

There are probably as many definitions of the term eGovernment as there are people working in that field. The definition used in Belgian federal eGovernment runs as follows:

"eGovernment is the continuous *optimization of service delivery and governance* by transforming internal and external relationships through technology, internet and new media" [8]. This optimization relies on a number of important principles. We only mention the two most important ones here.[5].

The first principle is that information shall be treated as a *strategic resource for all government activities*. On the Belgian Federal level this means, for instance, that information [8]:

- shall be modelled in a flexible way that maximally takes into accounts the users' needs.
- should be managed efficiently during its whole life-cycle. This means, inter alia, that information should be collected only once and maximally reused. In addition, a functional task division should be agreed on, to know which government entity *stores which data in authentic form*.
- information should be exchanged electronically where possible, based on a functional and technical interoperability framework and on the usage of common identification keys for all relevant entities.
- information should be processed in accordance with privacy and data protection regulation, and, more in general, be consistent and properly embedded in the law.

The main idea behind the mentioned *authentic storage of data*, is that government bodies should not collect the same information repeatedly from citizens or companies: The relevant data is collected only once and than verified, validated, stored and updated when needed.

From then on, other entities are supposed to request the information they need from these data repositories only. The government entities that are responsible to maintain these data repositories, commonly called "authentic sources", are "data managers". Data managers shall only communicate authentic data to the thereto authorized entities.

---

[5]Our description is mainly based on [8, 2], the federal portal (http://www.belgium.be) on the page 'about eGovernment' [14, 9]

If the data maintained in the authentic source is personal data (i.e. any information relating to an identified or identifiable natural person[6]), their disclosure is strictly limited due to privacy and/or data protection requirements.

A second important principle is the *integration of back-offices*. The term refers to the idea that government services are delivered in two phases. First the intake of the basic data for the service delivery, and a first part of the service delivery by the front-office (e.g., a government website), and then the completion of the service by the back-office [2].

The back-office evaluates if the client[7] is entitled to get the service or not, verifies the data received from the client at other entities, and/or communicates them to other entities. A large part of the service process is not visible by the client and should not necessarily be performed by the same government entity.

It can be performed by several departments of several administrations from different government levels, working together in some form of cooperation structure [2]. The result of the service process is presented to the client via one or more front-offices.

From a technical perspective the integration of back-offices is typically looked for through a (cross-border) *"Service Oriented Architecture"* (SOA).

In practice, identity management components (such as authentication services) are often integrated as basic service components of such a SOA in eGovernment. These services are then compiled with other services to so-called value-added services [15].

3   Identity Management in eGovernment

Identity Management (IDM) is the definition, designation and administration of identity attributes as well as the administration of the choice of the partial identity to be (re-) used in a specific context, to manage the access to and the usage of online applications, services and resources [18, 12][8].

It includes the management of identity attributes by their owners (user-side IDM) and/or by those parties with whom the owners interact (services-side IDM). The infrastructure used for the definition, designation and administration of these identity attributes is the identity management system.

There are several strong drivers to implement Identity Management (IDM) in eGovernment, such as, for instance:

---

[6]Art. 1 Directive 95/46/EC of the European Parliament and of the Council of 24 Oct 1995 on the protection of individuals with regard to the processing of personal data on the free movement of such data, Official Journal of the European Communities, L 281, 23 Nov 1995, 31-50.

[7]As explained in section 3.1 of FIDIS deliverable 5.4 (in press), the notion to see a citizen as a client of the "business of government" was introduced a few decades ago. It is strongly present in current Belgian eGovernment, where citizens and enterprises are being treated as government's clients (see for example the used terminology on the federal portal (www.belgium.be) (in the section "about eGovernment")).

[8]Definition from Wikipedia, available at: http://en.wikipedia.org/wiki/Identity_management.

- a reduction of the cost of the organization's system (e.g., optimization of user management via account creation),
- an increased efficiency, transparency and effectiveness of the organization's activity,
- an improvement of the functionality or experience (e.g., via single sign on), and
- a reduction of the operational risk of the organization's activity.

There are also a number of good reasons for not implementing IDM systems in eGovernment. IDM systems rely on input from many different areas and levels both within, across and potentially from outside the organization. Their implementation is not an easy task. In addition, it is also clear that the usage of IDM systems creates additional risks (for example because of the cross-context exchange of personal data, which implies additional data protection and privacy risks and the additional exposure to security risks).

Depending on the goals of the eGovernment project, it is usually good to start with a risk assessment of the organization's activity. Such an assessment starts with the evaluation of the need for identity management mechanisms to protect information, applications and the infrastructure of the organization.

These mechanisms can be understood in terms of a lifecycle: (1) create an identity of an entity, (2) authenticate the identity, (3) grant the appropriate permissions to that entity, (4) monitor and incorporate accountability mechanisms, and finally (5) audit and assess the IDM processes [16].

In order to perform this lifecycle, we typically need the following components of an IDM system:

- registration,
- identification,
- authentication,
- authorization and access control,
- user management,
- accountability,
- audit, and
- data storage and communication.

Not all IDM systems contain all these components. It is also important to realize that, since they are all part of the mentioned lifecycle, they are also strongly interconnected.

In sum, we can conclude that in eGovernment identity management is an integral part of the general data management architecture of a SOA where identity management mechanisms help:

- to manage risks (e.g., operational risks related to unauthorized disclosure of personal data etc.),
- to enhance trust and
- to provide more efficient, more secure and more effective services to the government's clients (citizens, businesses etc.).

4 Privacy and data protection in identity management for eGovernment

The implementation of IDM in eGovernment can, but does not necessarily take into account privacy and/or data protection requirements.

As mentioned in the introduction section, when governmental processes are being re-engineered to eGovernment services, *privacy principles are often not rated high in the basic architecture design.*

There are a number of good reasons why this is problematic, especially in eGovernment. One of them is that the usage of ICT in governmental processes creates new, substantial risks, which should be adequately answered *to maintain the power balance between the citizen and the state with regard to personal data.*

Indeed, one should not forget that the fundamental right to privacy[9] protects the fundamental political value of a *democratic constitutional state.*

This means that it guarantees individuals their freedom of self-determination, their right to be different and their autonomy to engage in relationships, their freedom of choice, their autonomy as regards for example - their sexuality, health, personality building, social appearance and behavior, and so on.

With other words, privacy guarantees each person's uniqueness, including alternative behavior and the resistance to power at a time when it clashes with other interests or with the public interest. It therefore plays an essential role in *regulating the power balance* between governments and their citizens in regard to a very important government' resource: information [10, 3, 2].

When privacy and data protection requirements are left out from the IDM architecture, the latter typically includes *user identification,* and data exchange is typically based on the common usage of *globally unique* identification keys.[10]

This creates important risks: when personal data from one context can be linked to personal data from another context (internal or external to the government sphere), it *can* result in detailed profiles about natural persons and a significant lack of privacy. Even though such interconnections can be unauthorized or illegal, it is not excluded that they will take place anyway.

The key question we have to ask ourselves is therefore whether – to protect the fundamental right to privacy and to make sure the European data protection principles are being respected – it suffices to rely on procedures to be applied by the administrative staff, if, at the other hand, massive data aggregation and

---

[9]which was codified, inter alia, in article 8 of the European Convention on Human Rights and article 22 of the Belgian Constitution

[10]This is for example the case in Belgium, where data exchange mainly relies on the usage of the National Registry Number of the person to whom the exchanged data relates. Since decades, a unique identifier is being assigned to Belgian citizens at their first registration in the National Registry. Since the advent of Belgian eGovernment, this identifier has become *globally* unique because it is now used to refer to that person *across several government contexts.* It is thus not limited to one or more particular spheres of government' activity. Other "relevant" entities (such as enterprises, foreigners etc.) hold a similar, globally unique identifier.

linkage of databases is at least being facilitated through the unrestrained usage of ICT in eGovernment.

We believe the answer is no. We are convinced that if a substantial erosion of privacy is made possible through eGovernment, governments must take all necessary countermeasures, including technical ones. We will come back to this below.

As mentioned supra, several approaches to counter such a privacy erosion can be imagined. Research on the topic of privacy and identity management often suggests to tackle privacy erosion through a translation of privacy and/or data protection rules into code (cf. ideas by L. Lessig) [4].

Yet, research that aims at incorporating privacy and data protection rules in the IDM architecture also usually focuses on *maximum privacy*. The enhancement from a privacy perspective is mainly based on the notion that the protection can and should be put in the hands of the person the user trusts most: *himself*.

A privacy-enhancing application design therefore supports both "user-controlled data release" as well as "user-controlled data linkage" [13].[11]

Discussions we've had with government managers so far seem to indicate that this type of privacy enhancements may be over-ambitious for eGovernment. They do not see enough incentives to implement such an IDM system *on a large scale* for systematic exchange of personal data in eGovernment.

This is understandable to some extent, because privacy is not an absolute fundamental right: not one single aspect of privacy takes absolute precedence over other rights and interests. Never does an individual have absolute control over an aspect of his/her privacy.[12]

Privacy can thus be restricted when balanced against other interests (rights of others, law enforcement, public health, etc.) and under a number of conditions

---

[11]This 29th edition of this terminology paper makes an explicit distinction between user centric privacy enhancing identity management, and (general) privacy enhancing identity management. Contrary to the above mentioned PRIME project, the latter does not include user centricity as such. It focuses on unlinkability as a privacy enhancing technology. In Prof. Pfitzmann and Mrs. Hansens's view, a Privacy-Enhancing IDM system can therefore be defined as an IDM system that, given the restrictions of a set of applications, sufficiently preserves unlinkability (as seen by an attacker) between the partial identities and corresponding pseudonyms of an individual [13]. Although we can in principal agree to take user centricity out of the definition of (general) PE-IDM, it would lead us too far to further go into detail on these terms here. More information on that topic, however, can be found in the deliverables of WP16 of the FIDIS project.

[12]This is nicely illustrated by the fact that the European Court of Human Rights (ECHR) recognizes different sorts of human rights. The ECHR recognizes some so called 'hard core' or absolute rights that must be respected even in times of emergency when derogations to other rights are justified (article 15 2 ECHR). Next to this there are 'normal rights' (e.g., article 5 and 6 ECHR) which can be derogated from in times of emergency (article 15 1). Finally the ECHR counts four rights which can be legitimately restricted in terms of emergency but also under some specified conditions (article 8-11 ECHR, the conditions for permissible restrictions are listed in the second paragraphs of these Articles). Privacy is one of these 'restrictable rights'. See [10].

(such as, the legality of the restriction, the link with a pressing social need and the proportionality between the restriction and these needs) [6].

Tasks government entities carry out in the public interest undoubtedly justify to some extent limitations of the right to privacy and the foreseen exceptions of the general data protection rules.

It is self-evident that these exceptions and limitations also effect the privacy components of a data and identity management architecture used in eGovernment. Concretely, this means that a privacy-enhanced (or maximised) identity management architecture which implements *user-controlled context-dependent role and pseudonym management* will often not be a realistic option in eGovernment, where privacy coexists with a number of strong other interests and exceptions.

This does not mean, however, that there is no alternative available. The underlying idea – which is not further developed here – is that there are indeed less far-going ways to increase privacy and data protection through code in eGovernment. The research objective is obviously not to be only compliant with privacy and data protection regulation, but where possible also to go one or more steps beyond and thereby re-equilibrate the power balance between the citizen and the State.

Explained in terms of the types of IDM systems set out in deliverable 3.1 of the FIDIS project [5], we believe there is concrete research to be done in investigating privacy enhancements of a type 1 IDM system (i.e., services-side and used inter alia for accounting and user management) in eGovernment instead of putting the focus on a type 3 IDM system.[13]

5   Why privacy friendly IDM in the basic architecture used in eGovernment?

Even though there might be a lack of drivers to implement a IDM system that focuses on maximum privacy on a large scale in eGovernment (PE-IMS, as described above), there are very good reasons to incorporate at least some degree of privacy and data protection requirements in the basic data architecture design used in eGovernment. These drivers are, for example:

- the reduction of the operational risk of the organization's activity due to data protection and privacy requirements,
- an increased trust in the eGovernment project, since users get more transparency and a way to enforce their privacy and data protection rights,
- the auditability of compliance with the regulation and/or authorizations received to exchange a particular set of data.

We believe these and other drivers need to be made explicit via research, to be convincing enough for government managers to change some of their priorities on privacy and data protection in eGovernment.

---

[13]FIDIS type 3 IDM systems typically include user-controlled context-dependent role and pseudonym management.

For the limited purposes of this paper, we believe it is useful to say a few words on the first driver we've pointed out: *risk management.*

Risk is a well-known concept in the industry, but is less known in a government context. It can be defined as the likelihood that an unwanted incident will occur and the impact that could result from the incident [21]. Its basic principles can be summarized as follows:[21, 11].

- Both businesses and governments have to achieve well-known objectives, within a well-known context of acceptable risk.
- Sustainable results can only be achieved when both industry and operational risks are being managed and thus kept under control.
- Industry risk refers to the risk inherent to the performed activities (e.g., the customer insolvency for a bank).
- Operational risk refers to the risks caused by inadequacy or failure in the day to day business (e.g., illness of the personnel, theft of goods, non-compliance with legislation etc.).

Organizations that manage their industry and operational risks assess what the loss might be if something goes wrong, and whether they can absorb that loss if it indeed goes wrong. These decisions are typically based on information provided by trusted third parties (audits etc.). Risk assessment is the process of identifying and evaluating such risks.[21, 11].

Managing risks thus leads to concrete actions, for example subscribing insurances, the provisioning of sufficient financial means or accepting risks and communicating these decisions to the stakeholders.

Operational risks very often result from legal or sector-specific obligations. For example, in the banking sector, banks are forced to provision a large part of the money they dispose of to contain the risk of bankruptcy. Other obligations for example arise from privacy and data protection regulation.

If we accept that the unrestrained usage of ICT in eGovernment at least potentially creates a substantial risk of privacy erosion for the persons to whom the data relates, this is an operational risk that needs to be identified, and which should result in a concrete *risk decision.*

A risk assessment of an eGovernment project could for example result in the decision to accept the risks related to a potential eGovernment "privacy-gate scandal" and the negative publicity, court cases, loss of electorate, burning decisions of the privacy commission etc. that goes with it.

We do not think it would be a wise decision to just accept that risk, because of the *objective liability provision* contained in the data protection regulation.

Before we go any further, we need to explain 3 legal rules:

1. *Objective risk liability:* Article 23 of the European Data Protection Directive, as transposed in article 15bis of the Belgian Data Protection Act[14] states

---

[14]Law of 8 December 1992 on Privacy Protection in relation to the Processing of Personal Data, Belgian State Gazette 18 Mar 1993, as modified by the law of 11 December 1998 implementing Directive 95/46/EC, Belgian State Gazette 3 Feb 1999, and the law of 26 Feb 2003, Belgian State Gazette 26 Jun 2003.

that *the data controller* – this is the entity that alone or jointly with others determines the goals and the means of the processing of personal data – *is in principle liable for the damages caused to the data subject as a result of a processing or any act that is not compatible with the Data Protection legislation.* He may only be exempted from this liability, if he proves that is not responsible for the event that gave rise to the damages. This is an exception to the normal liability rules, following which, to hold someone accountable, one has to prove the existence of a fault, damages and a causal link between them (art. 1382 of the Belgian Civil Code).

The mentioned data protection article is an "objective" risk liability provision, because there is no need to prove the fault of the data controller to hold him/her accountable for a certain action: the mere fact that he/she infringed the data protection law leads to liability, of course only if there is a causal link between the damages and this infringement of the law.

2. *Privacy in the data protection law:* Article 2 of the Belgian Data Protection law introduces a subjective right for natural persons to *respect for their private life* (read: privacy) *with regard to the processing of personal data that concern him / her.*

   Similarly, article 1 of the Data Protection Directive states that *Member States shall protect the fundamental rights and freedoms of natural persons, and in particular their right to privacy with respect to the processing of personal data.*[15].

   Concretely, based on this article, one can say that the obligation to respect the right to privacy is also applicable to data controllers. We will come back to this below.

3. *Obligation to take the appropriate technical and organizational measures:* Article 16 of the Belgian Data Protection Law and article 17.1 of the Data Protection Directive contain an obligation to take *appropriate technical and organizational measures* to protect the processed personal data against:
   - accidental or unlawful destruction or accidental loss, alteration, unauthorized disclosure or access, in particular where the processing involves the transmission of data over a network, and
   - *against all other unlawful forms of processing.*

   Such measures shall ensure a level of security appropriate to the risks represented by the processing and the nature of the data to be protected, having regard to the *state of the art* and the cost of their implementation. The Belgian article further specifies to whom it applies (inter alia to data controllers) and foresees the possibility to explicate these obligations by means of a Royal Decree.

By jointly reading these 3 legal rules, it becomes clear that, (1) if we accept the fact that the unrestrained ICT usage in eGovernment at least potentially

---

[15]The main difference between both texts is that only the Belgian article creates a concrete (subjective) right for natural persons which is usable in court to tackle infringements committed by other natural persons. This is the so-called horizontal action of the right to privacy. Both texts apply, however, also to vertical relations between governments and the natural persons that fall under their jurisdiction.

creates a substantial risk of privacy erosion for the persons to whom the data relates and (2) if a government wants to avoid the mentioned liability risk, all adequate organizational and technical measures should be taken to avoid unlawful forms of data processing, which also means having respect for the privacy regulation mentioned in section 4 (second bullet point).

Also, as explained in the third bullet point, the "adequateness" of such measures is evaluated by having regard to the state of the art. The latter could, *given the maturity of the research on privacy and identity management*, refer to the incorporation of at least some degree of privacy and data protection in the basic eGovernment architecture design.

If an eGovernment architecture does not take such privacy enhancing measures into account, one should realize that – in case something happens –, data controllers or entities acting on their behalf can be held accountable, *even without a concrete or proven fault*, if it appears that the eGovernment architecture was not adequate to protect the personal data at stake.

Whether a concrete IDM architecture is adequate or not is easy to evaluate. Nevertheless, it is clear that the usage of privacy enhancing *technologies* are increasingly being perceived – also on the political level – as a suitable way to enhance the level of privacy and data protection in an organization's activity.[16]

In sum, to answer the question asked before, namely whether it suffices to rely on procedures to be applied by the administrative staff, if, at the other hand, massive data aggregation and linkage of databases is at least being facilitated through the unrestrained usage of ICT in eGovernment.

We believe the answer is NO, because it becomes more and more likely that Privacy Enhancing Technologies are necessary to comply with the above mentioned obligation to take all appropriate technical and organizational security measures.

6   Conclusion

The starting point of this paper was the establishment of two facts: first, that the unrestrained usage of ICT in eGovernment creates a substantial privacy erosion and second, that privacy principles are often not rated very high in a basic eGovernment architecture design.

The question we asked ourselves is whether – to protect the fundamental right to privacy and to make sure the European data protection principles are being respected – it suffices to rely on procedures to be applied by the administrative staff, if, at the other hand, massive data aggregation and linkage of databases is

---

[16]See for instance, the recent communication of the European Commission on the Promoting Data Protection by Privacy Enhancing Technologies (PETs) on this topic: *"To pursue the objective of enhancing the level of privacy and data protection in the Community, the Commission intends to clearly identify the need and technological requirements of PETs and further promote the development of these technologies [...] and their use by industry and public authorities, involving a vast array of actors, including its own services, national authorities, industry and consumers."*[17]

at least being facilitated through the unrestrained usage of ICT in eGovernment. The goal of this paper is to explain why we believe this is not the case.

After a general introduction on eGovernment and identity management (sections 2 and 3), we explained that there are several approaches to tackle this privacy erosion and that research on privacy and identity management that wants to implement privacy and data protection *via code*, usually focuses on *maximum privacy*. This means that it usually includes *user-controlled data release and user-controlled data linkage via context-dependent role and pseudonym management*.

We explained that this might be a tad too much for eGovernment, because (1) privacy is not an absolute right, (2) there are a number of valid, competing interests in eGovernment and (3) there seem to be a general lack of drivers for governments to restrain from technical capabilities on the personal data they are processing.

We suggested to follow another approach to implement privacy and data protection requirements in the basic eGovernment architecture design. We made clear that there is concrete research to be done in investigating privacy enhancements of an organizational IDM system (i.e., services-side and used inter alia for accounting and user management, also called FIDIS type 1) in eGovernment.

The Privacy enhancements as such were not described in the paper. We only pointed out that such enhancements would probably have to (1) especially address the interest of natural persons to control, or at least significantly influence the processing of data about him/her-self, and (2) integrate at least some degree of privacy and data protection requirements in the basic IDM architecture design.

In the last section of the paper we identified a number of reasons to choose for a so-called "privacy-friendly identity management system" which does exactly that. One of these reasons is *operational risk management*.

We've explained that – from a risk management perspective – the obligation to take *adequate* organizational and technical measures is a strong driver to implement a "privacy-friendly IDM system".

Indeed, the adequateness of such measures is, inter alia, evaluated by taking into account the state of the art. The latter could, given the maturity of the research on privacy and identity management, refer to the incorporation of at least some degree of privacy and data protection in the basic eGovernment architecture.

In our view, it would therefore definitely be a too large risk to take, to only rely on procedures to be applied by the administrative staff to protect privacy and to make sure the European data protection principles are being respected in eGovernment.

References

1. Boutonnet M. Le Principe de Prcaution en Droit de la Responsabilit Civile, Librairie Gnrale de Droit et de Jurisprudence, Paris, 2005.

2. De Bot D. Privacybescherming bij e-government in België – Een kritische analyse van het Rijksregister, de Kruispuntbank van Ondernemingen en de elektronische identiteitskaart. Vandenbroele, Brugge, 2005.
3. De Bot D. Verwerking van persoonsgegevens, Kluwer, Antwerpen, 2001.
4. Lessig L.Code version 2.0. Basic Books, New York, 2006.
5. Bauer M., Meints M., and Hansen M. Fidis Deliverable 3.1., Available at: http://www.fidis.net 15 Sep 2005, last visited: 20 Aug 2006
6. Buchta A., Dumortier J., and Krasemann H. The Legal and Regulatory Framework for PRIME, in FISHER-HUEBNER S, ANDERSSON CH and HOLLEBOOM TH (eds.), PRIME D 14.1.a: Framework V1, Available at: https://www.prime-project.eu/prime_products/reports/fmwk/pub_del_D14.1.a_ec_wp14.1_V4_final.pdf, 13 Jun 2005, last visited: 13 Jun 2005.
7. De Hert P. Titel II De Wet 8 Dec 1992 met betrekking tot de verwerking van persoonsgegevens, Apr 2005, in P. DE HERT (ed.), Privacy en Persoonsgegevens, Politeia, Brussels, 2005.
8. Deprest J. and Robben F. eGovernment: the approach of the Belgian federal administration. Available at: http://www.ksz.fgov.be, Jun 2003, last visited: 20 Jun 2006
9. Deprest J. and Strickx P. eGovernment initiatives. Available at: $http://www.ibbt.be/egov/pres/9._{JAN}Deprest_2005.10.26-e Gov_update_initiatieven.ppt$, 26 Oct 2005, last visited: 20 Sept 2006
10. Hildebrandt M., Gutwirth S., and De Hert P. Fidis Deliverable 7.4, Implications of profiling practices on democracy and rule of law, Available at: http://www.fidis.net, 5 Sep 2005, last visited: 15 Sep 2006.
11. Huyghens C.H. IDM in the risk universe, liability, methodology, standards, Available at: https://projects.ibbt.be/idem/uploads/media/2005.12.20.idem.workshop1.risk.pdf, 20 Dec 2005. last visited: 20 Dec 2005.
12. Leenes R. and Fischer-Huebner, S. PRIME Framework version 2. Available at: http://www.prime-project.eu, Jul 2006, last visited: 23 Aug 2006
13. Pfitzmann A. and Hansen M. Anonymity, Unlinkability, Unobservability, Pseudonymity, and Identity Management - A Consolidated Proposal for Terminology. Version 0.29. Available at: http://dud.inf.tu-dresden.de, Jul 2007, last visited: 31 Jul 2007
14. Robben F. eGovernment, presentation available at: http://www.law.kuleuven.be/icri/frobben/presentations/20060327b.ppt, 27 Mar 2006, last visited: 1 Apr 2006.
15. Robben F. E-government in the Belgian social sector coordinated by the Crossroads Bank for Social Security, presentation available at: http://www.law.kuleuven.be/icri/frobben/presentations/20060623nl.ppt, 23 Jun 2006, last visited: 22 Mar 2007.
16. Slone S. Identity Management. A white paper. Available at: http://www.opengroup.org, Mar 2004, last visited: 11 Nov 2004
17. Weitzner D, et al. Transparency and End-to-End Accountability: Requirements for Web Privacy Policy Languages', A position paper for the W3C Workshop on Languages for Privacy Policy Negotiation and Semantics-Driven Enforcement, available at: http://www.w3.org/2006/07/privacy-ws/papers/, Oct 2006, last visited: 17 Oct 2006.
18. Identity Management Systems (IMS). Identification and Comparison Study', Available at: http://www.datenschutzzentrum.de, Sep 2003, last visited: 7 Jul 2005

19. Report   on   Privacy   Enhancing   Technologies,   performed   for
    the   Danish   Ministry   of   Science   and   Innovation.   Available   at:
    http://www.vtu.dk/fsk/ITC/Rapportvedrprivacyenhancingtechlologies.pdf,
    28 Mar 2005, last visited: 15 Oct 2005
20. Modinis   IDM   Terminology   Paper,   Available   at:
    https://www.cosic.esat.kuleuven.be/modinis-idm/, 23 Nov 2005, last visited: 22
    December 2005
21. IDA Authentication Policy. Basic policy for establishing the appropriate au-
    thentication mechanisms in sectoral networks and projects, Available at:
    http://ec.europa.eu/idabc/servlets/Doc?id=19281, Jul 2004, last visited: 20 Oct
    2006.

Generic Predefined Privacy Preferences for Online Applications

Mike Bergmann

Technische Universität Dresden, Germany

Abstract. Every day users disclose various kinds of personal data using the Internet for daily activities. The disclosed data in summary may draw a perfect picture of them. Up to now it is difficult for end users to decide what to disclose and what to hide. We try to support the user in this task and propose a limited set of applicable predefined privacy preferences taking privacy principles into account. We will apply these preferences for typical online activities to evaluate and to enhance them. We elaborate the dependencies and correlations between the privacy preferences and application scenarios. As a final result and based on the proposed privacy preferences we introduce a privacy-enhancing data disclosure splitting guiding the user step by step through the process of data disclosure.

1   Introduction

Nowadays electronic communication and electronic business get more and more established. Every day users disclose personal data using the Internet for daily activities like checking timetables of public transport, doing shopping, using translation services, etc.

In the offline world, for instance, paying with cash in a shop, where the cashier does not know you, would allow you to anonymously buy goods and services. In the online world, submitting various personal data items like the item of interest, the payment and shipping information may allow to trace and to link the user's activities and may reveal user's privy preferences. Shopping becomes a privacy issue.

To enforce the right of informational self–determination in the digital world, it seems necessary to enable the user to control data disclosure and also the circumstances of the disclosure. The privacy principle of data minimization, i.e. the avoidance of the data disclosure and minimisation of the amount of data to be disclosed as a method to lower the probability of data misuse, becomes important. Privacy policies, stated by the service providers and communicated to and negotiated with the users, are introduced to express these needs and to formalize online business processes.

In the next section, we list related work relevant for our research interest. In section 3, we develop a predefined set of privacy preferences for online transactions based on today's legal and user requirements. Further on in section 4, we discuss the application of the proposed privacy preferences for typical online applications. We complement this by user interviews. We split the complex

Please use the following format when citing this chapter:

Bergmann, M., 2008, in IFIP International Federation for Information Processing, Volume 262; The Future of Identity in the Information Society; Simone Fischer-Hübner, Penny Duquenoy, Albin Zuccato, Leonardo Martucci; (Boston: Springer), pp. 259–273.

e–business process into subtasks to provide some possibilities to implement the data minimization principles. Finally the sketched wizard approach in section 5 offers a privacy–enhanced data disclosure process with further potential for user interface simplification.

2   Related work

One of the established privacy policy standards is P3P [1]. It allows expressing privacy policies in a standardized form and allows user agent based policy analysis using P3P standard terminology. A very interesting HCI approach in this context is the implementation of P3P using the bird metaphor, the so called privacy bird[2]. However, as problems we have to mention the change of privacy policies afterwards without notice and the limited negotiation capabilities. After the development of P3P, many privacy-related policy languages have been proposed [3]. Also the World Wide Web Consortium continues its work in the privacy policy area and has recently established an Interest Group on Policy Languages as part of the Privacy Activity. This group is called PLING - Policy Languages Interest Group. Its objective is the discussion and coordination of policy languages and W3Cs metadata framework. This group "will primarily focus on policy languages that are already specified and broadly address the privacy, access control, and obligation management areas; it is not expected to engage in the design of new policy or rule languages. The Interest Group will work towards identifying obstacles to a joint deployment of such languages, and suggest requirements and technological enablers that may help overcome such obstacles." [4].

However, privacy enhancing technologies, based on complex concepts like these privacy policies, communication mixes, credentials, certificates and pseudonyms, are often not easily understood by users[5]. Additionally, a user normally has to deal with various email accounts, public/private key pairs, (cell-) phones and credit card numbers, GPS navigation devices etc. This increases the complexity, too.

In [6] were analysed the user's protection goals. Based on these goals a set of complex user interfaces is proposed to address these goals. In [7] an approach is sketched to further simplify the process of privacy policy selection by using a town map–like approach to create a relationship between different kinds of privacy preferences and their representations in the topology of a artificial town map. There are various other approaches, like the role concept at [8] and the already mentioned P3P policies [1] etc. The PRIME project[1] is presenting a slightly different approach, combining roles and policies [9]. However, the management of dedicated privacy preferences, assigned to dedicated activities, remains difficult.

---

[1] The PRIME project receives research funding from the European Community's Sixth Framework Program and the Swiss Federal Office for Education and Science. For further information see https://www.prime–project.eu/.

3   Introducing Predefined Privacy Preferences

It is a common understanding that privacy and usability can be antagonistic requirements in system design. Functional requirements are primary, usually as secondary we meet security requirement, and if generally present we meet privacy requirements behind these. Beside this, sometimes the legal privacy obligation to inform the user conflicts with the usability of the corresponding application.

For example it is not user-friendly if a system bothers the user with long explanations and never-ending terms and conditions and privacy policy documents enforcing acceptance by simply waiting until the user scrolled down the page finding the accept button at the very end of the page. However, privacy is a fundamental right of any individual in our democratic society and needs to be protected.

To assist the users to manage privacy it is important to define privacy relevant context properties on one hand and offering privacy preserving concepts, visible, perceptible and understandable by the user on the other hand. Article 6 of the EU Directive 95/46/EC [10] requires purpose binding and the necessity of data processing as significant factors to formulate a legally compliant services side privacy policy. We derive the following definitions:

Privacy policy describes the services side's official statement about the concrete data items being collected, their concrete purposes and the retention period, planned or potential data transfers possibly including further particulars. It may also contain information about the system in place to manage and protect the collected data.

As the corresponding counterpart to express client side privacy requirements we introduce the construct of privacy preferences and their instances:

Privacy preferences in summary represent the data release policy (i.e. the policy under which a user would release data) and privacy requirements a user expresses concerning possible interactions with others. They contain statements about the accepted amount of specified data items for dedicated purposes, contain conditions for transferring dedicated data items to other 3rd parties and contain statements on user-controlled linkability of different actions, i.e., for whom which user actions must, should or could be linkable or not linkable and the expected obligations and reputation[2] of the potential data receiver. The privacy preferences will be later on matched to the privacy policy of the prospective data receiver.

The privacy preferences and the privacy policy could be understood as a plug–socket system. The privacy preferences represent the plug, requiring dedicated assets, expressed by some dedicated pins (the preferences). If the privacy policy, the socket, has the corresponding holes, the plug fits. If the socket offers

---

[2] Obligations are e.g. the expected data retention period, secured connection, recurring audits etc. Reputation could be expressed e.g. as membership on a white list, owner of privacy seals, user experience, etc.

more additional holes (additional privacy pledges) the plug fits, too. There is no privacy conflict. But if the plug has more or other pins than the socket accepts, the system does not fit. We could see that as a privacy conflict.

Based on these definitions and with respect to the different kinds of applicable pseudonym types (transaction pseudonym, role–relationship pseudonym, role pseudonym resp. relationship pseudonym, person pseudonym [11]) now we construct privacy preferences, taking data protection law requirements, and in particular the data minimization principles, into account. We start with the most privacy friendly one and decrease the level of privacy protection in discrete steps. External definitions of what are the minimal data requirements for dedicated purposes (e.g. by data protection authorities) assist the user to follow the data minimization principles. The user selects parts of these general preferences and applies it to the concrete application case before starting the disclosure as the basis for the privacy policy negotiation. To make it even more comfortable we assemble a collection of four predefined privacy preferences:

(α) **No PII:** Personal Identifying Information (PII) are not released, transaction pseudonyms are used, i.e. user actions are linkable by the service provider only within a dedicated transaction. The user may decide afterwards to connect transaction pseudonyms to become linkable. Reading a weblog or editing a Wikipedia entry anonymously [12] (see also the blog scenario description in section 4) are examples where such privacy preference could be applied[3].

(β) **No PII, but linkable:** PII are not released. Transactions are linkable by the service provider using the provided (role–) relationship pseudonyms as defined in [11]. However the communication itself works pseudonymously. Data about personal preferences (and pseudonyms) might be released (which are not directly identifying the user). Prominent examples are web mailers, various news panels (see the email application scenario in section 4) etc. The more data becomes linkable, the more difficult it becomes for the user to remain not identifiable.

(γ) **Disclose only necessary PII:** Only PII to fulfil the purpose of primary service are released. No "sensitive" data should be disclosed[4]. Beyond that, a strict "no further transfer" policy should be applied to other recipients to avoid data leaking. To take the today's distributed service architectures[5] into account we extend it to "trusted[6]" communication partners with the user's explicit consent only. The communication becomes linkable. A well

---

[3] We assume the standard TCP/IP connection is anonymized, e.g. using JAP [13] and no other user identification (via cookies etc.) is possible.

[4] Sensitive in the meaning according to the definition of Art. 8 [10] and additionally according to the perception of the user. The personal data should contain a corresponding sensitivity flag that a user could apply.

[5] Distributed service architecture with dedicated partners for order fulfilment, goods delivery and payment processing.

[6] What "trusted" means for a user, has to be specify in the privacy preferences. It could be some personal reputation, the presence of privacy seals, trusted hardware

known example where these privacy preferences could be applied is to buy a book online (see the e–shopping application scenario in section 4).

(δ) **Disclose additional PII:** Personal data may be released also for additional services[7]. Data are released only to "trusted" communication partners according to the user's trust policy. Transfer to other recipients should be controlled (e.g. only with the user's explicit consent) or only transfer to "trusted" recipients. "Sensitive" data are excluded. An example is a participation in a customer care program to get bonus points or other benefits.

Table 1 shows the concrete privacy preferences. The first column is numbering the preferences. The second column contains a short description about the data that should be released, the third column states whether the user acts anonymously, pseudonymously or identifiably, the fourth column contains the data release policy applied to the data.

	PII	Relationship	Purpose and Transfer
α	no PII	anonymous	not applicable
β	no PII, but user name, password, further additional non–identifying personal data	pseudonymous	only for current purpose[8] and no transfer
γ	sufficient (but not sensitive) PII	pseudonymously or real identity	only for current purpose and strict no further transfer
δ	additional (but not sensitive) PII	pseudonymously or real identity	for additional purposes and strict no further transfer

Table 1. The predefined privacy preferences

In α and β, PII are not disclosed at all. However, personal data that are indirectly released, such as a collection of search strings, a click stream, some special personal preferences like favourite colour, interests etc. may lead to a significantly reduced anonymity set and therefore to an re–identification of the subject [14].

---

etc. A more simple approach could just trust all partners fulfilling the same or stricter privacy policies.

[7] Additional means the data are not necessary to fulfil the primary service intent, i.e. data are requested to offer additional services, like for marketing or advertisement, for suggesting related topics, collecting bonus points etc. This does not mean a full or uncontrolled data disclosure

[8] "Current purpose" is defined [1] as the usage for completion and support of activity for which data was provided; Information may be used by the service provider to complete the activity for which it was provided, whether a one-time activity such as returning the results from a Web search, forwarding an e–mail message, or placing an order; or a recurring activity such as providing a subscription service, or allowing access to an online address book or electronic wallet.

In the next section, we will instantiate the discussed privacy preferences in context to concrete applications to apply the proposed concrete privacy preferences and compare them to the services side privacy policies.

4   Applying the Predefined Privacy Preferences

Applying the four pre–defined privacy preferences we have to define suitable online applications. An internal PRIME privacy preferences survey [15] was performed to elaborate the current situation and to help finding these suitable online applications[9]. The survey confirmed the expectation that users percept Internet business scenarios as more privacy invasive as e.g. mobile phone applications or native desktop applications. The survey furthermore elaborated, which are the most popular online services in general and which are the usually required data items to disclose[10] for such services in particular.

According to the results of the study we selected the online applications, listed below, for our further elaboration. We have to mention that these examples are not covering the whole variety of online applications and not ordered yet. They do not exclude each other and may be combined. The user should be able to define the missing preferences based on our predefined privacy preferences.

e–shopping: Applicable for buying physical and digital goods. The amount of PII to disclose depends on the services, usually *reliable PII*[11] are required for shipping and billing purpose. e–shopping in general is used *pseudonymously, but identifiable*. The applied privacy policy limits PII usage to the stated *current purpose* with possible *transfer to associated 3rd parties*, applying the same privacy policy as for the service, to fulfil the business processes. Normal e–shopping accounts like accounts at Amazon or Apple iTunes are examples for this.

Social network: Applicable for social networks about music, photo, video sharing etc. There are *no PII* necessary, but is expected to increase the trustworthiness from the perspective of other peers. In general a *pseudonymous, non-identifying* account is used. The applied privacy policy is less strict compared to e–shopping. The data often are intentionally used for *additional purposes* too, like statistical, marketing etc. The data could be *transferred to associated 3rd parties*. Prominent examples are Skype, YouTube, MySpace, SecondLife etc.

Download: To download software (but also MP3 files, videos, pictures etc.) if payment is not mandatory. *No PII* are required, but often requested.

---

[9] 35 persons from various countries of the European Union took part in the survey. We are aware of the fact that this small number of participants in general, and the PRIME project members in particular are not representative for this kind of survey, but it holds as a starting point for further research.

[10] We analyse the concrete PII request only. Further content, released by the data subject, like the text itself in a blog for instance, is not taken into account.

[11] We could require certified PII, but this is less usual in the explored scenarios.

The data are therefore not sensitive and could be fictive (false name, e–mail, phone number etc.) Ideally an *anonymous* account is used. The privacy policy may have some additional marketing aspect included, consequently the purpose is extended to *marketing purpose* with possible *transfer to 3rd parties*.

Blog: Read, edit and create new comments in a news forum or blog. There is *no PII* identifying the user. The usage is performed under *pseudonym or even anonymously*. The applied privacy policy often states *further purposes* beside the current purpose and *allows transfer* to 3rd parties.

e–mail: Used to access so called free–mail or e–mail accounts to write e–mails, to configure the spam filter and to fill the address book. There are *no PII* required, but during usage the collectable data could become identifying, especially address data, contact information, personal interests and other[12]. The applied privacy policy allows *additional purposes and transfer* to associated 3rd parties. The released data could be *sensitive*[13]. Prominent examples are Yahoo or Google mail services for instance. Especially the "Google Mail" privacy policy [16] does not comply with our understanding of a user– and privacy–friendly data handling policy[14].

Membership: To get access to restricted resources like special web pages etc. *PII* is required. The access is provided *pseudonymously*, but based on the PII the user could be identified. The service privacy policy limits the PII usage to the *current purpose* with *no transfer* to 3rd parties. Examples are automotive and sports club membership etc.

Further: Application scenarios like *infrastructure, licensing, collaboration, news* are of less frequent usage and fit into one of the above mentioned scenarios. We do not list them here separately.

Application	PII usage and account requirements	Purpose	Transfer	coverd by
Download	no PII, anonymous	additional	to other parties	α
Blog	no PII, pseudonymous	additional	to other parties	β
e–mail	no PII, pseudonymous	additional	to trusted 3rd parties	β
Membership	PII, identifying	current	not allowed	γ
e–shopping	PII, identifying	current	to trusted 3rd parties	γ
Social network	PII, identifying	additional	to trusted 3rd parties	δ

Table 2. The application's typical privacy policies and the applied privacy preferences

---

[12] We assume that all content is encrypted so the content itself could not be read.

[13] Could be for instance information about health status, about membership in an alcoholism self–helping group etc.

[14] Besides this, the Google privacy policy bases on different legal grounds (US law instead of European law). But as the Google services are really widely distributed used and accepted we took such non–European application scenarios also into account.

Table 2 groups the selected example applications mentioned above. It shows the association of the predefined privacy preferences from section 3 with the privacy policies of the online applications. It shows that the predefined privacy preferences cover the sketched applications. However we made the following implicit assumptions about some of the parameters:

- Transfer of PII to 3rd parties, not applying the same privacy policy as the service (lets call it *suspicious party*), is excluded. This means, in case of an involvement of an strange party (e.g. by the presence on a black list or by simply being unknown to the user), the user has to decide about the relationship to the 3rd party. Doing so the user could either accept the new party (and thereby transfer the situation towards a valid predefined preferences application) or reject the service.
- As transfer to "any party" is not provided for, if PII is affected, we have to state that some services are not covered at all by the proposed privacy preferences. If the user releases PII to such services, like the Google e–mail service for instance, the privacy preferences settings do not fit [16].
- There is no pre–configuration for sensitive PII. In case sensitive PII is affected, the user has to decide it separately and manually to take the sensitivity into appropriate consideration. So we intentionally excluded it from the predefined privacy preferences. The same holds for other special service conditions and configurations.

In this section we elaborated the introduced predefined privacy preferences and associated them to privacy policies of typical online applications. We discussed the necessity of PII, the usual purpose binding and data transfer policy for each example. In the following section we will show, how the predefined privacy preferences (γ) can be applied in practice. Further on we discuss a further potential privacy enhancement by splitting data disclosure requests into their basic data disclosure elements. A concrete example implementation is given.

5   Predefined Privacy Preferences Implementation

A conventional e–shopping application contains various subtasks. Subtasks for instance are *Order, Payment* and *Shipping*. If there are further 3rd parties involved, more subtasks may be defined (address verification, certification, subcontracting etc.). To perform the shopping process, quite a lot of data are necessary. Applying the discussed "strict no further transfer" policy, as discussed in section 3, privacy preferences γ, service scenarios become impossible because of the need to transfer PII to 3rd parties to fulfil the service. To solve this contradiction we split the data disclosure into subtasks.

5.1   Privacy enhancing data disclosure splitting

Usually there is no need for the shop vendor to know the customer's address or payment information. If we split the business process into the three mentioned separate parts *Order, Payment* and *Shipping*, like shown in Table 3, every involved party gets the data needed. The separation of processes on the need-to-know basis for enhancing the users privacy has been proposed also in academic concepts (e.g., Chaum 1985 [17]; Pfitzmann/Waidner/Pfitzmann 1990/2000 [18]; Clauß/Köhntopp 2001 [19]) as well as in practical specifications such as the Secure Electronic Transaction standard (SET 1997 [20]) or as a use case in the Liberty Alliance project (Foll 2007 [21]), which is developing specifications for federated identities and identity-based Web services.

In Figure 1 we sketched a possible communication flow in case we split the data disclosure process as described. The subtasks are interconnected by each other by so called transaction IDs. Using different IDs for different subtasks we avoid an unintended linkability between the involved parties. The benefit of the split for the user is obvious. The data are only disclosed to the party related to the business and limited to the purpose for which the data was released and could be tailored for the very special business purpose. Also from the service provider's point of view it becomes much easier to be legally compliant – if less data are collected less data have to be protected etc. In our example very few personal details at all should be disclosed to the shop. Table 4 explains the details.   In

Ordering a book at www.bookstore.net:

Data	Communication Partner	Policy
Pseudonym (e.g. customer number), item of interest e.g. ISBN	Merchant/Service provider, for example www.bookstore.net	Only for "current" purpose, in our case selling a book; no further transfer, secure data storage not longer as legally required

Payment with credit card

Data	Communication Partner	Policy
Credit card number, expiry date, real name, amount of money	Payment service provider, for instance www.cash.eu	Only for "current" purpose, in this case payment; no further transfer, secure data storage not longer as legally required

Delivery of the good to a specified address

Data	Communication Partner	Policy
Address of the client and the (covered, hidden) good, i.e. the item of interest is not known	Shipping service provider, for instance www.ups.com	Only for "current" purpose, in our example to deliver the good; no further transfer, secure data storage not longer as legally required

Table 3. Business process splitting into subtasks

summary, splitting the business process into subtasks offers the benefit that only the minimal amount of data is released to all involved parties. Instead of sending all data to the shop (which then would have to transfer data to payment and shipping providers), the shop gets only to know the list of ordered items from the

Step	Description	Communication Details
1	The user makes the initial request to place an order. He sends an identifier of the resource to be ordered. In our case he requests a book using the ISBN Number.	the ISBN Number to address the resource.
2	The service provider informs the user about the access conditions for the resource. As far as the final cost may depend on other facts (like shipping in this example), first he informs about all possible shipping partners.	Transaction IDs ('A' and 'B') as the identifying handles; Description of the next step and further on a list of accepted third parties like DHL, UPS, FedEx etc.
3	The user contacts the shipping provider of his choice and requests a transport commitment token (credential).	Transaction ID 'A' to enable partners to link the process and the address details of the sender and recipient.
4	In this simplified version the shipping provider contacts the service provider directly using the address details to get additional parameters (like weight and size) to calculate the costs.	The shipping provider sends a parameter request using the Transaction ID 'A' for authentication and a list of required parameters.
5	The service provider sends the desired parameters back.	Transaction ID 'A' for linkability and list of concrete parameter details.
6	As we use a simplified version the shipping provider sends the token directly to the service provider. In a more privacy enhanced version the shipping provider may send the token to the user and the user forwards it to the service provider. A more general example may get the payment directly from the user; it just copies the payment steps, see below. The benefit is that the request (see step 2) could contain all necessary information (cost, size, weight etc.) and does not need further communication for parameter updates.	Transaction ID 'A' for authentication, the shipping credential (like an "e–Stamp" to certify and to prove the successful shipping arrangement) and the concrete costs for shipping.
7	Repeats step 2 with details about the payment procedure. The service provider provides additional payment parameters (the concrete costs) directly. Applying this to step 2 could make step 4 and 5 obsolete.	Transaction ID 'B' for assigning the payment to the transaction; Payment information and accepted payment partners.
8	The user contacts his payment provider to send a dedicated amount of money to the service provider.	Transaction ID 'B' for authentication; Details like Sender, Receiver of the payment and amount of money to pay.
9	The payment provider issues the corresponding credential (like a cheque) and send it to the service provider.	Transaction ID 'B' for authentication; Payment credential.
10	After the service provider received all necessary access tokens, in our case payment and shipping credentials, the physical good is shipped to/picked up by the shipping provider.	Transaction ID 'A' for linkability; the final delivery.

Step	Description	Communication Details
11	An order confirmation is sent to the user.	Transaction ID 'A' and 'B' for linkability.
12	The shipping company delivers the good. The payment provider should deliver the payment. This is not shown in this example.	Transaction ID 'A' for authentication and the delivery itself. The order process is finished.

Table 4. Communication Details for Figure 1

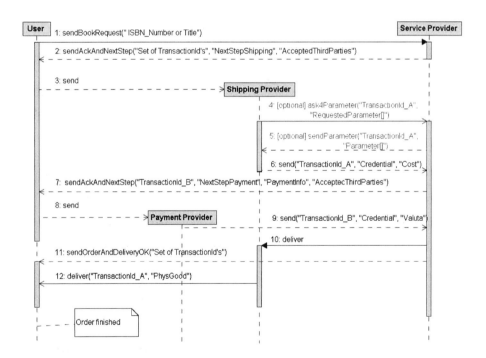

Fig. 1. A possible sequence diagram for our split scenario

user, while the shipping providers received the address data and the payment provider receives the payment details directly from the user. This implements the strict no-transfer policy that we have foreseen for the predefined privacy preference (see γ). It helps to increase the privacy in general and to fulfil the privacy principle of data minimization in particular.

5.2   The "Wizard–like" Approach

In the introduction we promised to structure identity management processes towards enhancing privacy and to simplify the user interactions regarding privacy and identity management at the same time. However in the previous section, we have split the action "buying a book" into tree different actions with different service providers (see Figure 1). At first glance it seems to contradict to the idea of simplification. We solve this issue by introducing a wizard–like approach assisting and guiding the user through the decision making process. The assistant presents a sequence of decision requests according to the privacy preferences of the end user to compile a finally instantiated privacy policy. A short pilot user test confirmed that users percept the splitting into subtasks as simplifying the process and increasing the transparency. Further user tests should examine this statement in more detail.

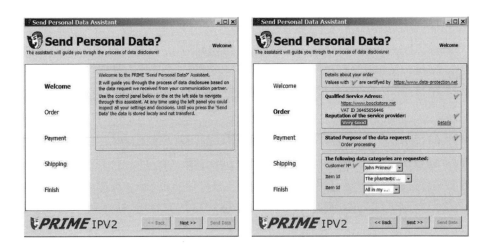

Fig. 2. An example "Send Personal Data" Assistant

As shown in Figure 2 the assistant informs the user about the overall procedure. It collects all the required PII, shows the dedicated purpose of the data request and allows to walk through the different stages to check the settings, made before. It possibly shows also available information about the service provider (e.g. seals or reputation data), about the requested certificates as well as the data handling policies and obligations. In our example the dialogue contains sections with the statements about data recipient, stated purposes and required personal data. The wizard in Figure 2 receives the dedicated data request provided by the service provider. Using the predefined privacy preferences here, offers the advantage that users do not have to define their preferences themselves from the scratch, but jut have to chose one of the predefined ones. It instantiates our privacy preferences (γ) for an e-shopping application could then warn the users if for instance more data is requested than needed for the specific service. Thanks to the predefined preferences it becomes easy to gather and maintain the user's privacy requirements even for users not primarily interested in privacy.

6   Conclusion

In this paper we provide a set of predefined privacy preferences, helpful for deriving applicable instances of dedicated privacy preferences for various online applications. The user could simply choose from these instead of defining privacy preference by hand repeatingly. By using the predefined preference the system could then warn the users if the service provider does not behave as predefined in the preferences.

Besides this, we proposed an approach for structuring privacy–related data disclosure processes in a more privacy–friendly way then before. The developed wizard-based UI approach is guiding the user through this process. The special focus to the strict "no transfer, only for the stated purpose" policy enhances the privacy of the user.

Further user acceptance tests will help to improve and fine–tune this approach. Additional tests to check whether the wizard approach really simplifies the data disclosure and privacy policy understanding will supplement the work.

7   Acknowledgment

Thanks to our colleagues for the helpful comments. Special thanks to the team of the Technische Universität Dresden, namely Andreas Pfitzmann, Sebastian Clauß and Thomas Kriegelstein, to Simone Fischer-Hübner and John Sören Pettersson from the Karlstad University, Sweden, to Lothar Fritsch from Johann–Wolfgang–Goethe–University Frankfurt/Main, to Marit Hansen and Jan Schallaböck from Unabhängiges Landeszentrum für Datenschutz Schleswig-Holstein, the PRIME–internal survey participants and all others contributors for the very helpful discussion.

References

1. W3C.   Platform for Privacy Preferences, April 2002.   Online available at http://www.w3.org/TR/P3P/.
2. L. Cranor. P3P: Making privacy policies more useful. *IEEE Security and Privacy*, pages 50–55, 2003.

3. Marit Hansen and Ammar Alkassar. A study on network protocols and privacy-aware communication. Technical report, FIDIS Deliverable D3.8, Frankfurt/Main, November 2007.

4. W3C Policy Language Interest Group. PLING Charter. available online at http://www.w3.org/Policy/2007/ig-charter.html.

5. A. Whitten and J.D. Tygar. Why Jonny Cant Encrypt: A Usability Evaluation of PGP 5.0. In *Proceedings of the Ninth USENIX Security Symposium*, 1999.

6. Gritta Wolf and Andreas Pfitzmann. Properties of protection goals and their integration into a user interface. In *Computer Networks: The International Journal of Computer and Telecommunications Networking*, volume Volume 32, pages 685–700, New York, NY, USA, May 2000. Computer Networks, Elsevier North-Holland, Inc.

7. Mike Bergmann, Martin Rost, and John Sören Pettersson. Exploring the feasibility of a spatial user interface paradigm for privacy-enhancing technology. In *Proceedings of the Fourteenth International Conference on Information Systems Development*, Karlstad, August 2005. Springer-Verlag.

8. Sebastian Clauß and Thomas Kriegelstein. Datenschutzfreunliches Identitätsmanagement. *DuD Datenschutz und Datensicherheit*, 27:297, 2003.

9. John Sören Pettersson, Simone Fischer-Hübner, Ninni Danielsson, Jenny Nilsson, Mike Bergmann, Sebastian Clauß, Thomas Kriegelstein, and Henry Krasemann. Making PRIME usable. In *Symposium on Usable Privacy and Security*, Carnegie Mellon University, Pittsburgh, PA, USA, July 2005. Carnegie Mellon University.

10. Council of Europe. Data Protection Directive 1995/46/EC of the European Parliament and of the Council of 24 October 1995 on the protection of individuals with regard to the processing of personal data and on the free movement of such data. Online available at http://eur-lex.europa.eu/LexUriServ/LexUriServ.do?uri=CELEX:31995L0046:EN:HTML.

11. Andreas Pfitzmann and Marit Hansen. Anonymity, unobservability, and pseudonymity - a proposal for terminology. In *Proceedings of WS on Design Issues in Anonymity and Unobservability*, Designing Privacy Enhancing Technologies, LNCS 2009, Proceedings of the Fourteenth International Conference on Information Systems Development, Heidelberg, August 2001. LNCS. Revised version 0.29 of July, 31st 2007; Anonymity, Unlinkability, Undetectability, Unobservability, Pseudonymity, and Identity Management - A Consolidated Proposal for Terminology; available at http://dud.inf.tu-dresden.de/Anon_Terminology.shtml.

12. Wikipedia. Help:Contents/Getting started – Wikipedia, The Free Encyclopedia, 2007. [Online accessed 19-May-2007] http://en.wikipedia.org/wiki/Help:Contents/Getting_started.

13. O. Berthold, H. Federrath, and M. Köhntopp. Project "Anonymity and Unobservability in the Internet". In *Proc. Workshop on Freedom and Privacy by Design / Conference on Freedom and Privacy 2000*, pages 57–65, Toronto/Canada, April 4-7 2000. ACM.

14. Michael Barbaro and Tom Zeller Jr. A face is exposed for AOL searcher No. 4417749. *New York Times Online*, August 2006. http://www.nytimes.com/2006/08/09/technology/09aol.html?ex=11754 00000&en=fd9b0c3b15c36970&ei=5070.

15. Mike Bergmann. PRIME internal privacy preferences survey about privacy concerns and conditions. In *Technical Report TUD-FI07-04-Mai 2007*, Technische Universität Dresden, Saxony, Germany, May 2007. Technische Universität Dresden. http://dud.inf.tu-dresden.de/~mb41/publications/TUD-FI07-04_Mai2007.pdf.

16. Google Inc. Google Mail Privacy Policy, 2007. Online; accessed 20-May-2007; http://mail.google.com/mail/help/intl/en-GB/privacy.html.
17. David Chaum. Security without identification: Transaction systems to make big brother obsolete. In *Communications of the ACM*, volume 28, No. 10, pages 1030–1044, October 1985.
18. Birgit Pfitzmann, Michael Waidner, and Andreas Pfitzmann. Rechtssicherheit trotz Anonymitt in offenen digitalen Systemen. *Datenschutz und Datensicherung DuD*, 14/5-6:243–253, 305–315, 1990. translated into English: Secure and Anonymous Electronic Commerce: Providing Legal Certainty in Open Digital Systems Without Compromising Anonymity, IBM Research Report RZ 3232 93278) 05/22/00, IBM Research Division, Zurich (May 2000).
19. Sebastian Clauß and Marit Köhntopp. Identity management and its support of multilateral security. *Computer Networks*, 37:205–219, 2001.
20. SET Secure Electronic Transaction LLC. The set standard specification, May 1997. originally at http://www.setco.org/set_specifications.html; now mirrored at http://www.cl.cam.ac.uk/research/security/resources/SET/.
21. Fulup Ar Foll. Liberty Alliance From Usecases to Specifications, Jan 2007.

Workshop: Legal Identity and Identification Aspects

Data Protection and the Use of Biometric Data in the EU

Annemarie Sprokkereef

Institute of Communications Studies (ICS) Leeds University UK
and Tilburg Institute for Law, Technology and Society (TILT),
Faculty of Law, Tilburg University: Warandelaan 2, 5000 LE Tilburg, NL
a.c.j.sprokkereef@uvt.nl

Abstract. This article is concerned with the legal approach to the regulation of biometrics in European policy making. It is observed that the latter is based mainly on a data protection perspective. From this data protection point of view, the handling of biometric data in the EU would benefit from a more stringent application of the purpose binding principle. Further, it is demonstrated that more thorough impact assessments could become the cornerstone for legal assessments of the application of data protection principles in individual biometric projects such as EURODAC. The conclusion is that the current approach to informational trends and biometrics will have to develop beyond *personal* data protection towards a more comprehensive notion of *societal* data protection through privacy enhancing data and identity management. Within this wider framework, data protection should be able to deal with the use of biometrics and multiple layers and concepts of privacy created by the information society as it is developing.

1 Introduction

Biometrics has become the key element of new EU policies aimed at increasing safety, interoperability, availability and efficient border control. This technology identifies people by means of their biological characteristics. As individual body characteristics are used for identification or authentication purposes, biometrics is considered the most far reaching means of personal identification [1]. The shift to the use of biometrics opens new possibilities on the one hand, and introduces complications on the other. Possibilities lie e.g. in the biometric options to authenticate someone without identifying him or her, whilst complications relate to the reliability of biometrics and the impossibility to replace someone's biometrics as well as the presence of biometric features in the public domain. Although the full implications of the use of biometrics on a large scale are still relatively unclear, most newly issued EU travel documents contain face scans on a RFID chip by now [2], and in the near future fingerprints stored in this way will become mandatory too [3]. In addition, some biometric data are already stored on databanks, and European wide data systems that include biometrics are put forward as policy objectives for the medium and longer term.

Please use the following format when citing this chapter:

Sprokkereef, A., 2008, in IFIP International Federation for Information Processing, Volume 262; The Future of Identity in the Information Society; Simone Fischer-Hübner, Penny Duquenoy, Albin Zuccato, Leonardo Martucci; (Boston: Springer), pp. 277–284.

In general, and compared to the past, public and private collection and use of personal data is widespread. In response to this trend, there has been an increase in the laws and policies that regulate the collection of personal information and the way this information is processed and distributed [4]. As regards the regulation of biometrics, a plurality of approaches ranging from the legal to the technical can be identified. In general terms, this plurality has been conceptualized by political scientists as a shift from government to governance [5]. National governments as well as international bodies, and commercial stakeholders as well as data protection interest groups, play a role in the regulation process [6, 7]. Thus, privacy protection and biometrics are evolving as a domain of multi-level governance. The question is how biometrics, identity protection and data protection interrelate. Identity protection needs and biometrics protection needs are not the same, and distinctions between technical and legal approaches should be made, as well as the overall impact of both of them on society assessed. Just as intellectual property and the Internet, data protection is fast becoming a global issue regulated by states, but also by a variety of societal forms of governing such as international (voluntary) standards [8], self regulation, privacy protective technologies and education. In this process, the role of biometrics, particularly in how it creates obstacles and opportunities for privacy enhancing data and identity management, should be explored.

2   Functions of Biometrics

Basically, the purpose of using a biometric is inspection and this can take only three basic forms: authorization (checking the right of a person), authentication (checking the genuineness of a document) or verification (checking whether a person is the person claimed to be).

However, biometrics can be used for different functions, and these in turn can be carried out with an endless number of practical applications varying from small scale to large scale systems involving millions of individuals. These applications might be developed to carry out only one of the three basics forms of inspection but are also often designed to combine purposes. Indeed, applications with combinations of purposes have diverging impacts on individuals and communities involved. The verification purpose is generally regarded to create the most risks for privacy and security of the individual because it invariably needs a data base to check against. The following functions are the most commonly encountered in biometric applications at this moment in time: [9]

1. verification of an individual; is a person the person he claims to be in situations were access is requested or documents are issued.
2. identification; establishing the true identity of a person
3. personal approval; a formal way to obtain a person's approval or consent after verification that he or she is the person he or she claims to be.
4. biometric on card administration to compensate for a human disability; linking processes and data without human intervention.

5. reliable provision of services; through the use of a biometric a person can be validated by the system, a reliable ink between the data and the process can be established and a service can be provided or continued without human intervention.

3   Legal Implications of Biometrics as an "Anchor"

It has been argued that the introduction of biometrics constitutes a fundamental change as it creates an "anchor" for identity in the human body, to which data and information can be fixed [10]. This biometric anchor makes it conceivable to develop a global mechanism for government-sanctioned proof of identity. As a UNESCO report has recently concluded: biometrics as "a globally unique identifier could seem to be the answer for according a person official digital existence in the Information Society". [11] However, trust in the reliability of the technology in making this anchor almost invulnerable to human mistake or fraud is mistaken. It should be clear that there are in fact no such things as 'infallible' biometrics. Even when the latter were the case, the safety of a system is only as strong as its weakest link, and therefore biometrics would still depend on total system safety. In fact, biometric techniques still have variable accuracy rates. In that context, especially false positives give rise to a range of legal issues when biometrics are used in law enforcement. Biometrics do therefore pose a challenge to the current legal framework currently governing the handling of personal data or personal particulars.

Technically speaking, the extent to which the data can be traced back to a persons' other data determines whether the data are regarded as personal particulars. A distinction is thus often made between personal particular, anonymous and semi-anonymous biometrics [12]. Personal particular biometrics can with reasonable effort be traced back to the person who has provided the biometrics. Semi-anonymous biometrics is referred to when only the issuer of a biometric identifier knows the identity of the person whose biometric feature is registered, and no one else. In the case of anonymous biometrics the person who has provided the biometrics cannot, with reasonable effort, be traced.

Data and information relating to a person, therefore, do not necessarily have to be traced back to a biometric feature. Some applications with a maximum of PET (privacy enhancing technology) characteristics establish no –or an untraceable- link between the biometric and other data [13]. The overall impact of biometrics on privacy is therefore not that clear cut as sometimes argued. [14] It is beyond discussion that the data and the information fixed to a particular biometric can vary from system to system. Therefore the impact of the use of biometrics on the privacy of the individual involved, or on the character of the (information) society as a whole, will also vary according to the type of system chosen. Systems that maximise de-centralisation of biometric data and technically prevent interoperability with other data systems for example pose a completely different threat to breaches of privacy than multi country systems incorporating databases with data from millions of individuals. The basic question to be answered here is as follows: can data protection principles be applied consistently to legal rules on the fixing of data and information to a biometric or is the introduction of biometrics in fact an innovation that requires a new legal approach? In other words: will the large scale use of biometric data require a readjustment of the legal framework because privacy can no longer be the core value that should determine the regulation of data handling?

4   Legal-Normative Approach

Lipps et al. [15] have argued that the most common non-technical perspective used actively to approach informational trends in general has been what they call "legal-normative". This perspective derives especially from data protection legislation. The literature on biometrics has indeed also been mostly legal-normative [16, 17]. It focuses on the implications of the use of biometric identifiers for the *individual* citizen's privacy. Core values that should be protected following this approach are the principles of purpose specification and proportionality [18]. Minimal collection of personal data and maximum anonymisation of these data then become the norm.

These principles have been consolidated in European data protection law through data protection directive 95/46/EC. Although the term 'biometrics' does not appear in the Directive, it is seemingly indisputable that their processing involves 'capturing, transmitting, manipulating, recording, storing or communicating sound and image data relating to natural persons' in the sense of the Directive. Hence, the Directive applies to processing involving such data and it equates 'personal data' with any information relating to an identified or identifiable natural person ('data subject'); an identifiable person is one who can be identified, directly or indirectly, in particular by reference to an identification number or to one or more factors specific to his physical, physiological, mental, economic, cultural or social identity.

Although not all biometrical data is sensitive in common knowledge terms or in data protection terms, they are collected and stored in order to identify persons. The Directive does not apply to anonymous data, but the definition of the latter is very strict. The notion of 'identifiable' in the European Directive is, unlike other international data protection texts, very extensive. Data that at first glance does not 'look' like personal data can very often lead to an individual. It is not because a processor wants data to be anonymous, that data is anonymous. The definition of 'identifiable' is so broad that data can be considered personal as long as the controller himself is still able to identify the persons behind the data. In view of the technical difference made between anonymous and semi-anonymous biometrics (see above) it is clear the Directive will consider semi-anonymous biometrics as falling under the directive.

5   Use of Biometrics in EU Policies

I will briefly sketch what the experience with the introduction of biometrics in the context of the EU seems to indicate so far. In the policy deliberations and the legislative process the introduction of biometrics has been justified for security reasons and held against the light of data protection principles in that context [19]. As already discussed above, the implications of the use of biometric identifiers on an individual's privacy have been addressed in this process. This implicit weighing of an individual's privacy against safety concerns regarding society as a whole have resulted in a relatively lenient interpretation of the proportionality principle in relation to the handling of biometric data by European authorities [20]. The European Parliament and the European Data Protection Supervisor have criticized the lack of large scale evaluation and impact assessment on recent initiatives involving biometrics [21, 22, and 23]. It can be sustained that the EU has gradually extended the use of biometric technology in its information systems, but has not shown itself equally committed to strict rules on evaluation and limitation of purpose [24]. This general observation applies to EURODAC, VIS (Visa Information system); SIS (Schengen information system) and the European biometric passport. An example that can be given here is the recent proposal of the JHA (Justice and Home Affairs) Council to give law enforcement authorities' access to EURODAC [25]. The Standing Committee of Experts in International Immigration, Refugee and Criminal law has written a note objecting to this proposal [26]. The Committee holds that individuals can no longer rely on the principle that information submitted to one authority will not be used by different, foreign authorities as well. They then give four reasons why the use of EURODAC information (including biometric data such as fingerprints) should not be extended to law enforcement authorities: infringement of the principle of purpose limitation, stigmatising asylum seekers, proliferating unreliable information and endangering persons in need of protection. [27] This example illustrates how future data protection comes under considerable pressure as a result of the relatively open ended approach to the limitation of purpose principle. When it comes to collecting and storing biometrics of European citizens, visitors or residence permit holders in the EU, an extensive legal interpretation of the original purpose for which the data were collected may well lead to a use that was not foreseen by those providing a sample. In view of the fact that many samples will have been given on a non-voluntary basis, and   the legal basis for profiling and surveillance differ considerably from country to country, this leave the individual in the dark about what will eventually be done with his or her biometrics. It also invites a fundamental rethink on the impact of these seemingly open ended uses of biometrics on society a whole. Combining and comparing biometric data by a whole range of authorities might fundamentally challenge our conception of privacy and anonymity [28]. This in turn leads to questions about who will end up making checks on whom. [29]

Impact assessments of new biometric polices have taken place after the need for a societal impact assessment had been identified in a study commissioned by the European Commission [30]. Most have reportedly (because they have not been published in full) concentrated on individual impact assessment such as a European pilot studies using biometrics (for example the BIODEV I visa experiment conducted by Belgium and France in 2004/2005). In view of the above identified trend to allow new and additional government agencies access to the (biometric) information collected, and the observation that the EU is introducing its biometric schemes at an ever larger scale, it is clear that any assessment of the impact of biometrics should transcend individual privacy. Privacy can be regarded as an individual value, but is also an important value for society as a whole. Privacy is more than anything the foundation for values held in common, such as a free and equal society, sociability, trust, and democracy. This requires a paradigm shift from considering the effects on individuals (the basic test for privacy protection till now) to considering the impact on society as a whole.

6   Summary: Towards a Legal Perspective Encompassing Societal Impact

It is held here that an assessment of the impact on society however can fit into the normative-legal perspective on biometrics. Obviously, a straightforward objective of minimal collection of personal data can no longer be upheld in the global information society as it is emerging. Aided by a large range of new technologies, in this society personal information is pervasive, and collected by public and private organizations and individuals continuously [31]. The more important it has therefore become to use that same technology to protect privacy, and where necessary the law, to lie down the rules and enforce compliance.

There is no reason why the data protection principles of anonymity, proportionality and purpose binding could not be upheld when it comes to the handling of biometric data by European governments. Probably, the key in which the traditional core administrative identity is stored will shift from a-numerical to biometric in the near future. Biometrics do not necessarily have to be used in a privacy invading manner. Technical possibilities to use biometrics as a PET (privacy enhancing technology) should be exploited to maintain high standards of privacy protection. [32]. The legal approach to informational trends and biometrics will have to develop beyond *personal* data protection towards a more comprehensive notion of *societal* data protection through privacy enhancing data and identity management. Compulsory impact assessments before proposed European legislation can be adopted have already been called for and could form part of such a societal approach. Within this wider framework, data protection should be able to deal with the use of biometrics and multiple layers and concepts of privacy created by the information society as it is developing.

References

1. I. van der Ploeg, The Illegal Body: 'Eurodac' and the Politics of Biometric Identification, Ethics and Information Technology, 1, 295-302 (1999).
2. D. Darquennes, and Y. Poullet, RFID : Quelques Réflections Introductives á un Débat de Société, Revue du Droit des Technologies de l'Information, 26, 255-279 (2006).
3. P. de Hert, W. Schreurs and E. Brouwer, Machine-Readable Identity Documents with Biometric Data in the EU: Overview of the Legal Framework, Keesing Journal of Documents and Identity, 21, 3-10 (2006).
4. C. Prins, Making Our Bodies Work for Us: Legal implications of Biometric Technologies, Computer Law & Security Report, 14(3), 159-165 (1998).
5. Governance Project EUI, Florence (May 30, 2007), http://www.eu-newgov.org/index.asp.
6. J. Lodge, European Governance 2015: Popping the Digital Bubble, in: New Spaces of European Governance, edited by J. Melchior (University of Vienna, Vienna, 2006) pp. 19-46.
7. J. Lodge, EJustice, Security and Biometrics: the EU's Proximity Paradox, European Journal of Crime, Criminal Law and Criminal Justice 13(4), 533-564 (2005).
8. C. Chatwin, A History of ICAO Doc 9303: The Development of International Standards for Travel Documents, Keesing Journal of Documents and Identity, 23, 16-22 (2007).
9. Netherlands Biometrics Forum, Rotterdam (May 30, 2007) www.biometrieforum.nl.
10. The Surveillance Studies Network, A Report on the Surveillance Society For the Information Commissioner (London, 2006), p 9.
11. UNESCO, Information for all Programme (IFAP), Ethical Implications of Emerging Technologies: a Survey edited by M. Rundle and C. Conley (UNESCO, Paris, 2007) p40.
12. R. Koorn, et al, Privacy Enhancing Technologies Witboek voor Beslissers (Ministerie van Binnenlandse Zaken en Koninkrijksrelaties, The Hague, December 2004).
13. Netherlands Biometrics Forum, Biometrics. Cut out for us? (Netherlands Biometrics Forum Rotterdam, 2007) p9.
14. R. Hes, et al, At Face Value: on Biometrical Identification and Privacy (The Hague, Registratiekamer, september 1999) pp 48-56.
15. M. Lips, J. Taylor and J. Organ Identity Management as Public Innovation: Looking beyond ID cards and authentication systems, in: Information and Communication Technology and Public Innovation: Assessing the ICT-Driven Modernization of Public Administration, edited by V. Becker et al (Amsterdam: IOS Press, 2006), pp 204-216.
16. P. J.A. de Hert, Biometrics: Legal Issues and Implications. Background paper for the Institute of Prospective Technological Studies, DG JRC (Seville, European Commission, 2005).
17. R. Thomas, Biometrics, International Migrants and Human Rights, European Journal of Migration and Law 7, 377-411 (2005).
18. P. de Hert and A. Sprokkereef, An Assessment of the Proposed Uniform Format for Residence Permits: Use of Biometrics, CEPS Briefing Note for the European Parliament's Committee on Civil Liberties, Justice and Home Affairs, (Brussels, May 30, 2007); http://www.libertysecurity.org/article1193.html.
19. T. Balzacq and S.Carrera (Ed), Security versus Freedom: A Challenge for Europe's Future (Ashgate, 2006).
20. See Thomas reference 17 above.
21. European Data Protection Supervisor, Opinion on the Proposal for a Council Regulation Amending Regulation (EC) 1030/2002 Laying Down a Format for Residence Permits for Third Country Nationals. Brussels, 16th Oct 2006: (May 30, 2007); www.edps.europa.eu.

22. 2006 Budapest Declaration on Machine Readable Travel Documents, FIDIS, Budapest); http://www.fidis.net/press-events/press-releases/budapest-declaration/.

23. Council of the European Union, Briefing 19 Sep 2007, Interinstitutional file: 2006/0088, 12665/07, p1, http://www.statewatch.org/news/2007/sep/eu-biometric-visas-12665-07.pdf.

24. A. Sprokkereef and P. de Hert. Ethical Practice in the Use of Biometrics Identifiers within the EU. Law, Science and Policy, 3, 177-201 (2007).

25. EURODAC is a European Union wide electronic system (including a fingerprint database), for details on SIS, VIS and EURODAC in general see: http://ec.europa.eu/justice_home/index_en.htm. On this particular point consult: COM (2007) 299 final, Report from the Commission to the European Parliament and the Council on the evaluation of the Dublin system, http://eur-lex.europa.eu/LexUriServ/site/en/com/ 2007/com2007_0299en01.pdf, p 11.

26. Standing Committee of Experts on International Immigration, Refugee and Criminal Law, CM0712-IV, Note on the Proposal of the JHA Council to Give Law Enforcement Authorities Access to EURODAC, the Hague, 18 Sep 2007, http://www.statewatch.org/ news/2007/sep/eurodac-meijers-committee.pdf.

27. 27. Op cit p 2 and 3.

28. See reference 11.

29. See reference 10.

30. European Joint Research Centre, Institute of Prospective Technological Studies DG JRC. Biometrics at the Frontiers: Assessing the Impact on Society. Technical Report EUR 21585 (Seville, European Commission, 2005).

31. D. Bailey, The Open Society Paradox; Why the 21st Century Calls for more Openness-not less (Potomac Books, 2004).

32. European Biometrics Forum, Security and Privacy in Large Scale Biometric Systems. Report commissioned by the EC-JRC/IPTS (European Commission Joint Research Centre Technical Report, Oct. 2007 http://is.jrc.es/documents/SecurityPrivacyFinal Report.pdf).

Keynote Session 4:

ICT Implants
The Invasive Future of Identity?

Mark N. Gasson

Department of Cybernetics
University of Reading
Reading, Berkshire, UK
m.n.gasson@reading.ac.uk

Abstract. Is the human body a suitable place for a microchip? Such discussion is no longer hypothetical – in fact in reality it has not been so for some years. Restorative devices such as pacemakers and cochlear implants have become well established, yet these sophisticated devices form notably intimate links between technology and the body. More recent developments in engineering technologies have meant that the integration of silicon with biology is now reaching new levels - with devices which interact directly with the brain. As medical technologies continue to advance, their potential benefits for human enhancement will become increasingly attractive, and so we need to seriously consider where this may take us. In this paper, an attempt is made to demonstrate that, in the medical context, the foundations of more advanced implantable enhancement technologies are already notably progressed, and that they are becoming more science fact than is widely considered. A number of wider moral, ethical and legal issues stem from enhancement applications and it is difficult to foresee the social consequences, the fundamental changes on our very conception of self and the impact on our identity of adoption long term. As a result, it is necessary to acknowledge the possibilities and is timely to have debate to address the wider implications these possibilities may bring.

1 Introduction

The ability to form direct, bi-directional links with the human brain will open up the potential for many new application areas. Scientists predict that within the next thirty years neural interfaces will be designed that will not only increase the dynamic range of senses, but will also enhance memory and enable "cyberthink" - invisible communication with others and technology [1]. But are these claims realistic, and should they be taken seriously? Here we will look at how a fundamental shift in thinking may pave the way for greater developments in this field, and review the current state-of-the-art of implantable technology, its potential as an enhancement tool, and the likelihood that people would undergo implantation.

Please use the following format when citing this chapter:

Gasson, M.N., 2008, in IFIP International Federation for Information Processing, Volume 262; The Future of Identity in the Information Society; Simone Fischer-Hübner, Penny Duquenoy, Albin Zuccato, Leonardo Martucci; (Boston: Springer), pp. 287–295.

2 Emerging technologies and the coming years

It is clear that not all future visions will be accurate, and this goes for those debated by scientists as much as anyone else. A clear case-in-point is the assertion that, by now, Artificially Intelligent machines, with intellect to match our own, will be a great cause for concern. These, to date, have evidently failed to materialize. In a shift in approach, 'Emerging Technologies' is a new way of thinking which considers the convergence of fields such as nanotechnology, biotechnology, information technology, cognitive science, robotics, and artificial intelligence. It is considered that the next wave of disruptive technologies will actually be a result of this domain fusion rather than from any one field in isolation. Already the foundations of implantable technology are being investigated and developed for medical applications, and progress is becoming less hampered by our lack of understanding of brain functionality. It is clear that this application area is one which can be greatly enhanced through this new emerging technology phenomenon.

However, we must also consider what the state-of-the-art is currently. The relatively new trend for low-tech implants has recently risen in the public consciousness, although less publicized developments of high-tech implants in the medical domain have been progressing for several decades. Indeed, a significant drive behind the development of so called Information Communicating Technology (ICT) implant devices is medical – i.e. restoring deficient human abilities.

2.1   ICT implants for Restorative application

There is a fair range of 'restorative' devices already in clinical use, although many, such as artificial joints, could not through their function alone be considered ICT devices. Others, such as the artificial pacemaker, have actually become notably sophisticated in recent years with integrated movement sensors to adjust heart rate based on estimated demand, internal logging of biological data, and RF communication with the outside world. Of greater interest is the development of technologies which are able to interact with us on a neural level. The most ubiquitous sensory neural prosthesis is by far the cochlear implant [2]. Where destruction of cochlea hair cells and the related degeneration of auditory nerve fibers has resulted in sensorineural hearing loss, the prostheses is designed to elicit patterns of nerve activity via a linear array of electrodes implanted in the deaf patient's cochlea that mimics those of a normal ear for a range of frequencies. Current devices enable around 20 percent of those implanted to communicate without lip reading and the vast majority to communicate fluently when the sound is combined with lip reading. Its modest success is related to the ratio of stimulation channels to active sensor channels in a fully functional ear, with recent devices having up to 24 channels, while the human ear utilizes upwards of 30,000 fibers on the auditory nerve. With the limitations of the cochlear implant in mind, the artificial visual prosthesis [3] is certainly substantially more ambitious. While degenerative processes such as retinitis pigmentosa selectively affect the photodetectors of the retina, the fibers of the optic nerve remain functional, so with direct stimulation of the nerve it has been possible for the recipient to perceive simple shapes and letters. However, the difficulties with restoring full sight are several orders of magnitude greater than those of the cochlear implant simply because the retina contains millions of photodetectors that need to be artificially replicated, and so this technology remains in development.

While both cochlear implants and retina stimulators operate by artificially manipulating the peripheral nervous system, less research has been conducted on direct electrical interaction with the human central nervous system, and in particular the brain. Work on animals [4, 5] has demonstrated how direct brain stimulation can be used to guide rats through a maze problem, essentially by reinforcement, by evoking stimuli to the cortical whisker areas to suggest the presence of an object, and stimulation of the medial forebrain bundle (thought to be responsible for both the sense of motivation and the sense of reward) when the rat moves accordingly. Early work to translate this research to humans demonstrated radical (and occasionally dubiously interpreted) changes in mood and personalities when such 'pleasure centers' were stimulated [6, 7]. This period saw some seventy patients implanted with permanent micro-stimulators to treat a variety of disorders with reportedly good success, although the indiscriminant use of the procedure and significant failure rate saw it largely condemned. This may have been in part because the disorders targeted were psychiatric rather than neurologic, and it was not until the 1980s, when French scientists discovered that the symptoms of Parkinson's disease (PD), with better understood anatomical pathology, were treatable using Deep Brain Stimulation (DBS), that research again picked up pace. However, difficulties in accurately targeting structures deep in the brain, lack of safe durable electrodes, problems of miniaturizing electronics and power supply limitations meant that such therapy was not readily available for several more years.

Recently there has been a resurgence of interest in the surgical treatment of movement disorders such as PD. This is because of the disabling side effects of long term treatment with L-dopa, a chemical precursor to dopamine which can cross the blood-brain barrier and metabolize in the brain to address insufficient dopamine levels, thought to be a primary cause of PD. Also many movement disorders, such as multiple system atrophy or dystonia, do not respond to dopaminergic treatment at all. A limited range of DBS systems have been made commercially available and are now in clinical use despite their significant cumulative costs. Deep brain electrodes are routinely implanted into the thalamus, pallidum or sub-thalamic nucleus to alleviate the symptoms of Parkinson's disease, tremors of multiple sclerosis and dystonia. In pain patients, electrodes are implanted into the sensory thalamus or periventricular / periaqueductal grey area (see e.g. Fig. 1). The depth electrodes are externalized for a week to ascertain effect prior to internalization. A control unit and battery is implanted in the chest cavity and the electrode connections internalized after this time if good symptom relief is realized, at a cost of around £12,000.

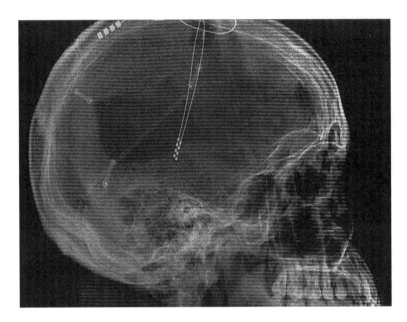

Fig. 1. A lateral X-Ray of the head of a 38-year-old showing two Deep Brain Stimulation leads implanted in the sub-cortical thalamus area.

At present DBS is used to stimulate deep brain structures continuously at high frequencies (typically 100-180Hz for movement disorders and 5-50Hz for pain). Such high frequency DBS is probably effective because it takes command of the local networks and prevents them from relapsing into the slow synchronous cycles that may cause the symptoms of the disorder. The corollary of this is that when entrained to continuous deep brain stimulation the basal ganglia neurons are probably unable to perform their normal functions. However, the success of DBS as a treatment for the symptoms of movement disorders, combined with an improved understanding of the pathophysiologic basis of neuropsychiatric disorders has now seen renewed interest in the application of DBS for these conditions [8].

The ability of electrical neural stimulation to drive behavior and modify brain function without the recipient's cognitive intervention is evident from this type of device. Further, it has been demonstrated how electrical stimulation can be used to replace the natural percept, for example the work by Romo et al. [9]. However, in all cases these devices operate in a unidirectional fashion - the ability to form direct bi-directional links with the human nervous system certainly opens up the potential for many new application areas. However, bi-directional neural implants are very much experimental. Whilst they have much potential in the areas of prosthetics, major developments have been slow in coming. Recent research in the area of DBS has shown that by recording brain activity via the implanted electrodes it is possible to detect characteristic signal changes in the target nuclei prior to the event of tremor, and so stimulation based on a prediction of what the brain will do is possible [10]. The development of such technologies, which are able to decode the brain's function, are clearly of great value.

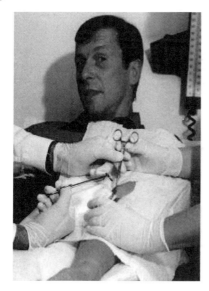

Fig. 2. A 2cm long RFID tag (shown right) is invasively implanted into a healthy volunteer during a research program conducted in 1998.

2.2   Application of ICT implants for Enhancement

On Monday, August 24th, 1998, a groundbreaking experiment was conducted by Prof. Warwick's group at the University of Reading in the UK (see Fig. 2). At the heart of this work were the sub-dermal implantation of a Radio Frequency IDentification (RFID) tag[1] and the augmentation of the infrastructure at the university's Department of Cybernetics with RF nodes such that the system was able to track him, via the tag, as he roamed the building. The possibilities using this technology were, even at that time, not greatly limited, however the system was restricted to simple profiling of his behavior. From this automated customization of his environment was possible, such as unlocking doors, turning on lights and brewing his coffee on arrival.

While the public response to this work was varied, from suggestions that this was the work of the devil,[2] to awe of the technological possibilities, acknowledgement of

---

[1] In brief, RFID tags wirelessly communicate data to reader devices from which typically the power is supplied wirelessly to the tag. The data, in the simplest devices, is a unique code which identifies the tag, and thus the object, if known, to which it is attached.

[2] Revelation 13:16-18 "He [the beast] also forced everyone, small and great, rich and poor, free and slave, to receive a mark on his right hand or on his forehead, so that no one could buy or sell unless he had the mark, which is the name of the beast or the number of his name". Such scaremongering is in keeping with the flawed logic which demonstrates that

the prophetic merit largely mirrored that of academic musings on the scientific value. Few could appreciate the idea that people may actually be open to having such devices implanted if there was some net benefit in doing so. Equally, few entertained the realization that, at that time, RFID technology was on the cusp of becoming cost effective enough to essentially become ubiquitous.

Some six years later, implantable identifying RFID tags were commercialized by 'VeriChip' and approved by the FDA in the USA for human use. It was proposed that these devices could essentially replace 'medic alert' bracelets and be used to relay medical details when linked with an online medical database. Such devices have subsequently been used to allow access to secure areas in building complexes, for example the Mexican Attorney General's office implanted 18 of its staff members in 2004 to control access to a secure data room, and nightclubs in Barcelona, Spain and The Netherlands use a similar implantable chip to allow entry to their VIP customers, and enable automated payments.

By 2007, reports of people implanting themselves with commercially available RFID tags for a variety of applications have become a familiar occurrence (see e.g. Fig. 3). The broad discussion on security and privacy issues regarding mass RFID deployment has picked up pace, and security experts are now specifically warning of the inherent risks associated with using RFID for the authentication of people[3]. Whilst the idea that RFID can be used to covertly track an individual 24-7 betrays a fundamental misunderstanding of the limitations of the technology, there are genuine concerns to address. The use of implanted RFID tags in this scenario is especially thwart with issues because being implanted forms a clear, permanent link with the individual and makes compromised tags hard to revoke.

Concerns for those who have decided to have an RFID tag implanted are valid, although an assumption is that such procedures will never become compulsory and so most people will remain unaffected. However, while mass deployment of RFID technologies is well documented, especially in the context of commerce, it should be noted that, through non-nefarious means, it is possible that people could become implanted with RFID unknowingly. This is mostly related to safety issues regarding passive medical devices such as hip replacements and breast implants whereby being able to determine the exact manufacturing details non-invasively could be advantageous. This is especially valuable when manufacturing faults are subsequently discovered and devices of unknown provenance have been used. Thus embedding an RFID enabled device before it is surgically utilized would enable this function, but result in the wider issues of having RFID implanted. Further, following the polemic on silicone-gel breast implants [12], a device based around RFID technology,

---

the common barcode contains a hidden '666', e.g. as described by Relfe in her 1982 book "The New Money System: 666".

[3] RFID technology is still in its infancy and resource-constraints in both power and computational capabilities make it hard to apply well understood privacy protection techniques that normally rely heavily on cryptography (see [11] for more information). For instance a 'man-in-the-middle' attack would make it possible for an attacker to steal the identity of a person (i.e. tag identifier), while widely published techniques for RFID tag cloning make utilizing this information technically feasible.

designed to be located inside the breast, which detects rupture has been developed, and many are investigating the benefits of being able to non-invasively monitor the condition of a medical device, such as a heart valve, using this type of technology.

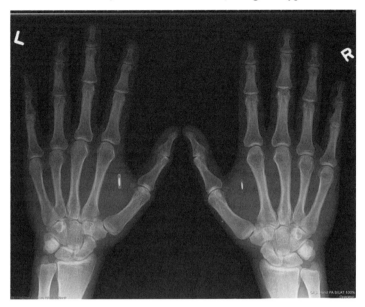

Fig. 3. An individual with two RFID implants: His left hand contains a 3mm by 13mm EM4102 glass RFID tag that was implanted by a cosmetic surgeon, his right hand contains a 2mm by 12mm Philips HITAG 2048S tag with crypto-security features, implanted by a GP using an animal injector kit [13].

Exact numbers of those who have received this type of low-tech implantable technology are not known, but it is clear that the figure is rising, and, with familiarity, public acceptance will surely grow. Because we largely dismissed such uses of the technology as improbable some ten years ago, a lack of timely debate on the wider implications means that we are now faced with the prospect of addressing them whilst the technology gets a foot-hold. Not least of all, this certainly leaves some open identity management questions which technologists must now address. It is not hard to imagine that dealing with technical and wider issues retrospectively will be immensely more difficult.

Having seen the applications which RFID has found despite earlier pessimism, we should consider the application of the more advanced medically orientated technologies on healthy individuals, i.e. enhancement rather than restoration, as a distinct probability. Reports of this pioneering step are rare, although in a notable echo of 1998, the University of Reading in the UK has been active in this area. On March 14th, 2002, an array of one hundred individual needle electrodes was surgically implanted into the median nerve fibers of the left arm of Prof. Warwick, a healthy volunteer [14, 15]. This study demonstrated, in a rudimentary fashion, a range of applications, from nervous system to nervous system communication, feedback control of robotic devices and augmented sensory capabilities.

To date there are no well reported studies involving implantation in the central nervous system of healthy volunteers. There is, however, some largely anecdotal evidence of the occasional positive side effect that DBS in patients has had. In one such case, a graphic designer, who received DBS surgery for a severe Tourettes disorder, found that stimulation through one specific electrode could actually make her more creative. Indeed, when this electrode was used, her employer noted an improvement in color and layout in her graphic design work [16]. The application of this type of effect in the long term clearly cannot be discounted, and so nor can the translation of medical devices to this area.

Society in general has come to accept restorative technologies such as pacemakers and DBS systems which have become notably advanced in their function. However, it is clearly timely to have debate regarding the potential use of this technology in individuals with no medically discernable need. A number of wider moral, ethical and legal issues stem from such applications [17] and it is difficult to foresee the social consequences of adoption long term which may fundamentally change our very conception of self and sense of identity. Intervention with regard to the possible negative impacts should clearly take place at an early point such that we are not left relying on purely legal measures.

3 Conclusions

We are already seeing simple passive technologies such as RFID being implanted in humans, and these alone introduce challenging identity and identity management related questions. Issues relating to the implementation of more advanced enhancing ICT implants are immense, and in most cases tangible solutions to technical problems are still yet to be found. However, technological advancement is a part of our evolution, and the significant next step of forming direct bi-directional links with the human brain is moving inexorably closer. It is understandable to think that since the technology has not yet and may not be perfected there is no need to address the incipient legal, ethical and social issues that the development of these devices may bring. However, the basic foundations of advanced ICT implant devices are being developed for clear medical purposes, and it is reasonable to assume that few would argue against this progress for such noble, therapeutic causes. Equally, as has been demonstrated by cosmetic surgery, we cannot assume that because a procedure is highly invasive people will not undergo it. So, while we may be some way away, there is clear evidence that devices capable of significant enhancement will become reality, and most probably applied in applications beyond their original purpose. Thus, clear consideration needs to be given now to the fundamental moral, ethical, social, psychological and legal ramifications of such enhancement technologies. It is not too soon to start real debate.

References

1. McGee, E.M. and Maguire, G.Q. (2007) 'Becoming borg to become immortal: regulating brain implant technologies', Camb Q Healthc Ethics, Summer;16(3), pp. 291-302.
2. Zeng, F.G. (2004) 'Trends in cochlear implants', Trends Amplif., 8(1), pp. 1-34.
3. Hossain, P., Seetho, I.W., Browning, A.C. and Amoaku, W.M. (2005) 'Artificial means for restoring vision', BMJ, 330, pp. 30-3.
4. Olds J and Milner P M. (1954) 'Positive reinforcement produced by electrical stimulation of septal area and other regions of rat brain', J. Comp. Physiol. Psychol. 47, pp. 419-27.
5. Talwar, S. K., Xu, S., Hawley, E. S., Weiss., S. A., Moxon, K. A., and Chapin, J. K. (2002) 'Rat navigation guided by remote control', Nature, 417, pp. 37-8.
6. Moan, C.E., and Heath, R.G. (1972) 'Septal stimulation for the initiation of heterosexual activity in a homosexual male', J. Behavior Therapy and Experimental Psychiatry 3, pp. 23-30.
7. Delgado, J.M. (1977) 'Instrumentation, working hypotheses, and clinical aspects of neurostimulation', Applied Neurophysiology 40 (2–4), pp. 88-110.
8. Wichmann, T. and DeLong, M.R. (2006) 'Deep Brain Stimulation for Neurologic and Neuropsychiatric Disorders', Neuron, 52:1, pp. 197-204.
9. Romo, R., Hernandez, A., Zainos, A., Brody, C. D., Lemus, L. (2000), 'Sensing without touching: psychophysical performance based on cortical microstimulation', Neuron, 26, pp. 273-8.
10. Gasson, M.N., Wang, S.Y., Aziz, T.Z., Stein, J.F., and Warwick, K. (2005) 'Towards a Demand Driven Deep-Brain Stimulator for the Treatment of Movement Disorders', MASP2005, 3rd IEE International Seminar on Medical Applications of Signal Processing, London, UK, pp. 83-86, 3-4 November, 2005.
11. Fischer-Hübner, S., and Hedbom, H. (eds) (2007) 'A Holistic Privacy Framework for RFID Applications', FIDIS. Available at: http://www.fidis.net/
12. Kessler, D.A. (1992) 'The basis of the FDA's decision on breast implants'. New Engl. J. Med. 326, pp. 1713–1715.
13. Graafstra, A. (2007) 'Hands On', *IEEE Spectrum*, 44:3, pp. 18-23.
14. Gasson, M.N., Hutt, B.D., Goodhew, I., Kyberd, P., and Warwick, K. (2005) 'Invasive Neural Prosthesis for Neural Signal Detection and Nerve Stimulation', International Journal of Adaptive Control and Signal Processing, Vol.19:5, pp. 365-75.
15. Warwick, K., Gasson, M.N., Hutt, B.D., Goodhew, I., Kyberd, P., Andrews, B.J., Teddy, P., and Shad, A. (2003) 'The Application of Implant Technology in Cybernetic Systems', Archives of Neurology, Vol.60(5), pp. 1369-73.
16. Cosgrove, G. R. (2004) 'Neuroscience, Brain, and Behavior V: Deep Brain Stimulation', Transcript – session 6, June 25, The President's Council on BioEthics. http://www.bioethics.gov/transcripts/june04/session6.html
17. Rodotà, S., and Capurro, R. (eds) (2005) 'Ethical Aspects of ICT Implants in the Human Body', Opinion of the European Group on Ethics in Science and New Technologies to the European Commission, pp. 18-23D.

Workshop: Privacy-Enhancing Technologies

Using Identity-Based Public-Key Cryptography with Images to Preserve Privacy

Sebastian Pape and Nabil Benamar

Databases and Interactive Systems Research Group, University of Kassel
Wilhelmshöher Allee 73, 34121 Kassel
{pape,benamar}@db.informatik.uni-kassel.de
http://www.db.informatik.uni-kassel.de/

Abstract. We propose a public-key signature and encryption application which strongly relies on identity-based public-key cryptography. By alternately using obvious identity information like names and essential image data of the involved parties as public keys we preserve all advantages gained by identity-based public-key schemes, mainly including the absence of a public-key infrastructure [1]. On the other hand, all parties obtain only obvious and necessary information about other involved parties.

1 Introduction

The purpose of our application is to avoid tickets written on paper and particularly to remove those bondings, where a customer's name is printed on his ticket and he has to show his passport, that the controller can check the equality of the name on the ticket and the one in the passport. The controller's next step then usually is to compare the customer's appearance with the picture in his passport. In many cases the passport is only a sort of translation from the customer's name to his picture. Thus, the customer's name, address, identity number and so on are not needed here, the controller only wants to check if the person who claims a service is legitimated. Our approach aims at an portrait-based legitimation of customers with mobile devices like PDAs or cell phones. While there are several identity based applications, we found none which uses stand-alone pictures or essential parts of them to protect the customer's privacy. We give a sketch of our idea and some references in Sect. 2.1 how to derive the keys.

For the customer's purposes of course it would be desirable to have anonymous commercial transactions, e.g. by using anonymous digital credentials [2]. Otherwise there is a commercial demand to identify the customer, e.g. when charging fees for altering a booking or considering discount systems like the German Railways' one. The latter costs an annual fee and grants a discount on all train tickets during this year in return. Needless to say that German Railways don't want their customers to share those discount cards. When looking at the examples above or at customer retention systems and considering today's courses of business, tickets have to be bound to a specific customer so that the transfer of

Please use the following format when citing this chapter:

Pape, S. and Benamar, N., 2008, in IFIP International Federation for Information Processing, Volume 262; The Future of Identity in the Information Society; Simone Fischer-Hübner, Penny Duquenoy, Albin Zuccato, Leonardo Martucci; (Boston: Springer), pp. 299–310.

privileges, discounts or tickets is impossible. Therefor our aim was to bind tickets to a specific customer without using bureaucratic identity information like name, address, credit card number, any other customer number and so on. We explain in Sect. 2.5 why we suggest to rely on face-recognition here and do not think that the customer's face is as worthy of protection as other identity information like finger prints or name and address. To avoid reinventing the wheel we based our application solely on identity-based public-key cryptography.

Given that customers should be able to hold arbitrary devices, no tickets are stored on their mobile device(s). This design avoids unnecessary bondings to specific devices. The customer only needs to setup each of his devices once and is then able to switch them at his choice. Therefore, the tickets have to be stored in one (or more) database(s). But central ticket storage involves a drawback: Other persons – including the party providing the database – should not be able to browse the tickets of any customer. Third persons should only gain information with the customer's knowledge and control, e.g. when he proves his tickets valid to a train conductor. This leads to a database where all (most) information is encrypted with the appropriate customer's key. Since the customer has to decrypt his ticket before showing it, it has to be assured that he is not able to change or misuse the ticket's data.

As abovementioned a trivial example for our application is selling and controlling train tickets. Another example is the sale of soccer tickets. Regarding the last soccer world championchip all tickets contained RFID chips with an unique identifier which linked the ticket to the customers' identification information, e.g. name, date of birth, identity card number. Irrespective if all this information is really necessary it would be quite complicate to prove if a person belongs to a specific ticket. The guard has to read the ticket's unique number, lookup the customer's identification information in a database and then prove via the picture on the customer's identity card that he really belongs to the ticket. When looking at the current state of soccer, e.g. in Italy, there may be a need to personalise tickets, to keep hooligans out of the stadiums. But we claim that if there is really identification information necessary like name or identity card number to achieve this goal, it is needed when selling the ticket and not needed when entering the stadium. The guard does not need to know who wants to watch the soccer game, he only has to be sure, that the ticket is not passed to another person. We state more examples and wherein they differ later on.

2   Scenario, Terms and Our Contribution

There is a customer C who buys or receives a ticket t from a dealer D. Later on C has to prove the validity of his ticket to a Guard G. We only consider cases where C has face-to-face contact to D and G. Note that D could be any kind of salesman, e.g. for train, soccer or concert tickets or he even could be a doctor writing out prescriptions while G could be a controller or a pharmacist, respectively. An more abstract possibility would be to have personalised tokens which prove properties like "over 18", "valid driving license" or " European citizen". We store the tickets in a database, but an adequate setup does not necessarily include a central database. As long as D writes to the same database G reads from, it is satisfactory to have subgroups sharing one database for each task. For example one database stores train tickets and another one contains recipes.

We would also like to emphasise, that the roles of guard and dealer are not fixed. Regarding to our first scenario of train tickets and personal discounts, the attribute "gets discount" could also be stored as a ticket at the database. Then the dealer would first act as guard and control the discount ticket, before granting the discount when selling a ticket.

The customer's public and private keys are denoted by c_{pub} and c_{priv}, respectively. Analogous notations correspond to the dealer's and the guard's keys. Since all participants possess public-key pairs, we assume they communicate through a secure channel and do not need to consider authentication and encryption any further. The following section describes how each of the involved parties have to construct their public keys and which way their private keys are constructed by a trusted third party TTP.

2.1   Key Generation

In identity-based encryption or signature schemes the public key can be an arbitrary string. A trusted third party holds a secret master-key and then generates private keys corresponding to the respective public key string. We first describe how we construct the public keys and then suggest corresponding identity-based schemes.

Public Keys. Since it should be easy for any of C's counterparts (D or G) to get his public key, c_{pub} is derived from the customer's face. Following [3] automatic face-recognition involves three subtasks. The detection of faces, feature extraction and identification and/or verification. Regarding our purpose we only need the first subtasks, namely face detection and feature extraction. Despite face recognition and especially feature extraction is not perfect, enormous progress has been made. Therefore we cannot expect to get precisely the same data each time a picture of the same face is captured, but we assume that by feature extraction we receive data that for the same person remains reasonable close with each measurement. There are different efforts how to utilise this data for cryptographic purposes. Either by using fuzzy identity-based encryption [4], which has an error-tolerance property to allow decryption if and only if the sampled key is close to its original. Or by using fuzzy extractors proposed in [5] which provide the same output, even if the input changes, but remains reasonably close to the original. Dodis et al. also claim that their fuzzy extractors output is nearly distributed uniformly which renders it suitable as key in cryptographic applications. Since we will see in Sect. 2.4, that each customer needs a unique key to locate his tickets at the database we prefer the latter.

Generating the public keys for dealers and guards does not need the same effort.

All dealers and guards use their obvious identity information (e.g. name, address or a symbolic name) as public key d_{pub} respective g_{pub}. That way the customer can easily construct the dealers' and guards' public keys.

Private Keys. As already stated in identity-based public-key cryptography private keys are computed by a trusted third party TTP, which has to approve the identities of the particular party. There are two different needs for keys in our application. While C needs a pair of en- and decryption keys, D and G need signature key pairs. At first we address the customer's en- and decryption.
While there where several proposals, e.g. [6, 7], Boneh and Franklin [8] provided the first usable scheme for identity-based encryption. Their scheme relies on bilinear maps on elliptic curves, namely the Weil pairing and performs probabilistic encryption of arbitrary ciphertexts. Later research of identity-based encryption schemes is also mostly based on bilinear Weil or Tate pairings. We suggest to use their scheme not only because there already exists a well documented toolkit[1]. Let us now take a look at appropriate signature schemes for D and G. While there where quite early solutions for satisfactory id-based signature schemes [9, 10], we suggest to use the scheme from Cha and Chen [11] based on the hardness of the computational Diffie-Hellman problem since it shares the same system parameters and the same private/public key pairs with [8] and is claimed to be as efficient as Boneh's and Franklin's scheme.

2.2 Setup

Knowing how to construct private/public key pairs from the previous section, the setup for our application is quite easy. First of all the trusted third party TTP has to generate its master-key corresponding to the used cryptosystems. Then each participant (C, D and G) has to get his private key from TTP (Fig. 1). The trusted third party approves that customers and dealers qualify and that the customer's public key is really derived from his face. Note that it may be possible to fully automate the process of generating c_{priv} likewise existing passport photograph automates. It is also worth mentioning, that following the previous section all participants are able to use their key pairs for signatures and en-/decryption.

2.3 Creation of Tickets

At first D has to construct c_{pub} by taking a picture of him and deriving the public key exactly as described in Sect. 2.1. As soon as D creates a ticket t, he includes c_{pub} and signs it with his private key d_{priv} and then encrypts the result with c_{pub}. Now D has to store $encr_c(sign_d(t, c_{pub}))$ in the common database as shown in Fig. 2. Note that for ticket creation the customer does not need his device. Although depending on the level of trust C has on D, D may has to prove that he

---

[1] see http://www.voltage.com/ibe_dev/index.htm

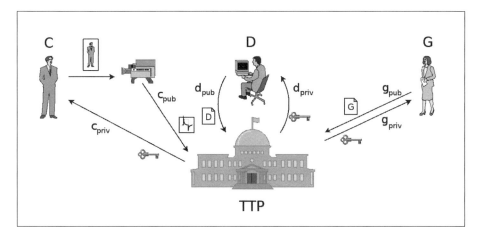

Fig. 1. Setup

really inserted the ticket in the database. Assuming D is a doctor, C might trust
D will insert the ticket in the database while C may want some evidence when
buying train, soccer or concert tickets. Due to the fact that no deterministic two-
party contract-signing protocol can achieve fairness [12], a trusted third party
may be present here. Since the usual setup probably is, that C is at D's facility
and has no (straight) access to TTP, a convenient solution could be the so-
called optimistic approach [13, 14]. When using optimistic protocols TTP can be
regarded as offline, since TTP comes only into play if a problem appears, e.g. a
technical failure or a cheating party. Thus, using the optimistic protocol for fair
exchange D may return a signed receipt to C while receiving C's payment. This
procedure is almost equivalent to today's traditional processing. Alternatively
any other fair protocol involving a trusted third party operating the database
may be used instead.

Since the tickets are stored encrypted, they are stored in relation to C's public
key to make it possible to recover them later on. There is also little additional
(plain text) information (e.g. a date or a place) stored to reduce the number of
tickets C has to decrypt later when showing his ticket (see Sect. 2.4).

2.4   Validation of Tickets

When C has to prove to G that he is the owner of a valid ticket, G first derives
c_{pub} from C's face - exactly in the way D obtained C's private key in the previous
section. Next G receives all tickets from the database associated with c_{pub} and the
additional information and passes all matching data sets to C. Thus, C obtains
a set of tickets of the form $enc_c(sign_d(t, c_{pub}))$. C is then able to decrypt the
encrypted tickets and returns to G the unencrypted but signed ticket $sign_d(t, c_{pub})$
suitable for this situation. An overview of the procedure is depicted in Fig. 3.
Note that C probably does not need to decrypt all tickets since he can benefit

Fig. 2. Creation of tickets

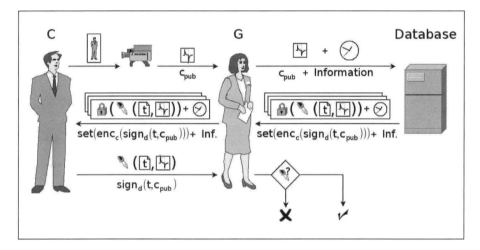

Fig. 3. Validation of tickets

from the additional information and start decrypting the more likely tickets first.

2.5 Privacy Discussion

Using Identification Information Derived from the Customer's Face.
As mentioned above we assume that the customer has face-to-face contact to the
dealer and the guard. To get worse he not only has face-to-face contact to them,
he usually enters their environment (shop, train, stadium, etc.). Furthermore
state-of-the-art advances and produces cheaper, smaller and increasingly powerful devices. On account of this we assume it is almost impossible for the customer
to prevent guard and dealer from installing hidden cameras and secretly taking
pictures of the customer. We do not think that pictures or extracted essential
information from them is less sensitive information than e.g. fingerprints, iris or

retinal scans or gene checks. But when looking at biometric personal identification the customer can not prevent misbehaving dealers or guards from collecting information which does not rely on his cooperation or even knowledge. Besides face recognition, e.g. voice recognition and analysis of odour or gait fall in this category. Therefore we claim that we can make responsible use of such analysis since we do need regulations by law in any case - independent whether we make use of it or not. Furthermore if our application is used in conjunction with anonymous payment (like cash) and we assume misbehaving dealers or guards, they do not get information about the customer's name, address and so on like they get the traditional way. This may sound contradictory, but in our opinion the real privacy risk in face recognition systems is up to the connection of other sensitive information with the data from face recognition systems. As we explained in Sect. 2.3 almost any data at our database is stored encrypted.

Let us assume a dealer or guard misbehaves, who naturally has access to the stored data at the company's database. The public key of a customer is derived from essential information from the customer's face. Therefore an adversary can conclude how many tickets are stored for this user. He has also access to the sparse additional information stored with the tickets while all other information is stored encrypted. The adversary also may take additional pictures and store all information which has to be presented in plain text to him, namely ticket purchases or validations. The worst case is that all guards and dealers of a company are instructed to additionally store the customer's ticket information in plain text. Of course they can do that, too regarding traditional ticket creation and validation. But here furthermore the ticket is issued to a name or a unique identifier which is related to the customer's name. As already stated, we assume a misbehaving dealer or guard is able to secretly take a picture of the customer, which he easily can link to the identifier or name of the customer assuming traditional ticket schemes. Hence with the proposed application we are at least not worse off than before, since we give only sparse information away and prevent dealers and guards from constructing a database with face recognition information linked to names or other identifiers. Although we can think of some cases where having bureaucratic identity information like name and address is far more crucial than having identity information in the form of a picture. For example when an adversary wants to collect more information it is easier to use world wide web search engines in conjunction with a name than with a picture. Even if we assume that customers are willing to disguise themselfs and we assume that face recognition can not cope with it, at least the guard has a good chance of taking a picture, when the customer has to remove his camouflage to prove that he really belongs to the picture at his identity card. Thus disguising is only helpful, if the customer dos not want to use tickets.

Additional Plaintext Information. As described above, the encrypted data stored in the database includes additional plain text information. This may be necessary if some customers hold many tickets. Since in the majority of cases G holds a mobile device and at least C's power is limited, it is useful to lower the number of tickets transferred. There is only sparse information that can be used here, because if we made C storing information he would better keep the ticket itself. However, depending on the amount of tickets it is possible to use time ranges here. Note that – independent of the kind of information stored – this is a trade-off to improve efficiency by compromising privacy since this information is stored unencrypted.

Regarding the Dealer's Anonymity. G may also be able to learn which dealer(s) C prefers since he has to verify their signature. This may be circumvented by using group signature schemes. We propose a variation of our application which makes use of identity-based group signatures in Sect.3.1. The idea of group signatures is to provide anonymity to the dealer, G is only able to verify that a member of a specific group (dealer) signed the ticket. The trusted third party acts as a group manager and is able to revoke anonymity in the case of abuse. In this case the anonymity of the dealer is valuable for C's privacy, since the guard may draw various conclusions from the fact which dealer(s) C prefers.

Compromised Private Keys. Even if the private key of a customer is compromised no one else can use his tickets, because the adversary would already fail when he has to provide the public key via the already in Sect. 2.1 explained procedure. Moreover the customer is able to get a reissued private key from the trusted third party, thus his already paid tickets are not lost. Hence compromised private keys are only relevant to the customer's privacy. Depending whether the adversary has access to the database the compromised key may let him decrypt all tickets of the customer. In case of a lost key the customer could only aim for a re-encryption of all existing tickets with an uncompromised key. A general protection for the customer is to renew his key in a short intervall as described in Sect. 3.2.

2.6   Security Aspects

First of all it has to be ensured that C is unable to forge tickets. Since all tickets are signed by D it is infeasible for C to create tickets as long as the underlying cryptosystem holds. C is also not able to pass tickets to other customers, because the tickets are bound to c_{pub}.

Due to the fact that D is able to write to the common database, D is a more sensitive party. If D wants to insert forged tickets to the database he still has the same problem as mentioned above. Entries in the database have to be signed correctly – otherwise G will not accept the ticket later. As anyone can imagine signing tickets with his own key may be no wise decision if D wants to cheat. However, D must be prevented from deleting tickets and flooding the database with invalid entries. The former can easily be achieved by adapting the database's interface. The latter would require an additional database layer. Since all entries to the database are encrypted the integrity of new entries can not be checked. By using an additional signature of the encrypted record it is possible to track which dealer inserted invalid entries to the database. When C decrypts data he is then able to complain about invalid entries and the untrustworthy dealer's license can be removed. Note that C's claim can be easily proved here, since the encrypted entry has to be stored in the database.

Accounting G's capability is quite interesting in spite of the fact he is only able to read the database. G is able to change data he read from the database before he hands it to C. Given that G is always able to decline C's legitimation – even if C turns over a valid ticket, his only intention could be accusing D of cheating. On the one hand this may easily be prevented if the database provider (or the dealer) additionally signs the set of data he sends to G. On the other hand this accusation cannot be held up for long, simply because any other honest guard can prove the opposite.

Since any combination of cheating parties that involves the guard benefits from the fact, that G is able to manipulate the legitimation test, the only combination of parties cheating in common that makes sense to consider is the pair of customer and dealer. But even if C and D make common cause with each other, the ticket still has to be signed by the dealer since G proves that later. The only way they could cheat would be if D issues a ticket to C, but instead of transmitting it to the database he hands it to C. When C has to prove to G that he has a valid ticket, he discards the set of tickets from G and shows the ticket he received from D to G. If this flaw can be exploited depends on the exact procedure charges are payed from D and is beyond the scope of this paper - not only because if paper tickets are used, D could easily print an extra ticket.

Thus, we claim our application is secure against forgery as long as the underlying cryptosystem holds and the guard really examines the tickets. The latter is no drawback since dishonest guards or controllers cancel almost any real world ticket system.

3   Variations

As already stated in Sect. 2.5 we also propose two slight variations of our application.

3.1   Using Group Signature Schemes for Dealer and Guard

If we want to prevent the guard from learning which dealers the customer prefers, we have to use a group signature scheme. Thus all dealers or guards belonging to the same organisation use the same public key, e.g. "Dealer of German Railways" or "Soccerclub's guard". There are several approaches for id-based group signatures [15, 16] based on bilinear pairings which could be used instead of [11]. The price we have to pay here is, that we cannot share the system parameters and the private/public key pairs with [8], which might be annoying but is feasible.

3.2 Key Revocation

The main advantage of identity-based public-key cryptography is that the distribution of public keys is quite easy, because they can be derived from identity information (e.g. the customer's picture in our application) and therefore no directories with files of public keys need to be kept. But there is a price to pay. In traditional public-key schemes certification revocation lists are used to deal with the consequences of compromised keys. However when using identity-based public-key cryptography a traditional certification revocation list would give its main advantage away. The first generalised method for key revocation in identity-based public-key cryptography was described in [8]. By adding a period of time (e.g. the current year) to a public key it contains an implicit preset expiration date. The public key c_{pub}^{rev} for this variation therefore would be a concatenation of c_{pub} and the expiration date: $c_{pub}^{rev} = c_{pub}||expiration - date$. While public keys can still be derived quite easily this way, the trusted third party has to renew the private key each time the period is over. Note that this is no real key revocation since the customer has to sit an wait until his key expires and despite of whether the key should be revoked or not a regular (and frequent) key renewal is necessary. Otherwise buying tickets and getting a new private key is commutative since the customer does not need his private key when purchasing a ticket, because he only has to decrypt his ticket, when showing it to the guard. However this design of public keys necessitates a short renewal interval to reduce the impact of lost or broken keys. Thus it is inevitable to relieve the customer from the burden of receiving a private key in short time periods from the trusted third party. Dodis et al. [17–19] introduce the idea of a private key-generator-device which generates the actual private key from a secret master key in non id-based cryptography. Hierarchical identity-based encryption schemes [20, 21] however allow the trusted third party do delegate key generation to some lower-level trusted party. As the name hierarchical indicates, there can be several levels of delegation and when a key-generator of a specific level is compromised higher-level key generators are not put at risk. [22] then combines hierarchical identity-based cryptosystems with the idea of private key generators and suggest that, e.g. each time a mobile phone's battery is recharged it recharges its stored private keys from such a private key generator. That way it is possible to have short renewal intervals, without making the customer revisiting the trusted third party daily.

If we use c_{pub}^{rev} as customer's public key in combination with short renewal intervals, our application changes slightly, because we can omit the additional plain text information stored with each ticket.

4   Conclusion and Drawbacks

By using the above setup implicit key management is given as known by identity-based public-key systems and almost no unnecessary information is revealed to any party. Since the customer knows at least the symbolic identity of salesmen, doctors, controllers, pharmacists and so on he easily derives the corresponding public keys without gaining additional knowledge. Vice versa because the customer's public key is derived from a picture of him all groups mentioned above learn nothing more about him than they could see anyway when negotiating face-to-face. Note that TTP is only involved when setting up the system. The trusted third party is not needed during the communication phase although it could be useful if the customer does not trust his dealer (see Sect. 2.3).

As stated in Sect. 2.6 none of the participating parties is able to cheat and as long as the underlying cryptosystem holds our application can be regarded as secure.

However, there are some drawbacks. Given that both dealer and guard need the ticket's plain text information it is impossible to prevent them from keeping their own records. Nevertheless, this is not a major drawback since today's real world scenario already allows that. Depending on the situation the customer may even want to keep them informed (e.g. doctor, pharmacist).

Finally the proposed application removes the bonding between a customer's name and a service and makes it possible to bind tickets to a picture, so the customer reveals no more information than obvious in face-to-face communication. Even if an undesirable face-to-identity dictionary exists this application may be usefull, since access to this dictionary hopefully will be restricted to governmental authorities. In conjunction with anonymous payment [23] our application gives consideration to the user's privacy needs while also including commercial issues and provides personally bound electronic tickets which do at least not reveal more information than todays transactions.

5   Acknowledgements

We would like to thank all our colleagues for helpful discussions, especially Heiko Stamer for his numerous annotations.

References

1. A. Shamir, Identity-based cryptosystems and signature schemes, Advances in Cryptology-Crypto 84, LNCS 196, pages 47–53, Springer-Verlag, 1984.
2. D. Chaum, Security without identification: transaction systems to make big brother obsolete. Communications of the ACM, 28, 1030-1044, 1985.
3. W. Zhao, R. Chellappa, J. Phillips, A. Rosenfeld, Face Recognition: A Literature Survey ACM Computing Surveys, pages 399–458, 2003.
4. A. Sahai and B. Waters, Fuzzy Identity Based Encryption. In Advances in Cryptology – Eurocrypt, volume 3494 of LNCS, pages 457–473. Springer Verlag, 2005.
5. Y. Dodis, L. Reyzin, A. Smith, Fuzzy extractors: How to generate string keys from biometrics and other noisy data, In Proceedings of the International Conference on Advances in Cryptology (EUROCRYPT '04), Lecture Notes in Computer Science, Springer Verlag, 2004.
6. H. Tanaka, A Realization Scheme for the Identity-Based Cryptosystem CRYPTO '87: A Conference on the Theory and Applications of Cryptographic Techniques on Advances in Cryptology, Springer-Verlag, pages 340–349, 1988.

7. S. Tsuji and T.Itoh, An ID-based cryptosystem based on the discrete logarithm problem, IEEE Journal of Selected Areas in Communications, Vol.7, No.4, pp.467–473, 1989.
8. D. Boneh, M. Franklin, Identity-Based Encryption from the Weil Pairing, SIAM Journal on Computing, vol. 32, issue 3, pages 586–615, 2003.
9. A. Fiat, A. Shamir, How to prove yourself: practical solutions to identification and signature problems Proceedings on Advances in cryptology, In Proceedings of CRYPTO '86, Springer-Verlag, pages 186–194, 1987.
10. U. Fiege, A. Fiat, A. Shamir, Zero knowledge proofs of identity In Proceedings of the nineteenth annual ACM conference on Theory of computing (STOC '87), ACM, pages 210–217, 1987.
11. J. C. Cha, J. H. Cheon, An Identity-Based Signature from Gap Diffie-Hellman Groups, PKC '03: Proceedings of the 6th International Workshop on Theory and Practice in Public Key Cryptography, Springer-Verlag, pages 18–30, 2003.
12. S. Even, Y. Yacobi, Relations among public key signature systems, Technical Report 175, pages 148-153, Computer Science Dept, Technion, Israel, March, 1980.
13. N. Asokan, M. Schunter, M. Waidner, Optimistic Protocols for Fair Exchange, In 4th ACM Conference on Computer and Communications Security, pages 7–17, 1997.
14. H. Bürk, A. Pfitzmann, Value exchange systems enabling security and unobservability, In Computers and Security, vol. 9 ,pages 715–721, 1990.
15. Z. Chen, and J. Huang, and D. Huang, and J. Zhang and Y. Wang, Provably secure and ID-based group signature scheme, In Proceedings of the 18th International Conference on Advanced Information Networking and Applications (AINA 2004), volume 2, 384-387, 2004.
16. V. K. Wei, T. H. Yuen, F. Zhang, Group Signature Where Group Manager, Members and Open Authority Are Identity-Based, In Proceedings of the Information Security and Privacy, 10th Australasian Conference, ACISP 2005, Springer Verlag, pages 468–480, 2005.
17. Y. Dodis, J. Katz, S. Xu, and M. Yung, Key-insulated public key cryptosystems, Proc. Eurocrypt'02, LNCS 2332, pages 65-82, Springer-Verlag, 2002.
18. Y. Dodis, M. Franklin, J. Katz, A. Miyaji, and M. Yung, Intrusion-resilient public-key encryption, Proc. CT-RSA'03, LNCS 2612, pages 19-32, Springer-Verlag, 2003.
19. Y. Dodis, M. Franklin, J. Katz, A. Miyaji, and M. Yung, A generic construction for intrusion-resilient public-key encryption, Proc. CT-RSA'04, LNCS 2964, pages 81-98, Springer-Verlag, 2004.
20. C. Gentry, A. Silverberg, Hierarchical ID-Based Cryptography, Advances in Cryptology – Asiacrypt'2002, Lecture Notes on Computer Science 2501, Springer-Verlag, pages 548–566, 2002.
21. J. Horwitz, B. Lynn, Towards Hierarchical Identity-Based Encryption, Advances in Cryptology – Eurocrypt'2002, Lecture Notes on Computer Science 2332, Springer-Verlag, pages 466–481, 2002.
22. Y. Hanaoka, H. Hanaoka, J. Shikata, H. Imai, Identity-Based Hierarchical Strongly Key-Insulated Encryption and Its Application, Cryptology ePrint Archive, Report 2004/338, 2005.
23. David Chaum, Blind signatures for untraceable payments, Advances in Cryptology, Proceedings of CRYPTO '82 (David Chaum, Ronald L. Rivest, and Alan T. Sherman, eds.), Plenum Press, 1983.

Traffic Flow Confidentiality in IPsec:
Protocol and Implementation

Csaba Kiraly[1], Simone Teofili[2], Giuseppe Bianchi[2],
Renato Lo Cigno[1], Matteo Nardelli[1], and Emanuele Delzeri[2]

[1] University of Trento,
{kiraly,locigno,matteo.nardelli}@dit.unitn.it
[2] University of Rome Tor Vergata,
{giuseppe.bianchi,simone.teofili,emanuele.delzeri}
@uniroma2.it

Abstract. Traffic Flow Confidentiality (TFC) mechanisms are techniques devised to hide/masquerade the traffic pattern to prevent statistical traffic analysis attacks. Their inclusion in widespread security protocols, in conjunction with the ability for deployers to flexibly control their operation, might boost their adoption and improve privacy of future networks. This paper describes a TFC protocol integrated, as a security protocol, in the IPsec security architecture. A Linux-based implementation has been developed, supporting a variety of per-packet treatments (padding, fragmentation, dummy packet generation, and artificial alteration of the packet forwarding delay), in an easily combinable manner. Experimental results are reported to demonstrate the flexibility and the effectiveness of the TFC implementation.

1 Introduction

Extensive literature work demonstrates that the traffic pattern generated during on-line communications carries plenty of information, which can be gathered through specially devised "statistical traffic analysis attacks". These attacks operate irrespective of the deployed encryption means, and allow the extraction, from the statistical analysis of the generated packet sizes and of their inter-arrival times, of valuable confidential information such as the employed applications [1], the application layer protocols [2], the physical devices used [3], or the web page accessed [4,5]. To perform these attacks, a signature for the protocol or the web site to be recognized is typically pre-computed as a set of statistical parameters describing packet size and/or packet inter-arrival time distributions. Flow classification can be performed by matching the actual statistics with the pre-stored signatures. Quite interestingly, accurate flow classification may be obtained even by looking only at its very first packets [2,6]. Statistical traffic analysis attacks have been also employed for the purpose of

This work was supported by the EU IST 6th Framework Program project Discreet, IST No. 027679

Please use the following format when citing this chapter:

Kiraly, C., Teofili, S., Bianchi, G., Lo Cigno, R., Nardelli, M. and Delzeri, E., 2008, in IFIP International Federation for Information Processing, Volume 262; The Future of Identity in the Information Society; Simone Fischer-Hübner, Penny Duquenoy, Albin Zuccato, Leonardo Martucci; (Boston: Springer), pp. 311–324.

breaching security (such as for gathering passwords transmitted over encrypted sessions [7,8]), and for performing passive [9] or active [10] attacks to anonymization (mix) networks, aimed at uncovering the identity of the communicating parties.

To duly protect the privacy of the users, "Traffic Flow Confidentiality" (TFC) mechanisms are necessary. These mechanisms are devised to alter or mask the statistical characteristics of the traffic patterns. Specifically, they operate by combining basic per-packet treatments, which include, but are not restricted to, i) pad their size and/or fragment them to achieve pre-determined packet size statistics (for instance equalizing the size of all transmitted packets or achieving a random packet size distribution), ii) add extra forwarding delay to alter the packet inter-departure time distribution, and iii) generate dummy packets to fill gaps between subsequently transmitted "real" packets and thus contribute to alter the traffic pattern statistics.

The contribution of this paper is twofold. First, we propose a TFC approach embedded as a sub-layer (a separate, self-contained, TFC protocol) of IPsec. We believe that the inclusion of TFC mechanisms in existing and widely deployed standards may significantly improve their adoption. Second, our approach is not bound to provide a "specific" traffic masking pattern, but rather aims at providing a flexible platform, endowed with a set of packet treatment primitives upon which the system deployers may easily configure the traffic masking patterns they deem more appropriate for achieving a given privacy/performance trade-off.

To the best of our knowledge, our approach differs from existing literature in this field as:

i)   it supports a vast choice of packet level modifications (including arbitrary modification of packet size through padding or packet aggregation, as well as through fragmentation[2], artificial alteration of the packet forwarding delay, and "traffic padding" through the suitable insertion of dummy packet), in order to prevent traffic analysis attacks, and in contrast to other protocols that aim to protect against one or another specific attack with a limited set of modifications;

ii) it is developed as a flexible suite of easily composable tools rather than as a pre-programmed specific traffic masking technique (for instance, the frequently employed traffic CBR-ization, i.e. transforming traffic into continuous bit rate pattern composed of packets with maximum size);

iii) it is designed to improve not only the security of the communication but also to protect the privacy of the communicating entities. The proposed protocol provides protection either against statistical traffic analysis aiming to break into a system [7,8], as well as against attacks that use traffic pattern analysis to violate user privacy [4,5];

---

[2] Indeed, fragmentation is a technique traditionally neglected as a tool for traffic masking, as most of the approaches proposed in the past are based on traffic padding and/or dummy packet generation. Conversely, we believe that fragmentation is a highly effective tool as i) it has a very low overhead if compared with padding or dummy packet generation, and ii) it may be selectively employed on the packets, such as the very first in the flow [1,5,6], which are found to provide most of the information useful for the classification algorithms.

iv) it is deployed as an additional protocol part of the generic IPsec security architecture (thus reutilizing Security Association and Policy management of the IPsec framework), rather than being integrated in a specific Mix-like solution [11,12,13]; and

v) it is already implemented in Linux as part of the packet transformation framework introduced in the 2.6 kernel.

The rest of this paper is organized as follows. Section 2 briefly reviews related works and relevant standards. Section 3 details the design of the TFC system as an IPsec sub-layer and discusses relevant implementation issues. Section 4 experimentally demonstrates the operation of the TFC protocol and its associated control solutions. Finally, conclusions are drawn in section 5.

2   State of the Art

Traffic Flow Confidentiality was identified as one of the fourteen security services already in the ISO/OSI Security Architecture (ISO 7498-2) [17]. The standard identifies the physical, network and application layers as candidates for implementing TFC functionality. Albeit being identified already in the late '80s, security protocols did not focus on TFC for long time as the use of Statistical Traffic Analysis as a basis for attacks was little investigated. Recently, as Traffic-Analysis-based attacks gained ground, TFC-like features appeared in newer version of several security protocols and related products.

TLS 1.0 and 1.1 [18] allows for a padding length up to 255 bytes to be added. Unlike earlier SSL versions where the use of padding was restricted to the smallest integer multiple of the block cipher's block length, TLS allows for any length up to 255 bytes, as long as it results in a length being an integer multiple of the block length. As RFC 4346 states: "lengths longer than necessary might be desirable to frustrate attacks on a protocol that are based on analysis of the lengths of exchanged messages".

Version 3 of the IPsec Encapsulated Security Payload [14] introduced arbitrary size packet padding. The newly introduced padding is still limited in its use: there is no field containing the length of the padding or the length of the original datagram, therefore, padding can only be added if the encapsulated PDU contains a specification of the length of the datagram. This prevents the use of padding for several very important protocols, one for all: TCP.

Our TFC protocol overcomes the limitations present in both of these protocols by supporting arbitrary packet padding for any type of encapsulated datagram. It also provides support for more advanced tools such as fragmentation, aggregation, timing and dummy packets.

Some of the low-latency anonymous routing networks also try to address the issue of statistical traffic analysis by providing limited TFC-like functionality. Tarzan [13] uses the CBR approach by establishing bidirectional, time-invariant packet streams between nodes of the network. This "brute force" approach is supported by our protocol, even if we think that a CBR covert traffic is too costly in terms of resulting overhead and as such should only be used in highly critical cases. In fact, we argue that, a more selective (hence lightweight) use of dummy packet insertion may eventually provide a better performance-protection trade-off. Freedom (see [19] section 4.3.3) removed TFC from its last version 2.1. While this might be interpreted as a sort of position statement against TFC, the authors themselves claim that the limited methods they have used in previous versions are necessary, but not sufficient to protect against some attacks, and that they plan to study the problem of traffic analysis in subsequent versions[3]. Tor [12] uses fragmentation and padding to fixed size cells. Designers of Tor choose not to adopt other TFC mechanisms in the currently available version, postponing the problem until there is a proven and convenient design that improves anonymity. We believe that (especially in the absence of an "all-for-one" widely accepted traffic masking solution) a clever strategy is to decouple the TFC functionality from the anonymous routing platform, provide a separate protocol specifically devised to provide TFC, and use this as a hop-level component of anonymous routing networks.

Several papers addressing the issue of traffic analysis attacks point to the use of traffic flow confidentiality measures stronger than simple padding. [20] discusses the use of dummy packets and packet delaying in anonymous routing networks both against external and against internal attackers. In [21] a strong traffic analysis attack for global adversaries is presented against real-time anonymization networks that use only packet delaying. In [22] another attack is shown to work on the current implementation of Tor. These papers point towards the use of more advanced TFC techniques such as delaying, cover traffic and stream independence as a possible solution. [16] presents a website fingerprinting attack, but also discusses padding strategies as a countermeasure against such attacks. Authors simulated padding modifying their nonprotected traces, and found packet padding to be an effective defense against their attack.

3   TFC sub-layer design and implementation

To overcome the drawbacks of previous solutions, we have designed TFC as a separate IPsec sub-layer, thus maintaining backward compatibility with traditional IPsec implementations. The TFC sub-layer is implemented through a neat separation between i) the TFC control logic, namely the algorithms devised to transform a traffic pattern into another one, ii) their protocol support, accomplished through the specification of a TFC header, and iii) the set of basic mechanisms employed by this control logic to modify characteristics at the packet level. Basic TFC mechanisms can be conveniently categorized as follows:
a) Packet forming: devised to alter the packet size; they include packet padding, packet fragmentation, and packet aggregation (multiplexing);

---

[3] Development of Freedom was finished after this version due to the company ceasing operation, and due to the success of the similar Tor system.

b) Dummy packet management: devised to generate and discard dummy packets, in order to alter the traffic pattern;

c) Packet timing: devised to alter the forwarding latency of packets adding extra per-packet delay.

Our TFC implementation is developed inside the Linux Kernel 2.6, and leverages the XFRM framework [15] deployed for integrating the TFC processing in the IP/IPsec networking stack[4]. Being developed as an IPsec sub-layer, the TFC protocol can easily take advantage of all the existing ESP functionalities (confidentiality, data integrity and authentication), as well as Security Association and Security Policy management.

Packet Forming

To support the three packet forming mechanisms, we have designed an IPsec Header Extension, the TFC Header (Fig. 1), for the encapsulation of the datagram. The TFC header is internal to the IPsec ESP payload, and it conveys the necessary information to restore the original packet (padding removal, reassembly, de-multiplexing). A next header code should be reserved in the ESP trailer to indicate to the receiver that the protocol contained in the ESP payload is TFC: in our experimentation we used the value 253, reserved by IANA for experimentation and testing. The next header field in the TFC header identifies the protocol carried in the payload.

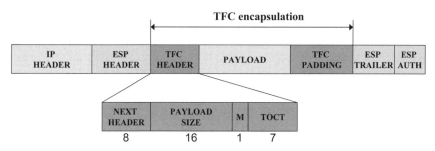

Fig. 1: TFC header format

Packet padding (see Fig. 2) is the traditional (albeit naïve[5]) approach to alter the packet size statistics. The TFC header manages padding simply by explicitly carrying the packet payload size information in a dedicated field. We point out that this allows

---

[4] In additional details, TFC, just like other IPsec security services, is managed through Security Associations, i.e. we have developed a new Security Association type for TFC similarly as what was done for the ESP and AH SAs. This allows controlling TFC through standard security policies included in the IPsec Security Policy Database (SPD). We use the Netlink interface and XFRM SA and SP databases to implement these features. For additional implementation details, please refer to the Discreet Project Deliverable D3102 – available upon request from the authors.

[5] Indeed, statistics taken on real IP flows show a high variance in the packet size, and thus padding to the maximum possible size introduces a massive overhead. Moreover, studies such as [1,5,6] seem to imply that most of the traffic classification mechanisms use the size information contained in the first few packets of a session which are those that convey the protocol fingerprint, making it less important to `heavily' pad subsequent traffic.

overcoming the significant drawback of the "implicit" padding function proposed in the current version of IPsec, which impedes its usage for inner protocols which do not provide an explicit indication of the payload size (e.g. TCP).

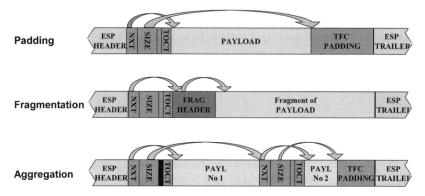

Fig. 2: Padding (using the payload size field); Fragmentation (using fragment header); Aggregation (using the M flag)

Packet fragmentation allows splitting a large packet into smaller packets, and hence avoids the need to add a very large amount of per-packet overhead in the presence of many small packets and a few large ones. The fragmentation feature of the IP header (see Fig. 1) cannot be used for our scope, since it is external to the ESP encryption and thus visible to observers. Therefore, fragmentation should be handled explicitly by our protocol. Instead of placing our own fragmentation related fields in the TFC header structure, we chose to support fragmentation by using an extension header, reusing the structure of the IPv6 fragment header[6] (see Fig. 2). Fragments are reassembled at the end of the overlay link, before the packet is handed out to upper protocols.

Packet aggregation allows multiplexing packets into a bigger datagram, thus increasing the size of the packet through useful information and not through wasted padding bytes. Packet multiplexing is supported by introducing a flag in the TFC header. If this flag is set, after the defined length of the payload, another TFC header and payload follows instead of padding. With this mechanism, several payloads (even fragments) can be transferred in one datagram.

Finally, the TFC header is also exploited to deliver a field, called TOCT (Type of Confidentiality Treatment) which enables to carry information about the type of treatment the packet may be subjected to, when multiple IPsec links are used in a multi-hop fashion, and especially for building IPsec-based mix networks. For reasons of space this operation is not described in this paper.

Dummy Packets

---

[6] With this choice, we reduce header size when fragmentation is not in use. Moreover, we facilitate implementation of the TFC protocol by exploiting existing implementations of the fragment header and fragmentation functionality in current networking stacks.

The use of dummy (artificially generated) packets is frequently referred to as "traffic padding". It allows filling traffic gaps and avoids disclosing inactivity periods (i.e., provide unobservability). Moreover, dummy packets are a powerful instrument to alter the traffic pattern statistics, especially when real packets, due to quality of service constraints, cannot be delayed to an extent that allows proper reshaping of the traffic profile. Finally, dummy packet generation is a technique extensively studied for (and employed in some implementations of) anonymization networks to counteract correlation and several types of active attacks (see e.g. [13]).

Protocol support for dummy packet management is straightforward, setting the next header code to "dummy". In our implementation the value 59 is employed, as this value has been standardized in the IPsec ESP specification. For a more homogeneous implementation of the TFC tools we use the dummy packet value 59 inside the inner TFC header, rather than inside the ESP trailer.

Packet Timing

Information extracted from packet inter-arrival times is a usual source for statistical traffic analysis methods [1,5,10]. To counter these attacks, scheduling algorithms (externally programmed in the "control logic" module discussed next – see Fig. 3) should alter the forwarding time of packets.

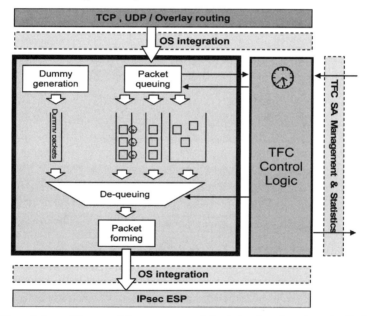

Fig. 3: TFC module architecture. Management and Statistics interface (not detailed it the article) reutilizes management components of the generic IPsec framework

Our implementation supports two methods to alter the packet delays. A first "event-driven" method allows a packet, upon its arrival (top arrow in Fig. 3), to be associated with a specific, possibly packet-dependent, delay. The packet is then delivered inside the TFC module queues[7] only when the associated timer elapses. A second "timer-driven" method allows de-queuing packets stored inside the TFC module queues at scheduling instants computed according to an algorithm controlled by the Control Logic module. Note that in the case queues are empty, a dummy packet will be de-queued from the dummy packet buffer and delivered.

Implementation complexity is delegated to the control logic implementation, as packet delivery is internally accomplished through appropriate setting of standard Linux timers which drive the invocation of a de-queuing primitive. Trivial methods, such as fixed or random packet clocking, may be easily replaced by adaptive clocking algorithms which explicitly take into account the status of the queues and the related congestion level (although, to the date of writing, the effectiveness of such adaptive approaches in terms of performance/privacy gains and trade-offs is still to be assessed).

Control Logic

The "intelligence" of the system is implemented in a separate control logic module, which can combine the TFC basic mechanisms arbitrarily. For the time being, in order to provide flexibility, we have implemented batching, CBR (Continuous Bit rate), random padding, and random delay algorithms. The ease of such implementation shows the flexibility of the proposed framework, as well as its amenability to implement new algorithms.

We believe that a significant asset of our work is the accomplished decoupling between the algorithmic logic devised to masquerade/shape the traffic pattern, and its underlying implementation as a set of basic tools. This decoupling allows the network deployer to configure (or eventually directly program in the control logic) the most appropriate TFC algorithm suited for its purposes. For instance, in an anonymization network such as Tarzan [13] (which may be built on top of IPsec tunnels extended with the proposed TFC functionalities) the user activity is "well known" but it is necessary to modify the flow fingerprint in order to avoid correlation attack. Conversely, in a point to point connection (e.g., user to proxy) the main goal is to avoid protocol or web site fingerprinting, which may be more adequately countered with different masking algorithms. This versatility of the TFC mechanism also allows for the selection of different protection levels based on user preferences. A simple protection based on packet size modifications can be used for example to achieve a low level of protection. Packet timing can be added to improve the protection in exchange of some performance loss. Finally, the use of dummy packets can be turned on to provide an even higher level of protection, and the control logic can still control the amount of extra packets, from e.g. introducing extra dummy packets randomly amounting to the 10% of original data packets (a strategy that causes only negligible network load increase) to a CBR strategy (which provides perfect protection at the price of a constant load irrespective of the original traffic).

---

[7] Multiple queues may be internally deployed to differentiate packets incoming from different streams, where a stream may be defined either as a classification rule on the incoming packets, and/or in dependence of the different TFC Security Association mapped over the same IPsec ESP Security Association.

4   Demonstration

Fig. 4: Test setup

In what follows we demonstrate the flexibility of the TFC protocol as a protection means against website fingerprinting attacks. We chose website fingerprinting as an example where different levels of protection can easily be shown; however we emphasize that this is only one of the situations where Traffic Flow Confidentiality, as a basic security service, has importance. As we have discussed previously, timing based attacks on security protocols, traffic classification attacks, as well as traffic analysis attacks on mix networks all call for a TFC security service, and with different configurations of our TFC protocol (i.e., different control logics configured through SAs and paired with the appropriate SPs), security/privacy of these systems can also be enhanced.

To demonstrate the TFC protocol, we set up a test environment (Fig. 4) similar to the one used in [5] and [16]. We analyze how the information content of traffic dumps can be reduced, while performance degradation remains limited.

In our scenario, a client downloads web pages from normal, unmodified web servers (we use http://www.cnn.com/, http://www.nytimes.com/ and http://www.reuters.com/ for our experiments). To protect against traffic classification attacks, the client creates an IPsec protected tunnel to an exit node. Two ESP SAs and two TFC SAs are set up to cover the traffic of the bi-directional communication[8].

In this setup, protection is provided against attackers eavesdropping on links between the client and the exit node, while traffic is not protected from the exit node or on links between the exit node and the server. We emphasize that this is only an example of the many uses of TFC Security Associations. Being an IPsec security protocol, it can also be used in other network architectures, including security gateway to security gateway tunnels, end-to-end connections (using TFC in transport mode), or cascaded or encapsulated tunnels in anonymizer networks.

The client downloads a full web page, with all of its inline content, using the Firefox browser. We record traces of the packets traveling on the tunnel, repeating the experiment 10 times. We do not consider crypto analysis, therefore, according to our model, the only useful information for the attacker are: the packet length, packet time (and packet inter-arrival time) and the packet direction.

---

[8] Throughout our tests, we were using symmetric configuration for the SAs, but of course parameters (as well as the control logic) used in the two directions may differ.

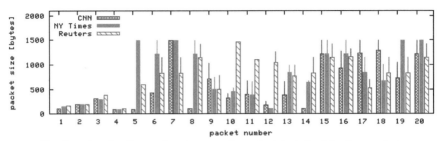

Fig. 5: packet size fingerprints (mean and standard deviation) for three websites.

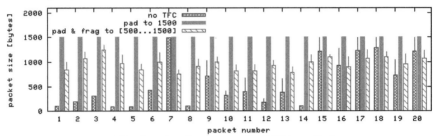

Fig. 6: packet size pattern after TFC is applied

First, we examine protection against attacks based on packet cardinality and properties of individual packets. A usual way of calculating the distance of traffic patterns is to examine properties (size, time or packet inter-arrival time) of the first n packets, calculating the distance as a function (typically sum) of individual distances (according to some distance metric) for the 1st, 2nd, ..., n^{th} packets.

Fig. 5 shows the size of the first 20 packets for the three sites when no TFC is applied. The filled bars represent the mean packet size, the thin bars the standard deviation. It can be seen how each site has its own characteristic packets (packets where the mean size is different from other sites' mean value, and where standard deviation is low). A traffic analysis tool can recognize these packets and match traffic patterns based on these values.

Fig. 6 shows the size of the first 20 packets after various protections are turned on (we show this only for one website in order to keep the figure readable). This figure demonstrates that the implementation of our protocol is working as expected, but also how characteristic packet sizes can be removed from the trace. Padding all packets to the MTU makes the packet size information uniform over all packets and, what is more important, over all traces. The other control logic determines a random size between 500 and 1500 bytes with uniform distribution, and uses padding and fragmentation to achieve this size. It can be seen (and also follows from the independence of the random value from the original packet size) that the introduced noise is enough to make packet size information useless.

Fig. 7 shows packet inter-arrival times (PIAT) for the three sites. Characteristic values can also be seen in these patterns. In Fig. 8 we show how the introduction of a minimum PIAT, or the introduction of dummy packets with a CBR logic changing the pattern. The first method removes only part of the characteristic values; large PIAT

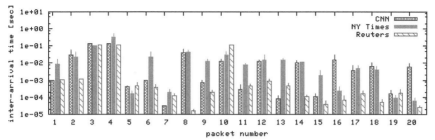

Fig. 7: packet inter-arrival times for the first 20 incoming packets for three websites.

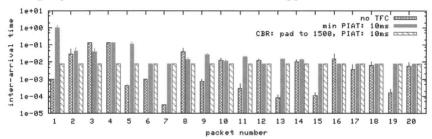

Fig. 8: packet inter-arrival times for CNN after TFC is applied.

values remain almost intact. With the introduction of dummy packets, these can also be changed: CBR with its constant PIAT represents the extreme of the use of dummy packets by removing all information from PIAT values.

How much protection these TFC strategies give? Which control logic to apply? In the figures shown until now, it can easily be seen even visually how information is removed from traffic traces. To really quantify the amount of protection, either an attack should be replicated or an information theoretical measure of the remaining characteristic information should be developed. Such an evaluation is out of the scope of this paper.

However, in Fig. 9 we show a representation, which, according to our knowledge was not used for website fingerprinting attacks before, and provides some insight into the level of protection. While packet counting and packet number based algorithms (such as [2,5,16]) can be fooled using a simple control logic (without randomization and without dummy traffic), looking at Fig. 9, it can easily be seen that the traffic pattern mapped into the "cumulative length" - "elapsed time" space remains somewhat characteristic of the site.

The top figure shows how the download of the three sites can be differentiated if no TFC is applied. For example, the main page of CNN and the NY Times contains the same amount of data and loads almost in the same time, however, differences in the structure of these sites dictate diverse download curves.

On the one hand, we can see that these curves remain (visually) recognizable even after padding (see middle figure) or after simple modifications to timing (see the bottom figure). It is not trivial how this resemblance can be used in automated recognition, but it shows that these simple control logics might not be enough once more sophisticated attacks are developed.

On the other hand, it comes trivially that CBR control logic would change each of the curves into a straight line, and therefore makes attacks based on these curves useless.

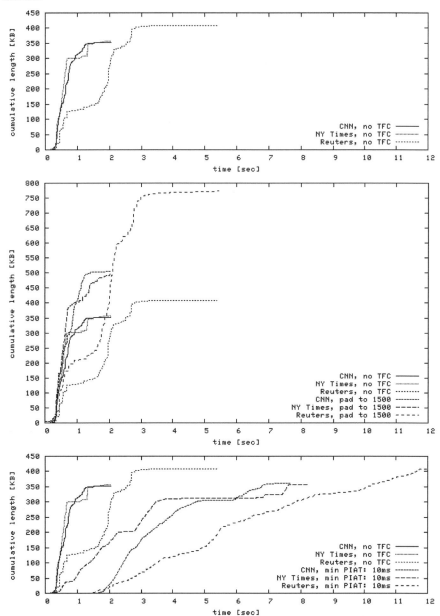

Fig. 9: Download of three web pages with different control logics: (top) representative download curve for each site; (middle) effect of padding on the curves (unmodified curves shown to ease comparison); (bottom) effect of PIAT variation on the curves.

Fig. 9 shows the performance drawback of each control logic as well. The end-point of each line shows the overhead in user perceived page download time and in traffic amount. For example, without TFC, the CNN page downloads in 2 seconds and generates 350 kbytes of traffic. The same download with packets padded to maximum size requires 2 seconds and 500 kbytes (this implicitly means that the tunnel was not the bottleneck). The introduction of a 10ms minimum PIAT limits burst speed to about 140 kbytes/sec, which, with page sizes in these days, reduces user experience considerably (the whole page is downloaded in 7-8 seconds).

These differences justify our choice of separating the control logic from the basic tools. In fact, whenever TFC is required, the appropriate control logic should be selected based on the attack model, performance requirements and the setting in which TFC is applied.

5   Conclusions

As shown by many recent papers, statistical traffic analysis techniques provide good results based on packet size and packet inter-arrival time statistics. We have designed the TFC IPsec security service to protect against such attacks, discussed its implementation and demonstrated its effectiveness.

Our approach goes well beyond current protocols and even beyond protections that were studied against statistical traffic analysis attacks. It provides a variable level of protection that makes the protocol applicable in various systems, introducing fragmentation, aggregation and packet inter-arrival time variation to balance the protection-performance tradeoff.

We further remark that fragmentation, as a technical tool to alter the traffic pattern's statistics, has received little attention in past work which typically implemented traffic flow confidentiality means through packet padding and dummy packet generation. However, literature work on IP flow classification [2] and on web site finger-printing [6] appear to suggest that a significant amount of the information used by the classifiers is brought by a few packets (frequently the initial ones in the session), whose size is quite different from the remaining ones in the session. This implies that fragmentation (eventually in conjunction with other tools) may be an extremely effective limited-overhead traffic flow confidentiality tool.

Our future work includes the evaluation of different (deterministic and stochastic, traffic independent and adaptive) control logics.

References

1.   L. Bernaille, R. Teixeira, and K. Salamatian, "Early Application Identification", Proceedings of the 2nd ADETTI/ISCTE CoNEXT Conference, Portugal, 2006.
2.   M. Crotti, F. Gringoli, P. Pelosato, L. Salgarelli, "A statistical approach to IP-level classification of network traffic", IEEE ICC 2006, 11-15 Jun. 2006.

3. T. Kohno, A. Broido, K. C. Claffy. "Remote physical device fingerprinting", in IEEE Symposium on Security and Privacy, pp. 211–225. IEEE Computer Society, 2005.

4. A. Hintz, "Fingerprinting Websites Using Traffic Analysis", Privacy Enhancing Technologies, PET 2002, S. Francisco, USA, April 2002

5. G. D. Bissias, M. Liberatore, D. Jensen, B. N. Levine, "Privacy Vulnerabilities in Encrypted HTTP Streams", PET 2005, Cavtat, Croatia, May 30-June 1, 2005.

6. L. Bernaille, R. Teixeira, "Early Recognition of Encrypted Application" Proc. PAM, April 2007.

7. D. X. Song, D. Wagner, X. Tian, "Timing analysis of keystrokes and timing attacks on SSH", 10th USENIX Security Symposium, 2001.

8. B. Canvel, A. Hiltgen, S.Vaudenay, M. Vuagnoux, "Password Interception in a SSL/TLS Channel", CRYPTO2003, Aug 2003, Santa Barbara, USA

9. Y. Zhu, X. Fu, B. Graham, R. Bettati, W. Zhao "On Flow Correlation Attacks and Countermeasures in Mix Networks", PET 2004, May 2004

10. X.Wang, S. Chen, S. Jajodia, "Tracking anonymous peer-to-peer VoIP calls on the internet", ACM Conf. on Computer and Communications Security, November 2005.

11. G. Danezis, R. Dingledine, N. Mathewson, "Mixminion: Design of a Type III Anonymous Remailer Protocol", 2003 IEEE Symp. on Security and Privacy, May 2003.

12. R. Dingledine N. Mathewson, P. Syverson, "Tor: The Second-Generation Onion Router", 13th USENIX Security Symp. Aug 2004.

13. M. J. Freedman, R. Morris, "Tarzan: a Peer-to-Peer Anonymizing Network Layer", ACM Conf. on Computer and Communications Security, Washington, DC, November 2002.

14. S. Kent, "IP Encapsulating Security Payload (ESP)", RFC 4303, December 2005.

15. M. Kanda, K. Miyazawa, H. Esaki, "USAGI IPv6 IPsec development for Linux", Int. Symp. Applications and the Internet Workshops (SAINT) 2004. pp. 159-163, Jan. 2004.

16. M. Liberatore, B. N. Levine, "Inferring the Source of Encrypted HTTP Connections", CCS2006, October 2006

17. ISO, "Information processing systems -- Open Systems Interconnection -- Basic Reference Model -- Part 2: Security Architecture", ISO 7498-2, 1989

18. T. Dierks, E. Rescorla, "The Transport Layer Security (TLS) Protocol Version 1.1", RFC 4346, April 2006

19. A. Back, I. Goldberg, A. Shostack, "Freedom 2.1 Security Issues and Analysis", May 2001

20. P. Syverson, G. Tsudik, M. Reed and C. Landwehr, "Towards an Analysis of Onion Routing Security", Workshop on Design Issues in Anonymity and Unobservability Berkeley, CA, July 2000

21. G. Danezis, "The trac analysis of continuous-time mixes", Privacy Enhancing Technologies (PET 2004), May 2004

22. S. J. Murdoch, G. Danezis, "Low-Cost Traffic Analysis of Tor", In Proceedings of the 2005 IEEE Symposium on Security and Privacy, May 2005.

On the Fundamentals of Anonymity Metrics

Christer Andersson and Reine Lundin

Karlstad University, Department of Computer Science
Universitetsgatan 2, 651-88 Karlstad, Sweden
{christer.andersson, reine.lundin}@kau.se

Abstract. In recent years, a handful of anonymity metrics have been proposed that are either based on *(i)* the number participants in the given scenario, *(ii)* the probability distribution in an anonymous network regarding which participant is the sender / receiver, or *(iii)* a combination thereof. In this paper, we discuss elementary properties of metrics in general and anonymity metrics in particular, and then evaluate the behavior of a set of state-of-the-art anonymity metrics when applied in a number of scenarios. On the basis of this evaluation and basic measurement theory, we also define criteria for anonymity metrics and show that none of the studied metrics fulfill all criteria. Lastly, based on previous work on entropy-based anonymity metrics, as well as on theories on the effective support size of the entropy function and on Huffman codes, we propose an alternative metric – the scaled anonymity set size – that fulfills these criteria.

1 Introduction

Anonymity can be defined as follows: "anonymity of a subject from an attacker's perspective means that the attacker cannot sufficiently identify the subject within a set of subjects, the anonymity set" [12]. This definition underlines both that anonymity can be quantified on a relative scale and that there might be a (situation-dependent) threshold where anonymity begins. Anonymity both involves *(i)* maintaining unlinkability between user / application data and the corresponding user with whom these data is concerned (data level anonymity) and *(ii)* hiding with whom a user is communicating (communication level anonymity). *Sender anonymity* means that a message cannot be linked to the sender of that message, while *recipient anonymity* implies that a message cannot be linked to the receiver(s) of that message [12]. The scope of the paper is limited to sender anonymity, although most ideas are valid also for recipient anonymity.

This paper discusses *anonymity metrics*, metrics that can be applied to measure the degree of anonymity in a certain scenario. State-of-the-art anonymity metrics are normally based on either *(i)* the number participants in the given scenario, *(ii)* the probability distribution in an anonymous network regarding which participant is the sender / receiver, or *(iii)* a combination thereof. In this paper, we first discuss the basics of measurements and anonymity metrics. Then, a basic model for anonymity attacks is proposed and some recent anonymity metrics

Please use the following format when citing this chapter:

Andersson, C. and Lundin, R., 2008, in IFIP International Federation for Information Processing, Volume 262; The Future of Identity in the Information Society; Simone Fischer-Hübner, Penny Duquenoy, Albin Zuccato, Leonardo Martucci; (Boston: Springer), pp. 325–341.

are presented. Thereafter, we define a set of "typical" scenarios for anonymous communication and quantify the degree of anonymity in these scenarios using the earlier introduced metrics. In the scenarios, the Crowds [14] system, a theoretically well studied and intuitive protocol, is used for providing anonymous communication. On the basis of this evaluation of the scenarios – and taking elementary properties of each anonymity metric into account – we thereafter propose a set of criteria that an anonymity metric should meet and assess whether the studied anonymity metrics fulfill these criteria.

A result from the evaluation of the criteria is that although some metrics fulfill most criteria, there is no anonymity metric that fulfill all criteria. Using existing entropy-based anonymity metrics [4, ?] as a starting point, we therefore propose and evaluate an alternative anonymity metric that better fulfills the stated criteria. We denote this anonymity metric the *scaled anonymity set size*, and to explain the underlying semantics of this metric, we use concepts such as Huffman codes / Huffman trees [3] and the effective support size of the entropy function [9].

This paper has the following structure. Section 2 introduces Crowds and presents a model for anonymity attacks. It also explains the basics of measurements and introduces a set of state-of-the-art anonymity metrics. Section 3 evaluates the behavior of these anonymity metrics when applied in a number of scenarios using the Crowds system. This section also proposes a set of criteria for anonymity metrics and evaluates the studied anonymity metrics against these criteria. As no metric fulfills all criteria, Section 4 proposes and explains an alternative entropy-based metric designed to meet these criteria – the scaled anonymity set size. Finally, Section 5 concludes the paper.

2   Preliminaries

2.1   Introduction to Crowds

This paper later presents four scenarios building on the *Crowds* system [14] – a mechanism for anonymous web browsing based on traffic forwarding through virtual paths. For this reason, this section contains a brief description of Crowds. The anonymity set in Crowds is denoted a *crowd*, and all users in the crowd run a *jondo* application. Also, a *blender* application administrates user membership and key distribution. Paths in Crowds are created randomly: first, a user extends the path to a random jondo, which, in turn, flips a biased coin (based on the probability of forwarding, p_f) to determine whether the path should be ended (i.e., the request is submitted to the web server), or extended to another jondo which repeats the same procedure.

2.2   A Model for Anonymity Attacks

An *anonymity attack* entails an attacker $\mathcal{A}$ trying to uniquely link an observed message (or set of messages) $\mathcal{M}$ to a user u_i in the anonymity set $\mathcal{U} = \{u_1, u_2, ...,$

u_n} by gathering knowledge about the system, the user base $\mathcal{U}$, and $\mathcal{M}$. Each of these entities have a set of attribute types / values. The system has attributes such as $a_i = \{application,\ \text{"Crowds"}\}$ and $a_j = \{p_f, \frac{3}{4}\}$. One essential attribute in the system is the probability distribution $\mathcal{P} = (p_1, p_2, \ldots, p_n)$, where p_i denotes the probability that u_i is the sender of $\mathcal{M}$. $\mathcal{U}$ has attribute sets about its users (or their devices), such as $a_i = \{name,\ \text{"Bob"}\}$ and $a_j = \{IP,\ 192.168.10.20\}$. Lastly, $\mathcal{M}$ shares several attribute types with $\mathcal{U}$, although they are initially empty. Now, an anonymity attack can be described as follows:

1. Initially, $\mathcal{A}$ can be assumed to know at least the public parameters of the system and some information about the users in $\mathcal{U}$.[1] $\mathcal{A}$ initially possess no knowledge about the sender. Hence, $\mathcal{P}$ is initially uniform.
2. Now, $\mathcal{A}$'s objective is to either passively observe or actively trigger events to learn information about $\mathcal{M}$. The triggering can be accomplished using arbitrary active attacks, such as a predecessor [18], intersection [13], or Sybil attack [6]. If $\mathcal{A}$ is successful, the events may enable him to learn one or more attribute values of $\mathcal{M}$'s attribute types, or at least restrict the corresponding value domains.
3. Then, $\mathcal{A}$ analyzes the collected attribute values of $\mathcal{M}$, together with the attributes of the system and the users in $\mathcal{U}$. $\mathcal{A}$'s objective is to calculate a new (less uniform) $\mathcal{P}'$. The way $\mathcal{P}'$ is calculated varies from scenario to scenario; in the included scenarios we base our calculations on the internal structure of Crowds [14].
4. $\mathcal{A}$'s goal is to map a single user in $\mathcal{U}$ to $\mathcal{M}$. Depending on $\mathcal{P}'$, there are three possible next steps: *(i)* if there is a $p_i \in \mathcal{P}'$ that is equal (or very close) to 1, the attacker succeeds; *(ii)* if any of $\mathcal{A}$'s resources are exhausted, he fails; else *(iii)* if $\mathcal{P}'$ cannot bind one u_i to $\mathcal{M}$ with a specifically large likelihood, repeat step two.

When assessing a system's resistance against anonymity attacks, an analyst can simulate these steps. In step three, the analyst can use an anonymity metric to determine the degree of anonymity. In the next section, we discuss the basics of measurement and anonymity metrics and give examples of anonymity metrics.

2.3 Anonymity Metrics

The Basics of Measurements. *Measurement* can be defined as "a mapping from the empirical world to the formal, relational world. Consequently, a *measure* is the number or symbol assigned to an entity by this mapping in order to characterize an attribute" where "the real world is the *domain* of the mapping, and the mathematical world is the *range*" [7]. One important rule is the *representation condition* which asserts that "a measurement mapping M must map entities into numbers and empirical relations into numerical relations in such a way that the empirical relations preserve and are preserved by the numerical relations" [7]. Lastly, a *metric* is a standard of measurement.

---

[1] Compare for example with the information distributed by the blender in Crowds [14].

Introduction to Anonymity Metrics. An anonymity metric is a mapping from the empirical world (the domain) to the mathematical world (the range), in which numbers or symbols are assigned to entities in a system to describe the degree of anonymity. The *domain* is the knowledge of the attacker $\mathcal{A}$ about the studied entities in the real world – the system and its anonymity set $\mathcal{U} = \{u_1, u_2, ..., u_n\}$. $\mathcal{A}$ may both be a real attacker or a model defined to test the resistance of a system against anonymity attacks. The system can both be a real world instance or a theoretical model. The *mapping* itself can be seen as a function behaving according to set of rules. An important parameter in the mapping is the probability distribution vector $\mathcal{P} = (p_1, p_2, ..., p_n)$ among the users in $\mathcal{U}$ regarding which user is the sender in a communication. Finally, the *range* is the set of possible values from the mapping. Here, there are many options, as different anonymity metrics use different units for presenting the degree of anonymity.

Examples of Anonymity Metrics. Below, we introduce some common metrics.

- *Anonymity set size:* a classic degree is the anonymity set size, $|\mathcal{U}| = n$. The concept of anonymity set was introduced in [2].
- *Crowds-based metric:* in this metric, the degree of anonymity A_i of a user u_i is measured on a continuum between `provably exposed` (0) and `absolute privacy`[2] (1), were $A_i = 1 - p_i = \bar{p}_i$ [14] (p_i is the probability that u_i is the sender). The continuum includes the intermediary points: `possible innocence` (the probability that u_i is *not* the sender is non-negligible, thus $A_i \geq 0 + \delta$, where $\delta > 0$); `probable innocence` (p_i that u_i is the sender is less than $1/2$, thus $A_i \geq 1/2$); and `beyond suspicion` (u_i is not more likely than any other $u_j \in \mathcal{U}$ to be the sender, and thus $A_i = \max\{A_1, A_2, ..., A_i, ..., A_n\}$ among $\mathcal{U}$).
- *Source-hiding property:* here, Θ is defined as the greatest probability you can assign to any user u_i of being the sender of a message, thus $\Theta = \max(\mathcal{P})$ [17]. Naturally, $\frac{1}{n} \leq \Theta \leq 1$, where $\Theta = \frac{1}{n}$ denotes maximum anonymity.
- *Entropy-based metrics:* in Serjantov / Danezis's metric [15], "the effective anonymity set size" $\mathcal{S}$ is defined as the Shannon entropy $H(\mathcal{P})$ [16] regarding which user in $\mathcal{U}$ sent a message, with $\mathcal{S} = -\sum_{i=1}^{n} p_i log_2(p_i)$, where $0 \leq \mathcal{S} \leq log_2(n)$. Díaz *et al.* [4] instead calculate the degree of anonymity $d = \frac{H(\mathcal{P})}{log_2(n)}$, where $0 \leq d \leq 1$. Both $\mathcal{S}$ and d output a max degree of anonymity when $\mathcal{P}$ equals the uniform distribution.

2.4   Measuring the Uniformness of Probability Distributions

To study how an anonymity metric behaves when the probability distribution $\mathcal{P}$ change, a function $d(\mathcal{P}, U)$ is needed, where U is the uniform distribution. Such

---

[2]The latter means that the attacker cannot distinguish between a situation where a potential sender participated in a communication and a situation where he did not [14].

a function $d(\mathcal{P}, U)$ should by some means quantify the distance (or quotient) between $\mathcal{P}$ and U. There are several alternatives for $d(\mathcal{P}, U)$, such as $d(\mathcal{P}, U) = H(U) - H(\mathcal{P})$ or $d(\mathcal{P}, U) = \frac{H(\mathcal{P})}{H(U)}$. Another option that we think could be used as well is to calculate $d(\mathcal{P}, U)$ as the Euclidean distance (ED) in n-space, according to the following:

$$d(\mathcal{P}, U) = \sqrt{\sum_{i=1}^{n}(p_i - \frac{1}{n})^2} \tag{1}$$

Here, $\frac{1}{n}$ is the probability assigned to each of the n users for the uniform distribution. Intuitively, Equation (1) outputs the ordinary distance between the two points $\mathcal{P}$ and U when they are plotted in an n-dimensional space, where $0 \leq d(\mathcal{P}, U) \leq \sqrt{\left(\frac{n(n-1)}{n^2}\right)}$. For $n \to \infty$, $\left(\frac{n(n-1)}{n^2}\right)^{1/2}$ approaches 1. In Figure 1 to the right, ED in 2-space is plotted for one example distribution $\mathcal{P} = (\frac{2}{3}, \frac{1}{3})$.

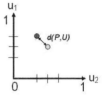

Fig. 1. ED in 2-space between $\mathcal{P} = (\frac{2}{3}, \frac{1}{3})$ and $U = (\frac{1}{2}, \frac{1}{2})$.

3   Evaluation of Anonymity Metrics

This section evaluates the degree of anonymity in a set of example scenarios using *Crowds* [14]. The scenarios involves a user communicating with an external web server through the Crowds network. The following parameters are varied in the scenarios: the number of users n, the number of rogue users c (where $c < n$), and p_f:

- In scenario one, $n = 10$, $c = 1$, and $p_f = 11/20$;
- In scenario two, $n = 1000$, $c = 10$, and $p_f = 11/20$;
- In scenario three, $n = 1000$, $c = 200$, and $p_f = 11/20$;
- In scenario four, $n = 1000$, $c = 200$, and $p_f = 3/4$.

Attacker Model. As Crowds does not provide anonymity against global observers or eavesdroppers directly observing the sender [14], we omit these entities from the attacker model, and instead only include *(i)* the c corrupted users and *(ii)* the web server. In the analysis, we assume that a corrupted user is succeeding the sender in the path.

3.1   Anonymity Evaluations

Below, we evaluate the erlier scenarios against the metrics introduced in Section 2.3. We provide the details of the calculations only for scenario one. For the entropy-based metrics and the source-hiding property, we need the probability distribution $\mathcal{P}$. From the perspective of the c corrupted users, $\mathcal{P} = (0.56, \frac{0.44}{8}, \frac{0.44}{8}, \frac{0.44}{8}, \frac{0.44}{8}, \frac{0.44}{8}, \frac{0.44}{8}, \frac{0.44}{8}, \frac{0.44}{8}, 0)$, while from the perspective of the web server $\mathcal{P}$ is uniform. The probability $p_i = 0.56$ is calculated as: $p_i = \frac{n - p_f(n-c-1)}{n} = \frac{10 - 0.55*8}{10} = 0.56$ [14].

- *Anonymity set size:* against the web server, this metric yields $|\mathcal{U}| = 10$ for $S1$ and $|\mathcal{U}| = 1000$ for $S2 - S4$. The corrupted users only count the honest users $\mathcal{U}' = \mathcal{U} - c$. Thus, in this case $|\mathcal{U}'| = 9$ ($S1$), $|\mathcal{U}'| = 990$ ($S2$), and $|\mathcal{U}'| = 800$ ($S3$, $S4$).
- *Crowds-based metric:* A_i against the web server is `beyond suspicion`, as all users in $\mathcal{U}$ are equally likely of being the sender. If expressing A_i as $1 - p_i$, we get $A_i = \frac{9}{10}$, as p_i that any u_i is the sender is $\frac{1}{10}$. Assuming that one of the c corrupted users succeeds the user u_i in the path, A_i against the corrupted users is `possible innocence`. This is because the following inequality does not hold [14]: $n \geq \frac{p_f}{(p_f - 1/2)} * (c + 1)$. Instead, the corrupted users can say with $p_i = 0.56$ that u_i is the sender (i.e., $A_i = 1 - p_i = 0.44$).
- *Entropy-based metrics:* according to Serjantov / Danezis [15], the effective anonymity set size against the corrupted users is calculated as $S = -\sum_{i=1}^{n}(p_i * log_2 p_i) = 1.83477 \approx 1.83$ bits. According to the metric proposed by Díaz et al. [4], the degree of anonymity is instead calculated as $d = \frac{H(\mathcal{P})}{log_2(n)} \approx 0.55$. Regarding the web server, Díaz et al.'s metric gives us $d = 1$, as $\mathcal{P}$ is uniform. Using Serjantov / Danezis's metric, we get $S \approx 3.32$ bits.
- *The source-hiding property:* the greatest p_i the corrupted users can assign to any u_i is $\max(\mathcal{P}) = 0.56$, and thus $\Theta = 0.56$. Against the web server, $\Theta = \max(\mathcal{P}) = \frac{1}{10}$.

In Table 1, we list the degrees of anonymity for the above scenarios. For comparison, we also include $d(\mathcal{P}, U)$ according to the Euclidean distance in n-space.

Table 1: Anonymity evaluation of scenarios (incl. Euclidean distance).

	Scen.	c corrupted users	Web server
Anonymity	S1	$|\mathcal{U}| = 9$	$|\mathcal{U}| = 10$
set size	S2	$|\mathcal{U}| = 990$	$|\mathcal{U}| = 1000$
	S3 & S4	$|\mathcal{U}| = 800$	$|\mathcal{U}| = 1000$
Crowds-	S1 & S3	`possible innocence`	`beyond suspicion`
based m.	S2 & S4	`probable innocence`	`beyond suspicion`
Entropy-	S1	$S = 1.83$ bits	$S = 3.32$ bits
based	S2	$S = 6.37$ bits	$S = 9.97$ bits
metric	S3	$S = 5.23$ bits	$S = 9.97$ bits
(Serjantov / Danezis)	S4	$S = 6.75$ bits	$S = 9.97$ bits
Entropy-	S1	$d = 0.55$	$d = 1$
based	S2	$d = 0.63$	$d = 1$

metric	S3	$d = 0.52$	$d = 1$
(Díaz et al.)	S4	$d = 0.68$	$d = 1$
Source-	S1	$\Theta = 0.56$	$\Theta = 1/10$
hiding	S2	$\Theta = 0.46$	$\Theta = 1/1000$
property	S3	$\Theta = 0.56$	$\Theta = 1/1000$
	S4	$\Theta = 0.40$	$\Theta = 1/1000$
Euclidean-	S1	$d(\mathcal{P},U) = 0.49$ (max: 0.95)	$d(\mathcal{P},U) = 0$
distance in	S2	$d(\mathcal{P},U) = 0.46$ (max: 0.995)	$d(\mathcal{P},U) = 0$
in n-space	S3	$d(\mathcal{P},U) = 0.56$ (max: 0.995)	$d(\mathcal{P},U) = 0$
	S4	$d(\mathcal{P},U) = 0.40$ (max: 0.995)	$d(\mathcal{P},U) = 0$

Some Observations from the Evaluation Results:

- All metrics except the anonymity set size consider probabilities. This is evident in the results as the difference in the degree of anonymity against the corrupted users and the web server is much less significant for the anonymity set size.
- Although stated in [15], we do not think that Serjantov / Danezis's metrics reflect the "effective anonymity set size" (as the endpoints do not overlap with those of the anonymity set size metric). We also think that the max anonymity (given n) should be made explicit. That is, S could be expressed as $H(P)$ out of $log_2(n)$ bits.
- Against the corrupted users, most metrics yielded the highest anonymity in $S4$.
- $d(\mathcal{P},U)$ according to the Euclidean distance in n-space seems to be fairly alike measuring distance based on entropy, although not exactly similar. Further analysis on the deviation between these different measures of $d(\mathcal{P},U)$ is left as future research.

3.2   Criteria for Anonymity Metrics

As it is essential that an anonymity metric gives an accurate picture about the degree of anonymity, we below state a set of criteria that an anonymity metric should meet.

- A user can be said to be de-anonymized when an attacker can, beyond reasonable doubt, pinpoint a user as the sender of an observed communication (step 3 in Section 2.2). Thus, the analyst must, in one way or another, consider probabilities.
    ⇒ *C1: An anonymity metric should base its analysis on probabilities.*

- The endpoints in an anonymity metric are "no anonymity" and "max anonymity". The meaning of 'max anonymity' can differ between different metrics. In metrics solely based on $\mathcal{P}$, max anonymity occurs when $\mathcal{P}$ is uniform and no anonymity occurs if: $\exists p_i \in \mathcal{P} \; ; \; p_i >> \max\{\mathcal{P} - p_j\}$, where $p_i \neq p_j$. A uniform $\mathcal{P}$ would yield (a special case of) beyond suspicion in the Crowds-based metric for any $u_i \in \mathcal{U}$. Yet, max anonymity for u_i in the Crowds-based metric – absolute privacy – does not correspond to max entropy, as $p_i = 0$ for u_i, and thus $\mathcal{P}$ is not uniform. Still, an anonymity metric should model these two endpoints in a theoretically sound manner.
  $\Rightarrow$ *C2: An anonymity metric must have well defined and intuitive endpoints.*
- Intuitively, the more uniform the $\mathcal{P}$, the more uncertain the attacker is. A metric should preserve this relation (recall the representation condition [13]). Thus, a degree of anonymity should increase if the uniformness of $\mathcal{P}$ increases, and vice versa.
  $\Rightarrow$ *C3: The more uniform the distribution $\mathcal{P}$, the higher the anonymity.*
- Assuming an unchanged uniformity of $\mathcal{P}$: the more the (honest) users in $\mathcal{U}$, the more the potential senders, and thus the higher the attacker's uncertainty. A metric should preserve this relation according to the representation condition. Thus, the degree of anonymity should increase if the number of users increases, and vice versa.
  $\Rightarrow$ *C4: The more the users in the anonymity set, the higher the anonymity.*
- By studying the degree of anonymity in a scenario, an analyst should be able to judge where in between the two endpoints (no & max anonymity) the current degree is. Thus, all values in the value domain of an anonymity metric should be well defined.
  $\Rightarrow$ *C5: The elements in the metric's value domain should be well defined.*
- An anonymity metric should use a scale preserving the ordering among elements, such as ordinal, interval, ratio, or absolute scale [13]. Further, it should be fined-grained enough to differ between seemingly similar, but not equivalent, scenarios.
  $\Rightarrow$ *C6: The value range of the metric should be ordered and not too coarse.*

Next, we evaluate the aforementioned anonymity metrics against these criteria.

3.3 Evaluation of Anonymity Metrics against Criteria

In Table 2, we assess whether the studied metrics fulfill the earlier stated criteria.

Table 2: Evaluation against criteria.

Anonymity set size metric	C1	-	Neither $	\mathcal{U}	= n$ nor $log_2(	\mathcal{U}	)$ consider (dynamic) probabilities.
	C2	-	As this is an absolute measure, the metric always outputs n, which can vary between 1 and ∞. Difficult to state a "good-enough" value for n.
	C3	-	Not fulfilled, as this metric does not consider probabilities.
	C4	+	Fulfilled, as the degree of anonymity is $	\mathcal{U}	= n$.
	C5	+	n simply entails the number of users in the anonymity set ($	\mathcal{U}	$).
	C6	+	Fulfilled, as this metric uses absolute scale.
Crowds-based metric	C1	+	Fulfilled, as output corresponds directly to the probability of being the sender an attacker can assign to the sending user in a system.
	C2	+	The metric varies between provably exposed and absolute privacy, where each intermediary category is semantically mapped to probabilities.
	C3	-	Not always true as individual probabilities are quantified.
	C4	+	In general fulfilled, assuming that the corresponding $p_i > 0$. Specifically, increasing n helps fulfilling $n \geq \frac{p_f}{(p_f - 1/2)} * (c+1)$ in the scenarios.
	C5	+	Categories are based on the underlying probability of being the sender.
	C6	-	Although ordinal scale is used, the output is fairly coarse.
Entropy-based metric (Serjantov / Danezis)	C1	+	Based on the entropy of the probability distribution.
	C2	-	The endpoints are 0 and $log_2(n)$. The latter is hard to calculate by hand.
	C3	+	Fulfilled, if we assume $d(\mathcal{P}, U) = H(U) - H(\mathcal{P})$.
	C4	+	Fulfilled. Note that the maximum increases with an increasing n.
	C5	-	States that an attacker on average has to find the answer for at least $H(P)$ binary questions to identity the sender which is not perfectly intuitive.
	C6	+	This criterion is fulfilled as ratio scale is used.
Entropy-based metric (Díaz et al.)	C1	+	Based on the entropy of the probability distribution.
	C2	+	Clear endpoints: 0 (no anonymity) and 1 (max anonymity).
	C3	+	Fulfilled, if we assume $d(\mathcal{P}, U) = \frac{H(\mathcal{P})}{H(U)}$.
	C4	-	This criterion is not fulfilled, as the resulting d is normalized.
	C5	+	Easy to interpret as d denotes the quotient between $H(\mathcal{P})$ and $H(U)$.
	C6	+	This criterion is fulfilled as ratio scale is used.
Source-hiding property	C1	+	Θ is directly based on the greatest probability in $\mathcal{P}$, as $\Theta = \max(\mathcal{P})$.
	C2	-	The use of an inverted scale is somewhat confusing (best case: $\Theta = 0$).
	C3	-	Although it can be expected to be true in many real scenarios, it may not coincide as the output is merely an individual probability.
	C4	+	Fulfilled, assuming corresponding $p_i > 0$ for added users.

		Θ is the max probability (of being the sender) any user in the anonymity set can be assigned of by the attacker. In real scenarios, it will probably often overlap with the probability assigned to the real sender.
	C5 +	
	C6 +	This criterion is fulfilled as ratio scale is used.

We can note in Table 2 above that no metric fulfill all criteria.

4   The Scaled Anonymity Set Size Metric

In Section 3.3, we saw that no anonymity metric fulfilled all criteria. For this reason, this section proposes an alternative entropy-based anonymity metric – the scaled anonymity set size metric – that is designed to fulfill these criteria.

Definition 1. *The scaled anonymity set size for a given distribution $\mathcal{P}$ is defined as:*

$$A = 2^{H(\mathcal{P})} \tag{2}$$

Equation (2) increases with an increasing uniformity of $\mathcal{P}$ and varies between 1 (when $\exists p_i \in \mathcal{P} \ ; \ p_i = 1$) and $n = |\mathcal{U}|$ (when $\mathcal{P}$ is uniform). The endpoints are intuitive as $max(A) = n$ equals the the actual size of the anonymity set and $min(A) = 1$ denotes a singleton set (i.e., the sender is identified). In the next sections, the underlying semantics of the scaled anonymity set size are explained. In particular, we show that $H(\mathcal{P})$ denotes a lower bound for the average number of yes-no questions an attacker needs to answer to identity the sender; thus, $2^{H(\mathcal{P})}$ is the the expected number of possible outcomes – or the effective support size of $H(\mathcal{P})$ (see below) – given this lower bound.

4.1   Theoretical Background

This section elaborates on the underlying semantics of the scaled anonymity set size by relating $H(\mathcal{P})$ and $2^{H(\mathcal{P})}$ to concepts such as Huffman codes, Huffman trees, expected number of questions (EQ), and the effective support size of the entropy (ESS).

Source codes and optimality. A *source code* is a mapping that assigns short descriptions (code words) to the most frequent outcomes of a data source (i.e., a random variable) and longer descriptions to less frequent outcomes. Source codes are often used in, e.g., data compression. Formally, the data source outputs symbols from an alphabet, where each symbol is associated with a weight stating the probability that it will be the next produced symbol by the data source. An *optimal* source code yields code words of minimum average length[3]. The following holds for optimal source codes, where L is the average length of the

---
[3]For more information on source codes and conditions for optimality, see for instance [3].

code words and $H(\mathcal{P})$ is the entropy of the probability distribution $\mathcal{P}$ (i.e., the weights) over the possible outcomes of the data source [16].

$$H(\mathcal{P}) \leq L < H(\mathcal{P}) + 1 \qquad (3)$$

Huffman codes. A classical optimal source code is the *Huffman code* [10]. The basic technique for producing Huffman codes is to create a binary tree, called a *Huffman tree*, from which the set of code words can be derived[4]. Each leaf in the tree corresponds to one possible outcome from the data source, and the code word corresponding to the data source is retrieved by traversing the tree from the root note to the given leaf node, while adding '0' to the code if a left branch is selected and '1' if a right branch is selected. See Figure 2 for an illustration, where the grey leaf nodes represent the possible outcomes and the digits to the left of the colons in the branch labels above the leaf nodes denote the respective code words for these possible outcomes.

The game of 20 questions and its relation to Huffman codes. In [3], the game of 20 questions is defined as the act of finding the most efficient series of yes-no questions to determine an object from a class of objects (assuming that we know the probability distribution $\mathcal{P}$ on the objects). It is shown in [3] that an optimal solution to this game is to create a Huffman tree based on $\mathcal{P}$ where the objects constitute the leaf nodes. Then, the strategy is to traverse the Huffman tree from the root node, and at each intermediary node ask the question "Is the sought object below the left branch or right branch?". Using this strategy, the average number of questions needed to identify the object, EQ, will coincide with the expected length L of the Huffman code (where the latter is determined by traversing the Huffman tree). Thus, Equation (3) can be rewritten as:

$$H(\mathcal{P}) \leq EQ < H(\mathcal{P}) + 1 \qquad (4)$$

Anonymity attacks and their relation to Huffman codes. The game of 20 questions (see above) corresponds directly to a situation when an anonymity attacker is trying to single out a sender from a group of users by using an optimal divide-and-conquer strategy on the user sets (i.e., binary search). If we assume that the attacker has derived $\mathcal{P}$, he can use the following strategy to identify the sender. First, he creates a Huffman tree, where the users in $\mathcal{U}$ constitute the leaf nodes in the tree (see Figure 2). The attacker then starts at the root node in the tree. Now, he needs to answer a series of yes-no questions of the type "is the sender in the group of users in the subtree below the left branch or below the right branch". By answering a certain number of such yes-no questions, the attacker will eventually end up in one of the leaf nodes in the tree, and now the sender is identified as the user corresponding to the current leaf node. As with the game of 20 questions, the expected number of yes-no questions that the attacker needs to answer, EQ, is bounded by $H(\mathcal{P})$ according to Equation (4).

---

[4]For more information on Huffman codes and Huffman trees, see for instance [3].

Support size and effective support size. In coding theory, the *support size* of a variable X with a probability distribution $\mathcal{P}$ is denoted $S(\mathcal{P})$. The support size is the size of the value domain of X (only counting outcomes whose corresponding $p_i \in \mathcal{P}$ are greater than zero). For example, if X is the outcome of a toss of a coin, $S(\mathcal{P}) = 2$. The support size is not affected by changes in $\mathcal{P}$ as long as the indvidual probabilities are not set to zero. If, for example, the coin was manipulated so that $\mathcal{P}' = (\frac{1}{10}, \frac{9}{100})$, $S(\mathcal{P}')$ would still yield two. On the other hand, the *effective support size* (ESS) for a variable X with probability distribution $\mathcal{P}$ outputs a value in the range $1 \leq ESS(\mathcal{P}) \leq S(\mathcal{P})$, depending on the degree of uniformity of $\mathcal{P}$, where $ESS(X) = 1$ if $\exists p_i \in \mathcal{P}$; $p_i = 1$ and $ESS(\mathcal{P}) = S(\mathcal{P})$ if $\mathcal{P}$ is uniform [9]. Grendar showed that it is appropriate to define $ESS(\mathcal{P}) = \exp(H(\mathcal{P}))$ for arbitrary log bases (and thus $ESS(\mathcal{P}) = 2^{H(\mathcal{P})}$ for log base two) [9]. The latter definition corresponds to the definition of the scaled anonymity set size metric. According to Grendar, $ESS(\mathcal{P})$ has a more natural meaning than the entropy $H(\mathcal{P})$, at least in the realms of statistics and probabilities.

On the semantics of the scaled anonymity set size. Above, we stated that the scaled anonymity set size represents the expected number of possible outcomes (alternatively: effective support size) given $H(\mathcal{P})$, which, in turn, is a lower bound for EQ – the expected number of yes-no questions an attacker needs to answer to identify the sender. This section presents a more intuitive explanation of the scaled anonymity set size. First, however, we prove the well known obsevation that the entropy of a variable X_1 with distribution $\mathcal{P}$, where $|X_1| = n$, equals the entropy of a variable X_2 with a uniform distribution, where $|X_2| = 2^{H(\mathcal{P})}$. Below, we state this property more formally in the context of anonymous communication (to improve clarity, the size of the user base is added as a parameter in the entropy expression for the remainder of this subsection).

Theorem 1. *The entropy $H(\mathcal{P}, n)$ of a probability distribution $\mathcal{P}$ over a user base $\mathcal{U}$ with n participants is equivalent to the entropy $H(U, n')$ of the uniform distribution U over a user base $\mathcal{U}'$ with $n' = 2^{H(\mathcal{P},n)}$ participants.*

Proof. [5]
The entropy $H(\mathcal{P}, n)$ in a user base $\mathcal{U}$ with n participants can be expressed as:

$$H(\mathcal{P}, n) = -\sum_{i=1}^{n} p_i log_2(p_i) \tag{5}$$

Now, $H(U, n')$ in a user base $\mathcal{U}'$ with $n' = 2^{H(\mathcal{P})}$ participants can be expressed as:

---

[5]This proof holds when $2^{H(\mathcal{P},n')}$ is an integer. Using differential entropy, Theorem (1) can be proved in a similar manner also for decimal numbers.

$$H(U, n') = -\sum_{i=1}^{n'} u_i log_2(u_i) = \tag{6}$$

$$-\sum_{i=1}^{2^{H(\mathcal{P},n)}} 2^{-H(\mathcal{P},n)} log_2(2^{-H(\mathcal{P},n)}) = \tag{7}$$

$$H(\mathcal{P}, n)2^{-H(\mathcal{P},n)} \sum_{i=1}^{2^{H(\mathcal{P},n)}} 1 = H(\mathcal{P}, n) \tag{8}$$

Upon the basis of Theorem 1 and its proof, we can state the following theorem.

Theorem 2. *The degree of anonymity according to the scaled anonymity set size in a user base $\mathcal{U}$ with n participants, $A = 2^{H(\mathcal{P},n)}$, is equivalent to the degree of anonymity $A = 2^{H(U),n'}$ in a user base $\mathcal{U}'$ with $n' = 2^{H(\mathcal{P},n)}$ participants, hence $A = 2^{H(\mathcal{P},n)} = 2^{H(U,n')} = n'$.*

Proof. This follows trivially from: $H(\mathcal{P}, n) = H(U, n') \Rightarrow 2^{H(\mathcal{P},n)} = 2^{H(U,n')} = n'$.

Informally, this means that a sender that participates in a communication where, for instance, $A = 10$ according to the scaled anonymity set size metric is as anonymous as he would be in a group of 10 users, where all users are equally likely of being the origin sender (regardless of the size of the original user base).

On the relationship between $A = 2^{H(\mathcal{P})}$ and EQ. Finally, to express a relation between $A = 2^{H(\mathcal{P})}$, $ESS(\mathcal{P})$, and EQ, we can rewrite Equation (4) as:

$$2^{H(\mathcal{P})} \leq 2^{EQ} < 2^{H(\mathcal{P})+1} \Rightarrow 2^{H(\mathcal{P})} \leq 2^{EQ} < 2 * 2^{H(\mathcal{P})} \tag{9}$$

From Equation (9) it follows that $1 \leq 2^{EQ} < 2n$, where $n = |\mathcal{U}|$. Thus, the theoretical minimum for the expected size of the solution space $2^{H(\mathcal{P})}$ (or effective support size) does not always match the *actual* expected solution space size 2^{EQ}. Yet, as $2^{H(\mathcal{P})} \leq 2^{EQ}$, the scaled anonymity set size never underestimates the effort an attacker must undertake to identity the sender. Still, in situations when $EQ > H(\mathcal{P})$, you could argue that it (and all other metrics based on entropy) "understates" the degree of anonymity, as in this case the theoretical minimum cannot be reached (as EQ is optimal).

Concluding notes. Above, we showed that entropy (and the scaled anonymity set size) are related to concepts such as optimal source codes and search trees, and, further, that the entropy gives a lower bound for how difficult it is to perform a binary search on the search space (see also [11] for more information). This means that entropy is well suited for quantifying security or anonymity in cases when the attacker conducts a binary search on the search space (i.e., uses a divide-and-conquer strategy), but it may be questionable whether entropy is a good measure in cases when the attacker conducts, e.g., a linear search on the search space (similar to a brute force attack). We suspect that in the context of anonymity attacks, the attacker behaves more intelligently than a simple (probability-based) linear search on the user base. Yet, we leave as future work asserting whether a model for anonymity attacks (such as the one in Section 2.2) corresponds to the anonymity attack based on Huffman codes described above.

4.2 Numerical Examples

Below follows two numerical examples in which we calculate the scaled anonymity set size and EQ. In these examples, we assume an attacker observing a system with five users. The attacker conducts attacks and, based on the information he learns from his attacks, calculates $\mathcal{P}$ regarding who is the sender in a particular communication.

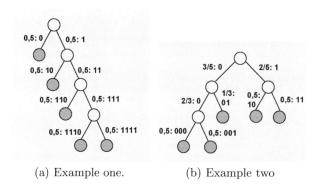

(a) Example one.   (b) Example two

Fig. 2. Huffman trees for examples one and two. The numbers to the left of the colons denote the probability for taking the given decision (left / right), while the right digits represent the code for the current position in the tree (0 = left and 1 = right). The leaf nodes represent the users.

Example one. Assuming that the attacker has calculated $\mathcal{P} = (p_{u_1} = \frac{1}{2}, p_{u_2} = \frac{1}{4}, p_{u_3} = \frac{1}{8}, p_{u_4} = \frac{1}{16}, p_{u_5} = \frac{1}{16})$, $H(\mathcal{P}) = 1,875$, and $A = 2^{H(\mathcal{P})} = 2^{1,875} = 3,67$ (max: 5). According to Equation (4), $H(\mathcal{P})$ denotes a lower bound for the expected number of yes-no questions the attacker needs to answer to identify the sender, while the reachable expected number of questions is given by EQ. The latter can be calculated by creating a Huffman tree based on $\mathcal{P}$ (left tree in Figure 2). Then, EQ can be calculated by using basic probability theory as $EQ = \frac{15}{8} = 1,875$. Hence, in this example $H(P) = EQ$.

Example Two. In this example, the attacker has obtained the (uniform) distribution $\mathcal{P} = (p_{u_1} = \frac{1}{5}, p_{u_2} = \frac{1}{5}, p_{u_3} = \frac{1}{5}, p_{u_4} = \frac{1}{5}, p_{u_5} = \frac{1}{5})$. Now, he can determine $H(\mathcal{P}) \approx 2,32$, $EQ = \frac{12}{5} = 2,4$ (see the right Huffman tree in Figure 2), and $A = 2^{H(\mathcal{P})} = 2^{2,32} = 5$ (max: 5). Thus, the maximum degree of anonymity is achieved in this example, and, contrary to the former example, the entropy $H(\mathcal{P})$ is here slightly lower than EQ.

4.3   Evaluation against Scenarios and Criteria

In Table 3, we calculate the degree of anonymity according to the scaled anonymity set size metric for the four scenarios defined in Section 3, while in Table 4 the scaled anonymity set size metric is evaluated against the criteria defined in Section 3.3. Table 3 shows that the ordering among the scenarios equals that of the Serjantov / Danezis metric [15]. Yet, we argue that the linear scale in the scaled anonymity set size metric more clearly shows that, e.g., A in scenario one is far lower than in the other scenarios. Further, Table 4 shows that all criteria are fulfilled for the scaled anonymity set size.

Table 3: Degrees of anonymity for the scaled anonymity set size.

	Scen.	c corrupted users	Web server
Scaled	S1	$A = 2^{H(\mathcal{P})} = 2^{1.83} = 3.6$ (for $n = 10$)	$A = 2^{log_2(10)} = 10$
anonymity	S2	$A = 2^{H(\mathcal{P})} = 2^{6.37} = 83$ (for $n = 1000$)	$A = 2^{log_2(1000)} = 1000$
set size	S3	$A = 2^{H(\mathcal{P})} = 2^{5.23} = 38$ (for $n = 1000$)	$A = 2^{log_2(1000)} = 1000$
	S4	$A = 2^{H(\mathcal{P})} = 2^{6.75} = 108$ (for $n = 1000$)	$A = 2^{log_2(1000)} = 1000$

Table 4: Evaluation of scaled anonymity set size against criteria.

Scaled	C1	+	Fulfilled, as this metric is based on probabilities.
anonymity	C2	+	Intuitive and well defined endpoints where A varies between 1 and n.
set size	C3	+	This criterion is fulfilled as A is based on the uniformity of $\mathcal{P}$.
	C4	+	Fulfilled, as max anonymity increases with n: $\max(2^{H(\mathcal{P})}) = 2^{log_2(n)}$.
	C5	+	$A = 2^{H(\mathcal{P})}$ is the size of the corresponding anonymity set in a user base where all users are equally likely of being the sender (see Theorem 2).
	C6	+	Fulfilled, as the scaled anonymity set size metric uses ratio scale.

4.4   Related Work on Quantifying Anonymity as $A = 2^{H(\mathcal{P})}$

To the authors' best knowledge, the consequences of quantifying the degree with which a user can be linked to a communication as $A = 2^{H(\mathcal{P})}$ have not previously been formally analyzed. However, in the context of anonymized databases, $2^{H(\mathcal{P})}$ have previously been proposed as measure of the risk of re-identification.

- In [8], Fischer-Hübner proposed to use $2^{H(\mathcal{X}_1,\ldots,\mathcal{X}_n)}$ as a measure of how many combinations of the value ranges of $\mathcal{X}_1,\ldots,\mathcal{X}_n$ that can be used for re-identification. A high value of $2^{H(\mathcal{X}_1,\ldots,\mathcal{X}_n)}$ means that the attacker is more likely to re-identify the user;
- Shortly after the pre-proceedings version of this paper was published, Bezzi proposed in [1] to use $2^{H(\mathcal{R}|s)}$ to quantify the number of different records in an anony-mized database that could correspond to the user, where $H(\mathcal{R}|s)$ denotes the conditional entropy between the anonymized and the original database. In this example, a high value of $2^{H(\mathcal{R}|s)}$ instead indicates a lower risk of re-identification for the user.

5   Summary & Outlook

In this paper, we discussed elementary properties of anonymity metrics. We defined a set of example scenarios for Crowds and quantified the degree of anonymity in these scenarios for some recent metrics. Based on the evaluation and measurement theory, we then defined a set of criteria for anonymity metrics, and assessed whether the studied metrics fulfilled these criteria. Lastly, we proposed to quantify anonymity as $A = 2^{H(\mathcal{P})}$ (denoted the scaled anonymity set size metric) and showed that this metric fulfilled the above criteria. Future work includes further analyzing the underlying semantics of scaled anonymity set size and other entropy-based metrics, formalizing a model for anonymity attacks and relating it to different optimal search strategies, as well as studying the correlation between different ways of quantifying the uniformity of probability distributions and their relation to different metrics.

Acknowledgements

Parts of this work have been funded by the EU FP6 project PRIME (Contract No. 507591) and the IST FIDIS (Future of Identity in the Information Society) Network of Excellence project (Contract No. 507512).

References

1. Michele Bezzi. An Entropy Based Method for Measuring Anonymity. In *Proceedings of the 3rd International Workshop on the Value of Security through Collaboration (SECOVAL 2007) in conjunction with the 3rd International Conference on Security and Privacy in Communication Networks (SecureComm2007)*, Nice, France, 17–20 Sep 2007. IEEE Xplore Digital Library.

2. David Chaum. The Dining Cryptographers Problem: Unconditional Sender and Recipient Untraceability. *J. Cryptography*, 1(1):65–75, 1988.
3. Thomas M. Cover and Joy A. Thomas. *Elements of Information Theory*. Wiley, 1991.
4. Claudia Díaz, Stefaan Seys, Joris Claessens, and Bart Preneel. Towards Measuring Anonymity. In Dingledine and Syverson [5].
5. Roger Dingledine and Paul Syverson, editors. *Proceedings of the 2nd Workshop on Privacy Enhancing Technologies (PET 2002)*, volume 2482 of *LNCS*, San Fransisco, CA, USA, Apr 2002. Springer-Verlag.
6. John R. Douceur. The Sybil Attack. In P. Druschel, F. Kaashoek, and A. Rowstron, editors, *Peer-to-Peer Systems: Proceedings of the 1st International Peer-to-Peer Systems Workshop (IPTPS)*, volume 2429, pages 251–260, Cambridge, MA, USA, 7–8 Mar 2002. Springer-Verlag.
7. Norman E. Fenton and Shari Lawrence Pfleeger. *Software Metrics – A Rigorous & Practical Approach*. PWS Publishing Company, 20 Park Plaza, Boston, MA 02116-4324, second edition, 1997.
8. Simone Fischer-Hübner. *IT-Security and Privacy: Design and Use of Privacy-Enhancing Security Mechanisms*, volume 1958 of *LNCS*. Springer-Verlag, May 2001.
9. Marian Grendar. Entropy and Effective Support Size. *Entropy*, 8(3):169–174, Aug 2006. Short note.
10. David A. Huffman. A Method for the Construction of Minimum-Redundancy Codes. *Proceedings of the Institute of Radio Engineers*, 40(9):1098 – 1101, Sep 1952.
11. Reine Lundin, This J. Holleboom, and Stefan Lindskog. On the Relationship between Confidentiality Measures: Entropy and Guesswork. In *Proceedings of the 5th International Workshop on Security in Information System (WOSIS 2007), held in conjuction with 9th International Conference on Enterprise Information Systems*, pages 135 – 144, Madeira, Portugal, 12–13 Jun 2007.
12. Andreas Pfitzmann and Marit Hansen. Anonymity, Unlinkability, Undetectability, Unobservability, Pseudonymity, and Identity Management - A Consolidated Proposal for Terminology v0.29, 31 Jul 2007.
13. Jean-François Raymond. Traffic Analysis: Protocols, Attacks, Design Issues, and Open Problems. In H. Federrath, editor, *Proceedings of Designing Privacy Enhancing Technologies: Workshop on Design Issues in Anonymity and Unobservability*, volume 2009 of *LNCS*, pages 10–29. Springer-Verlag, July 2000.
14. Michael Reiter and Avi Rubin. Crowds: Anonymity for Web Transactions. In *DIMACS Technical report*, pages 97–115, 1997.
15. Andrei Serjantov and George Danezis. Towards and Information Theoretic Metric for Anonymity. In Dingledine and Syverson [5].
16. Claude E. Shannon. A Mathematical Theory of Communication. *The Bell System Technical Journal*, 27:379–423, Jul 1948.
17. Gergely Tóth and Zóltan Hornák. Measuring Anonymity in a Non-Adaptive, Real-Time System. In David Martin and Andrei Serjantov, editors, *Proceedings of the 4th Workshop on Privacy Enhancing Technologies (PET 2004)*, pages 226–241, Toronto, Canada, 26–28 May 2004.
18. Matthew K. Wright, Micah Adler, and Brian Neil Levine. The Predecessor Attack: An Analysis of a Threat to Anonymous Communication Systems. *ACM Transactions on Information and System Security*, 7(4):489–522, Nov 2004.

A Model-based Analysis of Tunability in Privacy Services

Reine Lundin[1], Stefan Lindskog[1,2], and Anna Brunstrom[1]

[1] Department of Computer Science
Karlstad University
Karlstad, Sweden
`reine.lundin|anna.brunstrom@kau.se`
[2] Centre for Quantifiable Quality of Service in Communication Systems
Norwegian University of Science and Technology
Trondheim, Norway
`stefan.lindskog@q2s.ntnu.no`

Abstract. In this paper, we investigate the tunable privacy features provided by Internet Explorer version 6 (IE6), Mix Net and Crowds, by using a conceptual model for tunable security services. A tunable security service is defined as a service that has been explicitly designed to offer various security configurations that can be selected at run-time. Normally, Mix Net and Crowds are considered to be static anonymity services, since they were not explicitly designed to provide tunability. However, as discussed in this paper, they both contain dynamic elements that can be used to utilize the trade-off between anonymity and performance. IE6, on the other hand, was indeed designed to allow end users to tune the level of privacy when browsing the Internet.

1 Introduction

Many security services today only provide one security configuration at run-time, making it impossible to utilize the trade-off between performance and security, when user demands and/or the environment changes. Furthermore, the security configuration is often set by default, during setup or installation, i.e., before run-time, to achieve a high level of security, which may affect the performance of the system negatively. According to, for example, Pfleeger and Pfleeger [14], security services should be operating according to the principle of adequate security, which states that computer items must be protected only until they lose their value, and they must be protected to a degree consistent with their value. Hence, in situations where we want to make use of the trade-off between security and performance, tunable security services are needed. In this paper, a tunable security service is defined as a security service that has been explicitly designed to offer various security configurations that can be selected at run-time.

One important component of security is privacy, which by Westin [17] is defined as:

Please use the following format when citing this chapter:

Lundin, R., Lindskog, S. and Brunstrom, A., 2008, in IFIP International Federation for Information Processing, Volume 262; The Future of Identity in the Information Society; Simone Fischer-Hübner, Penny Duquenoy, Albin Zuccato, Leonardo Martucci; (Boston: Springer), pp. 343–356.

"Privacy is the claim of individuals, groups and institutions to determine for themselves, when, how and to what extent information about them is communicated to others."

Note, however, that the European view of privacy is slightly different than Westin's definition. In most European contries privacy protection is regarded as a basic right, not as a claim, and only individuals can have the right to privacy, not groups and institutions. A well-known aspect of privacy is anonymity. In [13] anonymity is defined as:

"Anonymity of a subject from an attacker's perspective means that the attacker cannot sufficiently identify the subject within a set of subjects, the anonymity set."

Hence, anonymity ensures that a user may use a resource without disclosing his or her identity.

A service that considers tunable privacy aspects is the web browser Internet Explorer version 6 (IE6) that is equipped with two mechanisms, cookie blocker and pop-up blocker, to safeguard the end users' spatial privacy [3] when browsing the web. Furthermore, to provide anonymity when browsing the web, the two services Mix Net, a network of mixes [1], and Crowds [16] could be used. The major difference between these two is that Mix Net provides anonymity by hiding the relation between incoming and outgoing messages for each mix, while Crowds provides anonymity by hiding one user's actions within the actions of many others. Even though Mix Net and Crowds were not explicitly designed as tunable anonymity services, they both contain dynamic elements that can be used to utilize the trade-off between anonymity and performance.

In this paper, IE6, Mix Net, and Crowds are analyzed using a conceptual model for tunable security services. The model was first proposed in [10], and it describes in a formal way the requirements for tunable security services. Thus, it provides a suitable tool to examine the tunability of privacy services.

The rest of the paper is organized as follows. In Section 2, the conceptual model for tunable security services used in the analysis is presented. Using this model, Sections 3–5 investigate IE6, Mix Net, and Crowds, respectively. Section 6 provides a discussion on tunable privacy and future work. Finally, Section 7 concludes the paper.

2   Conceptual Model

The conceptual model for tunable security services is described by the three sets:

- $T = \{\text{Tuner preferences}\}$
- $E = \{\text{Environmental descriptors}\}$
- $S = \{\text{Security configurations}\}$

and the function

$$TS : T \times E \to S \tag{1}$$

The TS function represents the mapping from tuner preferences, T, and environmental descriptors, E, to a particular security configuration, S. Hence, the TS mapping gives under which conditions the security configuration should be changed for the service. For example, when a device reaches a threshold in battery level the TS function could give that the security configuration of the device should be changed to increase the remaining time of the battery. Note that, for a security service to be a tunable security service S must contain at least two security configurations, otherwise the service will be static. The same will happen if both T and E are singular sets, since then $T \times E$ is a singular set as well.

Through the elements in T, the tuner preferences, a tuner entity can affect the security configurations in order to achieve desired trade-offs between security and performance. The tuner entities that set the tuner preferences of the security services typically exist on several layers, or phases of the system life cycle, such as system owner and/or end user. For example, a system owner might assign some tuner preferences for the provided service so that it fulfills the security policy of the company, while the end users in the same company are free to affect the rest of the preferences. The elements in T can be expressed at various abstraction levels, for example as low, medium, or high security, or by specifying frames or layers to encrypt in MPEG video streams [6, 11]. T might also be constructed from several parameters, each representing a different security objective such as confidentiality and integrity. In E, the environment and application descriptors that may influence the selection of security configurations are described. Possible elements in E include characteristics of equipment, threat model, energy consumption, and network load [4, 5, 9, 15]. The elements in S represent the possible security configurations of the tunable security service, such as encryption algorithm, MAC algorithm, key length(s), and key establishment algorithm.

In previous work, the above described conceptual model has successfully been used to examine the tunable features provided by seven different security services. Four services were analyzed in [10], the paper that introduced the model, and three additional services were evaluated in [8]. In this paper, we first apply the conceptual model when investigating the tunable privacy features provided within IE6. Then, we also apply the conceptual model when analyzing the two anonymity services, Mix Net and Crowds. Furthermore, since we only consider the privacy aspects of security, the term privacy configuration is used instead of security configuration in the rest of the paper.

3   Analyzing IE6

The first service to analyze is IE6, which is a web browser that is equipped with mechanisms to safeguard end users' privacy on the web[3]. The reason for describing IE6 as the first service is motivated by the fact that it is so commonly used today, and is therefore also quite well-known.

---

[3] See `http://msdn2.microsoft.com/en-us/library/ms537343.aspx` for a detailed discussion on privacy in IE6.

In IE6, two different blockers are provided to preserve end users' spatial privacy. One mechanism is referred to as the cookie blocker, and the other is referred to as the pop-up blocker. A cookie is a small file stored on the local computer and it is used as an identifier. Cookies are created by web sites to store information gathered about your visits to sites including, where you went, what you did, and any personal information you provided. Web sites may also have embedded links to other domains which set cookies. The latter type of cookies is known as third-party cookies. Cookies in relation with privacy is further described in [7]. The cookie blocker controlls how the browser handles cookies, and the pop-up blocker is aimed to prevent pop-up windows from appearing on the end users' screen.

3.1 Privacy Configurations (S)

The available privacy configurations in IE6 are based on the set of possible configurations of the cookie blocker, denoted CB, and the set of possible configurations of the pop-up blocker, denoted PB. Thus, the privacy configurations of IE6 can be expressed as: $S = CB \times PB$. With respect to cookie handling, six different privacy configurations are provided, ranging from "Block All Cookies" to "Accept All Cookies". The full set of cookie blocker options are as follows: $CB = \{BAC, Hi, MH, Me, Lo, AAC\}$, where the different options are abbreviations of "Block All Cookies", "High", "Medium High", "Medium", "Low", and "Accept All Cookies", respectively. The pop-up blocker feature, on the other hand, is simpler and could either be turned on or off. Thus, $PB = \{yes, no\}$.

3.2 Tuner Preferences (T)

The user interface provided in IE6 is illustrated in Fig. 1. In the figure, the cookie blocker is set to "Medium" and the pop-up blocker is turned on. As is shown in the figure, when selecting a cookie blocker option additional information about that particular choice is displayed. Furthermore, the IE6 service offers no abstraction of the privacy configurations. Hence, the privacy configurations are directly controlled by the tuners and, thus, $T = CB \times PB$.

Note that some web sites require that cookies can be stored and later retrieved from the client to work properly. This implies that web sites that are built on cookies may not be accessible as expected when the high privacy protection policies are used in IE6.

3.3 Environmental Descriptors (E)

There is no explicit use of environmental descriptors, since the privacy configuration is directly controlled by the tuner. Hence, the set of environmental descriptors contains the empty set in this case, i.e., $E = \{\emptyset\}$. However, the tuner can take the environment into account when selecting a privacy configuration.

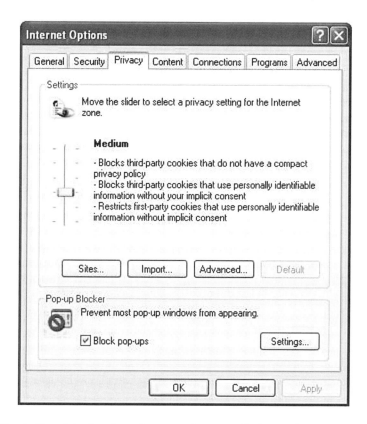

Fig. 1. User interface for privacy settings provided to end users in IE6.

3.4 The TS Mapping

The TS function is in this case the identity mapping

$$TS(t, \emptyset) = t \qquad (2)$$

where $t \in T$. The simplicity of the TS function is an effect of the direct tuner control of the privacy configurations. Thus, it is up to the tuner to select an appropriate privacy configuration.

4 Analyzing Mix Net

To achieve untraceable electronic mail David Chaum introduced the idea of mixes [1]. A mix is a special network station that has the basic task of hiding the relation between incoming and outgoing messages. Hence, a mix basically attains sender anonymity and unlinkability between sender and receiver. A network of mixes is called a Mix Net. In Fig. 2 a Mix Net chain, an ordered sequence of mixes, is illustrated.

Fig. 2. A Mix Net chain.

The major work for a single mix is to collect messages in a pool, decide when a subset of messages should be flushed from the pool, and decide which subset of the messages in the pool to flush. The flushing conditions divide the mixes into two types, timed mixes and threshold mixes [2]. Timed mixes flush on certain predefined time intervals and threshold mixes flush when they have collected a certain amount of messages. A combination of the two types also exists [12]. The subset of messages to flush is determined by the pool flushing algorithm. Below we will analyze mixes that have a deterministic pool flushing algorithm [2].

4.1 Privacy Configurations (S)

A deterministic pool flushing algorithm uses the number of messages in the pool, n, to determine the number of messages to send out, s. For such mixes, we can write $s = nP$, where P is the fraction of sent messages, obviously $1 \leq s \leq n$. Note, however, that the subset of sent messages are still randomly chosen from the pool, even if the number of sent messages is deterministic. See Fig. 3 for an illustration of a mix with a deterministic flushing algorithm.

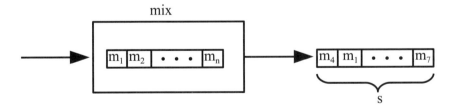

Fig. 3. A mix having n messages in the pool and flushing s messages.

The cycle of collecting and flushing messages is called one round. Furthermore, since a Mix Net consists of several mixes, we write s_{ij} to denote the number of sent messages in round i at mix j, $i \geq 1$ and $1 \leq j \leq m$. In a similar way, n_{ij} denotes the number of messages in the pool in round i at mix j. Now, since s_{ij} and n_{ij} are the only parameters that affect the privacy configurations, and also the performance, of a Mix Net with a deterministic pool flushing algorithm, we get the following privacy configurations $S = \prod_{j=1}^{m}(s_{ij} \times n_{ij})$.

4.2 Tuner Preferences (T)

For deterministic mixes the privacy configurations are directly controlled by the tuner, just as for IE6, since the system offers no abstraction of the privacy configurations. Furthermore, in a Mix Net there might be a tuner for each mix, which is the system owner of the mix. Hence, the set of tuner preferences is in this case equal to the set of possible privacy configurations, $T = \prod_{j=1}^{m}(s_{ij} \times n_{ij})$. Although not explicitly expressed in T, the selection of a privacy configuration represents a trade-off between the level of anonymity and the resulting overhead in terms of message delay in the system. Note, however, that it is the system owner for each mix that controls the anonymity level. Hence, the system owners are the tuners, not the end users.

4.3 Environmental Descriptors (E)

Exactly as for IE6, there is no explicit use of environmental descriptors when considering deterministic mixes, since the privacy configuration is directly controlled by the tuner. Hence, $E = \{\emptyset\}$.

4.4 The TS Mapping

The TS function is, hence, as for IE6, the identity mapping

$$TS(t, \emptyset) = t \tag{3}$$

where $t \in T$. Thus, it is up to the tuner to select an appropriate privacy configuration and to investigate the trade-off between anonymity and performance.

5 Analyzing Crowds

The basic idea of Crowds [16] is to provide anonymous web browsing by hiding one end user's web actions within the web actions of many others. The Crowds system consists of two main components. The Jondo proxy application, which the browser requests must be set to go through, and the Blender server for managing memberships. See Fig. 4 for an illustration of the Crowds system.

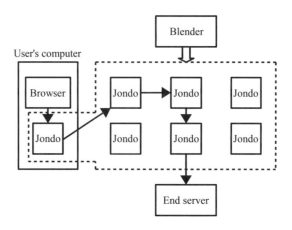

Fig. 4. The Crowds system.

5.1 Privacy Configurations (S)

One important parameter in Crowds is p_f, $0 \leq p_f < 1$. It gives the probability of forwarding a message, in the path creation process. When the first request arrives at a local Jondo, it forwards the request to another randomly selected Jondo in Crowds, possibly itself. The next Jondo, on the path, chooses to forward the request to another randomly selected Jondo in the Crowds system with probability p_f, or to submit the request to the end server with probability $1 - p_f$. This decision process, forward or submit, continues until a Jondo submits the request to the end server. Since the only parameter that gives the privacy configuration in Crowds is p_f, we get that $S = p_f$.

5.2 Tuner Preferences (T)

In [16], the authors defined six different anonymity levels (AL) for sender/receiver anonymity. Note that in the definitions below, the sender can be exchanged to receiver.

- A sender has absolute privacy (AP), if an observation gives the attacker no additional information.
- A sender is beyond suspicion (BS), if though the attacker can see evidence of a sent message the sender appears no more likely to be the originator of that message than any other potential sender in the system.
- A sender has probable innocence (PrI), if from the attacker's point of view the sender appears no more likely to be the originator than to not be the originator.
- A sender has possible innocence (PoI), if from the attacker's point of view there is a non trivial probability, $\delta > 0$, that the real sender is someone else.

- A sender is exposed (Ex), if the attacker can identify the sender but not necessarily prove it to others.
- A sender is provably exposed (PE), if the attacker can identify the sender and also prove the identity to others.

In this paper, we treat the ALs Ex and PE as equal. Furthermore, as will be discussed later, it is only possible to tune sender anonymity against attackers that are collaborating members. For this case, using the anonymity measure given in [16], the Crowds system can not be configured to guarantee BS and AP. Thus, $T = \{PrI, PoI, Ex\}$. However, as we will see, the Crowds system offers from the sender's perspective and under probabilistic assumption both AP and BS.

5.3   Environmental Descriptors (E)

Except from the p_f parameter, two further parameters, n and a, are needed to describe the Crowds system. The first parameter, n, represents the total number of Jondos in the Crowds system, hence, $n > 1$. The second parameter, a, on the other hand, represents one of the following three attacker types in the Crowds system.

1. A local eavesdropper (LE) is an attacker who can observe all communication to and from the computer of a specific Crowds member.
2. Collaborating members (CM) are attackers in the form of Crowds members that can pool their information and even deviate from the prescribed protocol.
3. The end servers (ES) are attackers to which web requests are directed.

Thus, $a \in A = \{LE, CM, ES\}$, and $E = n \times A$. When $a = CM$ we set $a = c$, the number of collaborating Jondos.

5.4   The TS Mapping

The sender/receiver ALs that are achieved by Crowds [16] are given in Table 1.

Table 1. Levels of anonymity offered by Crowds against different types of attackers.

Attacker	Sender Anonymity	Receiver Anonymity
LE	Ex	$\lim_{n\to\infty} P(BS) = 1$
CM	PrI if $n \geqslant \frac{p_f(c+1)}{p_f - \frac{1}{2}}$	$\lim_{n\to\infty} P(AP) = 1$
ES	BS	N/A

From Table 1 we see that for receiver anonymity against LE the probability of BS tends to one as the number of Jondos tends to infinity. However, receiver anonymity against LE can be both Ex and BS, depending on if the initiating Jondo finally sends the request by itself to the end server or not. If the initiating Jondo sends the request it will be unencrypted to the LE and receiver anonymity is Ex, otherwise the receiver has BS. The probability of the receiver, R, to be Ex against LE are

$$P_{R,LE}(Ex) = \frac{1}{n} \sum_{i=0}^{\infty} p_f^i (1 - p_f) \tag{4}$$

$$= \frac{1}{n}$$

Hence, $\lim_{n \to \infty} P_{R,LE}(Ex) = 0$ or $\lim_{n \to \infty} P_{R,LE}(BS) = 1$, as stated in Table 1.

For receiver anonymity against CM we have a similar situation. From Table 1 we see that the probability of AP tends to one as the number of Jondos tends to infinity, for a fixed number of CM. However, the receiver has AP if the path does not contain a CM and Ex otherwise, since all requests on a path are unencrypted to all crowds members on that path. The probability of the receiver, R, to have AP against CM are

$$P_{R,CM}(AP) = \sum_{i=0}^{\infty} \left(\frac{n-c}{n} \right)^{i+1} p_f^i (1 - p_f) \tag{5}$$

$$= 1 - \frac{c}{n - p_f(n - c)}$$

Hence, $\lim_{n \to \infty} P_{R,CM}(AP) = 1$, if c is fixed, as stated in Table 1.

For sender anonymity against CM, Table 1 only gives PrI when inequality (6) holds.

$$n \geqslant \frac{p_f(c+1)}{p_f - \frac{1}{2}} \tag{6}$$

However, in general for sender anonymity against CM three important cases can occur.

1. The sender, S, has AP if the path does not contain any CM. This happens with the same probability as $P_{R,CM}(AP)$, see equation (5). Thus,

$$P_{S,CM}(AP) = 1 - \frac{c}{n - p_f(n - c)} \tag{7}$$

2. The sender, S, is BS if he or she does not have a CM as an immediate successor, since the CMs suspect the immediate preceding Jondo more than the other Jondos. This situation occurs with probability

$$P_{S,CM}(BS) = \frac{c(n-c-1)}{n^2}(1 - p_f) \sum_{i=0}^{\infty} p_f^{i+1} \sum_{j=0}^{i} \left(\frac{n-c}{n} \right)^j \tag{8}$$

$$= \frac{p_f c(n-c-1)}{n(n - p_f(n-c))}$$

3. The sender, S, has X anonymity, where $X = PrI|PoI|Ex$ depending on the value of $P_{S,CM}(X)$, if he or she has a CM as an immediate successor. This situation occurs with probability

$$P_{S,CM}(X) = \frac{c}{n}(1 - p_f) \sum_{i=0}^{\infty} p_f^i + \frac{c}{n^2}(1 - p_f) \sum_{i=0}^{\infty} p_f^{i+1} \sum_{j=0}^{i} \left(\frac{n-c}{n}\right)^j \quad (9)$$

$$= \frac{c(n - p_f(n - c - 1))}{n(n - p_f(n - c))}$$

From the discussion above, Table 2 extends Table 1. In Table 2 all the possible ALs are included.

Table 2. Extended table of levels of anonymity offered by Crowds against different types of attackers.

Attacker	Sender Anonymity	Receiver Anonymity
LE	Ex	BS|Ex
CM	AP|BS|PrI|PoI|Ex	AP|Ex
ES	BS	N/A

It is only in situation three for sender anonymity against CM where it is possible with the value of p_f to guarantee the achieved anonymity. Thus, it is only possible to tune sender anonymity against CM. In [16], the authors derived and used an anonymity measure, $P(I|H_{1+})$, for sender anonymity against CM, where $P(I|H_{1+})$ is the probability that the path initiator is the first collaborator's immediate predecessor, given that there is at least one CM on the path. This is the same as

$$P(I|H_{1+}) = \frac{p(X)}{1 - p(AP)} \quad (10)$$

$$= 1 - p_f \frac{n - c - 1}{n}$$

$$= 1 - p_f N(n, c)$$

where $N(n, c)$ is the fraction of non-CMs in Crowds excluding your own Jondo. Note that in [16], the authors used another approach to calculate $P(I|H_{1+})$.

Using this measure, it is only possible to have $T = \{PrI|PoI|Ex\}$, since $AL = AP$ is excluded due to the fact that CMs are on the path, and $AL = BS$ is not possible, since

$$1 - p_f N(n, c) > \frac{1}{n} \quad (11)$$

Furthermore, by setting $P(I|H_{1+}) \leq \frac{1}{2}$, Reiter and Rubin [16] showed that Crowds offers PrI as long as inequality (6) holds, which can be rewritten to

$$p_f \geq \frac{1}{2N(n, c)} \quad (12)$$

This implies that we must have $N(n,c) \geq \frac{1}{2}$. Similarly, by setting $P(I|H_{1+}) \leq 1-\delta$, Crowds offers PoI as long as

$$p_f \geq \frac{\delta}{N(n,c)} \tag{13}$$

Finally, by setting $P(I|H_{1+}) = 1$ the AL is Ex. Thus $p_f = 0$.

Now, assume that we would like to minimize the delay in Crowds, under a given privacy constraint. Then, since the expected path length [16] is, $L = \frac{2-p_f}{1-p_f}$, the smallest value of p_f minimizes the delay. Thus, we get the following TS function.

$$\begin{aligned} TS(PrI,n,c) &= \frac{1}{2N(n,c)} \\ TS(PoI,n,c) &= \frac{\delta}{N(n,c)} \\ TS(Ex,n,c) &= 0 \end{aligned} \tag{14}$$

We have in this case assumed that $N(n,c) \neq 0$, otherwise Crowds will only offer Ex. In Fig. 5, we have plotted X with respect to p_f for $N(n,c) = 1$ ($n \to \infty$, c fixed) and $N(n,c) = 1/2$ when $\delta = \frac{1}{6}$. Note, however, that it is not possible for the system to achieve PrI as $N(n,c)$ becomes one half.

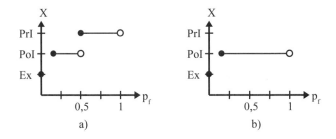

Fig. 5. X as a function of p_f for a) $N(n,c) = 1$ and b) $N(n,c) = 1/2$.

6 Discussion and Future Work

In this paper, three different services that provide privacy protection have been studied by using a previously proposed conceptual model for tunable security services. All three offer some form of privacy tunability. In the case of IE6, the degree of privacy protection is directly specified by the end user. The same holds for deterministic mixes, where the degree of anonymity is directly controlled by the mix owners. In Crowds, both end user preferences and environmental characteristics are taken into consideration when selecting a privacy configuration. A continuation of this work would be to investigate the tunable features in other privacy services.

The basic idea with tunable privacy services is to have the opportunity to utilize the trade-off between performance and privacy at run-time. However, to be able to select the most appropriate privacy configuration in a particular situation, both performance and privacy metrics must be studied further. A simple ordering of privacy configurations with respect to privacy and performance is sometimes sufficient, while finer grained metrics that also specify the difference between available configurations are needed in other situations. We believe that developing such metrics is a very challenging research task in this field.

From the three investigated privacy services, it is not trivial for the tuner to specify the most suitable configuration in a given situation. Hence, further research is clearly needed on end user privacy configurability in relation with usability, since very few end users are today able to make correct decisions on how to configure privacy services on their own computer. This is partly due to poor user interfaces and partly due to a lack of privacy awareness. More emphasis on the design of user interfaces for end user controlled privacy and more efforts on spreading knowledge about privacy will therefore considerably reduce the risk for the end users.

7   Concluding Remarks

In this paper, the tunable privacy features of IE6, Mix Net and Crowds have been analyzed. Both tuner preferences (T) and environmental characteristics (E) that influence the choice of a specific privacy configuration (S) have been identified. In addition, the mapping to a particular privacy configuration has been described through a mapping function, which is referred to as the TS function. This implies that some dynamic elements of each service have been identified and analyzed.

Acknowledgment

The work performed at Karlstad University was supported by grants from the Knowledge Foundations of Sweden with TietoEnator and Ericsson as industrial partners.

References

1. D. Chaum. Untraceable electronic mail, return addresses, and digital pseudonyms. *Communications of the ACM*, 4(2), February 1981. http://www.eskimo.com/~weidai/mix-net.txt.
2. C. Díaz. *Anonymity and Privacy in Electronic Services*. PhD thesis, Katholieke Universiteit Leuven, Leuven, Belgium, December 2005.
3. S. Fischer-Hbner and C. Andersson. Privacy risks and challenges for the mobile internet. In *Proceedings of the IEE Summit on Law and Computing*, London, November 2 2004.
4. C. T. R. Hager. *Context Aware and Adaptive Security for Wireless Networks*. PhD thesis, Virginia Polytechnic Institute and State University, Blacksburg, VA, USA, November 2004.

5. H. Johnson, L. Isaksson, M. Fiedler, and S. F. Wu. A decision system for adequate authentication. In *Proceedings of the International Conference on Networking, International Conference on Systems and International Conference on Mobile Communications and Learning Technologies (ICNICONSMCL'06)*, Washington, DC, USA, April 23–29, 2006. IEEE Computer Society.

6. Y. Li, Z. Chen, S. M. Tan, and R. H. Campbell. Security enhanced MPEG player. In *Proceedings of the 1996 International Workshop on Multimedia Software Development (MMSD'96)*, pages 169–176, Berlin, Germany, March 25–26 1996.

7. H. Lindskog and S. Lindskog. *Web Site Privacy with P3P*. Wiley Publishing, Indianapolis, IN, USA, 2003.

8. S. Lindskog, A. Brunstrom, and Z. Faigl. Analyzing tunable security services. In *Proceedings of the 3rd Swedish National Computer Networking Workshop (SNCNW 2006)*, Luleå, Sweden, October 26–27, 2006.

9. S. Lindskog, A. Brunstrom, Z. Faigl, and K. Tóth. Providing tunable security services: An IEEE 802.11i example. In *Proceedings of the first Workshop on Enterprise Network Security (WENS 2006)*, Baltimore, MD, USA, August 28, 2006.

10. S. Lindskog, A. Brunstrom, R. Lundin, and Z. Faigl. A conceptual model of tunable security services. In *Proceedings of the 3rd International Symposium on Wireless Communication Systems (ISWCS 2006)*, pages 531–535, Valencia, Spain, September 5–8, 2006.

11. J. Meyer and F. Gadegast. Security mechanisms for multimedia data with the example MPEG-I video, 1995. http://www.gadegast.de/frank/doc/secmeng.pdf.

12. U. Möller, L. Cottrell, P. Palfrader, and L. Sassaman. Mixmaster Protocol — Version 2, July 2003.

13. A. Pfitzmann and M. Hansen. Anonymity, unlinkability, undetectability, unobservability, pseudonymity, and identity management – a consolidated proposal for terminology. Draft, July 2007.

14. C. P. Pfleeger and S. L. Pfleeger. *Security in Computing*. Prentice Hall, Upper Saddle River, NJ, USA, 3rd edition, 2003.

15. P. Prasithsangaree and P. Krishnamurthy. On a framework for energy-efficient security protocols in wireless networks. *Computer Communications*, 27(17):1716–1729, 2004.

16. M. K. Reiter and A. D. Rubin. Crowds: anonymity for Web transactions. *ACM Transactions on Information and System Security*, 1(1):66–92, 1998.

17. A. Westin. *Privacy and Freedom*. Atheneum, New York, NY, USA, 1967.

Workshop: Social and Cultural Aspects of Identity

Digital Identity and Anonymity
Desi Manifestations and Regulation

Rowena Rodrigues

School of Law, University of Edinburgh
rowena_edw@yahoo.com

Abstract. This paper briefly introduces identity influences, the categorizations of identity and the concepts of anonymity and pseudonymity in India. It also makes a study of digital identity, anonymity and pseudonymity, the manifestations thereof, applications and concerns. It examines the regulation of digital identity vis-à-vis the IT Act 2000, case laws and the implementation of the Multi-purpose National Identity Cards (MNIC's) in India.

1 Introduction

India is not just a nation with the second largest population in the world and with the world's largest electorate; it is a country constantly in a state of growth and development. It produces supercomputers, launches satellites and has the second largest community of software developers in the world. India has a significant online presence [1] that is constantly growing and expanding and is beginning to face a number of challenges in respect of the digital realm, particularly in relation to identity, anonymity, pseudonymity and their regulation (which are the focal points of study of this paper).

To better comprehend what affects identity in India, we need to take a closer look at its past, present and development. India is a country that has been made and moulded by history of invasions, ruthless colonisation and consequent dramatic divisions. It is a melting pot of different cultures, customs, traditions, rites, rituals and languages. It is a country with a tapestry of assimilation and dissemination, of tolerance, influence and confluences. It is a country steeped in mythology, shrouded by religion and garbed by culture and tradition. On a political note, it is a democratic republic with a strong social welfare agenda.

2 Identity influences and categories

There have been many studies on identity in India [2-5]. Cohn [6] states that identity formation in South Asia was influenced by the British colonial census. Jodhka [7] affirms that public discussions and academic discourses on the question of identity in India have been influenced by Hall's views on identity-looking at identity in cultural terms-in terms of one, shared culture, a collective of true self hidden inside the many other more artifically imposed or superficial selves [8].

Please use the following format when citing this chapter:

Rodrigues, R., 2008, in IFIP International Federation for Information Processing, Volume 262; The Future of Identity in the Information Society; Simone Fischer-Hübner, Penny Duquenoy, Albin Zuccato, Leonardo Martucci; (Boston: Springer), pp. 359–374.

360   Rowena Rodrigues

Many writers support the view that while western societies are characteristic of individualism and a certain independence in relations amongst members of society, the case is different in many non-western/eastern societies where relationships (at different levels) play an important and pervasively influential part in all aspects of life [9]. There are strong affiliations, interrelationships and inter-dependencies along with a pervasive spirit of interconnectedness and belonging in such societies. Life and in consequence, the shaping of identities in non-western countries is very much affected and influenced by the bonds of tradition, custom, beliefs [10]. This was the case, and still remains true for modern India.

One key factor that affects identity is religion, perhaps controversially so, as India officially is a secular state with no state religion. Guha stresses how religious identities which are a manifestly accepted part and parcel of life, are not just that but are subject to much "social production and propagation" on a daily basis [11]. Religion is the mainstay of social life with Hinduism having the largest number of followers, followed by Christianity, Jainism, Sikhism, Islam etc.

Hinduism[1] and its philosophy in particular, has been (and is) a significant identity influence. It is characterised by the existence of a number of gods and goddesses, all governing different aspects of life. Central to it is the Brahmannical triad which represents a union in plurality of form. The triad comprises of Lord Brahma - the God of creation, Lord Shiva- the God of destruction and Lord Vishnu who represents the power of sustenance. This triad represents a plurality of identity and the self as well as at the same time represents a commonality and unification, not unlike the monotheism of the West. There are other gods like Lord Rama, who was immortalized for his 'perfect' nature in the epic Ramayana (not unlike what we often seek to achieve in Second Life [12] or through our avatars in other domains).

Identity and identification in India have also been affected and effectuated by the introduction and promotion of reservation policies [13-16] for the "weaker, disadvantaged" and marginalized sections of society. These policies cover seats in legislature, government jobs and even admissions to universities and colleges and the establishment of identity is primary to the availing of these benefits. Jenkins [17] emphasizes that "contemporary Supreme Court decisions have demonstrated the continuing legal reinforcement of official identity categories."

India is primarily a 'collectivist society' [18]. Many studies have demonstrated how the individual identity is not as important [19] as the group identity [20-22]. Common examples of cohesion are the caste system and the joint family [23]. While life in the cities and towns is more impersonal, life in rural India is characterized by everybody having a deep personal knowledge of the other- villages are small communities with very strong and habitually intimate social bonds.

Courts in India have been called on time and again to decide on matters of identity and identity fraud in relation to social status certificates, conversions, marriage etc. In Kumari Madhuri Patil v Additional Commissioner Tribal Development and others [24], a case of verification of identities, the Supreme Court outlined procedures for

---
[1] Hinduism basically advocates that there is one supreme god and that God is the supreme self in man.

verifying identities after stating that identity claims had to be judged on "legal and ethnological basis." In Mrs. Valsamma Paul v. Cochin University & Ors [25] the Supreme Court further stated that, "people have several identities which constantly intersect and overlap."

Thus, in the light of the above, we can see that identity plays out as a fluid dynamic in Indian society. It can be represented as a whole and a sub-set of the whole. The whole represented by the "indianness" of the self (the overarching national identity), which uniquely comprised a unification of different sub-identities for each individual. The different sub-identities may be sub-classed on the following basis[2]:

Region	e.g. North and South
State	e.g. Assamese, Goan, Maharashtrian, Gujarati, Punjabi
Religion	e.g. Hinduism, Islam, Christianity, Buddhism
Language	e.g. Hindi, Tamil, Telugu, Konkani, Malayalam
Caste	e.g. Brahmins, Kshatriyas, Vaishyas, Shudras
Class	e.g. Upper, average middle, middle, lower class
Family	e.g. Joshis, Iyers, Kulkarnis, Basus

At this stage, one may be compelled to make a comparison between India and the EU. Certainly, there are some strong similarities in identity issues and categorisations. Both India and the EU are made up of distinct states and diverse communities. However, there are some very important reasons why the case of India in identity issues is peculiar and to be considered on its own merits. First, in India although certain legislative powers are devolved to the states and union territories, they are all subject to a single uniformly applied constitution and the sovereignty of the country is democratically and "strongly centrally vested" (unlike the EU which arguably is said to have a weak centre, where only some level of sovereignty has been delegated by nations on specific subjects of interest). Second, as J L de Reede [26] points out, the "centralised judicial testing of primary judicial law" as can be carried out by the Supreme Court in India is virtually non-existent in the EU[3]. Third, we must also consider the level of development. And finally there are some stark differences in the play of identity issues – for instance, being identified as a member of the Scheduled Castes and Tribes[4] holds not just social significance but economic and legal repercussions too.

---

[2] This list is not comprehensive.

[3] Reede states that decentralized reviews do happen in the EU and the testing he talks about is in relation to "the basic constitutional principles in Europe".

[4] For definition see the Constitution of India, Article 366(24) and (25) and Arts. 341 and 342.

3   Anonymity and pseudonymity

In classical Hindu philosophy, one of the four stages of life[5] was the stage of vanaprastha, or withdrawing from the world and all its ties and becoming a forest dweller. People would completely renounce their material ties, become a sanyasi[6] and take on a state of non-existence or no identity, where their worldly existence did not matter or simply ceased to be order to attain moksha[7], which became the ultimate aim of existence.

People have often resorted to changing birth identities and taking on alternate identities. While this may not fit with how we strictly conceptualize anonymity or pseudonymity, it can be likened in some sense to assuming a 'false'[8] identity. For many, birth identities often came to represent a life of segregation, shame and despondency- brought on by stringent social categorizations and distinctions. Many dalits[9] and untouchables (as they were called)[10] abandoned their identities by actively adopting alternate ones through religious conversions to escape victimization, isolation and economic and social deprivation [28-30].

There are different degrees of anonymous and pseudonymous behavior evident in practice in India. One such example is the practice of women using veils to cover their head and face (a practice prevalent in many societies in India even today) particularly when they are outside their family home or in a public place.

In the field of art and architecture, artists and sculptors in India in the past did not ascribe their names to their art and the 'resolute anonymity' [31] of the individual Indian artisan, craftsman, printmaker or sculptor' was, and still remains in a number of cases, an accepted fact e.g. the artists that painted Ajanta caves [32].

In literature, the use of pseudonyms was prominent. Authors often adopted pen names as a matter of general practice, e.g. Munshi Premchand (a great Hindi novelist), Bonoful (author, playwright and poet Balāi Chānd Mukhopādhyāy), Firaq Gorakhpuri

---

[5] The four stages of life, applied to males belonging to the twice born Aryan castes, are: Brahmacharya (the instructive stage of life), Grahasta (being a householder), Vanaprastha (withdrawal from life and retreat into the forest) and Mokhsha (liberation from the cycles of rebirth).

[6] Sanyasi refers to one with no self-interest or craving for the material world and all in it.

[7] Liberation from the cycles of rebirth.

[8] Refers to the new identity as opposed to the old pre-determined one.

[9] The Dalit Freedom Network defines a dalit as being a "a person who comes from any lower caste, even though technically authentic Dalits are kept outside the caste system as unworthy to enter the social and religious life of society. They are generally considered to be polluted socially, poor economically and powerless politically. They are not allowed to touch caste Hindus and are therefore treated as 'untouchables'" [27].

[10] Untouchability is an offence punishable under law. See specifically, Art. 17, Constitution of India and the Protection of Civil Rights Act, 1955, originally called the Untouchability (Offences) Act 1955.

(noted contemporary Urdu poet). Perhaps, even interestingly some authors very often appended their pen names to their real names[11].

The examples above illustrate that in Indian society, individual identities were (and still in many cases are) not the end all. There was also a strong culture and practice of anonymity and pseudonymity, fitting well with the Indian tradition and culture of abdication of the self (into a state of anonymity).

4   Digital identity and anonymity: Manifestations, Applications and Concerns

4.1   Internet Usage

The Internet has come to represent a key factor influencing change and development in India. Applications of the Internet and digital technology vary from blogging, P2P, digital radio, online games[12], social networking to video conferencing, distance education, remote diagnosis and troubleshooting etc. The transmission of localized content and services has been made a priority by the government [34]. Take for instance, in Rajasthan, the Neyla village has an information kiosk called "Rajnidhi" which uses ICT to facilitate e-governance [35]. Madhya Pradesh has Gyandoot which connects many villages through Intranet and Soochanalaya kiosks [36]. Other examples are E-Choupal [37] and Tarahaat [38]. Thus digital technology touches not just the lives of the select few in the metropolitan cities and towns but has clearly made inroads into rural areas (nearly 70% of the Indian population lives in villages) [39].

Cyber cafés are the main mode of access to the Internet in suburbs, towns and metropolitan cities, primarily because home internet access is an expensive prospect since the Internet is still mostly traditionally accessible though dial up connections and broadband has not made the enormous difference it was expected to[13].

Given access, infrastructure and affordability issues, a single computer is often a multiple access point for Internet access. E Miller's report [42] on the basis of observations recorded in an Indian village evidences another form of digital identity. The report highlights how many residents of an area came to visit the house of an electrician and made use of his computer to send emails, surf the web, download material or simply entertain themselves. The electrician in this case was a kind of a conduit (an Internet service provider of sorts), proficient in English (the main

[11] For instance, Surendra Jha 'Suman', Baidyanath Mishra 'Yatri', Raghupati Sahay 'Firaq' Gorakhpuri

[12] However, gaming is not considered to be a part of mainstream culture and has often been actively discouraged [33].

[13] For a more comprehensive coverage of issues affecting the growth of information technology systems see [40-41].

navigatory language of the web). The legal implications of such informal and kind for kind relationships are yet to be established and are cause for further research.

Social networking sites are very popular and Indian users have successfully formed a number of web congregations. Google's Orkut [43] in fact has nearly 6.6 million registered Indian users (of its 49 million worldwide users). A lot of time is devoted to professional networking. Recruitment websites are doing booming business. Usenet groups like soc.culture.indian are widely subscribed to. Indians even resort to the Internet for religious purposes[14] and even subscribe to personalized astrological services.

Online matrimonial services are very popular[15]. These services often have separate domains for users of different castes, religion and classes e.g. there may be separate domains for Brahmin, Kshatriya, Punjabi, Sindhi or even Vaishya communities. This is evidence of how the strong caste and class influences of the offline world have permeated online and to even greater effect. One specific identity issue related to these matrimonial websites is the creation of profiles thereon. While normally one would register oneself for the use of these services, many times the profiles (containing personal details and photos) registered on these websites are done so by second or third parties (e.g. the mother/uncle of the prospective bride or groom) often with or without the consent of the profiled party. While the top few established companies do (in their effort to self-regulate) make adequate provisions for protection of privacy and identity misuse and theft, there are some that recklessly allow access to personal details of subscribed members without limit, and this is a definite concern that needs to be addressed.

The pre-dominance of the English language on the Internet has been highlighted as a hurdle to expression of lingual sub-identities [44]. Multimedia tools like webcams, microphones and digital telephony have helped overcome this difficulty and have ensured that non-English speaking users can stay connected and use the Internet. Orkut has introduced local language content to cater to its users needs[16].

Sen[17] talks about how our freedom in choosing our identities in terms of how others see us is extraordinarily unlimited and Indians have made this discovery and become empowered by the choices they can choose to make in respect of their identities- who they choose to be or not to be – on the Internet[18]. We can chose to be part of a community that is closely linked with what we represent in the offline social context or choose to join a different group altogether. In the real world, identity choices are often constrained by interpersonal recognition.

It is relevant at this point to show how open information and identity sharing is in India and what its influence on digital use is with the help of India's first knowledge village-Hansdehar [45]. The village website [45] purports to be a "web interface for all stakeholders involved in the development and upliftment of the village." The

---

[14] There are a number of sites offering services, along with forums and communities.

[15] e.g. Shaadi.com at http://www.shaadi.com/; Bharat Matrimony http://www. Bharatmatrimony.com/. Accessed 29 September 2007.

[16] Orkut is available in languages like Hindi, Bengali, Marathi, Tamil and Telugu.

[17] Sen, A. 2005. *The argumentative Indian*.

[18] Sen, A. 2005. *The argumentative Indian:* 351

village website not only has a citizens' directory, but also has a list of voters and a pensioners list. The Citizens Directory is very comprehensive in its coverage and contains personal data [46] like name, date of birth, age, occupation, sex etc. While this is an alarming proposition from the point of view of data protection and privacy culture and law that is well developed in Europe and other parts of the world, this is nothing to be astounded at in India, for reasons explained earlier as well (openness of knowledge and existence of the sharing principle) as also for the simple reason that the western concept of privacy (and data protection) is yet to trickle down to the grass root level. There is hardly any awareness of the value and marketability of information, as well as its potential for data theft.

A study by Kumaraguru and Cranor [47] contrasted data practices in the US and India. It was found that while a fourth of the US respondents in the study feared identity theft, the issue was by and large ignored by their Indian counterparts. It is evident that some sort of awareness of identity theft and issues concerning protection of personal information and privacy (particularly in the light of the outsourcing data scams) has been increased; there still is a lackadaisical attitude towards identity theft.

4.2   Digital anonymity

There is not much evidence to show extensive usage of online anonymous services. This could to some extent be attributed to the lack of awareness of the existence of services like anonymous remailers, anonymous web surfing services etc. Another factor that could explain this would be the time factor – the Internet is very often accessed at cyber cafés which bill users on a minute/hourly basis and users are generally too busy making the most of their limited time either entertaining themselves, corresponding and chatting with loved ones, satisfying their curiosity or applying for jobs to focus on shielding their identity or protecting their privacy through covering their digital trail. Some users simply do not bother because they think they have nothing to hide or are under the mistaken impression that the Internet is a medium that offers them the anonymity that the real world does not.

However, the relative anonymity and pseudonymity of the net (as perceived, though often not achieved) has come to represent empowerment (in terms of breaking traditional social barriers and distinctions impossible in real time), liberation and freedom to a great number of users. The level of conservativeness (as compared to western societies that are much more free and open), is still very high (even given the level of advancement). India is a land with a lot of taboos – e.g. anything related to sex, sexual health and intimacy is taboo. This has created a number of problems in the real world. With the relative anonymity of the Internet, a person with HIV can find the information, advice and help needed (through support groups, like sufferers), without being subject to discrimination and persecution (HIV and AIDS still carry high social stigma) [48-50].

Many people indulge in "anonymous" blogging to deal with social problems and issues (which in real time would attract or result in retribution - political, economic or social). The guise of web anonymity and pseudonymity is thus used to voice genuine grievances, disseminate information and express opinions on a matter of public concern as well as post comments [51]. One prominent example is the media criticism blogs – blogs that aim at exposing the corrupt practices in the local media.

Digital anonymity and pseudonymity has of late increasingly come to be associated with the bad and the ugly. Some anonymous bloggers have resorted to using their blogs as platforms to malign and defame. Pseudonymous users have used social networking services to generate ill feeling, hatred and communal discontent [52].

5   The regulation of identity

5.1   The IT Act

India passed the Information Technology Act 2000[19], the first substantial piece of legislation affecting electronic communications, primarily with a view to facilitate the conduct of ecommerce and e-governance. The Act, a welcome legislative initiative, while commendable in its features has come under severe criticism for not adequately addressing problems generated by the use of the Internet and other computer based services [53-55].

The Act seeks to "provide legal recognition for electronic forms of communication and transactions carried out by means of electronic data interchange and other means of communication, commonly referred to as electronic commerce." The Act also touches upon privacy,[20] breach of confidentiality, validifies digital signatures, creates information technology offences, sets out authorities to regulate the sector, and made consequential amendments to related existing laws.

One of the most significant criticisms leveled against the Act, and most relevant to the discussion at hand, is the provision that the Act makes for the interception of information transmitted through a computer resource if "necessary or expedient…in the interest of the sovereignty or integrity of India, the security of the State, friendly relations with foreign states or public order or for preventing incitement to the commission of any cognizable offence[21]". This provision has been questioned for its potential for misuse by corrupt and oppressive governments as a tool of victimization[22]. This fear is not unfounded given past events and historical developments.

There is no express concept of "personal data" in the Act – data in the Act is defined as being, "a representation of information, knowledge, facts, concepts or instructions which are being prepared or have been prepared in a formalized manner, and is intended to be processed, is being processed or has been processed in a computer system or computer network, and may be in any form (including computer

---

[19] 21 of 2000, entered into force on 17th Oct. 2000, *vide* G.S.R. 788 (E), 17th Oct. 2000.
[20] See Section 76 of the IT Act 2000.
[21] See Section 69 of the IT Act 2000.
[22] See Duggal, P. 2001. *Cyberlaw in India.*

printouts magnetic or optical storage media, punched cards, punched tapes) or stored in the memory of the computer[23]."

Chapters IX and XI of the Act create cyber crimes in relation to unauthorized access to computers, computer systems, computer networks or resources, unauthorized alteration, deletion, addition, modification, alteration, destruction, duplication or transmission of data, computer database, etc

5.2   Cases

India's first case of cyber stalking brought digital identity into the spotlight. A man misused a woman's identity in a chat room on the www.mirc.com website[24] and gave out her personal information like name, telephone number and address to other people resulting in the woman being personally harassed and troubled. The man was prosecuted under S.509 of the Indian Penal Code[25] after his IP address was traced.

Another similar case was that of the State of Tamil Nadu v Suhas Katti [56]. This case concerned the posting of obscene, defamatory and annoying messages about a divorcee woman in the Yahoo! message group. The perpetrator also forwarded emails to the victim for information through a false e-mail account which he had opened in her name. The woman got annoying phone calls from people who were under the misapprehension that she was soliciting. The accused was arrested and found guilty of offences under Ss. 469, 509 IPC and 67 of Information Technology Act 2000 and was successfully convicted and sentenced for the offence[26].

In Nasscom v. Ajay Sood & Others,27 the Delhi High Court declared phishing to be an illegal act entailing an injunction and the recovery of damages. The Court laid down the ambit of phishing and declared it to be a form of internet fraud where a person pretended to his advantage to be a legitimate association, like a bank or an insurance company in order to extract personal data from a customer such as access codes, passwords, etc. The Court further stated that phishing, was an illegal act and defined to specifically as being "a misrepresentation made in the course of trade leading to confusion as to the source and origin of the e-mail causing immense harm not only to the consumer but even to the person whose name, identity or password is misused."

The identity concerns of social networking sites (SNS) were brought home with a bang when a student was arrested for creating a classmate's profile and uploading her picture along with offensive messages [57].

While all the above cases show that the IT Act and criminal law is successfully being used (albeit limitedly) to prosecute and convict identity fraudsters and criminals, it can safely be concluded that as compared to developments in other parts

---

[23] Sec. 2 (1) (0), IT Act 2000

[24] www.mirc.com

[25] Act No. 45 of Year 1860.

[26] S. 67 of the IT Act 2000 deals with the publishing of information which is obscene in electronic form.

[27] 2005 (30) PTC 437

of the world, India's digital identity problems are still in their nascent stages. One reason for this could be that Indians do not attribute the same level of value to personal information associated with their identities, as perhaps do people in western societies where personal information is of immense economic value (but perhaps India will be heading the same way!). Another reason could be the relatively low usage of ecommerce. There is also the concern that some offences are not being reported[28] for lack of awareness on the part of digital users (particularly private users) and investigated for lack of awareness in the policing sector.

5.3   Multipurpose National Identity Cards (MNIC)

On 26 May 2007, in keeping with current trends of social sorting [58], the Government of India rolled out the Multi-purpose National Identity Cards (MNIC) at Pooth Khurd, Narela [59]. This heralds a step towards a state of definitive and conclusive identification and a dossier society [60] which of late seems to have increasingly become a global regulatory fad.

The MNIC Scheme aims at providing a "credible individual identification system and simultaneous use for multifarious socio-economic benefits and transactions within and outside the Government" for efficient e-governance [61].

The Citizenship Act 1955 was amended in December 2003 [59], to provide for compulsory registration of all citizens and issue of a national identity card. Prior to implementation, a pilot project had earlier been initiated in November 2003 to test the proposal in Assam, Delhi, Goa, Gujarat, Jammu & Kashmir, Rajasthan, Tripura, Uttar Pradesh, Uttarakhand, Tamil Nadu, West Bengal, Andhra Pradesh, and Pondicherry. Data, in targeted sectors of the pilot areas was collected using the census approach. Particulars of individuals above 18 years of age were ascertained and photographs and finger biometrics were collected.

The MNIC Scheme is to be supported by a Citizens Database, which in turn will be supported by 20 fully technologically equipped centres at the Tehsil/Block headquarters. Bharat Electronics Limited (BEL) has been entrusted with the back end management of these centres. The CPSUs [Consortium of Central Public Sector Undertakings comprising Bharat Electronics Limited (BEL), Electronics Corporations of India Limited (ECIL) and Indian Telephone Industries (ITI)] will handle the personalization of the cards [63].

The MNIC bears a unique 16 digit NIN (National Identification Number) for each citizen. It has a 16kb memory microchip. The cards will also contain a finger biometric. The card is secured with asymmetric and symmetric key cryptography, to protect it from falling prey to any tampering or cloning. The process envisaged by the Scheme was to consist of three steps: data collection through field surveys, collection of data and creation of a Citizens Database and verification and validation of the e-data against the collected data[29].

---

[28] A view supported by P Duggal, Supreme Court Advocate. See Gupta, V. No end to cybercrime. *Express Computer.* 19 November 2007.
[29] See Government of India Notice, 9/76/2006 CRD (MNIC).

The scheme has not been without its critics [64], and even local resistance [65], who argue that the cards give too much control to bureaucrats who may be able to misuse the system to their own ends particularly since there are no express legislative safeguards in place to deal with consequential problems. Sethi [66] goes so far as to state, and not without merit, that India is not ready for the upheaval that the implementation of the MNIC will bring and that this scheme is "part of a proclivity that seeks technological fixes to deal with vast socio-political and economic realities.

It is reported that experts have underlined the key difficulties in implementation of the cards to be the twin problems of illiteracy and lack of documents to support claims of residence [67]. There is a huge section of population in India with what can be termed as negligible 'provable' identity. There is a large migrant population that moves from place to place in search of work, and sets up temporary homes, works for a while and moves on again. In their journeys, they marry, have children and go through life one day at a time. Registration of birth, death and residence is probably the last thing on their mind when they barely eke out an existence [68]. How are such persons who hardly have the means to sustain themselves to prove their identity to meet the MNIC gold standard requirements? Are they lesser citizens of the country than someone who can prove their identity with documents? These concerns have been raised, but there is great concern that policy makers and the executive have failed to take these into consideration before implementing the MNIC scheme.

The MNIC scheme is also fraught with data protection and privacy implications – which have not been thought through, or legally catered for by appropriate safeguards. The government's proposal to link various databases to the NIN database[30] gives us an idea of what is to come and why the privacy conscious are worried.

Briefly, the legal issues that arise from the MNIC scheme can be summarised as follows:

1. Inaccuracies in collection, verification and confirmation of data [69].
2. False identities[31]
3. Data theft/security [70]
4. Data correction issues
5. Function Creep
6. Perpetuation of discrimination
7. Redressal mechanisms
8. Bureaucratic control over personal information without adequate judicial safeguards

Problems in regard to the first point raised above (the collection and verification of data) were evident at the pilot stage itself. In the Murshidabad district of Calcutta, it was reported that there was an alarming probability that 90% of the population had failed to show proof of nationality (one of the main criteria of the identification exercise) and a large number could not provide supporting documents [71]. In another incident, it was reported that around 400 Bengali and Persian speaking Iranis who came to India and settled here 70 years ago had not been covered.

---

[30] See proposed linkages at http://www.mit.gov.in/plan/ppt/national%20ID.ppt

[31] The electoral history of the country has seen identities (of living and dead persons) being faked and misused for political gain.

Our experience with the EPICs (Electronic Photo Voter ID Cards) in fact should have taught us a valuable lesson - even till the year 2005 it was reported that only 69% of the population had defect free cards, and even until lately (nearly 15 years since the cards were implemented, nearly a quarter of eligible voters still do not have one) [72].

What is perhaps the most frightful prospect given India's past history and pluralistic sensitivities is the extent of control that the MNIC database and its linkages will vest in the state and the bureaucracy. What is to stop a renegade government taking drastic measures, or indulging in a bit of ethnic cleansing [73-74] or even forcing all eligible men to undergo vasectomies against their wishes (as was done in the Emergency of 1975-1977) [75]?

5.4   Other developments

In late 2006, a news item revealed that the cyber crime cell of the Mumbai police had got Orkut to make an arrangement (albeit informal) called the Priority Reporting Tool, by which Orkut had endeavored not just to block forums and communities containing "defamatory" or "inflammatory" content[32] but in addition to provide the IP addresses from where such content had been generated [77].

Also last year, the Delhi police (after an increase in terror threats) issued orders to all cyber café proprietors to verify the identities of cyber café users and log details of their entry and exit [78]. There was a wave of criticism for this move, some even seeking to draw the conclusion that India was moving towards a China like regulation of the Net amidst expressions of fear of loss of civil liberties and freedom to browse, or perhaps (as recent reports show) it may just be an Orwellian homecoming [79]! In the same vein, it has been reported that cyber cafés in Mumbai will soon be subject to the CARMS (Cyber Access Remote Monitoring System) which will enable the monitoring of not just email, messaging, web browsing, file transfers but can also be deployed in a wide way to curb access to different sites [80].

6   Conclusion

The concepts of digital identity, anonymity and pseudonymity are still taking shape and developing in India. The Internet is a unique portal where individuals freely express, make and have experiences, share personal information and perhaps just be themselves. This paper has demonstrated how cultural, religious and social influences have made their way into the digital play of Indian identity, anonymity and pseudonymity.

With MNIC's, India has moved a level up in making personal information associated with identity more economically and politically valuable. Will this real time "gold standard" for identity find its digital equivalent or perhaps emanate some

[32] A PIL was filed against Orkut in this regard [76].

influence on digital users in terms of making them realize the value of their personal information? Perhaps this will curb the current traditional value and culture of "openness" explicitly manifest on the web, especially SNSs. Or maybe again it may not. It would all depend on how much economic value came to be attached to identities and identifiers.

But in all this, it is hoped that law will be able to address the underlying and resulting issues and problems effectively. Policy makers (often having other pressing primary concerns), still don't understand technology and the Internet enough to legislate keeping the interests of all stakeholders in mind [81], and the legal and academic community is still finding its feet in this area of law. It remains to be seen whether courts will remain the first port of call for identity issues and whether Indian courts will use international norms and decisions to guide them [82], take into account local peculiarities and enforce local solutions or try and find a middle path.

References

1. JuxtConsult Online Research & Advisory, India Online 2007. Report.
2. Paranjpe, A C. 1998. Self and identity in modern psychology in Indian thought. Springer.
3. Gottschalk, P. 2000. Beyond Hindu and Muslim: Multiple identity in narratives from village India. OUP.
4. Chakrabarty, B. 2003. Communal identity in India: Its construction and articulation in the twentieth century. OUP.
5. Singh, Y. 2000. Culture change in India: Identity and globalisation. Jaipur.
6. Cohn, B S. 1971. India: The social anthropology of a civilization. Englewood   Cliffs, NJ: Prentice-Hall.
7. Jodhka, S S (ed.). 2001. Community & identities: Contemporary discourses on culture and politics in India: 26.
8. Hall, S. 1990. Cultural identity and diaspora. In Identity: Community, culture, difference, ed. J Rutherford, 223.
9. Hofstede, G. 1980. Culture's consequences. Sage Publications.
10. Cohn, B S.1987. The census, social structure and objectification in South Asia. In An anthropologist among historians and other essays, 224-254. New Delhi: Oxford University Press.
11. Guha, S. 2003. The politics of identity and enumeration in India c. 1600–1990. Society for Comparative Study of Society and History, 148-167:50.
12. Second Life. Second Life is a 3D digital world that is the product of its residents' imagination, activity and maintenance. See http://secondlife.com/
13. Pai Panandiker, V A (ed.). 1997. The politics of backwardness: Reservation policy in India. New Delhi. Konark Publishers;
14. Wadwha, K K. 1975. Minority safeguards in India: Constitutional provisions and their implementation. New Delhi. Thomson Press (India) Limited;
15. Galanter, M. 1984. Competing equalities: Law and the backward classes in India. Delhi: Oxford University Press;
16. Nabhi's brochure on reservation and concession. 2001. New Delhi: Nabhi Publications; Reports of the Commissioner for Scheduled Castes and Scheduled Tribes.
17. Jenkins, L. D. 2003. Identity and identification in India: Defining the disadvantaged: 24.

18. Geert, H. 1991.Culture and organizations, software of the mind, intercultural cooperation and its importance for survival. McGraw-Hill.
19. Bharati, A. 1985. The self in Hindu thought and action. In Culture and the self: Asian and Western perspectives, ed. A. J. Marsella, 211.
20. Dumont, L. 1970. Homo Hierarchicus: The caste system and its implications. University of Chicago Press: 8-9;
21. Kakar, S. 1981. The Inner world: A psycho-analytic study of childhood and society in India, Delhi, 37;
22. Ramanujam, B.K., Toward maturity: Problems of identity seen in the Indian clinical setting. In Identity and adulthood, ed. S Kakar, OUP, 37-55: 54.
23. Encyclopedia Britannica Online. The joint family, 29 May 2007 http://www.britannica.com/eb/article?tocId=26070.
24. Kumari Madhuri Patil v. Addl.Commnr. Tribal Development (1994) 6 SCC 241.
25. Mrs. Valsamma Paul v. Cochin University & Ors. JT 1996 (1) SC 57
26. Reede, J L. de. 2006. Protection of basic constitutional features in India and Europe. Book review. European Constitutional Law Review. 2: 476–482.
27. http://www.dalitnetwork.org/go?/dfn/about/C20/#sc_st_or_scheduled_caste_scheduled_tribes
28. Stern, R.W. 1993. Changing India: Bourgeois revolution on the subcontinent: 78; BBC News. Dalits in conversion ceremony. 14 Oct. 2006, http://news.bbc.co.uk/1/hi/world/south_asia/6050408.stm.
29. Gupta, D. Killing caste by conversion. The Hindu, 13 Nov. 2001 http://www.hinduonnet.com/thehindu/2001/11/13/stories/05132523.htm.
30. Chandra, R & S. Mittra. 2003. Dalit identity in the new millennium. New Delhi, Commonwealth.
31. Rajadhyaksha, A. Presentation at the School of Oriental and African Studies (SOAS). University of London. 24 May 2007
32. Government of India, Visual Arts, paintings and sculptures, http://india.gov.in/knowindia/visual_arts.php. 27 Sep. 2007; Gupte, R & B. D. Mahajan. 1962. Ajanta, Ellora and Aurangabad caves. Bombay: Taraporevala & Co.
33. Badam, R.T. India tech institute curbs internet use. International Business Times. 21 March 2007. http://www.ibtimes.com/articles/20070321/india-internet.htm
34. See GoI. Ministry of Communications and Information Technology, Department of Information Technology, Information technology annual report 2006-07, Accessed 20 Nov. 2007. http://www.mit.gov.in/download/annualreport2006-07.pdf
35. The Society for Promotion of e-Governance, major e-governance projects, 23 Sep. 2007. http://www.egovindia.org/egovportals.html
36. www.gyandoot.nic.in
37. ITC. E-Choupal: ITC's rural development philosophy at work, http://www.itcportal.com/ruraldevp_philosophy/echoupal.htm. Accessed 1 Sep. 2007.
38. Tarahaat. http://www.tarahaat.com/. Accessed 30 Sep. 2007.
39. Census of India 2001
40. Background Report of the Working Group on Information Technology for Masses, http://itformasses.nic.in/page1.htm#bg5a.
41. Fischer & Lorenz. 2000. Internet and the future policy framework for telecommunications. A report for the European Commission. 31 January 2000: 61 http://europa.eu.int/ISPO/infosoc/telecompolicy/en/Fischer31a.pdf
42. Miller, E. Wireless internet access in rural south India: A report by Eric Miller" December 2000. http://ccat.sas.upenn.edu/~emiller/report.html

43. Orkut. http://www.orkut.com/. Accessed 29 September 2007.

44. Keniston, K. Panel on global culture, local culture, and vernacular computing: the excluded 95% in South Asia. http://web.mit.edu/~kken/Public/PDF/Panel%20on%20Global%20Culture.pdf

45. Smart Villages. http://www.smartvillages.org/hansdehar/people.htm. Accessed 29 Sep. 2007.

46. Art 2(a), Directive 95/46/EC of the European Parliament and of the Council of 24 October 1995 on the protection of individuals with regard to the processing of personal data and on the free movement of such data, OJ L 281, 23.11.1995: 31–50

47. Kumaraguru, P. and L. Cranor. 2005. Privacy perceptions in India and the United States: An interview study. http://www.cs.cmu.edu/~ponguru/tprc_2005_pk_lc_en.pdf. Accessed 15 Sep. 2007.

48. World Bank. HIV/AIDS in India. Aug 2007. http://siteresources.worldbank.org /INTSAREGTOPHIVAIDS/Resources/HIV-AIDS-brief-Aug07-IN.pdf.

49. BBC News. Bareth, N. Court puts on hold HIV decision. BBC News. 28 Sep. 2007. http://news.bbc. co.uk/1/hi/world/south_asia/7017573.stm.

50. BBC News. 'HIV stigma' drives India suicide. 3 Jul 2006. http://news.bbc.co.uk/1/hi/world/south_asia/5141100.stm

51. Glaser, M. Indian media blog shuts down after legal threats from Times of India. Online Journalism Review. Annenberg School of Journalism. University of Southern California. 15 March 2005. http://www.ojr.org/ojr/stories/050315glaser

52. PTI. Pune cops book Orkut user. The Times of India. 2 September 2007. http://timesofindia.indiatimes.com/Pune_cops_book_Orkut_user/articleshow/2331802.cms

53. Sreekala, G. Much hyped IT Act stays a dead letter. Times News Network. 20 July 2006. http://economictimes.indiatimes.com/News/Business_Law/General_Law/Much_hyped_IT _Act_stays_a_dead_letter/articleshow/1783026.cms.

54. Duggal, P. Cyberlaw in India: The Information Technology Act 2000 - Some perspectives. 6 Sep. 2001. http://www.mondaq.com/article.asp?articleid=13430&print=1.

55. Basu, S. & R Jones. March 2003. E-commerce and the law: A review of India's Information Technology Act 2000.Contemporary South Asia. 12(1): 7-24.

56. Singh, T. Cyber law and information technology. http://www.delhidistrictcourts. nic.in/CYBER%20LAW.pdf. Accessed 3 Sep. 2007

57. Nikade, N. Youth misuses classmate's profile, posts lewd scraps. Mumbai Mirror. 29 September 2006.

58. Lyon, D. November 2004. Identity cards: social sorting by database. Oxford Internet Institute. Internet issue brief No 3: 3

59. Ministry of Home Affairs. First tranche of multi-purpose national identity cards handed over to the citizens. Press Information Bureau. 26 May 2007. http://pib.nic.in/ release/release.asp?relid=28238

60. Mehmood, T. From chowkeydari act to biometric identification: Passages from the information state in India. International colloquium on information society. History and politics. Sarai CSDS. New Delhi. 29 Nov-2nd December 2006. http://www.sarai.net/ research/information-society/resources/texts-and-essays/from_chowkeydari_act.pdf

61. Office of the Registrar General India. 2003. Project review: Multi-purpose National Identity Card. E-censusIndia, Issue 17 http://www.censusindia.net/results/eci17.pdf

62. Citizenship (Registration of Citizens and Issue of National Identity Cards) Rules, 2003 were notified in the Government of India Gazette Vide GSR No. 937(E) dated 10 December 2003.

63. Ministry of Home Affairs. First tranche of multi-purpose national identity cards handed over to the citizens. Press Information Bureau. 26 May 2007. http://pib.nic.in/release/release.asp?relid=28238Ministry of Home Affairs, Press Release

64. SAHRD. Multi-purpose national identity: Protection or restriction of right. HRF/169/07. 13 July 2007. http://www.hrdc.net/sahrdc/hrfeatures/HRF169.htm

65. Vishwa Mohan. Multi-purpose smart cards arrive," *Times News Network.* 24 May 2007. http://timesofindia.indiatimes.com/Cities/Delhi/Multi-purpose_smart_cards_arrive/article show/2070343.cms; No need for a new ID care scheme: CPI-M tells poll panel.4 April 1998. *The Statesman.*

66. Sethi, A. December 2005. Peeking out of your pocket: India's national ID scheme is 'on schedule.' http://www.himalmag.com/2005/november/analysis_7.html

67. Merinews Network. I-cards for Indian citizens as govt. launches MNIC project. Merinews. 28 May 2007. http://www.merinews.com/catFull.jsp?articleID=125184

68. Prabhu, R. 2003. From national ID to global citizenry. Convergence Plus. http://www.convergenceplus.com/3rd%20scti%202003.html

69. Mehmood, T. 2005. Playing cards- identity cards and the politics of information. World Information City, Bangalore. 14- 19 Nov. 2005 http://www.sarai.net/research/ information-society/resources/texts-and-essays/playing_cards.pdf

70. Srinivasan, S. Now, for the born identity. The Economic Times. 1 Sep. 2007.

71. Purohit, D. Report taking shape amid infiltration buzz. The Telegraph Calcutta. 23 Aug. 2005. http://www.telegraphindia.com/1050823/asp/nation/story_5136259.asp

72. Misra, N. 186 million Indians without voter IDs. Hindustan Times, 15 May 2007. http://www.hindustantimes.com/storypage/storypage.aspx?id=df526e99-d0d6-4235-b3d6 -9f964ae0b445&&Headline=186+million+Indians+without+voter+IDs

73. Fussell, J. 2001. Group classification on national ID cards as a factor in genocide and ethnic cleansing. Presented on 15 Nov. 2001 to the Seminar Series of the Yale University Genocide Studies Program.

74. Longman, T. 2001. Identity cards, ethnic self-perception, and genocide in Rwanda. In Documenting individual identity: The development of state practices in the modern world. ed. J Caplan and J Torpey. Princeton University Press.

75. Tarlo, E. 2003. Unsettling memories: Narratives of the 'emergency' in Delhi. C Hurst & Co.

76. TNN. PIL seeks ban on Orkut. Times of India. 24 Nov 2006. http://timesofindia. indiatimes.com/Cities/Mumbai/PIL_seeks_ban_on_Orkut_/articleshow/548286.cms

77. Times News Network. Orkut's tell-all pact with cops. The Economic Times Online. 1 May 2007

78. IBN Live. Photo ID must for cyber cafe users. IBN Live. 21 July 2006. http://www.ibnlive.com/news/photo-identity-cards-for-net-users/16297-3.html

79. Varma, A. India's cops get Orwellian. LiveMint.com. 6 September 2007. http://www.livemint.com/2007/09/06000800/India8217s-cops-get-Orwelli.html

80. Menon, V. K. Virtual khabris to zoom-in on terrorists. Midday. 29 August 2007. http://www.mid-day.com/news/city/2007/august/163165.htm

81. Wolcott, P. 2003. Global diffusion of the internet I: India: Is the elephant learning to dance? Communications of the Association for Information Systems. Volume 11, 560-646: 627

82. Jolly George Varghese v. Bank of Cochin, [1980] 2 SCJ 358

ICT and Social Work: a Question of Identities?

Véronique Laurent

Cellule Interdisciplinaire de Technology Assessement
University of Namur, Belgium
vla@info.fundp.ac.be

Abstract. Computers and Information and Communication Technologies (ICT) have become, nowadays, part of the daily work environment of numerous enterprises and organizations. Social services organizations are concerned by those technological changes affecting various fields like, for instance, social help management, contact with public, communication between social workers, relationships with authorities. The integration of technologies in organizations generally raises many questions. Those questions concern worker's use, perception, trust and appropriation of ICT. Our paper will focus on a recent empirical research about computerization in Belgian Public Social Action Services (CPAS) undertaken by the University of Namur. The central issue raised in this research regards the potential impact of ICT on the professional identity of the social workers, questioning a potential cultural shock between new visions of social work endorsed by ICT programs and patterns and the traditional ones at work amongst the social workers. Using identity theory, structural approach of computerization and empirical data, we will try to analyze this central issue following different steps. This issue is very critical when considering that professional identity has crucial impact regarding the way social workers operate and the relationships they have with public concerned.

1   Introduction

Main objective of this contribution is to relate the potential impact of ICT on the professional identity of the social workers in CPAS. Using empirical data and an identity perspective, we will study the potential impact of ICT on the professional identity of the social workers, questioning a potential cultural shock between new visions of social work endorsed by ICT programs and patterns and the traditional ones at work among social workers.

This issue is very critical when considering that professional identity has crucial impact regarding the way social workers operate and the relationships they have with public concerned.

In a first part, we will describe universes and evolutions of poverty, social work and CPAS. Secondly, we will analyze the integration of technologies in those

Please use the following format when citing this chapter:

Laurent, V., 2008, in IFIP International Federation for Information Processing, Volume 262; The Future of Identity in the Information Society; Simone Fischer-Hübner, Penny Duquenoy, Albin Zuccato, Leonardo Martucci; (Boston: Springer), pp. 375–386.

services, according to the results we have collected about use and perception of ICT by workers. In a third part, we will confront the different dimensions of technology and social care, especially as far as social workers are concerned. Finally, we will conclude our paper with some practical recommendations questions for a more successful adaptation between frameworks of ICT and CPAS. We will also purpose some additional perspectives to our research.

We will mainly focus on workers and their perception of the situation. Detailed impacts of ICT like organizational changes and transformations in the job qualifications will not be covered here. Those concepts are further investigated in our book [1] and in literature about computer story and impacts [2].

2   Research methodology and identity perspective

2.1   Computerization in Belgian Public Action Services

CPAS exist are responsible of social help of citizens in each municipality (589 in Belgium). Each service has an independent juridical status, but must enforce everyday different decisions and laws coming from various levels of power (Belgian Federal State, regions, provinces, municipalities,...) [3].

Belgian Public Action Services are concerned about computerization. Indeed, those are frequently in contact with ICT, generally used in various fields like, for instance, communication with users, workers and organizations, human resources and management, secretarial work, treatments of users and of social documents, and accountancy. Computer firms, subsidiary powers and public authorities have developed the used applications. Since the 1st January 2006, CPAS have been constrained to use ICT, due to their obligation to be connected to a national computerized network of data-bank concerning users, so called the social security crossroad.

At the end of the year 2005, our research team was contacted by a delegation of CPAS from Wallonia[1] to undertake a holistic survey in order to identify the new challenges of computerization in their sector (262 CPAS) [4]. Our group was composed of two sociologists, one psychologist and three jurists.

Using an interdisciplinary point of view, we have tried to answer to new challenging questions concerning the relationship between computerization and social work. How are ICT used and perceived in CPAS? What are the impacts of using ICT in work and identity of social workers? Are the users of social services concerned by

---

[1] Belgium is divided into three regions and three different language speaking communities. The three regions are Wallonia, Brussels and Flanders. The three communities are the French speaking community, the Flemish speaking community and the German-speaking community. The link http://www.belgium.be is an useful starting point to get to know Belgium.

the digital divide? What can be the advantages of using ICT for people helped by social services? What are the legal challenges concerning ICT?

Our research was made from October 2005 to May 2007. Our methodology has been qualitative and quantitative. To collect our empirical data, we have, in a first step, made several visits and interviews in Belgian Public Action Services. In a second step, from February to March 2006, we have undertaken a large survey, sending a questionnaire to each person in charge of a CPAS[2] [4]. This survey has been conceived in close relationship with workers. In conclusion of our research, we have written a book, presenting our results and practical recommendations for the social work sector, scientists and public authorities [1].

2.2   Our identity perspective

One of the focus of this paper does concern professional identity of social workers. The concept of professional identity is wide and different frames of analysis can be adopted. Among those ones, we have chosen to adopt the theories of Henri Tajfel and John Turner about social identity [5].

In everyday life, each individual meets different social groups, deliberately chosen or not. A family, a sports group, a working group, a country can be some examples of different group constituting an individual's social identity. Following these authors, social identity will be understood as *"a part of individual's self-concept which derives from his knowledge of his membership of a social group (or groups) together with the value and emotional significance attached to that membership"* [5].

For Tajfel and Turner, social identity is not necessary linked to objective properties. You can, for instance, feel yourself belonging to the black community without having any black skin. You can also use intensively technologies without feeling like belonging to a group of ICT users. On the contrary, an individual's social identity is represented by his affective attachment to groups or social categories he wants to be connected.

The description of "what "is" a group" by an individual includes a range of between one to three components: *"a cognitive component in the sense of knowledge that one belongs to a group; an evaluative one, in the sense that the notion of the group and/or of one's membership of it may have a positive or a negative value connotation"*; and an emotional component *"in the sense that cognitive and evaluative aspects of the group and one's membership of it may be accompanied by emotions (such as love or hatred, like or dislike) directed towards one's own group and towards others which stand in certain relation to it."* [5]. How is technology integrated in professional identity of workers in social services? In our paper, we will examine and analyze those three above mentioned dimensions (cognitive, evaluative

---

[2] The population of our survey was persons in charge of CPAS in CPAS from wallonia. We received 131 answers: 50% of our population. However, only 126 questionnaires (48% of the Walloon CPAS) could be used within the framework of this study. Five questionnaires were not exploitable, fault of being correctly filled. More information about our methodology is in our survey report [4] and our book [1].

and emotional) according to the results We have collected in our research about use and perception of ICT.

3   The universe of social work and its evolution

Having specified our research framework and our identity perspective, we are going to describe and to precise the general context that surrounds the CPAS in order to better understand the mutual interactions between ICT and social action. Poverty, social work and Belgian Social Services have evolved in accordance with their times. We can detail this evolution in four main points.

3.1   From social care to social action

After their creation, in the seventies, public social services were practicing 'social care', granting care and a minimal income to people in need. Nowadays, the situation has changed. This concept of "social care" has disappeared, leaving space to the concept of "social integration" (1990), and now, to the concept of "social action" (2002). In this new context, it is increasingly required from people to use their own abilities to benefit from the social care and help from CPAS. Users are given responsibilities to change their position in society.

3.2   A greater diversification of social care activities

A second change regarding CPAS has been the greater diversification of social care activities since their creation. Indeed, due to the evolution of poverty and the changes in law, CPAS have been attributed additional and diversified missions: housing, debts mediation, management of old people's housing, family services, minor's protection, catering, … Those tasks are now added to the three basic missions of a CPAS: social assistance, medical care and social and medical activities.

3.3   A greater diversification of benefactors

A third trend is the greater diversification of benefactors of CPAS due to economic factors. A more diversified range of people from various background could, one day, be in need and then be confronted with social action. Citizen being not in conditions to receive financial help from CPAS can also benefit from their services, for example for information, old people's housing or family services.

3.4   A bigger interconnection with other actors

To conclude, important actors surrounding social action are more diversified. Indeed, CPAS are being increasingly interconnected with other actors of economic and social life like public authorities, associations, fundings authorities, companies, … Those are also increasingly working in cooperation.

4   The identity of social workers

In order to better understand the mutual interactions between ICT and social action, we are now going to analyze the identity of social workers. Methods and conceptions of social work in CPAS have been extended. Sociologists Guy Bajoit and Abraham Franssen [7] (1997-1998) have developed a typology regarding the four different profiles at work in social working. This typology has emerged from a research with social workers concerning the ways of perceiving their own role (see Fig. 1).

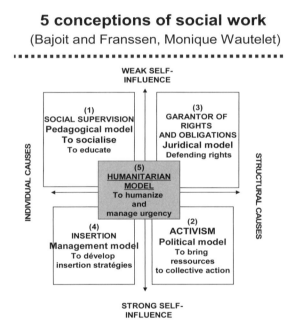

Fig 1. Five conceptions of social work

This typology is the result of crossing of two main axes. The first refers to the causes of marginality, perceived like being linked to individual causes or to structural causes. The second axis refers to the capacity of individuals to change their situation. A person can be seen like having a strong influence on his/her present condition (empowerment) or like having a weak influence on his/her own marginality. Four identity models of the social worker, being four ways of perceiving their own role, exist around these two axes.

(1)   Pedagogical model is based on charity and on rehabilitation. Benefactors are perceived as responsible of their own precariousness and as deprived

of abilities to improve their situation. Social worker is an agent of social control whose mission is to guarantee the respect of social norms.

(2)   Political model is related to the conception of social work in the seventies. Within this framework, the role of the social worker has become an agent of social transformation. Poverty is considered as a result of social domination. Social workers have adopted the idea that it is possible to fight against poverty while being organized collectively, speaking or being an actor in society. Benefactors are perceived as exploited or excluded. Social worker has a role of militant, bringing resources to collective action.

(3)   In the juridical model, benefactors are perceived as precarious due to structural causes (unemployment, diseases,…). Users are seen like irresponsible victims of a system, having right to an institutional solidarity. Social worker is regarded itself as a guarantor of rights and duties of benefactors.

(4)   To conclude, the management model perceives benefactors as responsible for their own situation while having obligation to be integrated in society. The role of social workers is to support autonomy of the benefactors while being agents of social control. A social worker has a role of social manager.

In addition of those four models, Monique Wautelet, a Belgian social assistant, has also worked on that subject and has created a fifth model, at the crossroad of the other: the humanitarian model [8]. This identity model is acts above all on the effects of a problem, without putting questions about its causes. The user is perceived like being in poverty and the role of social worker is to humanize and manage urgency.

Following those models, the identity of "social workers", through its cognitive (what social workers know about their professional group), evaluative (positive and negative value connotation of the group) and emotional components (emotions directed towards the group) can be perceived in different ways. We have observed the existence of those five models in CPAS of our research.

5   The place of ICT in social work

Due to national obligation to be connected to a computerized network, and particularly to the national social security crossroad, each CPAS is generally well equipped in ICT (PC, servers and internet connexions). Our central question is how ICT can affect the ways or working in CPAS and particularly the professional identities of the social workers in their three layers quoted above: cognitive, evaluative and emotional one.

5.1   Cognitive component of ICT

Workers have two spontaneous opposite knowing of computerization. On one hand, computerization is viewed as a tool, helpful for social action with different benefits: to gain time, increase speed in the treatment of documents, be more efficient, … On the other hand, computerization is viewed as a barrier for social action. In both cases, ICT are viewed as mandatory, requiring new skills and qualifications to use it and to integrate it in their every day work.

5.2   Evaluative component of ICT

The assessment of CPAS workers over computerization is overall rather positive, even if some risks regarding the quality of the social action are pointed out by the social workers. [4].

The efficiency of ICT has been mainly underlined. 96% of respondents agree or totally agree with the fact that computerization makes their work more efficient. 73% have the same position on the fact that ICT improves the internal communication and facilitates the exchanges of information. 74% agree or completely agree with the fact that ICT shortens the retrieval of documents and 84% think that ICT increases the capacity of action and resolution of problems by a better access of each worker to information.

Risks related to computerization are generally understated by CPAS. Indeed, only 22% agree or completely agree with the fact that ICT implies more control on the work of employees. 15% adopt the same position regarding the risk related to the decreasing of social skills and knowledge. Though, 36% consider that burdens social work since ICT programs are often viewed as too complex, needing long time of adaptation. The fact that ICT programs are numerous without any coordination between them increases this complexity and obliges to re-key the same data several times. Finally, for 26%, ICT decrease the freedom of the employees in the way they can manage social cases and related documents.

Some fears about ICT have been underlined in CPAS. Indeed, nearly 50% agree or completely agree with the fact that use of computer decreases the proximity between social worker and concerned public. 74% have the same opinion regarding the fact that data processing does not improve the relation between social workers and people being given social care.

To conclude, the normative feature of computerization is underlined since 82% consider as normal that, in our era of E-government, circulars or law related to them are sent via Internet.

5.3   Emotional component of ICT

Those rather positive opinions regarding ICT contrast strongly with the feeling shared by all the social workers who perceive ICT more as a mandatory external requirement than as an internal choice supported by a true process of negotiation and appropriation. This feeling can be better understood when knowing that most of the ICT programs at use in CPAS have been imposed by the various public authorities funding and surrounding the CPAS. This feeling is reinforced by the little mean at disposal to really appropriate those devices. Less than one third of the surveyed CPAS benefits from the presence of computer scientists to help them in their ICT appropriation and management (there were 46 computer scientists for 126 CPAS). Both feeling of obligation and lack of qualified people explain also that only 48% have developed a true ICT policy, which again reinforced their feeling of an 'external dictator' regarding their technological destiny [4].

5.4   A contrasted image of computerization

According to the survey, all the CPAS are not on the same level regarding their use and their perception of ICT. On the contrary, computerization seems better fit with certain professional profiles identified in the typology presented before.

Two profiles seem better match with the ICT's purposes and requirements. It is first of all the social management profiles motivated by goals of rationalization and efficiency both compatible with the aims of ICT. It is also the humanitarian profile stimulated by the social emergency and for whom ICT bring an image of rapidity and efficiency. In these two cases, computerization seems to be 'the tool of the situation', facilitating a more rational management and helping to react quickly to social emergencies.

On the contrary, technologies seems to be less in accordance with profiles like the pedagogical (1) and the militant one (2), based on personal and close relationships with the public aiming at empowering people and at fighting against social exclusion.

6   ICTs and social work : two opposite logics?

To explain the cautious assessment made by social workers on their ICT surroundings, one could make the hypothesis that a cultural shock exists between the initial logics that support the social work, on one hand, and, on the other, those at work with the computerization[3].

Comparing those two logics can help to understand difficulties encountered by some social workers regarding the integration of these news ways of working in their every day life. It can also explain a shift at work in some CPAS between those who adopt ICT and those who are left behind. Finally, it also explain some political games at work in the CPAS between clerical workers and social workers, the first ones gaining in power due to their larger involvement into ICT's matter. All those observations seem to lead to a certain digital divide into the CPAS world.

---

[3] The components of those logics have been created on basis of literature, observations, interviews, and our survey's results.

Table 1. Comparison between frameworks of ICT and of social work

Logics of computerization	Logics of social work
Standardization – rationalization of social care with the use of formatted programs or applications	Personalization of practices – case by case work
Information sharing due to computer servers, Internet, e-mail, …	Confidential work - each social worker has his own way of working
Written tradition - bureaucratization	Oral and proximity tradition
Speed - efficiency	Slow work with users
Quantitative judgments and global approach of reality (statistics)	Qualitative judgments (more individualized approach)

7   A limited cultural shock?

However, the mutual opposition of technology and social services is limited. Our epistemological approach refuses to adopt a strictly determinist position, considering technology "*as an objective external force that would have (relatively) deterministic impacts on organizational properties such as structure.*" [9]. On the contrary, we advocate for "*a structurational model of technology*" [9]. Our model of reference is Giddens'theory of structuration [10]: "*The theory of structuration recognizes that human actions are enabled and constrained by structures, yet that these structures are the result of previous actions*" [9]. Computerization is part of structures, having influences and being influenced by human workers or human actions.

The introduction of ICT in an organization is not sufficient in itself to change professional practices. This appropriation of technology has two conditions. It *"requires not only that the receiving ground has the necessary means to assimilate and use the object, but also a need of the object to answer questions or a difficulty which arises, even implicitly"* [11].

Workers can also manifest strategic attitudes of resistance. Generally, professionals of a sector cannot be completely constrained by ICT. They always have the freedom and possibilities of playing with the rules.

Eventually, computerization has its limits. It is, therefore, far from being extended to all the features of work in CPAS, and largely, of social work. Indeed, most of those workers use daily relational, listening and empathy qualities with their users. ICT are definitely not sufficient to replace the practices of social workers by machines….

8   Conclusion, practical recommendations and additional points of view

8.1   Conclusion

Main objective of this contribution was to relate the potential impact of ICT on the professional identity of the social workers in CPAS.

As underlined before, CPAS rather perceive computerization as an obligation than as a real project. The fast rhythm imposed by their public authorities for their computerization has not given time to adapt themselves to ICT, nor has it provided them with a sound policy to appropriate ICT to their identity. Meanwhile, our analysis shows that these difficulties are unequally perceived by CPAS, according to their means and their resources, but mostly according to their perception of social action.

Computerization seems to fit rather well with professional identity perceiving social action as a matter of efficiency and of emergency for which it is necessary to react with speed and effectiveness (like in the management and the humanitarian profiles). On the contrary, technologies seems to be less in accordance with professional identities for which social work is first of all a question of proximity , of personalized process of caring and of defense of excluded people (like in the political and the humanitarian profiles). For those professional identities, there exist a bigger 'cultural shock' between logics of ICT and logics of social work. Indeed, the bureaucratization related to ICT appears as incompatible with the personalized process they deploy with excluded people.

8.2   Recommendations

Many adjustments and dialogues are possible to avoid 'a marriage of convenience' between CPAS and ICT and to facilitate the appropriation of ICT by those services. However, many efforts have to be done to foster this appropriation. First of all, it seems that the traditional model of ICT imposition endorsed by the related public authorities should gain in maturity and effectiveness by a better consultation and a true negotiation with the concerned CPAS. On the other hand, CPAS should be encouraged to develop ICT policies regarding their needs, theirs projects and their capacities. To conclude, ICT appropriation is a training matter and, in this domain, a sound effort should be done in the learning programs that support the social workers education.

Nevertheless, the major change has to expect from the community of CPAS acting as a single demanding player since most of them share the same difficulties and constraints. This goes through three main recommendations:

- Our first recommendation would be to create a regional platform, federating CPAS. It would be an intermediary between CPAS, public authorities and computer companies. It could help social center to negotiate computer applications, and the development of their computerization.

- A second recommendation is to implement communities of practices for CPAS. Those communities would bring further solidarity between social services. CPAS could share their experience, computer perceptions and resources. Those communities could also allow CPAS to define common computer policy and could teach the employees the new challenges of computerization (use and maintenance of ICT, ethical and legal perspectives, …)
- Our third recommendation would be to create an external observatory for the computerization of CPAS. This observatory could report to public authorities the problems and lacks of means of CPAS concerning their computerization process. Public authorities could adapt their policy accordingly.

Acting as a community can give a chance to each CPAS to better master its ICT policy and to each of the concerned social worker to move from an ICT obligation to an ICT appropriate project.

8.3   Towards further researches?

Each research has unfortunately its own limits! Different additional perspectives could be an interesting complement to our research.

In a first time, it could be very interesting to compare our computerization research's results with those of social services in other countries or in other cultures. A comparison between ICT's integration in CPAS and in other associations or public organisations (hospitals, public administrations or municipalities, …) could also be useful. Secondly, a qualitative and quantitative analyse of benefactor's perceptions about computerisation of work in social services could be an enriching view for our study. Those perceptions could be added to another analyze: professional identity of other actors surrounding CPAS: public authorities, associations, subsidiary powers, companies, Third, our results need to be frequently updated. A longitudinal study would give interesting data to observe evolutions and changes in social sector.

Computers and ICT are evolving and increasing in social professions. The central message of this paper is that their deployment is not a fate. Human workers always have the possibility to be actors of their computerization. Therefore, our contribution could also be interesting for other kinds of organizations.

9   Acknowledgments

I would like to thank my research team: Claire Lobet-Maris, Françoise Navarre, Cedric Burton, Yves Poullet and Philippe Versailles. I also thank also my colleagues of the CITA and the summer school participants I have met in Karlstad for the interesting discussions we had. Their contributions have been very useful for the redaction of this article.

References

1. C. Burton, V. Laurent, F. Navarre, Y. Poullet, and P. Versailles, *Quand l'informatique rencontre l'action sociale… Regards pluridisciplinaires sur l'informatisation des CPAS* (Presses universitaires de Namur, Namur, 2007).
2. J. Agar, *The Government Machine: A Revolutionary History of the Computer* (MIT Press, Cambridge, 2003).
3. J.M Berger, *Mémento des CPAS* (Kluwer, Bruxelles, 2004).
4. C. Burton, V. Laurent, C. Lobet-Maris, F. Navarre and Y. Poullet, L'informatisation des CPAS, une informatique plurielle au service de l'action sociale, Rapport de résultats du questionnaire préparatoire au Colloque des Secrétaires de CPAS (Herbeumont, April 2006, http://www.fundp.ac.be/pdf/publications/57376.pdf).
5. H. Tajfel (dir.), *Differentiation between social groups, studies of the social psychology of intergroup relations*, (Cambridge, Academic Press, 1978), p 28.
6. R. Castel, Du travail social à la gestion sociale du non travail, *Revue Esprit*, (1998), pp. 28-45.
7. G. Bajoit, A. Franssen, Le métier d'assistant social, *Travailler le social*, n°17, 1997-1998, pp 36-70.
8. M. Wautelet, Le métier de travailleur social en CPAS : aujourd'hui et demain, *lecture at the Carrefours du Printemps de la Fédération des CPAS de l'Union des Villes et des Communes de Wallonie* (2004, http://www.fewasc.be/pages/news/news13.htm).
9. W. Orlikowski, The duality of technology: rethinking the concept of technology in organizations, *Organisation Science*, (vol 3, num 3, 1992), pp. 398-427, (p.399-403-404).
10. A. Giddens, *The constitution of society: Outline of the theory of structuration* (Oxford, Polity Press, 1984).
11. G. Chevalier, *Les services sociaux à l'épreuve de l'informatique* (European Science Foundation, Issy-les-Moulineaux, 2000), p. 95.

Workshop: Identifiers in eHealth

Putting Identifiers in the Context of eHealth
Introduction of a Model

Rieks Joosten[1], Diane Whitehouse[2], and Penny Duquenoy[3]

[1] TNO, Netherlands
rieks.joosten@tno.nl
[2] The Castlegate Consultancy, United Kingdom
diane.whitehouse@thecastlegateconsultancy.com
[3] Middlesex University, United Kingdom
P.Duquenoy@mdx.ac.uk

Abstract. eHealth is becoming an increasingly noteworthy domain in terms of public sector exploitation of information and communications technologies. Appro-priately identifying the users of electronic health systems is a major contem-porary challenge. The appropriate identification of eHealth systems' and ser-vices' users is one of its core areas of concern. This paper develops a particular problem statement that relates to the notion of identifiers in eHealth, outlines its conceptual background, and defines a set of solutions to the problem outlined. It lists a variety of use cases or examples against which the issues can be tested (these are further explored in a parallel paper [13]), and proposes some possibilities for future work. In particular, the paper de-scribes the results of a 2007 workshop that explored all of these notions. While the paper bases its orientations in a general European framework, the main examples and illustrations used by the authors come from experiences in the Netherlands.

1 Introduction

Probing the concept of identifiers, what they are, how they are used, and how they can be managed in an information systems environment – particularly one that has relevance to the eHealth domain – is the focus of this paper. The notion of a unique identifier, and what it is intended to do, is not difficult to understand. However, there is a considerable challenge in transferring an identifier that is unique from its own small context to a wider context or scope. A conceptual shift is required that can take into account the nature of the technologies with which we are surrounded whether in eHealth or in some other public sector services field. In this paper, therefore, we present an approach that takes a perspective based on the requirements of the computer system and its capabilities. The model presented here illustrates the various scoping difficulties involved (see also, [8, 10]).

The writing of this paper was stimulated by a workshop held at the IFIP WG 9.2, 9.6/11.7, 11.6/FIDIS summer school held in Karlstad, Sweden (August 6-10, 2007) on 'Identifiers and eHealth' run by Diane Whitehouse and Penny Duquenoy. As a result of the combination of persons present, particularly Rieks Joosten of TNO (Netherlands), the session focused on developing an underpinning model of

Please use the following format when citing this chapter:

Joosten, R., Whitehouse, D. and Duquenoy, P., 2008, in IFIP International Federation for Information Processing, Volume 262; The Future of Identity in the Information Society; Simone Fischer-Hübner, Penny Duquenoy, Albin Zuccato, Leonardo Martucci; (Boston: Springer), pp. 389–403.

identification that can be applied to the eHealth domain. The underlying purpose of the model is clearly explained in the second section of this paper that follows.

2 Purpose

The particular contribution of the workshop, and of the paper resulting from it, is to propose a model for identifiers, and a working procedure for using that model. When applying the contribution in a given setting, the following results can be expected:

1. ability **to distinguish identifier-related issues from non-identifier issues** in that particular context. This approach is necessary so as to verify that a selected issue is **actually identifier-related** and that the model can be used according to its intentions (rather than as a solution to larger, global, problems).

2. opportunity to obtain an absolutely **clear perspective on the particular problem's identifier-related issues**. While this opportunity is a pre-requisite for problem-solving, it is not a solution in itself (although, in some cases, it may suffice to see the proper solution).

With these two clear intentions, identifier issues in a particular situation can be addressed by the people/personnel responsible for the situation. It can enable them to understand the setting fully, and apply the relevant contextual and regulatory conditions, and so on. The actual solution of individual problems is outside the scope of our paper. The paper merely seeks to use **an example illustration** of the proposed model, and a suggested method for putting it to work.

The paper is intended to be the technical report of the outcomes of a particular summer school workshop. By applying the model to the eHealth sector, as we did in this workshop, the actual process of examining the various test cases shows how the model can unravel the complexities of combining data sets. As this possible transformation lies at the core of eHealth, it is crucial to understand where the problems arise. Having such a model or tool available may clarify the relationships between different systems of data organisation, and may help in resolving these difficulties. The paper particularly aims at helping to make software architects and designers more aware of the pervasive nature of identifiers, whether in eHealth or more widely, and helps to indicate how they should be handled. In terms of the personnel working in eHealth, it enables those concerned to understand the considerable complexities facing the domain. Hence, the paper does not solve particular problems. Rather it aims to clear a kind of 'fog', and to make issues clearer for the personnel in charge of a particular problem area.

We wish to emphasise that there are yet other domains in which this paper does not stray. The paper is not intended to survey the entirety of the identifier problems throughout the whole of the European Union, nor more widely internationally: even so, it does use as a particular illustration the eHealth context in a particular European country (the Netherlands). It is nevertheless evident that the example could be explored in terms of other European Member States. Surveys of the different Member States' approaches to identification issues have taken place under the aegis of other projects and initiatives, e.g., the European Commission co-financed i2health project. Nor does the paper provide a critical social, ethical, or legal review of the issues surrounding identifiers[1]. Overall, therefore, the paper does not seek to promote the notion of a unique personal identifier[2]. While it is clear that some Member States and some other international countries have chosen that particular approach[3], the orientation for direction on such issues is the domain of European, and Member States, policy-makers and decision-makers.

3 Background on eHealth

The domain of eHealth has grown from research and development initiatives undertaken in Europe from the 1960s onwards, and which have thrived especially during the past twenty-year period. eHealth has progressed from an area of theoretical exploration to one which is being put into practice today throughout a growing number of European countries. As the research team of the i2Health project on eHealth, an eTEN project co-financed by the European Commission, emphasised:

"Information and information technologies (ICT) are currently deployed on a broad scale in healthcare. European Member States are struggling to deploy promising eHealth services under high pressure .... The fundamental use case of eHealth is making medical information quickly available for a better and more efficient treatment of patients. ... eHealth can be reduced to a transmission of information on someone (who?) between actors (again who?). An appropriate implementation of identification management guarantees correct attribution of information and access control to guard privacy." [7]

eHealth comprises a wide range of organisational forms and technological applications. The domain is said to describe 'the application of information and communications technologies across the whole range of functions that affect the health sector' [2]. Each application has a different requirement for the quality of identification associated with it: whether the application is, for example, reimbursement, electronic booking, clinical information, electronic patient records (or 'patient summaries'), emergency data sets, ePrescribing, or some Internet-based publicly-available information.

---

[1] For readers interested in these issues, see the referenced European Directive 95/46/EC [3] and the FIDIS [5] project deliverable on profiling techniques in the field of ambient intelligence.

[2] Note that doing so would have been a proposition for a solution to a problem, which is explicitly not one of the results we expect of our model.

[3] Examples include the national registry number in Belgium, the BSN – the citizen's service number or social security number - in the Netherlands, and the social security number in the United States of America and also in Canada.

While individual European Member States are responsible for the provision of healthcare[4], it is becoming increasingly evident that the challenges facing national health systems are no longer separate dilemmas but rather problems that confront the whole of Europe. A focus on the issues surrounding patient, health professional, and institutional identification has expanded particularly as the different European Member States have progressed to focus on the provision of electronic healthcare (or medical) records for their respective individual citizens. As the potential connectedness and interoperability of Europe's health systems and services expands both organisationally and electronically, it is timely to ensure that the users of eHealth systems are appropriately identified. It is only right and proper that the appropriate person (or persons) is accessing, using, and manipulating the appropriate data at the appropriate time and in the appropriate place (this is an adaptation of a statement by Duquenoy et al. [4] and HEHIP [6]). These issues will increasingly come to the fore as cross-border provision of healthcare is promoted, and a launch of a large-scale pilot on eHealth interoperability takes place. In this paper, the example of a single country (the Netherlands) is used rather than using exemplars from the whole of the European Union.

4 Problem statement with regard to identifiers

Fundamental to the 2007 Karlstad summer school workshop was the notion that identifiers are key to eHealth, and somehow also seem to present a number of challenges. Given the perceived importance of the identifier issue, the original focus of the workshop, namely "the exploration of social and stakeholder-related issues related to identifiers in eHealth" was shifted towards "developing an underpinning model of identification that can be applied to the eHealth domain". Hence, the workshop was inductive in character: it involved a quest or search for the problem statement.

This section therefore explores some of the general characteristics of identifiers in the articulation of the problem that is needed to be addressed. Wherever possible, rather than selecting a generic workplace, organisation, or surveillance setting, we have deliberately chosen – as we did in the workshop – a healthcare context to illustrate the points made.

We have established a number of criteria for identifiers. This section explores two of these identifier criteria (IC), that is, IC1 and IC2, and the process used to develop them, which are explained in greater detail below. Sections 4 and 5 refine the criteria still further to arrive at IC3. IC4 is outlined briefly in section 9.

---

[4] Title XIII Public Health, Art. 152 of the European Community Treaty ensures a high level of human health protection in the definition and implementation of all Community Policies and activities.

To this end, we started a quest for a criterion[5] for identifiers based on an initial proposal criteria IC1) that: *an identifier is (1) a text that (2) names someone or something.* Throwing a number of test cases at these criteria helps us to make them increasingly strong and more effective. At the same time, we come to an understanding of some of the underlying issues that need to be addressed. A number of test cases follow. They lead to an enhanced identifier criteria (IC2).

4.1   Testing first criteria for identifiers

Our first test case is this: is the text "Donald Duck" an identifier[6]? According to IC1, identifiers must satisfy two requirements. First, an identifier must be a text and, secondly, it must name someone or something. "Donald Duck" satisfies both requirements: it is a text and it names a Disney character with whom we are all familiar.

Our second test case places us in a hospital ward where there is a patient called Jane Smith. According to IC1, the text "Jane Smith" is an identifier because it names this particular patient. Now suppose that another patient is brought in, and she happens to be called Jane Smith too. What occurs next is that the ward nurses would detect[7] the ambiguity of this name and as a result would start to concoct some form of consensus as to how to distinguish both patients. For example, they might come to call one of the patients "Jane", and the other one "Mrs. Smith" or "Jane with the grey hair". Whatever the consensus, the result is that, in the ward setting, both patients will be assigned (different) names that actually uniquely identify them. Note that "Jane Smith" has continued to be an identifier, at least according to IC1. However, the nurses started a process that resulted in there being other identifiers (according to IC1). They did this automatically and unconsciously to ensure that these identifiers would have the property of uniquely identifying the patients in the ward.

Apparently, the nurses (unconsciously) used a criterion for identifiers that incorporates this property of uniqueness. So we propose another criteria for identifiers, IC2: *an identifier is a text that names precisely one someone or something.* IC2 (which still works in the "Donald Duck" example). This example means dismissing "Jane Smith" as an identifier as soon as a second patient called "Jane Smith" enters the ward.

The ward nurses start a process to come up with new IC2-compliant identifiers as soon as there are patients in the ward without a compliant identifier[8]. Note that "Jane Smith" has remained a name for either patient, which implies that identifiers and

---

[5] We use a criterion (or criteria) rather than a definition. This is because the correctness of a definition may be disputed, but a criterion is something that anyone can simply apply.

[6] Although we use a fictional character to illustrate our test, we generally assume that the eventual identifier used will (if it is a name) be a factual and authentic name.

[7] This is an example of how the violation of a criterion leads to an action. This is a fundamental principle and is explained further in section 6.

[8] A consequence of using criteria for identifiers rather than definitions, is that violations of criteria may serve as triggers for processes that restore compliance. See section 6.

names are different things. The generally accepted idea that the terms "identifier" and "name" have the same meaning is hence flawed! The nurses' behaviour of automatically disambiguating patient identifiers by creatively thinking of different names for the patients is readily recognisable in other organisational settings. Apparently, it is something we humans do unconsciously. This does not mean however that, as human beings, we can actually and accurately describe what it is we are doing. To illustrate this point, everyone can tell that sentence this not proper English grammar to adheres, even though readers are unlikely to be able to list the grammatical rule(s) that are violated in the phrase.

This approach might explain why many information technology (IT) specification documents do not explicitly specify how the system should handle identifiers so as to guarantee the unique identification property; after all, their authors are only human. As a consequence, systems in the eHealth domain, as well as in other domains, may contain flaws related to identifiers, e.g., there will be systems that assume names and identifiers to be the same (which, as we have seen, is a flawed assumption).

From this last test case, we conclude that the identifier problem is one of automation design rather than of knowing or not knowing how to deal with identifiers. In particular, it is necessary, at least for software architects and designers, to have an explicit model of what constitutes an identifier at their disposal.

4.2 Testing enhanced criteria for identifiers

Let us return to the example of the two women who are both called "Jane Smith". We can easily think of names that they will be called in another setting, such as in their homes. There, they might be called "Jane" but they will also have other names such as "Mum" or "Darling". However, these last two names, while they are unambiguous in Jane's own home, are also used in other households; there they are unambiguous as well. In the setting of most (English language) households, the name "Mum" would unambiguously identify one person. So, here we see that one name can be associated with multiple identifiers, depending on the setting. Here too, people have an automatic way of dealing with identifiers. By being sensitive to the particular setting in which they find themselves and switching contexts unconsciously when necessary, people have no problem with the fact that a single name may have the property of uniquely identifying different people or things in different settings. People apparently make these kinds of adaptations all the time.

Looking at this case in another way, we see that while "Mum" has a unique identification property in a given household, this is no longer the case when we stretch the scope to include the entire street, city, or country. A text can be used as an identifier when we consider that a certain scope (setting) may no longer be an identifier and when the scope under consideration is enlarged.

This description might explain what happens in eHealth and other software applications. For example, a software application in a hospital is likely to have been designed for use in a particular setting (or scope). However, as the scope that the application has to function in grows (e.g. as a consequence of a hospital merger or if external parties have been given access to the particular hospital system), the application may not be able to follow suit. It may be the case that its identifiers are no longer identifiers in the new, enlarged scope and that it is also not equipped with the program code that allows the systems to resolve the issues in a similar way that human beings do unconsciously.

From this exploration of a number of tests of IC1 and IC2, we conclude that the identifier problem is also one of increasingly large, or rather, enlarging scopes rather than the previous small ones. In eHealth terms, this could not only be a problem when local systems are increasingly connected. It could also be a challenge when nationwide systems try to bring smaller systems together, and even – quite possibly – if European Member States were at some hypothetical point in time in the future ever to start to look at ways of integrating their health-related systems. With regard to the transfer of information, from hospital to hospital, for example, this paper deliberately does not – as already stipulated – address those legal or regulatory issues which might be relevant. [9,10]

To conclude, in the 2007 Karlstad summer school workshop, our quest for identifier criteria led us to the four following observations:

1. Human beings deal with identifiers mostly unconsciously. However, the architects and designers of software systems need a conscious, explicit idea of what identifiers are if they are to design software programs that exhibit similar behaviour to that of human beings.
2. Whether or not a text (label, name, number) is considered as an identifier depends on the setting (scope) in which it is used.
3. A text may identify (i.e., be the name of) different things in different settings.
4. An identifier may lose its unique identification property when the scope (setting) that it is defined or used in is enlarged.

In the following section, we outline how we proposed in the workshop to deal with the identifier challenges uncovered.

---

[9] Readers interested in these aspects may refer to the FIDIS [5] project deliverable which draws attention to the 'finality principle' and the 'legitimate purposes principle'. International transfer of data is covered by the 'safe harbour principle'. The notion of 'scope' used in this paper provides a formal of demarcation but one that is not necessarily related to legalities or the legitimacy principle, jurisdictions, or domains. The challenge of transferring information between two hospital jurisdictions are not identifier issues that arise when transferring information between two scopes – in the sense used in this paper.

[10] It might be more realistic to add the notion of introducing the person's date of birth. However, this model is not intended to determine whether it is right or wrong to use names and dates of birth as identifiers. Rather, the model is used to verify or validate the quality of a criterion that can distinguish identifiers from non-identifiers.

5 A proposal for a resolution of the problem statement: a new model

In this section, we set out to deal with the particular challenge of enlarged scope. Dealing with this problem leads us to outline two more identifier criteria, IC3 and IC4. IC3 is dealt with in detail here. IC4 is treated only briefly in section 9.

Steps towards a solution to this set of observations would be to make the relation between identifiers, scopes and texts (names, labels, and bit strings) explicit, to apply this model in various use cases to see whether it works, and to detect any possible or associated limitations. The model we propose is quite simple, and can be worded as identifier criterion IC3: *an identifier is a symbol*[11] *that, when interpreted in a given scope*[12] *(setting), uniquely identifies an entity.* We use the term 'identifier-symbol' for symbols that are part of an identifier. We define 'name' as a pair (s, e) where s is an identifier-symbol of some identifier that uniquely identifies entity e. A visual representation of this model is shown in Fig. 1 below:

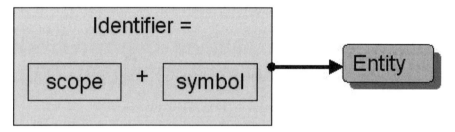

Fig. 1. An identifier is a symbol that, when interpreted in a given scope, uniquely identifies an entity.

Registration within a given scope (i.e., the creation of an identifier), means that the combination of this scope and a symbol (i.e., an identifier) is stored, and is linked to an entity[13]. Hence, the symbol is a name for that entity within the given scope. Within the scope of the hospital ward outlined in our second test case example, the new names of the two Mrs. Smiths were registered as the consensus developed on these two names was established. Likewise, symbols may be registered as identifiers in the databases of the various healthcare institutions that point to examples such as electronic health (or medication) records, and employees' files.

---

[11] As this model is intended for personnel such as information technology (IT) professionals, we prefer to use the term 'symbol' rather than 'text' so as to allow for other data types, such as pictures or photographs to be used as a symbol.

[12] Similarly, we prefer to use the term 'scope' over 'setting' as it aligns well with terminology used in design and programming languages. In particular, the term 'identifier scope' is well defined in programming languages, and it is our sense that the model might be an extension of what is used there already. In other circumstances (in the 2007 Karlstad summer school itself, for example), we used the term 'context'.

[13] An e.

Pursuing this particular model or criterion has several consequences:

1. Every identifier uniquely identifies an entity[14]. Note that in computers, entities can be files, database records, objects, etc. In eHealth, entities can be patients, medical staff, or hospital administrators. Also, note that this does not imply that every entity must have a unique id-symbol.

2. Interpretation of an identifier symbol, i.e., associating a meaning to that symbol, is specific to the setting (scope) in which this is done, and its meaning is the entity (associated with the identifier).

3. Within every scope, there must be guarantees for the unique identification property of its identifiers, i.e., guarantees that every identifier satisfies IC3 and continues to do so over time. Which guarantees are selected and how they are operated is a design decision. However, particular attention should be paid to the registration of symbols to ensure that not only the symbol (text label) itself and the entity it references are registered, but also the scope within which the symbol names that entity. Also, attention must be paid to the situation where symbols cross the borders of scopes, e.g., when a system receives a message containing symbols from another system in another scope, or if the scope is enlarged, e.g., the system is supposed to work with data from other resources.

4. Within a given scope, symbols may only be used reliably if they are an identifier-symbol within that very scope, or if the scope in which they are an identifier-symbol is explicitly known. If not, such symbols bear the risk of being interpreted ambiguously (i.e., not being identifier-symbols any more). Note that a violation of this rule can happen when the scope is enlarged – it is then no longer the same scope. Also, this may happen if the identifier's symbol is interpreted in a completely different scope.

5. If a system within a certain scope is required to handle a symbol that is part of an identifier from another ('foreign') scope, the software designers of that system must have defined a way to interpret this symbol in a way that is useful within the system's scope/setting. This can be done e.g., by means of a 'dictionary' (i.e., a translation table or a correspondence table) that, to use this analogy, translates the identifier-symbol of the first identifier into an identifier in the system's scope. Note that both identifiers may in fact point to the same or different entities. For example, both identifiers may point to a single patient. However, one of them may point to a patient while the other may point to the patient's electronic patient record. Whatever translation is useful depends on the purpose pursued. This, we feel, is the actual basis of the situation in which we deal properly with identifiers[15].

---

[14] An entity is something that has a separate and distinct existence and objective or conceptual reality. See http://www.webster.com/dictionary/entity/

[15] The model presented in this paper has already been used in an internal prototype tool by TNO for the translation of identifiers from one scope to another as a means of coming to grips with use cases. This tool has been developed at the same time as the model and has influenced its construction.

For the automated settings that can be found within computer systems (software applications), this means there must be symbol-registries, each entry of which is associated with exactly one scope and precisely one entity. Current database technology is capable of supporting this option; it is more a question of using it appropriately.

6 Conceptual background

This section describes in some detail the conceptual background to the problem statement we have developed. The way that we have treated the identifier problem here is rooted in the recently developed, yet still unpublished, technique called 'Ampersand' [11, 12]. The Ampersand method can be applied by anyone who can think conceptually, is familiar with relation algebra[16], and is capable of mapping the conceptual models onto reality. The method starts by making one or more statements (rules, criteria) about a given topic, e.g. IC1. The idea is that such statements are universal truths' within the context for which they are created. Usually, such statements are about concepts and the relations between such concepts. The statements together form a conceptual model or a conceptual pattern.

The universal truth of the conceptual model is challenged by throwing at it multiple use cases (cases that actually happen in practice). For every relevant use case, an attempt is made to map it onto the conceptual model. If the attempt succeeds, the model has passed yet another test. If it fails, then this forces us either to modify the model or to think about the topic in a different way. Both possibilities brings us further forward. Either the model becomes better and more robust or our understanding of the topic is enhanced.

This technique requires that the statements behind the conceptual model are not only represented in natural language (as IC1 through IC4 are), but are also represented in relation algebra (we have, however, omitted this algebraic representation in this paper). This latter representation ensures that the statements have a formal underpinning, which means that combining multiple conceptual models can be done with the aid of automated reasoning tools. Topics that have been modeled this way can consistently and fluently be related to other topics that have been modeled using the same method. Also, the relation algebra representations form a solid, mathematical basis from which both process and service designs can be created.

An important characteristic of this technique is that the universal truth statements can be operationalised. By this we mean that violations of such statements can be detected, in particular, in automated settings. Any such event is to be treated as a trigger for an action that changes the situation in which violations exist into a situation where this is no longer the case. This is illustrated already in the second test in section 4.2, where IC3 was violated when a second "Mrs. Smith" entered the hospital ward.

---

[16] Relation algebra is based in mathematics. For a short explanation, see e.g. http://en.wikiped ia.org/wiki/Relation_algebra. Relational algebra [1] differs subtly from relation algebra. Relational algebra has to do with databases.

This violation (that was unconsciously signalled by the nurses), caused them to come up with a solution that removed the violation and restored the truth of IC3. In fact, detecting violation of universal truth statements is a powerful mechanism for designing processes, which is covered in a paper that describes the use of the statements (rules) as the definition of a process [9]). This technique could be useful in eHealth for designing healthcare processes as a set of criteria that should become fulfilled during that process.

7 Results of the workshop

In a proposed associated paper [13], we outline some of the results that emerged during the workshop and immediately afterwards. A number of examples, some of which – but not all – are directly pertinent to the field of eHealth, may have become less problematic when viewed in the light of the proposed model. We chose six examples to illustrate the problem issues:
1. an application of a first set of questions about identifiers, scope, symbol and entity;
2. identification of patients in a hospital setting;
3. how to deal with an enlargement of scope (for example in hospital systems);
4. selecting among identifiers;
5. a particular challenge uncovered in Health Level 7 (HL7);
6. a number of possible software solutions to the problem statement outlined.

8 Discussion and conclusions

The focus of this workshop was on probing the concept of identifiers – what they are, how they are used, and how they can be managed in an information systems environment. As this paper has made clear, the notion of a unique identifier and what it is intended to do, is in itself not difficult to grasp. However, what is problematic is the transfer of an identifier that is unique in one small context to a wider context (or scope, to use the term of the model). Each human being has a set of characteristics that can be used to differentiate one person from another (and are used in our everyday lives). However, transferring these characteristics to the specific, and explicit, rules that are required by an information system is, as we have seen, not feasible – at least in the same way as they are used, adapted and extended by ourselves as human beings. The example of 'Jane Smith' in the hospital ward demonstrated this. A conceptual shift is needed, one that takes into account the characteristics and limits of the technologies with which we are working.

What we have presented here is an approach that takes a perspective based on the requirements of the system and its capabilities. This model illustrates the scoping issues. It allows us to see more clearly what is needed in an identifier when it is expected to cross the boundaries of a constrained setting to much broader settings –

i.e. when its scope is extended. By demonstrating, through the examples and cases we have used, the changing nature of uniqueness (from 'Donald Duck', to 'Mum', to 'Jane Smith') we have a more effective understanding of the criteria necessary for identifiers in these settings. Through this perception, we were able to see the challenge more clearly. The problem is one of automation design and the need to have an explicit model with which software architects and designers can work (cf., Section 4.1). For example, by noting that a change in scope or number of entities constitutes a violation of the criteria, it is possible to set out in technical terms the rules necessary to restore the situation (Section 5). Addressing the problem in this way allows the use of existing technical operations (e.g., symbol-registries) rather than devising new techniques.

In applying the model to the eHealth sector the process of examining the different cases showed how the model could begin to unravel the complexities of combining data sets. As controlled, reliable database accessibility is at the heart of eHealth, it is vital to understand where the problems arise, and to have some tool available that can highlight any conflicting or inconsistent relationships that arise between different systems of data organisation in order to attempt to resolve these difficult issues.

As we have said, the techniques and standards are already in place to support our identifier model. What remains to be done is twofold: firstly, to make software architects and designers aware of how pervasive identifiers really are and how they should be handled, in particular with respect to scoping and extending this IT-notion to organisational entities, organisations and even countries; and, secondly, to make eHealth and other business professionals aware of the pervasiveness of this issue, and the impact it must have if we are to work with identifiers effectively.

9 Future work

By its very nature this workshop adopted an exploratory approach, and thus could only scratch the surface of identifier challenges as they appear in eHealth. The model, as it currently stands, has limitations: it does not yet explicitly address the problem that identifiers may no longer have a unique identification property when the scope grows. Given the possibilities for such enlargement occurring, whether in the domain of eHealth or within other public sector domains, this is an issue that requires attention. In this respect we therefore need to pursue our quest further than we have been able to do in this paper.

During the workshop we also touched on the question of whether or not an identifier must actually reference an (existing) entity. An argument can be made that, if there is an identifier that references an entity and that entity ceases to exist, this should perhaps mean that the identifier is not declassified. If this situation were to be preferable over the currently suggested solution, the associated identifier criterion IC4: would read: *an identifier is a symbol that, when interpreted in a given scope (setting), identifies at most an entity*. The challenge of the further development of IC4 has been left open for further exploration. Therefore a useful exercise would be to explore the creation of models for similar cases within or outside eHealth. A possible topic for further work is the verification of whether or not an electronic patient file actually matches the patient that the electronic patient file is allegedly about or if an electronic patient file for a given patient actually exists. Further examples in the eHealth domain could include situations when a patient moves out of his/her country of residence or even what happens when a patient dies.

While identifiers have been addressed in this paper, identities have not. Apart from often being confused with identifiers, identities in the context of information and communication technologies are usually considered to be a set of attributes associated with a specific entity (person, thing). Additional challenges are those of the integrity (correctness, reliability) of the individual attributes, as well as whether all attributes should actually be associated to one and the same entity. Ongoing work on this issue is being undertaken in the FAIM project within TNO.

At the end of the workshop, we were pleased that such a simple model could be so powerful in explaining the use cases we threw at it. We feel that, to a great extent, the mutual learning gained by applying the model to the challenges we posed to it, in terms of examples, was a major factor in experiencing the model's power.

Others who lack such an experience may react quite differently. One participant of the summer school at which the workshop took place initially commented along the lines of "You just make the problem bigger by introducing such [a] model"[17]. Talking with him a bit more allowed him to clarify his statement. It put us in a position to see that what happened is that he realised the enormous amount of scopes that exist. The identifiers with the symbol "Mum", for example, show that just about every household must be considered as an individual setting. And this is only a single symbol!

Making a mental image of all these settings and their symbols can indeed be an overwhelming experience. However, seeing this large number of scopes does not mean that our model makes the problem bigger. These scopes have existed all along – we have not invented them. The only thing we have done is to enable people to become conscious of the wide variety of scopes, so that we can actually start to think about them in a rational way. This approach will equip us better to design appropriate software rather than to create designs that contain 'seat-of-the-pants' decisions. Metaphorically speaking, we clear the murky waters of the so-called 'identity swamp' so that we can actually see what challenges are out there to address. Apparently, we need to prepare people for this reality before (gently) revealing what is in the swamp... and the swamp is indeed large and requires considerable future work.

At the end of the eHealth and identifiers workshop, we experienced that the actual, practical use of this model changes the way in which we come to think about identifier problems (i.e., there was a conceptual change). This observation can be explained if our model is a good explicit model of what we human beings do unconsciously; it could generate some kind of 'Aha-erlebnis'[18].

---

[17] We are indebted to a number of attendees at the Karlstad August 6-10, 2007 summer school for their feedback in this regard.

[18] We use here the term developed by the early twentieth century German psychologist and theoretical linguist, Karl Bühler, which means a form of 'insight', 'enlightenment' or 'intuition'.

Future work thus might include making people aware of this model in a way that they can actually experience its workings, and to do so using even more specific examples associated with eHealth, e.g., in a workshop setting or in next year's summer school. In this respect, it would be useful to enhance the prototype tool for identifier translation so that it can enable people to acquire the learning experience that we shared together in the workshop.

Acknowledgments

We would like to acknowledge the internal TNO project FAIM support for work in development, and also the EC co-funded project i2Health for providing the starting-point for the workshop. Paul Eveson, Connecting for Health (UK), Marc Griffiths, The Castlegate Consultancy (UK), Wiltfried Pathuis, TNO (the Netherlands), and an anonymous reviewer have also provided useful evidence and criticism. Ultimately, responsibility for the content of the paper is, however, taken by the three authors.

References

1. Codd EF (1970) A Relational Model of Data for Large Shared Data Banks CACM, 13 (6), June 1970
2.   COM(2004)356 final (2004) e-Health – making healthcare better for European citizens: An action plan for a European e-Health area. Luxembourg, European Commission
3. Directive 95/46/EC (1995) of the European Parliament and the Council of 24 October 1995 on the protection of individuals with regard to the processing of personal data and on the free movement of such data. See in particular: Whereas 33; article 6.1 (b); article 8.
4. Duquenoy P, George C, Solomonides A (2007) What ELSE? Regulation and compliance in medical imaging and medical informatics. In: Proceedings of MIMI 2007: Medical Imaging and Informatics Conference, Beijing, China, 15-16th August, 2007
5. FIDIS (2007) project deliverable D7.3 Report on Actual and Possible Profiling Techniques in the Field of Ambient Intelligence. http://www.fidis.net/resources/deliverables/profiling/ Ac-cessed 5 January 2008
6. HEHIP (2003) A handbook of Ethics for Health Informatics Professionals. London, The Brit-ish Computer Society
7. i2Health (2007) (Interoperability Initiative for a European eHealth Area) project deliverable D3.1b Identification management in eHealth. http://www.i2-health.org/ Accessed 5 January 2008
8. Joosten R, Joosten S (forthcoming) Rules for Identity and Access Control. In: Fischer-Huebner S, Duquenoy P, Zuccato A, Martucci L (eds) Proceedings of the IFIP WG9.2, 9.6/11.7, 11.6/FIDIS Summer School on 'The Future of Identity in the Information Society'
9. Joosten S, Joosten R (2005) Specifying business processes by means of rules. In: Proceedings European Business Rules Conference. Amsterdam. June 2005

10. Joosten S, Joosten R (2007) Will rule based BPM obliterate Process Models?, to be published.
11. Joosten S, Joosten R, Joosten S (2007a) Ampersand: foutvrije specificaties voor B&I vraagstukken, Informatie jul/aug (42-50). This article is being translated into English.
12. Joosten S, Joosten R, Joosten S (2007b) Ampersand: Errorfree Specifications for Business-Information Problems, to be published. This article is the translation of the Dutch article cited above.
13. Joosten R, Whitehouse D, Duquenoy P (forthcoming) An identifier model applied to a health context: Results of a workshop (in preparation)

Workshop: Economical and Organisational Identity Aspects

Knowledge Based Organization

An identification model

Cristina Denisa Neagu

Business Information Systems Department,
Faculty of Economics and Business Administration
Al. I. Cuza Iasi University
Bvd. Carol I, Nr. 22, Iasi, 700505, Romania
dneagu@uaic.ro

Abstract. In the recent years, terms like knowledge society, intelligent, learning or knowledge based organizations are used more often. Related to these concepts, many studies underline the fact that organizations should act intelligently by learning and using their knowledge or by being just knowledge-based organizations. The majority of these studies are suffering from being too much philosophical in describing the organization of the future. This philosophical approach limits the possibility of comparison and analysis of organizations based on their potential of being more or less knowledge based. The purpose of this paper is to support the analysis of organizations based on their potential for acting intelligently. After the literature review, this paper provides a model for evaluating and identifying how much an organization could be included in the category of knowledge based organizations. It continues with the presentation of the proposed identification model and it concludes with the analysis results based on this model application in a Romanian company selected for the case study.

1 Introduction

The socio-economic life is based on knowledge and especially in the last years, knowledge have gained more attention being perceived as a strategic asset, as the key resource for organizations, knowledge which is further embedded in the products and services available on the market. In these conditions, concepts such as knowledge based organization, intelligent or knowledge creating company have gained a lot in number of studies related to them. Other concepts like the old one of the organizational structure suffer transformations and a relatively new concept like knowledge worker creates contradictions. Which type of the organizational structure is the best, the flatter one or the bureaucratic, hierarchical but flexible one? Who is knowledge worker, any specialist, expert in his domain of activity, no matter the education or only highly educated people?

Answering to these questions is highly required in indentifying what differentiates one organization from another which has the same physical assets. This paper purpose is to establish an order in the Pandora's Box of knowledge-based organization concept's complexity by answering to these questions in a more elaborated way.

Please use the following format when citing this chapter:

Neagu, C.D., 2008, in IFIP International Federation for Information Processing, Volume 262; The Future of Identity in the Information Society; Simone Fischer-Hübner, Penny Duquenoy, Albin Zuccato, Leonardo Martucci; (Boston: Springer), pp. 407–421.

1.1   Known results

Knowledge based organization have nowadays became widely an important research topic. Most researchers are focused on one or some of aspects related to this concept, such as: types of knowledge, organizational learning and organizational knowledge, knowledge assets and their specific processes which allow knowledge to be acquired, applied, stored, transferred and organizational strategies in order to support and / or improve the knowledge use inside and outside organization.

Several studies are underling the fact that knowledge is the primary resource in the organizations of the 21st century. Further more, the knowledge flows are becoming more important than the financial flows, the employees are revenue creators, the organizational hierarchical structure has fewer levels and so on. The managers are becoming leaders and they are focused on employee's career development and on supporting the organizational learning and continuum innovation. All these statements are insufficient for clarifying why one organization is "smarter" than another because they are highly and firmly connected to the philosophical approach. Furthermore, all the aspects mentioned above are presented partially and sometimes in a confusing way. In order to offer some clarification in this domain, we will use their integration in one identification model.

1.2   Our results

This paper tries, after the literature review, to identify the characteristics of knowledge based organizations and to provide a complete definition for this concept. Building on these characteristics, further criteria will be developed and integrated in an identification model which will allow analyzing and indentifying the potential of being knowledge based organization.

This model is called an identification model based on the fact that is limited to aspects such as: 1) human resources as knowledge workers; 2) the knowledge-creation processes; 3) the organizational culture and 4) the organizational structure; 5) the management and 6) the information infrastructure. It doesn't include a model for measuring the organizational knowledge assets; this is partially included in the intellectual capital evaluation models and it would be a subject for another paper.

Finally, the paper will apply this model on a Romanian organization where direct observation, unstructured interviews and questionnaire were used in order to get the real image of this organization and analyze it in order to identify its possible characteristics as knowledge based organization.

2   Preliminaries

2.1   Problem description

In the process of providing a more clear description of the knowledge based organization, we have started by analyzing, based on the literature addressing this concept, how the organization of the knowledge society should look like. We have selected several definitions as being related to the knowledge-based organization and have extracted the aspects which will be used (along with others) in the identification model.

Table 1 highlights the core aspects which should be analyzed, such as: human resources, knowledge-creation processes, organizational culture, structure and management. We consider that there is another vital aspect like the existence of an information infrastructure capable to support the employees and the knowledge creation processes and continuum flow of knowledge inside and between organizations.

Concerning the workforce inside this type of company, the employees should be *knowledge workers*, which could be tackled from two different perspectives. The permissive perspective (Drucker [7]; Collins [8]) is based on the principle that "no matter what we do we are all, in some form or other, knowledge workers". The restrictive perspective (Despres and Hiltrop [9]; Standfield [10]; Barrow and Loughlin [11]) includes in the category of knowledge workers only highly educated employees (for Davenport [12] secondary education is not enough to be a knowledge worker); knowledge work – involves using four main assets, such as: 1) knowledge; 2) relationship; 3) emotional; 4) time assets Standfield [10]. These assets are used in the process of knowledge creation based on the conversion of two main types of knowledge: explicit and tacit and the conversion processes are: socialization, externalization, combination and internalization (Nonaka [2]).

The knowledge workers are main actors in the knowledge creation inside the company and not only. The knowledge creation can effectively take place in an environment which promotes and supports communication, trust, freedom to innovate and improvise (Wiig [5]);

From the organizational structure point of view, a knowledge based organization could be 1) flatter with less hierarchical levels (see Drucker [13] and the symphony organization) or 2) hierarchical but flexible one combining three layers – bureaucratic layer with project team layers and knowledge layer (Nonaka [6]).

The management has the role to create and promote the vision and strategies for knowledge-conversion processes both internally and externally to the organization (Nonaka [6])

The communication and collaboration between knowledge workers in the knowledge-creation processes are and should be supported by the information and communication technologies. These are both conditions (involving knowledgeable users) and supporting tools (speeding up the information and knowledge transfer). Taking this into consideration, managers have to find and implement the right information infrastructure in order to ensure the knowledge creation and dissemination both inside and also externally by being involved in bigger knowledge networks from which knowledge can be acquired Maier [14].

Table 1. Possible definitions for the knowledge-based organization.

Concept	Definition	Elements
Knowledge based-organization Liebowitz [1]	"An entity that realizes the importance of its knowledge, internal and external to the organization, and applies techniques to maximize the use of this knowledge to its employees, shareholders, and customers"	Knowledge – important internally and externally
Knowledge creating company Nonaka [2]	Organization "that consistently create new knowledge, disseminate it widely throughout the organization, and quickly embody it in new technologies and products".	Consistent knowledge creation in entire organization and which is embodied in new technology and products
Learning organization Argyris and Schon [3], Senge [4]	"When members of the organization act as learning agents for the organization, responding to changes in the internal and external environments of the organization by detecting and correcting errors" "Organizations where people continually expand their capacity to create the results they truly desire, where new and expansive patterns of thinking are nurtured, where collective aspiration is set free, and where people are continually learning to learn together"	Employees – learning agents Detecting and correcting errors Employees learn together Collective aspiration is free
Intelligent organization Wiig [5]	"Organization which acts effectively in the present and its capable to deal effectively with the challenges of the future. Its meets its objectives by implementing its visions and strategies through its systems, policies and organizational structure".	Employees – based on their skills, have the freedom to innovate and improvise and have to act intelligently by using effective and active communication
Hypertext organization Nonaka [6]	The core feature of the hypertext organization is the ability to switch between the various context of knowledge creation, to accommodate changing requirements from situations both inside and outside the organization.	The organizational structure with two real layers (business units and project teams) and one conceptual (knowledge layer)

In our opinion, a knowledge based organization is an organization which 1) acts intelligently and successfully in its domain by learning and creating knowledge in a continuum way, 2) uses its knowledge (both the tacit – resident in employees' minds – and the explicit which is embedded in the work procedures, databases, etc.) 3) by creating and implementing the right organizational culture (characterized by freedom to innovate and experiment) 4) supported by a flexible organizational structure (hierarchic structure combined with multifunctional, efficient and ad-hoc created and efficient project teams) and 5) by the right combination of information and communication technologies in order to cover all four processes of knowledge conversion both internally and externally to the organization.

2.2   The identification model's components

"An organization is defined by the way in which the work is being done. The purpose of one organization is to get the work done. This requires a structure. Also, an organization is, above all, social. It is people. Its purpose must therefore be to make the strengths of people effective" Drucker [15].

Having this statement in our mind, we have decided to elaborate one model in order to identify if an organization has the features for being considerate as being knowledge based. The elements to be analyzed are: 1) the human resources; 2) the knowledge creation; 3) the organizational culture and 4) structure and 5) the management and 6) the information infrastructure.

The employees, *knowledge workers,* are the owners of the most important and valuable resource of one organization, knowledge. Their knowledge skills are highly important in identifying the possible knowledge-based feature of one company. In order to evaluate the employee's knowledge skills, we have combined the hierarchy of skills provided by Johnson [16]) and the skills provided by education:

Table 2. Knowledge worker's skills (adapted from Johnson [16]).

Knowledge skills	Education
Basic	Secondary + Tertiary + Life Long Learning
Professional	Secondary + Tertiary + Life Long Learning
Technological	Secondary + Tertiary + Life Long Learning
Information Problem Solving and Higher Thinking	Tertiary + Life Long Learning
Conceptual	Life Long Learning

The *knowledge creation* should take place through all four processes of knowledge conversion and their specific methods:

Table 3. Knowledge creation and its methods ([2], [6], [17], [18] [19]).

Conversion	Methods
Socialization	a) Apprenticeship; b) Shared experiences; c) On-the-job training; d) Joint activities; e) Physical proximity; f) Walking in the company; g) Informal meetings outside the workplace; h) Wandering outside the company
Externalization	a) Use of metaphors and analogies; b) Dialogue; c) Self-reflection
Combination	a) Use different data sources; b) Meetings and telephone conversations; c) Presentations; d) Using ICTs
Internalization	a) Learning-by-doing; b) Focused training with senior colleagues; c) Simulation/experiments; d) Self-reflection upon documents; e) Reflection with others

The *organizational culture* should promote the knowledge transfer between employees.

Table 4. Organizational culture (adapted from Goffee and Jones [20]).

Aspects of the culture	Scale
Sociability	1) Very weak; 2) Weak; 3) Neutral; 4) Strong; 5) Very strong
Solidarity	1) Very weak; 2) Weak; 3) Neutral; 4) Strong; 5) Very strong
Knowledge transfer	1) Very rarely; 2) Rarely; 3) Neutral 4) Regular; 5) Daily
Physical space	1) Highly closed; 2) Closed; 3) Neutral; 4) Open; 5) Highly open
Communication	1) Highly formal; 2) Formal; 3) Neutral; 4) Informal; 5) Highly informal
Flexible schedule	1) Very rarely; 2) Rarely; 3) Neutral 4) Regular; 5) Daily
Identity	1) High individualism; 2) Individualism; 3) Neutral; 4) Some similarities; 5) Strong similarities

The *organizational structure,* in mainly all companies, is still mainly hierarchical. In these conditions, we use Nonaka's point of view about the hypertext organization based on flexible structure and the role played by project teams in the knowledge-creation processes [6].

Table 5. Organizational structure.

Aspects	Scale
Use	1) Very rarely; 2) Rarely; 3) Neutral 4) Regular; 5) Daily
Flexibility	1) Highly rigid; 2) Rigid; 3) Neutral; 4) Flexible; 5) Highly flexible
Creation	1) Imposed by the procedures; 2) Imposed by the bosses; 3) At demand; 4) Voluntarily; 5) Ad hoc
Variety	1) One domain – one department; 2) One domain – more departments; 3) More domains and internal experts 4) One domain – internal experts – one external expert; 5) More domains – internal and external experts
Physical space	1) Highly functional; 2) Functional; 3) Neutral; 4) Weak structure; 5) Unstructured
Efficiency	1) Very weak; 2) Weak; 3) Neutral; 4) Good; 5) Very good

The *management* should move to a new direction in offering more freedom and training to organization's employees, but also has to take into consideration aspects such as:

Table 6. Management.

Aspects	Scale
Autonomy	1) High supervision; 2) Some supervision; 3) Neutral; 4) Some freedom; 5) High freedom
Empowerment	1) Highly subjective; 2) Subjective; 3) Neutral; 4) Objective; 5) Highly objective
Evaluation	1) Highly subjective; 2) Subjective; 3) Neutral; 4) Objective; 5) Highly objective
Incentives	1) Highly subjective; 2) Subjective; 3) Neutral; 4) Objective; 5) Highly objective

Accessibility to knowledge	1) Highly restrictive; 2) Restrictive; 3) Neutral; 4) Access under control; 5) Highly accessible
Communication	1) Mainly inside the department; 2) On the same level; 3) Both inside the department and on the same level; 4) Between different levels; 5) Mainly between levels and with external environment
Openness to ideas	1) Highly restrictive 2) Restrictive; 3) Neutral; 4) Some openness; 5) Highly open

The *information infrastructure* in one knowledge-based organization should contain information technologies able to cover all four knowledge conversion processes. The available technologies are grouped in table 7.

Table 7. ICTs for knowledge based organization (Nonaka [2] and Maier [14]).

Conversion	Technology
Socialization	Groupware, Expertise location, Knowledge Map Systems, Visualization tools, Instant Messaging, Email, Knowledge Portals
Externalization	Groupware, Newsgroups, Forums, Instant messaging, Email, Workflow systems, Artificial Intelligence, Knowledge Portals
Combination	Search Engines, Workflow, Innovation Supporting Tools, Competitive Intelligent tools, BI (Business Intelligence), Document and content management systems, ERP Systems, Intranet, Voice / Speech Recognition, Search Engine, Taxonomy, Knowledge Portals
Internalization	eLearning, Computer Based Training, Innovative supporting tools

2.3   Model's methodology and applicability

The model for identification of knowledge based organizations takes into consideration six strategic criteria such as: human resources, knowledge creation, organizational culture, structure, management and information infrastructure. Each criterion contains sub-criteria with two exceptions: human resources (levels of knowledge skills) and knowledge creation (knowledge-conversion processes).

The evaluation scale for the each of six criteria included in the model is from 1 to 5 and it was already presented in the model's description, except the one for the human resources. The scale is: 1) Very weak, 2) Weak, 3) Neutral, 4) Good, 5) Excellent. The value of each of the six criteria (except for human resources) is the average of value of each sub-criterion. The formula for identifying the staff skills for each level from the Jones model is: the staff covering the specific level skills as % from the company's workforce X 5/100. The human resources capacity to sustain a knowledge-based organization is identified through the next formula: Human resources skill level = 0.05 X Basic + 0.1 X Professional + 0.2 X Technological + 0.3 X Informational + 0.35 X Conceptual. The scale used to identify the level of knowledge creation inside the company is: 1) Never; 2) Occasionally; 3) Often; 4) Regular; 5) Daily.

The individual results of all six criteria have values between 1 and 5. The final result is an average of the values for all six aspects analyzed. The final evaluation scale is 1) Very limited knowledge-based, 2) Very weak, 3) Weak, 4) Good, 5) Excellent.

As it results from the evaluation scale, each organization is based on knowledge but the difference is the level of its dependency on knowledge showed by the value for each six criteria. For results lower or equal with 3, the organization is weakly knowledge based and has to develop strategies in order to transform its weaknesses in strengths.

This model could be used in the SWOT analysis in order to develop strategies for organizational development. The application of this model could explain why one organization is performing better than another one in the innovation process. Although it stays in the philosophical approach of the knowledge-based organization concept, by being mainly qualitative than quantitative, organizations could use this model in the initial phase of identifying their organizational intelligence. The model could be extended to a wider area of strategic assets which provides organizational uniqueness on the market and the organization's success in the knowledge society.

3   The Romanian case study

3.1   Company description

The company selected for the case study is a Romanian public organization, the biggest in the north-east of Romania. It has an organizational structure with five levels organized in three main divisions 1) economic, 2) technique and 3) production – which is the largest because it covers the company's main activity and the majority of employees.

The human resources structure is represented by 85% of employees with secondary education. 80 % of them are working at the operative level, mainly outside the office and they are part of the production division. The information infrastructure is available only for top and middle managers and administrative and technical staff (around 20% of the employees).

The analysis of the Romanian company was based on three methods, such as: questionnaire, direct observation and unstructured interviews. The questionnaire was used in the case of top and middle managers and administrative and technical staff. The direct observation and unstructured interviews were used in the case of employees from the operative level.

3.2   The analysis results in the case of managerial, technical and administrative departments

The questionnaire (response rate - 91.1 %.) was organized based on the identification model presented above and had six sections such as: 1) human resources, 2) organizational culture, 3) management, 4) knowledge sources 5) organizational structure and 6) information systems.

The managerial, technical and administrative departments have *human resources* with a low level of knowledge needed for using ICTs (2.87), but they have good information (4.55) and conceptual skills (4.34). Taking this into consideration, along with the model of Johnson [16], the average for the human resources in the case of departments mentioned above is 4.06 which imply that these employees are specific to and able to support a knowledge based organization.

Table 8. The analysis results for the managerial, technical and administrative departments.

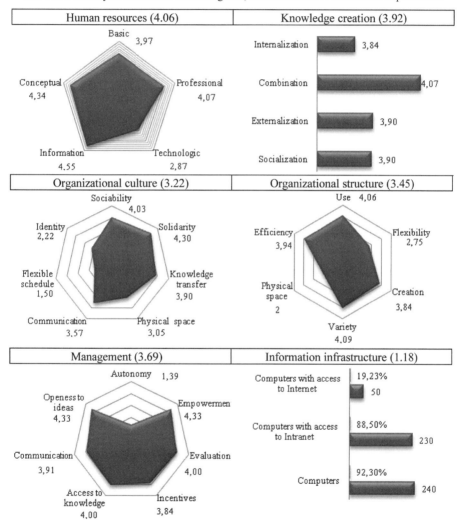

The *knowledge creation* (3.92) takes place, in this case, mainly through meetings and telephone conversations, presentation of projects and their results, use of scientific data (through ICTs or library's resources) and the knowledge is accumulated in documentations, which are also source of knowledge for new employees.

Knowledge is converted, at this level, mainly through combination (4.07), but also externalization and socialization (3.9).

The strengths of *organizational culture* (3.22) are: solidarity (4.3), sociability (4.03), and knowledge transfer (3.9). The weaknesses of the organizational culture are flexible working program (1.5) and identity (2.22). At this level, the *organizational structure* (3.45) needs improvements in order to support the knowledge based organization by focusing on increasing the flexibility of the teams (2.75) and the space allocated for their meetings (2). Teams have a good variety (employees with different backgrounds) (4.09) and the use of project teams is promoted (4.06) and the available teams have a good efficiency (3.94).

The *management* (3.69) in the managerial, administrative and technical departments has the capacity to sustain a knowledge based organization. The only weak aspect is the autonomy of employees in taking decisions (1.39).

The *information infrastructure* is at a very low level (1.18), unable to support a knowledge based organization. The analysis of the questionnaire for these criteria highlights the fact that employees understand and specify the need to implement: an organizational portal, an integrated electronic environment for supporting communication between employees, a specific area on the organizational portal dedicated to eLearning and an electronic journal with all employees, their domains of expertise and their contact details.

The average of the results for the six criteria is 3.25, which indicates that the Romanian company is a knowledge based organization but in the initial phase. The company has to invest mainly in the information infrastructure provided for its managerial, technical and administrative employees. Other aspects to be taken into consideration are organizational culture and a wider and efficient use of teams in order to increase the organizational structure's flexibility.

3.3   The analysis's results including the production departments

At the entire organizational level, including the production division which covers around 80% of the company's activity, the methods used in order to analyze the organization were direct observation and unstructured interviews. The analysis results are presented in table 9.

The level of *human resources* from the knowledge workers point of view is a very low level (1.24) and is determined by the fact that the activity inside the company involves mainly physical force and only 10% of employees have tertiary education. Furthermore, the majority of employees (around 80%) don't have the necessary skills for using ICTs.

The main *knowledge creation* (3.17) takes place through socialization (3.81), more precise through observation, imitation and apprenticeship. The second most important knowledge-conversion process is combination (3.03) which is specific to employees working in the managerial, technical and administrative departments.

The *organizational culture* (3) needs improvement in order to be able to support a knowledge based organization. The most important aspects which needs improvement is the knowledge transfer that could be solved through a highly promoted and motivated dissemination of knowledge in the entire organization.

The *organizational structure* (2.83) doesn't have the capacity to support a knowledge based organization because although is using teams for reaching specific objectives, these teams have a low efficiency, flexibility and diversity (are formed mainly from employees from the same department).

Table 9. Analysis results at the entire organizational level.

The *management* (3.57) at the Romanian company analyzed has the capacity and characteristics needed to support a knowledge-based organization because it supports empowerment, access to knowledge (documentation and organizational library), communication and openness to employees' ideas. The weaknesses are represented by autonomy and incentives.

418   Cristina Denisa Neagu

The *information infrastructure* (2.5) doesn't have the capacity to support a knowledge based organization because is limited to email, ERP and instant messaging (for around 20% employees).

The average of the results for the six criteria is 2.74, which indicates that the Romanian company is a very weak knowledge based organization. The areas in which the company has to invest are: human resources (developing their technological, informational and conceptual skills), the information infrastructure (in order to support all four processes of knowledge conversion) and the organizational structure (increasing the flexibility of activating in teams and providing the physical space needed for meetings).

3.4   Concluding remarks for the Romanian case study

The Romanian company was analyzed at two different levels: the core and the organization itself. The core is represented by the managerial, technical and administrative staff involved in creating, developing and using the organizational strategic assets for further development of the entire organization. The second level of analysis was the organizational one which took into consideration the rest 80% of employees involved in the production division.

It was important to analyze the organization at the core level because, in the case of an investment in the organizational infrastructure (we are concentrated here on the production infrastructure) then an important number of employees might loose their jobs or we will integrate in the core level.

Table 10. Comparison between managerial, technical and administrative departments and the entire organization.

Managerial, technical and administrative departments	Entire organization

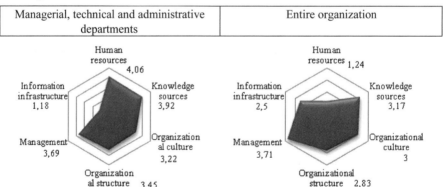

As shown in table 10, the *human resources* at the core level are higher qualified and specific for a knowledge-based organization than the human resources' skills at the entire organizational level.

The *knowledge creation* takes places mainly through combination (in the case of middle managers and administrative and technical staff) and socialization (in the case of operative employees).

The o*rganizational culture* is characterized by high solidarity and some similarities between employees.

The *organizational structure* is characterized by teams, mainly in the case of operative employees, but these teams don't have a high flexibility or diversity having as members employees from the same department;

The *management* supports autonomy and freedom in decision making mainly in the case of managers and administrative and technical staff. The management supports learning inside organization through training and access to library's resources;

The *information infrastructure* is very limited and cannot cover all the four processes of knowledge creation. This information infrastructure is mainly available for top and middle managers and administrative a technical staff.

The application of this model on the Romanian case study showed the company's weaknesses and where future strategies have to be developed in order to support the organization's development. From the knowledge skills point if view, company has to support training for developing technological, problem solving and conceptual skills. The company analyzed is concerned about developing these critical skills and is in the process of creating the needed infrastructure (training center) and available training programs (with internal experts and also with companies providing professional training).

The most critical aspect is the information infrastructure, which is not capable of supporting the four knowledge creation processes. It lacks in supporting the internalization. This process takes place inside the company through training provided by internal experts, learning from mistakes and on the job training. The existent information infrastructure is supporting mainly the activity of top and middle managers, the applications are not integrated at the company level (except the ERP solution) and communication is done mainly though email, telephones and classic mail. The actual information infrastructure doesn't support learning and knowledge transfer and these are the main elements which have to be solved in the near future. A project was proposed (it is in the analysis phase) for creating an integrated management solution which will be a web-based software and will incorporate, besides the workflow management (both internally and externally – collaboration with partners), important key features like eLearning, knowledge management based and visualization and optimization tools.

4   Conclusions

The knowledge society implies knowledge-based organizations with the culture and management which promote knowledge transfer and support knowledge workers to constantly create knowledge trough their daily work and use, store and transfer it through the right information and communication technologies.

This paper proposes an identification model in order to highlight the strong and weak elements of the organization for the creation, use and transfer of knowledge point of view. This model is very useful in the initial phase of the analysis in case the company intends to implement a knowledge management strategy. The model proposed could be applied by using methods like questionnaire, interviews and direct observation and it is very useful in the SWOT analysis in case one company wants to elaborate a strategy for its future development which relies of its internal knowledge and its knowledge networks available both internally and externally.

The identification model is also useful in combination with intellectual capital models needed in the company's evaluation from the intangible assets point of view. Together, these models could highlight the weaknesses and strengths at the organizational level and could explain the intangible results.

This identification model was applied in the case of the Romanian company which is committed to its development. The results have showed that it is knowledge-based in the initial phase and has plan improvements (the IT and human resources strategy) in order to reach at least the value 4 which means good knowledge based organization capable of surviving in a dynamic and complex environment specific to knowledge economy and society.

References

1. J. Liebowitz, Knowledge organization. What every manager should know, CRC Press, 1998, p.14
2. I. Nonaka, The Knowledge Creating Company in *Harvard Business Review on Knowledge Management*, 1998, pp.21-45
3. C. Argyris and D. Schon, Organizational learning – A Theory of Action Perspective, Addison-Wesley, 1978, p.29
4. P. Senge, The Fifth Discipline – The Art and Practice of the Learning Organization, Random House, 1990, p.3
5. K., M. Wiig, The Intelligent Enterprise and Knowledge Management, 2000, http://www.krii.com/downloads/intellig_enterprise%20&%20km.pdf
6. I. Nonaka, A dynamic theory of organizational knowledge creation", in *Organization Science*, 5 (1), 1994, pp.14-36
7. P. Drucker, The New Productivity Challenge, in *Harvard Business Review*, November – December 1991, p.71
8. D. Collins, Knowledge Work of Working Knowledge? Ambiguity and Confusion in the Analysis of the "Knowledge Age", Employees Relations, Vol. 19(1), 1997, p.45
9. C. Despres and J. M. Hiltrop, Human Resource Management in the Knowledge Age: Current Practice and Perspectives on the Future, Employee Relations, Vol. 17(1), 1995, pp. 9-23
10. K. Standfield, Intangible Management, Tools for Solving the Accounting and Management Crisis, Academic Press, 2002, p.9
11. M. J. Barrow and H. M. Loughlin, Towards a learning organization, Industrial and Commercial Training, 1992, vol. 24, no, 1, pp.3-7
12. Th. Davenport, Thinking for a Living – How to Get Better Performance and Results from Knowledge Workers, Harvard Business School Press, 2005, p.10
13. P. Drucker, The Coming of the New Organization, in Harvard Business Review on Knowledge Management, 1998, p.7

14. R. Maier, Knowledge Management Systems: Information and Communication Technologies for Knowledge Management, Springer, 2002
15. P. Drucker, The Organization of the Future, Jossey Bass, 1997, pp.1-5
16. D. Johnson, *KWRedux,* http://www.doug-johnson.com/dougwri/KWRedux.pdf, 2005
17. I. Nonaka, I., R. Toyama, and N. Konno, SECI, Ba and Leadership: a Unified Model of Dynamic Knowledge Creation, Long Range Planning 33, pp. 5-34
18. I. Nonaka and N. Konno, The Concept of Ba: Building a Foundation for Knowledge Creation, California Management Review, Vol. 40(3) 1998, pp. 40-54
19. I. Nonaka, B. Byosiere, C. Borucki, and Konno, N., Organizational Knowledge Creation Theory: A First Comprehensive Test, International Business Review, Vol 3(4), 1994, pp. 337-351
20. R. Goffee and G. Jones, Organizational Culture: A Sociological Perspective in Cooper, C.L., Cartwright, S., Earley, P.S., in The Organizational Handbook of Organization Culture and Climate, Willey, 2001, pp.3-20

Collaborative Knowledge Networks
Lessons to Learn from a Large Automotive Company

Nouha Taifi

eBusiness Management Section, ISUFI, University of Salento,
Via per Monteroni, 73100, Lecce, Italy,
nouha.taifi@ebms.unile.it

Abstract. The organizations nowadays have shifted their identities to an open and extended profile in which their operations are not only internal but also external to their organizations and management. Thus, in the actual unstable environment firms overlap their boundaries and create strategic alliances and collaborations with their suppliers, customers and partners. In this paper, we present the case of an organization that is applying this concept. As an extended enterprise, it continuously innovates and creates new products using its dynamic capabilities. It seeks to leverage its relationships with its customers and suppliers through net-works creation. In order to develop further toward being an extended enterprise, its actual focus is on a partnership with the organizations, constituting a Dealers' network- providing after sales services to customers as assisting, selling, and re-pairing cars. Our focus is on the dealers' network consisting of small and medium organizations that represent the automotive company and that are the intermediary among it and its customers. Through this research, we are elaborating a model rep-resenting the collaborative mechanisms among the automotive company and its dealers' network that leads to knowledge creation and sharing about the automobiles components and services of this extended enterprise. The collaborative knowledge network (CKN) contributes to the sustainability of the new product development (NPD) process of the automotive company.

1   Introduction

In the digital era, the extended enterprise is continuously creating new collaborations with external actors basically on information and communication technologies. Besides, it is aware of the importance of external actors in the creation of innovative products. By absorbing the knowledge of external actors, an organization changes its identity and become extended. Gathering external actors -especially professional and expert ones, in networks in which they can create and share their know-how and experience, is a critical step toward integrating strategic knowledge in the new product development of the extended enterprise that has absorptive and dynamic capacities to keep up with the complex business environment.

In this paper, we are presenting the case of a large automotive- extended enterprise that decided to take action and takes care of its dealers network that are external actors interacting directly with the customers of the EE. We first present a

Please use the following format when citing this chapter:

Taifi, N., 2008, in IFIP International Federation for Information Processing, Volume 262; The Future of Identity in the Information Society; Simone Fischer-Hübner, Penny Duquenoy, Albin Zuccato, Leonardo Martucci; (Boston: Springer), pp. 423–429.

literature review to clarify the reasons behind the importance of partnering with external actors for new product development and innovation, then we describe the CKN among the EE and its dealers' network, and finally we discuss the organizational, technological and strategic dimensions of these interactions presenting some challenges facing the CKN and also especially some important factors that leads to success which is the creation, sharing and integration of knowledge in the new product development process of the extended enterprise.

2   Literature review

The complexity and increasing turbulence of the environment leads the ex-tended enterprise to seriously strengthen its inter-firm relationships for knowledge creation and competitive advantage; this is a part of the management of its identity. The strategic alliances are important for business performance and innovation. Many scholars have studied the relationship among a firm strategic alliances and its innovative performance [1-3]. Thus, we consider the capabilities to manage strategic alliances and the related organizational capabilities of learning and communicating as key-enablers for the process of knowledge creation and sharing. The strategic alliances are efficient instruments allowing access to external re-sources and overlapping firm's boundaries [4], thus firms focus on knowledge acquisition and sharing through the network of partners. Strategic networks [5-6], as the strategic alliances, are composed of inter-organizational ties that are based on social, professional and exchange relationships. Therefore, collaboration at the inter-firm level is a critical vehicle for the exploration of novel technologies and capabilities. For instance, in automobile development studies, collaboration between firms enhances the knowledge exchange for exploratory problem-solving in product development process [4, 7-9]; organizations are not only competitive but also cooperative.

For the creation of competitive advantage, the involvement of external actors in the new product development extends the areas of innovation outside the firm; innovation is distributed across different actors –such as lead user [10-11]. Considered as co-creators, the external actors are regarded as partners and their knowledge is integrated in the innovation process of the extended enterprise [12] through an efficient collaboration in an environment based on trust and motivation. Besides, since innovation is a complex process, firms adopt systemic approaches to manage knowledge. Thus, it is a good strategy to adopt knowledge management systems to capture, create and use knowledge to enhance the organizational performance.

The process of knowledge exploration and exploitation is speeding up the new product development process and innovation may require the creation of organized entities representing the external actors such as research groups, communities of interest, communities of practice [13-14] and other organizational structures that are separated from the main organization but still connected to it [15]. The in-formation and communication technologies play the role of enablers of communication activities among the external actors- combined into entities- and the main organization.

Through the use of information and communication technologies, the interaction among the firm and its external actors groups is leveraged and new knowledge is integrated in the new product development process.

3   Case studies

3.1   Known Results

By applying the concept of the innovation funnel, the dealers' network know-how can be integrated in the NPD process, and by this increasing the innovative performance of the automotive company. The innovation funnel represents the innovation steps by which the product goes before being produced. The automotive company is following the fifth generation innovation model based on [16]. This model- Systems integration and Networking (SIN) model considers the creation of networks for the integration of new expertise and know-how in the innovation process. In fact, by creating networks among the dealers' network and NPD process of the automotive company, it is possible to improve the innovative performance of the extended enterprise.

Besides, as an extended enterprise, the automotive company has unclear boundaries and applies a win-win approach with its partners. For that, its interactions with the dealers' network take the shape of a collaborative knowledge net-work (CKN) [17] in which knowledge is created and shared. The CKN dedicated to learning and knowledge sharing allows the continuous development of the innovation process.

3.2   Research questions

Through this paper, we are elaborating a model representing the collaborative relationships among the automotive company and its dealers' network that leads to knowledge creation and sharing about the automobiles components and services of this extended enterprise.

To address this issue, this study framed the following research questions:

- How are the mechanisms involved in the interaction among the extended enterprise and the dealers' network?
- How do the collaborative tools and processes impact on the CKN?
- What are the successful outcomes and challenges of the CKN among the extended enterprise and the dealers' network?

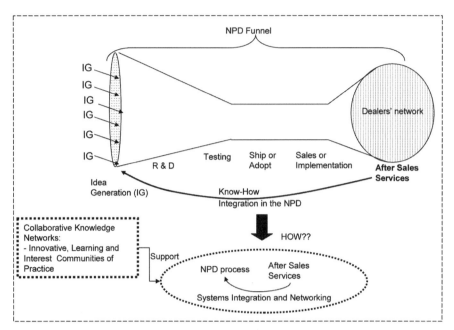

Fig. 1. Systems integration and networking among the NPD process and the after sales services organizations.

3.3   Research Method

Research into the CKN was undertaken using case study method [18]. Individuals involved in the management of the CKN were identified and interviewed using a semi-structured questionnaire. The reason behind choosing this type of interviews is to encourage the interviewees to provide detailed, elaborated answers. The interviewees are the top-managers responsible of the entire dealer's network, and the middle managers responsible of specific activities carried out within the CKN. Thus, data were representing different levels and perspectives of management.

Besides, we analyzed the state of the art of the interaction among the dealers' network and the automotive company. We noticed that the CKN among the automotive company and the dealers' network is mainly supported by information and communications technologies and professional trainings for knowledge sharing and learning. Through a questionnaire, dedicated to the members of the dealers' network, we investigated on the perceived ease of use and usefulness of those two previous main collaboration means in the development of the CKN. This questionnaire was dedicated to a significant representing sample from the very large population of the dealers' network.

4   Exploratory Results and Discussion

4.1   Collaborative knowledge network mechanisms

On one hand, most of the collaboration among the automotive company and its dealers' network is ICT-based. Many tools are used to satisfy different purposes creating a bi-directional knowledge sharing environment among the automotive company and the dealers' network. For instance, one of the IT tools, analyzed during the research, is dedicated to solving technical problems related to cars. An efficient procedure is followed in which one of the dealers' network members communicate interactively the car problem faced to the automotive company and this later gives feedbacks to the entire dealers' network in the form of e-service news, thus, spreading one CKN member knowledge in the whole CKN- this is a part of the codification strategy [19] of the automotive company in which it calls for a high codification infrastructure which results in more knowledge reuse via person-to-document exchange.

Another instance is when the automotive company provides the dealers' network, on a regular basis, with an updated IT tool for diagnosis analysis for the inconveniences in cars brought by customers in the dealers' workshops. These tools support the technicians in their labor on cars. Thus, through the diagnosis tool, the automotive company shared its knowledge with dealers about the way the inconveniences in cars might be discovered.

On the other hand, the CKN is profiting from professional trainings for knowledge sharing. The purpose of the professional trainings is to gather the members of the dealers' network, in a face-to-face manner, to share their knowledge with each other and especially to grasp and exchange new knowledge with the automotive company. The technicians of the dealer's network member are the main focus of these initiatives since they are the knowledge workers directly interested by the professional trainings. In fact, in addition to the IT tools mentioned in the first paragraph, the professional trainings are efficient means of creating, processing and enhancing the technical knowledge of the dealers' network knowledge workers.

4.2   Some success factors

There are many factors leading the CKN to be successful and innovative. From the organizational point of view, the CKN members are all from the same country which facilitate communication and avoid possible misunderstandings that might occur generally as a result of different cultures, and more specifically as a result of different work processes, different languages, and/or different types of leadership [20]. In fact, belonging to different enterprises and being geographically dispersed in their nation did not create any major obstacle to their collaborative knowledge network. As small and medium enterprises, and independent organizations from the automotive company, the dealers' network members take advantage of the ICT-based collaboration and of the sustainable opportunities offered by the automotive company to create an inter-organization collaboration based on trust and motivation.

4.3   Some challenges

The main issue that can probably slow down the CKN operations is the computer self-efficacy [21] of the dealers' network members. In fact, computer self-efficacy refers to a judgment of one's capability to use a computer. The dealers' network members are small and medium enterprises consisting of average skilled technicians in ICT use, thus, often their computer use is limited since their work-focus is mainly cars. However, the automotive company is aware of that and provides professional trainings and tutoring to facilitate the dealers' network members understanding of the importance of being able to use computers in their everyday work.

Besides, it is important to mention that the dealers' network members' perceived ease of use and usefulness of the IT tools provided for the collaboration in the CKN is critical for an efficient collaboration. Perceived usefulness is defined as the degree to which a person believes that using a particular system would enhance his or her job performance [22] and perceived ease of use, in contrast, refers to the degree to which a person believes that using a particular system would be free of effort [22]. These two concepts are directly connected with the computer self-efficacy level of the dealers' network but also with the efficiency of the IT tools provided by the automotive company. These two concepts give good insights on IT elements that might need some modifications for better outcomes.

Finally, concerning the CKN organizational structure, we noticed that the small and medium dealers enterprises have different connections' types with the automotive company; the medium enterprises are connected directly and have strong ties with the EE, whereas the small ones have weak ties with the automotive company since the medium ones play an intermediary role among them and the automotive company. According to [23], weak ties increase innovative capacities, allows a faster working process, and facilitates access to resources. However, the small dealers' enterprises still have some difficulties to access IT resources because of the medium ones' intermediary role.

References

1. Shan, G. Walker, and B. Kogut, Inter-Firm Cooperation and Start-up Innovation in the Biotechnology Industry, *Strategic Management Journal, A* 15(55), 387-394 (1994).
2. J. A. C. Baum, T. Calabrese, and B. S. Silverman, Don't Go it Alone: Alliance Network Composition and Startups' Performance in Canadian Biotechnology, *Strategic Management Journal, A* 21 (3), 267 – 294 (2000).
3. J. Lerner, and A. Tsai, Do Equity Financing Cycles Matter? Evidence from Biotechnology Alliances", *Journal of Financial* Economics, Elsevier, *A* 67(3), 411-446 (2003).
4. A. Takeishi, Knowledge Partitioning in the Inter-Firm division of labour: The Case of Automotive product development, *Organization Science, A* 13(3), 321-338 (2002).

5. R. Gulati, Alliances and Networks, *Strategic Management Journal*, *A* 19, 293-317 (1998).
6. R. Gulati, N. Nohria and A. Zaheer, Strategic Networks, *Strategic Management Journal*, *A* 21, 203-215 (2000).
7. K. B. Clark and T. Fujimoto, Product Development Performance: Strategy, Organization, and Management in the World Automobile Industry (Harvard Business School Press, Boston, (991)
8. J. H. Dyer and H. Singh, The Relational View: Cooperative Strategy and Sources of Inter-Organizational Competitive Advantage, *Academy of Management Review*, *A* 23(4), 660-679 (1998).
9. S. N. Wasti, and J.K. Liker, Collaborating with Suppliers in Product Development: A U.S. and Japan Comparative Study, *IEEE Transactions on Engineering Management*, *A* 46 (4), 444-46 (1999).
10. E. Von Hippel, The Sources of Innovation (Oxford University Press, London 1988).
11. H. Thomke and E. Von Hippel, Customers as Innovators: A New Way to Create Value (Harvard Business Review, 2002).
12. D. Teece, Managing Intellectual Capital (Oxford University Press, London, 2000)
13. S. Brown and J. Duguid, Organizational Learning and Communities of Practice: Toward a Unified View of Working, Learning and Innovation, *Organization Science*, *A*2 (1), 40-57 (1991).
14. E.C. Wenger and W.M. Snyder, Communities of Practice: The Organizational Frontier, *Harvard Business Review*, Jan-Feb, 139-145 (2000).
15. M. H, Zack, Developing a Knowledge Strategy, *California Management Review*, *A*41(3), Spring, 125-145 (1999).
16. R. Rothwell, Towards Fifth-Generation Process Innovation, International Marketing Review, 11(1), 7-31 (1994).
17. P. Gloor, Swarm Creativity – Competitive Advantage Through Collaborative Innovation Networks (Oxford University Press, 2006)
18. K. M. Eisenhardt, Building Theories from Case Study Research, *Academy of Management Review*, *A* 14 (4), 532-550 (1989).
19. M. Hansen, N. Nohria and T. Tierney, What's your Strategy for Managing Knowledge, Harvard business review, *A*77 (2), 106-116 (1999).
20. E. Wenger, R. McDermott, and W.M. Snyder, Cultivating Communities of Practice: A guide to Managing Knowledge (Harvard Business School Press, 2002).
21. D.R. Compeau and C.A. Higgins, Computer Self-Efficacy: Development of a Measure and Initial Test, *MIS Quarterly*, June (1994).
22. D.F. Davis, Perceived Usefulness, Perceived Ease of Use, and User Acceptance of Information Technology, *MIS Quarterly*, September (1989).
23. M. Granovetter, The Strength of Weak Ties: a Network Theory Revisited, *Sociology Theory*, *A*1, 201-233 (1989).

Workshop: Economical Aspects of Identity Management

Enterprise Identity Management
What's in it for Organisations?

Denis Royer

Johann Wolfgang Goethe University Frankfurt
Institute of Business Informatics
Chair of Mobile Business & Multilateral Security
denis.royer@m-chair.net

Abstract. When introducing enterprise identity management systems (EIMS), organisations have to face various costs for the planning, the implementation, and the operation of such systems. Besides the technological issues, it is important that organisational aspects are incorporated into the development of an enterprise identity management (EIdM) solution as well. Indeed, without a proper assessment of the costs and the organisational settings (e.g. stakeholders, processes), companies will not see the benefit for introducing EIdM into their IT infrastructure and their business processes. This paper proposes initial ideas for a generic approach for assessing the value of investing in the introduction of EIMS (Type 1 IMS), which can be used for decision support purposes and the planning phase. Furthermore, the organisational aspects are discussed and possible solutions for integrating all relevant parties into the planning process are presented.

1 Introduction

Enterprise Identity Management (EIdM) is becoming an increasingly important issue for companies and corporations [7]. Organisations have to take care of their user and access management (identity and access management (IAM)), in order to protect their systems from unauthorised access (involving security and privacy implications) and to lower their overall costs (e.g. for keeping account data up-to-date or for helpdesk activities). This is especially so, given the diverse IT infrastructures being used in everyday transactions (e.g. enterprise resource planning (ERP), document management (DMS), human resources management (HR)).

Furthermore, the *identity lifecycle* needs to be managed, since employees change departments or get promoted. Therefore, the following process steps need to be handled as well [12, 27]:

- ***Enrolment - creation of accounts for new employees:*** issuance of the credentials and setting of the access permissions needed by the new employee
- ***Management - maintenance of accounts:*** in a changing working environment (promotions, changes of departments) the "*user and access management*" needs to handle the changing access permissions for the enrolled users (in order to minimise liabilities)

Please use the following format when citing this chapter:

Royer, D., 2008, in IFIP International Federation for Information Processing, Volume 262; The Future of Identity in the Information Society; Simone Fischer-Hübner, Penny Duquenoy, Albin Zuccato, Leonardo Martucci; (Boston: Springer), pp. 433–446.

- ***Support - password management:*** issue new passwords or reset passwords that are "lost"
- ***Deletion - end of lifecycle:*** revoke or freeze user-accounts or entitlements

Based on the IMS categorisation presented by Bauer, Meints and Hansen [1], organisations use so-called *type 1* identity management systems (IMS). Supporting the lifecycle of identities on the organisational level, this group of systems fulfils the functions of authorisation, authentication, administration, and audit of the user accounts that need to be managed.

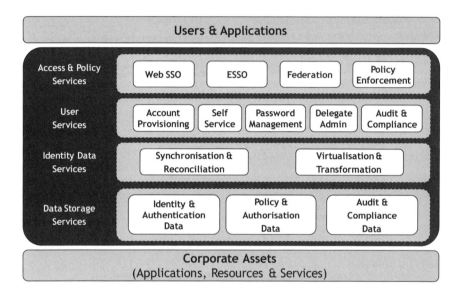

Fig. 1. EIdM technology framework based on Flynn [9].

At the technological level, a variety of technologies can be identified, belonging to the cluster of EIdM technologies, for example single-sign-on (SSO), meta-directories, public-key infrastructures (PKI), and IAM systems [9, 27]. Therefore, EIdM can be considered a framework of different technologies, rather than a product or an out-of-the-box solution (cp. Figure 1).

1.1 Driving Factors for EIdM

There are a variety of driving factors for introducing enterprise identity management systems (EIMS) into an organisation. Based on an explorative study (expert interviews), conducted by the author, the most prevalent factors appear to be (1) value creation goals, (2) IT risk management goals, and (3) compliance goals[1] (cp. Table 1). Without proper management of the identity lifecycle, companies may face losses in their productivity (increased costs for managing their IT infrastructure), risks associated with potential security leaks (resulting from incoherently managed user accounts) or ramifications for non-compliance against relevant laws and regulations [2]. However, the presented goals are not mutually exclusive. Table 1 gives an overview of the driving factors identified so far:

Table 1. Most prevalent factors for implementing IdM in organisations[2].

1. Risk Management / IT Security Goals
• Minimise liabilities
• Mitigate risks
• Make systems more secure
2. Value Creation Goals
• Efficiency goals (e.g. process optimisations)
• Lower overall costs
3. Compliance Goals
• Comply with relevant laws and regulations (e.g. Basel II or Sarbanes-Oxley Act (SOX)) [2]

1.2   Goal of this paper

Without a thorough cost-benefit analysis, no decision maker will invest in IT security related technologies such as EIdM. The question *"What's in it for Organisations?"* needs to be answered, using concrete methodologies that serve as a decision support instrument for the decision makers in an organisation. Consequently, the question *"How can investments into EIdM be evaluated?"* needs to be researched and answered as well. This paper strives to present initial ideas on how a generic approach can be constructed, which should help to consistently assess the value (including risks, costs, and benefits) of EIdM in organisations.

This paper is structured as follows: Following the introduction (1), the second section (2) discusses the underlying research approach needed to carry out the research in this field. The third section (3) introduces general cost and benefit aspects for the introduction of EIdM and some of the general problems encountered in EIdM projects. Next, the fourth section (4) describes the proposed evaluation process as a starting point for assessing the costs and benefits of such projects as a means for decision support. Here, the general prerequisites and the stakeholders are described as well. Furthermore, some of the organisational aspects are presented and discussed. The last section (5) summarises the findings and gives an outlook on further research questions.

---

[1] In this context, ***compliance*** refers to corporations and public agencies needs to ensure that personnel are aware of, and take steps to comply with relevant laws and regulations (e.g. Basel II or Sarbanes-Oxley Act (SOX)) [2].

[2] These factors are based on an explorative expert interview conducted by the author.

2 Research Approach

In order to answer the posed research question, a self-developed, 3-staged research approach, based on the design science framework by Hevner et al. [13], will be used. The (primary) artefact to be designed is a framework for assessing the value of EIdM in organisations (including its requirements and properties), including the approach described in this paper. The constructed design process itself is divided in 4 *sub-questions*, which are used to further structure the different stages:

- **Sub-Question 1:** Which are the methods that can be used to assess the value of EIdM?
- **Sub-Question 2:** Which of these methods applied in practice (that is, in the corporate field for decision support) and how?
- **Sub-Question 3:** What are the actual requirements and properties that are needed to assess the value of EIdM and how can they be formalised into a framework?
- **Sub-Question 4:** How can the framework (including its requirements and properties) be applied into a decision support instrument for the assessment of EIdM?

The individual stages and sub-questions are visualised in Figure 2. The *first stage* of the designed research approach deals with the problem identification and the analysis of the problem relevance of the presented research questions. Here the foundations for the further research will be laid out and discussed, including the hypotheses building.

The *second stage* depicts the actual design process and the creation of the researched artefact(s). Within this stage, the first 3 sub-questions (1-3) will be discussed. Sub-question 1 will begin with a literature review of the available methods to assess the value of EIdM and IT security investments in general (assessment of the "state-of-the-art"). This will help to identify the available methods and to assess their advantages and disadvantages. The next sub-question (2) will be answered by using expert interviews. The targeted experts will be practitioners in the field of EIdM, who will be asked which methods are actually used in real-life, and why certain methods are (not) used. Based on these results, the requirements for a framework to assess the value of investments into EIdM will be derived (based on the framework by Lee [16]). The synthesis of the results of the first 2 sub-questions is discussed in the 3rd sub-question. Here, the framework (the primary artefact), its requirements, and its properties for assessing the value of EIdM will be derived (representing the research contribution). Furthermore, a generalised outline for how the framework can be used in practice and design recommendations will be presented (secondary artefacts). The search process for the artefacts will be iterative, coupling feedback loops to the 1st and 2nd sub-question.

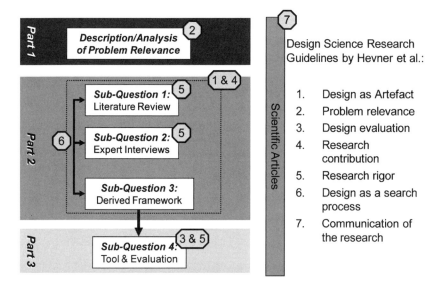

Fig. 2. Research approach based on the design science framework by Hevner et al. [13].

In order to validate the designed artefacts (design evaluation), the 4th sub-question (*3rd stage*) of the presented research approach will test the framework in practice. In order to do this, a prototypic decision support instrument for the assessment of the value for introducing EIdM will be implemented (instantiation of the framework). For the actual evaluation of the design, a combination of case study research and expert interviews is planned, analysing how the proposed evaluation framework improves the decision making process in practice.

The paper at hand discusses the *first stage*, including the analysis of the problem and its relevance. Furthermore, initial ideas and requirements (based on the initial literature review) for an evaluation process will be presented, which serve as a component of the evaluation framework.

3 Cost and Benefit Aspects for Introducing EIdM

According to an explorative study conducted by Deron, the costs for creating or deleting users-accounts are reduced by 50% when using an EIdM solution. The total costs for the user management are reduced by up to 63%, compared to manual management of the user accounts and the related transactions [6].

However, when introducing EIdM solutions, companies have to face significant costs. According to Deron's survey of 3,500 German small to mid-sized companies [6], EIdM projects can easily exceed €100,000 and more in total cost (for the actual EIdM solution being used, and the consulting necessary to implement and introduce such systems into the company).

From the author's point of view and based on the conducted literature review, there are additional factors that have to be taken into consideration as well. These include:

- EIdM itself is not a purely technology-driven topic since it directly intervenes with everyday processes, workflows, and the organisational structure of a company. So, when introducing EIMS, organisational factors have to be recognised as well:
  - Who is responsible for maintaining the accounts?
  - Who defines the necessary policies, and on what basis?
  - Who defines the necessary processes for managing the identity lifecycle?
  - Who enforces the policies being set?
- The nature of EIdM projects is diverse and there are various goals for introducing this technology (cp. Table 1). While the requirements for one project may include the overall increase of security, other projects are driven by issues such as compliance or provisioning. The projects' inherent requirements have to be gathered and analysed to come up with a more generalised view to cope with this variation.
- As stated before, EIMS are not products, but frameworks of different technologies (meta-directories, SSO, workflow management, etc.) that can be integrated into an (existing) IT infrastructure (cp. Figure 1). Therefore all projects are unique, which makes it difficult to come up with a general cost assessment for the implementation and introduction of EIdM [27].
- Last but not least, the costs associated with the lifecycle of an EIdM solution (lifecycle costs) need to be considered. These costs include items such as training, upgrading and integrating existing EIdM infrastructures, and migration of legacy systems, etc. [23].

So, while EIMS offer high cost saving potentials, they also have high investment costs associated with the planning, the implementation, and the operation.

4 Development of the proposed Evaluation Process

In order to perform a cost-benefit analysis, decision makers need concrete methodologies and evaluation processes to assess the value of EIdM investments (based on the widely used *return on investment (ROI)* business ration). Such methodologies need to fulfil several prerequisites. These include the incorporation of the driving factors for introducing EIdM (cp. Table 1).

Besides its many different technical and financial definitions, the ROI generally refers to the degree of how efficiency by which the capital invested into a project is used to generate profit [21, 23]. Looking at this, it is reasonable to expect that the higher the actual ROI of a project is, the higher will be its competitiveness (compared to other investment alternatives). The same applies to the likelihood that the project will actually be executed by the decision makers in an organisation.

From the viewpoint of the investment process, ROI analyses are performed for two general purposes:

(1)   For determining the degree of fulfilment after a project was executed. This is especially used as a measure for project performance.

(2)   As a decision support tool for comparing similar investment opportunities or the question, whether a project should be generally executed or not.

Here, we will focus on the latter point, of using ROI analyses as a decision support instrument.

4.1   EIdM, the IT Productivity Paradox, and the Return on EIdM Investments

One of the starting points for analysing the ROI of IT security related projects is the structure of the project itself. As shown initially, EIdM technologies need to be integrated on the process level of an organisation. The introduction of an EIMS will most likely have a huge impact on the whole organisation and its structure (changes in processes, etc.). Therefore, EIdM projects need to be analysed in a holistic manner, including factors such as people, structure, task, and technology.

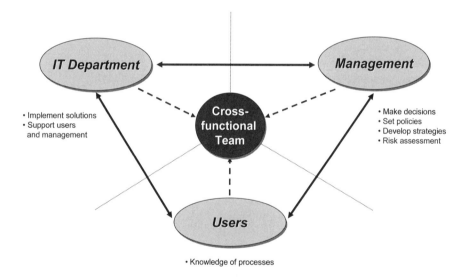

Fig. 3. Stakeholders involved in the process for introducing EIdM into an organisation and their roles (own representation based on Dos Santos [8]).

So while technology changes (or can be changed) rapidly, the organisational factors need to be taken into consideration as well. Without proper change management and the involvement of the stakeholders, it is unlikely that the strategic goals (cp. Table 1) and potentials of the expenditures for introducing EIdM can be achieved within a set time-frame [8, 17]. Even though companies invest in EIdM solutions to achieve the presented goals (e.g. risk mitigation), they may fail to see the *"big picture"* and therefore will not achieve the returns they aimed for. This leads to the effect referred to as the *IT productivity paradox* [4, 14, 26].

One of the ways to ameliorate the negative consequences of introducing EIdM is by *cross-functional teams*, integrating all the stakeholders into the process of introducing EIdM into an organisation. By doing this, strategic thinking throughout the organisation can be enabled, including all aspects and requirements, reframing the role of EIdM in the organisation, and overcoming possible language barriers in the communication between the stakeholders [8, 21]. The different groups and their roles/tasks are presented in Figure 3. Moreover, by having a general overview of all the affected processes and stakeholder groups, it is easier to identify the possible costs and benefits [24] which can be achieved by this type of technology.

Similar to the IT productivity paradox, the evaluation of IT security investments is also discussed widely in scientific literature [5, 17, 25]. Besides the various inherited problems of general IT investments, such as the described productivity paradox [4, 26], EIdM and IT security investments suffer from additional problems [17, 25]. These include the identification of (possible) revenues generated by an IT security investment or the optimal level of the total security investments. Furthermore, IT security investments are carried out to mitigate risks and to prevent possible losses [25]. If indeed the risks are mitigated and occurrences of security incidents and potential losses are prevented, it is difficult to assess whether an investment can be established cost-effective, due to the preventive nature of IT security investments.

In scientific literature several methods and frameworks are discussed that should help to assess the economic impact and the value of IT security investments, such as the return on security investments (ROSI) [5, 17, 25]. Depending on the taken approach, ROSI tries to monetarise IT security investments, for example by analysing the productivity losses associated to security breaches. However, extended metrics incorporating organisational settings and intangible factors seem necessary, in order to evaluate the return on EIDM investments. As laid out in the research approach, the analysis of these methods and frameworks will be subject of the future research in this field.

4.2   Prerequisites for an Evaluation Scheme/Process

Generally, when analysing IT investments, an evaluation scheme must fulfil several prerequisites in order to produce a sufficiently complete and thorough analysis of the subject's matter [22]. Based on the literature research, the presented prerequisites should help a cross-functional team to adequately build a decision support instrument:

- First, the underlying assumptions taken as a basis for an analysis need to be realistic. This can be achieved by analysing other EIdM projects in the same industry, using their results as a reference/benchmark for deducing the related costs.
- The modelling of the underlying environment should also take additional cost factors into account, such as development costs, migration costs, and other costs related to the lifecycle of the investment.
- Based upon the gathered data, it is important to determine the impact and interaction of the different parameters to get a complete picture of the cost effects being present in the analysed case.

- Evaluations using static finance-mathematical methods (e.g. ROI) should be avoided. A better way of determining the worth of an investment is to use dynamic methods, such as the internal rate of return (IRR) or the net present value (NPV) [10, 14]. While the static methods work with periodic mean values, the dynamic methods examine the actual present value over the complete runtime of an investment. The main difference is the consideration of the cash in- and outflows and their present value over time. This gives a more accurate view upon the development of the investment than just an average value [3, 25].
- Although a thorough collection and analysis of the present data is a good foundation for an evaluation, one has to deal with uncertainties in the development of the parameters [20]. In order to adequately forecast such effects, methods, such as the scenario technique presented by Geschka and Hammer, offer a good way to assess them [11], as they give a possible range for the actual outcome of an investment.
- For decision support, it is not possible to determine all data with 100% accuracy within an acceptable timeframe. Therefore some degree of compromise is necessary. So when preparing the data, one has to keep in mind that (most of the time) the results only need to be sufficiently accurate for decision making processes. Also, the methods used should incorporate into existing approaches, in order to minimise potential incompatibilities when building an evaluation scheme [21].
- Finally, the results have to be comprehensible for third parties, in order to allow the validation of the initial assumptions[10] and to support the decision making process. In order to achieve this, the methods for the assessment of the risks, the costs, and the benefits, need to be consistent/ standardised [21, 25].

4.3   Operationalisation of EIdM Projects

One of the initial steps of a cross-functional team is the operationalisation of the overall plan for introducing EIdM into an organisation. This is needed to cut down on complexity, as this approach helps to analyse the costs and benefits of manageable sub-projects. Moreover, a step-by-step introduction helps to minimise potential failures [21]. For this purpose, the author proposes the following steps to be taken for (preparing) an analysis:

1. Analyse the organisational environment in order to derive strategic goals for the introduction of EIdM (cp. Table 1).
2. Build a holistic view of the organisation based on the derived strategic goals, deriving a global plan for introducing EIdM.
3. Divide the global plan into smaller *sub-projects*, which can be executed step-by-step.
4. *Evaluate the sub-projects (see next section).*
5. Determine the sequence of the *sub-projects* based-on their return for the later execution of the plans.

The described process is visualised in Figure 4. The feedback loops introduced in steps 1 to 3 help to improve the results of the process itself.

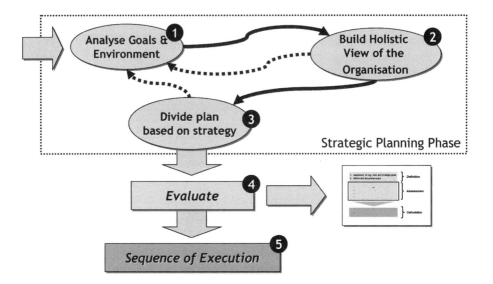

Fig. 4. Proposed process for an initial operationalisation of the project's structure.

4.4   Structure of the proposed Evaluation Process

As a next step, the actual analysis for the sub-projects is prepared. The proposed process is built upon the prerequisites and the operationalisation presented earlier (literature review), dividing it into 6 steps (cp. Figure 5):

- **Step 1:** assessment of the organisational view on EIdM in order to derive strategic goals for its introduction. What should be achieved by introducing EIdM?
- **Step 2:** define and document the project's scope (what should be analysed) based on the strategic determinates set earlier. (In order to avoid important facets being missed, this step should be used in a cycle with Step 1).
- **Step 3:** define all project costs including all investments in hardware and software, license fees, and labour (e.g. consulting).
- **Step 4:** document and estimate potential *tangible and intangible benefits*. For the tangible benefits, this includes all direct (budgeted) and indirect (unbudgeted) savings and gains. Examples are potential saving in optimised processes that lead to less support requests. Furthermore negative productivity needs to be included, especially since security measures could come at the cost of convenience [25]. For the intangible benefits, the question *"What else does the project help to achieve?"* needs to be answered as well. Possible aspects include being compliant with laws, offering interoperability, and extensibility. In either case, it is important to analyse the interdependencies between the

tangible and intangible benefits. Here, standardised methods are needed to determine the costs accordingly [25].

- **Step 5:** document the possible operational risks such as resources, schedule, staffing, and legal and determine what *tangible and intangible impacts* they may have on the analysed case.
- **Step 6:** calculation of the potential return, based on the tangible benefits *and* the potential impacts of the risks (e.g. by using metrics and models such as ROI or ROSI).

The proposed evaluation process is visualised in Figure 5. Compared to other models such as Pisello [19], it strives to offer the following enhancements: First of all, the *potential operational risks* associated to EIdM are incorporated. This is necessary, as *IT security investments*, such as EIdM, help to reduce/mitigate potential risks. This result is a more accurate view of the benefits which can be derived from these kinds of technologies [21].

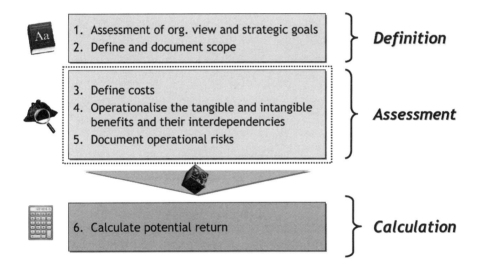

Fig. 5. Visualisation of the proposed evaluation process

Moreover, the presented process heavily relies on the documentation of the performed steps and the evaluation of the related operational risks, benefits, and the costs. Furthermore, this helps to identify the interdependencies between these aspects more easily and in a more consistent manner.

The documentation needs to be written in such a way that *all* involved parties can understand the used terminology and concepts. Common knowledge bases and glossaries are helpful to fulfil this requirement. In the opinion of the author, this helps 3rd parties not involved in the evaluation process (such as top level management) to comprehend and validate the results more easily.

4.5   Discussion

As part of the research approach outlined in section 2, the proposed evaluation process should help to assess the benefits and costs related to EIdM in a structured and standardised way (cp. [25]), introducing the associated risk into the process as an additional factor. As projects differ in their scope, a formalised process helps to keep track of the project-inherent factors, helping the decision makers to assess the introduction of EIdM technologies in a more transparent manner.

As previously indicated, the decisions made by a cross-functional team need to be made on the basis of the organisational overview, in order to determine the actions to be taken on the strategic, the tactical, and the operational levels of the organisation. Therefore all relevant stakeholders need to be involved as all groups play a vital role for assessing the overall EIdM strategy. Here, the affected (business) processes that interfere with the EIdM in an organisation are the focal point for examination. They need to be acknowledged, analysed, formalised and documented in an appropriate way to get an overview on what is needed and where.

It seems clear that formalised process models are needed, in order to support the decision makers when planning the EIdM strategy for an organisation. Such process models need to address the special requirements for EIdM solutions, such as the roles, the access permissions, the affects business process, and the lifecycle of the identities being present in an organisation. Also, this would help to better identity the risks associated with EIdM.

Besides formalised process models, evaluation frameworks are needed that help to assess the overall value of investments into EIdM. Also it is important that such a framework is extending the limited view of financial metrics (e.g. NPV, ROI, or ROSI) [14, 18], taking tangible and intangible factors and associated operational risks into consideration. Here, an IT Security/EIdM Balance Scorecard (BSC), derived from the classical BSC by Kaplan and Norton [15] may be an appropriate approach to develop an integrated evaluation framework.

5 Summary and Outlook

When introducing EIMS, organisations incur a variety of costs for the implementation and the related organisational aspects. This paper presents initial ideas for a formalised process for assessing and considering the associated operational risks, costs, and benefits related to EIdM projects in an organisation.

Based on the presented research approach (section 2), the evaluation process at hand is a first step to achieve this. However, future research needs to extend the work presented here. This especially includes concepts, such as an IT Security/EIdM BSC, which integrate tangible and intangible factors into the decision making process. Furthermore, such an instrument could be used to execute an EIdM project on the tactical level, bringing together the strategic and the operational perspectives.

Acknowledgements

The research at hand was funded by the European (6th Framework Program) Network of Excellence (NoE) FIDIS (Future of Identity in the Information Society). The author wants to thank all people that helped to improve the contents of this paper with their comments, their contributions, and their reviews.

References

1. Bauer, M., Meints, M. and Hansen, M., Deliverable D3.1: Structured Overview on Prototypes and Concepts of Identity Management Systems (FIDIS, 2005).
2. Berghel, H., The Two Sides of ROI: Return on Investment vs. Risk of Incarceration, Communications of the ACM, 48(4), pp. 15-20 (2005).
3. Blohm, H. and Lüder, K., Investition, Schwachstellenanalyse des Investitionsbereichs und Investitionsrechnung (Vahlen, Munich, 1995).
4. Brynjolfsson, E., The Productivity Paradox of Information Technology, Communications of the ACM, 36(12), pp. 67-77 (1993).
5. Cavusoglu, H., Mishra, B. and Raghunathan, S., A Model for Evaluating IT Security Investments, Communications of the ACM 47(7), pp. 87-92 (2004).
6. Deron GmbH, Identity Management Studie 2006/2007 (Deron, Stuttgart, 2007).
7. Dewey, B. I. and DeBlois, P. B., Current Issues Survey Report 2007, EDUCAUSE Quarterly, 30(2), pp. 12-31 (2007).
8. Dos Santos, B. L. and Sussman, L., Improving the return on IT investment: the productivity paradox, International Journal of Information Management, 20(6), pp. 429-440 (2000).
9. Flynn, M. J. (2007); http://360tek.blogspot.com/2006/07/enterprise-identity-services.html, accessed 27th of September 2007.
10. Franklin, C. J., The ABCs of ROI, Network Computing, 27th of April, pp. 93-95 (2002).
11. Geschka, H. and Hammer, R., Die Szenario Technik in der strategischen Unternehmensplanung, in: Strategische Unternehmensplanung - strategische Unternehmensführung, edited by Hahn, D. and Taylor, B. (Physica, Heidelberg, 1997), pp. 464-489.
12. Hansen, M. and Meints, M., Digitale Identitäten – Überblick und aktuelle Trends, Datenschutz und Datensicherheit (DuD), 30(9), pp. 571-575 (2006).
13. Hevner, A. R., March, S. T. and Park, J., Design Science in Information Systems Research, MIS Quarterly, 28(1), pp. 75-105 (2004).
14. Jonen, A. et al., Balanced IT-Decision-Card, Ein Instrument für das Investitionscontrolling von IT-Projekten, Wirtschaftsinformatik, 46(3), pp. 196-203 (2004).
15. Kaplan, R. S. and Norton, D. P., The Balanced Scorecard. Translating Strategy into Action (Random House, Boston, 1996).
16. Lee, A. S., Integrating Positivist and Interpretive Approaches to Organizational Research, Organisational Science, 4(2), pp. 342-365 (1991).
17. Magnusson, C., Molvidsson, J. and Zetterqvist, S., Value Creation and Return On Security Investmensts (ROSI), in: IFIP SEC 2007: New Approaches for Security, Privacy and Trust in Complex Environments, edited by Venter, H. et al. (Springer, Boston, 2007), pp. 25-35.
18. May, T. A., The death of ROI: re-thinking IT value measurement, Information Management & Computer Security, 5(3), pp. 90-92 (1997).

19. Pisello, T., Return on Investment for Information Technology Providers (Information Economics Press, New Canaan, 2001).
20. Potthof, I., Kosten und Nutzen der Informationsverarbeitung: Analyse und Beurteilung von Investitionsentscheidungen (DUV/Gabler, Wiesbaden, 1998).
21. Purser, S. A., Improving the ROI of the security management process, 23(6), pp. 542-546 (2004).
22. Rossnagel, H. and Royer, D., Investing in Security Solutions - Can Qualified Electronic Signatures be Profitable for Mobile Operators, Proceedings of the 11th Americas Conference on Information Systems (AMCIS), Omaha, Nebraska (2005).
23. Schmeh, K. and Uebelacker, H. (2006); http://www.heise.de/tp/r4/artikel/18/18954/ 1.html accessed 22.10.2007.
24. Solingen, R. v., Measuring the ROI of Software Process Improvement, IEEE Software, 21(3), pp. 32-38 (2004).
25. Sonnenreich, W., Albanese, J. and Stout, B., Return On Security Investment (ROSI) – A Practical Quantitative Model, Journal of Research and Practice in Information Technology, 38(1), pp. 45-56 (2006).
26. Wan, Z., Fang, Y. and Wade, M., A Ten-Year Odyssey of the "IS Productivity Paradox" - A Citation Analysis (1996-2006), Proceedings of the 13th Americas Conference on Information Systems (AMCIS), Keystone, Colorado (2007).
27. Windley, P. J., Digital Identity (O'Reilly, Sebastopol et al., 2005).

Privacy and Data Protection in a User-Centric Business Model for Telecommunications Services

Juan C. Yelmo, José M. del Álamo, and Rubén Trapero

DIT, Universidad Politécnica de Madrid,
Ciudad Universitaria s/n, 28040 Madrid, Spain
{jcyelmo, jmdela, rubentb}@dit.upm.es

Abstract. New business models have come up in different contexts such as the Internet and Telecommunications networks which have been grouped under the umbrella of the buzzword 2.0. They propose the opening up of service platforms in order to increase profits by means of innovative collaboration agreements with third parties. In this paper we go a step further and propose a business model for Telecommunications services where end-users actually become the collaborating third parties. This user-centric business model poses several privacy and data protection concerns that we analyze and for which we propose a solution.

1 Introduction

Many e-companies have been working for a long time just with their own close set of customers and resources. It was one of their treasures and they were reluctant to share them with other companies because they were afraid of losing profits to their competitors. Acting in such a way has lead to walled-garden business models. Their main drawback is that a huge engineering effort has to be spent both on development and marketing in order to get a new service up and running to the market.

On the other hand, new paradigms have arisen in different contexts such as the Internet and Telecommunications, which have been grouped under the umbrella of the buzzword 2.0: Web 2.0 [1], Telco 2.0 [2], Mobile Web 2.0 [3], and so on. Some of their common approaches are:

1. *The idea of a platform*; i.e. there is no hard boundary as in the walled-garden models, but rather, a gravitational core around which the business is created.
2. *Harnessing collective intelligence*; i.e. turn your customers and providers into a global brain, which could be used to enhance your business.
3. *Data is one of the assets a company owns*; notice that most of the time this information is about the company's customers.

Regarding the first point, there is nowadays a trend in Telecommunications and Internet domains towards partnership and the need to build technology platforms that enable third party providers to collaborate. Relevant examples of this trend are British Telecommunications (BT) Project Web21C [4] and Amazon Web Services [5]

Please use the following format when citing this chapter:

Yelmo, J.C., del Álamo, J.M. and Trapero, R., 2008, in IFIP International Federation for Information Processing, Volume 262; The Future of Identity in the Information Society; Simone Fischer-Hübner, Penny Duquenoy, Albin Zuccato, Leonardo Martucci; (Boston: Springer), pp. 447–461.

platforms, which allow external developers and businesses to build their own applications with a set of Web Services interfaces.

The most innovative case though, is the so called user-centric platform [6]. It allows users (not necessarily technically skilled) to create their own contents and applications (*mashups*) from the combination (composition) of different sources. There are currently few initiatives in user-centric platforms: on the Internet we can find Yahoo Pipes [7], and in the Telecommunications domain we can find the Open Platform for User-centric service Creation and Execution (OPUCE) [8].

User-centric environments support the fast development and supply of innovative services and this provides benefits for the different actors involved:

- The platform provider obtains some profit from the use of its own services and a percentage for the services created by end-users.
- End-users can create their own personalized services that fit their needs better.

Nonetheless, the combination of user-centric environments with social networks allows users to share their services within a community which will promote the most interesting ones at a minimum cost (viral marketing[1]), thus eliminating the main disadvantage of walled-garden business models i.e. development and marketing expenses.

The obvious question now is why should any end-user use my platform rather than someone else's? The answer points to the third idea of the 2.0 approach: data is one of the main assets of a company.

Companies have been collecting information about their customers which has been kept in information silos just for their own use. However, they can now use this information to boost their platforms and take advantage of the benefits the user-centric approaches provide, thus leveraging new and profitable business models. Moreover, in most cases they have even established a trust relationship with their customers, which may be also used as a powerful asset. Nonetheless, customers can also benefit from the use of their identity information with features such as personalization, customization, improved usability, better user experience and enhanced security.

On the other hand, in most countries there are laws which require companies to ensure security and privacy when revealing personal information about a customer, such as the 2002/58/EC [9] and the 95/46/EC [10] Directives, both of the European Union. Thus, we have arrived at a point where we could create open platforms that end-users would use to develop and consume innovative and profitable services as far as their privacy and identity information are protected.

This paper analyses the requirements with regard to privacy and data protection for a user-centric service creation and execution business model. In order to do so, a business model supporting user-centric service creation and execution is first proposed. Then the requirements for privacy and data protection for the business

---

[1] Viral marketing refers to marketing techniques that use pre-existing social networks to produce increases in brand awareness, through self-replicating viral processes, analogous to the spread of pathological and computer viruses. It can be word-of-mouth delivered or enhanced by the network effects of the Internet. [Source: Wikipedia].

model are analysed, and a solution is proposed. Finally, a case study where these ideas are applied is described.

2   Business models in user-centric service creation and execution environments

The Telecommunication Information Networking Architecture Consortium (TINA-C) states [11] that *a business model defines the different parties involved in service provisioning and their relationships*. In this section we first describe the requirements for a business model to support user-centric service creation and execution. Then we introduce existing business models for Telecommunications and analyze them regarding these requirements. Finally, we present the proposed business model, the participating entities and their relationships.

2.1   Requirements for the business models to support user-centric service creation and execution

End-user service execution – The first requirement is that end-user service execution should be allowed.

End-user service creation – The next requirement is that the business model should support end-user service creation. This will allow end-users to compose their own services from the set of services that is already offered within the platform.

End-user service provision – The business model should allow extensions to accommodate new players in the service provision. Once end-users create new services, they will probably want to provide them to other end-users.

End-user service recommendation – Finally, the business model should allow users to recommend services to other users. This will contribute to the success of a set of high value services from among the great amount of services that are to be created within the platform. These frequently recommended, high value services will actually provide added value to users, and might turn out to become a kind of killer services [12].

2.2   Existing Telecommunications business models

The following three approaches are currently being studied by telecoms operators in order to find the most appropriate business model for the service provision.

Walled garden – Business models for Telecommunications companies (telcos) have traditionally followed the *walled garden* paradigm [13]. The goal has always consisted of subscribers getting everything they wish (services and contents) in the operator's portfolio. Access to outer services is not allowed and third party service providers, if any, appear under the operator's brand name. The user experience is limited to choosing a service and paying for it under different billing plans. All revenues go directly to the telco from its customers. In this business model end-user service recommendation does not exist at all, since only the operator's selected services are offered to users following operator's criteria.

Bit pipe – The bit-pipe approach [14] describes the operator network as bit pipes that allow its customers to access services with neither constrains nor added value. The operator gets its revenue from the use of the network. Users may choose from the set of services offered by third parties. They pay for the services following the service provider terms and conditions, which may differ from provider to provider. The quality of service (QoS) is not checked by the operator, and thus not ensured. The management of identity information and the privacy and data protection is up to each service. Operators do not provide any mechanism to promote or recommend services, since they are not offered by them. In some cases, the third party providers include tools in their services to recommend them to other users (i.e. inviting friends by sending an e-mail with the recommendation). In any case end-user service recommendation may be performed, but out of the scope of the business model.

Semi-walled garden – Within this business model customers stay inside the operator's *walled garden* but they are free to choose and enjoy third party services and contents [15]. The revenue is divided between the operator and the provider. Operators offer value-added service enablers that are attractive to third party providers thus encouraging the partnership between them: some are related to the Telecommunications infrastructure (e.g. QoS, SMS service or setting up calls), and other to users' identity (e.g. authentication, presence, location or address books). The network operator, the service provider and content provider, all work together in a team to build a value chain that produces services which may be interesting to the end users and providing some revenue to each member in the chain. Similar to the walled garden case, it is the operator itself who carries out the service recommendation by suggesting as trusted and directly accessible from the service menu those services which belong to selected third parties. The order in which services are prompted to the users determines the actual service recommendation. This order is usually based on off-line agreements between the operator and the corresponding service providers.

The three business models are analyzed in **Table 1** with respect to the proposed requirements.

Table 1. Analysis of Telecommunications business models.

Requirement	Walled garden	Bit pipe	Semi-walled garden
End-user service execution	Yes	Yes	Yes
End-user service creation	No	No	No
End-user service provision	No	No	No
End-user service recommendation	No	Yes (externally)	No

None of the main business models for Telecommunications satisfy the requirements related to end-user service creation and provision. The best approach, the *semi-walled garden,* lets third parties to take part in the business by developing services that the customer could use within the framework provided by the *walled garden*, and that is a first step on the right path. However, the process to become a third party is long and tedious and is not feasible for end-users. Nevertheless, an evolution of the business model is needed which will make it possible also for customers to create, share and recommend their own services. This is the particularity of the business model we present; the fact that the customer performs now other roles in the business model apart from the service consumer.

2.3   A business model for user-centric service creation and execution

To begin with the description of the proposed business model we present the entities that participate: the operator and the customer. The operator provides the user-centric platform where end-users create and execute their services. It may also provide some services with basic functionality e.g. send an SMS, set up a call, retrieve a presence status or a location, and so forth. Customers may execute the services available, but also create their own. Some third party service providers might also participate, providing specialized contents or services on the operator's platform. In this case their relationship with the operator may be modelled using the semi-walled garden business model. In order to simplify our description we will not consider third party service providers.

The relationships between the different entities and their roles in the user-centric business model are detailed in the following figure.

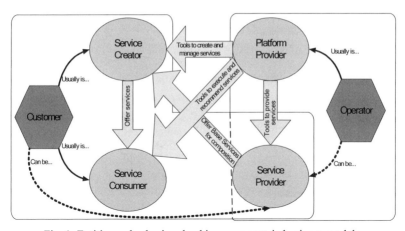

Fig. 1: Entities and roles involved in a user-centric business models.

The roles played by the different entities are: platform provider, service consumer, service creator and service provider. The customer may play the role of service consumer, service creator and service provider. The difference between service creator and service provider is that the former offers services to consumers, while the latter offers its services to other service creators for combination. The operator usually plays the role of platform provider, but as we said it could also provide its own service portfolio for combination thus becoming a service provider too.

The platform provider supplies all the features that enable the creation, the management, the provision, the execution and the recommendation of services. It is also involved in the economic flows between the different members (creators, providers and consumers).

Service creators find that a service is needed and useful (for themselves or for any other member of the community) and have the necessary skills and tools to create it from the set of services already available within the platform. Once the service is created and deployed on the platform it will be available to be used by other service consumers under different billing plans. Successful services may also be used as base services in further compositions, thus becoming service providers too.

To identify which value is perceived by the different actors, we define the value chain of the business. The actors that add value in this value chain are the operator that provides the platform, and the customer that creates services that can be provided. There are no intermediaries between the service creator and the service consumer, except the platform. Therefore the traditional value chain for service provisioning has been shortened to put creators in touch with consumers via a simplified channel (Fig. 2). This new channel should have the means and the tools to simplify both the creation and the consumption of new services.

Fig. 2: Value chain for the proposed business model.

Some of the benefits of the business model for different roles are briefly described below:

Customer value – The two main factors for the value perceived by the customer are the level of personalization of the services (very personalized since service creators are usually the final users themselves) and later, the chance of sharing them, making the platform a hugely connected network based on user-generated services. The services provided are valuable to all the users belonging to the community as long as they can be personalized more than just because of their own usefulness. In that sense, identity attributes such as age, gender, location or presence status are commonly used for personalization purposes.

Platform value – Traditional network businesses base their value on the number of participants that take advantages of their features. A user-centric platform is a network business as well, and thus it is important for its success to have as many members as possible. This will allow the flow of services being shared between service creators and service consumers to increase.

Figure 3 shows the flows of revenue between different roles. The consumer pays the platform (if needed this will be applicable only for premium services) for the use of one final service under different billing plans (monthly fee, pay per use, etc). It could be determined by means of the nature of the service. The service creator receives part of this revenue, which can be proportional to the number of users of their services (this is a revenue-sharing model, but their might be others depending on the service itself). Service providers perceive their revenues from the platform, for example by agreements on percentages for each mashup they are part of. If users perceive the service as valuable, the platform provider and the service creator receive

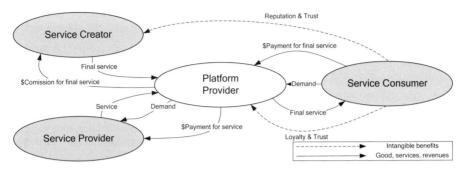

Fig. 3: Flows of revenue for the proposed business model.

intangible benefits such as customer loyalty (the former), reputation (the latter) or trust (both).

3 Privacy issues in the proposed business model

Proper management of identity information provides better usability and improves the user experience, which may be used to enhance user-centric service creation and execution platforms. It is also at the core of the relationship of the platform provider with its customers, both creators and consumers, and other companies such as the service providers; i.e. identity management is a must when enabling access to identity attributes. Moreover, it increases efficiency, enhancing security and open new revenue opportunities. Thus, the use of customers' identity information provides benefits for all the roles in the business model. Some examples are:

- Automated access to the service portfolio supported by single sign-on and dynamic service discovery and invocation, which enhances the usability of the platform and the consumers' user-experience.
- Service adaptability and context awareness, which allows services to react according to the circumstances under which they operate to offer better usability. These circumstances are usually based on consumers' identity attributes such as location, presence status or consumer's device.
- Service personalization, which allows service creators to customize pre-existing services and components based on personal attributes and user profiles.

The next section describes the specific requirements for the business model regarding privacy and data protection issues in terms of their legal and technical approaches. It also proposes a solution to fulfil these requirements.

3.1   Requirements

Proper identity management is essential in every new Telecommunications service that is implemented or provided in Europe. Furthermore, it is obligatory because of restrictions and legal constraints derived from several European Directives:

- European Union Data Protection Directive [16];
- European Union Electronic Communications Privacy Directive [9];
- European Union Data Retention Directive [10].

Within the Data Protection Directive, *personal data* is defined as information that relates to an identified or identifiable natural person. The *processing of personal data* is defined as any operation or set of operations that is performed on personal data, such as collecting, storing, disseminating, and so on. The different dimensions of data protection are:

1. Personal data must be collected for ***specified, explicit and legitimate purposes*** and not further processed in a way incompatible with those purposes.
2. Personal data must be ***adequate, relevant and not excessive in relation to the purposes*** for which they are collected and/or further processed. This can be seen as part of the privacy principle of data minimization, which can be seen in two ways:
    o   Avoid that private date might appear scattered in multiple places in the network.
    o   Ensure that a unique unit of private data is provided to a certain requester, and not a set of it which may include more private information that the one that is needed.
3. Personal data may be processed only if the data subject has ***unambiguously given her or his consent.***

In the proposed business model there are three roles which may process personal data, and thus may be affected by the Privacy and Data Protection Directives. The platform provider stores consumers' accounts and preferences so it is clear that it processes personal data. Service providers may provide personal information to service creators or use it for different purposes. Service creators may need to use service providers to fulfill some specialized task and thus they might need to provide identity information about the service consumers in order to compose new services.

Taking into account the Data Protection Directive, we can derive the specific requirements for each role:

1. The platform must explicitly state in a **privacy policy** the **purposes** of the personal data it processes. Service providers and service creators must also explicitly state in a privacy policy the purpose of the data it processes. We do not discard to include mechanisms to enforce the fulfillment of such policies, for instance, by using specific alternatives such as the Enterprise Privacy Authorization Language (EPAL) [17].
2. The platform must not release and the service providers/creators must not collect attributes that are irrelevant for the service in question. A special case is that when a service is not interested in the consumers' attributes but on their

authorization to access the service. In this case the platform should derive the authorization from the consumer's attributes without releasing any of them. In any other case the service provider must **explicitly specify the attributes that is processing**.

3. The platform must **ask for consumer consent** for the set of attributes it is processing. Each service must also ask for **consumer** consent for the set of attributes it is processing. When asking for **consumer** consent, the privacy policy that states the purpose and the relevance of the attributes must be available. Furthermore, the user must also be informed about which is the entity that is requesting the attributes (as it is stated in the Article 10 of [10]).

4. Consumers must be allowed to **query the set of identity attributes** the platform has got about them, and to **correct them** when they are not accurate. They must also be able to know which services are using their identity attributes, and **revoke consent** as desired.

The Directives also allocate compliance responsibilities according to the role that any given participant is performing. In that sense liability issues must be taken into account. Therefore:

5. The platform should provide a **liability disclaimer** to prevent misuse and abuses by service creators, service providers and service consumers. Service providers and service creators should also provide liability disclaimers for the use of their services.

3.2 Technical approach to fulfil the privacy and data protection requirements

As we have shown, the platform and the service provider are the roles directly affected by the privacy and data protection directives as they must implement privacy policies that state the identity attributes they use and reason for using them. They should also include liability requirements to prevent misuse and avoid abuses. These requirements are quite straightforward and they could be fulfilled beforehand. On the other hand, the requirements for the service creators must be automatically fulfilled by the tools supporting the creation process.

The approach we propose to fulfill the requirements is:

1. **Privacy policy**. Each service must have a privacy policy that states the identity attributes it uses and reason for using them.

2. **Privacy policy composition**. When a new service is created the policies of the individual components must be automatically aggregated in order to create a new privacy policy that states both the identity attributes it is processing and the purpose. The set of attributes the components are processing must be automatically aggregated and explicitly specified in the new privacy policy (following a concatenation approach for individual privacy policies).

3. **Dynamic management of customers' consent**. The previous point stated that the privacy policy for the new services will contain the set of identity attributes they are using. Thus, at runtime it is possible for the execution environment to retrieve this information, check whether the customer has

granted the service to use her personal information and, if not, explicitly ask her for consent previously to the service execution.

4. **Self management of identity attributes and consents**. As the platform knows from the privacy policies which attributes are being used, by which services and whether it is agreed by the customers or not, then it is feasible to present this information to the customers and allow them to modify it.

5. **Liability disclaims**. Each service must provide a liability disclaimer that disclaims responsibilities resulting from service misuse or abuse. This could be automatically provided by the platform.

To sum up, the platform must enforce each service having a privacy policy, must provide the means to draw up the privacy policies for the new services, and the means to ask consumers for explicit consent on the use of their attributes (at least in the first use of the service). It also must ensure that each service has a liability disclaimer. It is possible to have a unique liability disclaimer for all the services offered on the platform.

4   Case study: OPUCE

The OPUCE project is a research project within the European Union Sixth Framework Programme for Research and Technological Development. OPUCE aims to bridge advances in networking, communication and information technology services towards a unique service environment where personalized services are dynamically created and provisioned by the end-users themselves.

The general objective of OPUCE is to leverage the creation of a user-centric service ecosystem giving users the chance to create their own personalized services as is currently done on the Internet. Within this approach, service concepts are redefined. In OPUCE, services are envisaged as short-lived telecom services that end-users will create by orchestrating simpler services called base services. Base services are considered as functional units deployed by the operator, available on the OPUCE platform and offered to end users through Web Services interfaces.

Figure 4 introduces a detailed diagram of the OPUCE architecture. Its main elements are:

- A *Service Creation Environment* with a set of tools to be used by people or third parties to create services dynamically. It can be seen as a portal through which users can create, manage and share services. Actually, it consists of two portals: a user portal, to manage social networks, service subscriptions and configurations, etc; and a service portal, to manage the service edition, test, simulation, monitoring, etc. The Service Creation Environment also includes other general functions (access control, registration) and administration tools.

- A *Context Awareness* module to manage the adaptation and customization of services to the users' ambience conditions. In OPUCE two types of context aware adaptations are supported: explicit, when it is the service creator who specifies the service behaviour by taking into account user context information; and implicit, when the platform itself analyzes the service and adapts the execution dynamically.

- A *User Information Management* module to control the user's personal information (agenda, buddy list, presence information, device capabilities, potential use of certain services, etc.), identity management and AAA.
- A *Subscription Management* module to keep control of the user subscriptions to services. The information that this module stores is mainly consumed by other OPUCE modules (such as the context awareness or the user information modules).
- A *Service Lifecycle Manager* module which manages the lifecycle of all services created within the OPUCE platform.
- A *Service Execution Environment* which manages the execution of services and orchestrates base services following the logic created by the users when composing them.

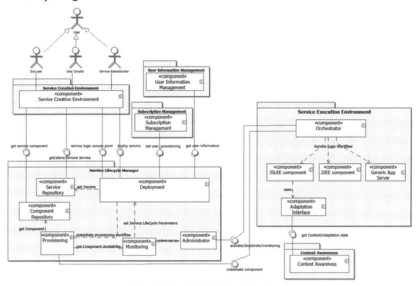

Fig. 4: The OPUCE architecture.

4.1   Privacy requirements fulfilment in OPUCE

A user-centric based service ecosystem requires major flexibility and dynamism in managing privacy and data protection compared to current service management systems. In order to automate the process between the creation and the execution of the services, the OPUCE platform needs a common way to describe the services completely. Therefore services are described using a service specification which contains all aspects of a service. Each aspect, called a facet, is further described in a separate XML-based specification [18] (Figure 5).

Up until now OPUCE has three sets of facets: functional facets include service logic, service interface, service semantic, etc; non-functional facets include service level agreements, quality of service, etc; and management facets include service lifecycle schedule, deployment and provisioning.

Facets are automatically generated and managed by the platform, without service creators taking further action except composing their services. For example, service creators use the Web visual editor to compose their services by orchestrating some of the available ones; the creation process is easy as they have to put together graphical building blocks representing the services they want to use. Then, the platform creates a service logic facet which contains the Business Process Execution Language (BPEL) [19] from the service orchestration. When the creation process has finished the service logic facet is stored in a repository. At the time of deployment, a service lifecycle management module moves the facet into a BPEL engine, where it is ready for execution. For further details on the service lifecycle management refer to [20].

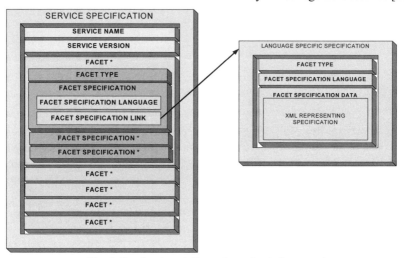

Fig. 5: Service description using a faceted approach.

A requirement derived from the privacy and data protection analysis for a user-centric environment business model is that each service must have a privacy policy. In that sense we see that a fundamental part of a service description is its privacy policy. Therefore a new facet is created: ***privacy policy facet***. This facet contains the privacy policy for the service which includes the set of identity attributes it is processing and the purpose. When a new service is created, a privacy policy facet is created by concatenating individual privacy policy of each base service.

In OPUCE each facet is described in a separate XML-based specification. This allows us to choose any XML-based language to express the privacy policy for the service as far as it complies with our requirements. The Platform for Privacy Preferences (P3P) [21] is a protocol developed by the World Wide Web Consortium (W3C) which defines an XML-based language through which services can describe their privacy policies in a machine readable format. Categories of information include different types of data being collected, the purpose(s) for collection, and which organizations will have access to the collected data. It covers enough of our requirements regarding privacy policies.

As for privacy policy composition, privacy policy facet for the composed services can be created in a similar way as the service logic facet is created i.e. at the time of creation it is made up of the privacy policy facets of the component services. The new facet is then stored in the repository.

At the time of subscription, the subscription management module would retrieve the privacy policy for the service and prompt users for consent on the use of their identity attributes. It must also ask the consumers for their acceptance of the liability disclaimer. The user information management is the module where this information is stored. At runtime, the service execution environment will check against the user information whether a user has given consent for a service to retrieve identity information. This allows OPUCE to fulfill the requirements regarding dynamic management of customers consent and liability disclaims.

Finally, customers can use the user portal to manage which personal information is being used by which services, and thus revoke consent as desired. Therefore, the last requirement can be fulfilled.

5   Conclusions

User-centric service creation and execution is becoming a new paradigm in the area of Telecommunications service provisioning. It poses several challenges resulting from the short lifecycles of the user-created services as well as the end-users' privacy and data protection in such a dynamic environment.

In this paper we have stated some of the basic requirements for a business model to support user-centric service creation and execution. The main business models in Telecommunications have been analyzed in the light of these requirements. As none of them fulfils the requirements we have proposed a new one describing the parties involved, their roles and their relationships.

For the proposed business model an analysis has been made regarding the privacy and data protection requirements in the European Union. In order to fulfil these requirements we have proposed a set of technical solutions based on the composition of individual privacy policies.

To demonstrate the feasibility of the proposed approaches, we have chosen a user-centric service creation and execution platform for Telecommunications which is currently under development. We have described the specific architecture of the solution and the processes that must take place. The final solution is based on the creation of XML-based service descriptions which include a facet that contains the privacy policy that applies to the service. Regarding service creation, whenever an end-user creates a new service its privacy policy will be generated automatically from the components' privacy policies. This privacy policy will be used at the time of subscription to get the end-users consent for the use of their identity attributes. Eventually, this information will be checked at the execution of the service to ensure privacy and data protection. Further work will tackle the improvement of the user interface for obtaining consents, with explicit mechanisms to inform the user about the privacy policy that will be applied, and asking for acceptance of the terms of the agreement.

Acknowledgements

This work is framed within the IST European Integrated Project OPUCE (*Open Platform for User-centric service Creation and Execution*), 6th Framework Programme, Contract No. 34101. We thank all our partners in the project for their valuable comments and proposals aiming at improving the conceptual model.

References

1. O'Reilly, T.: What is Web 2.0 - Design patterns and business models for the next generation of software. O'Reilly Media Inc, (Sep. 2005); http://www.oreillynet.com/pub/a/oreilly/tim/news/2005/09/30/what-is-web-20.html
2. STL Partners Ltd., Telco 2.0 Manifesto: How to make money in an IP-based world (May 2007); http://www.telco2.net/manifesto/
3. Jaokar, A. and Fish, T.: Mobile Web 2.0 (Futuretext, London, 2006)
4. Web21C SDK Developer Center (2007); http://sdk.bt.com/
5. Amazon Web Services (2007); http://www.amazon.com/
6. Caetano, J. et al, Introducing the user to the service creation world: concepts for user centric creation, personalization and notification. International Workshop on User centricity – state of the art. Budapest, Hungary (2007).
7. Yahoo Pipes Website (2007); http://pipes.yahoo.com/pipes.
8. OPUCE Website (2007); http://www.opuce.eu/.
9. Directive 2002/58/EC of the European Parliament and of the Council of 12 July 2002 concerning the processing of personal data and the protection of privacy in the electronic communications sector, Official Journal L 201, 37-47 (July 2002)
10. Directive 95/46/EC of the European Parliament and of the Council of 24 October 1995 on the protection of individuals with regard to the processing of personal data and on the free movement of such data, Official Journal L 281, Oct. 1995, pp. 31-50.
11. TINA-C Deliverable: TINA Business Model and Reference Points. Version 4.0. (1997)
12. Anderson, C.: The Long Tail: Why the Future of Business is Selling Less of More (Hyperion, New York, 2006)
13. Afuah, A., Tucci, C., Internet Business Models and Strategies (McGraw Hill, Irwin, 2001)
14. Cuevas, A., Moreno, J., Vidales, P., Einsiedler, H.: The IMS Service Platform - A Solution for Next-Generation Networks Operators to Be More than Bit Pipes. IEEE Communications Magazine, vol. 44, no. 8, Aug. 2006, pp. 75-81.
15. Baker, G. and Megler, V., The semi-walled garden: Japan's i-mode phenomenon (IBM pSeries Solutions Development, October 2001).
16. Directive 2006/24/EC of the European Parliament and of the Council of 15 March 2006 on the retention of data generated or processed in connection with the provision of publicly available electronic communications services or of public communications networks, and amending Directive 2002/58/EC, Official Journal L 105, Mar. 2006, pp. 54-63.
17. Powers, C. and Schunter, M. (Ed.): Enterprise Privacy Authorization Language (EPAL 1.2). Version 1.2. IBM Research Report (2003)
18. Sawyer, P., Hutchison, J., Walkerdine, J. and Sommerville, I.: Faceted Service Specification. Proceedings of Workshop on Service-Oriented Computing Requirements (SOCCER'05). Paris, France (2005).
19. Andrews, T. et al, Business Process Execution Language for Web Services. V. 1.1. (2003)

20. Yelmo, J.C., Trapero, R., Del Álamo, J.M., Sienel, J., Drewniok, M., Ordás, I., and McCallum, K.: User-driven service lifecycle management: Adopting Internet paradigms in telecom services. Prpceeding of the International Conference on Service Oriented Computing (ICSOC 2007), Vienna, Austria (2007)
21. W3C Recommendation: The Platform for Privacy Preferences (P3P). Version 1.0. (2002)

Printed in the United States of America